S0-BLE-781

Organizations: Theory and Design

PATRICK E. CONNOR

Oregon State University

Organizations: Theory and Design

SCIENCE RESEARCH ASSOCIATES, INC.
Chicago, Palo Alto, Toronto, Henley-on-Thames, Sydney

A Subsidiary of IBM

Acquisition Editor	David Bruce Caldwell
Project Editor	James C. Budd
Compositor	Typothetae
Illustrator	House of Graphics
Cover and Text Designer	Judith Olson

Printed in the United States of America

Library of Congress Cataloging in Publication Data

Connor, Patrick E.
Organizations: theory and design.

Includes index.
1. Organization. 2. Organizational effectiveness.
I. Title.
HM131.C7457 301.18'32 79–14823
ISBN 0–574–19380–4

10 9 8 7 6 5 4 3 2

To my parents,
Jean Barkman Connor
and
Francis Edward Connor,
with love and thanks

CONTENTS

FOREWORD

Organizations are complex social phenomena. This complexity is reflected in the eclectic nature of organization theory, the diversity of scientific research in the field, and the myriad of organization designs in the modern world. This book focuses on the macro level of organization theory and design and provides an integrated framework for better understanding through the linking of research, theory, and practice. It uses an open-systems perspective of organizations in interaction with their environments and develops contingency concepts, emphasizing that appropriate designs are those matching organizatonal goals and characteristics with constraints (environment, technology, and people).

Professor Connor has made a meaningful contribution by sifting, distilling, and integrating a vast amount of information. His introductions and conclusions provide helpful insights to facilitate comprehension and integration of salient concepts in the writings of experts in organization theory and design.

This book is more than a collection of random ideas and propositions. It is a carefully thought-out presentation of key concepts that shoud be helpful to serious students who want to understand organizations—the theory underlying their functioning and guidelines for designing better ones. It provides a comprehensive source of information on the current state of organization theory and design and also develops concepts and models for the extension of the field.

Fremont Kast
James Rosenzweig
Consulting Editors

PREFACE

About five years ago I decided that the world needed another book on organizations. That there were already a number of volumes did not dissuade me—they all seemed to have one of two basic problems. Either they attempted to describe organizations from a pretty narrow perspective—such as those that were based on a particular typology—or they were little more than dressed-up management books.

My graduate training at the University of Washington emphasized what has since come to be called *macro* aspects of organizational life. My inclination, therefore, was to try to describe some of those aspects—and to do so without relying on a single classification scheme or a set of POSDCORB-like prescriptions.

In October 1975 I chanced to attend a workshop on organizational design. The workshop was organized by Lou Pondy and Ken Rowland, sponsored by the TIMS College on Organization, and held at the University of Illinois. It developed into a wide-ranging examination of several notions—notions that may or may not have had much to do with organization design. The examination *process,* however, was stimulating. As a result, I came away from the workshop with a desire to bring an organization-design focus to my upper-division management and organization courses.

In the few years that followed, that focus took shape and is reflected in the structure of this book. Basically, the idea is this:

Question: Why do organization designers design?
Answer: To achieve various organization goals.
Question: Since nothing is free, what constrains designers' design options?
Answer: Where the organization is operating (that is, the environment), how its goods and services get produced (organizational technology), and the nature of the people doing the producing.
Question: What is it that designers design?
Answer: Various organizational properties and processes, such as work, structure, and control and decision processes, for example.
Question: So what results from all this?
Answer: The main outcomes are two: organizational climate and organizational effectiveness.

The book's main discussion, Sections Two through Five, reflects this question-and-answer litany. Having a high need for order, I have preceded that discussion with a section on basic organization-theoretic and organization-design concepts. My equally high need for closure suggested a concluding section, dealing with some applications and some "what-next?" considerations.

The reader will almost instantly recognize that this book is primarily informed by open-systems ideas. That is, the organization is treated principally as an open system—open to its environment, acquiring and processing resources, producing output, readjusting those processes, and so on. It is, of course, fashionable in some quarters to criticize systems ideas as bearing less fruit than promised. Still, I think they do help capture some of the action of organizational functioning. So, with no apologies, I have followed a fairly straightforward systems approach to organizational design.

The format of this book is text-reader: some of the discussion is mine; some is others'. Specifically, each chapter contains some introductory remarks, one to three articles (usually edited), and then a concluding statement (a summary-and-conclusion essay). The objective of the introductions is simple: to set the stage for the ensuing discussion and to provide a road map for what follows in the articles and concluding statement. A road map, of course, is a device by which readers may identify the path they are about to follow. Each road map identifies the purpose of the chapter, as well as the chain that ties the chapter's discussion together. Some of the introductory remarks are brief, some quite lengthy. The length depends on the amount of preliminary material that I believe it is necessary to present. In general such material contains definitions, reviews of earlier work, and so forth.

The objective of the concluding statements is somewhat more elaborate. Each is presented in the hope of providing the reader with a fairly brief summing up of what we appear to be able to say about the chapter's subject. Necessarily, each statement provides some integration of the articles that precede it, but none is limited to an integration of only those articles. Rather the concluding remarks attempt to be overall statements on the subjects.

Each major section contains one or more cases. The cases vary in length from brief (actually "incidents") to fairly long, running several pages. Settings for the cases also vary, ranging from nursing homes to manufacturing plants. Each case has been written or selected to provide an opportunity for the reader to focus on one or more fairly specific design issues appropriate to that section.

As will become apparent, this book is aimed at the advanced undergraduate or beginning graduate student. I have assumed that the reader has some familiarity with the concepts and terms covered in typical introductory courses in management, organizational behavior, or organization theory. Although most of the chapters contain some review of the subject at hand, it is never intended to be complete or comprehensive. Rather it is intended to remind the reader of the principal notions and vocabulary regarding that subject.

Finally, as with all perpetrators of books, I would like to note the support and assistance of several people. Professionally, Robert T. Golembiewski provided me with much help. His advice, encouragement, and efforts in behalf of this project are most gratefully acknowledged. Fremont E. Kast and James E. Rosenzweig were also instrumental in helping bring some partially formed ideas to fruition. The book's quality has also been greatly enhanced by the helpful reviews of Philip Birnbaum, Indiana University; Sandra Beldt, Georgia State University; Joel T. Champion, Air University, Department of the Air Force; Joseph Forest, Georgia State University; Theodore Herbert, University of Akron; Fremont E. Kast and James E. Rosenzweig, University of Washington; Jill Mellick, Golden Gate University; Cynthia Pavett, University of San Diego; John Seybolt, University of Utah; and Richard Steers, University of Oregon.

Additionally, my colleagues in the Management Department of Oregon State University have provided a large measure of stimulation and encouragement—especially Dennis R. Briscoe, Craig C. Lundberg, and J. S. Mendenhall. Discussions with them and with William G. Ouchi, together with their essays that are contained herein, contributed substantially. Oddly enough, all four people have moved to other universities, as noted in the Special

Acknowledgment section that follows. Whether their collaborating with me was instrumental in these moves is not known at this time. Special thanks are due Professor Barbara Karmel, Willamette University, who helped supervise the preparation of several cases in the text.

On a personal level, my parents, to whom this volume is dedicated, have helped me grow and mature in more ways than they know, and my gratitude is greater than they suspect. My family has also given me a great deal of support during this project. When people inquire, "You teach *how* many hours a week?", my wife informs them how a lot of the remaining hours get spent. And my children have been altogether understanding of the whole business; their presence contributed immeasurably.

To all these people, I say . . . thank you.

Patrick E. Connor
Corvallis, Oregon
November 1979

SPECIAL ACKNOWLEDGMENT

As noted in the preface, the purpose of the concluding statements in this book is to bring together a variety of ideas and information about each chapter's subject. Each concluding statement focuses on the design implications of that chapter's discussion—although it may not be *limited* to those implications.

Some of the concluding statements are written by people whose expertise is in that specific subject area—to ensure the best treatment possible. I would therefore like to take this opportunity to acknowledge—and especially thank—the following colleagues:

Professor J. S. Mendenhall, Western Michigan University. For reference purposes, his statement (Chapter 5) is entitled, "Technology and Organization Design."

Professor Dennis R. Briscoe, University of San Diego. For reference purposes, his statement (Chapter 6) is entitled, "Organization Design: The Human Factor."

Dean Craig C. Lundberg, State University of New York at Binghamton. For reference purposes, his statement (Chapter 7) is entitled, "Work as an Organization Design Variable."

Professor William G. Ouchi, University of California at Los Angeles. For reference purposes, his statement (Chapter 8) is entitled, "A Conceptual Framework for the Design of Organizational Control Mechanisms." Professor Ouchi's statement is an adaptation of a paper appearing in *Management Science*, volume 25 (1979).

A NOTE ABOUT REFERENCE MATERIALS

There is a wealth of material on organizations available in most college and university libraries: books, journals, bulletins, conference proceedings, and so forth. The student interested in the theory and design of organizations should not hesitate in consulting them.

Following are listed several journals commonly available. Some of them contain material that has been written primarily for researchers. Some are primarily for students and practitioners. The latter journals are indicated with an asterisk (*). Those and the journals marked with a dagger (†) should be considered "must" reading for the serious student.

MANAGEMENT JOURNALS

Academy of Management Journal
Academy of Management Review †
Business Horizons *
California Management Review *
Harvard Business Review *
Organizational Dynamics *

ORGANIZATIONAL PSYCHOLOGY

Journal of Applied Psychology †
Journal of Social Psychology
Organizational Behavior and Human Performance †

ORGANIZATIONAL SOCIOLOGY

American Journal of Sociology
American Sociological Review

OTHER JOURNALS

Administrative Science Quarterly †
Human Organization
Management Science
Organization Studies
Public Administration Review *

The above list, of course, is not meant to be exhaustive. But it does contain most of the journals that one encounters in studying organization theory and design. These journals will take the student far along the path toward understanding organizations.

SECTION ONE

Introduction

INTRODUCTION TO SECTION ONE

Designing organizations is a complicated undertaking. The intent of this introductory section is to examine some ideas—some assumptions, concepts, and relationships—that underlie that undertaking.

Section One is divided into two chapters. These chapters reflect the twin sets of ideas on which organization designing is based. Chapter 1, "Organization Theory," traces the development of organization and management theory as it has evolved over the past several decades. The chapter concludes by pointing out that despite some fashionable criticism, the open-systems view provides the most useful approach to understanding and designing organizations. In particular, open-systems thinking emphasizes the dynamics of resource flow and organization-environment relations. To be effective, designs must reflect the reality of these dynamics.

Chapter 2, "Designing Organizations," examines some themes and premises that underlie the designing function. Open-systems thinking is translated into organization-design concepts. The chapter looks at several factors that designs should encompass. We conclude our discussion by outlining the design model that guides this book. In short, this section identifies two sets of ideas: *organization theory* and *organization design.* It is these ideas that provide the foundation for the process of organizational designing.

1

Organization Theory

INTRODUCTORY REMARKS

Formal organizations are social instruments for accomplishing goals. Organization theory is the systematic study of those instruments and their operation. Although organizations have a long past, organization theory has a short history. Historians are able to describe organizations that existed in Sumer and Egypt over 6000 years ago. The systematic, comprehensive study of organizations, however, has its principal roots in the past century.

The purpose of this chapter is to bring us up to date on that study. More specifically, this chapter is aimed at developing some concepts—concepts that will then be useful for focusing on one of organizations' most important aspects—their design. As we mentioned in the preface, the format of this volume (and therefore this chapter) is text-reader. We open the chapter with these introductory remarks, which serve as a sort of preview. We then present two authors' statements about the study of organizations (the "Readings"), and close out the chapter with some concluding thoughts.

The Readings

By the term *organization* we mean a formal collection of people that has been created for the purpose of accomplishing collective goals on a relatively continuous basis. The collection is characterized by a relatively identifiable boundary, norms of behavior, primary groups, channels of communication, task-related activities, authority relationships, an incentive system, and so forth. The systematic study of organizations—organization theory—has developed rapidly. In this chapter's first selection, "The Short and Glorious History of Organizational Theory," Professor Charles Perrow traces this development. He shows thar its modern evolution began with classical administrative theory, which was the approach used by the "forces of darkness." Classical theory's prescriptive shortcomings, plus changing social, economic, and technical conditions, gave rise to the human relations school, whereby "forces of light" began to illuminate the conceptual and operational scene. The past two decades have witnessed various sociotechnical approaches, culminating today in the almost monopolistic dominance of general systems theory.

As Perrow notes, however, general systems theory is no cure-all, principally because it is difficult to translate into the day-to-day pragmatics of organizational management. Still, the general-systems approach does seem to provide fruitful opportunities for studying organizations. These opportunities were exploited by the late James D. Thompson in his work *Organizations in Action* (McGraw-Hill, 1967). This chapter contains the first of two selections from that important book. In "Strategies for Studying Organizations," Professor Thompson identifies uncertainty as the essential element underlying organizational behavior.

Organization theorists and managers who employ a closed-system perspective tend to ignore uncertainty as irrelevant. An organization that in fact confronts a fair amount of uncertainty, however, must deal with that uncertainty. To try to simply wish it away is foolish. In either situation, in what Thompson calls determinate or indeterminate conditions, the organization takes actions subject to the criteria of rationality. Thus managers, especially those who manage organizations operating under indeterminate (uncertain) conditions, attempt to *reduce* uncertainty, using various means to do so. And, says Thompson, it is this attempt that provides the underlying basis for all managerial action.

In short, Thompson shows that reducing uncertainty is a fundamental organizational imperative—one that provides a basis for understanding and explaining organizational action. Specifically it encourages us to pay systematic attention to various organizational properties. That is, if managers attempt to reduce or even completely forestall uncertainty, there must be some ways by which they can go about doing so. Put another way, they (managers) must manipulate certain organizational characteristics to best enable the enterprise to cope effectively with the uncertainty it faces.

Before we can plunge ahead and consider the ways organizational characteristics are manipulated—the alternative ways organizations are designed—we need to recognize that organizational variables, such as structure, decision patterns, control processes, and so forth, are highly interrelated. Thinking of the organization as an open system helps us maintain that recognition.

Conclusion

In summary, this chapter addresses three questions:

1. Where has organization theory come from and where is it now?
2. What are some fundamentals that underlie organizational/managerial action?
3. How do organizations deal with these fundamentals; that is, what organizational/managerial variables are critical for rational organizational designing?

THE SHORT AND GLORIOUS HISTORY OF ORGANIZATIONAL THEORY

CHARLES PERROW

From the beginning, the forces of light and the forces of darkness have polarized the field of organizational analysis, and the struggle has been protracted and inconclusive. The forces of darkness have been represented by the mechanical school of organizational theory—those who treat the organization as a machine. This school characterizes organizations in terms of such things as:

- Centralized authority
- Clear lines of authority
- Specialization and expertise
- Marked division of labor
- Rules and regulations
- Clear separation of staff and line

The forces of light, which by mid-twentieth century came to be characterized as the human relations school, emphasizes people rather than machines, accommodations rather than machinelike precision, and draws its inspiration from biological systems rather than engineering systems. It has emphasized such things as:

- Delegation of authority
- Employee autonomy
- Trust and openness
- Concerns with the "whole person"
- Interpersonal dynamics

THE RISE AND FALL OF SCIENTIFIC MANAGEMENT

The forces of darkness formulated their position first, starting in the early part of this century. They have been characterized as the scientific management or classical management school. This school started by parading simple-minded injunctions to plan ahead, keep records, write down policies, specialize, be decisive, and keep your span of control to about six people. These injunctions were needed as firms grew in size and complexity, since there were few models around beyond the railroads, the military, and the Catholic Church to guide organizations. And their injunctions worked. Executives began to delegate, reduce their span of control, keep records, and specialize. Planning ahead still is difficult, it seems, and the modern equivalent is Management by Objectives.

But many things intruded to make these simple-minded injunctions less relevant:

1. Labor became a more critical factor in the firm. As the technology increased in sophistication it took longer to train people, and more varied and specialized skills were needed. Thus, labor turnover cost more and recruitment became more selective. As a consequence, labor's power increased. Unions and strikes appeared. Management adjusted by beginning to speak of a cooperative system of capital, management, and labor. The machine model began to lose its relevancy.
2. The increasing complexity of markets, variability of products, increasing number of branch plants, and changes in technology all required more adaptive organization. The scientific management school was ill-equipped to deal with rapid change. It had presumed that once the proper structure was achieved the firm could run forever without much tampering. By the late 1930s, people began writing about adaptation and change in industry from an organizational point of view and had to abandon some of the principles of scientific management.
3. Political, social, and cultural changes meant new expectations regarding the proper way to treat people. The dark, satanic mills needed at the least a white-

Charles Perrow, "The Short and Glorious History of Organizational Theory," *Organizational Dynamics* (Summer 1973), pp. 2–15.

washing. Child labor and the brutality of supervision in many enterprises became no longer permissible. Even managers could not be expected to accept the authoritarian patterns of leadership that prevailed in the small firm run by the founding father.

4. As mergers and growth proceeded apace and the firm could no longer be viewed as the shadow of one man (the founding entrepreneur), a search for methods of selecting good leadership became a preoccupation. A good, clear, mechanical structure would no longer suffice. Instead, firms had to search for the qualities of leadership that could fill the large footsteps of the entrepreneur. They tacitly had to admit that something other than either "sound principles" or "dynamic leadership" was needed. The search for leadership traits implied that leaders were made, not just born, that the matter was complex, and that several skills were involved.

Enter Human Relations

From the beginning, individual voices were raised against the implications of the scientific management school. "Bureaucracy" had always been a dirty word, and the job design efforts of Frederick Taylor were even the subject of a congressional investigation. But no effective counterforce developed until 1938, when a business executive with academic talents named Chester Barnard proposed the first new theory of organizations: Organizations are cooperative systems, not the products of mechanical engineering. He stressed natural groups within the organization, upward communication, authority from below rather than from above, and leaders who functioned as a cohesive force. With the spectre of labor unrest and the Great Depression upon him, Barnard's emphasis on the cooperative nature of organizations was well-timed. The year following the publication of his *Functions of the Executive* (1938) saw the publication of F. J. Roethlisberger and William Dickson's *Management and the Worker,* reporting on the first large-scale empirical investigation of productivity and social relations. The research, most of it conducted in the Hawthorne plant of the Western Electric Company during a period in which the work force was reduced, highlighted the role of informal groups, work restriction norms, the value of decent, humane leadership, and the role of psychological manipulation of employees through the counseling system. World War II intervened, but after the war the human relations movement, building on the insights of Barnard and the Hawthorne studies, came into its own.

The first step was a search for the traits of good leadership. It went on furiously at university centers but at first failed to produce more than a list of Boy Scout maxims: A good leader was kind, courteous, loyal, courageous, etc. We suspected as much. However, the studies did turn up a distinction between "consideration," or employee-centered aspects of leadership, and job-centered, technical aspects labeled "initiating structure." Both were important, but the former received most of the attention and the latter went undeveloped. The former led directly to an examination of group processes, an investigation that has culminated in T-group programs and is moving forward still with encounter groups. Meanwhile, in England, the Tavistock Institute sensed the importance of the influence of the kind of task a group had to perform on the social relations within the group. The first important study, conducted among coal miners, showed that job simplification and specialization did not work under conditions of uncertainty and nonroutine tasks.

As this work flourished and spread, more adventurous theorists began to extend it beyond work groups to organizations as a whole. We now knew that there were a number of things that were bad for the morale and loyalty of groups—routine tasks, submission to authority, specialization of task, segregation of task sequence, ignorance of the goals of the firm, centralized decision making, and so on. If these were bad for groups, they were likely to be bad for groups of groups—i.e., for organizations. So people like Warren Bennis began talking about innovative, rapidly changing organizations that were made up of temporary leadership and role assignments, and democratic access to the goals of the firm. If rapidly changing technologies and unstable, turbulent environments were to characterize industry, then the structure of firms should be temporary and decentralized. The forces of light, of freedom, autonomy, change, humanity, creativity, and democracy were winning. Scientific management survived only in outdated text books. If the evangelizing of some of the human relations school theorists were excessive, and, if Likert's System 4, or MacGregor's Theory Y, or Blake's 9 × 9 evaded us, at least there was a rationale for the confusion, disorganization, scrambling, and stress: Systems should be temporary.

Bureaucracy's Comeback

Meanwhile, in another part of the management forest, the mechanistic school was gathering its forces and preparing to outflank the forces of light. First came the numbers men—the linear programmers, the budget experts, and the financial analysts—with their PERT systems and cost-benefit analyses. From another world, unburdened by most of the scientific management ideology and untouched by the human relations school, they began to parcel things out and give some meaning to those truisms, "plan ahead" and "keep records." Armed with emerging systems concepts, they carried the "mechanistic" analogy to its fullest—and it was very productive. Their work still goes on, largely untroubled by organizational theory; the theory, it seems clear, will have to adjust to them, rather than the other way around.

Then the words of Max Weber, first translated from the German in the 1940s—he wrote around 1910, incredibly—began to find their way into social science thought. At first, with his celebration of the efficiency of bureaucracy, he was received with only reluctant respect, and even with hostility. All writers were against bureaucracy. But it turned out, surprisingly, that managers were not. When asked, they acknowledge that they preferred clear lines of communication, clear specifications of authority and responsibility, and clear knowledge of whom they were responsible to. They were as wont to say "there ought to be a rule about this," as to say "there are too many rules around here," as wont to say "next week we've got to get organized," as to say "there is too much red tape." Gradually studies began to show that bureaucratic organizations could change faster than nonbureaucratic ones, and that morale could be higher where there was clear evidence of bureaucracy.

What was this thing, then? Weber had showed us, for example, that bureaucracy was the most effective way of ridding organizations of favoritism, arbitrary authority, discrimination, payola, and kickbacks, and, yes, even incompetence. His model stressed expertise, and the favorite or the boss's nephew or the guy who burned up resources to make his performance look good was *not* the one with expertise. Rules could be changed; they could be dropped in exceptional circumstances; job security promoted more innovation. The sins of bureaucracy began to look like the sins of failing to follow its principles.

Enter Power, Conflict, and Decisions

But another discipline began to intrude upon the confident work and increasingly elaborate models of the human relations theorists (largely social psychologists) and the uneasy toying with bureaucracy of the "structionalists" (largely sociologists). Both tended to study economic organizations. A few, like Philip Selznick, were noting conflict and differences in goals (perhaps because he was studying a public agency, the Tennessee Valley Authority), but most ignored conflict or treated it as a pathological manifestation of breakdowns in communication or the ego trips of unreconstructed managers.

But in the world of political parties, pressure groups, and legislative bodies, conflict was not only rampant, but to be expected—it was even functional. This was the domain of the political scientists. They kept talking about power, making it a legitimate concern for analysis. There was an open acknowledgment of "manipulation." These were political scientists who were "behaviorally" inclined—studying and recording behavior rather than constitutions and formal systems of government—and they came to a much more complex view of organized activity. It spilled over into the area of economic organizations, with the help of some economists like R. A. Gordon and some sociologists who were studying conflicting goals of treatment and custody in prisons and mental hospitals.

The presence of legitimately conflicting goals and techniques of preserving and using power did not, of course, sit well with a cooperative systems view of organizations. But it also puzzled the bureaucratic school (and what was left of the old scientific management school), for the impressive Weberian principles were designed to settle questions of power through organizational design and to keep conflict out through reliance on rational-legal authority and systems of careers, expertise, and hierarchy. But power was being overtly contested and exercised in covert ways, and conflict was bursting out all over, and even being creative.

Gradually, in the second half of the 1950s and in the next decade, the political-science view infiltrated both schools. Conflict could be healthy, even in a cooperative system, said the human relationists; it was the mode of resolution that counted, rather than prevention. Power became reconceptualized as "influence," and the distribution was less important, said Arnold Tannenbaum, than the total amount. For the bureaucratic school—never a clearly defined group of people, and largely without any clear ideology—it was easier to just absorb the new data and theories as something else to be thrown into the pot. That is to say, they floundered, writing books that went from topic to topic, without a clear view of organizations, or better yet, producing "readers" and leaving students to sort it all out.

Buried in the political-science viewpoint was a sleeper that only gradually began to undermine the dominant views. This was the idea, largely found in the work of Herbert Simon and James March, that because man was so limited—in intelligence, reasoning powers, information at his disposal, time available, and means of ordering his preferences clearly—he generally seized on the first acceptable alternative when deciding, rather than looking for the best; that he rarely changed things unless they really got bad, and even then he continued to try what had worked before; that he limited his search for solutions to well-worn paths and traditional sources of information and established ideas; that he was wont to remain preoccupied with routine, thus preventing innovation. They called these characteristics "cognitive limits on rationality" and spoke of "satisficing" rather than maximizing or optimizing. It is now called the "decision making" school, and is concerned with the basic question of how people make decisions.

This view had some rather unusual implications. It suggested that if managers were so limited, then they could be easily controlled. What was necessary was not to give direct orders (on the assumption that subordinates were idiots without expertise) or to leave them to their own devices (on the assumption that they were supermen who would somehow know what was best for the organization, how to coordinate with all the other supermen, how to anticipate market changes, etc.). It was necessary to control only the *premises* of their decisions. Left to themselves, with those premises set, they could be predicted to rely on precedent, keep things stable and smooth, and respond to signals that reinforce the behavior desired of them.

To control the premises of decision making, March and Simon outline a variety of devices, all of which are familiar to you, but some of which you may not have seen before in quite this light. For example, organizations develop vocabularies, and this means that certain kinds of information are highlighted, and others are screened out—just as Eskimos (and skiers) distinguish many varieties of snow, while Londoners see only one. This is a form of attention-directing. Another is the reward system. Change the bonus for salesmen and you can shift them from volume selling to steady-account selling, or to selling quality products or new products. If you want to channel good people into a different function (because, for example, sales should no longer be the critical functions as the market changes, but engineering applications should), you may have to promote mediocre people in the unrewarded function in order to signal to the good people in the rewarded one that the game has changed. You cannot expect most people to make such decisions on their own because of the cognitive limits on their rationality, nor will you succeed by giving direct orders, because you yourself probably do not know whom to order where. You presume that once the signals are clear and the new sets of alternatives are manifest, they have enough ability to make the decision but you have had to change the premises for their decisions about their career lines.

It would take too long to go through the dozen or so devices, covering a range of decision areas (March and Simon are not that clear or systematic about them, themselves, so I have summarized them in my own book), but I think the message is clear.

It was becoming clear to the human relations school, and to the bureaucratic school. The human relationists had begun to speak of changing stimuli rather than changing personality. They had begun to see that the rewards that can change behavior can well be prestige, money, comfort, etc., rather than trust, openness, self-insight, and so on. The alternative to supportive relations need not be punishment, since behavior can best be changed by rewarding approved behavior rather than by punishing disapproved behavior. They were finding that although leadership may be centralized, it can function best through indirect and unobtrusive means such as changing the premises on which decisions are made, thus giving the impression that the subordinate is actually making a decision when he has only been switched to a different set of alternatives. The implications of this work were also beginning to filter into the human relations school, through an emphasis on behavioral psychology (the modern version of the much maligned stimulus-response school) that was supplanting personality theory (Freudian in its roots, and drawing heavily, in the human relations school, on Maslow).

For the bureaucratic school, this new line of thought reduced the heavy weight placed upon the bony structure of bureaucracy by highlighting the muscle and flesh that make these bones move. A single chain of command, precise division of labor, and clear lines of communication are simply not enough in themselves. Control can be achieved by using alternative communication channels, depending on the situation; by increasing or decreasing the static or "noise" in the system; by creating organizational myths and organizational vocabularies that allow only selective bits of information to enter the system; and through monitoring performance through indirect means rather than direct surveillance. Weber was all right for a starter, but organizations had changed vastly, and the leaders needed many more means of control and more subtle means of manipulation than they did at the turn of the century.

The Technological Qualification

By now the forces of darkness and forces of light had moved respectively from midnight and noon to about 4 A.M. and 8 P.M. But any convergence or resolution would have to be on yet new terms, for soon after the political-science tradition had begun to infiltrate the established schools, another blow struck both of the major positions. Working quite independently of the Tavistock Group, with its emphasis on sociotechnical systems, and before the work of Burns and Stalker on mechanistic and organic firms, Joan Woodward was trying to see whether the classical scientific principles of organization made any sense in her survey of a hundred firms in South Essex. She tripped and stumbled over a piece of gold in the process. She picked up the gold, labeled it "technology," and made sense out of her otherwise hopeless data. Job-shop firms, mass-production firms, and continuous-process firms all had quite different structures because the type of tasks, or the "technology," was different. Somewhat later, researchers in America were coming to very similar conclusions based on studies of hospitals, juvenile correctional institutions, and industrial firms. Bureaucracy appeared to be the best form of organization for routine operations; temporary work groups, decentralization, and emphasis on interpersonal processes appeared to work best for nonroutine operations. A raft of studies appeared and are still appearing, all trying to show how the nature of the task affects the structure of the organization.

This severely complicated things for the human relations school, since it suggested that openness and trust, while good things in themselves, did not have much impact, or perhaps were not even possible in some kinds of work situations. The prescriptions that were being handed out would have to be drastically qualified. What might work for nonroutine, high-status, interesting, and challenging jobs performed by highly educated people might not be relevant or even beneficial for the vast majority of jobs and people.

It also forced the upholders of the revised bureaucratic theory to qualify their recommendations, since research and development units should obviously be run differently from mass-production units, and the difference between both of these and highly programmed and highly sophisticated continuous-process firms was obscure in terms of bureaucratic theory. But the bureaucratic school perhaps came out on top, because the forces of evil—authority, structure, division of labor, etc.—no longer looked evil, even if they were not applicable to a minority of industrial units.

The emphasis on technology raised other questions, however. A can company might be quite routine, and a plastics division nonroutine, but there were both routine and nonroutine units within each. How should they be integrated if the prescription were followed that, say, production should be bureaucratized and R&D not? James Thompson began spelling out different forms of interdependence among units in organizations, and Paul Lawrence and Jay Lorsch looked closely at the nature of integrating mechanisms. Lawrence and Lorsch found that firms performed best when the differences between units were *maximized* (in contrast to both the human relations and the bureaucratic school), as long as the integrating mechanisms stood halfway between the two—being neither strongly bureaucratic nor nonroutine. They also noted that attempts at participative management in routine situations were counterproductive, that the environments of some kinds of organizations were far from turbulent and customers did not want innovations and changes, that cost reduction, price and efficiency were trivial considerations in some firms, and so on. The technical insight was demolishing our comfortable truths right and left. They were also being questioned from another quarter.

Enter Goals, Environments, and Systems

The final seam was being mined by the sociologists while all this went on. This was the concern with organizational goals and the environment. Borrowing from the political scientists to some extent, but pushing ahead on their own, this "institutional school" came to see that goals were not fixed; conflicting goals could be pursued simultaneously, if there were enough slack resources, or sequentially (growth for the next four years, then cost-cutting and profit-taking for the next four); that goals were up for grabs in organizations, and units fought over them. Goals were, of course, not what they seemed to be, the important ones were quite unofficial; history played a big role; and assuming profit as the preeminent goal explained almost nothing about a firm's behavior.

They also did case studies that linked the organization to the web of influence of the environment; that showed how unique organizations were in many respects (so that, once again, there was no one best way to do things for all organizations); how organizations were embedded in their own history, making change difficult. Most striking of all, perhaps, the case studies revealed that the stated goals usually were not the real ones; the official leaders usually were not the real ones; the official leaders usually were not the powerful ones; claims of effectiveness and efficiency were deceptive or even untrue; the public interest was not being served; political influences were pervasive; favoritism, discrimination, and sheer corruption were commonplace. The accumulation of these studies presented quite a pill for either the forces of light or darkness to swallow, since it was hard to see how training sessions or interpersonal skills were relevant to these problems, and it was also clear that the vaunted efficiency of bureaucracy was hardly in evidence. What could they make of this wad of case studies?

We are still sorting it out. In one sense, the Weberian model is upheld because organizations are not, *by nature,* cooperative systems; top managers must exercise a great deal of effort to control them. But if organizations are tools in the hands of leaders, they may be very recalcitrant ones. Like the broom in the story of the sorcerer's apprentice, they occasionally get out of hand. If conflicting goals, bargaining, and unofficial leadership exists, where is the structure of Weberian bones and Simonian muscle? To what extent are organizations tools, and to what extent are they products of the varied interests and group strivings of their members? Does it vary by organization, in terms of some typological alchemy we have not discovered? We don't know. But at any rate, the bureaucratic model suffers again; it simply has not reckoned on the role of the environment. There are enormous sources of variations that the neat, though by now quite complex, neo-Weberian model could not account for.

The human relations model has also been badly shaken by the findings of the institutional school, for it was wont to assume that goals were given and unproblematical, and that anything that promoted harmony and efficiency for an organization also was good for society. Human relationists assumed that the problems created by organizations were largely limited to the psychological consequences of poor interpersonal relations within them, rather than their impact on the environment. Could the organization really promote the psychological health of its members when by necessity it had to define psychological health in terms of the goals of the organization itself? The neo-Weberian model at least called manipulation "manipulation" and was skeptical of claims about autonomy and self-realization.

But on one thing all the varied schools of organizational analysis now seemed to be agreed: organizations are systems—indeed, they are open systems. As the growth of the field has forced ever more variables into our consciousness, flat claims of predictive power are beginning to decrease and research has become bewilderingly complex. Even consulting groups need more than one or two tools in their kit bag as the software multiplies.

The systems view is intuitively simple. Everything is related to everything else, though in uneven degrees of tension and reciprocity. Every unit, organization, department, or work group takes in resources, transforms them, and sends them out, and thus interacts with the larger system. The psychological, sociological, and cultural aspects of units interact. The systems view was explicit in the institutional work, since they tried to study whole organizations; it became explicit in the human relations school, because they were so concerned with the interactions of people. The political science and technology viewpoints also had to come to this realization, since they deal with parts affecting each other (sales affecting production; technology affecting structure).

But as intuitively simple as it is, the systems view has been difficult to put into practical use. We still find ourselves ignoring the tenets of the open-systems view, possibly because of the cognitive limits on our rationality. General systems theory itself had not lived up to its heady predictions; it remains rather nebulous. But at least there is a model for calling us to account and for stretching our minds, our research tools, and our troubled nostrums.

Some Conclusions

Where does all this leave us? We might summarize the prescriptions and proscriptions for management very roughly as follows:

1. A great deal of the "variance" in a firm's behavior depends on the environment. We have become more realistic about the limited range of change that can be induced through internal efforts. The goals of organizations, including those of profit and efficiency, vary greatly among industries and vary systematically by industries. This suggests that the impact of better management by itself will be limited, since so much will depend on market forces, competition, legislation, nature of the work force, available technologies and innovations, and so on. Another source of variation is, obviously, the history of the firm and its industry and its traditions.

2. A fair amount of variation in both firms and industries is due to the type of work done in the organization—the technology. We are now fairly confident in recommending that if work is predictable and routine, the necessary arrangement for getting the work done can be highly structured, and one can use a good deal of bureaucratic theory in accomplishing this. If it is not predictable, if it is nonroutine and there is a good deal of uncertainty as to how to do a job, then one had better utilize the theories that emphasize autonomy, temporary groups, multiple lines of authority and communications, and so on. We also know that this distinction is important when organizing different parts of an organization.

We are also getting a grasp on the question of what is the most critical function in different types of organizations. For some organizations, it is production; for others, marketing; for still others, development. Furthermore, firms go through phases whereby the initial development of a market or a product or manufacturing process or accounting scheme may require a nonbureaucratic structure, but once it comes on stream, the structure should change to reflect the changed character of the work.

3. In keeping with this, management should be advised that the attempt to produce change in an organization through managerial grids, sensitivity training, and even job enrichment and job enlargement is likely to be fairly ineffective for all but a few organizations. The critical reviews of research in all these fields show that there is no scientific evidence to support the claims of the proponents of these various methods; that research has told us a great deal about social psychology, but little about how to apply the highly complex findings to actual situations. The key word is *selectivity:* We have no broad-spectrum antibiotics for interpersonal rela-

tions. Of course, managers should be sensitive, decent, kind, courteous, and courageous, but we have known that for some time now, and beyond a minimal threshold level, the payoff is hard to measure. The various attempts to make work and interpersonal relations more humane and stimulating should be applauded, but we should not confuse this with solving problems of structure, or as the equivalent of decentralization or participatory democracy.

4. The burning cry in all organizations is for "good leadership," but we have learned that beyond a threshold level of adequacy it is extremely difficult to know what good leadership is. The hundreds of scientific studies of this phenomenon come to one general conclusion: Leadership is highly variable or "contingent" upon a large variety of important variables such as nature of task, size of the group, length of time the group has existed, type of personnel within the group and their relationships with each other, and amount of pressure the group is under. It does not seem likely that we'll be able to devise a way to select the best leader for a particular situation. Even if we could, that situation would probably change in a short time and thus would require a somewhat different type of leader.

Furthermore, we are beginning to realize that leadership involves more than smoothing the paths of human interaction. What has rarely been studied in this area is the wisdom or even the technical adequacy of a leader's decision. A leader does more than lead people; he also makes decisions about the allocation of resources, type of technology to be used, the nature of the market, and so on. This aspect of leadership remains very obscure, but it is obviously crucial.

5. If we cannot solve our problems through good human relations or through good leadership, what are we then left with? The literature suggests that changing the structures of organizations might be the most effective and certainly the quickest and cheapest method. However, we are now sophisticated enough to know that changing the formal structure by itself is not likely to produce the desired changes. In addition, one must be aware of a large range of subtle, unobtrusive, and even covert processes and change devices that exist. If inspection procedures are not working, we are now unlikely to rush in with sensitivity training, nor would we send down authoritative communications telling people to do a better job. We are more likely to find out where the authority really lies, whether the degree of specialization is adequate, what the rules and regulations are, and so on, but even this very likely will not be enough.

According to the neo-Weberian bureaucratic model (it has been influenced by work on decision making and behavioral psychology), we should find out how to manipulate the reward structure, change the premises of the decision makers through finer controls on the information received and the expectations generated, search for interdepartmental conflicts that prevent better inspection procedures from being followed, and after manipulating these variables, sit back and wait for two or three months for them to take hold. This is complicated and hardly as dramatic as many of the solutions currently being peddled, but I think the weight of organizational theory is in its favor.

We have probably learned more, over several decades of research and theory, about the things that do *not* work (even though some of them obviously *should* have worked) than we have about things that do work. On balance, this is an important gain and should not discourage us. As you know, organizations are extremely complicated. To have as much knowledge as we do have in a fledgling discipline that has had to borrow from the diverse tools and concepts of psychology, sociology, economics, engineering, biology, history, and even anthropology is not really so bad.

STRATEGIES FOR STUDYING ORGANIZATIONS

JAMES D. THOMPSON

Complex organizations—manufacturing firms, hospitals, schools, armies, community agencies—are ubiquitous in modern societies, but our understanding of them is limited and segmented.

The fact that impressive and sometimes frightening consequences flow from organizations suggests that some individuals have had considerable insight into these social instruments. But insight and private experiences may generate private understandings without producing a public body of knowledge adequate for the preparation of a next generation of administrators, for designing new styles of organizations for new purposes, for controlling organizations, or for appreciation of distinctive aspects of modern societies.

What we know or think we know about complex organizations is housed in a variety of fields or disciplines, and communication among them more nearly resembles a trickle than a torrent (Dill, 1964; March, 1965). Although each of the several schools has its unique terminology and special heroes, Gouldner (1959) was able to discern two fundamental models underlying most of the literature. He labeled these the "rational" and "natural-system" models of organizations, and these labels are indeed descriptive of the results.

To Gouldner's important distinction we wish to add the notion that the rational model results from a *closed-system strategy* for studying organizations, and that the natural-system model flows from an *open-system strategy*.

CLOSED-SYSTEM STRATEGY

The Search for Certainty

If we wish to predict accurately the state a system will be in presently, it helps immensely to be dealing with a *determinate system*. As Ashby observes (1956), fixing the present circumstances of a determinate system will determine the state it moves to next, and since such a system cannot go to two states at once, the transformation will be unique.

Fixing the present circumstances requires, of course, that the variables and relationships involved be few enough for us to comprehend and that we have control over or can reliably predict all of the variables and relations. In other words, it requires that the system be closed or, if closure is not complete, that the outside forces acting on it be predictable.

Now if we have responsibility for the future states or performance of some system, we are likely to opt for a closed system. Bartlett's (1958) research on mental processes, comparing "adventurous thinking" with "thinking in closed systems," suggests that there are strong human tendencies to reduce various forms of knowledge to the closed-system variety, to rid them of all ultimate uncertainty. If such tendencies appear in puzzle-solving as well as in everyday situations, we would especially expect them to be emphasized when responsibility and high stakes are added.

Since much of the literature about organizations has been generated as a by-product of the search for improved efficiency or performance, it is not surprising that it employs closed-system assumptions—employs the rational model—about organizations. Whether we consider *scientific management* (Taylor, 1911), *administrative management* (Gulick and Urwick, 1937), or *bureaucracy* (Weber, 1947), the ingredients of the organization are deliberately chosen for their necessary contribution to a goal, and the structures established are those deliberately intended to attain highest efficiency.

Three Schools in Caricature

Scientific management, focused primarily on manufacturing or similar production activities, clearly

James D. Thompson, *Organizations in Action* (New York: McGraw-Hill Book Company, 1967), pp. 3–13.

employs economic efficiency as its ultimate criterion, and seeks to maximize efficiency by planning procedures according to a technical logic, setting standards, and exercising controls to ensure conformity with standards and thereby with the technical logic. Scientific management achieves conceptual closure of the organization by assuming that goals are known, tasks are repetitive, output of the production process somehow disappears, and resources in uniform qualities are available.

Administrative-management literature focuses on structural relationships among production, personnel, supply, and other service units of the organization; and again employs as the ultimate criterion economic efficiency. Here efficiency is maximized by specializing tasks and grouping them into departments, fixing responsibility according to such principles as span of control or delegation, and controlling action to plans. Administrative management achieves closure by assuming that ultimately a master plan is known, against which specialization, departmentalization, and control are determined. Administrative management also assumes that production tasks are known, that output disappears, and that resources are automatically available to the organization.

Bureaucracy also follows the pattern noted above, focusing on staffing and structure as means of handling clients and disposing of cases. Again the ultimate criterion is efficiency, and this time it is maximized by defining offices according to jurisdiction and place in a hierarchy, appointing experts to offices, establishing rules for categories of activity, categorizing cases or clients, and then motivating proper performance of expert officials by providing salaries and patterns for career advancement. Bureaucratic theory also employs the closed system of logic. Weber saw three holes through which empirical reality might penetrate the logic, but in outlining his "pure type" he quickly plugged these holes. Policymakers, somewhere above the bureaucracy, could alter the goals, but the implications of this are set aside. Human components—the expert officeholders—might be more complicated, but bureaucratic theory handles this by divorcing the individual's private life from his life as an officeholder through the use of rules, salary, and career. Finally, bureaucratic theory takes note of the outsiders—clientele—but nullifies their effects by depersonalizing and categorizing clients.

It seems clear that the rational-model approach uses a closed-system strategy. It also seems clear that the developers of the several schools using the rational model have been primarily students of performance or efficiency, and only incidentally students of organizations. Having focused on control of the organization as a target, each employs a closed system of logic and conceptually closes the organization to coincide with that type of logic, for this elimination of uncertainty is the way to achieve determinateness. The rational model of an organization results in everything being functional—making a positive, indeed an optimum, contribution to the overall result. All resources are appropriate resources, and their allocation fits a master plan. All action is appropriate action, and its outcomes are predictable.

It is no accident that much of the literature on the management or administration of complex organizations centers on the concepts of *planning* or *controlling*. Nor is it any accident that such views are dismissed by those using the open-system strategy.

OPEN-SYSTEM STRATEGY

The Expectation of Uncertainty

If, instead of assuming closure, we assume that a system contains more variables than we can comprehend at one time, or that some of the variables are subject to influences we cannot control or predict, we must resort to a different sort of logic. We can, if we wish, assume that the system is determinate by nature, but that it is our incomplete understanding which forces us to expect surprise or the intrusion of uncertainty. In this case we can employ a natural-system model.

Approached as a natural system, the complex organization is a set of interdependent parts which together make up a whole because each contributes something and receives something from the whole, which in turn is interdependent with some larger environment. Survival of the system is taken to be the goal, and the parts and their relationships presumably are determined through evolutionary processes. Dysfunctions are conceivable, but it is assumed that an offending part will adjust to produce a net positive contribution or be disengaged, or else the system will degenerate.

Central to the natural-system approach is the concept of homeostasis, or self-stabilization, which spontaneously, or naturally, governs the necessary relationships among parts and activities and thereby keeps the system viable in the face of disturbances stemming from the environment.

Two Examples in Caricature

Study of the *informal organization* constitutes one example of research in complex organizations using the natural-system approach. Here attention is focused on variables which are not included in any of the rational models—sentiments, cliques, social controls via informal norms, status and status striving, and so on. It is clear that students of informal organization regard these variables not as random deviations or error, but as patterned, adaptive responses of human beings in problematic situations (Roethlisberger and Dickson, 1939). In this view the informal organization is a spontaneous and functional development, indeed a necessity, in complex organizations, permitting the system to adapt and survive.

A second version of the natural-system approach is more global but less crystallized under a label. This school views the organization as a unit in interaction with its environment, and its view was perhaps most forcefully expressed by Chester Barnard (1938) and by the empirical studies of Selznick (1949) and Clark (1956). This stream of work leads to the conclusion that organizations are not autonomous entities; instead, the best laid plans of managers have unintended consequences and are conditioned or upset by other social units—other complex organizations or publics—on whom the organization is dependent.

Again it is clear that in contrast to the rational-model approach, this research area focuses on variables not subject to complete control by the organization and hence not contained within a closed system of logic. It is also clear that students regard interdependence of organization and environment as inevitable or natural, and as adaptive or functional.

CHOICE OR COMPROMISE?

The literature about organizations, or at least much of it, seems to fall into one of the two categories, each of which at best tends to ignore the other and at worse denies the relevance of the other. The logics associated with each appear to be incompatible, for one avoids uncertainty to achieve determinateness, while the other assumes uncertainty and indeterminateness. Yet the phenomena treated by each approach, as distinct from the explanations of each, cannot be denied.

Viewed in the large, complex organizations are often effective instruments for achievement, and that achievement flows from planned, controlled action. In every sphere—educational, medical, industrial, commercial, or governmental—the quality or costs of goods or services may be challenged and questions may be raised about the equity of distribution within the society of the fruits of complex organizations. Still millions live each day on the assumption that a reasonable degree of purposeful, effective action will be forthcoming from the many complex organizations on which they depend. Planned action, not random behavior, supports our daily lives. Specialized, controlled, patterned action surrounds us.

There can be no question but that the rational model of organizations directs our attention to important phenomena—to important "truth" in the sense that complex organizations viewed in the large exhibit some of the patterns and results to which the rational model attends, but which the natural-system model tends to ignore. But it is equally evident that phenomena associated with the natural-system approach also exist in complex organizations. There is little room to doubt the universal emergence of the informal organization. The daily news about labor-management negotiations, interagency jurisdictional squabbles, collusive agreements, favoritism, breaches of contract, and so on, are impressive evidence that complex organizations are influenced in significant ways by elements of their environments, a phenomenon addressed by the natural-system approach but avoided by the rational. Yet most versions of the natural-system approach treat organizational purposes and achievements as peripheral matters.

It appears that each approach leads to some truth, but neither alone affords an adequate understanding of complex organizations. Gouldner calls for a synthesis of the two models, but does not provide the synthetic model.

Meanwhile, a serious and sustained elaboration of Barnard's work (Simon, 1957a; March and Simon, 1958; Cyert and March, 1963) has produced a newer tradition which evades the closed- versus open-system dilemma.

A NEWER TRADITION

What emerges from the Simon-March-Cyert stream of study is the organization as a problem-facing and problem-solving phenomenon. The focus is on organizational processes related to choice of courses of action in an environment which does not fully disclose the alternatives available or the consequences of those alternatives. In this view, the organization has limited capacity to gather and process information or to predict consequences of alternatives. To deal with situations of such great complexity, the organization must develop processes for *searching* and *learning,* as well as for *deciding*. The complexity, if fully faced, would overwhelm the organization, hence it must set limits to its definitions of situations; it must make decisions in *bounded rationality* (Simon, 1957b). This requirement involves replacing the maximum-efficiency criterion with one of satisfactory accomplishment, decision making now involving *satisficing* rather than *maximizing* (Simon, 1957b).

These are highly significant notions, and it will become apparent that this book seeks to extend this "newer tradition." The assumptions it makes are consistent with the open-system strategy, for it holds that the processes going on within the organization are significantly affected by the complexity of the organization's environment. But this tradition also touches on matters important in the closed-system strategy: performance and deliberate decisions.

But despite what seem to be obvious advantages, the Simon-March-Cyert stream of work has not entirely replaced the more extreme strategies, and we need to ask why so many intelligent men and women in a position to make the same observations we have been making should continue to espouse patently incomplete views of complex organizations.

The Cutting Edge of Uncertainty

Part of the answer to that question undoubtedly lies in the fact that supporters of each extreme strategy have had different purposes in mind, with open-system strategists attempting to understand organizations per se, and closed-system strategists interested in organizations mainly as vehicles for rational achievements. Yet this answer does not seem completely satisfactory, for these students could not have been entirely unaware of the challenges to their assumptions and beliefs.

We can suggest now that rather than reflecting weakness in those who use them, the two strategies reflect something fundamental about the cultures surrounding complex organizations—the fact that our culture does not contain concepts for simultaneously thinking about rationality and indeterminateness. These appear to be incompatible concepts, and we have no ready way of thinking about something as half-closed, half-rational. One alternative, then, is the closed-system approach of ignoring uncertainty to see rationality; another is to ignore rational action in order to see spontaneous processes. The newer tradition with its focus on organizational coping with uncertainty is indeed a major advance. It is notable that the treatment by Crozier (1964) starts from the bureaucratic position but focuses on coping with uncertainty as its major topic.

Yet in directing our attention to processes for meeting uncertainty, Simon, March, and Cyert may lead us to overlook the useful knowledge amassed by the older approaches. If the phenomena of rational models are indeed observable, we may want to incorporate some elements of those models; and if natural-system phenomena occur, we should also benefit from the relevant theories. For our purposes, then, *we will conceive of complex organizations as open systems, hence indeterminate and faced with uncertainty, but at the same time as subject to criteria of rationality and hence needing determinateness and certainty.*

THE LOCATION OF PROBLEMS

As a starting point, we will suggest that the phenomena associated with open- and closed-system strategies are not randomly distributed through complex organizations, but instead tend to be specialized by location. To introduce this notion we will start with Parsons' (1960) suggestion that organizations exhibit three distinct levels of responsibility and control—*technical, managerial*, and *institutional*.

In this view, every formal organization contains a suborganization whose "problems" are focused around effective performance of the technical function—the conduct of classes by teachers, the processing of income tax returns and the handling of recalcitrants by the bureau, the processing of material and supervision of these operations in the case of physical production. The primary exigencies to which the technical suborganization is oriented are those imposed by the nature of the technical task, such as the materials which must be processed and the kinds of cooperation of different people required to get the job done effectively.

The second level, the managerial, *services* the technical suborganization by 1. mediating between the technical suborganization and those who use its products—the customers, pupils, and so on—and 2. procuring the resources necessary for carrying out the technical functions. The managerial level *controls,* or administers, the technical suborganization (although Parsons notes that its control is not unilateral) by deciding such matters as the broad technical task which is to be performed, the scale of operations, employment and purchasing policy, and so on.

Finally, in the Parsons formulation, the organization which consists of both technical and managerial suborganizations is also part of a wider social system which is the source of the "meaning," legitimation, or higher-level support which makes the implementation of the organization's goals possible. In terms of "formal" controls, an organization may be relatively independent; but in terms of the meaning of the functions performed by the organization and hence of its "rights" to command resources and to subject its customers to discipline, it is never wholly independent. This overall articulation of the organization and the institutional structure and agencies of the community is the function of the third, or institutional, level of the organization.

Parsons' distinction of the three levels becomes more significant when he points out that at each of the two points of articulation between them there is a *qualitative* break in the simple continuity of "line" authority because the functions at each level are qualitatively different. Those at the second level are not simply lower-order spellings-out of the top-level functions. Moreover, the articulation of levels and of functions rests on a two-way interaction, with each side, by withholding its important contribution, in a position to interfere with the functioning of the other and of the larger organization.

If we now reintroduce the conception of the complex organization as an open system subject to criteria of rationality, we are in a position to speculate about some dynamic properties of organizations. As we suggested, the logical model for achieving complete technical rationality uses a closed system of logic—closed by the elimination of uncertainty. In practice, it would seem, the more variables involved, the greater the likelihood of uncertainty, and it would therefore be advantageous for an organization subject to criteria of rationality to remove as much uncertainty as possible from its *technical core* by reducing the number of variables operating on it. Hence if both resource-acquisition and output-disposal problems—which are in part controlled by environmental elements and hence to a degree uncertain or problematic—can be removed from the technical core, the logic can be brought closer to closure, and the rationality, increased.

Uncertainty would appear to be greatest, at least potentially, at the other extreme, the institutional level. Here the organization deals largely with elements of the environment over which it has no formal authority or control. Instead, it is subjected to generalized norms, ranging from formally codified law to informal standards of good practice, to public authority, or to elements expressing the public interest.

At this extreme the closed system of logic is clearly inappropriate. The organization is open to influence by the environment (and vice versa) which can change independently of the actions of the organization. Here an open system of logic, permitting the intrusion of variables penetrating the organization from outside, and facing up to uncertainty, seems indispensable.

If the closed-system aspects of organizations are seen most clearly at the technical level, and the open-system qualities appear most vividly at the institutional level, it would suggest that a significant function of the managerial level is to mediate between the two extremes and the emphases they exhibit. If the organization must approach certainty at the technical level to satisfy its rationality criteria, but must remain flexible and adaptive to satisfy environmental requirements, we might expect the managerial level to mediate between them, ironing out some irregularities stemming from external sources, but also pressing the technical core for modifications as conditions alter. One exploration of this notion was offered in Thompson (1964).

Possible Sources of Variation

Following Parsons' reasoning leads to the expectation that differences in technical functions, or *technologies,* cause significant differences among organizations, and since the three levels are interdependent, differences in technical functions should also make for differences at managerial and institutional levels of the organization. Similarly, differences in the institutional structures in which organizations are imbedded should make for significant variations among organizations at all three levels.

Relating this back to the Simon-March-Cyert focus on organizational processes of searching, learning, and deciding, we can also suggest that while these adaptive processes may be generic, the ways in which they proceed may well vary with differences in technologies or in environments.

RECAPITULATION

Most of our beliefs about complex organizations follow from one or the other of two distinct strategies. The closed-system strategy seeks certainty by incorporating only those variables positively associated with goal achievement and subjecting them to a monolithic control network. The open-system strategy shifts attention from goal achievement to survival, and incorporates uncertainty by recognizing organizational interdependence with environment. A newer tradition enables us to conceive of the organization as an open system, indeterminate and faced with uncertainty, but subject to criteria of rationality and hence needing certainty.

With this conception the central problem for complex organizations is one of coping with uncertainty. As a point of departure, we suggest that organizations cope with uncertainty by creating certain parts specifically to deal with it, specializing other parts in operating under conditions of certainty or near certainty. In this case, articulation of these specialized parts becomes significant.

We also suggest that technologies and environments are major sources of uncertainty for organizations, and that differences in those dimensions will result in differences in organizations.

CONCLUDING STATEMENT

Well, what do we know about organization theory? Put another way, what ideas, concepts, models, theories, or whatever should we use to guide our thinking about organizational design? Be assured: all of us who study, manage, or otherwise deal with organizations do in fact use some model. The trick is to use one that works. Consider this analogy: the vast majority of us use a basic stimulus-response (S-R) model to explain, predict, and affect people's behavior. That is, most of us view people as doing those things for which they are positively rewarded. Now there is a wealth of evidence indicating that such a model is too simplistic. Nonetheless, most of us behave as if that model is correct. It is difficult to find the manager, parent, or teacher who does not use it. In short, most of us assume that people will behave in a way that will bring them some sort of need satisfaction.

Of course, not all people use an S-R model in dealing with others. Still, most people do use *some* conception, some "implicit personality theory" (Bonner, 1968). Thus, if a person, P, assumes another, O, is essentially devious and opposed to P's best interests, P's behavior toward O will reflect that assumption. Observers of and participants in organization and administration are no different. So people who study, work in, and design—*especially* design—organizations have some guiding conceptions of the organization. These conceptions tend to be rooted in two sets of assumptions. The first set is about the nature of the people who comprise an organization's membership. The second set is about the nature of the organization itself.

Since this chapter has examined different approaches taken by organization theorists over the past several decades, let us consider the two sets of assumptions that characterized those approaches.

ASSUMPTIONS ABOUT WORKERS

Earlier, Perrow described various approaches that have been important in the evolution of organization theory. Each approach has been based on certain assumptions about the nature of that social entity called *worker*. Let us consider them in a roughly chronological order.[1]

Classical Theory

The classicists—Weber (1958), Taylor (1911), Fayol (1949), Mooney and Reiley (1931), Gulick and Urwick (1937), to name the significant ones—held several identifiable assumptions about the human nature of workers. First, rights of property were considered most important, taking precedence over civil rights, for example. This assumption was reflected in the relationship between employer and employee. The view was that the employer owned real property, whereas employees owned their labor. Upon going to work for an organization, employees sold their labor for wages. The employer now owned the labor and, as owner, could dispose of it in any way seen fit.

1. Although we prefer labels slightly different from those used by Perrow, the flow and thrust of our analyses are the same.

Second, the classicists held what McGregor (1960) came to label a "Theory X" set of assumptions about people as workers:

- The worker dislikes work and tries to avoid it.
- Therefore, workers have to be coerced, threatened, and otherwise controlled by management.
- Such control is acceptable, because the average worker prefers to be directed, wishes to avoid responsibility, and in general has little ambition.

Third, the worker was assumed to be rational; that, is *goal directed*. As we shall see shortly, this assumption of rationality has carried on throughout the development of organization theory. However, to the classicists, worker rationality was rather simplistic, manifested along the single dimension of economics. In short, the worker was viewed as having the sole working objective of income maximization. Management's response to this assumption was to design organizational reward schemes that tied workers' incomes to their productivity. The piece-rate system is an illustrative outcome of this approach.

Finally, the classicists saw no inherent mutuality of interest between employee and employer. Mutual interest was created by economics—money became the binding force, tying worker and owner together. Owing to the direct relationship between productivity and income, the goals of the worker and those of the organization therefore were believed to converge.

Human Relations

The successors of Elton Mayo and his colleagues also held a number of assumptions about workers and employee-employer relationships. First, they did not seriously question that the worker was essentially an instrument of production, an instrument to be directed at the discretion of management. To be sure, the emphasis on efficiency that pervaded the Tayloristic approach to management was missing. Instead, observations, advice, and activities of the human relationists—especially the practitioners—were permeated with a philosophy of supposed humaneness: the worker is a social being whose needs have to be addressed. The humaneness was less than real, of course, because the human relationists' message to management was that satisfying these needs would lead to increased organizational effectiveness. In short, the message to management was the same as that of the classicists: help workers satisfy their needs and productivity will be high.

This brings us to the second assumption held by the human relationists, an assumption proving to be most basic to the whole movement. Like the classicists, proponents of the human-relations approach viewed the worker as rational. This rationality, however, was assumed to be multidimensional. That is, economic rationality was seen to be only one motivational drive among many. Mayo and his human-relationist successors concluded that for many workers in many organizational settings, needs for being liked, approved, and accepted by others are at least as motivating as economic ones. Although today we recognize its general validity, this assertion represented an important departure from the classical view of worker motivations.[2]

2. Taylor's (1911: 59) famous description of the ideal worker as phlegmatic and similar mentally to an ox did not represent the total complexity of his philosophy, yet it illustrates the popular view that his writings spawned.

Another conclusion of the early human-relations studies was that workers attempt to satisfy their social needs through participation in interpersonal interaction. The human relationists found that such participation occurred mainly through nonformal group membership. Thus the traditional administrative view of workers being motivated by economic rationality gave way to the observation that workers were motivated at least in part by social belonging, and that this motivation was typically satisfied through nonformal group membership.

The assumptions about workers characterizing the human relations movement has been nicely summarized by Leavitt (1958a : 291–303):

1. The worker has a multidimensional motivation structure.
2. Individual behavior must be explained in terms of the social setting at work.
3. Worker goals are not always identical to, or even compatible with, organizational goals; therefore, workers have to be influenced.
4. Participation in the decision-making process has a positive effect on morale.

In brief, proponents of the human relations movement argued that the worker was driven to accomplish a variety of goals: economic, social, and self. Further, worker behavior in service of these goals was conditioned by the presence, drives, and behavior of others. It was conditioned by the social system of which they were members.

Open Systems

What about the advocates of an open-system approach to management and organization? What assumptions do they hold about the human nature of the worker? The answer is unclear. Open-systems theory focuses at the macro level, dealing with the organization and interorganization relationships. Little attention is paid in the open-systems literature to the individual. The closest we come to such treatments is in textbooks that use an open-systems format. These works do not hold any unique view of the worker. Rather they tend to report conventionally accepted views: for example, Kast and Rosenzweig (1974) in their chapter, "Individual Behavior and Motivation," discuss perception, cognition, Maslow's (1943) hierarchy of needs, McGregor's (1960) Theory X and Theory Y, Herzberg's (1966) motivation-hygiene concept, the achievement motive (McClelland et al., 1953), and self-actualization. They devote approximately one-and-a-half pages to expectancy theory (Vroom, 1964; Steers and Porter, 1975). In short, open-systems advocates accept the idea that organizational members (workers and managers alike) have complex motivational structures. Because they focus on the organization as the analytical frame of reference, however, open-systems proponents show little distinctive interest in the individual beyond this point.

Organizational Humanism

There were several distasteful aspects of the human relations movement: its manipulative overtones, its acceptance of the organizational hierarchy as the rightful repository of legitimate power, and its unrealistic view of surface harmony as crucial (and conflict as dysfunctional) for organizational effectiveness. These characteristics gave rise to a philosophy incorporated in the tenets of humanism and democratic liberalism. The "organizational humanism" (Scott and Mitchell, 1976) movement gained its principal momentum in the 1960s and is best known for its emphasis on organizational development (OD). Unlike its contemporary, open-systems theory, organizational humanism does incorporate a number of assumptions about the nature of the worker. These assumptions form important foundational premises for this approach, and have been frequently examined, catalogued, and discussed (see, for example, Bennis, 1966; French and Bell, 1978; Golembiewski, 1972; Huse, 1975; Margulies and Raia, 1972; Miles, 1975; and Connor, 1977). The lists of assumptions produced usually resemble that elaborated by French and Bell (1978: 30–37):

1. Most individuals have drives toward personal growth and development.
2. Most people desire to make, and are capable of making, a higher level of contribution to the attainment of organizational goals than most organizational environments will permit.
3. One of the most psychologically relevant reference groups for most people is the work group, including peers and superordinates.
4. Most people wish to be accepted and to interact cooperatively with at least one small reference group and usually with more than one group.
5. Suppressed feelings adversely affect problem solving, personal growth, and job satisfaction.
6. The level of interpersonal trust, support, and cooperation is much lower in most groups and organizations than is either necessary or desirable.
7. Solutions to most attitudinal and motivational problems in organizations are transactional.
8. Policies and practices of the larger organization affect the small work group, and vice versa.
9. People have vast amounts of untapped potential and capability and desire to grow, to engage in meaningful collaborative relationships, to be creative in organizational contexts, and to be more authentic (Tannenbaum and Davis, 1969: 83).

As can be seen from this list, organizational humanists have taken the human-relations assumptions a significant step further. Two sets of humanistic values underlie this step. Commitment to traditional humanistic concerns of individual growth, development, dignity, worth, and meaning is expressed in all of organizational-humanism literature (Bennis, 1969; French and Bell, 1973: 65–68; Golembiewski, 1972; Huse, 1975; and Margulies and Raia, 1972: 3, 6). This is the primary set. Additionally the literature tends to emphasize collective behavior as the most effective means to both improved organizational performance and the goals of humanism (French and Bell, 1973; Tannenbaum and Davis, 1969). This collectivism is the secondary set. In short, organizational humanists view the worker as a person who is attempting to self-actualize, and who is making this attempt in the work place.

ASSUMPTIONS ABOUT THE ORGANIZATION

Just as the different organizational theories and schools reflect differing assumptions about workers, they also contain varying assumptions about the nature of the organization. We will consider them in the same order as before.

Classical Theory

As March and Simon (1958) describe, classical analysts conceptualized the organization using a machine analogy. By this analogy, specified administrative stimuli would produce predictable, routine, and mechanistic responses. Further, the advantage of the organizational machine was that it maximized rationality. Max Weber (1958: 214) said it as well as anyone:

> The decisive reason for the advance of bureaucratic organization has always been its purely technical superiority over any other form of organization. The fully developed bureaucratic mechanism compares with other organizations exactly as does the machine with the nonmechanical modes of productions.
>
> Precision, speed, unambiguity, knowledge of the files, continuity, discretion, unity, strict subordination, reduction of friction and of material and personal costs—these are raised to the optimum point in the strictly bureaucratic administration. . . . As compared with all collegiate, honorific, and avocational forms of administration, trained bureaucracy is superior on all these points. And as far as complicated tasks are concerned, paid bureaucratic work is not only more precise, but, in the last analysis, it is often cheaper than even formally unremunerated honorific service.

In short, as the passage illustrates, the concept of rationality was central to the Weberian analysis (Bendix, 1956; Weber, 1958; Parsons, 1960). Indeed, it was central to all of classical organizational theory. Weber, Fayol, Mooney and Reiley, Gulick and Urwick, the Gilbreths (1917), and Taylor all strove to describe a pattern of organizing that would maximize the production of organizational goods and services. Moreover, they made no bones about it. Fayol (1949), for example, delineated his several (explicit) "general principles of management." Urwick (1937) described the matter of organizing as a "technical problem," whose solution would maximize organizational goal attainment. And Taylor (1911) emphasized the *scientific method* as the best way to develop techniques for increasing productivity.

Human Relations

The classicists' "machine model" of the organization declined in importance under the empirical and ideological fire of the human relationists. Out of the studies and statements of the 1930s and '40s arose the notion that the organization should not be considered as a mechanistic "thing," but rather as a "complex pattern of relationships involving persons and their roles [by which the] social structure influences the individual, and the individual influences the social structure" (Bonner, 1968: 150–51).[3]

Further, stable organization implied "a degree of harmony and cooperation among the participants, a sharing of intention" (Haberstroh, 1966: 514). This view of the organization characterized by harmony, cooperation, and sharing of intention among organizational

3. One reason for classical theory's decline was a change in circumstances. The classicists' machine concept was probably appropriate to the times: low skills, routine technology, stable products, and so forth. As economic, technological, and environmental changes occurred, the concept became less and less appropriate.

members was compatible with the view of the worker characterized by a drive to participate in social relationships. Indeed, taken together these views facilitated the growing acceptance of the "informal organization" concept:

> . . . manifestations of informal organization are spontaneous phenomena which. . . cannot be prevented because they are the product of man's inherent desire to be a part of and belong to a group. [Roethlisberger, 1968: 99]

In short, the human-relations movement eventually evolved a set of assumptions that were relatively coherent. That is, the worker was viewed as desiring—and participating in—interpersonal relations, and the organization was considered to be a social system characterized by harmony and cooperative behavior. Assumptions of the human-relations movement about the organization have been summarized by Leavitt (1958a : 291–303):

1. The work-related social setting is affected by workers as well as managers.
2. Nonofficial small groups are real, and they affect and are affected by the formal organization.
3. Job roles are more complex than job descriptions suggest because of personal and social factors inherent in job functions. They are usually excluded in job analysis techniques, however.
4. The organization is a social system composed of numerous interacting parts.
5. Communication channels carry information relating both to the logical economic functioning of the organization and to the feelings and sentiments of the people who work in the organization.
6. Teamwork is essential for cooperation and sound technical decisions.
7. Participation in the decision-making process has a positive effect on productivity.

Open Systems

Open-systems theory is devoted to the discovery and analytical ordering of relationships among the universe of elements and processes.[4] The focus of open-system analysis can be at any of several levels, as identified by Boulding (1956):

1. The first level is that of the static structure. It might be called the level of *frameworks*. This is the geography and anatomy of the universe.
2. The next level of systematic analysis is that of the simple dynamic system with predetermined, necessary motions. This might be called the level of *clockworks*.
3. The next level is that of the control mechanism or cybernetic system, which might be nicknamed the level of the *thermostat*. The system maintains its equilibrium through self-regulation.
4. The fourth level is that of the "open system," or self-maintaining structure. This is the level at which life begins to differentiate itself from nonlife: it might be called the level of the *cell*.
5. The fifth level might be called the genetic-societal level; it is typified by the *plant*. The outstanding characteristic of these systems is a division of labor among cells to form a cell

4. This discussion borrows from Scott and Mitchell (1972) and from Connor and Becker (1975).

society with differentiated and mutually dependent parts (roots, leaves, seeds, etc.).

6. The sixth level is the "animal" level, characterized by increased mobility, teleological behavior, and self-awareness.
7. The next is the "human" level; that is, of the individual human being considered as a system.
8. Because of the vital importance for the individual of symbolic images, and behavior based on them, it is not easy to separate clearly the level of the individual human organism from the next level, that of social organizations. Nevertheless it is convenient for some purposes to distinguish individual humans as a system from the social systems which surround them, and in this sense social organizations may be said to constitute another level of organization.
9. To complete the structure of systems we should add a final turret for transcendental systems, the ultimates and absolutes and the inescapable unknowables, as they also exhibit systematic structure and relationship.

It is Boulding's eighth level, the social system, at which the open-systems approach to the study of organizations occurs. One of the earliest analysts to suggest a systemic approach to the study of organizations was Lawrence J. Henderson. Henderson illustrated the interdependence of system variables by means of the diagram shown in Figure 1–1 (Henderson, 1935: 14).

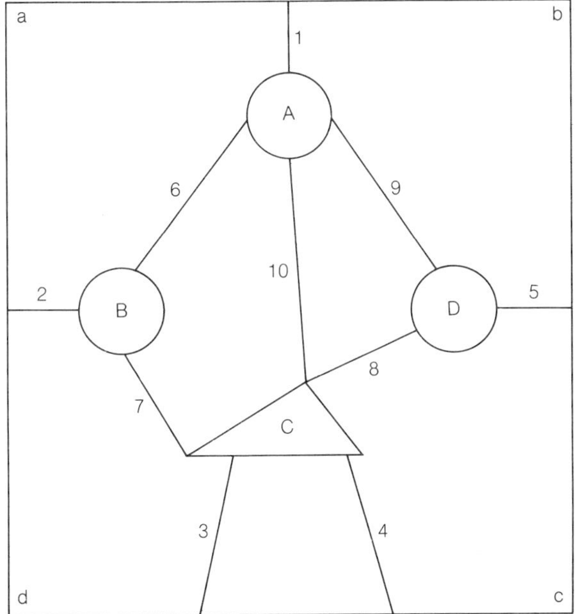

Figure 1-1. System interdependencies

Source: Lawrence J. Henderson, *Pareto's General Sociology* (Cambridge, Mass.: Harvard University Press), p. 14. Copyright © 1935 by the President & Fellows of Harvard College; renewed 1963 by Lawrence J. Henderson.

Henderson explains his diagram as follows (1935: 86):

> The four rigid bodies A, B, C, and D are fastened to a framework a, b, c, d by the elastic bands 1, 2, 3, 4, and 5. A, B, C, and D are joined one to another by the elastic bands 6, 7, 8, 9, and 10. Here the conditions of static equilibrium can be worked out mathematically, or determined empirically by introducing spring-balances into the bonds 1, 2, . . . 10, and reading the balances.
>
> Now imagine the point of attachment of 5 on the frame to be moving toward b, all other points of attachment remaining unchanged. What will happen? Consider A. There will be action on A by the path 5, 9, by the path 5, 8, 10, and by the path 5, 8, 7, 6. But in each case these actions do not cease at A, just as they do not previously cease at D. The first, for example, continues along the path 10, 8, and so back to 5. If we try to think of all this as cause and effect we must inevitably reach a state of confusion.

Henderson's concept of system interdependencies has been translated into organizational terms. First and most basically, open-systems theorists postulate that organizations acquire resources from the external environment, transform these input resources into output goods and services (by means of interdependent processes and actions), and dispose of the outputs in such a way as to facilitate the continual acquisition of additional inputs. This is illustrated in Figure 1–2.

This conceptualization may be elaborated, as we have seen done by James Thompson (1967), and may be illustrated in greater detail, as in Figure 1–3. Regardless of their precise form (and the various feedback loops have been left out of Figure 1–3 for visual clarity), systems models share a concept of the organization as a resource-processing entity operating under norms of rationality, which is a subsystem of larger subsystems (Parsons, 1956).

Organizational Humanism

As we have seen, proponents of organizational humanism are well known for their explication of values about the nature of workers. This development in organization theory is also founded on some relatively clear assumptions about the work place. Specifically, in conjunction with their assumptions about workers, organizational humanists assume that (French and Bell, 1973: 65–72; Scott, 1969: 45):

1. Group members, not just the leader, are critical to group effectiveness.
2. Managers are members of at least two work groups, as superordinates in one and as subordinate and peer in the other, and this multiple role situation is important to organizational effectiveness.

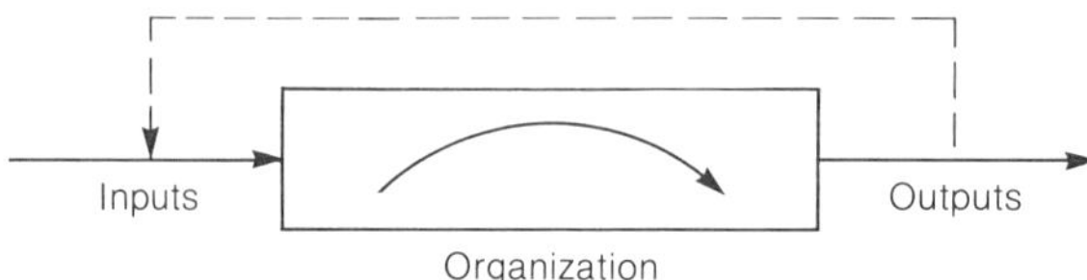

Figure 1-2. Systemic representation of the organization (a)

Source: From Patrick E. Connor and Boris W. Becker, "Values and the Organization: Suggestions for Research," *Academy of Management Journal,* Vol. 18, (Summer 1975), p. 553.

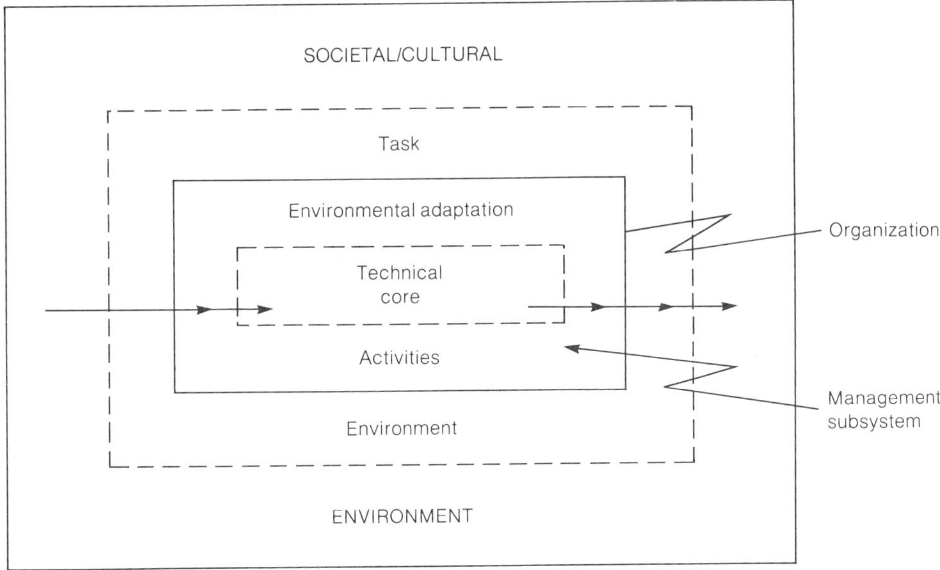

Figure 1-3. Systemic representation of the organization (b)

Source: From Patrick E. Connor and Boris W. Becker, "Values and the Organization: Suggestions for Research," *Academy of Management Journal*, Vol. 18, (Summer 1975), p. 553.

3. Organizational gains are basically the gains of people in them and the benefits (or satisfactions) flowing from these gains should be distributed as rapidly as possible to those responsible for them.
4. Those who are in organizations should be, in the last analysis, the source of consent for those who make policy and establish controls.
5. Win-lose conflict strategies are ultimately deleterious to overall organizational effectiveness.
6. Change in organizations should be the result of full awareness of alternatives and consensus by participants.

In addition to these, there are other assumptions underlying the philosophy and practice of organizational humanism (Connor, 1977): First, organizations are most realistically described using an open-systems model. Interdependencies among management, work group, task, individual, process, technology, and so on are seen as critical to effective organizational functioning. Moreover, these interdependencies form the basis for the organization's requiring a high level of interpersonal effectiveness on the part of its members (Golembiewski, 1972; Margulies and Raia, 1972; French and Bell, 1973: 74–83; Miles, 1975: 193–97).

Second, contemporary human and organizational values are both in transition and approaching significant convergence:

> Growing evidence strongly suggests that humanistic values not only resonate with an increasing number of people in today's world, but also are highly consistent with the effective functioning of organizations built on the newer organic mode. [Margulies and Raia, 1972: 11]

Organizational humanists assume not only that values of people and organizations are converging, but that this convergence is in the direction of a humanistic position (French and Bell, 1973: xiii; Margulies and Raia, 1972: 9–25). In general, this evolution is producing "a new concept of man, based on increased knowledge of his complex and shifting needs . . . ; a new concept of power, based on collaboration and reason . . . ; and a new concept of organization values, based on a humanistic existential orientation" (Bennis, 1966: 188). It is this perspective that leads organizational humanists to take a clear antibureaucratic (in the Weberian sense of the term) stance. Such classic bureaucratic prescriptions as rigid hierarchy, centralization of authority, and highly formal rules and regulations are considered inconsistent with humanistic goals. To organizational humanists,

> . . . The hierarchical form of organization . . . is inimical to, and destructive of, the human personality. Contemporary organizations fall into two major categories, the first of which is identified with the traditional and prevailing form of hierarchical organization, and the second of which is supportive of the needs and requirements of the human personality. [Wilcox, 1969: 54]

Finally, and once again most significant in terms of its actual impact on organizations, organizational humanists assume an essential rationality of organization and management. Indeed, organizational humanism is fundamentally rooted in the imperatives of organizational effectiveness. Most descriptions of the movement's principal manifestation, organization development (OD), emphasize the need for improving organizational performance (see, for example, French and Bell, 1973: xiv, 6–7, 33, 67, 72, 99; Margulies and Raia, 1972: 2–3, 17–23; Miles, 1975: 191–92). In fact, organizational humanists frequently focus their attention on calling for the development of improved social technologies (Lundberg, 1974: 1). For organizational humanism, the Tayloristic quest for the one best way (or set of ways) remains a viable paradigm within which organizational improvement rests. Job enrichment, job design, psychodrama, team building, organization grid, job-expectation technique, third-party intervention, process consultation—the list is long, but instructive. It is a list of techniques in the OD proponent's tool kit for improving performance; more variegated than Taylor's, of course, but still a tool kit.

Summary and Conclusion

We began this chapter by stating our intention to examine some organizational concepts. The purpose of such an examination, of course, is to provide a basis for dealing with the essence of this book: organizational design. Just as engineers require a knowledge of physics, organization designers require a knowledge of organization theory.

Our examination of organizational concepts has been composed of three parts. First, we traced the development of organization theory (Perrow). Second, we reviewed the currently most useful concept, the open-systems approach (Thompson). Finally, in this concluding statement we have detailed the important assumptions about the human nature of workers that underlay various organizational approaches.

With regard to the first part, the development of organization theory, we concluded that the open-systems approach is both dominant today and the most helpful approach for our purposes. Specifically it is systems thinking that guides this volume. No doubt you are familiar with the major ideas underlying an open-systems perspective of organizations and their management. Still, a brief review might be in order. Following is a list of key concepts, together with descriptions of their meanings.[5]

Subsystems or Components. A system by definition is composed of interrelated parts or elements. This is true for all systems—mechanical, biological, and social. Every system has at least two elements, and these elements are interconnected.

Holism, Synergism, Organicism, and Gestalt. The whole is not just the sum of the parts; the system itself can be explained only as a totality. Holism is the opposite of elementarism, which views the total as the sum of its individual parts.

Open Systems View. Systems can be considered in two ways: (1) closed or (2) open. Open systems exhange information, energy, or material with their environments. Biological and social systems are inherently open systems; mechanical systems may be open or closed. The concepts of open and closed systems are difficult to defend in the absolute. We prefer to think of open-closed as a dimension; that is, systems are relatively open or relatively closed.

Input-Transformation-Output Model. The open system can be viewed as a transformation model. In a dynamic relationship with its environment, it receives various inputs, transforms these inputs in some way, and exports outputs.

System Boundaries. It follows that systems have boundaries which separate them from their environments. The concept of boundaries helps us understand the distinction between open and closed systems. The relatively closed system has rigid, impenetrable boundaries; whereas the open system has permeable boundaries between itself and a broader suprasystem. Boundaries are relatively easily defined in physical and biological systems, but are very difficult to delineate in social systems, such as organizations.

Negative Entropy. Closed, physical systems are subject to the force of entropy which increases until eventually the entire system fails. The tendency toward maximum entropy is a movement to disorder, complete lack of resource transformation, and death. In a closed system, the change in entropy must always be positive; however, in open biological or social systems, entropy can be arrested and may even be transformed into negative entropy—a process of more complete organization and ability to transform resources—because the system imports resources from its environment.

Steady State, Dynamic Equilibrium, and Homeostasis. The concept of steady state is closely related to that of negative entropy. A closed system eventually must attain an equilibrium state with maximum entropy—death or disorganization. However, an open system may attain a state where the system remains in dynamic equilibrium through the continuous inflow of materials, energy, and information.

Feedback. The concept of feedback is important in understanding how a system maintains a steady state. Information concerning the outputs or the process of the system is fed back as an input into the system, perhaps leading to changes in the transformation process and/or future outputs. Feedback can be both positive and negative, although the field of cybernetics is based on negative feedback. Negative feedback is informational input which indicates that the system is deviating from a prescribed course and should readjust to a new steady state.

---

5. Fremont E. Kast and James E. Rosenzweig, "General Systems Theory: Applications for Organization and Management," *Academy of Management Journal*, vol. 15 (December 1972). © Copyright 1972 Academy of Management, Mississippi State University. Reprinted by permission.

Hierarchy. A basic concept in systems thinking is that of hierarchical relationships between systems. A system is composed of subsystems of a lower order and is also part of a suprasystem. Thus, there is a hierarchy of the components of the system.

Internal Elaboration. Closed systems move toward entropy and disorganization. In contrast, open systems appear to move in the direction of greater differentiation. elaboration, and a higher level of organization.

Multiple Goal-Seeking. Biological and social systems appear to have multiple goals or purposes. Social organizations seek multiple goals, if for no other reason than that they are composed of individuals and subunits with different values and objectives.

Equifinality of Open Systems. In mechanistic systems there is a direct cause and effect relationship between the initial conditions and the final state. Biological and social systems operate differently. Equifinality suggests that certain results may be achieved with different initial conditions and in different ways. This view sugggests that social organizations can accomplish their objectives with diverse inputs and with varying internal activities (conversion processes).

With regard to the latter point, we saw that the assumptions are dual in character, concerning (a.) the nature of workers, and (b.) the nature of the organizational work place. In essence, the historical development of organization theory has experienced a strengthening of one principal assumption: rationality. To be sure, worker rationality is now viewed as more complex than it once was; there even is reasonable consensus that organizational rationality is expressed along several dimensions. Despite evolutionary variations, however, it is clear that rationality is the dominant premise on which all contemporary concepts of organization are founded.

In the next chapter, we get to the heart of the matter: organizational design. What concepts, models, approaches, or schemes are helpful to effective organization design? It is quickly apparent that open-systems thinking dominates. Virtually all contemporary approaches to the design of organizations use it. The message is clear: *if managers want to design their enterprise to most effectively accomplish organizational missions, they must think in systemic terms—goals, constraints, resources, and outcomes.* The remainder of this book examines these variables in detail.

Questions for Review

1. What are the main differences Perrow perceives between the mechanical school of organization theory and the human relations school?
2. What are Perrow's major recommendations and cautions for management?
3. Thompson distinguishes two basic strategies for studying organizations. What are they? With which school of thought is each strategy most compatible?
4. Briefly summarize the main points of Thompson's paper.
5. What five assumptions *about the worker* are made by advocates of organizational humanism?
6. Describe four other assumptions (excluding those considered in question 5) that underlie the philosophy and practice of organizational humanism.
7. The human relations movement makes a considerable number of assumptions *about the organization.* What are they?
8. What are the various levels of focus of open-system analysis identified by Boulding?

9. What is *negative entropy?* How does it operate differently in an open system as opposed to a closed one?
10. How is *organization* defined in this chapter?

Questions for Discussion

1. What are some ways you see yourself using the S-R (stimulus-response) model in your daily life? Can you think of people or groups who generally or in certain situations do *not* do things for which they are positively rewarded? If you can, why do you think they choose not to "conform" to the S-R model?
2. Organizational humanists view a worker as a person who is attempting to self-actualize and who is making this attempt in the work place. Do you agree with this view? Use examples from your reading of current literature and/or your own experience to justify your position.
3. Perrow asks this rhetorical question: to what extent are organizations tools, and to what extent are they products of varied interests and group strivings of their members? How would you answer this difficult question?
4. Look up the exact meanings of these words in a good dictionary:
   a. holism
   b. synergism
   c. organicism
   d. gestalt

   How do you think each of these concepts fits in with—and contributes to—an open systems approach to organizations? Do any of these concepts seem irrelevant to you? Why?
5. This chapter's introduction poses a question: what are some fundamentals that underlie organizational-managerial action? What would be your own answer to this question? Does your answer conflict with those provided in the readings and the concluding statement? How does your answer differ?
6. List three positive and three negative qualities you see in using each of these theories to guide managerial action:
   a. classical
   b. human relations
   c. organizational humanism

   To which have you personally been exposed both in theory and in practice? Which do you believe most benefits the organization? The worker? In your opinion can these two be separated?
7. Are the means of resolution of conflict more important than preventing conflict altogether? Why or why not?
8. As Perrow describes it, the technological viewpoint suggests that "openness and trust, while good things in themselves, [do] not have much impact or perhaps [are] not even possible in some kinds of work situations." Do you agree or disagree with this statement? Has current organizational study and its application placed too much emphasis on these subjective qualities? Support your position with current reading and/or personal experience.
9. How do you cope with uncertainty on the personal level? How do you cope with it on the professional or organizational level? Do your methods differ? If so, Why?
10. Does it make sense to describe a fraternity or sorority as an open system? What will be the features of such a description?

2

Designing Organizations

INTRODUCTORY REMARKS

The purpose of this chapter complements that of Chapter 1 in which we explored various alternative ideas about organizations. Here we want to examine some ideas about their design. The principal theme sounded in Chapter 1's discussion was the open-systems approach. It is this approach that guides the present chapter, as well as the remainder of the book.

Also underlying this chapter and book is a basic premise: an organization is an open system with properties that can be specified and manipulated. These properties tend to fall into two categories—structure and process. McCaskey points out in the chapter's first selection that organization design is the managerial process of determining what the structures and processes of an organization will be.

Focusing on the Organization

Now, you may be accustomed to thinking of organizational issues and problems in terms of the people who populate the enterprise—members, clients, owners, and so forth. One may therefore ask: why bother examining organization structure and process, when it is *people* who cause and are affected by problems? Since this book focuses on the organization as the unit of analysis, rather than the people in or around it, we will attempt to answer that question. Or rather, we will call upon Charles Perrow to answer it:*

Organizations Are People

One of the enduring truisms of organizational analysis is that organizations are, after all, made up of people. Such a statement usually brings about a sagacious nodding of heads and a comfortable feeling of being on solid ground. But it is also true that organizations are inanimate things—they are filing cabinets, typewriters, machinery, records, mailing lists, or goods and services. This observation usually elicits no resounding thump on the table. Still, it raises a good question. Why are we so determined to equate organizations with people? It appears, at first glance at least, that most of the problems of organizations do arise from the people within them.

. . . People in this view, then, are the source of the problem, so this is the way organizations are defined. Furthermore, people can be changed or at least selected, whereas many other aspects of organizations seem to be beyond control. It is quite obvious what is wrong with people when they do things wrong. Jones is too conservative; Smith doesn't delegate authority; Brown is out only for himself. On these matters we are all experts. It is less simple . . . to determine what is wrong with the capital structure of the firm where Jones appears too conservative, or the psychiatric techniques employed in a mental hospital where Dr. Smith acts so dictatorially, or the uncertain political structure of the governmental bureau where Brown keeps shifting his alliances.

So let us alter the truism to say that visible organizational problems generally are exemplified by the people in the organizations and their relationships with one another. But this does not necessarily mean that in order to change these problems you have to change the people. For example, one of the persistent complaints in the field of penology, or juvenile correctional institutions, or mental hospitals, or any of the "people-changing" institutions is the need for better workers. Their problems, we hear, stem from the lack of high-quality personnel. More specifically, the types of individuals they can recruit as guards, or cottage parents, or orderlies typically have too little education, hold over-simplified views about people, tend to be punitive, and believe that order and discipline can solve all problems. Undoubtedly many with such attitudes work in prisons and hospitals just as there are many such people in steel mills, IBM, the Bureau of the Budget, universities, and all other types of organizations.

But [we] challenge this view by arguing that people's attitudes are shaped at least as much by the organization in which they work as by their preexisting attitudes. The very real constraints and demands presented by the job may dictate behavior which we call punitive; then we call the person punitive. In one study (Perrow, 1966) a number of applicants for positions as low-level supervisors in a juvenile correction institution were asked in an anonymous questionnaire about their opinions on the causes of delinquency, how delinquents should be handled, what was really wrong with delinquents, and whether or not they really differed much from other kids. The applicants' attitudes on the whole turned out to be quite enlightened and permissive. Some were subsequently hired by the institution, and after they had worked for a while they were again queried, as were all other personnel in the institution. It was found that the recent employees' opinions had markedly changed, and they now shared the views of the other personnel. They had become less permissive and took a punitive, unenlightened view regarding the causes of delinquency and the care and handling of delinquents. Thus, they had adopted the very attitudes about which the heads of these

*Adapted from *Organizational Analysis: A Sociological View,* by C. Perrow. Copyright © 1970 by Wadsworth Publishing Company, Inc. Reprinted by permission of the publisher, Brooks/Cole Publishing Company Monterey, California.

institutions had complained—only these were not the views they had brought with them. Considering the meager techniques for changing the character of delinquents, there was really little opportunity for the staff to do anything but adjust to the realities of the organization and the way it was run. Then they altered their attitudes to conform to the behavior expected of them. The truism, "organizations are people," is not much use in analyzing the problem of this institution.

It is difficult to change people directly through training programs and other psychological means; a good deal of backsliding is likely. Thus we will explore in this book other [factors] which might change people, or, more accurately stated, which would bring out different facets in people. It may not be the best strategy to argue that, since old Joe has a pretty tidy mind and is good with details, let us move him over to accounting and take him out of sales where imagination is needed. This may be true, but the question which should be asked first is whether sales is so organized that the only way Joe can get along there is by focusing on details. Might it not be true that if the organizational structure of the sales department, or its place in the company power structure, or the techniques it uses, were changed, then neither Joe nor anybody else would be concerned with detail but would be free to summon up initiative and imagination? Otherwise, you might put young Bill in there with all his initiative and imagination, and in a few years he would begin to look like old Joe. This is not to suggest that the many treatises on personnel selection are thus easily dismissed. The better ones note that it may be necessary to alter the structure of an organization and to redefine tasks because supermen are in short supply. Still, there is more to an organization than its people. It is clear that "organizations are people" is a shotgun approach to organizational problems—the target and the weapon are unselective.

Perrow's argument reflects the guiding theme of this book. As we have stated, formal organizations are social organisms that have identifiable properties, or characteristics. *Organization design is the process of specifying optimal combinations of organizational characteristics to achieve desired organizational outcomes.* Organizational characteristics, optimal combinations, and organizational outcomes form the content of the rest of this volume.

The Readings

Two selections make up the readings for this chapter. The first, by Michael B. McCaskey, provides an overview to the subject of organizational design. The author reminds us of three things. First, the organization is an open system; therefore internal interconnectedness is its hallmark, and optimal (rather than maximum) performance is its goal. Second, the familiar mechanistic-organic distinction drawn by Burns and Stalker (1961) is useful for designing purposes. (We will see this theme continued throughout most of the book.) Third, McCaskey reviews the basic design implication of the first two ideas: Lawrence and Lorsch's (1967) twin organizational processes of differentiation and integration. He concludes his overview with a brief review of some pertinent research findings. He also offers some suggestions for further work.

Chief among McCaskey's suggestions is that the dynamic, changing character of organizations should be more closely attended. Jay R. Galbraith provides such attention in the second selection. His view is that organizational tasks are performed under various degrees of uncertainty. Moreover, he says, the greater this uncertainty, the greater the amount of information that must be processed by organizational decision makers. For

Galbraith, therefore, organization design consists of choosing various strategies for processing information.

In choosing a proper strategy, organizational designers must decide what combination of integration mechanisms is best. Galbraith identifies three such mechanisms: coordination by rules or programs, the administrative hierarchy, and coordination by targets and goals. Having selected a combination, designers may then form their design strategy. What strategy is best will depend on the level of task uncertainty faced by the organization. Or more specifically, the choice will depend on whether decision makers wish to reduce their need to process information or increase their capability for doing so. The author describes four strategies: 1. creating slack resources, 2. creating self-contained tasks, 3. investing in vertical information systems, and 4. creating lateral relations. The first two serve the need to reduce. The second two help to increase organizational information-processing capabilities.

Again, the theme that Galbraith emphasizes is an important one: an organization operates under a given degree of uncertainty; organizational performance depends on its ability to deal with that uncertainty. That ability depends, in turn, on the organization's information-processing capability. Thus organization design involves choosing an information-processing strategy that is appropriate for the conditions under which the organization operates.

Conclusion

In summary, this chapter is concerned with the following questions:

1. What is organization design?
2. Why do organizations get designed?
3. What constrains designers' options?
4. What is it that designers design?
5. What results from the design process?

AN INTRODUCTION TO ORGANIZATION DESIGN

MICHAEL B. McCASKEY

How does a manager choose among organizational design alternatives? How does he, for example, decide how precisely to define duties and roles? Should decision-making be centralized or decentralized? What type of people should he recruit to work on a particular task force? Organization design tries to identify the organizational structures and processes that appropriately "fit" the type of people in the organization and the type of task the organization faces.

Organizational design determines what the structures and processes of an organization will be. The features of an organization that can be designed include: division into sections and units, number of levels, location of decision-making authority, distribution of and access to information, physical layout of buildings, types of people recruited, what behaviors are rewarded, and so on. In the process of designing an organization, managers invent, develop, and analyze alternative forms for combining these elements. And the form must reflect the limits and capabilities of humans and the characteristics and nature of the task environment (Simon, 1960: 2, 43).

Designing a human social organization is extremely complicated. An organization is a system of interrelated parts so that the design of one sub-system or of one procedure has ramifications for other parts of the system. Furthermore, the criteria by which a system design is to be evaluated (economic performance, survival capability, social responsibility, and the personal growth of organizational members) cannot be maximized simultaneously: the design of a human social organization can never be perfect or final. In short, the design of organizational arrangements is intended to devise a complex set of tradeoffs in a field of changing people, environment, and values.

Minor adjustments in organizational design are always being made during the life of an organization, but the times for major concentration on organizational design are: 1. early in the life of an organization, most likely after the basic identity and strategy have been largely worked out; 2. when significantly expanding or changing the organization's mission; or 3. when reorganizing.

Who designs the organization, organizational units, and task forces? Since organizational design concerns the arrangement of people and the division of tasks, a designer or planner has to have some influence or control over these variables. This task is most often handled by middle-level managers and up. However, the charter to design could be broadened to give organizational members at all levels more of a say in organizational design matters.

KEY CONCEPTS AND QUESTIONS

In approaching an organization design problem, some of the important questions to be answered are:

1. How uncertain is the task environment in which the organization operates?
2. In what ways should the organization be mechanistic and in what ways organic?
3. How should the subtasks be divided and how should the organization be differentiated? Should subsystems be organized by the *functions* people perform, by the *products* or services the company provides, or should some other form such as a matrix organization be used?
4. What kind of people are (or can be recruited to become) members of the organization? Under what conditions do they work and learn best?

5. How are activities to be coordinated and integrated? What mechanisms will be used, involving what costs?

Research and theory provide some findings that can be used as design guidelines, and we turn to consider them now.

Mechanistic Patterns of Organizing

Tom Burns' and G. M. Stalker's (1961) study of electronics firms and firms contemplating entering the electronics industry in Scotland and England contributed the important design principle of distinguishing between mechanistic and organic patterns of organizing.

Mechanistic organizational units are the traditional pyramidal pattern of organizing. In a mechanistic organizational unit, roles and procedures are precisely defined. Communication is channelized, and time spans and goal orientations are similar within the unit. The objective is to work toward machine-like efficiency. To that end the task is broken into parts that are joined together at the end of the work process. Authority, influence, and information are arranged by levels, each higher level having successively more authority, more influence, and more information. Decision-making is centralized at the top and it is the top levels that make appreciative judgments to determine what is important in the environment (Vickers, 1965). Top levels also determine the channels whereby the lower echelons will gather and process information.

Thus the social organization is designed as a likeness of a machine. People are conceived of as parts performing specific tasks. As employees leave, other parts can be slipped into their places. Someone at the top is the designer, defining what the parts will be and how they will all fit together.

Under what conditions is this pattern of organization appropriate? When the organizational unit is performing a task that is stable, well-defined, and likely to be programmable, or when members of the organization prefer well-defined situations, feel more secure when the day has a routine to it, and tend to want others to supply direction, the mechanistic pattern is applicable. Organization design findings show that, to the extent these conditions hold, a mechanistic form of organizing is more likely to result in high performance.

The mechanistic form is efficient and predictable. For people with a low tolerance for ambiguity it provides a stable and secure work setting. However, the mechanistic form is less flexible: once a direction and procedures have been set, it is hard to change them. Furthermore, mechanistic forms also entail the danger of stultifying their members with jobs that are too simple, with little responsibility, and no sense of worthwhile accomplishment.

Organic Patterns of Organizing

In contrast to mechanistic units, organic organizational units are based on a more biological metaphor for constructing social organizations. The objective in designing an organic unit is to leave the system maximally open to the environment in order to make the most of new opportunities. The demands of the task environment are ambiguously defined and changing, so people have multiple roles which are continually redefined in interaction with others. All levels make appreciations and there are few predetermined information channels. Decision-making is more decentralized, with authority and influence flowing to the person who has the greatest expertise to deal with the problem at hand. An organic organizational unit is relatively heterogeneous, containing a wider variety of time spans, goal orientations, and ways of thinking. The boundaries between the system and the environment are deliberately permeable, and the environment exerts more influence over the activities of the system than is true for the mechanistic unit.

An organic form is useful in the face of an uncertain task or one that is not well enough understood to be programmed. The organic form is also appropriate for people who like the disorder of an ambiguous setting, for people who prefer variety, change, and adventure and who grow restless when they fall into the same routine day after day. The organic form is flexible and responds quickly to unexpected opportunities. However, the organic form is often wasteful of resources. Not having precisely defined authority, control, and information hierarchies, time can be wasted in search activities that duplicate the efforts of other members.

Furthermore, the stress of uncertainty and the continual threat of power struggles can be exhausting.

Making the Choice

The choice of the most suitable form of organization is *contingent* upon the task and the people involved. There is no one form of organization that will work best in all situations, in all cultures, with every type of person. Organization design scholars using a contingency theory approach emphasize the need to specify the particular conditions under which a given form is most appropriate.

Note, too, that the same organizational unit can change its position on the organic/mechanistic continuum over time. The unit might start out being very mechanistically organized. But as the environment or staff change, the unit might move toward the organic end of the continuum. In fact, if the unit does not change its structures and processes to meet changed conditions, it is likely to suffer lower performance.

Even more important, one organization is likely to contain both organic units and mechanistic units at the same time. Burns and Stalker (1961) characterized whole organizations as mechanistic or organic; but Paul Lawrence and Jay Lorsch (1967) found that these descriptions more accurately described units of an organization. They researched and elaborated on a major contribution to organization design in the concepts of differentiation and integration (D&I).

DIFFERENTIATION

Differentiation, the creation or emergence of differences in the organization, can take place in several ways: 1. vertically—into levels; 2. horizontally—into sections, department, divisions, and so on; 3. division of labor—into occupational roles; and 4. patterns of thinking—differences between units in members' goals, time, and interpersonal orientations.

By differentiating, the organization gains the advantages of both economies of scale and people becoming experts in particular areas like production, accounting, contracting, and so on.

Lawrence and Lorsch found horizontal differentiation and the differentiation of patterns of thinking to be the most important types of differentiation for organizational design. The organization segments the environment into parts so that organizational units interact with different subenvironments. While marketing interacts with the media, ad agencies, legal departments, competitors' advertising, and the other elements that make up the marketing subenvironment, production is dealing with the machines, labor market, scheduling, cost consciousness, and safety regulations that pertain to their subenvironment. Furthermore, the structure and setting for each unit must supply the appropriate training and support for different job demands. Scientists, for example, need a milieu that will supply specialized information as well as support in projects that may take years to complete.

An important question in organization design, therefore, is how differentiated should the organization be? How should the environment be segmented and what activities should be grouped together? To what extent should the units differ in structures and procedures, types of people, and patterns of thinking?

Research indicates that business organizations in newer and more uncertain industries, like aerospace and electronics, need to be more highly differentiated because they face a greater range of subenvironments. As James Thompson (1967) argues, organizations try to shield their technical core from the uncertainties of the environment. The subenvironment of the core technology unit, then, will be relatively stable and call for more mechanistic patterns of organizing. The units having uncertain subenvironments (often the R&D subenvironment) will need to be more organically organized. Looking at the organization as a whole, the differences between the units will be significant because the range of unit organizational patterns extends from the mechanistic end to the organic end of the continuum.

Conversely, research indicates that organizations in older, more established, and more certain industries need to be less differentiated. They face a narrow range of subenvironments near the certainty end of the spectrum and will probably pursue the efficiency given by more mechanistic patterns of organizing. An organization in a relatively stable and certain environment benefits from having uniform rules and procedures, vocabulary, and patterns of thinking throughout the organization. The problem of integration for these organizations, therefore, is less demanding.

INTEGRATION

At the same time the organization is differentiated to work more effectively on tasks, some activities of organizational units must be coordinated and brought together, or integrated. The manager/designer must resist differentiating the organization too radically—the greater the differences between the units, the harder it is for them to coordinate activities with each other. If all the units have similar goals, values, and time horizons, messages and meanings are more likely to be clear. But when an organization is highly differentiated, people have to spend more effort translating and appreciating the frameworks of people in different units. Most people habitually think in their own terms, and it takes increased effort to move into another's frame of reference. The chances for misunderstandings increase in a highly differentiated organization.

The greater the differentiation, the heavier the burden on information processing and upon decision-making in the organization. This shows up in the array of techniques for coordinating the activities of a firm: 1. the use of rules and procedures along with the hierarchy of authority; 2. if two units are crucial and have trouble integrating, the appointment of a liaison (Lawrence and Lorsch, 1967b); and 3. the building of a new unit into the work flow to serve as an integrating department.

The list of coordinating mechanisms shows progressively more elaborate ways to achieve integration. With greater differentiation, an organization has to spend more effort integrating and use the more expensive devices.

So in addition to asking how much the organization should differentiate to meet environment and people requirements, another question must simultaneously be raised. How much differentiation, at that cost, can the organization successfully integrate? How should people be grouped to provide the best working conditions for individuals *and* to secure the most advantageous work flow for the whole organization? A manager/designer works for the best practical answer to these questions. Many times he may decide to stop short of differentiating to perfectly meet task environment demands because his staff would find it too great a strain or because it would be too costly. Research findings show that in uncertain environments, the most successful organizations are the most highly differentiated *and* the most integrated. The difficult design decision of how to differentiate and how to integrate is often framed as the choice between product or functional organization, or some newer form such as a matrix organization (Kingdon, 1973).

THE RESEARCH STUDIES

Table 2–1 summarizes a selection of research findings important for organization design theory. The studies were conducted mainly, although not entirely, with business firms. A wide range of methodologies has been used including historical study methods, an intensive case study of one division, a questionnaire survey of managers in different organizations, surveying and interviewing the top managers of all the business organizations in a given geographical area, and so on. All of the studies support a contingency approach to organizational design. Researchers found that explaining their data required them to specify the conditions upon which the use of a particular organization form was contingent.

In spite of different methods and vocabularies, certain patterns and continuities run through the findings. The design principle of distinguishing between mechanistic and organic forms is supported by the studies. Peter Blau's and Richard Schoenherr's (1971) findings based on all instances (53) of one type of government agency lends support to the Lawrence and Lorsch (1967c) findings based on a selected sample of ten business firms. Both studies found that environmental diversity is related to greater differentiation in the organization. Blau and Schoenherr found that differentiation raises the requirements for managerial manpower, and this is similar to Lawrence and Lorsch's (1967c) finding that greater differentiation requires more elaborate integrative devices. Furthermore, Jay Galbraith's (1973) research provides something of an

TABLE 2–1 EMPIRICAL RESEARCH FINDINGS ON ORGANIZATIONAL DESIGN

Researchers	Types of Organizations Studied	Selected Findings
Burns and Stalker (1961)	20 firms in U.K., including a rayon manufacturer, an engineering firm, several companies in electronics and others contemplating entry into electronics	"Mechanistic" management system suited to an enterprise operating under relatively stable conditions; "organic" required for conditions of change.
Chandler (1962)	Historical studies of DuPont, General Motors, Standard Oil of New Jersey, and Sears Roebuck, supplemented by brief reviews of over 70 other large American business companies	By trial and error a new structural form (decentralized, multidivisional form) developed to fit changed environmental conditions.
Woodward (1965)	100 English manufacturing firms	Patterns in management practice associated with how complex and how predictable production technology is.
Lawrence and Lorsch (1967)	10 U.S. companies in plastics, consumer food, and standardized container industries	1. High performing organizations are differentiated to meet environmental demands; diverse and uncertain environments require greater differentiation of the organization. 2. Differentiation and integration are antagonistic states; the more differentiated an organization is, the more elaborate the integrative devices must be. 3. Additional support for above findings.
Galbraith (1970)	Case study of the Boeing Aircraft Division	Structural changes to deal with greater task environment uncertainty related to the need to process more information.
Blau and Schoenherr (1971)	The 53 state employment security offices of the U.S. and territories	1. Increasing size generates structural differentiation in organizations along various dimensions at decelerating rates. 2. Structural differentiation in organizations raises requirements for managerial manpower. 3. Horizontal, vertical, and occupational differentiation are positively related to environmental diversity.
Duncan (1971)	22 decision-making units in 3 manufacturing organizations and in 3 R&D organizations	Structural profile used to make nonroutine decisions differs from that used to make routine decisions; suggests the same unit uses different organizing patterns over time.
Morse and Young (1973)	235 managers from 8 business organizations	Individuals working on certain tasks preferred controlling authority relations and had a low tolerance for ambiguity; individuals working on uncertain tasks sought independence and autonomy and were high in tolerance for ambiguity.

explanatory picture. His findings suggest that the need for more managerial manpower and more elaborate integrative mechanisms is related to the need for the organization to process more information.

Robert Duncan's (1971) findings that an organizational unit appears to change its structure over time simply reinforces managers' feelings that organization charts are often incorrect and out-of-date. This is a promising area of research for developing a more accurate picture of how and when changes in organization structure occur.

As the studies indicate, substantial progress has been made. However, some important questions remain to be answered.

WORK YET TO BE DONE

Our knowledge of organizational design is still growing. Some of the important subjects which need further research are:

1. We need a better understanding of the *dynamics* of an organization developing a good fit to its environment and its members. The processes that span organization and environment, such as planning and selecting, recruiting and socializing new members, need to be researched. In addition to learning more about the enduring structural patterns, we also need to learn about the ways in which organization and environment adjust to one another.

2. We must consider the assertion of power in the interaction of organizations and their environments. How do organizations seek to make the environment more favorable to their operations? How does the environment coerce or influence the organization to meet its demands? What are the consequences of one element gaining sizeable amounts of control over the other? We need to learn about the processes which mediate this contest for control and influence.

3. Up until now researchers have mainly relied upon the criterion of economic performance to assess good fit. Clearly, using economic criteria alone is too limited. How can we judge goodness of fit in terms of people outcomes? Moreover, what about the people who are content to follow orders from the organization? Some argue that we cannot be normative on this value question. If a person is satisfied to be passive and dependent on the job, who can insist that he take more control over his own work life? My view is that a democracy can hardly afford a work system which mainly trains people to be docile, to follow orders, and above all to be loyal to the organization. But others emphasize that many prefer following orders, and this is where the issue is joined.

4. A related issue is the possible conflict between efficiency and human needs. Some elements of organization design concern social engineering to devise the most efficient organization to accomplish a task. Other elements of organization design are concerned with the full growth and development of individuals. It is too optimistic to assume that efficiently designed organizations will always or even usually be conducive to human intercourse. Mammoth operations built to meet economies of scale considerations teach us that efficiently engineered operations can be inhumane. If we had better noneconomic measures of outcomes, maybe we could more accurately assess the design tradeoffs. As it stands now, much of organization design emphasizes an engineering approach, neglecting human growth aspects. Another challenge: How can we design organizations to meet both people and engineering concerns?

5. We also need to learn more about how facilities design supports or detracts from the intent of an organization design. How does the physical layout influence the pattern of social interaction? How does the visual display of information affect decision making? At what distance for what types of activities does physical separation of people or units greatly strain the organization's ability to integrate? How can facilities be designed so that physical spaces can be rearranged to fit changes in organizing patterns? Robert Propst, Fritz Steele, and Thomas Allen have begun work on some of these questions.

SUMMARY

A convenient guideline for reviewing what we know about designing organizations is the continuum from mechanistic to organic patterns of organizing. Most suited to stable, certain environments, and a staff that prefers stability, the mechanistic form is the traditional hierarchical pyramid that is controlled from the top and programs activities tightly. Most suited to an unstable, uncertain environment and people tolerant of ambiguity, the organic pattern of organizing is more collegial and stresses flexibility—in rules, decision-making authority, procedures, and so on. Of course, there are more than these two types of organizing patterns. They should be considered the ends of a continuum of types of organizing patterns.

An organization is likely to contain both organically and mechanistically organized units. How widely the units should range on the mechanistic/organic continuum is part of the question of differentiation. How great should the differences be between units in terms of structures, types of people, and patterns of thinking? Overall, organizations in mature and stable industries contain units that face more or less well-defined and certain subenvironments. Therefore, to meet environmental demands, the units should generally be more mechanistically organized and the organization as a whole will be less differentiated.

On the other hand, organizations in dynamic new industries must have some units organically organized to deal with an uncertain subenvironment. At the same time it should devise more mechanistic units (for example, production and accounting) to face more stable subenvironments. To cover that range of subenvironments, the manager/organization designer creates or allows to develop greater differences between the units. In addition, the organization tends to create more job roles (occupational differentiation) and more levels (vertical differentiation) in response to environmental diversity. The organization, therefore, becomes more highly differentiated.

The opposite tendency from differentiation is the need to integrate, to coordinate the activities of different parts of the organization. The greater the differentiation, the harder it is to integrate. The choice of a particular integrating mechanism, such as a liaison in addition to rules, signals the manager/designer's decision to expend a certain amount of effort to coordinate activities. Concurrent with designing the extent of differentiation in an organization, a manager must consider what effort at what cost will be needed to integrate those differences. The greater the differentiation, the more elaborate and costly are the mechanisms needed for integration.

Organizational design choices are tradeoffs between good fit to the task environment and people characteristics, to monetary and human costs, and to short-term and long-term consequences. Such a design is never perfect or complete. Organizational design seeks to build knowledge about and provide guidelines for designing more efficient and more human organizations.

ORGANIZATION DESIGN: AN INFORMATION PROCESSING VIEW

JAY R. GALBRAITH

THE INFORMATION PROCESSING MODEL

A basic proposition is that the greater the uncertainty of the task, the greater the amount of information that has to be processed between decision makers during the execution of the task. If the task is well understood prior to performing it, much of the activity can be preplanned. If it is not understood, then during the actual task execution more knowledge is acquired which leads to changes in resource allocations, schedules, and priorities. All these changes require information processing *during* task performance. Therefore *the greater the task uncertainty, the greater the amount of information that must be processed among decision makers during task execution in order to achieve a given level of performance.* The basic effect of uncertainty is to limit the ability of the organization to preplan or to make decisions about activities in advance of their execution. Therefore it is hypothesized that the observed variations in organizational forms are variations in the strategies of organizations to 1. increase their ability to preplan, 2. increase their flexibility to adapt to their inability to preplan, or, 3. to decrease the level of performance required for continued viability. Which strategy is chosen depends on the relative costs of the strategies. The function of the framework is to identify these strategies and their costs.

THE MECHANISTIC MODEL

This framework is best developed by keeping in mind a hypothetical organization. Assume it is large and employs a number of specialist groups and resources in providing the output. After the task has been divided into specialist subtasks, the problem is to integrate the subtasks around the completion of the global task. This is the problem of organization design. The behaviors that occur in one subtask cannot be judged as good or bad *per se.* The behaviors are more effective or ineffective depending upon the behaviors of the other subtask performers. There is a design problem because the executors of the behaviors cannot communicate with all the roles with whom they are interdependent. Therefore the design problem is to create mechanisms that permit coordinated action across large numbers of interdependent roles. Each of these mechanisms, however, has a limited range over which it is effective at handling the information requirements necessary to coordinate the interdependent roles. As the amount of uncertainty increases, and therefore information processing increases, the organization must adopt integrating mechanisms which increase its information processing capabilities.

1. Coordination by Rules or Programs

For routine predictable tasks March and Simon have identified the use of rules or programs to coordinate behavior between interdependent subtasks (March and Simon, 1958, Chap. 6). To the extent that job related situations can be predicted in advance, and behaviors specified for these situations, programs allow an interdependent set of activities to be performed without the need for inter-unit communication. Each role occupant simply executes the behavior which is appropriate for the task related situation with which he is faced.

2. Hierarchy

As the organization faces greater uncertainty its participants face situations for which they have no rules. At this point the hierarchy is employed on an exception basis. The recurring job situations are programmed

Jay R. Galbraith, "Organization Design: An Information Processing View," *Interfaces,* vol. 4, no. 3 (May 1974), pp. 28–36.

with rules while infrequent situations are referred to that level in the hierarchy where a global perspective exists for all affected subunits. However, the hierarchy also has a limited range. As uncertainty increases the number of exceptions increases until the hierarchy becomes overloaded.

3. Coordination by Targets or Goals

As the uncertainty of the organization's task increases, coordination increasingly takes place by specifying outputs, goals or targets (March and Simon, 1958, p. 145). Instead of specifying specific behaviors to be enacted, the organization undertakes processes to set goals to be achieved and the employees select the behaviors which lead to goal accomplishment. Planning reduces the amount of information processing in the hierarchy by increasing the amount of discretion exercised at lower levels. Like the use of rules, planning achieves integrated action and also eliminates the need for continuous communication among interdependent subunits as long as task performance stays within the planned task specifications, budget limits and within targeted completion dates. If it does not, the hierarchy is again employed on an exception basis.

The ability of an organization to coordinate interdependent tasks depends on its ability to compute meaningful subgoals to guide subunit action. When uncertainty increases because of introducing new products, entering new markets, or employing new technologies these subgoals are incorrect. The result is more exceptions, more information processing, and an overloaded hierarchy.

DESIGN STRATEGIES

The ability of an organization to successfully utilize coordination by goal setting, hierarchy, and rules depends on the combination of the frequency of exceptions and the capacity of the hierarchy to handle them. As the task uncertainty increases the organization must again take organization design action. It can proceed in either of two general ways. First, it can act in two ways to reduce the amount of information that is processed. And second, the organization can act in two ways to increase its capacity to handle more information. The two methods for reducing the need for information and the two methods for increasing processing capacity are shown schematically in Figure 2–1. The effect of all these actions is to reduce the number of exceptional cases referred upward into the organization through hierarchical channels. The assumption is that the critical limiting factor of an organizational form is its ability to handle the non-routine, consequential events that cannot be anticipated and planned for in advance. The non-programmed events place the greatest communication load on the organization.

1. Creation of Slack Resources

As the number of exceptions begin to overload the hierarchy, one response is to increase the planning targets so that fewer exceptions occur. For example, completion dates can be extended until the number of exceptions that occur are within the existing information processing capacity of the organization. This has been the practice in solving job shop scheduling problems (Pounds, 1963). Job shops quote delivery times that are long enough to keep the scheduling problem within the computational and information processing limits of the organization. Since every job shop has the same problem, standard lead times evolve in the industry. Similarly budget targets could be raised, buffer inventories employed, etc. The greater the uncertainty, the greater the magnitude of the inventory, lead time, or budget needed to reduce an overload.

All of these examples have a similar effect. They represent the use of slack resources to reduce the amount of interdependence between subunits (March and Simon, 1958, Cyert and March, 1963). This keeps the required amount of information within the capacity of the organization to process it. Information processing is reduced because an exception is less likely to occur and reduced interdependence means that fewer factors need to be considered simultaneously when an exception does occur.

The strategy of using slack resources has its costs. Relaxing budget targets has the obvious cost of requiring more budget. Increasing the time to completion

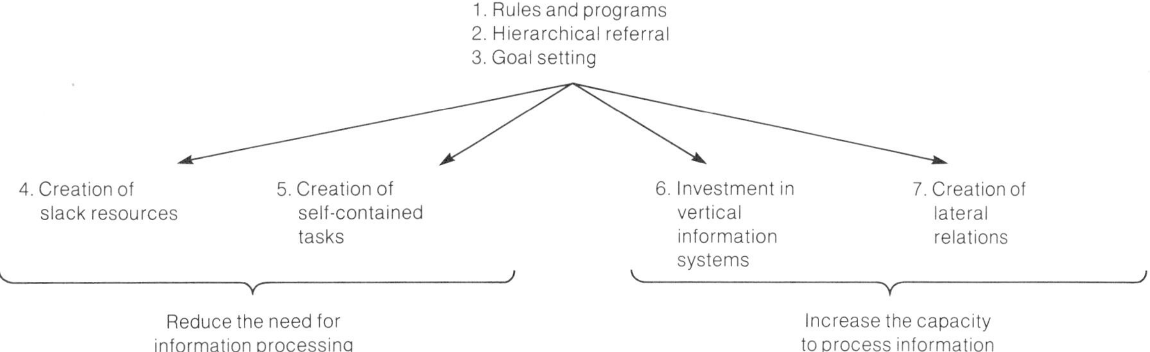

Figure 2-1. Organization design strategies

date has the effect of delaying the customer. Inventories require the investment of capital funds which could be used elsewhere. Reduction of design optimization reduces the performance of the article being designed. Whether slack resources are used to reduce information or not depends on the relative cost of the other alternatives.

The design choices are: 1. which factors to change (lead time, overtime, machine utilization, etc.) to create the slack, and 2. by what amount should the factors be changed. Many operations research models are useful in choosing factors and amounts. The time-cost trade off problem in project networks is a good example.

2. Creation of Self-Contained Tasks

The second method of reducing the amount of information processed is to change the subtask groupings from resource (input) based to output based categories and give each group the resources it needs to supply the output. For example, the functional organization could be changed to product groups. Each group would have its own product engineers, process engineers, fabricating and assembly operations, and marketing activities. In other situations, groups can be created around product lines, geograpical areas, projects, client groups, markets, etc., each of which would contain the input resources necessary for creation of the output.

The strategy of self-containment shifts the basis of authority from one based on input, resource, skill, or occupational categories to one based on output or geographical categories. The shift reduces the amount of information processing through several mechanisms. First, it reduces the amount of output diversity faced by a single collection of resources. For example, a professional organization with multiple skill specialties providing service to three different client groups must schedule the use of these specialties across three demands for their services and determine priorities when conflicts occur. But, if the organization changed to three groups, one for each client category, each with its own full complement of specialties, the schedule conflicts across client groups disappear and there is no need to process information to determine priorities.

The second source of information reduction occurs through a reduced division of labor. The functional or resource specialized structure pools the demand for skills across all output categories. In the example above each client generates approximately one-third of the demand for each skill. Since the division of labor is limited by the extent of the market, the division of labor must decrease as the demand decreases. In the professional organization, each client group may have generated a need for one-third of a computer programmer. The functional organization would have hired one programmer and shared him across the groups. In the self-contained structure there is insufficient demand in each group for a programmer so the professionals must do their own programming. Specialization is reduced but there is no problem of scheduling the programmer's time across the three possible uses for it.

The cost of the self-containment strategy is the loss of resource specialization. In the example, the organization foregoes the benefit of a specialist in computer programming. If there is physical equipment, there is a loss of economies of scale. The professional organization would require three machines in the self-contained form but only a large timeshared machine in the functional form. But those resources which have large economies of scale or for which specialization is necessary may remain centralized. Thus, it is the degree of self-containment that is the variable. The greater the degree of uncertainty, other things equal, the greater the degree of self-containment.

The design choices are the basis for the self-contained structure and the number of resources to be contained in the groups. No groups are completely self-contained or they would not be part of the same organization. But one product divisionalized firm may have eight of fifteen functions in the division while another may have twelve of fifteen in the divisions. Usually accounting, finance, and legal services are centralized and shared. Those functions which have economies of scale, require specialization or are necessary for control remain centralized and not part of the self-contained group.

The first two strategies reduced the amount of information by lower performance standards and creating small autonomous groups to provide the output. Information is reduced because an exception is less likely to occur and fewer factors need to be considered when an exception does occur. The next two strategies accept the performance standards and division of labor as given and adapt the organization so as to process the new information which is created during task performance.

3. Investment in Vertical Information Systems

The organization can invest in mechanisms which allow it to process information acquired during task performance without overloading the hierarchical communication channels. The investment occurs according to the following logic. After the organization has created its plan or set of targets for inventories, labor utilization, budgets, and schedules, unanticipated events occur which generate exceptions requiring adjustments to the original plan. At some point when the number of exceptions becomes substantial, it is preferable to generate a new plan rather than make incremental changes with each exception. The issue is then how frequently should plans be revised—yearly, quarterly, or monthly? The greater the frequency of replanning the greater the resources, such as clerks, computer time, input-output devices, etc., required to process information about relevant factors.

The cost of information processing resources can be minimized if the language is formalized. Formalization of a decision-making language simply means that more information is transmitted with the same number of symbols. It is assumed that information processing resources are consumed in proportion to the number of symbols transmitted. The accounting system is an example of a formalized language.

Providing more information, more often, may simply overload the decision maker. Investment may be required to increase the capacity of the decision maker by employing computers, various man-machine combinations, assistants-to, etc. The cost of this strategy is the cost of the information processing resources consumed in transmitting and processing the data.

The design variables of this strategy are the decision frequency, the degree of formalization of language, and the type of decision mechanism which will make the choice. This strategy is usually operationalized by creating redundant information channels which transmit data from the point of origination upward in the hierarchy where the point of decision rests. If data is formalized and quantifiable, this strategy is effective. If the relevant data are qualitative and ambiguous, then it may prove easier to bring the decisions down to where the information exists.

4. Creation of Lateral Relationships

The last strategy is to employ selectively joint decision processes which cut across lines of authority. This strategy moves the level of decision making down in the organization to where the information exists but does so without reorganizing around self-contained groups. There are several types of lateral decision processes. Some processes are usually referred to as the informal organization. However, these informal processes do not always arise spontaneously out of the needs of the task. This is particularly true in multinational organizations in which participants are separated by physical barriers, language differences, and cultural differences. Under these circumstances lateral processes need to be designed. The lateral processes evolve as follows with increases in uncertainty.

4.1 Direct Contact. Between managers who share a problem. If a problem arises on the shop floor, the foreman can simply call the design engineer, and they can jointly agree upon a solution. From an information processing view, the joint decision prevents an upward referral and unloads the hierarchy.

4.2 Liaison Roles. When the volume of contacts between any two departments grows, it becomes economical to set up a specialized role to handle this communication. Liaison men are typical examples of specialized roles designed to facilitate communication between two interdependent departments and to bypass the long lines of communication involved in upward referral. Liaison roles arise at lower and middle levels of management.

4.3 Task Forces. Direct contact and liaison roles, like the integration mechanisms before them, have a limited range of usefulness. They work when two managers or functions are involved. When problems arise involving seven or eight departments, the decision-making capacity of direct contacts is exceeded. Then these problems must be referred upward. For uncertain, interdependent tasks such situations arise frequently. Task forces are a form of horizontal contact which is designed for problems of multiple departments.

The task force is made up of representatives from each of the affected departments. Some are full-time members, others may be part-time. The task force is a temporary group. It exists only as long as the problem remains. When a solution is reached, each participant returns to his normal tasks.

To the extent that they are successful, task forces remove problems from higher levels of the hierarchy. The decisions are made at lower levels in the organization. In order to guarantee integration, a group problem solving approach is taken. Each affected subunit contributes a member and therefore provides the information necessary to judge the impact on all units.

4.4 Teams. The next extension is to incorporate the group decision process into the permanent decision processes. That is, as certain decisions consistently arise, the task forces become permanent. These groups are labeled teams. There are many design issues concerned in team decision making such as at what level do they operate, who participates, etc. (Galbraith, 1973, Chapters 6 and 7). One design decision is particularly critical. This is the choice of leadership. Sometimes a problem exists largely in one department so that the department manager is the leader. Sometimes the leadership passes from one manager to another. As a new product moves to the market place, the leader of the new product team is first the technical manager followed by the production and then the marketing manager. The result is that if the team cannot reach a consensus decision and the leader decides, the goals of the leader are consistent with the goals of the organization for the decision in question. But quite often obvious leaders cannot be found. Another mechanism must be introduced.

4.5 Integrating Roles. The leadership issue is solved by creating a new role—an integrating role (Lawrence and Lorsch, 1967b, Chapter 3).* These roles carry the labels of product managers, program managers, project managers, unit managers (hospitals), materials managers, etc. After the role is created, the design problem is to create enough power in the role to influence the decision process. These roles have power even when no one reports directly to them. They have some power because they report to the general manager. But if they are selected so as to be unbiased with respect to the groups they integrate and to have technical competence, they have expert power. They collect information and equalize power differences due to preferential access to knowledge and information. The power equalization increases trust and the quality of the joint decision process. But power equalization occurs only if the integrating role is staffed with someone who can exercise expert power in the form of persuasion and informal influences rather than exert the power of rank or authority.

*Ed. note: see the article by Lawrence and Lorsch in Chapter 10 of this volume.

4.6 Managerial Linking Roles. As tasks become more uncertain, it is more difficult to exercise expert power. The role must get more power of the formal authority type in order to be effective at coordinating the joint decisions which occur at lower levels of the organization. This position power changes the nature of the role which for lack of a better name is labeled a managerial linking role. It is not like the integrating role because it possesses formal position power but is different from line managerial roles in that participants do not report to the linking manager. The power is added by the following successive changes:

a. The integrator receives approval power of budgets formulated in the departments to be integrated.

b. The planning and budgeting process starts with the integrator making his initiation in budgeting legitimate.

c. Linking manager receives the budget for the area of responsibility and buys resources from the specialist groups.

These mechanisms permit the manager to exercise influence even though no one works directly for him. The role is concerned with integration but exercises power through the formal power of the position. If this power is insufficient to integrate the subtasks and creation of self-contained groups is not feasible, there is one last step.

4.7 Matrix Organization. The last step is to create the dual authority relationship and the matrix organization (Galbraith, 1971). At some point in the organization some roles have two superiors. The design issue is to select the locus of these roles. The result is a balance of power between the managerial linking roles and the normal line organization roles. Figure 2–2 depicts the pure matrix design.

The work of Lawrence and Lorsch is highly consistent with the assertions concerning lateral relations (Lawrence and Lorsch, 1967c, Lorsch and Lawrence, 1968). They compared the types of lateral relations undertaken by the most successful firm in three different industries. Their data are summarized in Table 2–2. The plastics firm has the greatest rate of

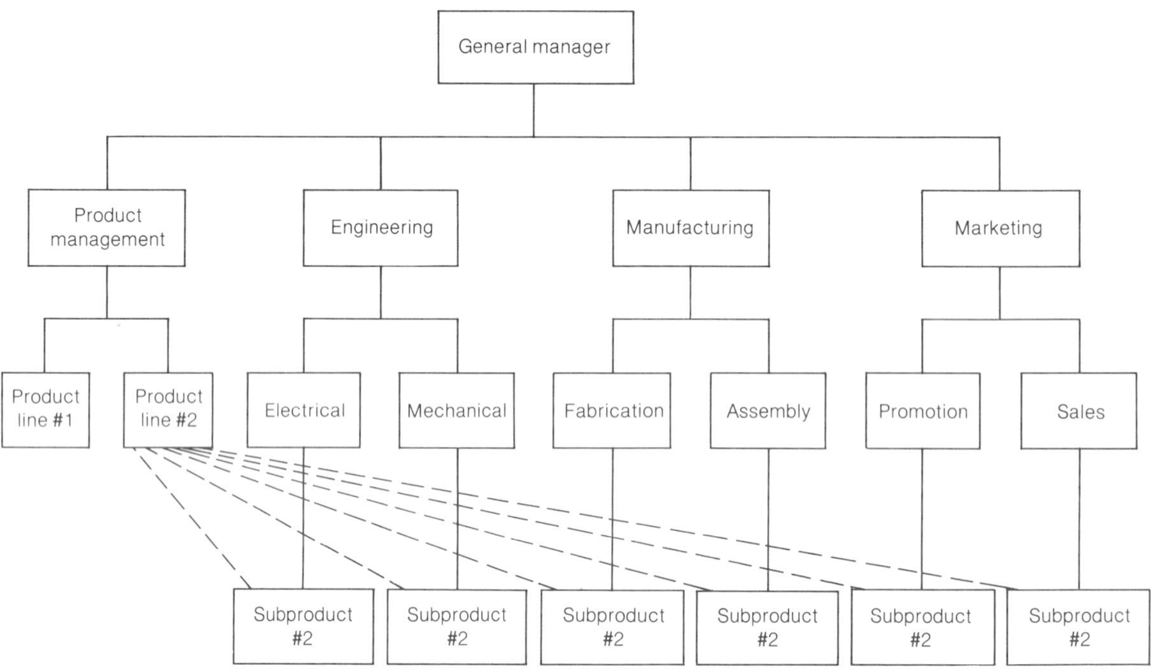

Figure 2-2. A pure matrix organization

TABLE 2–2 INTEGRATION IN THREE INDUSTRIES

	Plastics	Food	Container
Percent new products in last ten years	35%	20%	0%
Integrating devices	Rules Hierarchy Planning Direct contact Teams at 3 levels Integrating dept.	Rules Hierarchy Planning Direct contact Task forces Integrators	Rules Hierarchy Planning Direct contact
Percent integrators/managers	22%	17%	0%

SOURCE: Adopted from Paul R. Lawrence and Jay W. Lorsch, *Organization and Environment*. (Boston: Graduate School of Business Administration, Harvard University, 1967), pp. 86–138, and a paper by Lorsch and Lawrence (1968)

new product introduction (uncertainty) and the greatest utilization of lateral processes. The container firm was also very successful but utilized only standard practices because its information processing task is much less formidable. Thus, the greater the uncertainty the lower the level of decision making and the integration is maintained by lateral relations.

Table 2–2 points out the cost of using lateral relations. The plastics firm has 22 percent of its managers in integration roles. Thus, the greater the use of lateral relations the greater the managerial intensity. This cost must be balanced against the cost of slack resources, self-contained groups and information systems.

CHOICE OF STRATEGY

Each of the four strategies has been briefly presented. The organization can follow one or some combination of several if it chooses. It will choose that strategy which has the least cost in its environmental context. (For an example, see Galbraith, 1970.) However, what may be lost in all of the explanations is that the four strategies are hypothesized to be an exhaustive set of alternatives. That is, if the organization is faced with greater uncertainty due to technological change, higher performance standards due to increased competition, or diversifies its product line to reduce dependence, the amount of information processing is increased. *The organization must adopt at least one of the four strategies when faced with greater uncertainty.* If it does not consciously choose one of the four, then the first, reduced performance standards, will happen automatically. The task information requirements and the capacity of the organization to process information are always matched. If the organization does not consciously match them, reduced performance through budget and schedule overruns will occur in order to bring about equality. Thus the organization should be planned and designed simultaneously with the planning of the strategy and resource allocations. But if the strategy involves introducing new products, entering new markets, etc., then some provision for increased information must be made. Not to decide is to decide, and it is to decide upon slack resources as the strategy to remove hierarchical overload.

There is probably a fifth strategy which is not articulated here. Instead of changing the organization in response to task uncertainty, the organization can operate on its environment to reduce uncertainty. The organization through strategic decisions, long-term contracts, coalitions, etc., can control its environment. But these maneuvers have costs also. They should be compared with costs of the four design strategies presented above.

SUMMARY

The purpose of this paper has been to explain why task uncertainty is related to organizational form. In so doing the cognitive limits theory of Herbert Simon was the guiding influence. As the consequences of cognitive limits were traced through the framework, various organization design strategies were articulated. The framework provides a basis for integrating organizational interventions, such as information systems and group problem solving, which have been treated separately before.

CONCLUDING STATEMENT

What can we assume about organization design? To answer this question, let us back up and review a bit. In Chapter 1, concepts and ideas about organizations were examined. Out of that examination came a dominant theme: the organization is most usefully thought of as an open system. Into the organization flow *resources*, such as people, money, equipment, and so forth; *opportunities*, from new markets, skills, and technologies; and *demands*, from suppliers, labor unions, governmental regulatory agencies, and local communities. These resources, opportunities, and demands are transformed within the organization into the organization's *output* of goods and services. Finally, the outputs are disseminated into the surrounding environment.

In return, the organization receives resources—frequently in the form of profits or budgetary allocations—which it uses to acquire more inputs. And the cycle continues. As Katz and Kahn (1966: 16) put it, the organization is "an energic input-output system in which the energic return from the output reactivates the system." Figure 1–2 (reproduced here as Figure 2–3) suggested this cycle in schematic form.

We also saw in Chapter 1 that the input-output cycle intimately involves the environment within which the organization functions. We identified two major environments, noted in Figure 1–3 (Figure 2–4, here). The *task environment* is that part of the world outside the organization with which the organization comes into frequent, operating contact. Table 2–3 identifies the major people, interest groups, and organizations that make up the task environment.

The organization also operates in a larger context, termed the *societal/cultural environment*, whose principal components are also noted in Table 2–3. Designing and managing two shoe factories that are alike in all technical respects will still have some significant differences if one is located in Indianapolis and the other in Tokyo. Customs, traditions, cultural values and norms—all of these affect the organization. Designing and managing a medical clinic in Harlem will also differ from doing so in Beverly Hills.

We portray the task environment as part of the larger environment for a good reason: although societal/cultural factors do affect the organization, their effects are *experienced* by the organization in terms of task-environment factors. Consider, for example, that in the United States there have occurred at least two shifts in societal values within the last decade. One of these shifts can be described by the label *consumerism*. The other goes under the heading *ecology*. Both shifts have been experienced by organizations in terms of task-environment components.

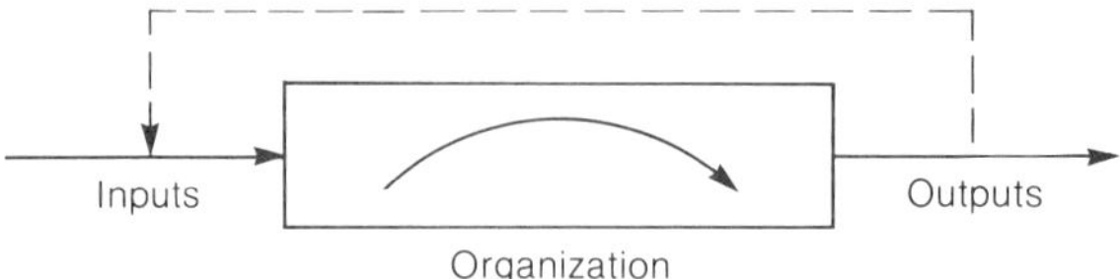

Figure 2-3. The organization as an input-output system

Source: From Patrick E. Connor and Boris W. Becker, "Values and the Organization: Suggestions for Research," *Academy of Management Journal*, Vol. 18, (Summer 1975), p. 553.

TABLE 2–3 ENVIRONMENTAL FACTORS

Task Environment	Societal/Cultural Environment
Consumers	Customs
Suppliers	Traditions
Regulators	Mores
Labor unions	Cultural norms
Financial sources	Values
Competitors	
Allies	

Customers sue organizations for damages incurred by shoddy or dangerous products. Government regulators levy fines against organizations for violating antipollution laws. Again, the point is that although the shift has been one of societal/cultural values, the organization experiences that shift in its dealings with the task environment. It is this environment with which the organization must transact resource-processing business.

SYSTEMS AND ORGANIZATION DESIGN

Viewing the organization as an open system is useful, because it aids our understanding of organizational processes—both those within the organization and those involved in its environmental transactions. Such a view is also useful, however, as a guide to organizational design. Namely, it focuses our attention on such organizationally related matters as environment, resource flow, output, and feedback processes. Compare these concepts with the classical, bureaucratic view, which focused on such matters as hierarchy, chain of

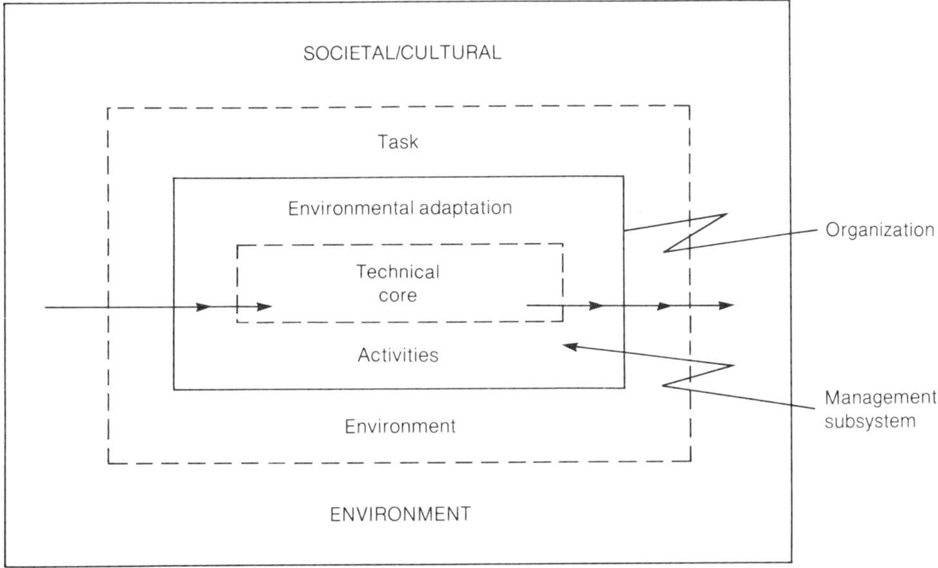

Figure 2-4. Systemic representation of the organization

Source: From Patrick E. Connor and Boris W. Becker, "Values and the Organization: Suggestions for Research," *Academy of Management Journal*, Vol. 18, (Summer 1975), p. 553.

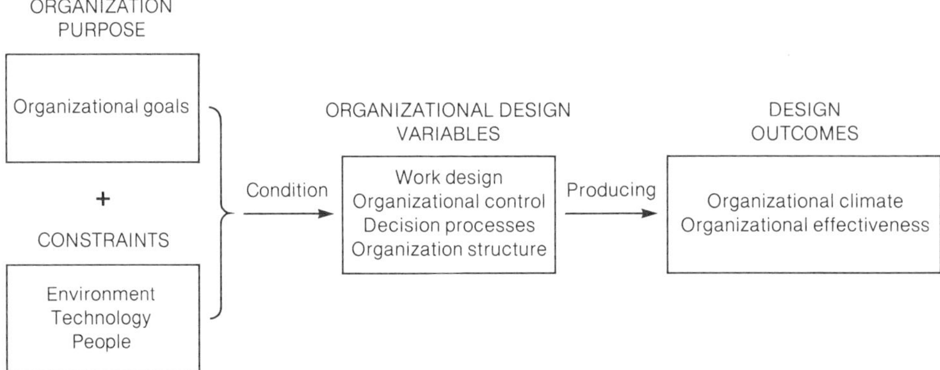

Figure 2-5. The process of organizational design

command, and span of control. It is not that these latter organizational properties are trivial—they just do not capture the dynamics of organizational functioning. *And it is the reality of these dynamics that organization designs must incorporate.*

Referring again to Figures 2–3 and 2–4, viewing the organization as an open system encourages some design-relevant questions:

1. Why do we acquire resources and process information?
2. What constrains our ability to acquire and process resources?
3. How are inputs transformed into outputs?
4. What are the outcomes of our efforts?

The first is a question of purpose, *goals,* or, more generally, organizational rationality. The second question concerns *constraints* on organizational designing. Question three asks, simply, "What are the *variables* that are designed?" The last question focuses on design results, or *outcomes.*

These four questions guide this book. They can be put into schematic form, as we have done in Figure 2–5. The rest of this chapter—and book—tracks through the figure, moving from left to right.

PURPOSE: ORGANIZATIONAL RATIONALITY

Several years ago Harold J. Leavitt (March 1965: 1144) wrote that one can view organizations as:

> . . . complex systems in which at least four interacting variables loom especially large: task variables, structural variables, technological variables, and human variables.

What Leavitt omitted from his brief list (although not from his subsequent discussion) is a fifth, driving variable: *rationality.* Organizational rationality embodies the concept of goals, and it is this concept that allows one to understand the interconnectedness of Leavitt's four variables, as illustrated in Figure 2–6.

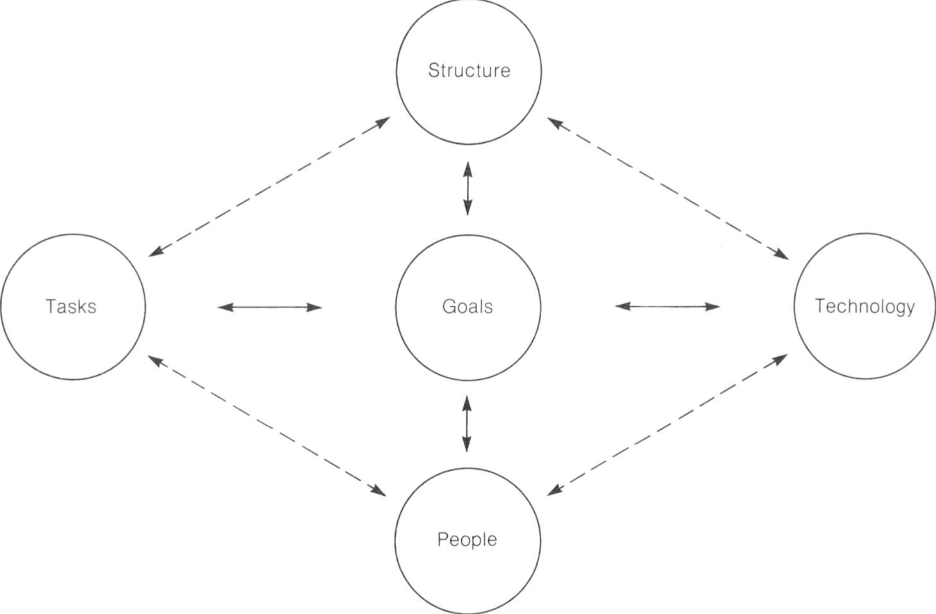

Figure 2-6. Internal organizational variables

Source: Adapted from Harold J. Leavitt, "Applied Organizational Change in Industry: Structural, Technological and Humanistic Approaches," in James G. March (ed.), *Handbook of Organizations*, Figure 1, p. 1145. © 1965 Rand McNally College Publishing Company. Reprinted by permission.

Rationality and Design

Rationality is especially useful for focusing on organizational design. Recall that in this chapter's introductory remarks we defined organizational design as the process of specifying optimal combinations of organizational characteristics to achieve desired organizational outcomes. This concept follows from the view that the organization is "an 'instrument'—that is, . . . a rationally conceived means to the realization of . . . goals" (Gouldner, 1959: 404)[1]. Indeed, the essential purpose of an organization is "the pursuit of relatively specific objectives on a more or less continuous basis" (W. R. Scott, 1964: 488). Thus, as Gross (1969: 277) observed,

> the central concept in the study of organizations is that of the organizational goal. . . . It is the presence of a goal and a consequent organizational effort so as to maximize the probability of attaining the goal which characterizes modern organizations.

The concept of goals, of course, is central not only to the study of organizations, as Gross said, but also to their design. For example, as we have noted elsewhere (Connor and Bloomfield, 1977), organizational rationality establishes a basis for organizational structure.

1. When we speak of organizational goals, more than outputs are being referred to. Organizations pursue a number of goals in addition to those relating to their products. Maintenance, personnel, environmental adaptation—these are just a few such goals. Refer to Chapter 3 for a more thorough discussion.

In particular, the framework of rationality relegates organizational structure to an instrumental role: structures are tools for effectively pursuing organizational goals[2]. More generally, the resurgence of contingency theories in the last decade reflects this idea. Organizations are designed, continually redesigned, and managed so as to best accomplish their purposes under prevailing conditions. Borrowing from engineering terminology, goals are the specifications to which organizations are designed.

ORGANIZATIONAL CONDITIONS: CONSTRAINTS ON DESIGN

The "prevailing conditions" referred to immediately above represent another idea central to organizational design. For a particular design to be considered appropriate, it must "fit," or be compatible with, the conditions under which the organization operates. Or putting it more actively, prevailing conditions are those factors that constrain organizational designers in the performance of their function.

A good way to think about design constraints is to remember that how the organizational instrument is designed will depend on, first, where it is to perform its mission (that is, accomplish its goals); second, how it is to do so; and third, who does it. Thus the major factors that constrain organizational designing are, respectively, the organization's environment, its technology, and the type of people who are its members. The goals/design/constraints relationship is suggested by Figure 2–7.

Following is a brief discussion of each of the principal design constraints.[3] (These constraints form the content of Section Three of this book.)

Environment

There have been several attempts by organization theorists to examine the effects of environmental conditions on organizational designs. Two of the most significant studies were those by Burns and Stalker (1961) and by Lawrence and Lorsch (1967).

The Burns and Stalker Study. Based on a comprehensive study of 20 industrial firms in the United Kingdom, Burns and Stalker concluded that environmental forces are felt directly by the organization. Specifically, they reported two major types of environment, *dynamic* and *static*. Dynamic environments are those characterized by rapid changes in markets, technology, economic conditions, and so forth. Static environments are characterized by relative stability in those conditions.

The importance of the Burns and Stalker study is this: They discovered that the organizational designs that were effective under dynamic environmental conditions differed from those that were effective under static environments. "Organic" organizations were designed to operate under dynamic conditions. Organic-organization managers deemphasize reliance on highly formalistic rules and centralized decision making, emphasizing collaboration and authority based on knowledge, rather than position.

In contrast, "mechanistic" organizations were designed to operate under static conditions. Mechanistic-organization managers rely on high formalization, high centralization, directives, and position-based authority.

2. Section Four, "Design Variables," is an elaboration of this general theme.

3. This discussion is based on Haimann, Scott, and Connor (1978: 255–58).

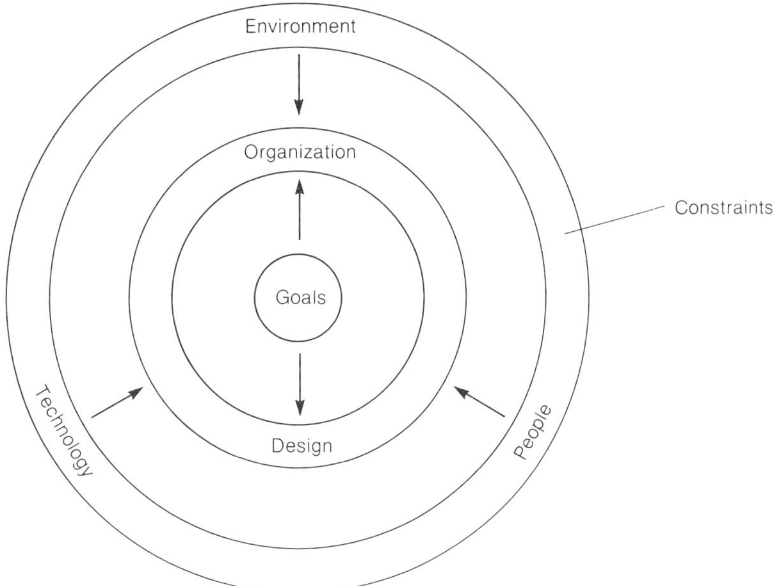

Figure 2-7. Designing the organization

Source: Theo Haimann, William G. Scott, and Patrick E. Connor, *Managing the Modern Organization*, 3rd. ed., (Boston: Houghton Mifflin Co., 1978), p. 254.

The Lawrence and Lorsch Study. Another important research project was that conducted by Lawrence and Lorsch, in which they examined organizations in the plastics, food, and container industries (Lorsch, 1965; Lawrence and Lorsch, 1967a, 1967b, 1967c; Lorsch and Lawrence, 1970). The authors set out to answer the following questions (1967b; 16):

1. How are the environmental demands facing various organizations different and how do environmental demands relate to the internal functioning of effective organizations?
2. Is it true that organizations in certain or stable environments make more exclusive use of the formal hierarchy to achieve integration, and, if so, why? Because less integration is required, or because in a certain environment these decisions can be made more effectively at higher organization levels or by fewer people?
3. Is the same degree of differentiation in orientation and in departmental structure found in organizations in different industrial environments?
4. If greater differentiation among functional departments is required in different industries, does this influence the problems of integrating the organizations' parts? Does it influence the organizations' means of achieving integration?

In essence, the Lawrence and Lorsch research supported and extended that by Burns and Stalker. Put briefly, managers of effective organizations in different environments used different means of coordination. Traditional techniques of coordination—rules, procedures, plans, and the chain of command—were effective when the organization operated under static environmental conditions. Systems techniques—teams, specifically designated "coordinators," and task forces—were effective when the organization operated under dynamic environmental conditions.

The theme underlying both research studies, as well as that of many of their successors, is that of uncertainty. As Thompson discussed earlier, and as both McCaskey and Galbraith emphasize in this chapter, organization designers must design their organization to cope with the degree and nature of the environmental and task uncertainty that it confronts. (These and related ideas are elaborated in Chapter 4.)

Technology

Without going into as extensive a discussion as with environment, we note a second critical factor on which organizational design is contingent: task technology. Basically technology is a term used to denote the way in which work is performed. Any task has a dominant technology, whether it be putting pockets on a piece of clothing, teaching a class of 50 management students, or putting a job hunter in touch with a company that is hiring.

Organization designers attempt to design their organization in a way that is compatible with its technology. More specifically, they take into account the *complexity* of the organizational technology. Technological complexity is concerned with such characteristics as the task's routineness, the number of separate variables involved, the predictability of results, and so forth. The fundamental rule is this: the more complex the technology, the more organic the organizational design needs to be. Note that once again the concept of uncertainty is important. Technological complexity and organic design are both concepts that embody this idea. (This theme is expanded in Chapter 5.)

People

A third critical design constraint is the organization's membership. Particularly significant are such human properties as motivational structures, degree of commitment to organizational purposes and practices, and the values that underlie people's perceptions, needs, drives, motivations, and behavior.

An aspect of an organization's membership that is especially important as a design constraint is its overall degree of *cosmopolitanism*. Basically "cosmopolitans" are people who are oriented to their profession, its other members, and the profession's work standards—scientists are a good example. In contrast, "locals" relate—are oriented—much more directly to their local situation; usually such people are high on organizational loyalty (Merton, 1968; Gouldner, 1957).

As brought out in Chapter 6, the relevance of cosmopolitanism for organizational design is that generally the higher people's cosmopolitan orientation, the more they value such things as decentralization, autonomy, knowledge-based authority, and so forth. The manager of basic research scientists would be ill-advised to design the organization in a highly mechanistic fashion.

THE ORGANIZATION AS INSTRUMENT: DESIGN VARIABLES

As we mentioned, the third question raised earlier asked, "what is it that is designed?" In other words, what organizational properties are manipulated so as to allow the organization to operate most effectively under its environment-technology-people constraints? It is impossible, of course, to give a totally comprehensive answer to this question. One would be required to list every organizational variable imaginable. And since many such variables are multidimensional, the list would be extraordinarily long.

Still, we can identify some major *groupings* of organizational properties that provide the designer with some opportunities for variation. Van de Ven (1976), for example, suggests that there are three principal design-variable groupings. These include structural factors, such as specialization and standardization; work flow; and administrative processes, such as decision making and information flow. Galbraith (1973), as we have seen, emphasizes that the design of information processes is particularly critical to effective organizational performance. (Almost any textbook or conceptual journal article you pick up will exhibit some model of that social instrument called *organization.*)

Basic Design Variables

Not wanting to write an infinitely long book (after all, think of the time it would take to read), we have opted for a fairly straightforward approach. We have chosen to tackle the question of what design variables to treat by using the systems perspective of resource flow. Specifically: resources flow into the organization, tasks are performed on them, those tasks are analyzed and controlled with respect to the guiding imperative of organizational rationality, and resources and activities are then reallocated. All this takes place within (and is facilitated by) the overall structural framework of the organization. Thus we focus on the variables of, respectively, *work design, organizational control, decision processes,* and *organization structure.* These variables are treated in Chapters 7–10.

DESIGN OUTCOMES

So what? We have said that the imperative guiding the design function is organizational rationality. Still, how do we know a good design when we see one? In other words, what *outcomes* should result to allow the designer to conclude that a good job was done?

There are two schools of thought. One says that a design is good if it helps the organization produce its goods and services in the most efficient manner possible (Becker and Neuhauser, 1975). The other school says there are two major outcomes. First, a design should contribute to fostering a *climate* that encourages organizational members to develop and grow to their human capacities. Climate, of course, refers to the overall character of the organization. Dimensions of organizational climate include such things as systems of pay and other rewards, working conditions, leadership styles, degree of employee discretion, and so forth (Hellriegel and Slocum, 1976: 12–13). Second, a design should contribute to the organization's achieving all of its *goals*—both output and such support goals as are appropriate (Gross, 1969; Perrow, 1961a).

For us, the second school of thought makes the most sense. According to this view, there are two major organization-design outcomes: climate and effectiveness. These topics are treated in Chapters 11 and 12, respectively.

SUMMARY AND CONCLUSION

The purpose of Chapter 1 was to present a conceptual, organization-theoretic basis for the rest of this text. Open-systems thinking—with its emphasis on inputs and outputs, resource flows, and organization-environment interactions—seems best suited for our purposes.

This chapter, on the other hand, focuses our attention on organization design. Organization design is defined as the process of specifying optimal combinations of organizational characteristics to achieve desired organizational outcomes. We began the examination in the introductory remarks with the reminder that dealing with organizational properties, rather than being restricted to dealing with people, is a legitimate and often fruitful approach. Next we took an overview of the subject (McCaskey), focusing on two important distinctions: mechanistic-organic organizational forms and differentiation-integration processes. Third, we examined the critical role that uncertainty plays in organization design (Galbraith).

Finally, in the concluding statement, we have developed an organization-design framework that will be used to structure the remainder of this volume. Beginning with the idea that the organization is a rationality-seeking (that is, *goal*-seeking) open system, we noted some important *constraints* that condition the *design variables* that designers vary, and the design *outcomes* that result.

Having discussed some important ideas and concepts underlying organization design, we move on in the next Section to a discussion of the rationale guiding designers' activities: The accomplishment of organizational goals.

Questions for Review

1. McCaskey lists criteria by which a system design is to be evaluated. What are they?
2. In the opinion of McCaskey and others, there are certain times for major concentration on organizational design. What are these times?
3. What are the major characteristics of a mechanistic organizational unit as specified by McCaskey?
4. What are three of the areas of organizational design that McCaskey believes need further research?
5. According to Galbraith, there are two methods for reducing the need for information, and two methods for increasing processing capacity. What are these four methods?
6. What are the main differences between *managerial linking roles* and *integrating roles* as defined and outlined by Galbraith? What are the successive changes involved in making this differentiation?
7. A diagrammatic representation of an open-system organization may be made using a core and radiating concentric areas. What are these areas, starting with the core and moving outwards?
8. What are the schools of thought on evaluating a good design?
9. How is *organizational design* defined in this chapter?
10. What are some of the important questions that need to be answered in approaching an organization design problem?

Questions for Discussion

1. Perrow argues that "people's attitudes are shaped at least as much by the organization in which they work as by their pre-existing attitudes." Do you agree? In the light of this chapter's discussion, plus your own experience or observation, evaluate this statement. Use concrete examples to support your position.
2. "A democracy can hardly afford a work system which mainly trains people to be docile, to follow orders, and above all to be loyal to the organization," states McCaskey. Do you think a democracy and such a system can and do co-exist? Do you agree with McCaskey's statement? Support your argument.
3. Galbraith assumes that the critical limiting factor of an organizational form is its ability to handle nonroutine, consequential events that cannot be anticipated and planned for in advance. Is this a valid assumption in your opinion? If not, what would you define as the critical limiting factor? If you agree with Galbraith, summarize at least two arguments he uses to support his assumption.
4. Would you prefer to work in an organic or mechanistic organizational unit? For you, what would be three positive and three negative effects of working in each of these environments?
5. Would you rather deal with the stress of uncertainty or the stress of boredom in the organizational environment? Why? Under what conditions might you change your mind?
6. Why do you think certain people exhibit an apparently higher tolerance for ambiguity than others? In what ways might this benefit someone? In what ways might this be a liability?
7. Within a college or university, what areas do you think are better suited to mechanistic patterns of organizing? Which are better suited to organic patterns? Draw a continuum of the major areas within your own school and place each area on that continuum, ranging from fully mechanistic to fully organic. What is it about these areas that caused you to place them where you did?
8. What would be some of the differences in the societal-cultural environments encountered in running a pharmacy in central Chicago and in a small, midwestern town? Do *these* differences validate an organization's need to consider task-environment factors? Explain.
9. According to Perrow, the belief that "organizations are people" is a truism. Do you agree? If you agree, support your position from your reading of this chapter. If you disagree, support your position by other current reading and/or experience.
10. What problems would a manager previously working in an organic open-system organization be likely to encounter in joining a mechanistic organization? Should he or she attempt to change the newly joined organization or just "fit in"?

Cases for Discussion

CASE: KITCHEN WORKERS

Priscilla Alexander is kitchen supervisor of the Chester A. Arthur Community College student union building. She is talking about the workers and the work situation as it prevails in her department.

"The employees in this department are mostly working here because it is the best job they can get. Most of them would quit tomorrow if they thought they had any chance of getting a better job. We pay better wages than most institutional jobs in this area—other than big hospitals and universities, that is. Our work facilities are better than most of the schools I have seen and are far better than any of the nonschool institutions (such as retirement homes and the downtown hotel, for instance). The employees have no legitimate complaints about the conditions on this job.

"As I said, most of them aren't capable of holding down a better job. I have to watch them constantly to make sure that the work gets done the way I want it done. The chief cooks on the shifts are supposed to supervise the other cooks and the kitchen helpers on their shifts, but they don't seem to be putting much effort into it. I never see them getting on any of their people to make sure that things get done. You know, the type people that take this kind of job don't have much ambition, and you have to really keep on them—give them a bit of a kick to urge them along—in order to get anything out of them.

"The turnover in help isn't as bad here as some other places I have been. I guess that we have a complete turnover about once a year. Probably a little more often than that, if you include just the helpers. Right now, the only two people who have been here more than a year, other than myself, are the chief cook and one of her assistant cooks from the weekend shift, and they are both only part-time workers."

Questions

1. What assumptions is Ms. Alexander making about her workers?
2. How are these assumptions probably affecting her own managerial work?
3. What can be done to improve the situation?

CASE: ADMINISTRATOR IN THE MIDDLE

Frederick Tyler, administrator of the Mountain View Convalescent Center, is discussing the effects of the cost-reimbursement system for patients receiving welfare benefits.

"When I submitted my last breakdown of costs to the Welfare Department to justify the payment rate, I made sure that there were no unrelated costs included; even borderline cases were not claimed. It still amounted to an average of $23.87 per patient-day. Now I get the award letter from Welfare saying, in effect, 'Congratulations, all of your costs are adequately justified. We are awarding you $20.50 per patient-day.' This leaves me with a deficit of $3.37 per welfare patient-day, which is, in effect, a tax imposed for the privilege of doing what we're required to do to maintain our good standing in the community—that is, accept welfare recipients as patients on a no-profit basis.

The information contained herein has been collected for the sole purpose of providing material for discussion, not to demonstrate correct or incorrect handling of managerial or organizational situations.

"The problem now is what to do about it. We've already decided to raise the rates for the private patients by amounts varying from $1.50 to $2.50 per day and averaging $1.60 per day. That's about the most we can raise our prices and stay at all competitive. Even if a larger raise was possible, we've already informed the private patients what their new rates will be, so we couldn't very well change it now. We had hoped that this increase would ease some of our other problems.

"The owners have been complaining that they aren't receiving adequate dividends on their investment and have made it clear that they expect an increase during the next year. Furthermore, we need to make some capital expenditures. The kitchen needs some additional equipment and some of the existing equipment replaced. Also, some of our patient-care equipment needs replacing. Finally, I wanted to give raises to some of our lower paid workers, particularly the kitchen helpers, the aides, and the orderlies, who now receive less than the minimum wage required of other businesses.

"The increase in the deficit on welfare patients uses up most of the increase in private patient rates. Most of the remainder will go to increase the dividend rate of the owners. That has to take first priority. Next, I'll have to set up priorities for capital expenditures. The owners refuse to allow us to use debt financing in any form for capital improvements. At this point, I'm not sure how much will be available for capital improvements. I am reasonably sure, however, that the wage increases will have to wait until next year when we can possibly get another raise in private patient rates.

"You can see the problems brought on when the Welfare Department requires the privately owned nursing home to subsidize the welfare patient. The profits from this type operation are inadequate to support the subsidy."

1. Who are the "publics" with whom the administrator must deal?
2. How would you diagram the various relationships involved here?

TASK: Design a strategy to help Mr. Tyler solve his problem.

CONSTRAINTS: The proportion of welfare patients is to remain at its present level (20 percent).

SECTION TWO

Designs for What? Organizational Purpose

INTRODUCTION TO SECTION TWO

Put simply, the reason people try to design organizations, rather than simply let them develop willy-nilly, is to improve their ability to accomplish the purposes for which they exist. Whatever else they may be, organizations are social devices for doing things. The things they do, of course, vary widely in our society: produce shoes, cure the ill, educate the young, provide sanctuary for the troubled, deliver health care to the isolated, and on and on. Even a single organization may pursue a variety of subpurposes. Your college, for example, undoubtedly offers courses, produces research, and provides services to the community along a variety of dimensions. More than that, it must afford opportunities to satisfy the various demands of its students, staff, faculty, and administrative members. All such activities reflect, and are reflected in, organizational goals. And, therefore, it is to accomplish such goals that organizational designs are created, modified, discarded, and refined.

Section Two consists of just one chapter, ''Organizational Goals.'' In a sense, goals serve as a constraint on design decisions. Indeed, as we shall see, this is a major theme in the chapter's second article, ''On the Concept of Organizational Goals,'' by Herbert A. Simon. Treating it as a constraint, therefore, the subject could have been included in Section Three, along with environment, technology, and people. It is our belief, however, that goals serve more than simply as a constraint. The pursuit of goals is the *raison d'etre* of the organization. Its importance is therefore more than just a limitation on design. The chapter on goals has been separated from the others to emphasize this importance.

3

Organizational Goals

INTRODUCTORY REMARKS

As we saw in Chapters 1 and 2, there are many approaches to thinking about and studying complex organizations. Despite their variety, however, most approaches subscribe to the view that *rationality* is fundamental to organizational action. Thus for the majority of people, the organization is a social instrument designed and operated to perform tasks and to satisfy needs and wants of various kinds—in short, to accomplish goals. Indeed, most definitions of *organization* either explicitly or implicitly include goal seeking as a principal element.

We share in this consensus. Accordingly we begin our consideration of organization design by focusing on its purpose: to accomplish organizational goals. It should be noted, incidentally, that we are not distinguishing between *goals* and *objectives* in the ensuing discussion. Everything said in the following pages can be applied equally to both.

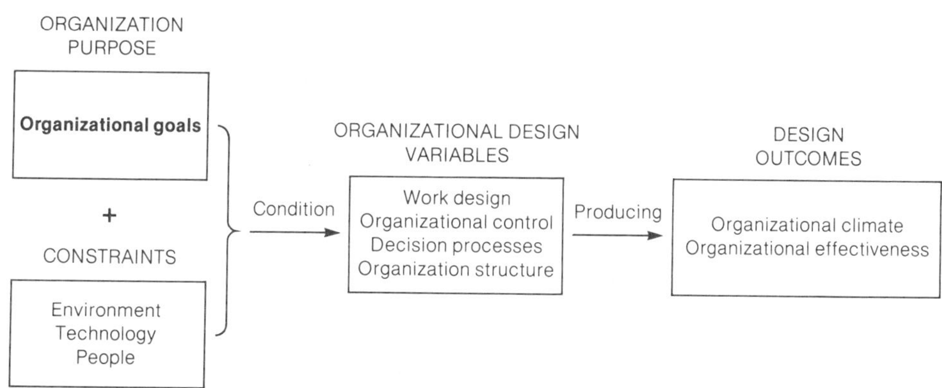

Organizational level, time frame (short run versus long run), and other typical goal-objective distinctions can be safely ignored as immaterial to this discussion.

Goals: What Are They?

There are two major schools of thought regarding organizational goals. The first is that it is not an issue with which students of organizations need be concerned. In this view, the concept of goals simply sets the stage for inquiry into other matters, such as how subordinates can be made to conform with management's desire for increased productivity (Perrow, 1968: 305). What is more, the concept is seen by some to have been analytically fruitless. People have spent more energy trying to understand and operate organizations using a goals concept than it has been worth (Georgiou, 1973). The second view (and that of this volume) is that organizational goals are real, possess certain properties, and provide analytical benefits. To determine the nature of those properties and examine their benefits, one must answer the following questions: what are goals, where do they come from, and what is their impact on the organization and its design? We consider these questions throughout the chapter.

Since the complexity of the subject is considerable, as we have already seen, the nature of organizational goals has never been described very crisply. Still, we can point to a couple of important aspects. The first concerns their relevance for the organization; the second, their relevance for management.

Goals and Organizational Domains

Three decades ago, economists suggested that other organizational goals besides profit might be at least as important as it was. Similarly sociologists have tended to view organizations as "complex institutions with evolving goals and a 'character' of their own" (Perrow, 1968: 305). Etzioni (1961a: 71), for example, has defined organizational goals as "a state of affairs which the organization is attempting to realize." He also acknowledges that organizations frequently serve more than one goal. However, such goals are (1961a: 265):

> . . . often set by a social unit . . . or external goal-setting collectivity . . . other than the organization itself. In addition, organizations which are committed to one paramount goal must often pursue quite different subgoals or tasks in order to achieve it.

Thompson (1967) has suggested that the organization also deliberately engages the environment, rather than simply reacting to it, as implied by Etzioni's statement. In particular, proposed Thompson, the organization establishes a *domain.* Domain "consists of claims which an organization stakes out for itself" (1967: 26). These claims are asserted in terms of the following: range of products produced, population of customers (actual and potential) served, and services rendered.

> Thus universities are universities, but their domains may range considerably; some offer astronomy courses, others do not; some serve local populations, others are international; some offer student housing and graduate education, others do not. No two firms in the oil industry are identical in terms of domain. Some refine petroleum and market gasoline and other derivatives; others buy and market gasoline and oil. Some operate in a regional territory; others are national or international. Some provide credit cards; others are cash and carry. [Thompson, 1967: 26]

Thompson points out that the *legitimacy* of an organization's domain depends on more than the organization's claim. It must be granted by other members of the task environment (suppliers, competitors, customers, regulators, and so forth). The point to this, of course, is that legitimate domains reflect organizational intentions and aspirations. In short, they reflect organizational goals.

Goals as Decision Constraints

Actually, goals do more than merely reflect organization-environment relationships. They also show up in specific managerial actions. This, at least, is the approach taken by Simon (1957a; 1964), presented in this chapter's second reading. Relying on his ideas, Cyert and March (1963: 117) define organizational goals as "a series of independent aspiration-level constraints." In particular, these constraints are imposed on the organization by members of the organizational coalition. We recall that the term *coalition* is used because the enterprise is seen as "a coalition of participants with disparate demands, changing foci of attention, and limited ability to attend to all organizational problems simultaneously" (Cyert and March, 1963: 43).

This approach suggests that organizational goals should be viewed in terms of their relation to decision making. Specifically, say Cyert and March, there are two kinds of organizational variables—those that affect goals and those that affect expectations about goal achievement. Variables that affect goals are: 1. the composition of the organization's membership, 2. the division of labor in decision making, and 3. the nature of problems facing the organization. Variables that affect goal expectations include: 1. the organization's past goals, 2. the organization's past performance, and 3. the past performance of other comparable organizations (1963: 115).

In any event, the importance of goals is how they affect decision making (Cyert and March, 1963; Simon, 1964). Goals establish decision boundaries, determine mixes of resources and activities to be employed, and otherwise limit the decision maker's options in a given situation. In short, organizational decision making is concerned with discovering "causes of action which satisfy a whole set of constraints" (Simon, 1964: 20). The constraints are organizational goals.

The Readings

Two articles have been selected for this chapter. Although many articles, papers, and books have been written about organizational goals, these two seem especially useful to our interest in designing organizations. In the first, "Organizational and Individual Objectives," Professor Fremont Kast provides us with a comprehensive treatment of the subject. Employing a perspective that treats the organization as an open system, he focuses at three levels: 1. the environmental level—the goal constraints imposed on the organization by society; 2. the organizational level—the goals of the organization as a system; and 3. the individual level—the goals of organizational participants. Kast then discusses three aspects of goals that are important to organizational design: 1. integrating individual and organizational goals; 2. setting and implementing goals; and 3. managing goal conflicts.

But be warned: the subject of goals is one of the most complex in organization theory. Kast's discussion meets this complexity head on. Thus while we have streamlined the article quite a bit from its original form, a fair amount of complexity remains. Thinking about the organization as an open system, with different levels (environment, organizational, managerial, individual) helps.

The debt Kast's treatment owes to the analysis of Barnard (1939), March and Simon (1958), and Simon (1964) is considerable. The question of whether organizations—or the people who populate them—have goals, the matter of means-ends relationships, and the basis on which people pursue goals are considerations taken up in this chapter's second article, "On the Concept of Organizational Goals," by Professor Herbert Simon. In particular, he notes that organizational goals are different from individual goals in important ways.

Simon also explains (and for us this is probably his most important contribution) that organizational goals should be thought of as sets of constraints that apply to decision-making processes. Constraint-sets reflect the *inducements* and *contributions* important to organizational members. That is, Simon's view is that people contribute to organizational production on the basis of having received adequate inducement to do so.

Finally, Professor Simon points out that organizations are characterized by a variety of goals, whose pursuit occurs simultaneously.

Conclusion

In summary, this chapter is concerned with the following questions:

1. What exactly do we mean by the term, *organizational goals?*
2. What kinds of goals do organizations pursue?
3. How do goals affect organization design?

ORGANIZATIONAL AND INDIVIDUAL OBJECTIVES

FREMONT E. KAST

Formal organizations are contrived social systems designed to accomplish specific purposes. The tendency to organize or cooperate in interdependent relationships is basic in human nature. Within the past several centuries, the growing importance of large groups or organizations has been one of the most pervasive phenomena (Stinchcombe, 1965). Organizations have been created in order to achieve objectives that could not be accomplished by the individual or more informal groups. Getting to the moon, staging a massive effort to meet our health problems, and creating a multinational business require complex and sophisticated organizations. However, although organizations are created by man to help him accomplish his purposes more effectively, they may generate many conflicts and problems.

There are many different definitions of organizations, but all reveal certain common elements. Organizations are oriented toward accomplishing goals. Knowledge and techniques are used in achieving these goals. Organization implies structuring and integrating activities—that is, people working or cooperating together in interdependent relationships. The notion of interrelatedness suggests a social system. Therefore we can say that *organizations* are 1. *goal-oriented,* people with a purpose; 2. *psycho-social systems,* people interacting together; 3. *technological systems,* people using knowledge and techniques; and 4. *an integration of structured activities,* people working together.

Throughout this discussion organizations will be considered as sociotechnical systems in interaction with their environment. Traditional management and organization theory used a highly structured, closed-system approach. The bureaucratic model emphasized the development of a rational organization structure based on authority. Scientific management concentrated on improving the performance of technical tasks. Both took a very limited and closed view of the organization.

Modern theory has moved toward the open-system approach. Drawing on the contributions of many modern writers, we can view an organization as an open, socio-technical system composed of a number of subsystems, as illustrated in Figure 3–1. The open-system view recognizes that the organization is in dynamic interaction with its environment and receives inputs, transforms these inputs in some way, and returns outputs.

The organization can be viewed as an aggregate of several major subsystems. The organizational *goals and values* are one of the more important. The *technical system* refers to the knowledge required to transform inputs into outputs. Every organization has a *psycho-social* system that consists of individual behavior and motivation, status and role systems, group dynamics, and influence systems. The *organization structure* can be considered as another major subsystem intermeshed

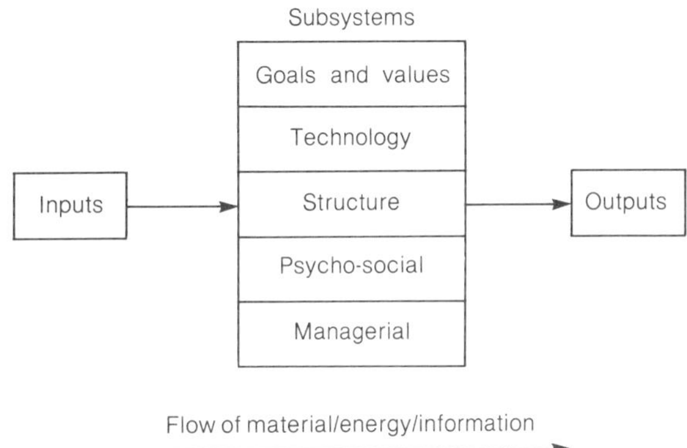

Figure 3-1. The organization as an open socio-technical system

Fremont E. Kast "Organizational and Individual Objectives," *Contemporary Management: Issues and Viewpoints,* ed. Joseph W. McGuire (Englewood Cliffs, N.J.: Prentice-Hall), pp. 150–80. © 1974, Prentice-Hall, Inc. Adapted by permission.

between the technical and the psycho-social subsystems. Structure is concerned with the ways in which the tasks of the organization are divided (differentiated) and with the coordination of these activities (integration). The *managerial system* spans the entire organization by directing the technology, organizing people and other resources, and relating the organization to its environment.

This open-systems view sets the framework for considering organizational and individual goals. The goals and values subsystem is of key importance in relating the organization to its environment, in determining the nature of the technology and structure, and in establishing the relationships among people in the organization.

What Are Goals?

Simply stated, goals are the desirable results of organizational or individual activities. In this sense, goals include objectives, purposes, missions, deadlines, standards, targets, quotas, and so on. However, the concept of a "goal" has acquired a variety of meanings, depending on the perspective of the writer. It is sometimes used to legitimize the role of the organization in society (the goal of General Motors is to make automobiles), or to provide a motive for the organization's activity (General Motor's goal is to make a profit). A goal may also be a specific accomplishment, such as manufacturing so many automobiles during a given time period. In another sense, goals may be considered as the set of constraints that the organization must satisfy; i.e., making profits for the stockholders, meeting governmental safety standards, pacifying the environmentalists, and satisfying customers. [Editor's note: See the following article by Simon.]

We need a more elaborate definition of goals that encompasses these various perspectives. Gore (1964: 184–85) says that goals are:

> The objects toward which organizations direct their energies and concerns. If organization is a means of accomplishing ends beyond the capacities of individuals, goals are collective ends translated into socially meaningful terms. Often represented as being defined by action, goals also influence organized activity. . . .

One of the major problems in the analysis of organizational goals is the distinction between the *official* goals and the actual *operational* goals. Official goals are often stated in broad, ambiguous terms to legitimize the activities of the organization. For example, the official goal of a mental institution may be to treat mental illness. However, the operational goals are those actually pursued. The mental hospital may provide little in the way of treatment and be geared instead to custodial care of patients.

> The type of goals most relevant to understanding organizational behavior are not the official goals, but those that are embedded in major operating policies and the daily decisions of the personnel. . . . These goals will be shaped by the particular problems or tasks an organization must emphasize, since these tasks determine the characteristics of those who will dominate the organization [Perrow, 1961: 854].

In studying organizational and individual goals, we face many additional conceptual difficulties. Do organizations have goals or are goals the composite of individual goals? How are goals established and modified? Who establishes the goals? Despite these and other questions we can agree on the importance of goals in organizational analysis. The efforts to achieve goals affects the ability of the organization to receive resource inputs from the broader society and thus legitimize its existence. They focus the attention of participants on actions that are organizationally relevant. They provide the standards for measuring success. They help determine the technologies and tasks required and also provide the basis for specialization of effort, authority patterns, communication and decision networks, and other structural relationships. The nature of the goals vitally affect the psycho-social relationships within the organization. In effect, the goals set the basic character of the organization. Perrow (1970: 171–72) says:

> They reflect more readily the uniqueness of organizations and the role of specific influences within the more general technological and structural categories. For goals are the product of a variety of influences, some of them enduring and some fairly transient. To enumerate some of these

influences: *The personality of top executives, the history of the organization, its community environment, the norms and values of the other organizations with which it deals (e.g., the "mentality of the steel industry"), the technology and structure of the organization, and ultimately the cultural setting.* [emphasis added—ed.]

Management is vitally affected by the nature of organizational and individual goals. Chief executives generally establish the broad institutional goals that help relate the organization to its environment. Management then translates these broad goals into operational objectives. It provides means of control to measure the extent of goal accomplishment. It must continually deal with goal conflicts and find ways of satisfying the interest of many internal and external groups. Thus, management is vitally concerned with goal formation and implementation, and conflict resolution. But it is not omnipotent. Many goals and constraints are imposed on the organization by the external society and internal participants.

This [article] will look more completely at a number of the issues raised in this introduction. The following topics are considered.

- Organizational Goals—Three levels of analysis
- Environmental Determinants of Organizational Goals
- Organizational Systems Goals
- Individual and Organizational Goals
- Integration of Individual and Organizational Goals
- The Role of Management in Setting and Implementing Goals
- Managing Goal Conflicts

Organizational goals can be considered from three primary perspectives: 1. the environmental level—the goal constraints imposed on the organization by society; 2. the organizational level—the goals of the organization as a system; and 3. the individual level—the goals of organizational participants. There obviously may be many goal conflicts among these three levels. However, there must also be a certain degree of goal compatibility if the organization is to survive. Each of these three levels is considered in detail in the following discussion. However, it is first necessary to consider whether or not organizations have goals distinct from those of individual participants.

Organizations have already been defined as specific goal-seeking systems. This *reification* of the organization—attributing a concrete reality to a social system—is reflected in much of the thinking about organizational goals. Perhaps the origins of this view stem from the classical economic theory of the firm, which considered the organization as a single entrepreneur—the goals of the firm and the entrepreneur are identical. Similarly in public agencies, the classical approach assumed that goals were determined by legislative action and the primary function of the agency was goal implementation. However, in reality there are many organizational participants—stockholders, executives, staffs, and other employees whose individual goals shape the activities of the organization. But we are left with a dilemma. If we do not accept the entrepreneural goal as the organization goal, what is the organization goal? Cyert and March (1963: 26) set forth this problem as follows:

1. People (i.e., individuals) have goals; collectivities of people do not.
2. To define a theory of organizational decision making, we seem to need something analogous—at the organization level—to individual goals at the individual level.

They also suggest a solution to this problem by conceptualizing the organization as a coalition.

> In a business organization the coalition members include managers, workers, stockholders, suppliers, customers, lawyers, tax collectors, regulatory agencies, and so on. In the governmental organization the members include administrators, workers, appointive officials, elective officials, legislators, judges, clientele, interest-group leaders, and the like. In the voluntary charitable organization there are paid functionaries, volunteers, donors, donees, and others. [Cyert and March, 1963: 27]

These organizational members have different and frequently conflicting goals. Thus the actual goals of the organization result from a continuous bargaining-learning process by coalition members.

This approach is followed throughout this article.

Organizations *do have* multiple goals that arise out of the continual learning-bargaining process of internal and external coalition members. These goals are frequently not officially stated and are often in conflict. There may be inconsistencies and ambiguities. The *goal set* of the organization is continually changing as a result of this learning-adapting process.

> In practice, goals are often set in a complicated power play involving various individuals and groups within and without the organization, and by reference to values which govern behavior in general and the specific behavior of the relevant individuals and groups in a particular society. [Etzioni, 1964: 7–8]

The question remains, Who are the various members of the coalition and how do they influence the goal structure of the organizations? The open-systems model will be utilized as a framework for discussing this question. The organization is a subsystem of the broader society but it also contains internal subsystems of groups and individuals. We will therefore consider a hierarchical order moving from the environment, to the organization, to the individual levels. The boundaries between these systems levels are not absolute and there is a high degree of interaction among them.

ENVIRONMENTAL DETERMINANTS OF ORGANIZATIONAL GOALS

The open-system view suggests that the organization receives resource inputs, transforms these inputs, and then returns outputs to the environment. The university receives appropriations, research grants, and students; transforms these inputs through its teaching, research, and service activities; and turns out trained graduates of many types, new research information, and a great variety of services. Every organization is in constant interaction with its environment. Even more important, it depends on this environment for its very survival. The goals that society prescribes for the organization are of vital importance.

An important conceptual model for viewing the relationship between the organization and the broader society has been developed by Talcott Parsons (1951). He used a systems viewpoint to conceptualize society as a complex of interlocking systems ranging from individual personalities and small groups, through more complex organizations, to whole societies. The organization is a subsystem of the broader society and its goals must be legitimized by that society. He says (1956: 238):

> It seemed appropriate to define an organization as a social system which is organized for the attainment of a particular type of goal; the attainment of that goal is at the same time the performance of a type of function on behalf of a more inclusive system, the society.

In this view the organization can survive only by meeting certain goals imposed by the society that legitimizes its activities. The organization is viewed as an instrument to accomplish society's goals, whether it be a business firm or some other organization.

> In achieving its generalized objectives of stability and growth, in providing for its current activities and future-oriented projects, and in making its routine and strategic decisions, society makes use of the business firm as an instrument. [Chamberlain, 1968: 139]

We have suggested that the broader socio-cultural environment imposes certain constraints on organizations to insure that they accomplish social purposes. This legitimizes the activities of the organization and requires it to set its operational goals within this framework. We will now turn to the next level of analysis—the organizational systems goals.

ORGANIZATIONAL SYSTEMS GOALS

Organizational systems goals pertain to the purposes and desired conditions of the organization as a distinct entity (Perrow, 1970: 144). Self-perpetuation, a high rate of profit, stability of operations, growth, satisfaction of participants, enhancement of position in its field, technological leadership and innovation—all are examples of systems goals. Systems goals are thus those states or conditions to which the organization aspires.

It was suggested earlier that organizations have multiple goals rather than a single goal and that this goal set is determined by bargaining among coalition members. Organizational goals cannot be understood merely by accepting officially stated goals but only by observing the actual policies of the organization and how they are implemented. Typically, official goals are stated in broad and ambiguous terms to allow for substantial discretion in operational goals. Organizations, like other open systems, exhibit equifinality—they generally have many alternative means for accomplishing systems objectives (Katz and Kahn, 1966: 26–27). The organization has substantial discretion concerning the goals that it attempts to reach and also many alternative transformation functions to accomplish them. It must operate within the constraints established by environmental forces and by the need to maintain the contributions of individual participations (to be discussed in more detail later).

The Organization as an Adapting, Goal-Satisficing System

It was suggested earlier that organizations are learning, adapting systems that have multiple, sometimes conflicting, goals. This view is in contrast to that of the organization as a rationally oriented, single-goal maximizing system. Cyert and March (1963) provided the most comprehensive treatment of this approach in *A Behavioral Theory of the Firm.* They developed a comprehensive behavioral theory of organizational decision-making, one part of which is consideration of organizational objectives. For our purposes here their most essential views of organizational goals are:

Organization as a Coalition

The organization is a coalition of individuals and subgroups. These coalition members have both common and conflicting interests. The inducements necessary to ensure the participation of these individuals and groups make for a variety of organizational goals. The goals of these coalition members are constraints on the organization.

> Basic to the idea of a coalition is the expectation that the individual participants in the organization may have substantially different preference orderings (i.e., individual goals). That is to say, any theory of organizational goals must deal successfully with the obvious potential for internal goal conflict inherent in a coalition of diverse individuals and groups. [Cyert and March, 1963: 27]

Formulating Goals Through Bargaining

The actual operational goals of the organization are formed through the process of bargaining for inducements by the various coalition members. These "side payments" or inducements for participation take many forms: money, authority and power, personal satisfaction, and so on. Thus stockholders require profits, employees want decent wages and favorable working conditions, managers require power and prestige, customers demand quality products. Because the coalition and power of the various members change over time, the goals of the organization are continually shifting to reflect these changes.

Satisficing Multiple Goals

Goals of coalition members are frequently in conflict. Therefore it is never possible to maximize the goal of any individual or group. Rather, the organization seeks to satisfy the goals of all coalition members in order to maintain their participation.

Modifying Goals Through Experience

Individuals and organizations have aspiration levels for the attainment of their objectives. These aspiration levels are influenced by past performance in relationship to goals, past aspiration levels, and comparisons with reference groups. The individual or the organization attempts to satisfy goal aspirations that can be changed in terms of past learning experiences. As an individual example, the university student who is successful in his studies may raise his aspirations—he may decide to go on to graduate school. Similarly, the organization that has achieved its sales goals within a given year will usually adjust its sights upward. Lack of success in goal achievement usually results in a downward adjustment in aspirations—both for the individual and for the organization.

Sequential Attention to Goals

With a multiple, frequently conflicting goal set, the organization cannot maximize all its goals. Generally, individuals and organizations devote sequential attention to goals. They endeavor to upgrade accomplishment of goals that have not yet been satisfactorily attained. (Students will sacrifice many other goals to cram for final examinations.) Organizations will embark on cost reduction programs or safety programs without considering all the consequences in terms of downgrading other goals. In the Cyert and March model, particular goals receive attention only when achievement falls below the aspiration levels. This is one way for the organization to minimize goal conflict. Much of the time, the conflict remains latent because the focus is on different goals at different periods of time.

Organizational Slack

The concept of organizational slack is useful in understanding how organizations maintain equilibrium in the face of multiple goal demands and changing conditions. Slack can be defined as the difference between total organizational resources and the payments necessary to maintain the contributions of the coalition members. When environmental conditions are very favorable, the coalition members' aspiration levels do not rise so rapidly as the available resources. These excess resources become organizational slack. Conversely, when environmental conditions become unfavorable, the slack becomes a cushion, permitting the organization to survive in the face of adversity. Conceptually, slack helps the organization maintain a dynamic equilibrium in the face of environmental turbulence.

Managing the Coalition

The primary executive function is to manage the coalition. Management, because of its authority position in the hierarchy and ability to allocate resources, has the key role of balancing the pressures from the various coalition members. It must satisfy their goals sufficiently well to retain their active participation. Management does not direct all organization activities toward the maximization of one omnipotent goal—such as profit maximization. Rather, it operates within the constraints of demands for goal satisfaction from many groups. *It must strive to maintain the dominant coalition to insure the survival, growth, and well-being of the organization.* [emphasis added—ed.]

The Cyert-March model suggests why organizations have difficulty in setting forth specific overall goals. It is frequently impossible to get all members of the coalition to agree on specific objectives unless the overall objectives are stated in ambiguous, general, and rather broad terms. Most university presidents proclaim their organizational goals to be creation of knowledge through research, dissemination of knowledge through teaching, and service to the community. These statements are sufficiently vague to keep all coalition members happy. However, they don't help much in explaining why certain universities consistently make the top ten in the national football poll whereas others are recognized for their intellectual contributions.

MEANS-ENDS CHAIN

We have suggested that overall goal statements are usually very general. They are not operational in that there are no established criteria for determining how particular programs or activities contribute to these goals. These broad statements of purpose must be translated into operational objectives. Understanding the means-end chain helps us to see how broad goals are translated into operational objectives.[1]

In analyzing goals it is also necessary to decide how they are to be accomplished, or what *means* will be used to attain them. In the organization, the relationship between means and ends is hierarchical. Goals established at one level require certain means for their accomplishment. These means then become the subgoals for the next level, and more specific operational objectives are developed as we move down the hierarchy. A fire department's primary goal is to reduce fire losses by such means as preventing and extinguishing fires. These means then logically become the goals of the next level in the organization and lead to the creation of a fire prevention unit and a fire fighting

1. For further discussion of means and ends see Simon, *Administrative Behavior,* pp. 62–66; March and Simon, *Organizations,* pp. 190–93; Joseph A. Litterer, *The Analysis of Organizations* (New York: John Wiley & Sons, 1965), pp. 139–42; Martin K. Starr, *Management: A Modern Approach* (New York: Harcourt Brace Jovanovich, Inc., 1971), p. 208; and R. W. Morell, *Management: Ends and Means* (San Francisco: Chandler Publishing Company, 1969), pp. 5–37.

unit. The means for carrying out these units' goals might be the establishment of specific programs for locating water hydrants, educating the public, and geographically decentralizing fire stations.

The hierarchy of goals and the means-end chain have important implications for organizational structure. Generally, the division of labor and functional specialization within the organization is based on the means-ends chain. The business organization may have a sales department, finance department, and production department that have specific subgoals related to their functional areas.

Goals at Different Levels

Through the means-ends chain general goals are translated into increasingly specific operational goals. Complex organizations have several administrative levels with differing goals and activities. Parsons (1960: 60–69) suggests that there are three levels in the hierarchical structure of complex organizations: the technical or production level, the managerial or intermediate level, and the institutional or community level.

The *institutional* level relates the activities of the organization to its environmental system. The goals at this level are broad and provide substantial flexibility concerning the means for their attainment.

The second level, the *managerial,* coordinates and integrates the task performance of the technical system to meet requirements set forth by the institutional level. The goals at this level are still fairly broad but can be stated in operational terms where performance can be measured, such as sales and production goals, budgets, and goals for program activities.

The third level concerns the *technical* subsystems that are involved in actual task performance. The goals at this level are usually very specific, short term, and measurable.

As we move from the institutional to the technical levels, goals and the means for their accomplishment become more specific, short-range, and measurable. The organization attempts to reduce the uncertainties in its basic technical operations by setting forth specific goals and means of accomplishing them. The managerial level performs a vital mediating function between the institutional and technical levels. [As we saw in Chapter 1, Thompson (1967: 12) suggests this role]:

> If the organization must approach certainty at the technical level to satisfy its rationality criteria, but must remain flexible and adaptive to satisfy environmental requirements, we might expect the managerial level to mediate between them, ironing out some irregularities stemming from external sources, but also pressing the technical core for modifications as conditions alter.

Interdepartmental Goal Conflict

In addition to differentiating and specifying subgoals through the means-ends chain on a hierarchical basis, subgoals are established for different functional units within the organization. In the correctional institution there are certain subunits whose primary responsibility is the confinement of inmates, whereas other subunits are charged with rehabilitation. In the business firm, the sales department's goal is to increase sales, the production department's goal is efficient, low-cost production, and the R & D department's goal is the development of new products. There is substantial differentiation of activities based on subgoals for different functional units. This leads to differences in structure, attitudes, and behavior; time perspectives; and interpersonal orientations for these different subunits (Lawrence and Lorsch, 1967c).

This differentiation frequently leads to substantial interdepartmental conflicts within the organization. Maximizing the goal accomplishments of one functional department may entail sacrificing the goals of another department. Thus, maximizing the confinement goal in correctional institutions may be in direct conflict with other subunits that are seeking to rehabilitate inmates. This, again, is another reason why the goal structure of the organization is never perfectly rational. The actual goals of the organization are a result of the power interplay among different organizational units and individuals. They are also continually being modified by environmental forces. The goal set is continually modifying and changing to reflect these forces.

Goal Displacement

One of the most difficult problems involves measuring how effectively goals are being met. When goals can be precisely stated, as frequently is the case at the technical level, goal accomplishment can be relatively simple. However, with more general goals, the measurement becomes more difficult. For example, how do we measure how effective the university is in disseminating and creating knowledge? By number of graduates? By analysis of their life-time earnings? By the volume of research publications? By the win-loss record of the football team?

Another of the difficulties that organizations face is overmeasuring specific quantitative goals and underemphasizing more abstract, less easily measured goals.

There are other forces that distort the goal structure of organizations. One of the more important is displacement of goals. *Goal displacement* stems from the need for the organization to differentiate activities and from the process of downward delegation of authority and responsibility. Sills (1970: 227) describes this process as follows:

> In order to accomplish their goals, organizations establish a set of procedures or means. In the course of following these procedures, however, the subordinates or members to whom authority and functions have been delegated often come to regard them as ends in themselves, rather than means toward the achievement of organizational goals. As a result of this process, the actual activities of the organization become centered around the proper functioning of organization procedures, rather than upon the achievement of the initial goals.

Through this process, the official goals of the organization are neglected in favor of goals associated with building or maintaining the organization. Many writers on organizations have noted this process. Michels (1949), in his study of socialist parties and labor organizations in Europe, pointed out how the original goal of creating a democratic society was displaced by the desire to maintain the organization and the position of the leaders. The original means become the actual ends of organizational activity. Merton says that goals are displaced because the bureaucratic organization affects participants' personalities and causes them to adhere rigidly to rules and regulations for their own sake. "Adherence to the rules, originally conceived as a means, becomes transformed into an end-in-itself; there occurs the familiar process of *displacement of goals,* whereby an instrumental value becomes a terminal value" (Merton, 1957: 199).

This phenomenon of goal displacement is most apparent in those situations in which the organizational goals are abstract and intangible.

> *Intangible goals* are expressions of intended states of affairs that do not adequately describe the desired states or the activities that would constitute their achievement. Such intangible goals do not provide adequate guidance for group action, and as a consequence, more tangible substitutes are developed. [Warner and Havens, 1968: 540]

Participants stress adherence to rules and regulations (means) rather than adherence to the more abstract and less measurable goals. This problem is apparent in many social welfare agencies. For example, strict adherence to the rule of no welfare payments if there is an employable male in the household may actually create many adverse social and family problems and defeat the overall goals of the agency.

This problem is not easily resolved. If organizational members are bound by rigid role prescriptions, rules, and regulations to guide their activities, and strong sanctions are used to enforce adherence, goal displacement will occur.[2] The organization might work to more adequately develop the means-ends chains so that individual activities are related to ends. Attempts to translate the intangible, abstract goals into more meaningful desired states of affairs can be helpful. One such approach, management by objectives, will be discussed in a later section.

INDIVIDUAL AND ORGANIZATIONAL GOALS

We turn now to the third level of analysis: the goals of individual participants and their relationship to organizational goals. Organizations are established to accomplish human purposes, purposes that could not be accomplished by individual action. It would be simple to assume that organizational goals and individual

2. For an insightful discussion of goal displacement and related issues see Michel Crozier, *The Bureaucratic Phenomenon* (Chicago: The University of Chicago Press, 1964), pp. 175–208.

participant goals are complementary. This, in effect, was the assumption in classical economic theory and most traditional management theories. Employees were compensated through monetary and other inducements for their participation in meeting organizational goals. This simple assumption of compatibility failed to recognize many bases for conflict between organizational and individual goals. First, man is much more complex than the rational economic man assumption. He has many needs and aspirations that are not easily met in purely economic terms. Second, the organizational goal set is not ideally rational; it is bounded by many discontinuities and ambiguities, as we saw in the preceding section.

The early human relationists saw the need for greater emphasis on human satisfaction as well as on organizational technical effectiveness. Although they saw the need for ensuring greater human satisfaction, the need was viewed as a *means* for achieving better organizational goal accomplishment. Management should turn from emphasizing satisfaction of lower level physiological and safety needs and instead direct its attention toward satisfying higher-level social, status, and self-actualization needs in order to obtain more effective employee participation *toward accomplishing organizational goals.* Human satisfaction was a *means* to the organizational *ends.*

[However, we raise a critical issue] when we question whether or not organizational goals and human needs are compatible.

> Thus, one of the major dilemmas of organizational psychology arises because policies and practices which insure organizational effectiveness often may leave an individual's needs unsatisfied, or worse, may create problems above and beyond the ones the person brought with him. He may become alienated, insecure, and bitter if the organization fails to fulfill minimum needs for security, maintenance of self-esteem, and opportunities to grow and develop. [Schein, 1970: 10]

We should not overemphasize the possible conflicts between organizational goals and human satisfaction. As Etzioni (1964: 2) suggests,

> Within limits, happiness heightens efficiency in organizations and, conversely, without efficient organizations much of our happiness is unthinkable. Without well-run organizations our standard of living, our level of culture, and our democratic life could not be maintained. Thus, to a degree, *organizational rationality and human happiness go hand in hand.* But a point is reached in every organization where happiness and efficiency cease to support each other. Not all work can be well-paid or gratifying, and not all regulations and orders can be made acceptable. Here we face a true dilemma.[45]

In the following discussion, we are not going to assume either that (1) organizational and individual goals are compatible, or that (2) organization and individual goals are contradictory. To a major extent they are both. Without a minimum degree of compatibility, organizations could not exist. But, total agreement is impossible and conflicts do exist.

The Inducement-Contribution Concept

The Barnard-Simon inducements-contributions model provides a basis for understanding the relationship between personal motives and organizational goals.* The basic aspects of this model are (March and Simon, 1958: 84):

1. An organization is a system of interrelated social behaviors of a number of persons whom we shall call the *participants* in the organization.
2. Each participant and each group of participants receives *inducements from* the organization in return for which he makes *contributions* to the organization.
3. Each participant will continue to participate in an organization only as long as the inducements offered him are as great or greater (measured in terms of *his* values and in terms of the alternatives open to him) than the contributions he is asked to make.
4. The contributions provided by the various groups of participants are the source from which the

**Ed. note:* This model is the basis of the Simon article, immediately following.

organization manufactures the inducements offered to participants.

5. Hence, an organization is "solvent"—and will continue in existence—only as long as the contributions are sufficient to provide inducements in large enough measure to draw forth these contributions.

The individual will continue to participate in the attainment of organizational goals only as long as the organization provides inducements that meet his personal goals. This inducement may be direct if the goals of the organization have direct personal value for the individual—such as church membership or participation in a voluntary charitable organization—or indirect if the organization offers personal rewards—money, status, position—to the individual in return for his contribution. The latter case is probably true for most employees in business organizations.

In this model, once the individual has made the decision to participate, he accepts an organizational role. Thereafter, his role-enacting behavior is determined by the organizational goals rather than his personal motivations (Simon, 1964: 11–19). The role prescriptions require that his actions be guided primarily by organizational goals.

> By whatever means the individual was originally motivated to adopt the role in the first place, the goals and constraints appropriate to the role become a part of the decision-making program, stored in his memory, that defines his role behavior. [Simon, 1964: 11–19][3]

Reciprocation Between Individual and Organization

Others have suggested an even stronger bond between the individual and the organization. There is a psychological contract between the individual and the organization that fulfills the goals of each. Levinson suggests that in modern industrial society there has been a loosening of family, small social group, and other psychological ties and that the work organization becomes increasingly important to man. "In a man's movement from one neighborhood or community to another, the work organization is his thread of continuity and may well become a psychological anchor point for him" (Levinson, 1965: 373).

This view is somewhat similar to the inducement-contribution model, but recognizes even further the psychological needs for affiliation that the organization provides. It suggests that the psychological bond between man and organization helps provide goal integration.

The importance of reciprocation becomes apparent when the psychological contract is broken. When the aerospace industry suffered a severe downturn, organizations discharged many long-term employees, including managers and professionals. These employees had developed a high degree of loyalty and attachment to their organizations and the results of the lay-offs were devastating (both psychologically and economically). We might hypothesize that the stronger the bonds of reciprocation, the more severe the problems of adjustment for the individual when these bonds are destroyed. Many managers, engineers, scientists, and other professionals had great difficulty accepting the fact of their dismissal.

Internalization of Goals

Internalization of organizational goals occurs when the individual develops a personal *commitment* in meeting organizational goals. This internalization is one of the most effective means of integration for it removes conflicts between organizational goals and individual motivation through the development of an organizational personality.

> In this way, through his subjection to organizationally determined goals, and through the gradual absorption of these goals into his own attitudes, the participant in organization acquires an "organizational personality" rather distinct from his personality as an individual. The organization assigns to him a role; it specifies the particular values, facts, and alternatives upon which his decisions in the organization are to be based. [Simon, 1959: 1964]

Although this internalization represents the ideal match between organizational goals and individual

3. Simon recognizes that this concept is an abstraction and that personal motivations do have an important impact on role-enacting behavior. However, he sees this separation of organizational role from personal goals as being very useful in understanding organizational decision making.

motivations, it is rarely fully achieved. Few participants make a full commitment toward meeting organizational goals. There may be conflicts among the organizational role and other roles that the individual tries to fulfill. This conflict is particularly apparent among scientists and other professionals. Traditionally, in professions such as medicine and law, activities were carried out in a nonorganizational context in close interpersonal relationship with clients. Early literature on professionalism focused on the pattern of behavior of these independent professionals and how this differed from that of bureaucrats or "organization men." This traditional view of independence and autonomy is no longer appropriate for most modern scientists-professionals. They are affiliated with businesses, hospitals, governmental agencies, large law firms, and other complex institutions. "No profession has escaped the advancing tide of bureaucratization" (Vollmer and Mills, 1966: 264).

DESIGN PROBLEM # 1: INTEGRATING INDIVIDUAL AND ORGANIZATIONAL GOALS

Many modern writers interested in organizational behavior are concerned with the problem of integrating individual and organizational goals. This section will examine very briefly some of the suggestions for more effectively meeting both organizational goals and individual needs.

Power Equalization

Most modern behavioral scientists emphasize the importance of more democratic, less authoritarian, less hierarchically structured organizations as a means for integrating individual and organization goals. They stress the need for "power equalization" among organizational participants. McGregor's Theory *Y*, Likert's interaction-influence system, Argyris' emphasis on self-actualization, Shepard's collaborative-consensus system, and Bennis' suggestion of the inevitability of democracy in organizations all have an underlying emphasis on power equalization, participation, and more democratic leadership styles as a basis for integrating organizational and individual goals. They have a humanistic orientation that places high value on participant satisfactions rather than purely economic-technical rationality.

Power equalization and more participative, democratic organizations are thus fundamental for many writers. The question remains, however, how they can be accomplished.

Changing the Individual, Group, and Organization

Many behavioral scientists advocate restructuring and organizational change as a means for integrating individual and organizational goals. In their attempts to change individuals, groups, and organizations for better goal integration, they have developed many new approaches. Laboratory or T-group training is an attempt to make the individual more aware of his own behavior and the way he is perceived by others. This "people changing approach" helps the individual develop new attitudes, understanding, and behavior patterns. In the early development of laboratory training, individuals were sent to special training centers away from their organizations. More recently, these programs are taking place "in house" within the organizational setting.

The Management Grid developed by Blake and Mouton (1964) incorporates many of the laboratory training approaches but integrates them with the organizational efficiency goals. Their grid recognizes the need for (1) concern for production, and (2) concern for people. The goal of their program is to bring about the system on their grid that they describe as, "A basic aim of 9,9 management, then, is to promote the conditions that integrate creativity, high productivity, and high morale through concerted team action" (1964: 42).

The Management Grid is one example of the approach toward integrating individual and organizational goals that can be termed *organization development.* Organization development programs emerged from the theory, research, and experiences at the National Training Laboratory (NTL) with their earlier emphasis on laboratory training (sensitivity or T-group). Organization development has taken as its main objective the resolution of the conflict between the organization goals and individual needs. As Beckard (1969: *v*) suggests,

> Enterprise managers today are deeply concerned with the dilemma of how to (a) fully mobilize the energy of the organization's human resources toward achievement of the organization's performance objectives, and (b) at the same time, so organize the work, the work environment, the communications systems, and the relationships of people that individuals' needs for self-worth, growth, and satisfaction are significantly met at work.

Ideally, through the use of such a program the individual internalizes the organizational goals and a high level of reciprocation is realized.

These approaches—laboratory training, the management grid, and organization development—recognize the inevitability of goal conflicts and establish a means of confronting conflicts based on interpersonal and group processes. Goal integration is not left to chance but is actively sought through a clearly planned and long range action program of change. "Planned change" is the by-word, with the behavioral scientists serving as the "change agent."

Human Asset Accounting

The search for ways of relating individual and organizational goals ultimately involves the problem of measuring organizational performance. There are many problems associated with measuring how effective an organization is in accomplishing its goals (see Yuchtman and Seashore, 1967). The problems of measuring the achievement of participant goals within the organization are even more difficult.

There is a growing concern that traditional financial accounting measures only certain aspects of the performance of the organization and does not adequately consider many other vital factors. Likert (1967), for example, suggests that in evaluating organizational performance, much greater consideration should be given to the psycho-social system of the organization. Although there are many statements suggesting that "our people are our most important asset," there is little or nothing done in the traditional managerial accounting and reporting system to reflect this viewpoint. The typical balance sheet, profit and loss statements, and budgetary system do not reflect the value of the human assets nor the organization's effectiveness in accomplishing participant's goals. Likert and others have suggested the need for a system of human asset accounting that would measure the current value of human asset and also indicate whether these are increasing or decreasing.[4] There are many difficulties associated with integrating human asset accounting within traditional accounting systems that cannot be covered in this brief discussion. However, this can be a very important development in measuring organizational goal accomplishment. Organizations and individuals do stress those goals that are measurable and for which they can be held accountable. A well-developed system of human asset accounting would provide the organization with more definitive and quantitative information on how effective it was in meeting participant's goals and would provide the basis for more effectively integrating organizational goals and human satisfactions.

These, then, are just a few of the current steps taken to deal with the issue of integrating individual and organizational goals. The issues are complex and progress has not been rapid. However, these developments do indicate important trends for the future. We will next look more specifically at the role of management in goal setting and implementing and in conflict resolution.

DESIGN PROBLEM # 2: SETTING AND IMPLEMENTING GOALS

Goals result from the learning-adapting response of the organization and are influenced by the various coalition members. Management plays a major role in actually setting operational goals and providing the resources for their implementation. The managerial system is the

4. For further discussion, see R. Lee Brummet, William C. Pyle, and Eric G. Flamholtz, "Human Resource Accounting in Industry," *Personnel Administation,* vol XXXII, no. 4 (July–August 1969), pp. 34–46; Rensis Likert and David G. Bowers, "Organizational Theory and Human Resource Accounting," *American Psychologists,* vol. XXIV, no. 5 (May 1969), pp. 585–92; and John Grant Rhode and Edward E. Lawler III, "Human Resource Accounting: The Accounting System of the Future?" in Marvin Dunnett (ed.), *Work in the Year 2001* (Belmont, Calif.: Wadsworth Publishing Company, 1979).

key decision-making and integrating force for the organization. It must respond to environmental forces and to demands of internal participants in order to maintain a viable coalition. In the complex organization, power is dispersed to the various internal and external groups and top management is constrained in setting and implementing goals. Thompson suggests that the role of administration is co-alignment of these various forces:

> The basic function of administration appears to be co-alignment, not merely of people (in coalitions) but of institutionalized action—of technology and task environment into a viable domain, and of organizational design and structure appropriate to it. Administration, when it works well, keeps the organization at the nexus of the several necessary streams of action. Paradoxically, the administrative process must reduce uncertainty but at the same time search for flexibility. [Thompson, 1967: 157–58]

This suggests that management has a vital role to play in charting the organization's course and in responding to various forces. However, it is a mistake to suggest that the goals of management and the goals of the organization are one and the same. Certainly, management is one of the major elements in the coalition, but it is not the only element. Management's power is never absolute. In the past we have mistakenly attributed the only goal of the business organization to be the profit maximization goal of owners. We should not make a similar mistake by associating organizational goals and managerial goals as one and the same.

> The professional manager [responds] to a *different* set of influences (including his own motivations) from the owner-manager. Because of these differences in actual (rather than publicized) goals, the behavior of the organizations are different (Monsen, 1969: 47).

Setting General and Specific Goals

At the institutional level in most organizations, statements of objectives tend to be very general. Frequently, there is a demand that these goals be made clearer. For example, it is frequently suggested that [universities] should be able to specify more clearly broad goals, thus ensuring support from constituent groups and greater efficiency in accomplishment. Yet, there may be some functionality in maintaining a degree of vagueness in the overall organizational goals. If goals are stated in general terms, there is room for organizational participants to fill in details according to their own perception. Ultra-precision can destroy flexibility and make it more difficult for individuals and organizations to adapt to changing conditions. Some vagueness makes it possible to work toward goals by many different means. It may also facilitate compromise on the part of participants with diverse value systems. As long as people can read into organizational goal statements their own interpretation of the ends to be achieved, compromise is feasible. Thus tacit agreement is often reached with regard to both ends and means. At the institutional level, mediation and compromise are essential ingredients in coordinating activity.

However, it is necessary to translate these broad, general goals into more specific objectives at the organizational and technical levels. A major part of the managerial function is to translate these broad goals into more specific operational objectives for various functional areas and participants within the organization. This process helps to simplify the complexities and ambiguities and to reduce uncertainties.

Management by Objective

Many approaches have been utilized to integrate functional and individual goals with overall organizational goals. "Management by objective" attempts to structure this relationship by setting forth established individual objectives and relating these to overall goals.

Management by objective was first popularized by Drucker who suggested (1954: 53) that "Objectives are needed in every area where performance and results directly and vitally affect the survival and prosperity of the business." He stressed the importance of establishing clearly defined objectives that guide and measure the performance of managers. Over the past 2 decades many business corporations have adopted management by objective programs (Wikstrom, 1968). Many of these programs started initially as a managerial performance-appraisal mechanism. However, many organizations have advanced to a much broader approach encompassing long-range planning, a system of control, and a primary basis of integrating the objectives of the organization with the objectives of individual managers. Although "management by objective" sounds deceptively simple, in practice organizations adopting this approach have had to spend considerable time in modifying their structure and managerial system in order to make it effective.

Studies of specific management-by-objective programs suggest that such programs do improve communications, increase mutual understanding, improve planning, create more positive attitudes toward the evaluation system, help in utilizing management abilities, and promote innovation (Carroll and Tosi, 1970). However, there are also many problems associated with these programs. Many organizational adjustments are necessary if the program is to be successful. It requires long-term effort and is not a short-run panacea. It includes only managerial personnel and does not provide for other employees. In particular, it is often difficult to encompass the efforts of many staff groups within such a program. There is a tendency for managers to direct their efforts toward meeting only those objectives on which they are measured. Other, less quantifiable, objectives may be short-changed. It is often difficult to set forth clearly definable objectives under conditions of rapid change or environmental turbulence. There are many difficulties tying performance appraisal into the program. Finally, there may be many difficulties in requiring objective accomplishment under uncertain and adverse conditions. Executives of companies that have established a management-by-objectives program declare that the program worked very well when environmental and competitive forces were favorable. However, during a business downturn, many managers thought they were held strictly accountable for accomplishing objectives over which they had limited control. Their programs did not adequately respond to new environmental conditions and instead of being a basis for positive motivation, the programs became a source of major conflict.

In spite of these difficulties, management-by-objective programs have been used successfully by a number of business organizations to integrate organizational and individual goals. Similar programs seem to be catching on in other types of organizations. For example, within school systems similar types of programs have been advocated for setting goals and measuring accomplishment.

DESIGN PROBLEM # 3: MANAGING GOAL CONFLICTS

A rising level of conflict within our organizations and in other social interactions is an apparent phenomenon in modern society. Part of this conflict arises because of different perceptions of the need for organizational and social change. Existing goals and values are being seriously challenged and we have not developed new mechanisms for resolving conflict and integrating diverse goals.

The increased awareness, education, and desire to influence the direction of our organizations and our society by many people are partial causes of this social conflict. Ways (1970) suggests that more people in our society are demanding the right to participate in *all* matters that affect their lives and they increasingly have the *power* to demand participation. "The general trend of twentieth-century society, particularly in the U.S., is toward a wider distribution of power, a broadening of participation by individuals in controlling their own lives and work" (Ways, 1970:174). With differing individual and group values and goals, these demands for greater participation are bound to lead to greater conflicts within organizations and in society in general.

It should be emphasized that these conflicts do not always arise because of differences in goals. They are frequently the result of different perceptions of reality, different role requirements for individuals within organizations, and conflicts over means rather than ends. Nevertheless, management and administration in all types of social institutions must deal with these conflicts and find new ways to solve them.

CONCLUSION

Throughout this [article] we have suggested many approaches for conflict resolution. Much of the work of the behavioral scientists is directed toward changing the organization to be more compatible with participant goals (and also changing participant values, attitudes, and behavior to be more compatible with organizational goals). Laboratory training, organization development, management by objective, and other specific programs take this approach.

In conclusion, we return to the basic dilemma with which we began this article. Every organizational activity, from the small informal group to the large-scale business, governmental, or religious organization, requires that the individual subordinate some of his independence and discretion to organizational requirements. He pays a price for his involvement in the hope of obtaining off-setting benefits. Although the organization is a means for the fulfilling of the individual's goals, it also requires him to direct his activities toward its ends. Any assumption that the business or any other organization should be able to satisfy *all* the goals of its participants and still accomplish its goals is in direct conflict with the requirements of organized behavior.

Management must use effective motivation to secure cooperation from organizational participants and should give greater recognition to the satisfaction of higher-level needs. Total reliance on monetary rewards, fringe benefits, and employment security as the only vehicle for motivation drastically limits the inducements that the organization can offer. Yet it does not follow automatically that management can and should take on the responsibility for total fulfillment of all participant goals. The objectives of uniformity and efficiency in the business organization mitigate against the operation of a truly democratic administration. Without democratic processes, the corporations attempting to satisfy all human goals could easily become paternalistic, monolithic structures. When the business organization, with its hierarchical structure and less than full power-equalization, seeks to meet the total goals of the individual, it runs the grave risk of completely subordinating the individual's freedom—not only in his work life but in his total life. Perhaps we would do better to recognize that man has many goals, some fulfilled by his participation in the business organization, some by other organizations such as educational institutions, churches, social groups, and families; some will not be fulfilled but will continue to be powerful motivators to higher levels of achievement.

ON THE CONCEPT OF ORGANIZATIONAL GOAL

HERBERT A. SIMON

Few discussions of organization theory manage to get along without introducing some concept of "organization goal." In the classical economic theory of the firm, where no distinction is made between an organization and a single entrepreneur, the organization's goal—the goal of the firm—is simply identical with the goal of the real or hypothetical entrepreneur. In general, it is thought not to be problematical to postulate that individuals have goals. If it is not, this solution raises no difficulties.

When we are interested in the internal structure of an organization, however, the problem cannot be avoided in this way. Either we must explain organizational behavior in terms of the goals of the individual members of the organization, or we must postulate the existence of one or more organization goals, over and above the goals of the individuals.[1]

The first alternative is an attractive one. It protects us from the danger of reifying the organization, of treating it as a superindividual entity having an existence and behavior independent of the behavior of its members. The difficulty with this alternative is that it is hard to carry off. The usual way it is attempted is by identifying the phrase "organization goals" with "goals of the firm's owners" or, alternatively, "goals of the firm's top management," or "goals of those who hold legitimate authority to direct the organization."

But this solution raises new difficulties, for we often have occasion to observe that the goals that actually underlie the decisions made in an organization do not coincide with the goals of the owners, or of top management, but have been modified by managers and employees at all echelons. Must we conclude, then, that it is the goals of the latter—of subordinate managers and employees—that are governing organizational behavior? Presumably not, because the kinds of behavior taking place are not those we would expect if the managers and employees were consulting only their personal goals. The whole concept of an informal organization, modified by, but not identical with, the goals either of management or of individual employees, becomes hazy and ambiguous if we follow this path.

Let us see if we can find a way between this Scylla and the Charybdis of reification. The first step toward clarification is to maintain a distinction between goals, on the one hand, and motives, on the other. By *goals* we shall mean value premises that can serve as inputs to decisions. By *motives* we mean the causes, whatever they are, that lead individuals to select some goals rather than others as premises for their decisions. In the next section we shall develop the concept of goal, defined as above. In subsequent sections we shall undertake to explicate the notion of *organization goal* and to clarify the relations between organization goals and personal motives.

Before we can define "organization goals" we shall have to be clear on what we mean by "goals of an individual." We shall begin by considering the latter question.

GOALS AND DECISIONS: MULTIPLE CRITERIA

Our discussion of goals will be much simplified if we have a definite model before us of the situation we are considering. In recent years in the field of management science or operations research, we have learned to build formal models to characterize even quite elaborate and complex decision situations, and to use these models to reach "optimal" decisions. Since many of these models make use of the tool of linear programming, we will

1. The present discussion is generally compatible with, but not identical to, that of my colleagues, R. M. Cyert and J. G. March, who discuss organizational goals in Ch. iii of *A Behavioral Theory of the Firm* (Englewood Cliffs, N.J.: Prentice-Hall, 1963). Their analysis is most germane to the paragraphs of this paper that treat of motivation for goals and organizational survival.

Herbert A. Simon, "On the Concept of Organizational Goal," *Administrative Science Quarterly*, vol. 9, no. 1 (June 1964), pp. 1–22.

employ a linear programming framework to describe the decision situation.

The optimal-diet problem is a typical simple linear programming problem. We are given a list of foods, and for each item on the list its price, its calory content, and its proportions of each of the minerals and vitamins relevant to nutrition. Then we are given a set of nutritional requirements, which may include statements about minimum daily intake of minerals, vitamins, and calories, and may also put limits on maximum intake of some or all of these components.

The diet problem is to find that sublist of foods and their quantities that will meet the nutritional requirements at least cost. [That sublist] is called an *optimal* diet.

What is the goal of the diet decision? It would be an appropriate use of ordinary language to say that the goal is to minimize the cost of obtaining an adequate diet, for [that] condition is the criterion we are minimizing. This criterion puts the emphasis on economy as the goal.

Alternatively, we might direct our attention primarily to the *constraints*, and in particular to the nutritional requirements. Then we might say that the goal is to find a nutritionally satisfactory diet that is economical. Although we still mention costs in this statement, we have clearly shifted the emphasis to the adequacy of the diet from a nutritional standpoint. The primary goal has now become good nutrition.

Under some circumstances, we can, however, restrict the set of diets that deserve consideration. Suppose that all the nutritional constraints are minimal constraints, and that we would always prefer, *ceteris paribus,* a greater amount of any nutritional factor to a smaller amount. We will say that diet A is "dominated" by diet B if the cost of diet B is no greater than the cost of diet A, and if diet B contains at least as much of each nutritional factor as does diet A, and more of at least one factor. We will call the set of diets that is undominated by other diets in that set the *Pareto optimal set.*

Our preference for one or the other of the diets in the Pareto optimal set will depend on the relative importance we assign to cost in comparison with amounts of nutritional factors, and to the amounts of these factors in relation with each other. If cost is the most important factor, then we will again choose the diet that is selected by [the cost] criterion. On the other hand, if we attach great importance to [a particular] nutritional factor, we will generally choose a quite different feasible diet—one in which the quantity of [that factor] is as great as possible. Within the limits set by the constraints, it would be quite reasonable to call whatever criterion led us to select a particular member of the Pareto optimal set our goal. But if the constraints are strong enough, then the constraints will have as much or more influence on what diet we finally select than will the goal. For example, if we set one or more of the nutritional requirements very high, so that only a narrow range of diets also satisfy the budget constraint, then introducing the cost minimization criterion as the final selection rule will have relatively little effect on what diet we choose.

Under such circumstances it might be well to give up the idea that the decision situation can be described in terms of a simple goal. Instead, it would be more reasonable to speak of a whole set of goals—the whole set, in fact, of nutritional and budgetary constraints—that the decision maker is trying to attain. To paraphrase a familiar epigram: "If you allow me to determine the constraints, I don't care who selects the optimization criterion."

MULTIPLE CRITERIA IN ORGANIZATIONS

To show the organizational relevance of our example it is only necessary to suppose that the decision we are discussing has arisen within a business firm that manufactures commercial stock feeds, that the nutritional requirements are requirements for hogs and the prices those of available feed ingredients, and that the finished feed prices facing the firm are fixed. Then minimizing the cost of feed meeting certain nutritional standards is identical with maximizing the profit from selling feed meeting those standards. Cost minimization represents the profit-maximizing goal of the company.

We can equally well say that the goal of the feed company is to provide its customers with the best feed possible, in terms of nutritional standards, at a given price, i.e., to produce feeds that are in the Pareto optimal set. Presumably this is what industry spokesmen mean when they say that the goal of business is not profit but efficient production of goods and services. If we had enlarged our model to give some of the prices that appear in it the status of constraints, instead of fixing them as constants, we could have introduced other goals, for example, the goal of suppliers' profits, or, if there were a labor input, the goal of high wages (Simon, 1957b: 170-82).

We may summarize the discussion to this point as follows. In the decision-making situations of real life, a course of action, to be acceptable, must satisfy a whole set of requirements, or constraints. Sometimes one of these requirements is singled out and referred to as the goal of the action. But the choice of one of the constraints, from many, is to a large extent arbitrary. For many purposes it is more meaningful to refer to the whole set of requirements as the (complex) goal of the action. This conclusion applies both to individual and organizational decision making.

SEARCH FOR A COURSE OF ACTION

Thus far, we have assumed that the set of possible actions is known in advance to the decision maker. In many, if not most, real-life situations, possible courses of action must be discovered, designed, or synthesized. In the process of searching for a satisfactory solution, the goals of the action—that is, the constraints that must be satisfied by the solution—may play a guiding role in two ways. First, the goals may be used directly to synthesize proposed solutions *(alternative generation)*. Second, the goals may be used to test the satisfactoriness of a proposed solution *(alternative testing)*.[2]

We may illustrate these possibilities by considering what goes on in the mind of a chess player when he is trying to choose a move in a game. One requirement of a good move is that it put pressure on the opponent by attacking him in some way or by preparing an attack. This requirement suggests possible moves to an experienced player (alternative generation). For example, if the opponent's king is not well protected, the player will search for moves that attack the king, but after a possible move has been generated in this way (and thus automatically satisfies the requirement that it put pressure on the opponent), it must be tested against other requirements (alternative testing). For example, it will not be satisfactory if it permits a counterattack that is more potent than the attack or that can be carried out more quickly.

The decisions of everyday organizational life are similar to these decisions in chess. A bank officer who is investing trust funds in stocks and bonds may, because of the terms of the trust document, take as his goal increasing the capital value of the fund. This will lead him to consider buying common stock in firms in growth industries (alternative generation). But he will check each possible purchase against other requirements: that the firm's financial structure be sound, its past earnings record satisfactory, and so on (alternative testing). All these considerations can be counted among his goals in constructing the portfolio, but some of the goals serve as generators of possible portfolios, others as checks (Clarkson, 1963).

The process of designing courses of action provides us, then, with another source of asymmetry between the goals that guide the actual synthesis and the constraints that determine where possible courses of action are in fact feasible. In general, the search will continue until one decision is found, or, at most, a very few alternatives. Which [decision] is discovered and selected may depend considerably on the search process, that is, on which requirements serve as goals or generators, in the sense just defined, and which as constraints or checks.

In a multiperson situation, one man's goals may be another man's constraints. The feed manufacturer may seek to produce feed as cheaply as possible, searching, for example, for possible new ingredients. The feed, however, has to meet certain nutritional specifications. The hog farmer may seek the best quality of feed, searching, for example, for new manufacturers. The feed, however, cannot cost more than his funds allow; if it is too expensive, he must cut quality or quantity. A sale will be made when a lot of feed is feasible in terms

2. For further discussions of the role of generators and tests in decision making and problem solving, see A. Newell and H. A. Simon, "The Processes of Creative Thinking," *Contemporary Approaches to Creative Thinking*, H. E. Gruber, G. Terrell, and M. Wertheimer, eds. (New York: Atherton, 1962), particularly pp. 77–91.

of the requirements of both manufacturer and farmer. Do manufacturer and farmer have the same goals? In one sense, clearly not, for there is a definite conflict of interest between them: the farmer wishes to buy cheap, the manufacturer to sell dear. On the other hand, if a bargain can be struck that meets the requirements of both [then in another sense] they do have a common goal.

In later paragraphs we shall state some reasons for supposing that the total sets of constraints considered by decision makers in different parts of an organization are likely to be quite similar, but that different decision makers are likely to divide the constraints between generators and tests in quite different ways. Under these circumstances, if we use the phrase organization goals broadly to denote the constraint sets, we will conclude that organizations do, indeed, have goals (widely shared constraint sets). If we use the phrase organization goals narrowly to denote the generators, we will conclude that there is little communality of goals among the several parts of large organizations and that subgoal formation and goal conflict are prominent and significant features of organizational life. The distinction we have made between generators and tests helps resolve this ambiguity, but also underlines the importance of always making explicit which sense of goal is intended.

MOTIVATION FOR GOALS

If by motivation we mean whatever it is that causes someone to follow a particular course of action, then every action is motivated—by definition. But in most human behavior the relation between motives and action is not simple; it is mediated by a whole chain of events and surrounding conditions.

We observe a man scratching his arm. His motive (or goal)? To relieve an itch.

We observe a man reaching into a medicine cabinet. His motive (or goal)? To get a bottle of lotion that, his wife has assured him, is very effective in relieving the itch of mosquito bites. Or have we misstated his motive? Is it to apply the lotion to his arm? Or, as before, to relieve the itch? But the connection between action and goal is much more complex in this case than in the previous one. There intervenes between them a means-end chain (get bottle, apply lotion, relieve itch), an expectation (that the lotion will relieve the itch), and a social belief supporting the expectation (that the wife's assurance is a reliable predictor of the lotion's efficacy). The relation between the action and the ultimate goal has become highly indirect and contingent, even in this simple case. Notice that these new complications of indirectness are superimposed on the complications we have discussed earlier—that the goal is pursued only within limits imposed by numerous side constraints (don't knock over the other bottles in the medicine cabinet, don't brush against the fresh paint, and so on).

Our point is identical with the point of the venerable story of the three bricklayers who were asked what they were doing. "Laying bricks," "Building a wall," "Helping to erect a great cathedral," were their respective answers. The investment trust officer whose behavior we considered earlier could answer in any of these modes, or others. "I am trying to select a stock for this investment portfolio." "I am assembling a portfolio that will provide retirement income for my client." "I am employed as an investment trust officer." Now it is the step of indirectness between the second and third answers that has principal interest for organization theory. The investment trust officer presumably has no "personal" interest in the retirement income of his client, only a "professional" interest in his role as trust officer and bank employee. He does have, on the other hand, a personal interest in maintaining that role and that employment status.

ROLE BEHAVIOR

Of course, in real life the line of demarcation between personal and professional interests is not a sharp one, for personal satisfactions may arise from the competent performance of a professional role, and both personal satisfactions and dissatisfactions may result from innumerable conditions that surround the employment. Nevertheless, it is exceedingly important, as a first approximation, to distinguish between the answers to two questions of motive: "Why do you keep (or take) this job?" and "Why do you make this particular investment decision?" The first question is properly answered in terms of the personal motives or goals of the occupant of the role, the second question in terms of goals that define behavior appropriate to the role itself.

Corresponding to this subdivision of goals into personal and role-defined goals, organization theory is sometimes divided into two subparts: 1. a theory of motivation explaining the decisions of people to participate in and remain in organizations; and 2. a theory of decision making within organizations comprised of such people (March and Simon, 1958: 83–111).

In the motivational theory formulated by Barnard and me, it is postulated that the motives of each group of participants can be divided into *inducements* (aspects of participation that are desired by the participants) and *contributions* (aspects of participation that are inputs to the organization's production function but that generally have negative utility to participants). Each participant is motivated to maximize, or at least increase, his inducements while decreasing his contributions, and this motivation is a crucial consideration in explaining the decision to join (or remain). But "joining" means accepting an organizational role, and hence we do not need any additional motivational assumptions beyond those of inducements-contributions theory to explain the ensuing role-enacting behavior.

THE ORGANIZATIONAL DECISION-MAKING SYSTEM

Let us limit ourselves for the present to situations where occupational roles are almost completely divorced from personal goals. If we now consider the organizational decision-making programs of all the participants, together with the connecting flow of communication, we can assemble them into a composite description of the organizational decision-making system—a system that has been largely abstracted from the individual motives that determine participation.

In the simplest case, of a small, relatively unspecialized organization, we are back to a decision-making situation not unlike that of the optimal diet problem. The language of "goals," "requirements," "constraints," that we applied there is equally applicable to similarly uncomplicated organizational situations.

In more complicated cases, abstracting out the organizational decision-making system from personal motives does not remove all aspects of interpersonal (more accurately, interrole) difference from the decision-making process. For when many persons in specialized roles participate in making an organization's decisions, the total system is not likely to be monolithic in structure. Individual roles will differ with respect to the number and kinds of communications they receive and the parts of the environment from which they receive them. They will differ with respect to the evaluative communications they receive from other roles. They will differ in their search programs. Hence, even within our abstraction, which neglects personal motives, we can accommodate the phenomena of differential perception and subgoal formation.

To make our discussion more specific, let us again consider a specific example of an organizational decision-making system—in this case a system for controlling inventory and production. We suppose a factory in which decisions have to be made about 1. the aggregate rate of production, that is, the work force that will be employed and the hours employees will work each week, 2. the allocation of aggregate production facilities among the several products the factory makes, and 3. the scheduling of the sequence in which the individual products will be handled on the production facilities. Let us call these the aggregate production decision, item allocation decision, and scheduling decision, respectively. The three sets of decisions may be made by different roles in the organization; in general, we would expect the aggregate decision to be handled at more central levels than the others. The real world situation will always include complications beyond those we have described, for it will involve decisions with respect to shipments to warehouses, decisions as to which products to hold in warehouse inventories, and many others.

Now we could conceive of an omniscient Planner (the entrepreneur of classical economic theory) who, by solving a set of simultaneous equations, would make each and all of these interrelated decisions. Decision problems of this kind have been widely studied during the past decade by management scientists, with the result that we now know a great deal about the mathematical structures of the problems and the magnitude of the computations that would be required to solve them. We know, in particular, that discovery of the optimal solution of a complete problem of this kind is well beyond the powers of existing or prospective computational equipment.

In actual organizational practice, no one attempts to find an optimal solution for the whole problem. Instead, various particular decisions, or groups of decisions, within the whole complex are made by specialized members or units of the organization. In making these particular decisions, the specialized units do not solve the whole problem, but find a "satisfactory" solution for one or more subproblems, where some of the effects of the solution on other parts of the system are incorporated in the definition of "satisfactory."

For example, standard costs may be set as constraints for a manufacturing executive. If he finds that his operations are not meeting those constraints, he will search for ways of lowering his costs. Longer production runs may occur to him as a means for accomplishing this end. He can achieve longer production runs if the number of style variations in product is reduced, so he proposes product standardization as a solution to his cost problem. Presumably he will not implement the solution until he has tested it against constraints introduced by the sales department—objections that refusal to meet special requirements of customers will lose sales.

Anyone familiar with organizational life can multiply examples of this sort, where different problems will come to attention in different parts of the organization, or where different solutions will be generated for a problem, depending on where it arises in the organization. The important point to be noted here is that we do not have to postulate conflict in personal goals or motivations in order to explain such conflicts or discrepancies. They could, and would, equally well arise if each of the organizational decision-making roles were being enacted by digital computers, where the usual sorts of personal limits on the acceptance of organizational roles would be entirely absent. The discrepancies arise out of the cognitive inability of the decision makers to deal with the entire problem as a set of simultaneous relations, each to be treated symmetrically with the others (see Dearborn and Simon, 1958).

An aspect of the division of decision-making labor that is common to virtually all organizations is the distinction between the kinds of general, aggregative decisions that are made at high levels of the organization, and the kinds of specific, item-by-item decisions that are made at low levels. We have already alluded to this distinction in the preceding example of a system for controlling inventory and production. When executives at high levels in such a system make decisions about "aggregate inventory," this mode of factoring the decision-making problem already involves radical simplification and approximation. For example, there is no single, well-defined total cost associated with a given total value of aggregate inventories. There will generally be different costs associated with each of the different kinds of items that make up the inventory (for example, different items may have different spoilage rates or obsolescence rates), and different probabilities and costs associated with stock-outs of each kind of item. Thus, a given aggregate inventory will have different costs depending on its composition in terms of individual items.

To design a system for making decisions about the aggregate work force, production rate, and inventories requires an assumption that the aggregate inventory will never depart very far from a typical composition in terms of individual item types. The assumption is likely to be tolerable because subsidiary decisions are continually being made at other points in the organization about the inventories of individual items. These subsidiary decisions prevent the aggregate inventory from becoming severely unbalanced, hence make averages meaningful for the aggregate.

The assumption required for aggregation is not unlike that made by an engineer when he controls the temperature of a tank of water, with a single thermometer as indicator, knowing that sufficient mixing of the liquid in the tank is going on to maintain a stable pattern of temperature relations among its parts. Without such a stable pattern it would be infeasible to control the process by means of a measurement of the average temperature.

If one set of decisions is made, on this approximate basis, about aggregate work force, production rate, and inventories, then these decisions can be used as constraints in making detailed decisions at subsidiary levels about the inventory or production of particular items. If the aggregate decision has been reached to make one million gallons of paint next month, then other decisions can be reached as to how much paint of each kind to make, subject to the constraint that the production quotas for the individual items should, when added together, total one million gallons (see Holt et al., 1960).

This simple example serves to elucidate how the whole mass of decisions that are continually being made in a complex organization can be viewed as an organized system. They constitute a system in which 1. particular decision-making processes are aimed at finding courses of action that are feasible or satisfactory in the light of multiple goals and constraints, and 2. decisions reached in any one part of the organization enter as goals or constraints into the decisions being made in other parts of the organization.

There is no guarantee that the decisions reached will be optimal with respect to any overall organizational goal. The system is a loosely coupled one. Nevertheless, the results of the overall system can be measured against one or more organizational goals, and changes can be made in the decision-making structure when these results are adjudged unsatisfactory.

Further, if we look at the decision-making structure in an actual organization, we see that it is usually put together in such a way as to insure that the decisions made by specialized units will be made in cognizance of the more general goals. Individual units are linked to the total system by production schedules, systems of rewards and penalties based on cost and profit goals, inventory limits, and so on. The loose coupling among the parts has the positive consequence of permitting specific constraints in great variety to be imposed on subsystems without rendering their decision-making mechanisms inoperative.

THE DECISION-MAKING SYSTEM AND ORGANIZATIONAL BEHAVIOR

In the previous sections great pains were taken to distinguish the goals and constraints (inducements and contributions) that motivate people to accept organizational roles from the goals and constraints that enter into their decision making when they are enacting those organizational roles. On the one hand, the system of personal inducements and contributions imposes constraints that the organization must satisfy if it is to survive. On the other hand, the constraints incorporated in the organizational roles, hence in what I have called here the organizational decision-making system, are the constraints that a course of action must satisfy in order for the organization to adopt it.

There is no necessary *logical* connection between these two sets of constraints. After all, organizations sometimes fail to survive, and their demise can often be attributed to failure to incorporate all the important motivational concerns of participants among the constraints in the organizational decision-making system. For example, a major cause of small business failure is working capital shortage, a result of failure to constrain actions to those that are consistent with creditors' demands for prompt payment. Similarly new products often fail because incorrect assumptions about the inducements important to consumers are reflected in the constraints that guide product design. (It is widely believed that the troubles of the Chrysler Corporation stemmed from the design premise that car purchasers were primarily interested in buying a good piece of machinery.)

In general, however, there is a strong empirical connection between the two sets of constraints, for the organizations we will usually observe in the real world—those that have succeeded in surviving for some time—will be precisely those which have developed organizational decision-making systems whose constraints guarantee that their actions maintain a favorable balance of inducements to contributions for their participants. The argument, an evolutionary one, is the same one we can apply to biological organisms. There is no logical requirement that the temperatures, oxygen concentrations, and so on, maintained in the tissues of a bird by its physiological processes should lie within the ranges required for its survival. It is simply that we will not often have opportunities for observing birds whose physiological regulators do not reflect these external constraints. Such birds are soon extinct.[3]

3. The relation between the functional requisites for survival and the actual constraints of the operating system is a central concept in W. R. Ashby's notion of a multistable system. See his *Design for a Brain*, 2d ed. (London: Chapman, 1960).

Thus, what the sociologist calls the functional requisites for survival can usually give us good clues for predicting organizational goals; however, if the functional requisites resemble the goals, the similarity is empirical, not definitional. What the goals are must be inferred from observation of the organization's decision-making processes, whether these processes be directed toward survival or suicide.

CONCLUSIONS

We can now summarize our answers to the question that introduced this paper: What is the meaning of the phrase "organizational goal"? First, we discovered that it is doubtful whether decisions are generally directed toward achieving *a* goal. It is easier, and clearer, to view decisions as being concerned with discovering courses of action that satisfy a whole set of constraints. It is this set, and not any one of its members, that is most accurately viewed as the goal of the action.

If we select any of the constraints for special attention, it is (a) because of its relation to the motivations of the decision maker, or (b) because of its relation to the search process that is generating or designing particular courses of action. Those constraints that motivate the decision maker and those that guide his search for actions are sometimes regarded as more "goal-like" than those that limit the actions he may consider or those that are used to test whether a potential course of action he has designed is satisfactory.

When we come to organizational decisions, we observe that many, if not most, of the constraints that define a satisfactory course of action are associated with an organizational role and hence only indirectly with the personal motives of the individual who assumes that role. In this situation it is convenient to use the phrase *organization goal* to refer to constraints, or sets of constraints, imposed by the organizational role, which has only this indirect relation to the motives of the decision makers.

If we examine the constraint set of an organizational decision-making system, we will generally find that it contains constraints that reflect virtually all the inducements and contributions important to various classes of participants. These constraints tend to remove from consideration possible courses of action that are inimical to survival. They do not, of course, by themselves often fully determine the course of action.

In view of the hierarchical structure that is typical of most formal organizations, it is a reasonable use of language to employ organizational goal to refer particularly to the constraint sets and criteria of search that define roles at the upper levels. Thus it is reasonable to speak of conservation of forest resources as a principal goal of the U.S. Forest Service, or reducing fire losses as a principal goal of a city fire department. For high-level executives in these organizations will seek out and support actions that advance these goals, and subordinate employees will do the same or will at least tailor their choices to constraints established by the higher echelons with this end in view.

Finally, since there are large elements of decentralization in the decision making in any large organization, different constraints may define the decision problems of different positions or specialized units. For example, "profit" may not enter directly into the decision making of most members of a business organization. Again, this does not mean that it is improper or meaningless to regard profit as a principal goal of the business. It simply means that the decision-making mechanism is a loosely coupled system in which the profit constraint is only one among a number of constraints and enters into most subsystems only in indirect ways. It would be both legitimate and realistic to describe most business firms as directed toward profit making—subject to a number of side constraints—operating through a network of decision-making processes that introduces many gross approximations into the search for profitable courses of action. Further, the goal ascription does not imply that any employee is motivated by the firm's profit goal, although some may be.

This view of the nature of organization goals leaves us with a picture of organizational decision making that is not simple. But it provides us with an entirely operational way of showing, by describing the structure of the organizational decision-making mechanism, how and to what extent over-all goals, like "profit" or "conserving forest resources" help to determine the actual courses of action that are chosen.

CONCLUDING STATEMENT

Where does all this leave us as far as organizational goals are concerned? We have seen that there are several aspects to the subject. What can we add? Let us conclude the discussion by emphasizing three things: the nature and characteristics of goals, their "mix" in the organization, and their inherent importance to the organization and its effective design.

TYPES OF GOALS

Despite the diverse analyses that the subject of organizational goals has received, at least one consistent theme has been sounded: organizations are characterized by several *types* of goals. It is important for us to know about some of these goal types, because they will help us relate goals to organizational design. And it is to this relationship that we are headed.

It would be futile—and not particularly useful, for that matter—to try to report every attempt that has been made to describe the various types or categories of goals that organizations pursue. We can, however, do so for the principal ones. Table 3–1 summarizes the attempts reported here.

Parsons

One of the first attempts to specify the types of goals pursued by organizations was that of Talcott Parsons (1956; 1960: 45–46). As a sociologist, Parsons views organizations as social systems, whose existence forms an integral part of the larger society. He therefore classifies organizations in terms of their principal societal functions. What is a function for the larger society is a goal for the organization:

- *Production.* An orientation toward production is one toward producing goods and services that are consumed by society.

TABLE 3-1 SELECTED GOAL TYPES

Parsons (1956, 1960)	Etzioni (1961)	Cyert and March (1963)	Gross (1965)	Katz and Kahn (1966)	Gross (1969)	Perrow (1970)
1. Production 2. Political 3. Integrative 4. Pattern maintenance	1. Control (order-oriented) 2. Economic 3. Cultural	1. Production 2. Inventory 3. Sales 4. Market share 5. Profit	1. Performance goals a. Producing output b. Satisfying interests c. Acquiring resources 2. Structural goals a. People b. Nonhuman resources c. Subsystems d. Internal relations e. External relations f. Coordination	1. Productive (economic) 2. Maintenance 3. Adaptive 4. Managerial-political	1. Output goals 2. Support goals a. Adaptation b. Management c. Motivation d. Position	1. Societal 2. Output 3. System 4. Product 5. Derived

- *Political.* Some organizations, and some subunits of one organization, are oriented toward political goals. Such organizations seek to generate and allocate power within the society.
- *Integrative.* These goals reflect attempts to settle conflicts and motivate people to fulfill society's expectations. Courts and political parties are two of the more obvious examples of organizations oriented primarily to integrative goals.
- *Pattern Maintenance.* Some organizations, or organizational subunits, pursue goals that contribute to continuity for the society. Churches, museums, schools, and libraries are especially active in pursuing pattern-maintenance goals.

Etzioni

For Etzioni (1961) organizations are different primarily because they have different types of control and compliance. Thus a prison, a manufacturing firm, and a church differ in important respects, because the kinds of *control* exercised are coercive, remunerative, and normative, respectively. On the other hand, the fundamental kinds of *compliance,* or obedience of members to organizational authority, are alienative, utilitarian, and moral, respectively. If we think about the organizations named and their members (convicts, workers, and ministers, for example), the attractiveness of Etzioni's reasoning is apparent. According to Etzioni, the types of organizations named have different goal orientations. These he calls *control, economic,* and *cultural.*

Cyert and March

As we have noted, Cyert and March (1963) see the organization as a collection of coalitions. Specifying a coalition with precise clarity is next to impossible, since people tend to float from one coalition to another under different circumstances. Still, coalition members can be identified in a general sort of way:

> In a business organization the coalition members include managers, workers, stockholders, suppliers, customers, lawyers, tax collectors, regulatory agencies, etc. In the governmental organization the members include administrators, workers, appointive officials, elective officials, legislators, judges, clientele, interest group leaders, etc. In the voluntary charitable organization there are paid functionaries, volunteers, donors, donees, etc. [Cyert and March, 1963: 27].

For Cyert and March, goals are formed through bargaining. Bargaining occurs among the various subcoalitions that comprise the overall organizational coalition. Because of the form that bargaining takes, the goals that are developed tend to have the following attributes (1963: 32):

1. They tend to be inconsistent, both with each other and in terms of overall policy.
2. Some goals are stated in terms of aspiration levels that serve as constraints ("we must allocate 10 percent of our total budget to research").
3. Some goals are stated in nonoperational terms. Nonoperationality, of course, reduces the chance of a goal being seen as inconsistent with another goal. The less well-specified a goal, the more leeway can be given to its interpretation.

Cyert and March emphasize the importance of goals as constraints on organizational decision making. In particular, goals constrain decisions dealing with a business firm's price, output, and general sales strategies. Accordingly five goals are seen to be critical to organizational success (1963: 40–43).

- *Production.* This is a goal that pertains both to the overall level of production and to the variability of that level.
- *Inventory.* This goal reflects the desires of coalition members to achieve and maintain a level of finished-goods inventory that will allow the firm to cope with changing demand for the output.
- *Sales.* Various members of the organizational coalition make demands that the organization meet some general criteria of sales effectiveness. The sales goal reflects these demands. This goal is simply an aspiration regarding the level of sales. It may be in terms of dollars, units, or both.
- *Market share.* This goal either supplements or substitutes for a sales goal. Market share concerns coalition members' demands for comparative success (vis-à-vis competitors, for instance) and growth.
- *Profit.* Finally, the authors assume that coalition members desire a profit. That is, members want to accumulate resources, both for continued operation of the firm and for rewarding investors and creditors. This goal is usually linked closely to pricing and resource-allocation decisions.

Katz and Kahn

In 1966 a major volume on organization theory was published. Entitled *The Social Psychology of Organizations,* the work by Katz and Kahn is about organizations as open systems. In their attempt to formulate a conceptual basis for analyzing organizational structure and functioning, the authors look at organizations as subsystems of the larger society. They especially focus on the type of activity in which the organization is engaged (1966: 110–13). There are four principal types, and as in Parsons' (1956, 1960) analysis, they have strong goal connotations. The goal categories consist of the following: *productive/economic, maintenance, adaptive,* and *managerial/political.*

The authors see most organizations as primarily oriented to one or another of these goals. On the other hand, as an open-systems perspective reminds us, most organizations direct some effort toward the accomplishment of all the goals.

B. Gross

Bertram Gross (1965) also uses an open-systems perspective. As one interested in administrative theory, however, he is also concerned with the rational commitment of organizational resources—that is, with administrative planning.

For Gross, the organization is composed of conflicting groups and interests.[1] Interaction and conflict revolve around two sets of goals, performance and structural:

- *Performance.* Performance goals involve such efforts as producing outputs, satisfying interests, efficiently using resources, investing in the organizational system, acquiring resources, observing codes, and behaving rationally.

1. While Gross does not say so, one suspects that his "groups" and "interests" are similar to Cyert and March's (1963) coalitions.

- *Structural.* These goals have to do with organizational subsystems, internal relationships, values, and coordination.

Gross argues that effective planning requires managers to seek a balance between clarity and vagueness in identifying those goals to which organizational resources are being committed in the planning process. Further he reminds us that effective management (and thus effective organizational performance) depends in large measure on a balance among various—sometimes conflicting—goals.

E. Gross

Edward Gross (1969) offers yet another set of goal categories. Following in the tradition of Parsons (1956, 1960), he notes that pursuing goals is the *raison d'être* of organizations. This pursuit distinguishes formal organizations from communities, families, youth groups, and the like.

Gross begins his treatment by reexamining Merton's (1957) classic description of bureaucratic personality. He argues that many people have taken the idea of "bureaucratic" behavior (in the stereotyped, red-tape sense) to include any behavior that is not aimed at producing output. Frequently, however, circumstances require that a great deal of behavior be aimed at serving purposes other than output. Chatting and joking in a committee meeting, for example, are behaviors not directly aimed at producing output, but instead serve various group-maintenance functions (Bales, 1958). Based on this sort of analysis, Gross concludes that organizations are characterized by output-oriented goals (the conventional view of goals), and *in addition* goals that can best be thought of as supportive in nature. He offers an empirically based view that there are five major types of organizational goals:

- *Output.* Output goals are reflected in some product or service that intentionally affects the organization's external environment.
- *Support.* Support goals include the following: *Adaptation,* reflecting the organization's need to come to terms with the environment(s) in which it exists. *Management,* reflecting decisions as to who should run the organization, the need to handle conflict, and the determination of priorities. *Motivation,* reflecting the organization's requirement for satisfaction and loyalty among members. *Position,* reflecting the organization's requirement to maintain its position in terms of the kind of place it is in comparison to other organizations.

These five goal types (output plus the four support goals), concludes Gross, describe the ways in which organizational resources and energies are expended. Thus, depending on their resource-utilization patterns, organizations possess more or less complex goal structures. We will develop Gross' idea of goal structure later in this concluding statement. What we call "goal mix" will be seen as an idea that is useful for designing organizations.

Perrow

The final set of goal types we should review is that presented by Perrow (1970). He observes that organizations are subject to many influences, including the personalities of key executives, community environment, norms and values of organizations with which one deals, and ultimately the cultural setting. As a result of these multiple influences, an organization pursues multiple and varying goals. Perrow distinguishes five major categories:

- *Societal.* Goals that concern the fulfillment of society's various needs.
- *Output.* These are goals that concern the organization's different outputs.
- *System.* Goals that determine the manner in which the organization will function are called system goals. The emphasis is on growth, stability, profits.
- *Product.* Product goals deal with the characteristics of the output, particularly its quality and style.
- *Derived.* Derived goals describe the manner in which the organization uses the influence and power that it generates in pursuit of other goals.

Types of Goals: Summary

Why have we spent so much time considering no less than seven separate sets of goals? There are two reasons. First, these are serious attempts by serious scholars to discover the ways in which organizational resources are spent. We should be familiar with these attempts.

Second, all of these typologies—summarized in Table 3–1—remind us that organizations do not pursue just one major goal, such as profit or growth. Rather they pursue a variety of goals, many of which are only indirectly related to their outputs. And although differing in their specifics, the different sets of goal types share a common basis. They all reflect the idea that the organization is an open system—responding to environmental demands and opportunities, acquiring resources, producing outputs, and so on. In short, the sets of goal types all point to various directions in which organizational resources are spent. It is this latter point that leads us to issues of organizational design.

THE IMPORTANCE OF GOALS

Let us recall why we are concerned with goals. As we have noted, the essential character of organizations is "the pursuit of relatively specific objectives on a more or less continuous basis" (Scott, 1964: 488). Thus "the central concept in the study of organizations is that of the organizational goal. . . . It is the presence of a goal and a consequent organization of effort so as to maximize the probability of attaining the goal which characterizes modern organizations" (Gross, 1969: 277). Put simply, the organization is a social instrument established and designed to perform a task. Organizational rationality—and therefore goals—is inherent to such an entity.

Being central to the existence and functioning of the organization, goals are important for their relationships with other organizational variables. As Scott (1964: 290) has put it, "the specific goals pursued will determine in important respects the characteristics of the structure" of the organization. We have stated that the theme of this book reflects this idea. Organizations are designed, continually redesigned, and operated to best accomplish their purposes under whatever conditions may prevail. Goals are the specifications to which the organization is designed.

We conclude this Statement by summarizing some important characteristics of organizational goals and noting their relationship to various organizational properties and processes.

THINKING ABOUT GOALS: RECOMMENDATIONS

To get a grasp on the concept of goals, it is helpful to remember some of its important aspects. In particular there are three questions that must be answered for organizational designs to reflect accurately the goals they are supposed to serve: What are goals, where do they come from, and how are they formed? Let us deal with these questions in order.

What They Are

Probably the best approach to thinking about organizational goals comes from Simon (1964), who maintains that they are rooted in courses of action taken by organizational members. A similar view is suggested by Etzioni (1964) and Perrow (1970). For them a "real" or "operative" goal—one that actually is being pursued by all or some part of the organization—is a state of affairs that the organization strives to realize by actively directing resources toward it.

The idea of a real or operative goal is a useful one. It says that a goal exists if there is both intention on the part of someone, and action, in the form of resources being expended (Gross, 1969). Both intention and action are necessary. Otherwise there is no goal. Managers, for example, who say "I want my department to have a better safety record next year" (intention), and then do nothing about it (no action), have not expressed a goal; they have made a wish statement.

On the other hand, an activity or other form of resource expenditure (action) in the absence of any purpose (intention) does not reflect an organization's goal either. It is an organizational accident.

Taking these ideas together, we see that a useful way of thinking about organizational goals is the following:

> Organizational goals represent a future state toward which all or part of the organization is striving. This striving is reflected in activities of members and the utilization pattern of organizational resources.

Obviously many activities occur in any organization. This means that organizational resources are utilized in many ways for many purposes. As we have seen, however, there is a developing body of evidence suggesting that only a few *types* of activities and resource-utilization patterns occur.

These approaches to describing types of organizational goals share two important properties. First, each recognizes that organizations are characterized by a *variety* of goals. As ongoing social systems, organizations contain activities and resources directed to many purposes. But significantly, these purposes can be grouped into a small number of well-defined categories, or types. Second, output goals constitute only one type of goal. Although most explicitly articulated by Edward Gross (1969), in all cases the dichotomization of organizational goals into "output" and "support" goals is clear.

As to what goals are, therefore, we offer two recommendations. First, consider goals as involving both intention and action. That is, a goal is real if it is actively pursued through the expenditure of resources, and if it is done on purpose. Second, remember that organizations pursue a small variety of goals. Thus the best way to think about goals is to think about various types of goals.

In the Readings and in this Statement we have offered several classification schemes. Personally, we recommend the types described by Gross (1969). First, they have come out of an extensive research project and therefore have some empirical basis. Second, they make a great deal of intuitive sense: organizations do produce *output,* they do spend resources to *adapt* to or cope with their surroundings. Further, they almost always contain activities and units, such as management teams, who spend time and effort in the *management* of the enterprise; they engage in efforts aimed at the *motivation* of organizational members, and they attempt to develop values, norms, and climates that contribute to a characteristic organizational *Weltanschauung* (*position*). Third, Gross' types lend themselves nicely to dealing with problems of organizational design.[2]

Readers are obviously free to choose the scheme that makes the most sense to them—or even generate their own. In any event, it is clearly no longer sufficient to think only in traditional terms of long-range versus short-range, or strategic versus tactical goals. Organizations spend scarce money, time, equipment, and other resources for producing their products. They also spend scarce resources in a variety of ways *not* directly involved in producing those products.

Where They Came From

The second question relevant to design concerns the source of organizational goals. Remember the old argument about where authority comes from? The classical writers contended that it comes from the top: an organization's owners give authority to top management, who in turn delegate it on down the hierarchy. This is known as the top-down view. Then Barnard (1938) and Simon (1947) came along and argued that a leader's authority is based on its acceptance by the followers. This is the bottom-up view.

A similar argument has permeated the literature on goals. The traditional view is a top-down one: top management sets goals which are then pursued in varying detail by organizational members on down the line. The opposite view, although not as explicit as the former, is that goals merely reflect what people do. What people do depends on a variety of factors—not just what top management dictates. This is a bottom-up sort of view.

So where *do* goals come from? The approach by March and Simon (1958), Cyert and March (1963), and Simon (1964) seems the most helpful. We have already discussed this approach at some length. Consequently we will be content with a brief reminder: organizational members form loosely-connected coalitions, coalitions that center around shared interests and activities.[3] Organizational goals—states or conditions that resources are being deliberately spent to attain—reflect these shared interests and activities. Hear the experienced voice of a university president:

> This job can beat a man down. There is no way to survive it without a sense of humor; there may also be no way to survive it happily without chucking it every once in a while. Organization charts show the president of a college on top, just a step below the financial angels. In actuality, a president is at the center of a web of conflicting interest groups, none of which can ever be fully satisfied. [John R. Coleman, quoted in the *Wall Street Journal,* April 24, 1974, p. 16]

2. For an example of an organizational redesigning project that used this set of goal types, see Connor and Bloomfield (1977). This article is also reproduced in Chapter 13 of this volume.

3. See Thompson (1967: 51–82) for an elaboration of this idea, with particular emphasis on organizational design implications.

How They Are Formed

The means by which specific goals are formed are not thoroughly understood. There appear to be three distinct processes (Barrett, 1970), some or all of which may operate in a particular situation. Referring to Fig. 3–2, goal formation involves activities and states that contribute to the satisfaction of individual needs and drives (*A*) and those that contribute to creating the organization's primary outputs (*B*). *C* is that subset of activities and states that contribute to both (Barrett, 1970: 3-5).

In *exchange* processes, the individual contributes to the pursuit of overall coalition goals. In return, coalitions contribute to the individual's goals. Figure 3–3 illustrates this relationship. *Socialization* processes involve individuals' taking on some coalition goals as their own (shown in Figure 3–4).

The third process involves a mutual *accommodation* between the individual and one or more coalitions. The means by which the individual contributes to coalition goals are chosen so as to allow the individual's personal goals to be pursued simultaneously. Figure 3–5 illustrates this process.

However organizational goals are formed, it is clear that they are not all pursued with equal vigor at the same time. It is true, of course, that the organization may direct resources at a single ultimate goal (profit or growth, for example). Still, pursuing a variety of different subgoals may be a necessary mediating step. This is especially true in a large, multiunit organization, in which specialized units may pursue goals that are different from—but necessary to—the achievement of one or more major organizational goals.

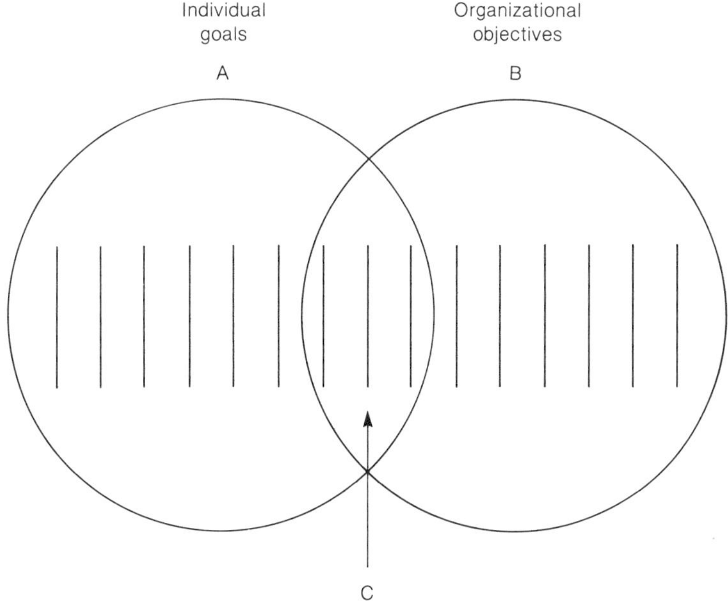

Figure 3-2. Integrating individual and organizational goals

Source: Jon H. Barrett, *Individual Goals and Organizational Objectives* (Ann Arbor: The University of Michigan Institute for Social Research, 1970), p. 5.

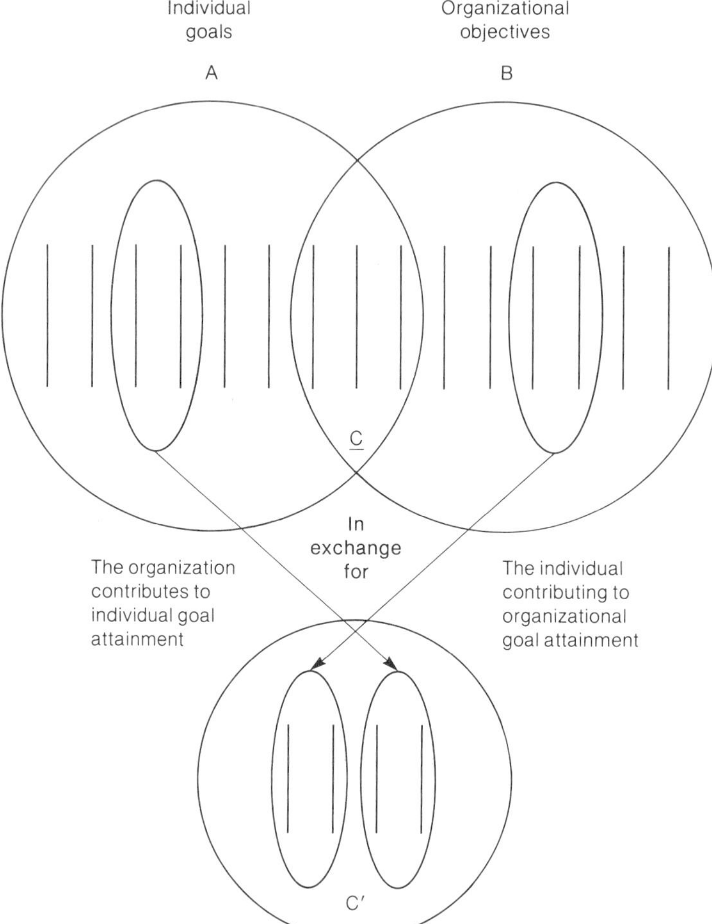

Figure 3-3. Goal integration: exchange process

Source: Jon H. Barrett, *Individual Goals and Organizational Objectives* (Ann Arbor: The University of Michigan Institute for Social Research, 1970), p. 7.

The sequence with which an organization or its subunits pursues a goal will vary with changes in either external or internal pressures and conditions. For example, as coalition members seek to establish organizational or subunit goals, conflicts occur. These are usually resolved through compromise and sequential attention to goals (March and Simon, 1958; Etzioni, 1960; Cyert and March, 1963; Simon, 1964; Perrow, 1970). In essence, although the organization is attempting to realize several goals, it does not pursue them all with the same vigor at all times.

We recall that coalitions often contain members who are located at the same or different levels of the hierarchy (or both). Since organizational goals are formed as a reflection of coalition interests, we have an answer to the question posed earlier, about where goals come from: they derive from the coalitions, neither exclusively from the top nor the bottom.

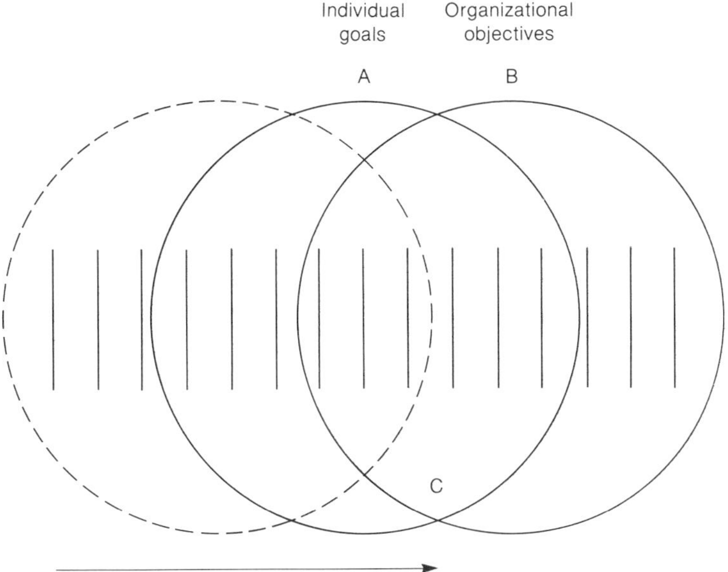

Figure 3-4. Goal integration: socialization process

Source: Jon H. Barrett, *Individual Goals and Organizational Objectives* (Ann Arbor: The University of Michigan Institute for Social Research, 1970), p. 9.

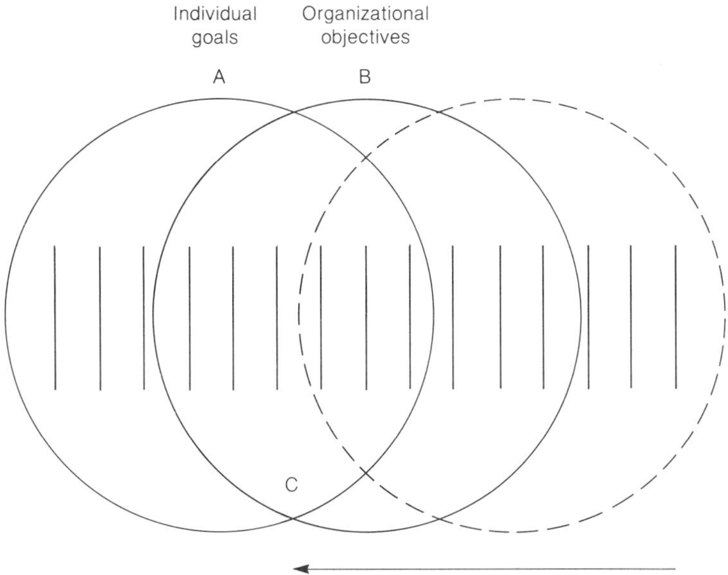

Figure 3-5. Goal integration: accommodation process

Source: Jon H. Barrett, *Individual Goals and Organizational Objectives* (Ann Arbor: The University of Michigan Institute for Social Research, 1970), p. 13.

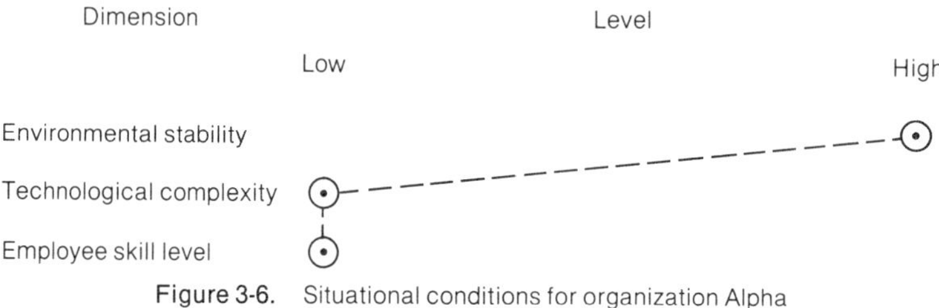

Figure 3-6. Situational conditions for organization Alpha

GOALS AND ORGANIZATIONAL DESIGN

The question that needs to be answered now is, "so what?" What does knowing about organizational goals tell us about organizations—that is, about organizational design? We can begin to get at answers to this question by employing the idea, noted earlier, that an organization has a structure, or mix, of goals that it pursues.

The Mix of Goals

We started this Statement by portraying goals as falling into a small number of categories or types. This approach leads to the following observation: organizations vary in the relative emphasis given to those different categories. That is, organizations differ in the degree to which they direct activities and resources toward the pursuit of goals within each class. This phenomenon is particularly apparent with respect to support goals. For example, some organizations, depending on the nature of the environmental situation in which they operate, direct relatively more activities and resources toward the pursuit and achievement of "adaptation" goals and relatively less toward "motivational" goals. We call this set of relative emphases—which is actually a set of relative priorities—the organization's *goal mix* (Connor and Bloomfield, 1977).

As a concept, goal mix tells us about the importance that an organization attaches to each goal type. As we suggested, this set of relative importances usually reflects the situation within which the organization functions. Let us consider two extreme examples. In the first situation, the organization—call it Alpha—is operating under environmental conditions that are relatively stable. Social, political, and economic pressures have changed little in recent years, and show no sign of changing much in the forseeable future. Furthermore, the products that Alpha produces are unsophisticated, requiring a relatively low level of technology—i.e., requiring on the part of the employees a great deal of work that is repetitive, predictable, small in its scope, and altogether routine. Thus the employees themselves require a low level of specialized skill and education. Figure 3–6 indicates Alpha's situation.

In such an organization as Alpha, we would expect an emphasis on "output" goals.[4] That is, Alpha's management would doubtless expend a large share of the organization's resources in trying to produce its outputs as efficiently and with as little slack, or unused resources, as possible. March and Simon's (1958) "machine model" of the organization would describe Alpha very well. With environmental, technological, and employee characteristics being as

4. As we mentioned earlier, we prefer to use the typology set forth by Gross (1969). "Output" goals is one type.

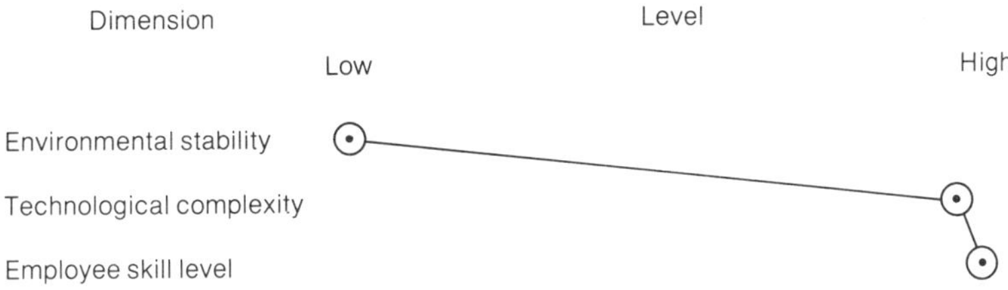

Figure 3-7. Situational conditions for organization Beta

simple and predictable as they are, there is little need for many organizational resources to be spent on the support-class goals.

If, for a second organization, Beta, conditions are sketched that are relatively opposite to those experienced by Alpha, it can be seen that different goals are emphasized. Beta operates under socio-political-economic conditions that are fairly dynamic: continually changing, frequently in unpredictable ways. Furthermore, the products of Beta are numerous and complex, involving a large number and variety of organizational resources to be assigned, scheduled, and coordinated. These products require nonroutine efforts to produce, requiring Beta's employees to exercise the sophisticated skills they have acquired in their extensive professional training. Beta's situation is represented in Figure 3–7.

Beta, it is clear, needs to attend much more closely to dealing with changing environmental demands and maintaining high morale among its highly skilled employees than does Alpha. We would therefore expect that Beta would emphasize "support" goals much more than does Alpha. In brief, it is apparent that environmental, technological, and employee characteristics will have great impact on an organization's goal mix. Probable goal mixes of Alpha and Beta can be illustrated, as in Figure 3–8, in which the goal types described by Gross (1969) are used.

Goal Mix and Structural Design: Alpha and Beta

In general, the complexity of organizational structure is directly proportional to the complexity of the organizational goals. For example, organizations that have very specific

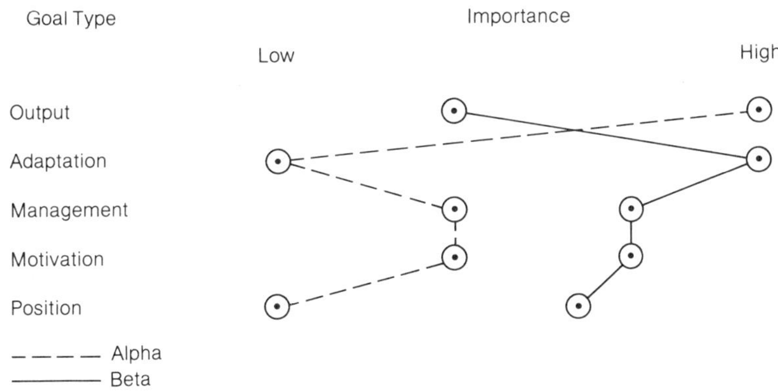

Figure 3-8. Organizational goal mix: Alpha and Beta

goals tend to have a relatively centralized authority structure (Scott, 1964: 493). On the other hand, consider an organization that is pursuing a highly complex set of goals. Such an organization will have a correspondingly complex structure. A multitude of levels, departments, teams, and task forces will be necessary to facilitate the accomplishment of those multiple goals (Thompson, 1967: 51–82).

Thus we would expect organization Alpha to have a relative high level of *formalization* (many rules), since rules and regulations would serve to facilitate the performance of tasks with a minimum of wasted energy.[5] Specifically, demands of both outside conditions and task requirements are stable, predictable, and routine. Responses to these demands can—and should—be equally stable, predictable, and routine. Rules and regulations help to create these responses.

Second, the nature of the demands, together with the low skill requirements of the employees, makes decentralization (the use of judgment and discretion by subordinates) unattractive. So, Alpha's level of *centralization* should be relatively high.

Finally, Alpha is able—at least as far as our example goes—to have relatively few administrative levels (*low vertical differentiation*) and many subordinates reporting to an administrator (*high horizontal differentiation*). This recommendation is consistent with those preceding. The routineness of the tasks, the lack of discretionary behavior, the extensive rules governing task performance: these all mean that one manager can supervise a relatively large number of people.

In brief, then, the conditions in which Alpha operates indicate that the organization will most likely have a relatively short and fat shape, a high degree of formalization governing task behavior, and a high level of centralized decision making.

Different design conclusions are called for in the case of organization Beta. For Beta, high *formalization* could prove disastrous. Probably Beta's managers will see to it that necessary guidelines are established; within these guidelines, however, employees will, owing to task and environmental requirements, exercise some discretion. Thus the level of *decentralized* decision making should be considerably higher than that in Alpha. Regarding *differentiation,* it turns out that many organizations in circumstances similar to Beta's find it most effective to assign a relatively few number of individuals to a supervising manager. This arrangement is helpful for two reasons. First, the typical manager is unable to effectively supervise a large number of people performing a variety of complex tasks. Second, the relationship between a supervisor and a subordinate, especially if both are skilled professionals, is likely to be one of colleagues, rather than strictly superior-subordinate. Having only a few subordinates allows a manager to enjoy the benefits of such a relationship (Blau and Scott, 1962).

In short, the conditions in which organization Beta operates suggest that it will most likely have a relatively tall and thin shape, a low degree of formalization governing task behavior, and a low level of centralized decision making.

The differences between organizations Alpha and Beta can be illustrated by their structural-design profiles, as shown in Figure 3–9.

The point of the foregoing example, then, is this: there are important differences between organizations Alpha and Beta in their settings, or *contexts* (cf. Pugh et al., 1963). These

5. This and the next few paragraphs are based on Theo Haimann, William G. Scott, and Patrick E. Connor, *Managing the Modern Organization,* 3rd. ed. (Boston: Houghton Mifflin Co., 1978), pp. 258–60.

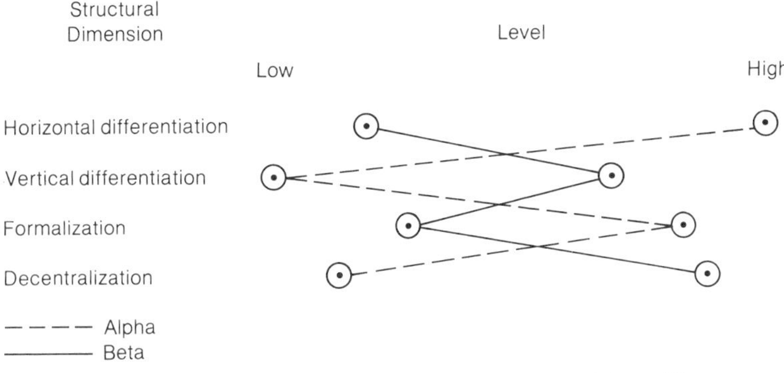

Figure 3-9. Structural-design profiles of organizations Alpha and Beta

differences are seen by comparing Figures 3–6 and 3–7. Further, these differences are reflected in different goal mixes (Figure 3–8) and different structural design profiles (Figure 3–9).

We do not mean to imply by the examples of Alpha and Beta that there is any one best way to design an organization, given a particular goal mix. There are probably several mix-design combinations that will prove successful for organizations. Rather, to paraphrase Perrow (1960: 174) the design issue is to ensure that such factors as environmental forces, technology, people, structure, and goals are all in harmony. This is what good organizational design is all about.

SUMMARY AND CONCLUSION

We began this chapter by recalling in the introductory remarks that the basic design premise is organizational rationality. Put simply, this premise is that organizations are established, designed, and operated to perform tasks and to satisfy various needs and wants—in short, to accomplish goals.

We then explored a variety of organizational goal characteristics (Kast), focusing at three levels: environmental, organizational, and individual. Three design problems were then discussed in that same article: integrating individual and organizational goals, setting and implementing goals, and managing goal conflicts. Next we examined (Simon) the role that goals play in constraining organizational (and individual) decision processes.

Finally, in the concluding statement we focused on the character and importance of organizational goals. Various goal types were described, goal-formation processes were discussed, and the impact of goal priorities for organizational design was explored.

Having begun the discussion of organizational design by focusing on its basic purpose, we turn now to an examination of some factors that constrain designers' options. As noted in the example of organizations Alpha and Beta, designers especially need to take into account the nature of the environment in which organizational coalitions are pursuing their goals, the techniques and methods it must use, and the people it has available to use them. These constraints—environment, technology, and people—form the content of the next section.

Questions for Review

1. According to Cyert and March, there are variables that affect goals, and there are variables that affect goal expectations. What are these variables?
2. What are the four elements used by Kast to define what an organization is?
3. Kast defines the main differences between organizational goals at each of the levels used by Parsons:
   a. institutional-level goals
   b. managerial-level goals
   c. technical subsystems goals

   What are these differences?
4. Kast reviews Cyert and March's views of organizational goals. What are the main points within their view that distinguish their work from others?
5. Outline the basic aspects of the Barnard-Simon inducements-contributions model.
6. What are some of the pros and cons of MBO programs designed to integrate functional and individual goals with overall organizational goals?
7. Cyert and March, Etzioni, and Katz and Kahn define organizational goals using different bases. What are these? What organizational goals arise from each of these?
8. What are the major categories of goal types postulated by Perrow? By Gross?
9. Why are goals important?
10. We described three processes for integrating individual and organizational goals: the exchange, socialization, process, and accommodation processes. Describe the differences between these.

Questions for Discussion

1. In his opening paragraph, Kast contends that "the tendency to organize or cooperate in interdependent human relationship is basic in human nature." Do you agree? Why? What do you understand by the phrase, "basic in human nature"? Is this encouraged in the American educational system?
2. "A goal is real if it is actively pursued through the expenditure of resources, and if that expenditure is done on purpose." How accurately does this statement reflect the hypotheses of some of the major theorists mentioned in this chapter? How accurately does it reflect your definition of a "real"goal?
3. Using the definition of a goal that seems soundest to you, examine your own current or past academic and professional life situations and assess what elements truly possess real goals, as you define them.
4. Are you familiar with an organization that clearly reflects the differences between official and operational goals? How do these vary in this particular organization? What effect does this variation have on the organization? Does it have any direct effect on you?
5. What do you deduce to be the goals of your university? Describe them, using one particular theoretical system discussed in this chapter. In your opinion, does the university succeed in meeting these goals? How do you know whether the institution is effective or not? What criteria would you use to evaluate its effectiveness?

6. Kast refers to Merton's view that "goals are displaced because the bureaucratic organization affects participants' personalities and causes them to adhere to rules and regulations for their own sake." To what degree have you found or observed this to be true?
7. In an organizational setting, should human satisfaction be a means to an end or an end in itself? Why? Which theorists do you think might support your view?
8. "No profession has escaped the advancing tide of bureaucratization," it has been said. What does this mean? Is this as universally true as the statement would have us believe? If so, what are the implications for the future of organization design?
9. It has been said that "objectives are needed in every area where performance and results directly and vitally affect the survival and prosperity of the business." Are they really needed in every area? Where do you think objectives are needed? Do any of the goal "typologies" discussed in this chapter help you respond to these questions?
10. Evaluate March and Simon's inducement-contribution theory in terms of its relevance to organizational design. How do you react to the theory as a student? How might you react to the theory as an employee?

CASES FOR DISCUSSION

CASE: BATES, BARKER & COMPANY (A)

The Bates, Barker & Company, a major advertising firm located in New York City, offers two major professional services to its clients. It offers plans for the contents of an advertising campaign (slogans, layouts, basic selling points) and plans for the media (radio, television, newspapers, magazines, billboards) required to reach the best audience most efficiently. In addition, the company offers services such as aid in marketing and distribution of products and marketing research to test advertising effectiveness. Company income is derived by the various media or from fees paid directly by the client, usually a large production or commercial enterprise. The firm was formed into a number of departments, each concerned with a professional specialty—the members of each department having a certain professional training in common. Individuals within each department were assigned work on the accounts of one or more clients.

Work on each client's account was coordinated by account management, consisting of account executives and account supervisors (senior account executives). The account supervisors reported to a vice-president who headed the Account Management Branch. Account executives were each assigned to one account. They acted as liaison between client and company and as coordinators of specialists within the agency who worked on their clients' accounts. Account supervisors controlled the work of a number of account executives.

The Creative Branch, headed by a vice-president, was concerned with the actual creation and production of advertisements and commercials. Members of the Copy Department wrote the scripts for radio or television commercials or wrote the copy (written parts) of printed advertisements. Members of the Art Department planned layouts of printed advertisements and arranged for the provision of appropriate illustrations if required. The Newspaper/Magazine Production and TV/Radio Production Departments took the rough advertisements produced by Copy and Art, put them in finished form, and arranged for their appearance in the mass media. For Newspaper/Magazine Production this meant arranging for reproductions of mats of advertisements to be made and forwarded to newspapers or magazines at the desired time. TV/Radio Production involved the preparation of filmed or taped commercials for distribution to local broadcasters.

The Marketing Branch, headed by a vice-president, was concerned with the actual diffusion of advertising and of its effects. Members of the Media Department estimated which means of mass communication and which specific organs of communication (particular television programs, newspapers and the like) might reach the largest numbers of potential buyers of a product for the least cost and with the most impact. Media buyers then arranged for the purchase of air time or print space if their plans were approved by the clients. The Merchandising Department helped to sell the clients' products by making exhibits, recommending new packages or means of distribution. The Research Department used survey research techniques to estimate potential markets and to attempt to evaluate advertising effectiveness. The Research Department included complete field and data processing sections.

The Bates, Barker organization could be viewed as several systems of control and communication each interweaving with the others in complex and subtle ways. In the Bates,

"Bates, Barker & Company" (*A-E*), adapted from *Bates, Barker & Company,* an unpublished case by Craig C. Lundberg. © 1964. Reprinted by permission of the University of Western Ontario.

Barker & Company, three main systems could be distinguished by the casewriter before reorganization: the organizational system, the client-centered systems, and the professional systems.

The organizational system (organization chart) showed the three vice-presidents and the Traffic, Personnel, and Financial Departments having line responsibilities to the executive vice-president. The executive vice-president had line responsibility to the president, who in turn reported to the board of directors. Through these channels flowed messages of company maintenance, internal policy, personnel changes, and information about general organizational attitude in regard to clients. There is little in their contents to distinguish these messages from organizational communications in any other bureaucracy[1] of similar size.

Most messages funnelled through the organizational system flowed vertically. However, at the higher levels of the organization, horizontal communication tended to be more frequent as top management consulted with each other on matters of general firm interest.

Client-centered systems were each concerned with contacts with and services for a given client. Account supervisors and account executives were the persons designated to act as the firm's liaison with clients. In reality, a large amount of direct communication was also maintained by others in the firm with their opposite numbers in the client organizations. For instance, agency research personnel had frequent contact with the market research departments of clients; copywriters often were called directly by the advertising managers of the client for whom advertisements were being written. In addition to such relatively unstructured contact, creative workers and research personnel often presented their work directly to clients at meetings and had to defend the firm's policy at these meetings.

One account executive described his situation: "Control! Control! How the hell can I keep track of five or six prima donnas? Each of them (firm professionals in different specialties) tries to play up his big idea to the client and half the time I don't know about it until a couple of hours later. If I were stronger I would make the whole pack of them come to me first and get approval first. Yes, before they did anything."

A few members were drawn from each specialty department in order to cooperate on work for a given client. An examination of company files by the casewriter revealed that a relatively large amount of personnel had been transferred from one account to another.

The professional systems were each located within one of the professional departments—Copy, Research, Art, and so on. Each department was organized hierarchically with a director, perhaps an assistant director, and one to three other levels of responsibility. Professional communications were mainly concerned with questions of shared knowledge and technique; communications of a professional nature were widespread and pervasive within each department. Many friendships were based on similar professional backgrounds; additionally, aid and advice were shared, and matters of professional interest were disseminated through departmental meetings and seminars.

Control in each professional system was exercised in two main ways—through control of professional promotions within the department and through supervision of work done by subordinates. For instance, in the preparation of a major advertising campaign for an important client, the head of the Copy Department would oversee the copywriters producing the advertisements. Using for legitimation a combination of organizational authority and claimed professional competence, he would scrutinize almost every word of the advertisements and would not let them be seen by those out of the department until he was satisfied.

Because of the different (although interrelated) characteristics of each of these systems of

1. *Bureaucracy* is used here in its technical meaning, referring to a large-scale formal organization designed upon principles of hierarchy of authority, rational procedures, and division of labor.

communication and control, a piece of work done by a specialist had a value—and sometimes a different value—in regard to each system. For instance, an advertisement written by a copywriter had one value in the organizational system, another in the account (client-centered) system, and yet another among his fellow copywriters. Although there was probably some interrelation, the bases of these judgments usually differed. For instance, a copywriter's advertisement might please the client and yet be considered a sloppy piece of work by his colleagues. Or the results of a survey might horrify a client and yet could be a first-rate professional job. As one research supervisor said:

> The most discouraging part of this is that the account executives always want our findings to show positive results. You know: that our advertising is the best and that it's selling soap. That it's better than last year's. But a lot of our research either shows nothing really positive or sometimes shows that our advertising is worse. There's a lot of pressure to fudge around. I think my biggest job is to show people the truth, not to tell them what they want to hear.
>
> Remember, nobody cares how good our research is except us—the client and the company only want results. We're in business to sell soap and not to do sophisticated research; that is, as far as they're concerned.

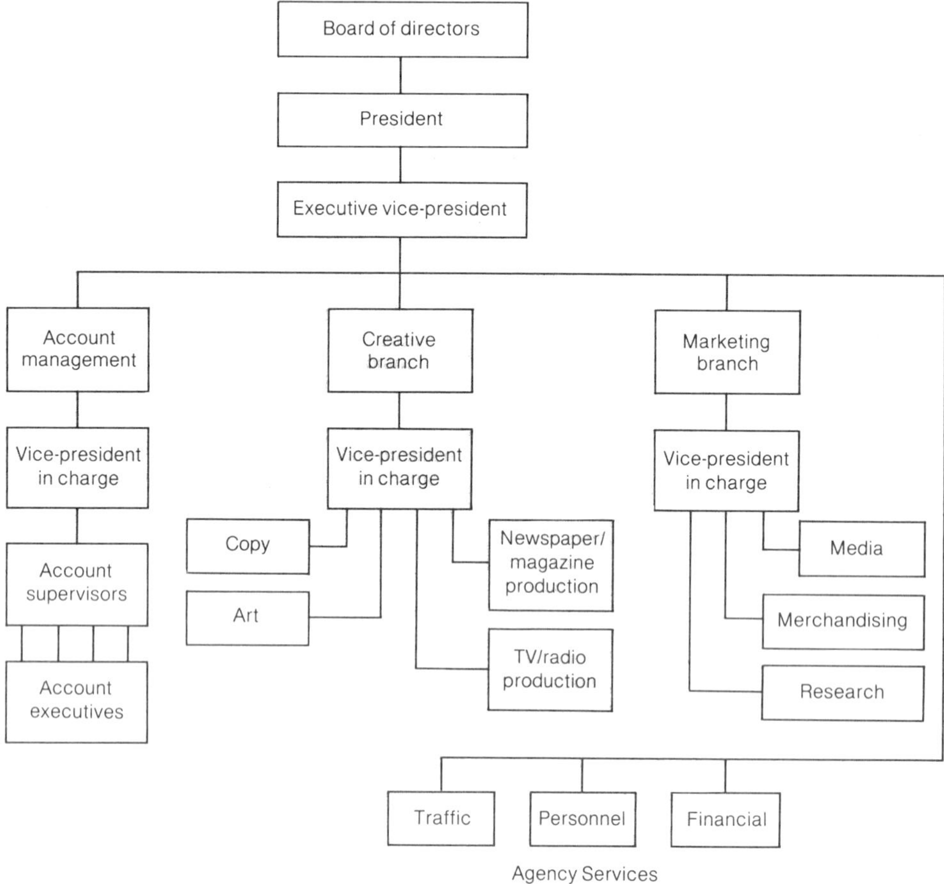

EXHIBIT I
Bates, Barker & Company
Organizational chart (before reorganization)

In 1963, a short period of time after the above had been written, Bates, Barker & Company experienced a rapid turnover in the major accounts handled by them. This turnover put a strain on the organization which prompted the top management to reconsider its objectives. This action in turn prompted an increased consciousness of a need for "flexibility" in the firm. A company reorganization was one of the solutions advanced by top management to increase this flexibility. It was also hoped that this organizational change would result in increased cooperation and communication between specialists of different types.

INSTRUCTIONS

1. Given the present organization (Exhibit 1), how would you reorganize the company to meet management's objective of increased flexibility? Draw an appropriate chart.
2. Given the present client-centered system (Exhibit 2), how would you reorganize it to meet management's objectives of increased flexibility, cooperation, and communication? Draw an appropriate diagram.
3. What action, other than reorganization, would you recommend that management take to achieve its objectives?

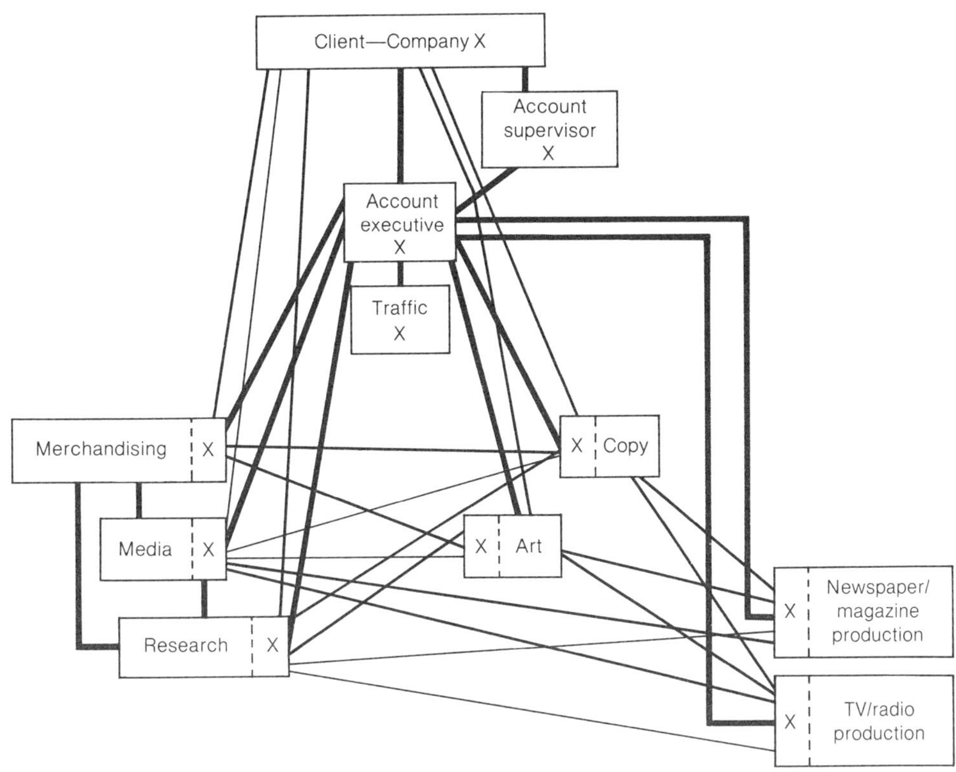

Note: Width of connecting lines roughly indicates amount of contact.

EXHIBIT 2
Bates, Barker & Company
Client-centered organization (for client Company X)

CASE: BATES, BARKER & COMPANY (B)

The Creative Branch was reorganized as a first step toward management goals. The various creative departments (Art, Copy, the Production Departments) were dissolved; in their stead were formed several composite creative groups, each group being assigned the work of one or more specific clients. The memorandum noting this change stated that:

> This reorganization will allow our creative people to concentrate on and be responsible for all the creative work of the clients to which they will be assigned. We are certain that this change will allow us to give our clients more effective service.[1]

Shortly after the change in the Creative Branch, a similar reorganization of the Marketing Branch was undertaken. The stated purpose of this further change was to

> form marketing groups composed of small numbers of different marketing specialists who will work together on the problems of a few clients. These marketing groups will be similar to the groups recently formed by our "creative brethren."
>
> . . . they will allow the different specialists in the Marketing Branch to be more closely coordinated and thus give clients better and quicker service. . . This reorganization will improve communications not only within the Marketing Branch but also with the Creative Branch and Account Management.[2]

In brief, the existing service departments were disbanded and their personnel were formed into heterogeneous marketing or creative groups to help fulfill the goal of more tightly integrated client service. Service was now provided by formal, permanent client-oriented groups in place of less structured, shifting client assignments.

Each group was assigned to a group supervisor, who was to be responsible both for internal coordination of work in his group and external coordination of contacts and communication. "External communication" is used here both in the sense of external to the agency (clients), and external to the specific group (communication with other service groups).

One of the physical changes made in the Bates, Barker & Company was the moving together of personnel of the service groups into contiguous offices.

INSTRUCTIONS

1. Draw the reorganized chart of the Bates, Barker firm.
2. What implications will the reorganization have? Specifically attempt predictions about:
   a. the control of agency-client contacts.
   b. professional communications.
   c. communications between service groups.
   d. the group supervisor's method for evaluating the performance of his subordinates.
   e. efficiency of the operations.
3. How successfully do you believe management will be achieving its aims by reorganizing? Explain.

---

1. Paraphrase (by the casewriter) of a staff memorandum, Bates, Barker & Company.
2. Paraphrase (by the casewriter) of a staff memorandum, Bates, Barker & Company.

CASE: BATES, BARKER & COMPANY (C)

Several important changes in the communication and control systems of the Bates, Barker & Company were observed by the casewriter after reorganization (see Exhibit 3). Among these changes were:

1. Control increased over direct contact between agency personnel and clients.
2. Professional communication decreased sharply.
3. Communications between members of different service groups both decreased and were more closely controlled as compared with communications between members of former specialty departments.

Control of Agency-Client Contact

With a group supervisor coordinating the activities of each service group, the problem of control of client communications had been greatly simplified. Now, a group supervisor performed primary coordination on account work with the agency; he served as an

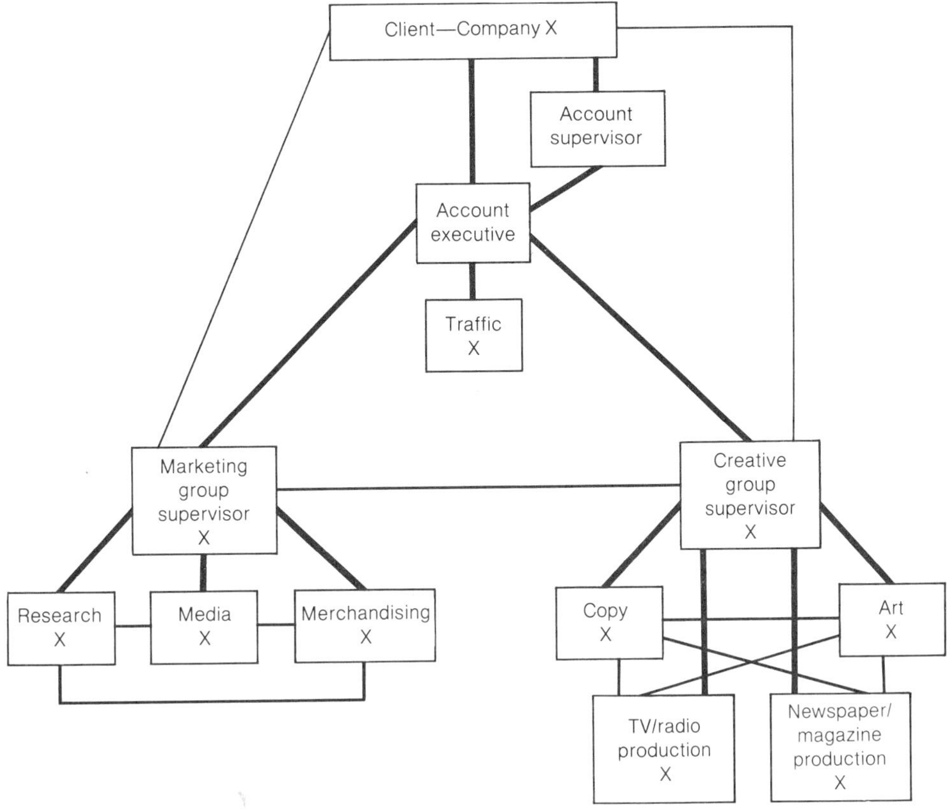

Note: Width of line roughly indicates amount of contact.

EXHIBIT 3
Bates, Barker & Company (C)
Client-centered organization (for Company X)

organizational censor who would not let any client communication out until it satisfied him. This meant that client contact could now be limited to account personnel and to group supervisors. Although this control was not as complete as had been planned, the amount of direct contact between agency personnel below the level of group supervisor and client personnel had diminished considerably. Relationships between client and agency were then restricted to fewer people whose efforts were more tightly coordinated.

Decrease in Professional Communication

One of the physical changes made in the Bates, Barker & Company was the moving together of the personnel of the several service groups into contiguous offices. This act, which symbolized the breakup of the old specialized departments, also served to make intraprofessional communication more difficult.

In addition to actual physical dispersion, reorganization signified that displays of particular skill or virtuosity not connected with satisfying a client's needs would no longer meet with any institutional approval. In other words, professional competence as judged by nonprofessionals, rather than virtuosity as judged by other professionals, was rewarded.

Decrease in Communication Between Service Groups

As was the case for intraprofessional communication, communication between client-centered service groups had decreased sharply since agency reorganization. Partly because of physical distance and partly because of the increased emphasis on the client, the tendency had been for communications to cluster within each client-centered group. In effect, Bates, Barker & Company was now a group of semi-autonomous small advertising agencies which were coordinated and connected only at the higher levels of management.

With each of the service groups separated both in space and in function, news and gossip flowed slowly among groups. As interest gradually became focussed on the service groups, this partial stoppage of information became even more complete. Official organizational channels of communication began to assume more importance as bearers of information about the condition of the agency. These channels were selective, however. Good news—approved and optimistic news—was emitted by management and circulated through organizational channels. Unpleasant news, such as firings of personnel as a result of temporarily poor business conditions, tended to be suppressed.

In order to allow for passage of gossip and professional information, several informal and semi-covert channels of communication developed in the months following reorganization. At Bates, Barker & Company these "new" channels had existed before as part of the organization: now they were superfluous. The semi-secrecy of such communications at first was occasion for somewhat shocked jokes. Later, the very fact of their being not sanctioned meant that each person who participated in such communications subverted organizational goals. To this extent, the need for opening of such gossip and information channels marked an alienation from the organization and a movement toward divided loyalties, doubts, and guilts.

Problems in Evaluating Performance of Subordinates

Another situation which perturbed some company group supervisors soon after reorganization was that, within each of the heterogeneous service groups, there was often no meaningful basis of comparison of performance from one individual to the next. In the former professional groupings, work could be judged by comparison with the similar work of other professionals. But it was difficult to assess the competence of a copywriter as compared with an artist, or a survey researcher with a person who buys television time. To judge the competence or usefulness of an individual in a client-centered service group it became necessary either to judge on personal factors—enthusiasm, friendliness, glibness, or their appearances—or else to compare the individual with his opposite number in another group (a practice not encouraged organizationally). Many of the client's criteria of worth—for instance, how well a client responds to an individual—could no longer be used because of the limitation of client contact to relatively few members of service groups.

Finally, the change in organization marked a shift from dual evaluations of work (both professional and client-centered) toward the single criterion of client satisfaction. This shift was organizationally useful in view of the relationship of the agency to its environment; an advertising agency must depend on clients' satisfaction for its existence. However, this shift meant that judgments of individual output were now usually made by those who did not share an outlook with professionals. This tended to make such valuations seem somewhat impersonal and strange. Further, because non-professionals are often unable to appreciate specialized skills, the feeling grew that expediency rather than the intricacies of craft was the deciding factor in judgment (which was so in many cases).

Increase in Efficiency of the Operations

The immediate effect of reorganization was that efficiency of operation did increase if efficiency is expressed as coordinated manipulation and transmission of work and information. More or less routine matters were handled with fewer delays, mistakes, or omissions than before. In addition, clients now knew that, whenever one of the agency contact people stated fact or policy, this was an official and relatively final agency opinion. Thus, there seemed to be an immediate increase in the possibilities for rapport between each client and the agency which did not exist before. This effect had continued in the year since the beginning of the reorganization and, in organizational terms, seemed to be a useful innovation.

At first, most of the personnel below top management levels tended to be worried and confused about themselves and their positions when reorganization was announced. This searching for some sort of anchor point was particularly acute during the time when offices were rearranged into service-group clusters. After this initial period, reactions among members of the agency varied in two ways which were associated with two major types of personal orientation to work and the company.

One group (which we shall call "careerists") tended to think of their work in terms of organizational status and of work and friendship patterns as means to achieve material and social status. Most friendships of this sort were so called business friendships, that is, contacts and luncheon friendships which are the foundation of possible personal and business advantages.

The other group (called "craftsmen" here) were concerned with their careers as well but viewed them in a somewhat different light. Craftsmen tended to think of careers in terms of the actual work and the satisfactions derived from creative production. And although some friendships are cultivated for the purpose of promotion, craftsmen generally tended to choose as acquaintances those who were also interested in the work done and its content. content.

In brief, craftsmen and careerists were differentiated by the things which characterized their commitments to their work life. Careerists were committed to organizational status and power and to the use of institutional and personal means to achieve this. Craftsmen were committed to their work and the direct satisfactions derived from it and to the sharing of intraprofessional friendships.

INSTRUCTIONS

1. Predict the possible behaviors the "craftsmen" and "careerists" will exhibit as a response to the new organization.
2. How quickly will the "craftsmen" and the "careerists" respond to the new organization?
3. What reasons might the "craftsmen" and "careerists" use to explain their behaviors?
4. How severe will the "craftsmen's" and "careerist's" responses to the new organization be?

CASE: BATES, BARKER & COMPANY (D)

For the careerists, reorganization meant that the objects and contents of their business relationships changed somewhat but the essential course of their actions changed little. That is, different people's decisions became binding and their work passed through new channels before it was finally approved. Immediately after reorganization most careerists spent a few anxious weeks assessing the effects of the changes on their chances for advancement within the company. A few careerists left the company a month or two after reorganization, mainly because they had been removed from protectors or because of budding conflicts with new superiors. Most of those who remained seemed to adjust to the organization changes with little apparent thought or bother—new communications with important people were soon arranged and new contacts were found and cemented.

Initial reactions of the craftsmen to reorganization were essentially the same as those of the careerists. Most of them were concerned about the safety of their jobs and about the compatibility of their new bosses. Added to these fears, however, were additional ones about losing the friendship and support of their professional friends and colleagues. In a sense, the craftsmen had clothed themselves with a sort of institutional mystique of craft. Many of them feared that they would not be respected for their professional skills as much as in their previous departments and that they might not do as well in the more general types of duties to be demanded in client-centered service groups.

These immediate fears were to some extent groundless. Most professionals continued to do the same sort of work and there were few cases in which they needed to fear for their jobs. Group supervisors proved incompatible with their new subordinates in only a few cases.

However, after several months many craftsmen found that they were becoming increasingly dissatisfied with their work. Mainly, the changes outlined previously affected these craftsmen to a much greater extent than they did careerists, the changes being alienation from professional colleagues and from the professional meaning of the work. This feeling of separation was summarized by a copywriter (craftsman) who left about five months after he had been assigned to a creative group:

> "I left because of the nitpicking of my copy. I left because nobody there who could get to the client stood up to him for anything. And I left because once I wrote something it was out of my hands more than at any other place I had ever been."

When the personal and interpersonal effects of the reorganization on agency members was examined, the results were somewhat different. One of the most immediate effects of reorganization was a feeling of loss and separation among many of the personnel. Old friendship patterns reinforced by close location and shared training and experiences were suddenly threatened. As one researcher (a craftsman) said shortly after the formation of marketing service groups:

"I feel lonely since we have moved offices. There's nobody to talk to except about business. You know, before this happened we used to have other research people look over our work and we used to talk about all sorts of other things. I don't know why it is but I can't seem to warm up to other people in this group.

"Another thing, what do these people know about research? I can't talk to them about what I do. So what do I talk about—sales figures?"

One young researcher (a careerist) summed up his feelings about the Research Department as follows:

"Sure there have been lots of changes but it doesn't make any difference to me. I just do my job, smile at my boss, and when I come home at night, it doesn't make any difference to me."

A year after reorganization was completed, a fair number of the craftsmen in the Bates, Barker & Company had moved on to other jobs, mainly because of dissatisfaction with their jobs at the company. Those who stayed often did so with grumbling and complaint. Many seemed to be less closely tied to the company—they were more critical; they seemed to take less interest in their work and in Bates, Barker & Company's fate.

These changes which occurred in the Bates, Barker & Company after reorganization were rather complex. In general, there had been a lessening of integration within the organization. This decrease in integration had taken place mainly among the craftsmen who began to grow away from the company within a few months after reorganization and had continued in this state of mind up to the time of writing (about a year after the beginning of reorganization). Careerists, however, seemed to have been affected relatively little.

INSTRUCTIONS

1. Explain the difference (if none show why) between your prediction and what actually occurred.
2. Knowing what you do know about the case now what would you as an administrator do?
3. Discuss how a manager can:
   a. Initiate and sustain organizational change.
   b. Measure organizational change.
   c. Measure the success of organizational changes.

SECTION THREE

Constraints on Organizational Designs

INTRODUCTION TO SECTION THREE

It would be nice, probably, if organization designers could fasten on the goals they wish their organizations to achieve—like railroad engineers fixing their eyes on a point down the track—and then design their organizations to those goals. Needless to say, organization designing is not that straightforward. For one thing, as we saw in the last chapter, goals are not fixed points off in the distance, attainable by means of a clearly specified path.

The other reason why designing an organization is more complex than guiding a train along parallel steel rails is this: the factors that affect—that is, constrain—designers' options are rather varied and complex. The purpose of this section is to examine three of the most potent constraints that affect designers' ability to exercise their responsibilities. We open the section with Chapter 4, "Environment." This chapter focuses on the ways in which organization designs may be constructed so as to match up with the requirements, demands, and opportunities that environmental conditions provide.

Chapter 5, "Technology," examines the means by which resources are processed in organizations. Further, the articles and concluding statement identify ways in which organization designs need to take technological characteristics into account.

The last chapter in this section is Chapter 6, "People." In this chapter we explore the impact that an organization's membership may have on designers' options. Chapter 6 points out the futility of considering people as some sort of passive resource to be utilized. People bring a dynamic of their own into the organizational setting—a dynamic that organization designers must respect if they are to be effective.

In summary, the last section asked "*what* are organizations designed to do?" This section asks "*where* are they going to do it, *how* are they going to do it, and with *whom?*" Organizational goals was, of course, the focus of the former question. Environment, technology, and people make up the focal points for the latter.

4

Environment

INTRODUCTORY REMARKS

We have seen that organizations have to be designed to do something—namely, to achieve their goals. The nature of an organization's goal mix, therefore, is an important factor that organization designers must take into account.

Also of importance to organizational design is the context—the *environment*—in which the organization is attempting to pursue its goals. Both the task environment and the societal/cultural environment, discussed in Chapter 2, are sources of demands, opportunities, problems, and resources for the organization. If the organization is to survive and prosper, it must respond to its environment. That is, it must develop structures and

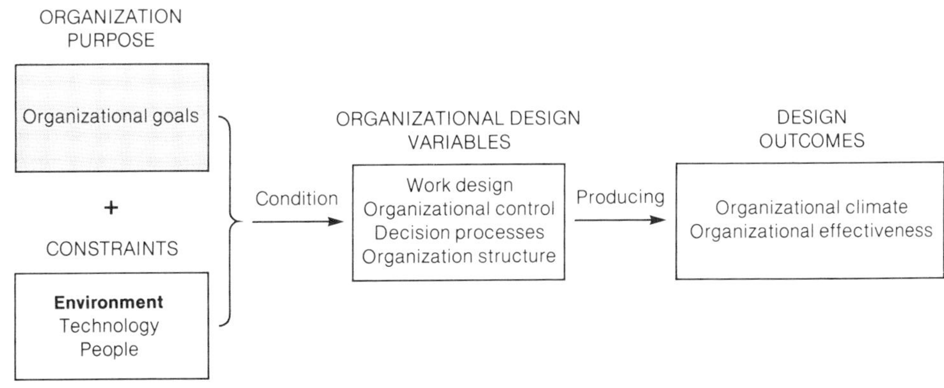

processes to meet those demands, take advantage of its opportunities, solve the problems it confronts, and acquire and process the resources it requires:

> An organization can survive so long as it adjusts to its situation; whether the process of adjustment is awkward or nimble becomes important in determining the organization's degree of prosperity. [Thompson and McEwen, 1958: 25]

The purpose of this chapter is to examine ways in which organizations are affected by environmental conditions. Further, the chapter explores ways in which organizations make their responses to those conditions.

ORGANIZATIONAL ENVIRONMENT: WHAT IS IT?

In order to see how organizations cope with environmental demands and opportunities, and design their structures and processes accordingly, it will be useful to examine the basic nature of the constraint.[1] Our examination focuses on three critical aspects: organizational boundaries, organizational domains, and specific characteristics, or dimensions, that are useful in distinguishing one set of environmental conditions from another.

Organizational Boundaries: Are There Such Things?

Most people will answer "yes" to the following questions: Are there people, processes, and activities that can logically be thought of as existing *inside* a particular organization? and Are there such things *outside* that organization? Such an affirmative answer suggests that to most people organizations have boundaries. Thus we usually draw pictures of organizations with solid lines around them (refer to Figures 1–2, 1–3, 2–3, and 2–4 for samples).

Still, we also acknowledge that organizations are systems—systems that are open to resources, demands, pressures, and other phenomena "outside." So the question arises: if we think of organizations as sort of social ecosystems, isn't it arbitrary at best, and even incorrect at worst, to think of some phenomena as being outside—and some inside—an organization? Should the president of a state university consider the legislature as "outside" the university organization? How helpful is it for a production supervisor to view the quality-control staff as "outside" his or her organization? This, in short, is the problem of boundary definition. Specifying the boundary of an organization is akin to specifying the boundary of a cloud (Starbuck, 1976). The lines are fuzzy—especially when there is a great deal of movement, change, and other turbulence.

In dealing with organizations, of course, the problem is even worse than with clouds. To the degree that an organization is interdependent with other organizations, its "boundaries" are even fuzzier and more ambiguous. Thus the task of merely discussing something called *organizational environment* is made difficult by the problem of deciding where the organization leaves off and the environment begins.

However, our purpose here is not to consider various philosophical nuances of the subject. We are interested in organization design. Therefore, let us use the following approach: *environmental phenomena are those that occur outside the set of roles and authority relationships*

1. This section follows the lead of Miles, Snow, and Pfeffer (1974); its treatment is indebted to their analysis.

that comprise the organizational framework. To say that organizations are interdependent with some such phenomena, or that certain organizational members are charged with reacting to, or even affecting, those phenomena, does not refute the meaning of external environment. Rather such a statement recognizes an organization-design reality: organizations contain roles and mechanisms to deal with phenomena that are *perceived* to be "external" (Weick, 1969). It is that perception that guides design decisions. Thus the philosophical point—the point as to whether something called an external environment exists—is moot. The managerial perception of that environment is real. Its design consequences are therefore real.

Organizational Domains

For design purposes we can (and should, for that matter) feel comfortable with the idea that organizations have boundaries. We must, however, focus our attention a little more closely if that idea is to be helpful. Specifically we should focus on that part of the external environment in which the organization purports to operate. It does little good (for making design decisions, at least) to try to examine every aspect of the larger society, culture, or civilization in which the organization is located. Such elements are not unimportant, of course. But their impact on design decision is indirect at best. Thus we begin to narrow our focus by examining what Levine and White (1961) and Thompson (1967) call the organization's *domain.*

The Nature of Domain

We have discussed the notion of domain before, in Chapter 3. Recall that by the term *organizational domain* we mean the claims that the organization has staked out for itself. These claims are asserted in terms of the following: 1. the range of products (goods or services) the organization produces; 2. the population of actual or potential customers served; and 3. services rendered.

By establishing a domain, the organization determines its pattern of *interdependence* with various environmental elements (Miles et al., 1974). By staking out the kinds of claims mentioned above, the organization places itself in mutually dependent interaction with suppliers, customers, regulatory agencies, unions, competitors, allies (such as in industry associations), and so forth:

> For example, if the organization decides to be a general hospital, it defines a pattern of interdependence with environmental elements that may be distinctly different from a hospital specializing in only a few major ailments. [Miles et al., 1974: 250]

The interdependence with which the organization must deal is of two types: input and output. On the input side, the organization depends on suppliers of necessary resources. These suppliers may be other business firms from whom the organization acquires raw material; financial institutions from whom needed capital is procured; or unions, which serve as a source of labor. On the output side, the organization may depend on institutions that provide transportation channels by which the organization's output may be dispersed. Similarly, the organization must form working relationships with distribution agencies, such as the stores in which its products are sold. And for the transportation and distribution organizations, of course, the organization under discussion provides an input. Thus are *mutual* dependencies established.

[Incidentally, now is as good a time as any for a reminder: when we speak of an *organization,* we mean anything from the whole multinational conglomerate to the cost-accounting department. Thus General Motors, as a total organization, has boundaries, establishes a domain, and is designed. It is equally true that the cost-accounting department in the AC Sparkplug Division has a boundary, establishes a domain vis-à-vis the rest of the Division, and is designed. After all, the cost-accounting department must acquire resources (in the form of a budget, personnel, and equipment, for instance) and deliver a product. Further, that product must be accepted by its "customers" (top management). In other words, whenever we speak of designing an organization we mean designing a department, field office, division, or whatever.]

Domain Legitimacy

For an organization simply to assert the existence of a domain is not sufficient. That assertion must be agreed to by those groups and institutions who are affected. Thompson (1967: 28) put it this way:

> The establishment of domain cannot be an arbitrary, unilateral action. Only if an organization's claims to domain are recognized by those who can provide the necessary support . . . can a domain be operated.

A group of physicians can, of course, get together and form an organization (a clinic, for example) that specializes in the treatment of rare tropical diseases. However, if those physicians decide to locate their clinic in Seattle or Toronto, there will likely be little demand for their product. Their claim of domain will be unaccepted. On the input side, a state college may find it impossible to persuade taxpayers (through the legislature) to fund a program of study that has no perceived relevance to that state. The licensing difficulty encountered a few years ago by proponents of acupuncture is a case in point. In this instance, the relevant regulatory agency did not agree that the claim to domain was legitimate.

Domain Legitimacy: Who Decides?

The examples noted above—the physicians' clinic, the state college, and the practice of acupuncture therapy—suggest that there are certain people, groups, and institutions outside the organization that pass judgment on the organization's claim to a domain. The result of passing such judgment is that the claim is or is not granted legitimacy.

Arising from these examples is a logical question: just who decides whether or not an organization's claim to a domain is legitimate? The answer is: the *task environment.* We recall from Chapter 2 that the task environment is that part of the world outside the organization with which it comes into frequent operating contact. Table 4–1 again identifies the major people, interest groups, and organizations that comprise the task environment. Task-environment elements must judge the organization to be offering something desirable. Otherwise, they will not legitimize its claim to a domain (Thompson, 1967: 28).

Basic to the relationship between the organization and its task environment is a process of *exchange.* In essence, as we have seen in our examples, the organization offers a source of

TABLE 4-1 ELEMENTS OF THE TASK ENVIRONMENT

Consumers
Suppliers
Regulators
Labor unions
Financial sources
Competitors
Allies

employment, an opportunity for invested capital to flourish, and a set of goods and services that are needed or desired. In turn, the task environment provides labor, financing, and consumers.

As we continually emphasize, the design problem for the organization is to develop mechanisms to deal successfully with this exchange process—in other words, mechanisms to manage these interdependencies. In the next section we review the major strategies available to designers to effect this management. First, however, we need to specify those characteristics or dimensions of the environment (that is, of the task environment) that must be taken into account in determining effective design strategies.

Environmental Dimensions

There have been several attempts by researchers to identify the environmental dimensions that matter for organizational design. As we noted in Chapter 2, among the first was that by Burns and Stalker (1961). Based on a comprehensive study of 20 industrial firms in the United Kingdom, they discovered that environments could be identified as to their relative "dynamic" or "static" character. The relevant dimension, therefore, was the *degree of change*—in markets, technology, economic conditions, and so forth. This continuum still provides a theme underlying most attempts to specify the state of organizations' environment.

Subsequent to Burns and Stalker's work, various analysts have attempted to elaborate on the dynamic-static theme. In 1965 Emery and Trist focused on two major aspects: the extent of environmental change experienced, plus the degree to which an organization is interconnected with other organizations. As a result of their analysis, the authors identified four types of organizational environment:

- *Placid, randomized.* In this sort of environment, opportunities and problems are relatively unchanged. Further, they are randomly distributed. Thus the organization somewhat meanders through its environment, encountering fairly undemanding, although not especially predictable, phenomena.
- *Placid, clustered.* The difference between this and the preceding type of environment is that the opportunities and problems tend to cluster together, rather than being randomly distributed in space and time.
- *Disturbed, reactive.* In this type of environment there are other, similar organizations attempting to do the same sorts of things (and thus competing for resources, customers, and so forth). Further, managers of an organization must assume that what they know about opportunities and problems is equally known to the other organizations. Thus

TABLE 4-2 DIMENSIONS OF ENVIRONMENT

Dimension	Description
Complexity	Reflects the number of environmental elements experienced by the organization
Diversity	Reflects the variety of environmental elements experienced by the organization
Change	Concerns the degree to which environmental elements experienced by the organization tend to vary over time
Uncertainty	Refers to the degree to which changes in environmental elements are unpredictable

SOURCE: Stephen M. Shortell, "The Role of Environment in a Configurational Theory of Organizations," *Human Relations*, vol. 30, 1977, pp. 275–302. New York: Plenum Publishing Corp.

"each will wish to improve its own chances by hindering the others, and each will know that the others not only wish to do likewise, but also know that each knows this" (1965: 26).

- *Turbulent field.* This type of environment also contains organizations that compete against each other (with the same foreign-intriguelike problem of "do they know that we know that they know. . . ."). In addition, however, environmental elements such as the marketplace, technology, economic conditions, and legal requirements are dynamic, changing in unpredictable ways.

Emery and Trist then go on to discuss various design strategies that organizations employ to operate successfully under each type of environmental condition. We will incorporate their analysis in the following section.

Environmental Dimensions Identified

In the 15 or so years since Emery and Trist's work, several authors have attempted to specify environmental dimensions that are relevant to organization design. Too many such attempts have been made for us to cover adequately here.[2] Rather than develop a long list of those attempts, therefore, we will focus on those dimensions that capture most of what seems to be important. Accordingly, we may identify four critical dimensions of organizational environment: *complexity, diversity, change,* and *uncertainty* (Duncan, 1972; Shortell, 1977). Table 4–2 presents a brief description of each dimension's characteristics.

Organization designers need to be aware of three aspects of these dimensions. First, it is useful to think of the dimensions as a group, in terms of common combinations. Thus, again relying on the dynamic-static theme, it is reasonable to expect that an organization might face an environment that simultaneously contains a large variety of factors that change, frequently in unpredictable fashion. This combination would describe a dynamic environment; the opposite combination, of course, would describe a static environment.

Second, we can do better than simply divide the world into two kinds of environment, dynamic and static, as appealing as such a division might be.[3] Thus while it is useful to think

2. The interested reader is referred to the following works: Thompson (1967), Lawrence and Lorsch (1969), Terreberry (1968), Pugh et al. (1969), Perrow (1970), Duncan (1972), Khandwalla (1972), Osborn and Hunt (1974), Kimberly (1975), Meyer (1975), Aldrich and Pfeffer (1976).

3. Mark Twain is reputed to have said, "There are two kinds of people in the world: people who divide the world into two kinds of people, and people who don't." You have no doubt observed that organization theorists tend to belong to the first group.

of the dimensions as a group, it is also helpful to focus on them separately. Mechanisms necessary to help an organization cope with just one or two unpredictably changing elements will differ, both in kind and variety, from those necessary to deal with a large variety of unchanging elements. The dynamic-static categories do not help much in describing these two environmental circumstances.

Third, regardless of the "configuration" of the environment confronting an organization, its designers need to be concerned with how *dependent* the organization is and each of the elements it faces. In other words, they must pay particular attention to the relative importance of the various dimensions identified above. As Shortell (1975: 7) illustrates:

> . . . two teaching hospitals may have equally [dynamic] environments in terms of a large number of dissimilar, unpredictable and rapidly changing factors to consider, but hospital A may be in a state in which the comprehensive health planning agency strictly reviews plans for expansion while hospital B may be in a state where such review is perfunctory or practically nonexistent. Thus hospital A would be more dependent on its environment in that its freedom to decide its future growth is more circumscribed than hospital B's. Likewise, it is possible for organizations operating in relatively [static] environments to vary in regard to dependence on that environment. For example, two local ice cream shops may have equally [static] environments in terms of a few, similar, predictable and seldom changing factors to consider, but if shop A does not have the capacity to make its own ice cream and shop B does, then A is more dependent on delivery by its suppliers than B.

Environmental Dimensions: Summary

In brief, then, organizations operate in environments that can be described in terms of a number of distinct dimensions. We have identified four: complexity, diversity, change, and uncertainty. It is frequently useful for our purposes to think of these dimensions as forming combinations that fall somewhere on a continium ranging from dynamic to static. However, it may be even more helpful to remember that the dimensions are distinct, with distinct implications for organizational design.

The Readings

Organizations' survival and prosperity essentially depend on the success of their strategies for dealing with two things: environmental uncertainty and interdependence with other organizations. The selection of a strategy—and its success, of course—depends in turn on various organizational structure and process characteristics that are designed. This theme is sounded in both of this chapter's readings.

The first selection is by Professor Jeffrey Pfeffer, "Beyond Management and the Worker: The Institutional Function of Management," in which he discusses the role that managers play in relating their organization successfully to environmental demands and opportunities. Pfeffer notes that, as an open system, the organization is affected by events outside its boundaries. In short, the organization must interact with other organizations—that is, manage its interdependence. Further, this interaction is outside its control—and thus is an important source of uncertainty. The author describes six strategies available to the organization in conducting this interaction. The strategies are: 1. merger, 2. joint ventures, 3. cooptation, 4. movement of key personnel among interacting organizations, 5. regulation, and 6. political activity. Most organizations employ some combination of these strategies.

The second reading is a recent article by Aldrich and Herker, "Boundary-Spanning Roles and Organization Structure." By the term *boundary-spanning roles,* the authors are referring to those persons and tasks necessary to helping the organization interact and deal with environmental events. In particular, Aldrich and Herker examine three aspects of the problem: 1. the specific functions served by boundary-spanning roles, 2. various organizational mechanisms—subunits, for example—that are designed to perform the boundary-spanning functions, and 3. the ways in which such roles vary from situation to situation.

Central to the authors' analysis is a key element to the whole issue of organizational design. To survive and prosper within its environmental constraints, the organization must deal with a critical resource: *information.* Specifically, the organization must acquire necessary information on a regular basis, process it, and interpret it for decision-making purposes. This was the theme struck early in the book (refer especially to Galbraith's article in Chapter 2) and continues throughout. Organizations contain functions that are designed to perform this information-handling chore. These functions are called boundary-spanning roles.

A brief warning about the Aldrich-Herker article: it is fairly sophisticated, involving some complex language. The reader is urged to attend closely to the analysis, however. The examples, illustrations, and hypotheses presented should clarify any ambiguities. Aldrich and Herker's article is not an easy one, but it is important, and the examples and hypotheses should help.

Conclusion

In summary, this chapter is concerned with the following questions:

1. What is it about the environment in which the organization operates that is important for organizational design?
2. What strategies do organizations follow in dealing with their environmental conditions?
3. What effects do environmental demands and opportunities have on specific design characteristics? That is, what characteristics get designed to help the organization deal with its environment?

We have already discussed the issue raised by the first question. The articles by Pfeffer and Aldrich-Herker lay the foundation for answering the second two questions. We will address them more specifically in the concluding statement.

BEYOND MANAGEMENT AND THE WORKER: THE INSTITUTIONAL FUNCTION OF MANAGEMENT

JEFFREY PFEFFER

Theory, research, and education in the field of organizational behavior and management have been dominated by a concern for the management of people *within* organizations. The question of how to make workers more productive has stood as the foundation for management theory and practice since the time of Frederick Taylor. Such an emphasis neglects the institutional function of management. While managing people within organizations is critical, managing the organization's relationships *with other organizations* such as competitors, creditors, suppliers, and governmental agencies is frequently as critical to the firm's success.

Parsons (1960) noted that there were three levels in organizations: (a) the *technical level,* where the technology of the organization was used to produce some product or service; (b) the *administrative level,* which coordinated and supervised the technical level; and (c) the *institutional level,* which was concerned with the organization's legitimacy and with organization-environment relations. Organization and management theory has primarily concentrated on administrative level problems, frequently at very low hierarchical levels in organizations.

Practicing managers and some researchers do recognize the importance of the institutional context in which the firm operates. There is increasing use of institutional advertising, and executives from the oil industry, among others, have been active in projecting their organizations' views in a variety of contexts. Mintzberg (1973) has identified the liaison role as one of ten roles managers fill. Other authors explicitly have noted the importance of relating the organization to other organizations (Pfeffer and Nowak, n.d.; Whyte, 1955).

The purposes of this article are: (a) to present evidence of the importance of the institutional function of management, and (b) to review data consistent with a model of institutional management. This model argues that managers behave as if they were seeking to manage and reduce uncertainty and interdependence arising from the firm's relationships with other organizations. Several strategic responses to interorganizational exchange, including their advantages and disadvantages, are considered.

INSTITUTIONAL PROBLEMS OF ORGANIZATION

Organizations are open social systems, engaged in constant and important transactions with other organizations in their environments. Business firms transact with customer and supplier organizations, and with sources of credit; they interact on the federal and local level with regulatory and legal authorities which are concerned with pollution, taxes, antitrust, equal employment, and myriad other issues. Because firms do interact with these other organizations, two consequences follow. First, organizations face uncertainty. If an organization were a closed system so that it could completely control and predict all the variables that affected its operation, the organization could make technically rational, maximizing decisions and anticipate the consequences of its actions. As an open system, transacting with important external organizations, the firm does not have control over many of the important factors that affect its operations. Because organizations are open, they are affected by events outside their boundaries.

Second, organizations are interdependent with other organizations with which they exchange resources, information or personnel, and thus open to influence by them. The extent of this influence is likely to be a function of the importance of the resource obtained,

Jeffrey Pfeffer, "Beyond Management and the Worker: The Institutional Function of Management," in *Academy of Management Review* 1976, pp. 36–46.

and inversely related to the ease with which the resource can be procured from alternative sources (Jacobs, 1974; Thompson, 1967). Interdependence is problematic and troublesome. Managers do not like to be dependent on factors outside their control. Interdependence is especially troublesome if there are few alternative sources, so the external organization is particularly important to the firm.

Interdependence and uncertainty interact in their effects on organizations. One of the principal functions of the institutional level of the firm is the management of this interdependence and uncertainty.

THE IMPORTANCE OF INSTITUTIONAL MANAGEMENT

Katz and Kahn (1966) noted that organizations may pursue two complementary paths to effectiveness. The first is to be as efficient as possible and thereby obtain a competitive advantage with respect to other firms. Under this strategy, the firm succeeds because it operates so efficiently that it achieves a competitive advantage in the market. The second strategy, termed "political," involves the establishment of favorable exchange relationships based on considerations that do not relate strictly to price, quality, service, or efficiency. Winning an order because of the firm's product and cost characteristics would be an example of the strategy of efficiency; winning the order because of interlocks in the directorates of the organizations involved, or because of family connections between executives in the two organizations, would illustrate political strategies.

MANAGING UNCERTAINTY AND INTERDEPENDENCE

The organization, requiring transactions with other organizations and uncertain about their future performance, has available a variety of strategies that can be used to manage uncertainty and interdependence. Firms face two problems in their institutional relationships: (a) managing the uncertainty caused by the unpredictable actions of competitors; and (b) managing the uncertainty resulting from non-competitive interdependence with suppliers, creditors, government agencies, and customers. In both instances, the same set of strategic responses is available: *merger,* to completely absorb the interdependence and resulting uncertainty; *joint ventures; interlocking directorates,* to partially absorb the interdependence; the movement and *selective recruiting of executives* and other personnel, to develop interorganizational linkages; *regulation,* to provide government enforced stability; and other *political activity* to reduce competition, protect markets and sources of supply, and otherwise manage the organization's environment.

Because organizations are open systems, each strategy is limited in its effect. While merger or some other interorganizational linkage may manage one source of organizational dependence, it probably at the same time makes the organizations dependent on yet other organizations. For example, while regulation may eliminate effective price competition and restrict entry into the industry (Jordan, 1972; Pfeffer, 1974a; Posner, 1974), the regulated organizations then face the uncertainties involved in dealing with the regulatory agency. Moreover, in reducing uncertainty for itself, the organization must bargain away some of its own discretion (Thompson, 1967). One can view institutional management as an exchange process—the organization assures itself of needed resources, but at the same time, must promise certain predictable behaviors in return. Keeping these qualifications in mind, evidence on use of the various strategies of institutional management is reviewed.

Merger

There are three reasons an organization may seek to merge—first, to reduce competition by absorbing an important competitor organization; second, to manage interdependence with either sources of input or purchasers of output by absorbing them; and third, to diversify operations and thereby lessen dependence on the present organizations with which it exchanges (Pfeffer, 1972b). While merger among competing organizations is presumably proscribed by the antitrust laws, enforcement resources are limited, and major consolidations do take place.

In analyzing patterns of interorganizational behavior, one can either ask executives in the organizations involved the reasons for the action, or alternatively, one can develop a hypothetical model of behavior which is then tested with the available data. Talking with organizational executives may not provide the real reasons behind interorganizational activity since (a) different persons may see and interpret the same action in different ways, (b) persons may infer after the fact the motives for the action or decision, and (c) persons may not be motivated to tell the complete truth about the reasons for the behavior. Much of the existing literature on interorganizational linkage activity, therefore, uses the method of empirically testing the deductions from a hypothetical model of interorganizational behavior.

The classic expressed rationale for merger has been to increase the profits or the value of the shares of the firm. In a series of studies beginning as early as 1921, researchers have been unable to demonstrate that merger active firms are more profitable or have higher stock prices following the merger activity. This literature has been summarized by Reid (1968), who asserts that mergers are made for growth, and that growth is sought because of the relationship between firm size and managerial salaries.

Growth, however, does not provide information concerning the desired characteristics of the acquired firm. Under a growth objective, any merger is equivalent to any other of the same size. Pfeffer (1972b) has argued that mergers are undertaken to manage organizational interdependence. Examining the proportion of merger activity occurring within the same two-digit SIC industry category, he found that the highest proportion of within-industry mergers occurred in industries of intermediate concentration. The theoretical argument was that in industries with many competitors, the absorption of a single one did little to reduce competitive uncertainty. At the other extreme, with only a few competitors, merger would more likely be scrutinized by the antitrust authorities and coordination could instead be achieved through more informal arrangements, such as price leadership.

The same study investigated the second reason to merge: to absorb the uncertainty among organizations vertically related to each other, as in a buyer-seller relationship. He found that it was possible to explain 40 percent of the variation in the distribution of merger activity over industries on the basis of resource interdependence, measured by estimates of the transactions flows between sectors of the economy. On an individual industry basis, in two-thirds of the cases a measure of transactions interdependence accounted for 65 percent or more of the variation in the pattern of merger activity. The study indicated that it was possible to account for the industry of the likely merger partner firm by considering the extent to which firms in the two industries exchanged resources.

While absorption of suppliers or customers will reduce the firm's uncertainty by bringing critical contingencies within the boundaries of the organization, this strategy has some distinct costs. One danger is that the process of vertical integration creates a larger organization which is increasingly tied to a single industry.

The third reason for merger is diversification. Occasionally, the organization is confronted by interdependence it cannot absorb, either because of resource or legal limitations. Through diversifying its activities, the organization does not reduce the uncertainty, but makes the particular contingency less critical for its success and well-being. Diversification provides the organization with a way of avoiding, rather than absorbing, problematic interdependence.

Merger represents the most complete solution to situations of organizational interdependence, as it involves the total absorption of either a competitor or a vertically related organization, or the acquisition of an organization operating in another area. Because it does involve total absorption, merger requires more resources and is a more visible and substantial form of interorganizational linkage.

Joint Ventures

Closely related to merger is the joint venture: the creation of a jointly owned, but independent organization by two or more separate parent firms. Merger involves the total pooling of assets by two or more organizations. In a joint venture, some assets of each of several parent organizations are used, and thus only a partial pooling of resources is involved (Bernstein,

1965). For a variety of reasons, joint ventures have been prosecuted less frequently and less successfully than mergers, making joint ventures particularly appropriate as a way of coping with competitive interdependence.

The joint subsidiary can have several effects on competitive interdependence and uncertainty. First, it can reduce the extent of new competition. Instead of both firms entering a market, they can combine some of their assets and create a joint subsidiary to enter the market. Second, since joint subsidiaries are typically staffed, particularly at the higher executive levels, with personnel drawn from the parent firms, the joint subsidiary becomes another location for the management of competing firms to meet. Most importantly, the joint subsidiary must set price and output levels, make new product development and marketing decisions and decisions about its advertising policies. Consequently, the parent organizations are brought into association in a setting in which exactly those aspects of the competitive relationship must be jointly determined.

The difference between mergers and joint ventures appears to be that mergers are used relatively more to cope with buyer-seller interdependence, and joint ventures are more highly related to considerations of coping with competitive uncertainty.

Co-optation and Interlocking Directorates

Co-optation is a venerable strategy for managing interdependence between organizations. Co-optation involves the partial absorption of another organization through the placing of a representative of that organization on the board of the focal organization. Corporations frequently place bankers on their boards; hospitals and universities offer trustee positions to prominent business leaders; and community action agencies develop advisory boards populated with active and strong community political figures.

As a strategy for coping with interdependence, co-optation involves some particular problems and considerations. For example, a representative of the external organization is brought into the focal organization, while still retaining his or her original organizational membership. Co-optation is based on creating a conflict of interest within the co-opted person. To what extent should one pursue the goals and interests of one's organization of principal affiliation, and to what extent should one favor the interests of the co-opting organization? From the point of view of the co-opting organization, the individual should favor its interests, but not to the point where he or she loses credibility in the parent organization, because at that point, the individual ceases to be useful in ensuring that organization's support. Thus, co-optation requires striking a balance between the pressures to identify with either the parent or co-opting institution.

Furthermore, since co-optation involves less than total absorption of the other organization, there is the risk that the co-opted representative will not have enough influence or control in the principal organization to ensure the desired decisions. Of course, it is possible to co-opt more than a single representative. This is frequently done when relationships with the co-opted organization are particularly uncertain and critical. Co-optation may be the most feasible strategy when total absorption is impossible due to financial or legal constraints.

Interlocks in the boards of directors of competing organizations provide a possible strategy for coping with competitive interdependence and the resulting uncertainty. The underlying argument is that in order to manage interorganizational relationships, information must be exchanged, usually through a joint subsidiary or interlocking directorate. While interlocks among competitors are ostensibly illegal, until very recently there was practically no prosecution of this practice. In a 1965 study, a subcommittee of the House Judiciary Committee found more than 300 cases in which direct competitors had interlocking boards of directors (House of Representatives, 1965). In a study of the extent of interlocking among competing organizations in a sample of 109 manufacturing organizations, Pfeffer and Nowak (n.d.) found that the proportion of directors on the board from direct competitors was higher for firms operating in industries in which concentration was intermediate. This result is consistent with the result found for joint ventures and mergers as well. In all three instances, linkages among competing organizations occurred more frequently when concentration was in an intermediate range.

Analyses of co-optation through the use of boards of directors have not been confined to business firms. Price (1963) argued that the principal function of the boards of the Oregon Fish and Game Commissions was to link the organizations to their environments. Zald (1967) found that the composition of YMCA boards in Chicago matched the demography of their operating areas, and affected the organizations' effectiveness, particularly in raising money. Pfeffer (1973) examined the size, composition, and function of hospital boards of directors, finding that variables of organizational context, such as ownership, source of funds, and location, were important explanatory factors. He also found a relationship between co-optation and organizational effectiveness. In 1972, he found that regulated firms, firms with a higher proportion of debt in their capital structures, and larger firms tended to have more outside directors. Allen (1974) also found that size of the board and the use of co-optation was predicted by the size of the firm, but did not replicate Pfeffer's earlier finding of a relationship between the organization's capital structure and the proportion of directors from financial institutions. In a study of utility boards, Pfeffer (1974b) noted that the composition of the board tended to correlate with the demographics of the area in which the utility was regulated.

The evidence is consistent with the strategy of organizations using their boards of directors to co-opt external organizations and manage problematic interdependence. The role of the board of directors is seen not as the provision of management expertise or control, but more generally as a means of managing problematic aspects of an organization's institutional environment.

Executive Recruitment

Information also is transferred among organizations through the movement of personnel. The difference between movement of executives between organizations and co-optation is that in the latter case, the person linking the two organizations retains membership in both organizations. In the case of personnel movement, dual organizational membership is not maintained. When people change jobs, they take with themselves information about the operations, policies, and values of their previous employers, as well as contacts in the organization. In a study of the movement of faculty among schools of business, Baty et al. (1971) found that similar orientations and curricula developed among schools exchanging personnel. The movement of personnel is one method by which new techniques of management and new marketing and product ideas are diffused through a set of organizations.

Occasionally, the movement of executives between organizations has been viewed as intensifying, rather than reducing, competition. Companies have been distressed by the raiding of trade secrets and managerial expertise by other organizations. While this perspective must be recognized, the exchange of personnel among organizations is a revered method of conflict *reduction* between organizations (Stern, Sternthal, and Craig, 1973). Personnel movement inevitably involves sharing information among a set of organizations.

If executive movement is a form of interfirm linkage designed to manage competitive relationships, the proportion of executives recruited from within the same industry should be highest at intermediate levels of industrial concentration. Examining the three top executive positions in twenty different manufacturing industries, the evidence on executive backgrounds was found to be consistent with this argument (Pfeffer and Leblebici, 1973b). The proportion of high level executives with previous jobs in the same industry but in a different company was found to be negatively related to the number of firms in the industry. The larger the number of firms, the less likely that a single link among competitors will substantially reduce uncertainty, but the larger the available supply of external executive talent. The data indicated no support for a supply argument, but supported the premise that interorganizational linkages are used to manage interdependence and uncertainty.

The use of executive movement to manage noncompetitive interorganizational relationships is quite prevalent. The often-cited movement of personnel between the Defense Department and major defense contractors is only one example, because there is extensive movement of personnel between many government departments and industries interested in the agencies' decisions. The explanation is frequently proposed that organizations are acquiring these personnel because of their expertise. The expertise explanation is frequently difficult to separate from the alternative that personnel are being exchanged to enhance interorganizational relationships. Regardless of the motivation, exchanging personnel inevitably involves the transfer of information and access to the other organization. It is conceptually possible to control for the effect of expertise—in other words, taking expertise into account, is there evidence that recruiting patterns reflect the influence of factors related to institutional management?

Regulation

Occasionally, institutional relationships are managed through recourse to political intervention. The reduction of competition and its associated uncertainty may be accomplished through regulation. Regulation, however, is a risky strategy for organizations to pursue. While regulation most frequently benefits the regulated industry (Jordan, 1972; Pfeffer, 1974a), the industry and firms have no assurance that regulatory authority will not be used against their interests. Regulation is very hard to repeal. Successful use of regulation requires that the firm and industry face little or no powerful political opposition, and that the political future can be accurately forecast.

The benefits of regulation to those being regulated have been extensively reviewed (Posner, 1974; Stigler, 1971). Regulation frequently has been sought by the regulated industry. Currently, trucking firms are among the biggest supporters of continued regulation of trucking. Since the Civil Aeronautics Board was created in 1938, no new trunk carriers have been started. Jordan (1970) found that air rates on intrastate (hence not regulated by the CAB) airlines within California are frequently 25 percent or more lower than fares on comparable routes of regulated carriers. Estimates of the effects of regulation on prices in electric utilities, airlines, trucking, and natural gas have indicated that regulation either increases price or has no effect.

The theory behind these outcomes is still unclear. One approach suggests that regulation is created for the public benefit, but after the initial legislative attention, the regulatory process is captured by the firms subject to regulation. Another approach proposes that regulation, like other goods, is acquired subject to supply and demand considerations (Posner, 1974). Political scientists, focusing on the operation of interest groups, argue that regulatory agencies are "captured" by organized and well-financed interests. Government intervention in the market can solve many of the interdependence problems faced by firms. Regulation is most often accompanied by restriction of entry and the fixing of prices, which tend to reduce market uncertainties. Markets may be actually allocated to firms, and with the reduction of risk, regulation may make access to capital easier. Regulation may alter the organization's relationships with suppliers and customers. One theory of why the railroads were interested in the creation of the Interstate Commerce Commission (ICC) in 1887 was that large users were continually demanding and winning discriminatory rate reductions, disturbing the price stability of railroad price fixing cartels. By forbidding price discrimination and enforcing this regulation, the ICC strengthened the railroads' position with respect to large customers (MacAvoy, 1965).

Political Activity

Regulation is only one specific form of organizational activity in governmental processes. Business attempts to affect competition through the operation of the tariff laws date back to the 1700's (Bauer, de Sola Pool, and Dexter, 1968). Epstein (1969) provided one of the more complete summaries of the history of corporate involvement in politics and the inevitability of such action. The government has the power of coercion, possessed legally by no other social institution. Furthermore, legislation and regulation affect most of our economic institutions and markets, either indirectly through taxation, or more directly through purchasing, market protection or market creation. For example, taxes on margarine only recently came to an end. Federal taxes, imposed in 1886 as a protectionist measure for dairy interests, were removed in 1950, but

TABLE 4-3 ADVANTAGES AND DISADVANTAGES OF STRATEGIES OF INSTITUTIONAL MANAGEMENT

Strategy	Advantages	Disadvantages
Merger	Completely absorbs interdependence	Requires resources sufficient to acquire another organization May be proscribed by antitrust laws, or infeasible for other reasons (e.g., a governmental unit cannot be absorbed by a firm)
Joint ventures	Can be used for sharing risks and costs associated with large or technologically advanced activities Can be used to partially pool resources and coordinate activities	Is available only for certain types of organizations, though less restricted than merger (COMSAT, for instance, brings together government and business)
Cooptation	Relatively inexpensive	May not provide enough coordination or linkage between organizations to ensure performance Coopted person may loose credibility in original organization
Personnel movement	Relatively inexpensive Almost universally possible	Person loses identification with original organization, lessening influence there Linkage is based on knowledge and familiarity, and on a few persons at most, not on basic structural relationships
Regulation	Enables organization to benefit from the coercive power of the government	Regulation may be used to harm the organization's interests
Political activity	Enables organization to use government to modify and enhance environment	Government intervention, once legitimated, may be used against the organization as well as for its benefit

a law outlawing the sale of oleo in its colored form lasted until 1967 in Wisconsin.

As with regulation, political activities carry both benefits and risks. The risk arises because once government intervention in an issue on behalf of a firm or industry is sought, then political intervention becomes legitimated, regardless of whose interests are helped or hurt. The firm that seeks favorable tax legislation runs the risk of creating a setting in which it is equally legitimate to be exposed to very unfavorable legislation. After an issue is opened to government intervention, neither side will find it easy to claim that further government action is illegitimate.

In learning to cope with a particular institutional environment, the firm may be unprepared for new uncertainties caused by the change of fundamental institutional relationships, including the opening of price competition, new entry and the lack of protection from overseas competition.

CONCLUSION

The institutional function of management involves managing the organization's relationships with other organizations. Table 4–3 presents strategies of institutional management with their principal advantages and disadvantages. From observation of organizational activities, the most common response to interdependence with external organizations seems to be the attempt to develop some form of interorganizational linkage to ensure the continuation of favorable relationships with important organizations in the environment.

All such interfirm linkages have costs, with the most fundamental being the loss of the organization's autonomy. In return for the certainty that one's competitors will not engage in predatory price cutting, one must provide assurances about one's own behavior. For example, co-optation involves the possibility of acquiring the support of an external organization, but at the same time the firm gives up some degree of privacy over its internal information and some control over its operations and decisions.

Variables affecting responses to the organization's environment can be specified. Actions taken to manage interdependencies are related to the extent of the interdependence and its importance to the organization. The response to competitive interdependence is related to measures of industry structure, and particularly to the necessity and feasibility of developing informal, interorganizational structures. Two important issues remain. First, is effective institutional management associated with favorable outcomes to the organization? Second, given the importance of institutional management, why are some organizations more successful than others at this task?

The effect of institutional management on firm performance is difficult to measure, and seldom has been examined. To examine the effect of successful institutional management, an outcome measure is needed. Profit is only one possibility, because there is evidence that the reduction of uncertainty may be sought regardless of its effect on profit (Caves, 1970). Whatever criterion is chosen is affected by many factors. To attribute a result to institutional management, other causes must be controlled. Nevertheless, institutional management receives a great deal of management attention in some firms, and a firm's interorganizational relationships may be important to its success and survival.

Of even more fundamental interest is the question of why some firms are able to develop more effective strategic responses to their institutional environments. It is possible that effective institutional management requires fundamentally different structures of top management, or the development of excess managerial capacity, or the development of particular types of information systems. It is easier to find successful institutional management than to identify critical variables enabling it to develop in the first place. For example, some universities have better relationships with their state legislatures than do others. It is possible to retrospectively infer explanations as to why this is so. What remains to be done is to explain those factors that could be designed into an organization initially to ensure effective institutional management in the future.

Considering its probable importance to the firm, the institutional function of management has received much less concern than it warrants. It is time that this aspect of management receives the systematic attention long reserved for motivational and productivity problems associated with relationships between management and workers.

BOUNDARY-SPANNING ROLES AND ORGANIZATION STRUCTURE

HOWARD ALDRICH
DIANE HERKER

A minimal defining characteristic of a formal organization is the distinction between members and nonmembers, with an organization existing to the extent that some persons are admitted, while others are excluded, thus allowing an observer to draw a boundary around the organization (Thompson, 1962: 139–46).[1] Defining organizations in terms of boundaries also allows a definition of the role of formal authority in an organization: authorities are persons who apply organizational rules in making decisions about entry and expulsion of members (Aldrich, 1971: 283). In this sense, organizational behavior (OB) has always contained an implicit "open systems" view, although few theorists or researchers have studied boundary maintaining or boundary crossing (Aiken and Hage, 1972).

The definition and location of a specific boundary may be possible only given a specific conceptual and empirical context. This article takes the existence of boundaries as given, while treating *boundary-spanning* activity as problematic. Specifically, it examines 1. functions served by boundary roles, 2. the generation of boundary units and roles relating organizations to their environments, and 3. the environmental and organizational sources of variation in the structure of boundary roles.

Although most investigators agree on the importance of focusing on relations between organizations and their environments, there is little agreement on the degree of autonomy of action organizations have. At the extreme are two positions: a natural selection model, laying heavy emphasis on the dominance of environmental constraints on behavior, and a strategic choice or resource dependence model, emphasizing the active role organizational administrators play in shaping outcomes. As these two macro-theoretical positions are reviewed elsewhere (Aldrich and Pfeffer, 1976), and there is no prospect of reconciling them in this paper, we concentrate on propositions and hypotheses of the middle range.

FUNCTIONS OF BOUNDARY ROLES

Two classes of functions are performed by boundary roles: information processing and external representation. Information from external sources comes into an organization through boundary roles, and boundary roles link organizational structure to environmental elements, whether by buffering, moderating, or influencing the environment. Any given role can serve either or both functions.

The Information Processing Function

In focusing on the information processing function, we are following the lead of Dill (1962), who suggested that the environment of an organization could be treated as information available to the organization through search or exposure. Terreberry argued that viable organizations are characterized by "an increase in the ability to learn and to perform according to changing contingencies in the environment"(1968: 660).

Boundary role incumbents, by virtue of their posi-

[1]The senior author thanks his colleagues. Sam Bacharach and Robert Stern, for admirably fulfilling their roles as good listeners and trenchant critics. Richard Hall, Jeff Pfeffer, Steve Rosell, and Dave Whetten also contributed to the clarity of the argument. Sandra Miller of the Centre for Environmental Studies, London, provided valuable assistance in the preparation of the paper.

This review could not have been written without the foundation laid by James D. Thompson, and our debt to him should be evident to those familiar with his work.

Abridged from Howard Aldrich and Diane Herker, "Boundary-Spanning Roles and Organization Structure,"*Academy of Management Review* 1977, pp. 217–30.

tion, are exposed to large amounts of potentially relevant information. The situation would be overburdening if all information originating in the environment required immediate attention. Boundary roles are a main line of organizational defense against information overload (Brown, 1966; Meier, 1965). Expertise in selecting information is consequential, since not all information from the environment is of equal importance. External information can be conceptualized in terms of a three-part hierarchy, corresponding to Parsons' (1956) distinction between three levels of authority in organizations: strategic, managerial, and technical information (Brown, 1966: 325). Their relative importance varies by type of environment and technology; e.g., in stable homogeneous environments and organizations with highly routine technology, strategic information is less important.

The process by which information filters through boundary positions into the organization must be examined. Boundary roles serve a dual function in information transmittal, acting as both filters and facilitators. Information overload would still be a problem if all relevant information had to be immediately communicated to internal members. Accordingly, boundary role personnel selectively act on relevant information, filtering information prior to communicating it (Cyert and March, 1963; March and Simon, 1958). They act autonomously on some information, and consolidate, delay, or store other information, thus alleviating the problem of overloading communication channels (although perhaps incurring other costs to the organization in the process). Information is summarized and directed to the organizational units that need it.

Boundary role personnel may act on information requiring an immediate response, as when a sales department responds to a customer inquiry about product specifications. They may store information for future use, as when a purchasing department files information on a new supplier's products, to be referred to at re-order points. Boundary personnel in marketing may uncover trends in the demand for their organization's products which will have a major impact on the mix of resources required, and communicate this information to purchasing. Boundary units may also summarize information and communicate it to other units on a regularized basis (Mathieson, 1972).

The expertise of boundary role occupants in summarizing and interpreting information may be as important to organizational success as expertise in determining who gets what information, depending upon the uncertainty in the information processed. Information to be communicated often does not consist of simple verifiable "facts." If the conditions beyond the boundary are complexly interrelated and cannot be easily quantified, the boundary role incumbents may engage in "uncertainty absorption"—drawing inferences from the perceived facts and passing on only the inferences (March and Simon, 1958: 189).

Consider the case of a lobbyist formulating a report on a bill and amendments that will differentially affect the operations of his or her organization. The lobbyist will have to summarize information about the bill's progress, testimony in hearings, and apparent predispositions of committee members and other legislators, as well as making the entire situation meaningful to his or her superiors. If these superiors cannot understand the interrelationships and implications of the raw data, they will not be able to use the information. Some simplification is necessary and the relationships of events in Washington to organizational operation will have to be clearly specified. In short the lobbyist must put the information in usable form (Wilson, 1973).

Innovation and structural change are often alleged to result from information brought into the organization by boundary personnel (Bennis, 1966; Hage and Aiken, 1970). All complex organizations have a tendency to move toward an internal state of compatibility and compromise between units and individuals within the organization, with a resultant isolation from important external influences (Campbell, 1969b). This trend can jeopardize the effectiveness and perhaps the survival of the organization, *unless* the organization is effectively linked to the environment through active boundary personnel. By scanning the environment for new technological developments, innovations in organizational design, relevant trends in related fields, etc., boundary personnel can prevent organizations from becoming prematurely ossified and mismatched with their environments (Child, 1969).

This review of the information processing function of boundary roles may be summarized in the following hypothesis:

H1: *An organization's ability to adapt to environmental contingencies depends in part on the expertise of boundary role incumbents in selecting, transmitting and interpreting information originating in the environment.*

The External Representation Function

External representation can be viewed in terms of an organization's response to environmental influence. Environmental constraints and contingencies can be adapted to in at least three ways: (a) by internal structural differentiation to match the pattern of the relevant environment, which requires information about environmental characteristics; (b) by gaining power over the relevant elements of the environment, manipulating it to conform to the organization's needs; and (c) a compromise position, the use of boundary personnel in "normal" boundary spanning roles. Included under the external representation function are all the boundary roles that involve resource acquisition and disposal, political legitimacy, and a residual category of social legitimacy and organizational image.

Boundary roles concerned with resource acquisition and disposal include purchasing agents and buyers, marketing and sales representatives, personnel recruiters, admissions officers, and shipping and receiving agents. In these roles the organization is represented to the environment, because the normal flow of authoritative commands is from the core of the organization to these boundary roles. The behavior of personnel in these roles is supposed to reflect the policy decisions of decision makers in line roles.

This usual flow of directives to boundary roles presents two problems for boundary personnel. First, much of the information they attend to has an external origin, and it occasionally becomes apparent that policy directives are based on information that is no longer relevant. This poses a dilemma for the conscientious boundary spanner, especially in organizations with a high degree of decentralization—should behavior be immediately modified to correspond to latest developments, or should action be delayed until the information has "gone through channels"? Second, as Strauss (1962) pointed out in his study of purchasing agents, some boundary personnel are not satisfied with their subordinate position on the vertical axis of the organization, given their self-evident horizontal location of equality with other departments. Thus, dissatisfied boundary spanners take the initiative to increase their power vis-à-vis other units. For example, personnel officers suggest changes in job descriptions before agreeing to post them; admissions or intake staff develop their own criteria of "worthy" applicants (Blau, 1957); and purchasing agents make informal compacts with salespersons from outside firms to push products which their production department "really" needs (Strauss, 1962).

Boundary roles involved with maintaining or improving the political legitimacy of the organization not only represent the organization but also mediate between it and important outside organizations. The term *mediate* refers here to aspects of the boundary role involving negotiations that will eventually affect the power of the organization vis-à-vis another organization or group. Kochan (1975) notes that city governments have created collective bargaining units as a response to threats to the city's control over its employees. The role of the corporate lawyer is perhaps the most clear example of the necessity and difficulty of preserving at least an equal balance of rights and responsibilities between business organizations (MacAulay, 1963).

Boundary-spanning personnel can help maintain the legitimacy of the organization by providing information to important client groups, specially adapted for them. Aldrich and Reiss (1971) note that police officers on the beat transmit an image of city law enforcement capabilities to small *businesspersons* independent of the *businessperson's* attitudes toward the police themselves. Information transmittal is facilitated because both police and small business are exposed to environmental forces that make their commonality of interest highly salient. Adair's (1960) study of the use of Navaho Indians as health aides for their own communities found that the Indians functioned as mediators in their boundary roles, drawing the doctor and the Navaho patient closer together. The Indian health worker offers a different side to each party involved, finding a middle ground to settle discords between them. Detached school workers perform the same sort of representation function for school systems.

Maintaining the organizational image and enhancing its social legitimacy are less a matter of mediating contacts than of simply making the organization visible. Advertising and public relations specialists try to influence the behavior of target groups in ways that benefit the focal organization, without bargaining or negotiating with the target group. The flow of intra-organizational influence to these roles is much more one-sided than in the boundary roles described above; one apparent consequence is a high rate of turnover.

One function of boards of directors and public advisory commissions is to link the organization to target groups in the environment in a highly visible way, so that they will feel their interests are being represented. Thus, women and blacks are being appointed in increasing numbers to corporate boards, and students now serve as trustees on university boards. Fulfilling this function requires recruiting people who are already members of or in contact with specific target groups.

These three varieties of external representation functions can be related to organizational effectiveness in the second hypothesis:

H2: *An organization's ability to cope with environmental constraints depends in part on the ability of boundary role incumbents to achieve a compromise between organizational policy and environmental constraints, to choose strategic moves to overcome constraints, or to create conditions in which the organization's autonomy is seldom challenged.*

CREATION OF BOUNDARY ROLES

By definition all organizations have some boundary-spanning roles, if only at the level of the organization head or chief executive. But some have an elaborate set of boundary roles while others have only a few. In some cases boundary roles are formalized into full-time organizational positions, while in others they are only part-time activities. This section examines the generation and formalization of boundary roles as explicit organizational roles, with references to organizational size and technology, and various characteristics of organizational environments. To understand the process of boundary spanning *behavior,* an interactive model of the kind developed by Adams (1976) is needed, but such models are highly specific to the particular pair-wise relationship being examined. Here we are concerned with the general features of the boundary role while recognizing that actual behavior in boundary roles will vary from context to context.

The extent to which organizational positions involve interaction with external elements varies greatly. Many positions outside the technical core involve some extraorganizational interaction, but only a few involve intensive interaction.

The number of formally designated boundary spanning roles in an organization is partially dependent on organizational size (Aiken and Hage, 1972). A small organization is able to survive with a fairly simple structure, with relatively few differentiated roles and functions. (Blau and Scott, 1962; Child, 1973; Child, n.d.). Its structure may be less formalized and more amenable to restructuring to achieve and maintain a satisfactory position vis-à-vis its environment. A small organization might be willing and able to rely on information brought to it informally by its members. This tendency is more marked among organizations that have highly committed members or that are not highly dependent on their environment for survival (Aldrich, 1972), such as a small religious sect (Harrison, 1972). As organizational and environmental complexities increase, organizations can no longer afford non-differentiated boundary spanning activities.

Technology and Boundary Role Differentiation

Holding size constant, boundary spanning units or roles should be expected to increase as a proportion of all roles as organizations differentiate in response to the interaction of technology and environment, and under the direct impact of environmental pressure. In the following discussion, technology is treated as a source of internal differentiation generating boundary roles to the extent that varying technology types create different patterns of organization-environment interaction.* Thompson's categories of mediating, long-linked and intensive technology capture the implications of various technology types for the generation of boundary roles (Thompson, 1967: 15–18).

Organizations with a *mediating technology* link clients or customers with each other, as in the case of banks, insurance companies, or the post office; or they link clients with other organizations, thus serving a "people-processing function" (Hasenfeld, 1972). Such organizations should have the highest proportion of boundary roles, as boundary roles are their line roles. The wholesaler of small consumer goods has boundary personnel who purchase goods from producers and sell them to organizations which, in turn, sell them to organizations which, in turn, sell them to retail customers. An investment banking firm contracts with a client to put together a "package" of investment instruments that satisfy financial needs and then sells the "package" to other organizations with funds to invest. Boundary personnel similarly serve a line function in the people processing component of organizations such as schools and government agencies.

A study of organizations using a mediating technology in the book publishing and record producing industries found that they allocated a large proportion of their personnel to boundary spanning roles, on the input side to contract for and supervise the production of raw material, and on the output side to promote the cultural products and achieve optimal distribution (Hirsch, 1972). These boundary roles also monitored the environment and provided information quickly to managers and executives, apparently as a strategy to help the organization hold its position in a very uncertain environment.

Organizations with a *long-linked technology* attempt to buffer most of their units and roles from the environment, and have a lower proportion of boundary roles. Since the various organizational units are serially interdependent, there are many boundary roles between intra-organizational components, but the focus here is on roles at the external boundary. Specific boundary roles are important for such organizations. First, long-linked technology gains maximum efficiency through standardized production of large volumes of output (to take advantage of economies of scale) and so such organizations need an effective marketing and sales force (Keller et al., n.d.; Pfeffer and Leblebici, 1973b). Second, Thompson (1967: 40) argues that "organizations employing long-linked technologies and subject to rationality norms seek to expand their domains through *vertical integration,*" and thus the legal and accounting departments of such organizations interact fairly intensively with potential acquisitions in the environment (Pfeffer, 1972a).

Organizations using an *intensive technology,* which depends on the object being worked on, also buffer most of their roles from the environment. They often achieve this by temporarily drawing the object or the client into the organization. In intensive technology organizations concerned with people-changing activities, the client is temporarily assigned an organizational role, and must change behavior to suit norms which preclude appealing to his or her environmental role relative to the organization. The boundary personnel who engage in initial interaction with potential clients affect the organization's subsequent internal operations if they have the power to admit or reject clients; e.g., the physician associated with a hospital or the admissions officer at a private college. By detecting a violation and making an arrest, a police officer provides the rest of the criminal justice system with raw material to be processed (Reiss, 1971).

Thompson argues that these organizations seek to expand their domains by incorporating the object worked on, with "total institutions" [e.g., prisons and mental institutions] (Goffman, 1961) placing an almost impenetrable boundary around clients. The people-changing organizations that use an intensive technology (e.g., hospitals) have one characteristic that opens them to environmental influence—their high degree of professionalization. Aiken and Hage (1968) assert that professionals in organizations engage in a great deal of boundary-spanning contact because of the need to maintain contact with a professional reference group and keep abreast of changing technology in their field.

*Ed. note: See Chapter 5.

In intensive technology organizations not concerned with people-changing activities, the clients often become a temporary part of the organization's administrative structure and thus need a liaison person to represent them, as in the construction industry (Thompson, 1967: 44). Thus, while it is clear that mediating technology organizations have proportionately more boundary spanning roles than other organizations, the relative ranking of organizations with long-linked and intensive technology cannot be determined without further empirical research.

H3: *Organizations using a mediating technology will have the highest proportion of boundary roles, while organizations using long-linked and intensive technologies will have a smaller proportion of boundary roles.*

H4: *Organizations using long-linked or intensive technologies will departmentalize and otherwise separate boundary spanning units from their core technical units.*

Environment and Boundary-Role Differentiation

Environmental pressures are responsible for much of the observed differentiation in organizations, after technology is taken into account. Some theories of organization-environment interaction posit that maintenance of a high degree of internal organizational complexity occurs only in response to environmental pressures that tolerate nothing less (Aldrich and Pfeffer, 1976; Campbell, 1969). The concentration of important environmental elements into an organized form may promote a matching organizational response, in the form of more boundary units or more formalized and centralized boundary-spanning activities (Pfeffer and Leblebici, 1973a). Kochan (1975: 7) points out that:

> A number of collective bargaining researchers have noted the proliferation of specialized labor relations units in city governments in response to the increased unionization of public employees.

Wilson (1973) discusses the growth of lobbying efforts of unions, trade associations, and other organizations representing vested interests, in response to the growth in power of the federal government. The consumer, ecology, and other movements have brought pressure on corporations, which have responded by establishing public relations units to deal with pressure groups. The same type of response occurred among public agencies in the President's Office for Consumer Affairs and similar offices in HEW, HUD, etc. (Nadel, 1971).

H5: *Organizations in environments where important elements are concentrated will have a higher proportion of boundary roles than organizations in environments where important elements are dispersed.*

Heterogeneous environments should evoke more organizational boundary spanning units and roles, as organizations "seek to identify homogeneous segments and establish structural units to deal with each" (Thompson, 1967: 70). Separate units, whether established on the basis of heterogeneity in a client population or in the geographical domain served, lead to a higher proportion of boundary roles than in organizations of comparable size serving a homogeneous domain. Hospitals establish separate units for obstetrics, contagious diseases, and out-patient services. Auto manufacturing firms respond to heterogeneity in client income distribution by divisionalizing operations around products with different selling prices, but not necessarily costs (Chandler, 1962).

H6: *Organizations in heterogeneous environments will have a higher proportion of boundary roles than organizations in homogeneous environments.*

Stable environments, which presumably call for less frequent monitoring, should evoke fewer boundary roles than unstable environments, although much depends on whether change is occurring at a constant or variable rate (Thompson, 1967: 71–72). In the cultural industry (books, records, films) where fashions change rapidly, we would expect to find proliferation of boundary roles on both input and output sides of the organization (Hirsch, 1972). In organizations producing for a stable market, we would expect most roles to be related directly to the production process, although an unexpected shift in the market can change the situation dramatically. Some theorists have argued that the most salient characteristic of organizational environments today is their rate of change (Terreberry, 1968), a purported trend which should cause an increase in the proportion of boundary spanning roles in most organizations.

H7: *Organizations in rapidly changing environments will have a higher proportion of boundary roles than organizations in stable environments.*

A final dimension to be considered is the extent to which the environment is rich or lean in resources (Aldrich, 1971; Benson, 1971; Emery and Trist, 1965). In rich environments, holding competition constant, we would expect to find fewer boundary roles, since environmental search and monitoring would be less critical for organizational survival than in environments where lack of resources prevents the accumulation of a "resource cushion." At a time of international or interorganizational hostility, the environment becomes less rich in information and so nations and organizations have to allocate more roles to their boundaries to make use of what little information is available (Wilensky, 1967).

H8: *Organizations in lean environments will have a higher proportion of boundary roles than organizations in rich environments.*

Environment and Boundary-Role Formalization

If internal complexity is associated with environmental pressures and demands, organizational boundary roles will be officially recognized full-time roles, especially if decision makers recognize the existence of such contingencies. Whether boundary roles will be thus formalized depends upon organizational recognition of potentially costly contingencies that may arise from failure to maintain effective links to elements in the environment. But such recognition need not be based on intelligence that organization itself has accumulated, as professional education (e.g., M.B.A. programs), professional and trade publications (e.g., *Business Week),* and informal inter-firm contact all keep organizational decision makers abreast of new developments in the design and administration of formal organizations (Benson, 1971; Pfeffer and Leblebici, 1973b; Starbuck, 1976). The following discussion focuses on direct, rather than indirect, recognition of environmental contingencies and constraints.

Most large organizations formally designate such roles as labor negotiators and corporate lawyers responsible for transactions in the labor relations sector, since strikes and law suits might cripple an organization. Labor contracts are negotiated for fairly long periods of time and the organizational costs of mistakes in boundary-spanning negotiation with unions are fairly high. Smigel's (1960) discussion of staff recruitment in large Wall Street law firms indicates that firms became aware of a variety of changes in their environment, including the small output of prestigious law schools, students' wariness of accepting positions with large firms, and the increasing demand for trained lawyers. One result was creation of the formal position of "hiring partner" to scan the potential output of top ranking law schools, sell students on advantages of employment in the firm, and thus improve recruitment of desirable graduates.

The more critical the contingency, the more attention is paid to explicit formalization of the role and selection of an incumbent. This is particularly evident with regard to the composition of boards of directors of large organizations, as Pfeffer (1972a: 222) argues that organizations:

> use their boards of directors as vehicles through which they co-opt, or partially absorb, important external organizations with which they are interdependent.

Price (1963), in a study of state wildlife governing boards, found that one major function of board members was to serve as a buffer group between the full-time staff and the public. Zald (1969: 99) points to the external representation functions of boards of directors:

> They promote and represent the organization to major elements of the organizational set, for example, customers, suppliers, stockholders, interested agencies of the state, and the like. That is, they defend and support the growth, autonomy and effectiveness of their agencies vis-à-vis the outside world.

Another critical contingency for large corporations involves managing reciprocal relations with other large firms; a trade relations person is alerted to look for opportunities to cooperate with other firms when it could be to their mutual advantage. Perrow (1970: 122) notes that:

> the practice of reciprocity is so extensive that about 60 percent of the top 500 corporations have staff members who are explicitly assigned to trade relations. Of course, any smart sales executive or top executive can serve in this capacity. However, it is striking that the practice is sufficiently common to justify so many special positions among the giants.

Pursuing leads on possible acquisition of other companies is an important function assigned to corporate development units. Aguiler (1967: 47) notes that the high volume of acquisition leads generated by this staff:

> demonstrates how the formalization of a search procedure can significantly increase a company's relative involvement with a particular kind of information.

H9: *Boundary roles are most likely to be formalized when crucial environmental contingencies have been explicitly recognized by organizational decision makers, or the organization is structured in a way that facilitates the adoption of structural innovations through imitation and borrowing from other organizations or other external sources.*

ROUTINIZATION, DISCRETION, AND POWER

The degree of role specificity (Hickson, 1966) of boundary roles varies considerably, with some being highly routinized and others highly nonroutine. Thompson (1962) identified two conditions leading organizations to increase specificity of control over boundary role personnel. First, organizations that provide services for large numbers of persons and thus face many nonmembers (relative to members) at the boundaries of the organization must either substantially increase the number of personnel in boundary positions or else routinize the tasks of existing staff so they can handle a higher volume of work. Second, organizations using a mechanized production technology which places a premium on large runs of standardized products depend upon a large volume of standardized transactions per member at the organization's output boundary. Pressures for routinization are somewhat lessened when the nonmembers dealt with have little or no discretion to participate in a relationship. Later Thompson identified a third condition, in that stable environments are likely to produce boundary roles governed by rules, whereas unstable environments are likely to increase flexibility in the specificity of boundary role routines (Thompson, 1967: 71).

Purchasing agents and sales personnel interact frequently with suppliers and buyers and usually deal with fairly homogeneous groups of organizations and individuals. A high frequency of interaction and homogeneity of elements at the boundary allows behavior in these roles to be highly routinized (Guetzkow, 1966: 24; Thompson, 1967: 111). Routinization is reflected in the existence of standard purchase and sales forms or contracts, standard operating procedures for soliciting and accepting bids, and standard operating procedures for calling on customers and closing sales. A classic example is the retail salesperson who knows the one proper way to record a cash sale and the one proper way to record a credit transaction.

Routinization of roles at the organization's boundary not only increases efficiency in handling predictable relationships and large numbers of repetitive transactions, but also serves a social control function. The programmed nature of these activities is partial insurance of boundary spanner consistency with organizational procedures, norms, and goals. Members who interact freely with nonmember groups, particularly homogeneous sets, are likely to develop attitudes consistent with those of the nonmembers, rather than of their focal organization. The existence of standard operating procedures partially protects the organization against attitudes and behaviors that are not consistent with organizational objectives.

Mathiesen's study of prison staff members identified the boundary role of "social worker" as a position that was difficult to routinize (1972: 76):

> Though almost all staff members claimed there were few or no specific rules or regulations guiding their communications, the social workers appeared particularly vehement about it, and included relations to official organizations. They stressed that here they had to be extremely flexible; that they had to organize the work on a day-to-day basis and according to the unique circumstances of the individual case.

Telephoning was preferred to the use of letters, and when complex cases arose, face-to-face meetings were arranged. Boundary roles (once created) that deal with heterogeneous elements must contain a minimal degree of routinization to maximize flexibility in dealing with special cases.

The degree to which boundary roles are routinized thus is a function of both the need to adapt to environment contingencies and constraints, and the need to control behavior of potentially deviant members. Routinization can serve as a social control mechanism when the organization does not or cannot assume normative commitment of members to organizational procedures. Similar mechanisms would be the use of uniforms to reinforce organizational identification, or frequently shifting employees between boundary roles and core roles to prevent development of identification with elements in the environment (Guetzkow, 1966: 21).

H10: *Boundary role routinization will vary directly with the volume of repetitive work, the predictability of outcomes, the homogeneity and stability of the environment, and the need to control the behavior of organizational members.*

Power in Boundary Roles

Thompson (1967) noted that where the environment is heterogeneous and shifting and where contingencies are important to the organization, boundary personnel are expected to exercise discretion and develop expertise, and to the extent they are successful in recognizing contingencies, they may become powerful within the organization. The potential power position of boundary spanners was evident in discussion of their information-processing function. The information that filters into the organization through boundary positions is often not raw data, but the inferences of boundary role incumbents. This type of information is difficult for anyone removed from the boundary to verify. The process of uncertainty absorption is a case of creation of organizational intelligence; and once created, intelligence tends to be accepted (Wilensky, 1967).

The organization thus relies upon the expertise and discretion of its boundary role personnel. They have a gatekeeper's power, and may become even more powerful if they make correct inferences and if the information is vital for organizational survival (March and Simon, 1958). Their power is further enhanced to the degree that the nature of the task assigned the boundary role makes routinization of the role difficult, if not impossible.

Labor negotiators provide an example of a boundary role that is difficult to routinize, thus leading to de facto concentration of power in the role. Even though negotiators may deal with fairly homogeneous groups, the outcomes are not highly predictable and the costs to the organization may be high. Therefore, negotiators require some degree of discretionary power. Their power is enhanced to the extent that the group they are negotiating with is powerful.

> Specifically, a number of components of union power that derive from the tactics or activities of the union—involvement in city elections, use of strike threats in bargaining—all are associated with a higher degree of power in the boundary unit in city governments. [Keller and Holland, 1975: 27]

H11: *The power of boundary role incumbents will vary inversely with boundary role routinization, and directly with their own expertise in accomplishing role requirements and with the costliness and unpredictability of interorganizational transactions.*

Organizational dependence on boundary role personnel raises the issue of their commitment to and integration into the organization. The least costly monitoring mechanism is for the organization to rely on the professional identification and ethics of the boundary personnel. More obtrusive strategies include attempts to indoctrinate boundary personnel in organizational policies, norms, and goals, prior to their engaging in interorganizational contacts. Rotation of members among boundary roles is another active strategy, although it has costs in terms of disrupting local adaptations that have been made by boundary spanners. An organization might grant powerful boundary personnel higher positions within the organizational structure to reinforce commitment, although such positions may be a result of the power these members develop through successful interaction on behalf of the organization: e.g., the common practice of picking top management out of the sales division of an organization.

Many studies emphasize the stress and conflict felt by personnel in boundary roles (Katz and Kahn, 1966; Organ, 1971), but overlook the positive potential inherent in their role accumulation prospects. Sieber (1974) has recently argued that multiple relationships with diverse role partners provide numerous sources of gratification, rather than strain, to individuals such as boundary personnel. He notes that role rights and privileges may accumulate more rapidly than duties, that overall status security may be enhanced by means of buffer roles, that multiple roles can serve as resources for status enhancement and role performance, and finally that multiple roles may enrich one's personality and enhance one's self-conception. While this article is not addressed to the issue of costs and benefits to individuals who occupy boundary roles, the positive side of the boundary-spanning activities should be seen as a counter to the negative image currently portrayed in the literature.

Two recent studies in a research and development organization and a large manufacturing company report positive correlations between boundary-spanning activity and several dimensions of job satisfaction. These studies also found very small or insignificant correlations between role conflict, role ambiguity, and boundary spanning activity. The authors argue that boundary spanning jobs, to the extent they enable role incumbents to reduce uncertainties for others, permit boundary spanners to gain power, improve their bargaining position, and hence increase their job satisfaction and perhaps even gain better jobs.

IMPLICATIONS

The picture of boundary-spanning roles portrayed in this article has two implications for the study of formal organizations. *First*, this view of organization-environment interaction is a decidedly disaggregated one, in contrast to current literature which sees organizations responding as "wholes" to environmental influence. We treat boundary-spanning roles as the critical link between environmental characteristics and organizational structure, with the further stipulation that organizations face multiple environments and thus can have a variety of boundary roles of units with different structural characteristics. This implies, for example, that when an investigator studies the impact of interorganizational dependence on organizational structure, the place to begin is with its impact on boundary-spanning roles in the immediate vicinity of the dependence relationship, rather than with the structure of the organization as a whole (Aldrich, 1977; Mindlin and Aldrich, 1975).

Second, more empirical studies are needed of how personnel in boundary spanning units or roles carry out their duties, and in particular how such role performance varies under different environmental conditions and over time. This would mean more studies of the type carried out by Mintzberg (1973), on the day-to-day behavior of managers, or Mathiesen (1972) on the day-to-day behavior of staff members in two Scandinavian prisons. Both studies make extensive use of nonparticipant observation and detailed first-hand knowledge of the actual, rather than self-reported, behavior of those persons studied. The cumulation of such studies would enable us to understand the process by which boundary spanning roles are generated, elaborated, and used by their incumbents.

CONCLUDING STATEMENT

So what can we say about organizational environment? Or, more accurately, how do environmental conditions constrain designers' options, and how do they respond? Basically the issue boils down to that described by Kast (1974: 156):

> The environment imposes many constraints on the organization. It can limit the amount of inputs the organization receives and also accept or reject the outputs. It can restrict many of the internal activities of the organization (for example, safety regulations, zoning restrictions, working standards, etc.). . . .
>
> At the same time that the society imposes certain goal constraints on the organization, it also serves as a field of exploration for the organization. "To society, the firm is an instrument to be used. To the firm, society is a field to be exploited"(Chamberlain, 1968: 144). This is particularly true for business firms operating in a market economy. Environmental changes, such as technological developments and population expansion, provide new opportunities for the firm (Chandler, 1962). [Indeed, the] survival of the organization depends on its ability to adapt to and utilize social resources. Seashore and Yuchtman (1967: 393) say: "We define the effectiveness of an organization as its ability to exploit its environment in the acquisition of scarce and valued resources to sustain its functioning."

We have already examined the nature of that environment, in our introductory remarks. Organizational strategies for exploiting it, and corresponding effects on organizational design are the subjects addressed in this statement.

MANAGING THE ENVIRONMENT: ORGANIZATIONAL STRATEGIES

The relationship between the organization and its environment is an uneasy one, at best: "the environment creates uncertainty, and uncertainty threatens the rational process which is at the heart of every organization" (Ouchi and Harris, 1976: 130). In addition, as we have seen (Chapter 2), environmental uncertainty is joined by the problem of interdependence in threatening the rational process.

Organizations attempt to reduce their uncertainty and interdependence. They do so either by actively engaging the environment, acquiring a measure of control over—or at least some intelligence about—parts of it, or by sealing themselves off from its effects (Thompson, 1967). There are several sets of strategies that organizations use in making these attempts. Since Pfeffer has already described them in some detail in this chapter, we will be content with a brief summary.[1]

Types of Strategies

Based on the work of several researchers and analysts, we can identify four major types of strategies that organizations employ in managing their environmental relationships.[2] Table 4–4 summarizes the types and their characteristics.

1. The reader is urged to review Pfeffer's article, remembering its point: organizations use a variety of strategies to cope with environmental uncertainty and interdependence.

2. See Selznick (1949), Thompson and McEwen (1958), Chandler (1966), Fouraker and Stopford (1968), Pfeffer (1972a, 1972b, 1973), Pfeffer and Leblebici (1973a), Miles et al. (1974), and Ouchi and Harris (1976).

TABLE 4-4 ORGANIZATIONAL STRATEGIES FOR MANAGING ENVIRONMENTAL ELEMENTS

Strategy	Examples
Direct engagement	Long-term contracts, mergers, joint ventures, cooptation
Indirect influence	Co-optation, lobbying
Cooperation	Conformity to industry norms, sharing of information, restraint of cut-throat competition
Diversification	Establishment of new product line, movement to new community

Direct Engagement

The first strategy, and probably the most common one, we may call *direct engagement*. Organizations employing this type of strategy attempt to meet environmental elements head-on. They enter into long-term contracts with suppliers, consumers, or labor unions, for example. They merge or engage in joint ventures with other organizations. They may also attempt to co-opt, or partially absorb, an environmental element, such as by placing a representative of another organization on the board of directors.

Indirect Influence

A second type of strategy may be termed *indirect influence*. In a sense, co-optation is a form of this strategy. A co-opted director, for example, cannot be expected to reduce directly the organization's uncertainty or interdependence. Still, he or she sometimes is able—and expected—to ease the way where possible.

A more common strategy of indirect influence involves third parties, such as trade associations. Such groups' offices are used to lobby governmental agencies about desired (or undesired) legislation or regulatory policies. They also provide a vehicle by which environmental intelligence may be shared among member organizations.

In neither of the examples above does an organization directly confront its important environmental elements directly. Rather, it participates in a well-established process of indirect influence. Much of the "political activity" that Pfeffer described earlier falls into this category.

Cooperation

There is a third type of strategy for coping with environmental uncertainty and interdependence. We may label this type *cooperation*. Phillips (1960), for example, describes firms in oligopolistic industries behaving as if they were members of a small group, conforming to group norms and coordinating their activities (reported by Miles et al., 1974). Even competitors are known to come to the aid of an organization that has suffered a severe setback. Perrow (1970: 124) reports the example of a firm whose factory was destroyed by fire. Competitors filled the firm's orders, made $600,000 in new machinery available, and generally assisted the organization in its recovery. Such action, incidentally, is not limited to this country. The *Wall Street Journal* (March 24, 1975) ran a story some time ago reporting the extensive managerial and financial aid given to the developer of the rotary engine Mazda by several other Japanese firms.[3] Perrow (1970: 125–26) also reports a reciprocal-type instance in which a firm declined an opportunity to expand into a foreign country. Management's reason? Another firm had already established itself in that country,

3. This *WSJ* article is reprinted in Connor (1978: 37-40).

and management was concerned that their moving in would be considered unseemly by the industry. As Perrow (1970: 126) notes: "It is upon such complex political as well as economic considerations that some seemingly irrational decisions are made in apparently rational organizations."

Diversification

When an organization finds that it is unable to excel at the environmental game in which it is playing and is unable to change the rules, it may decide to change games. Thus a fourth strategy involves moving into a different environmental circumstance. Usually this strategy involves some sort of diversifying—of product, consumer, community, or even industry. In short, one way that an organization can reduce the amount of uncertainty and interdependence with which it must cope is to move or expand into an environment that contains less. In 1976, for example, Mobil Oil company purchased the parent company of Montgomery Ward. By such a purchase Mobil was able to temper the increasing hostility of the "oil" environment (especially from government sources) with the more placid elements of the durable goods industry. *Diversification* is the process that describes such a strategy.

Having said that organizations use a variety of strategies to deal with their important environmental elements, we now need to examine the ways in which those elements and strategies are translated into design terms. In other words, what mechanisms do organizations adopt to help them cope with the environmental dimensions of complexity, diversity, change, and uncertainty?

ENVIRONMENT AND ORGANIZATION DESIGN

One of the most significant studies to examine the effects of environmental conditions on organizational designs was that conducted by Lawrence and Lorsch. As we noted in Chapter 2, they investigated organizations in the plastics, food, and container industries (Lorsch, 1965; Lawrence and Lorsch, 1967a, 1967b; Lorsch and Lawrence, 1970). The basic thrust of their research was to answer this question: "*Do organizations operating in different environments vary in the way they* differentiate *their activities, and do they vary in the methods they use to* integrate *those activities?*"

While the question is a cumbersome one, it introduces Lawrence and Lorsch's contribution to our understanding of organization design. Their concepts of differentiation and integration summarize two of the most critical, if not the most critical, processes of organization. To put the matter simply: when people organize their efforts—to build a pyramid, educate the young, or defend their nation—the first thing they do is divide up the work ("You tote the barge, I'll lift the bale, and Fred will put his shoulder to the wheel"). This process is called *differentiation*. People differentiate their labor into various tasks. Thus we see organizations with engineering departments, manufacturing departments, and sales departments. In turn, the manufacturing department contains a metal shop and a paint shop.

Differentiation is not enough, however. Ultimately the divided-up labor has to result in some common outcome: a pyramid, a college graduate, a victory. Organizations therefore have to have the means to bring their divided-up activities together so that common objectives are served. This latter process is called *integration*. As the reader is aware, and as we discuss more fully in Chapter 10, there are many ways that organizations use to effect integration. The most basic, of course, is the hierarchy itself. That is, one of the ways to

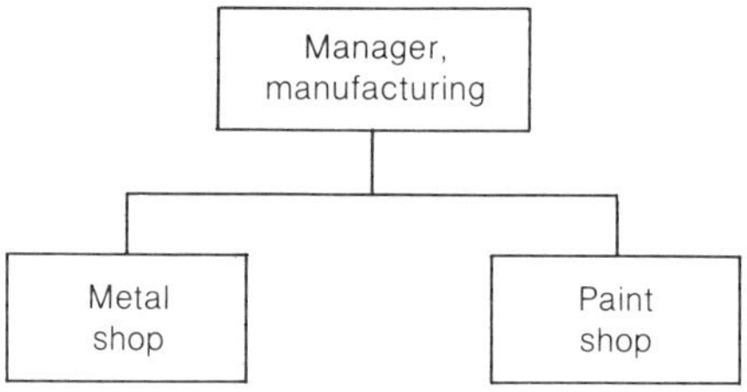

Manager, manufacturing

Metal shop

Paint shop

Figure 4-1. Integrating with the hierarchy

improve the chances that the metal shop and paint shop activities will ultimately result in the accomplishment of common goals is to create a position called "Manager of Manufacturing" (illustrated in Figure 4–1). The essence of this job is to integrate the activities that have been differentiated into metal shop and paint shop tasks. In addition, of course, there are other methods. Schedules and plans, for example, are also commonly used to integrate such activities.

Environment, Differentiation, and Integration

Before the discussion carries us too far, let us repeat the point: Lawrence and Lorsch found that differentiation and integration processes varied among firms operating in different environmental circumstances. Specifically, they identified three principal subenvironments: the *market* subenvironment, the *technoeconomic* subenvironment, and the *scientific* subenvironment.[4] These subenvironments correspond to the three major functions of the firms under study: sales, production, and research.

Next Lawrence and Lorsch focused on two aspects of their subenvironments. These were aspects that seemed to be important in effecting organization-design decisions. The environmental aspects they specified were: 1. degree of uncertainty and 2. degree of diversity (Lorsch, 1970).[5] The authors found what they expected; environments differed among the plastics, food, and container industries in terms of both uncertainty and diversity. Further, organizational responses differed correspondingly:

> For example, each of the ten organizations was dealing with a market subenvironment (the task of the sales organization), a technoeconomic subenvironment (the task of the manufacturing unit) and a scientific subenvironment (the task of the research or design unit). Each of these subenvironments within any one industry had a different degree of certainty of information about what needed to be done. How similar or different these parts of any environment were on the certainty-uncertainty continuum determined whether that environment was relatively homogeneous or diverse. For example, in one of the environments studied, the container industry, all parts of the environment were relatively certain and the environment was characterized as homogeneous. On the other hand, in a second environment, the plastics industry, the parts of the environment ranged from a highly certain technoeconomic sector to a very uncertain scientific subenvironment and the total environment was characterized as more diverse. As suggested above, the degree of differentiation in an effective organization was found to be related to the diversity of the environment. Thus in the economically effective container industry there was less

4. There can be no doubt—Mark Twain was right.
5. These aspects are virtually identical to two of the environmental dimensions we identified earlier.

differentiation than in an effective plastic organization. The less effective organizations in these industries did not meet the environmental demand for differentiation so well. [Lorsch, 1970: 6]

What about the other side of the coin? Did the organizations also differ as to integration methods? Again, the answer is "yes." Lawrence and Lorsch found that the organizations under study employed a large variety of integrating mechanisms. That variety included reliance on hierarchical relationships, specially designated individual coordinators ("integrators"), cross-unit teams, and even whole departments of integrators—that is, people whose basic role was coordinating tasks and outputs among several organizational subunits.

In short, Lawrence and Lorsch found that environmental conditions had a marked impact on organization design. Specifically, environmental conditions were strongly related to both the degree of differentiation and the degree of integration. Additionally, and this is most crucial, organizations operating under different environmental conditions employed different *methods* of integration. Table 4–5 summarizes these relationships.

SUMMARY AND CONCLUSION

This chapter has explored the importance of environmental conditions for organization design. The basic theme has been that the environment constrains designers' options. We began our discussion by examining the nature of "organizational environment." That examination considered such properties as organizational boundaries and domains. We then identified four characteristics of organizational environments that seem to be important for organization-design purposes. These characteristics were: *complexity, diversity, change,* and *uncertainty.* Table 4–2 described these dimensions.

Turning to the readings, we encountered Pfeffer's examination of what he calls managers' "institutional function." This function, it turns out, is to help the organization

TABLE 4-5 ENVIRONMENTAL FACTORS AND ORGANIZATIONAL DESIGN CHARACTERISTICS OF EFFECTIVE ORGANIZATIONS

			Integrative Devices		
Industry	*Environment Diversity*	*Actual Differentiation*	*Actual Integration*	*Type of Integrative Devices*	*Special Integrating Personnel as % of Total Management*
Plastics	High	High	High	Teams, roles, departments, hierarchy, plans and procedures	22%*
Foods	Moderate	Moderate	High	Roles, plans, hierarchy, procedures	17%*
Container	Low	Low	High	Hierarchy, plans and procedures	0%*

*This proportion was constant for the high and low performer within these industries.

SOURCE: Jay W. Lorsch, "Introduction to the Structural Design of Organizations," from Gene W. Dalton and Paul R. Lawrence (eds.), Jay W. Lorsch, (collab.) *Organizational Structure and Design* (Homewood, Illinois: Richard D. Irwin, © 1970), p. 13.

cope with external phenomena that confront it. Pfeffer focused on two results of this confrontation: uncertainty and interdependence. He then identified various strategies that organizations use to fulfill their institutional function. Those strategies include mergers, joint ventures, interlocking directorates, selective recruiting of executives, regulation, and political activity.

Next, Aldrich and Herker discussed an important organizational property, the boundary-spanning role. According to the authors, mechanisms are established to relate the organization to its environment; these mechanisms perform two principal functions, 1. acquiring, interpreting, and disseminating information about environmental conditions, and 2. acquiring and disposing of resources, as well as representing the organization to sources of external legitimacy. The authors then examined the various ways that environmental factors affect the creation of those mechanisms, or boundary roles.

In the concluding statement we have attempted to pull together a variety of information, knowledge, and speculation about the environment and its impact on organization design. We first summarized the argument that organizations use different strategies for coping with environmental uncertainty and interdependence. There appear to be four major types of strategies, which we labeled *direct engagement, indirect influence, cooperation,* and *diversification.*

We concluded the statement by noting some specific ways in which organization designs are affected by environmental conditions. Using Lawrence and Lorsch's (1967a; 1967b) research as a framework, we noted that environments have a dual impact, affecting both organizational differentiation and integration processes. Specifically the degree to which organizations differentiate and integrate tasks is related to the uncertainty and diversity of relevant subenvironments. Moreover, the *form* that organizational integration takes is constrained by subenvironmental conditions.

In conclusion, therefore, we can picture the designs of organizations Alpha and Beta—organizations we conjured up in Chapter 2—as varying because of differences in their environmental situations. Organization Alpha was described as operating in a fairly "static" (Burns and Stalker, 1961) environment. We might then suggest that it would score relatively low on our environmental dimensions of complexity, diversity, change, and uncertainty. Beta, on the other hand, confronted by somewhat "dynamic" conditions, would score rather higher on those same dimensions. Figure 4–2 illustrates the two circumstances.

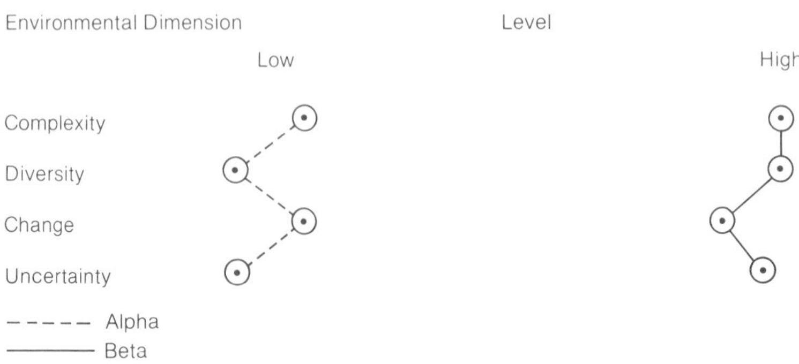

Figure 4-2. Environmental circumstances: organizations Alpha and Beta

Differences between Alpha and Beta's designs would correspond to their environmental differences. The first organization would be, on balance, relatively bureaucratically structured, with centralized—and somewhat programmed—decision making: in short, rather "mechanistic" (Burns and Stalker, 1961) in design. Beta, in contrast, would have to manage its higher degrees of uncertainty and interdependence by developing a more "organic" design. Figure 4–3 illustrates these differences.

Thus we conclude this chapter by emphasizing its principal message: to be effective, organization designs must take into account the nature of the environment in which the organization is operating. Designers must ask themselves such questions as the following (Khandwalla, 1977: 343):

1. What is the nature of the society or community in which the organization must operate? Are resources (labor, capital, consumers, suppliers, etc.) scarce?
2. How about the organization's domain? Are there a lot of elements that must be taken into account, or just a few? Do they all behave relatively similarly, or are they all different?
3. What about the specific industry? Is it highly competitive? Expanding or contracting? Does it fluctuate much, and if so does it do so with any degree of predictability?
4. What is the nature of the organization's particular situation? Is it a powerless organization within its industry or a dominant member of it? Is it an organization that is closely regulated by the parent organization, or is it quite autonomous? If the former, how severely is it competing (for funds, etc.) with other organizations in the parent organization? Is it subject to some special pressures and disabilities, such as those arising from a disadvantageous location, or from inexperience due to its relative youth, or from difficult access to the market because of its being relatively unknown? Or is it the beneficiary of some special advantages such as those that come from a particularly favorable location, a great deal of experience with its markets, a good reputation? Does the organization produce a great diversity of outputs or relatively homogeneous outputs?

Questions such as these can help organization designers evaluate the ways in which the environment constrains their options. Of course, environmental conditions are not the only design constraint. The differences in the designs of Alpha and Beta depicted in Figure 4–3 ignore—or at least do not explicitly include—two additional constraints: the nature of the organization's technology (or technologies), as well as the people who populate the organization. We turn to these matters in the next two chapters.

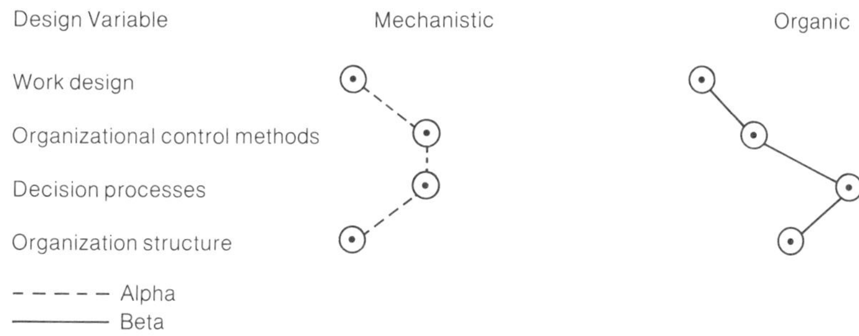

Figure 4-3. Organization design differences between Alpha and Beta

Questions for Review

1. What are the types of organization environment identified by Emery and Trist in their 1965 study?
2. Briefly describe Shortell's four critical dimensions of organizational environment.
3. As outlined by Pfeffer, what are the effects of joint ventures on competitive interdependence and uncertainty?
4. What are the main advantages and disadvantages of each of the strategies of institutional management described by Pfeffer?
5. There are three main focal points to Aldrich and Herker's discussion. Briefly outline these.
6. What are five of the hypotheses put forward by Aldrich and Herker?
7. What situations, according to Aldrich and Herker, are causally connected to a higher proportion of organizational boundary roles?
8. What conditions does Thompson specify that lead to organizations' increasing specificity of control over boundary personnel?
9. How do organizations attempt to sustain and augment the commitment and integration of boundary-role personnel?
10. Summarize the most prevalent organizational strategies for managing environmental relationships. Give at least one example for each.

Questions for Discussion

1. Pfeffer describes two fairly opposing theories about regulation: first, that regulation is created for the public benefit, but after the initial legislative attention, the regulatory process is captured by the firms subject to regulation. Second, that regulation, like other goods, is acquired subject to supply and demand considerations. Using one organization or one industry, compare the appropriateness and relevance of these two theories.
2. Two important issues are raised by Pfeffer in his concluding statements:
   a. Is effective institutional management associated with favorable outcomes to the organization?
   b. Given the importance of institutional management, why are some organizations more successful than others at this task?

   Taking into account that there are no simple answers to these questions, what would be some preliminary areas you might explore in developing an hypothesis or hypotheses about these issues?
3. Defining organization in terms of boundaries permits the following observation about organizational power: people have power who apply organizational rules in making decisions about entry and expulsion of members." Do you agree with this observation of formal authority? Why should entry and expulsion be theoretically and causally connected to boundaries.

4. All complex organizations, Aldrich and Herker maintain, "have a tendency to move toward an internal state of compatability and compromise between units and individuals within the organization with a resultant isolation from important external influences." In reviewing what you have studied thus far, would you agree with this satement or not? Support your position. What is the relevance of this statement for your present work and/or study?
5. What industries might have a large allocation of personnel in boundary-spanning roles? What makes these industries more dependent on personnel in these roles than other industries are? Are there any industries that exhibit no apparent need for boundary spanners?
6. This chapter's introduction poses the question: isn't it arbitrary at best, and even incorrect at worst, to think of some phenomena as being outside—and some inside—an organization? Has your reading of this chapter changed your views on this?
7. What are the several environmental elements with which your college or university must deal—and successfully? Rather than producing a list of 20 to 10,000 items, develop a set of categories that contains the important elements.
8. Using the information provided in this chapter, how would you describe the strategies used in your university to deal with its various environmental elements?
9. Do you know of a particular business or industry that is currently experiencing difficulty in establishing a domain? Why do you think it is experiencing this difficulty?
10. The job of "boundary spanner" is clearly not an easy one. Would it challenge you? In what type of industry would you be interested in performing this function? How do you perceive yourself functioning in this role? What criteria would you set for the dissemination of information?

5

Technology

INTRODUCTORY REMARKS

We saw in the last two chapters that organization designers must take into account the goals of their enterprise, as well as the nature of the environment in which it operates. In addition, however, they need to recognize that the means by which organizational outputs are produced—the organization's technology—also affects their design decisions. This chapter examines ways to think about the concept of technology, plus the impacts it can have on organization design.

We have seen that as an open system the organization acquires inputs, processes them, and produces outputs. The point of this chapter is that there are organizational consequences of using different technologies to move inputs through the processing unit, or technical core. Given this broad view of technology, it becomes fairly obvious that if one organization

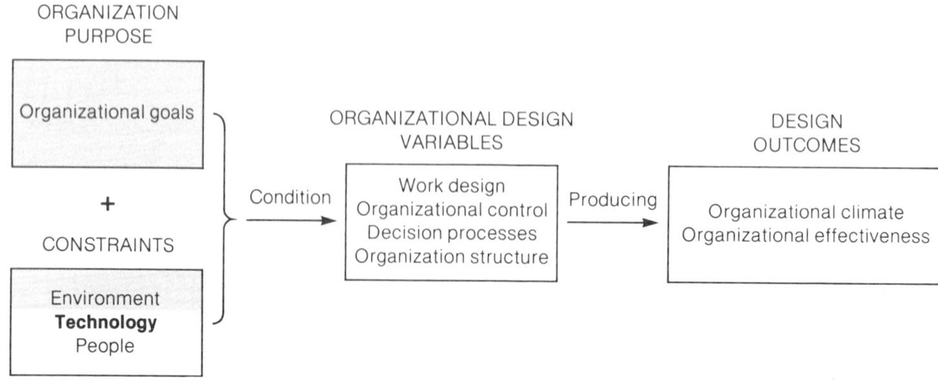

applies the various technologies it has chosen to use in its processes better than a second, the first organization will be more effective in achieving its goals. Expressed more simply, this chapter presents the idea that *the technologies an organization chooses to use to accomplish its goals partially determine how the organization should be designed.* A schematic expressing this idea looks like this:

TASK
STRUCTURE
TECHNOLOGIES⟶DESIGN⟶ORGANIZATIONAL SUCCESS
CONTROL
DECISION MAKING
PROCESSES

TECHNOLOGY: WHAT IS IT?

As in the case of the last chapter, these introductory remarks aim at laying a foundation—a foundation to serve two purposes: to preview the two articles that follow, and to set the stage for discussing how technology affects or constrains organization designers' options. We begin, therefore, by examining the nature of the constraint.

Definitions of Technology

The idea of technology presented earlier is broad and vague. Consequently, further definition of its meaning as applied to an organizational context will be helpful. Technology means different things to different people. For example, Thompson and Bates (1957) define technology as "the set of man-machine activities which together produce a desired good or service." Michael Fullan (1970) defines technology as "the manual and machine operations performed on an object in the process of turning out a final product." Marshall Meyer (1972) defines technology as "how an organization divides work among its members and the tools and machinery it uses in its tasks." Robert Dubin (1961) defines technology as "the tools used and the specialized ideas needed in getting particular kinds of work done." Finally, Charles Perrow (1967) defines technology as "the actions that an individual performs upon an object, with or without the aid of tools or mechanical devices, in order to make some change in that object," while Hage and Aiken (1969) avoid the problem by discussing technology in terms of its degree of routineness.

Actually, most of these definitions of technology do not differ too much from one another. In fact, most definitions of technology have one or more of several elements in common:

1. "Operations" technology represents the techniques used in workflow activities and includes the tools, machines, and other capital equipment mentioned in the definitions above, plus the manner in which an input is sequenced through the processing unit.
2. Definitions of technology also include "materials" technology, which refers to the basic characteristics of the input itself. Inputs might be hard or soft; uniform or not uniform; human, animal, or inanimate; but as the inputs fall into different categories, different technologies are used to alter them.
3. Finally, several definitions include the concept of "knowledge" technology or how much is known and understood concerning the inputs; that is, whether the input is well or poorly understood or is analyzable or unanalyzable. [Hickson et al., 1969]

What all this means is that when technology is referred to in an organizational context, the three basic subconcepts of "operations," "materials," and "knowledge" should be called to mind. It should also be recalled that each of these types of technologies has a different kind of organization design which is appropriate. However, while knowing that different kinds of technologies call for different kinds of organization designs is a useful sort of knowledge, it would be even more useful to be able to specify what type of design is appropriate with what type of technology. Several organizational typologies have been created which attempt to accomplish this task.

Types of Technology

An organizational typology consists of a method by which organizations with similar characteristics can be grouped together and distinguished from organizations with dissimilar characteristics. The technology being operated by an organization or one of its subunits (division, department, functional subgrouping) represents one useful method of classification.

Joan Woodward

One of the first organizational typologies using technology as the major variable was developed by Joan Woodward (1965). This typology showed that major elements of organization design differed by the type of organizational technology. Moreover, Woodward found organizational success to be dependent on the organization's using a design appropriate to its technology. The typology itself consists of three different types of technology as independent variables: production runs consisting of one or only a few *units*, *mass production*, and *continuous production*. Examples of unit and small batch production are machine-shop operations, ship building, and building construction. The prototypic example of a mass production technology is the assembly line, whereas the refining of gasoline and the production of many chemicals and fertilizers represent continuous production technologies. Differences in organization by type of technology found by Woodward are shown in Table 5–1.

James D. Thompson

A few years after Woodward presented her typology, James D. Thompson developed a three-variable typology that he felt was applicable to all types of organizations, not just

TABLE 5-1 WOODWARD'S (1965) TECHNOLOGY AND STRUCTURAL DIMENSIONS

Structural Dimensions	Technology		
	Unit	*Mass*	*Continuous*
Median scalar levels*	4	5	7
Median span of supervision	23	48	15
Median direct to indirect labor	9:1	4:1	1:1
Median line to staff labor	8:1	5½:1	2:1
Formalization	Low	High	Low
Centralization (job decisions)	Low	High	Low

SOURCE: Joan Woodward, *Industrial Organization: Theory and Practice* (London: Oxford University Press, 1965).

*Includes supervisory (management) levels plus one level of nonsupervisory employees.

manufacturing. This chapter's first article indicates that this typology consists of long-linked, mediating, and intensive technologies. Thompson's *long-linked* technology is very similar to Woodward's mass production category. A long-linked sequence is one in which Operation C can be performed only after Operation B, which can be done only after Operation A has been completed. Diagrammatically the long-linked sequence is as follows:

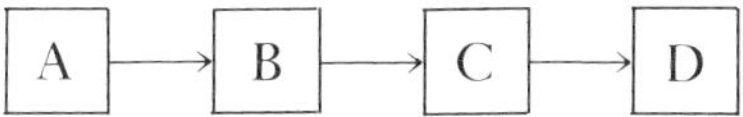

An assembly line, of course, is an excellent example of the long-linked concept, but the concept can also be applied to the channels of distribution in marketing:

SUPPLIERS⟶MANUFACTURER⟶WHOLESALER(S)⟶RETAILERS

A *mediating* technology is one in which the organization brings together parties having complementary needs. Banks bring together depositors and borrowers. Agents, for instance in real estate or insurance, bring together buyers and sellers. The ombudsman brings together those with complaints with those who have the power to resolve the complaints. Many governmental bureaucracies such as Social Security, the I.R.S., social service agencies, and the Employment Service operate mediating technologies.

An *intensive* technology is one in which a variety of techniques and technologies are drawn upon in order to accomplish a goal. The intensive care ward of a hospital is one example of this type of technology. The construction of the B-1 bomber or a NASA space shuttle are other examples. A commando raid to free hostages represents still another application of an intensive technology.

Charles Perrow

The final typology to be examined was developed by Charles Perrow (1967). This typology is quite different from the two preceding; there are two reasons for this difference: it is multidimensional rather than unidimensional, and it consists of four organizational types rather than three. As is shown in the second article for this chapter, Perrow's typology has two independent variables—*exceptions* and the *analyzability of problems*. Perrow's idea is that a given technology has either relatively few or relatively many exceptions. This is similar to the concept that organizational technologies vary as to how routine they are. The schematics below illustrate the similarity.

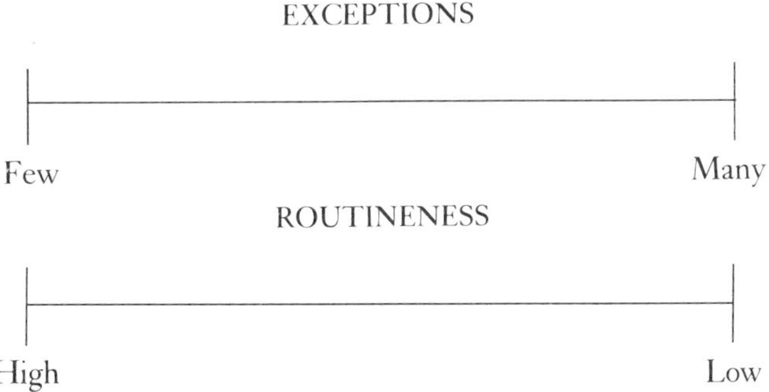

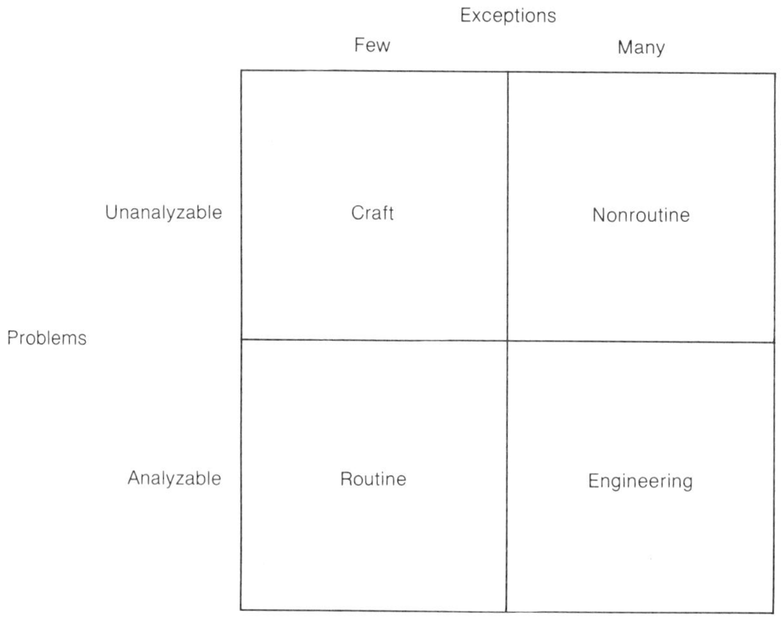

Problems \ Exceptions	Few	Many
Unanalyzable	Craft	Nonroutine
Analyzable	Routine	Engineering

Figure 5-1. Perrow's technology model

Perrow, however, does not limit himself to the characteristic of "exceptions" (or "routineness"). He describes a second dimension based on the analyzability of the problems faced by organizational decision makers. Thus in Perrow's scheme, the nature of the organization is contingent upon the interaction of the two technology variables, as shown in Figure 5–1. The differences in organizations that Perrow expects to find among the cells of his model are discussed in his article.

Interpreting Technology Types

Now that these three typologies have been presented and examined to a limited degree, a few additional comments about them are in order. First, it is clear that technology is not the only variable that influences organization design. Research by Blau (1970), and Hickson, Pugh, and Phesey (1969) indicates that size also influences design. Moreover, it was seen (Chapter 4) that the external environment also has influence on the organization (Burns and Stalker, 1961; Lawrence and Lorsch, 1967).[1]

Second, there is not a lot of empirical support for the various typologies. Woodward's typology has been supported by Fullan (1970), who found predictable differences (although not the same as Woodward's) in the design of automobile plants, the printing industry, and oil refining plants. Fullan attributed differences in worker attitudes—toward each other, management, strikes, and absenteeism—to differences in technology. A study by Zwerman (1970), designed to replicate Woodward's, was also supportive. On the other hand,

1. A contingency note: It could well be that the Lawrence and Lorsch study measures the rate of change in organizational technology, rather than the general environment.

research by Hickson et al. (1969), which was also intended to replicate Woodward's study on a broader sample of organizations, failed to do so. As mentioned above, this study concluded that size had a greater influence on organization design than did technology.

There has been even less research on the Thompson and Perrow typologies. Frost and Mahoney's (1974) study is supportive of the Thompson typology. There have been no studies which have examined the entire Perrow typology. However, Hage and Aiken's (1969) research supports the routineness (exceptions) dimension as do studies by Hall (1962), Udy (1958), and Burns and Stalker (1961). All of these studies indicate that organizations become more bureaucratized as their technologies become more routine (have fewer exceptions).

Third, it is probably unrealistic to apply a particular typological category to an entire organization. To present an extreme example, try to fit General Motors into any single category of any of the typologies. The manufacturing plants are clearly mass production /long-linked/routine. But where do the research facilities, the lobbying departments, and the long-range planning departments fit? The point here is that any given organization may operate multiple technologies in their technical cores, different technologies at the managerial level, and still different technologies for dealing with the environment.[2] Obviously no single typology is adequate to describe "the" organizational technology.

The solution to this problem is to follow the lead of Lawrence and Lorsch (1967) and Delbecq and Van de Ven (1974) and describe departmental, or subunit, technologies. This approach gives the analyst a solid method of specifying the design of individual departments and subunits. However, designers are still left with the problem of how to go about coordinating the several technologies, which are normally housed in different departments. We will deal with this issue in the concluding statement, since it is a natural lead-in to our examination of technology and organization design. First, however, let us see what Thompson and Perrow have to say.

The Readings

We begin with an excerpt from James D. Thompson's work, *Organizations in Action* (1967). In this discussion, Thompson lays out his idea that three types of technology are found in organizations. As we have noted, he used the following labels for the types: *long-linked, mediating,* and *intensive.* The author goes on to describe the actions of organizations as they attempt to operate under what he calls *norms of rationality.* Basically, says Thompson, organizations seek to "seal off" their technical cores from the disturbing influences of environmental uncertainty. Methods used in sealing off include the following: buffering, smoothing, anticipating, and rationing. As Thompson puts it, "these are maneuvering devices which provide the organization with some self-control despite interdependence with the environment."

A different, although complementary perspective on organizational technology is offered by Charles Perrow in the second article, "A Framework for the Comparative Analysis of Organizations." We have also noted that for Perrow, organizational technology involves two main dimensions: the number of exceptions (few, many) encountered in the work

2. On this latter point, the reader is reminded of the discussion in Chapter 4, especially the articles by Pfeffer and by Aldrich and Herker.

process and the analyzability (analyzable, unanalyzable) of the search process required to resolve those problems that do occur. He then describes four prototypic organizations based on the interaction of the two independent variables. A *routine* organization should be found when few exceptions occur, and the search process is highly analyzable. A *nonroutine* organization should be found when many exceptions occur and the search process is unanalyzable. *Engineering* organizations should be found when many exceptions occur in the work process, but procedures to locate solutions to the problem are analyzable. *Craft* organizations flourish under the opposite conditions: few exceptions in the work process, and unanalyzable search processes in the event of problems. Solutions in this case are located on a trial and error basis.

Having described four types of technologies, Perrow then illustrates how power between the technical (managerial) level of the organization and the supervisory (first, foremen) level will vary with technology. The craft organization is described as being decentralized, the nonroutine organization as being flexible and polycentralized, the engineering organization as being flexible and centralized, and the routine organization as being formal and centralized. Perrow does not deal with success issues directly but implicitly assumes that organizations that are designed congruently with their technologies will be more successful than those that are not so designed.

Conclusion

In summary, this chapter poses several questions, as follows:

1. What exactly is "organizational technology"?
2. What are the major types of technology that organizations use?
3. How is technology related to the accomplishment of organizational goals?
4. Further, how is technology related—as a design constraint—to the other design constraints, environment and people?
5. How does technology affect the design variables: work design, organizational control, decision processes, and organization structure?
6. Finally, how does technology affect organizational outcomes of climate and effectiveness?

RATIONALITY IN ORGANIZATIONS

JAMES D. THOMPSON

Instrumental action is rooted on the one hand in *desired outcomes* and on the other hand in *beliefs about cause/effect relationships*. Given a desire, the state of man's knowledge at any point in time dictates the kinds of variables required and the manner of their manipulation to bring that desire to fruition. To the extent that the activities thus dictated by man's beliefs are judged to produce the desired outcomes, we can speak of technology, or *technical rationality*.

Technical rationality can be evaluated by two criteria: instrumental and economic. The essence of the instrumental question is whether the specified actions do in fact produce the desired outcome, and the instrumentally perfect technology is one which inevitably achieves such results. The economic question in essence is whether the results are obtained with the least necessary expenditure of resources, and for this there is no absolute standard. Two different routes to the same desired outcome may be compared in terms of cost, or both may be compared with some abstract ideal, but in practical terms the evaluation of economy is relative to the state of man's knowledge at the time of evaluation.

We will give further consideration to the assessment of organizational action in a later chapter, but it is necessary to distinguish at this point between the instrumental and economic questions because present literature about organizations gives considerable attention to the economic dimension of technology but hides the importance of the instrumental question, which in fact takes priority. The cost of doing something can be considered only after we know that the something can be done.

Complex organizations are built to operate technologies which are found to be impossible or impractical for individuals to operate. This does not mean, however, that technologies operated by complex organizations are instrumentally perfect. The instrumentally perfect technology would produce the desired outcome inevitably, and this perfection is approached in the case of continuous processing of chemicals or in mass manufacturing—for example, of automobiles. A less perfect technology will produce the desired outcome only part of the time; nevertheless, it may be incorporated into complex organizations, such as the mental hospital, because desire for the possible outcome is intense enough to settle for possible rather than highly probable success. Sometimes the intensity of desire for certain kinds of outcomes, such as world peace, leads to the creation of complex organizations such as the United Nations to operate patently imperfect technologies.

VARIATIONS IN TECHNOLOGIES

Clearly, technology is an important variable in understanding the actions of complex organizations. In modern societies the variety of desired outcomes for which specific technologies are available seems infinite. A complete but simple typology of technologies which has found order in this variety would be quite helpful. Typologies are available for industrial production (Woodward, 1965) and for mental therapy (Hawkes, 1962) but are not general enough to deal with the range of technologies found in complex organizations. Lacking such a typology, we will simply identify three varieties which are 1. widespread in modern society and 2. sufficiently different to illustrate the propositions we wish to develop.

The Long-Linked Technology[1]

A long-linked technology involves serial interdependence in the sense that act Z can be performed only

1. The notions in this section rest especially on conversations some years ago with Frederick L. Bates. For a different but somewhat parallel analysis of workflows, see Dubin, 1959.

James D. Thompson, *Organizations in Action* (New York: McGraw-Hill, 1967), pp.14–24. © 1967 McGraw-Hill Book Company. Reprinted by permission.

after successful completion of act Y, which in turn rests on act X, and so on. The original symbol of technical rationality, the mass production assembly line, is of this long-linked nature. It approaches instrumental perfection when it produces a single kind of standard product, repetitively and at a constant rate. Production of only one kind of product means that a single technology is required, and this in turn permits the use of clear-cut criteria for the selection of machines and tools, construction of workflow arrangements, acquisition of raw materials, and selection of human operators. Repetition of the productive process provides experience as a means of eliminating imperfections in the technology; experience can lead to the modification of machines and provide the basis for scheduled preventive maintenance. Repetition means that human motions can also be examined, and through training and practice, energy losses and errors minimized. It is in this setting that the scientific-management movement has perhaps made its greatest contribution.

The constant rate of production means that, once adjusted, the proportions of resources involved can be standardized to the point where each contributes to its capacity; none need be underemployed. This of course makes important contributions to the economic aspect of the technology.

The Mediating Technology

Various organizations have, as a primary function, the linking of clients or customers who are or wish to be interdependent. The commercial bank links depositors and borrowers. The insurance firm links those who would pool common risks. The telephone utility links those who would call and those who would be called. The post office provides a possible linkage of virtually every member of the modern society. The employment agency mediates the supply of labor and the demand for it.

Complexity in the mediating technology comes not from the necessity of having each activity geared to the requirements of the next but rather from the fact that the mediating technology requires operating in *standardized ways,* and *extensively;* e.g., with multiple clients or customers distributed in time and space.

The commercial bank must find and aggregate deposits from diverse depositors; but however diverse the depositors, the transaction must conform to standard terms and to uniform bookkeeping and accounting procedures. It must also find borrowers; but no matter how varied their needs or desires, loans must be made according to standardized criteria and on terms uniformly applied to the category appropriate to the particular borrower. Poor risks who receive favored treatment jeopardize bank solvency. Standardization permits the insurance organization to define categories of risk and hence to sort its customers or potential customers into appropriate aggregate categories; the insured who is not a qualified risk but is so defined upsets the probabilities on which insurance rests. The telephone company became viable only when the telephone became regarded as a necessity, and this did not occur until equipment was standardized to the point where it could be incorporated into one network. Standardization enables the employment agency to aggregate job applicants into categories which can be matched against standardized requests for employees.

Standardization makes possible the operation of the mediating technology over time and through space by assuring each segment of the organization that other segments are operating in compatible ways. It is in such situations that the bureaucratic techniques of categorization and impersonal application of rules have been most beneficial (Weber, 1947; Merton, 1957a).

The Intensive Technology

This third variety we label *intensive* to signify that a variety of techniques is drawn upon in order to achieve a change in some specific object; but the selection, combination, and order of application are determined by feedback from the object itself. When the object is human, this intensive technology is regarded as "therapeutic," but the same technical logic is found also in the construction industry (Stinchcombe, 1959) and in research where the objects of concern are nonhuman.

The intensive technology is most dramatically illustrated by the general hospital. At any moment an emergency admission may require some combination of dietary, x-ray, laboratory, and housekeeping or hotel services, together with the various medical specialties, pharmaceutical services, occupational therapies, social work services, and spiritual or religious services. Which of these, and when, can be determined only from evidence about the state of the patient.

In the construction industry, the nature of the crafts required and the order in which they can be applied depend on the nature of the object to be constructed and its setting; including, for example, terrain, climate, weather. Organized or team research may draw from a variety of scientific or technical skills, but the particular combination and the order of application depend on the nature of the problem defined.

The development of military combat teams, with a multiplicity of highly skilled capacities to be applied to the requirements of changing circumstances, represents a shift toward the intensive technology in military operations (Janowitz, 1959).

The intensive technology is a custom technology. Its successful employment rests in part on the availability of all the capacities potentially needed, but equally on the appropriate custom combination of selected capacities as required by the individual case or project.

Boundaries of Technical Rationality

Technical rationality, as a system of cause/effect relationships which lead to a desired result, is an abstraction. It is instrumentally perfect when it becomes a closed system of logic. The closed system of logic contains all relevant variables, and only relevant variables. All other influences, or *exogenous variables*, are excluded; and the variables contained in the system vary only to the extent that the experimenter, the manager, or the computer determines they should.

When a technology is put to use, however, there must be not only desired outcomes and knowledge of relevant cause/effect relationships, but also power to control the empirical resources which correspond to the variables in the logical system. A closed system of action corresponding to a closed system of logic would result in instrumental perfection in reality.

The mass production assembly operation and the continuous processing of chemicals are more nearly perfect, in application, than the other two varieties discussed above because they achieve a high degree of control over relevant variables and are relatively free from disturbing influences. Once started, most of the action involved in the long-linked technology is dictated by the internal logic of the technology itself. With the mediating technology, customers or clients intrude to make difficult the standardized activities required by the technology. And with the intensive technology, the specific case defines the component activities and their combination from the larger array of components contained in the abstract technology.

Since technical perfection seems more nearly approachable when the organization has control over all the elements involved,

> *Proposition 5.1:* Under norms of rationality, organizations seek to seal off their core technologies from environmental influences.

ORGANIZATIONAL RATIONALITY

When organizations seek to translate the abstractions called technologies into action, they immediately face problems for which the core technologies do not provide solutions.

Mass production manufacturing technologies are quite specific, *assuming* that certain inputs are provided and finished products are somehow removed from the premises before the productive process is clogged; but mass production technologies do not include variables which provide solutions to either the input- or output-disposal problems. The present technology of medicine may be rather specific if certain tests indicate an appendectomy is in order, if the condition of the patient meets certain criteria, and if certain medical staff, equipment, and medications are present. But medical technology contains no cause/effect statements about bringing sufferers to the attention of medical practitioners, or about the provision of the specified equipment, skills, and medications. The technology of education rests on abstract systems of belief about relationships among teachers, teaching materials, and pupils; but learning theories assume the presence of these variables and proceed from that point.

One or more technologies constitute the core of all purposive organizations. But this technical core is always an incomplete representation of what the organization must do to accomplish desired results. Technical rationality is a necessary component but never alone sufficient to provide *organizational rationality,* which involves acquiring the inputs which are taken for granted by the technology, and dispensing outputs which again are outside the scope of the core technology.

At a minimum, then, organizational rationality involves three major component activities: 1. input activities, 2. technological activities, and 3. output activities. Since these are interdependent, organizational rationality requires that they be appropriately geared to one another. The inputs acquired must be within the scope of the technology, and it must be within the capacity of the organization to dispose of the technological production.

Not only are these component activities interdependent, but both input and output activities are interdependent with environmental elements. Organizational rationality, therefore, never conforms to closed-system logic but demands the logic of an open system. Moreover, since the technological activities are embedded in and interdependent with activities which are open to the environment, the closed system can never be completely attained for the technological component. Yet we have offered the proposition that organizations subject to rationality norms seek to seal off their core technologies from environmental influences. How do we reconcile these two contentions?

> *Proposition 5.2:* Under norms of rationality, organizations seek to buffer environmental influences by surrounding their technical cores with input and output components.

To maximize productivity of a manufacturing technology, the technical core must be able to operate as if the market will absorb the single kind of product at a continuous rate, and as if inuts flowed continuously, at a steady rate and with specified quality. Conceivably both sets of conditions could occur; realistically they do not. But organizations reveal a variety of devices for approximating these "as if" assumptions, with input and output components meeting fluctuating environments and converting them into steady conditions for the technological core.

Buffering on the input side is illustrated by the stockpiling of materials and supplies acquired in an irregular market, and their steady insertion into the production process. Preventive maintenance, whereby machines or equipment are repaired on a scheduled basis, thus minimizing surprise, is another example of buffering by the input component. The recruitment of dissimilar personnel and their conversion into reliable performers through training or indoctrination is another; it is most dramatically illustrated by basic training or boot camp in military organizations (Dornbusch, 1955).

Buffering on the output side of long-linked technologies usually takes the form of maintaining warehouse inventories and items in transit or in distributor inventories, which permits the technical core to produce at a constant rate, but distribution to fluctuate with market conditions.

Buffering on the input side is an appropriate and important device available to all types of organizations. Buffering on the output side is especially important for mass-manufacturing organizations, but is less feasible when the product is perishable or when the object is inextricably involved in the technological process, as in the therapeutic case.

Buffering of an unsteady environment obviously brings considerable advantages to the technical core, but it does so with costs to the organizations. A classic problem in connection with buffering is how to maintain inventories, input or output, sufficient to meet all needs without incurring obsolescence as needs change. Operations research recently has made important contributions toward this problem of "run out versus obsolescence," both of which are costly.

Thus while a fully buffered technological core would enjoy the conditions for maximum technical rationality, organizational rationality may call for compromises between conditions for maximum technical efficiency and the energy required for buffering operations. In an unsteady environment, then, the organization under rationality norms must seek other devices for protecting its technical core.

> *Proposition 5.3:* Under norms of rationality, organizations seek to smooth out input and output transactions.

Whereas buffering absorbs environmental fluctuations, smoothing or leveling involves attempts to reduce fluctuations in the environment. Utility firms—electric, gas, water, or telephone—may offer inducements to those who use their services during "trough" periods, or charge premiums to those who contribute to "peaking." Retailing organizations faced with seasonal or other fluctuations in demand, may offer inducements in the form of special promotions or sales during slow periods. Transportation organizations such as airlines may offer special reduced fare rates on light days or during slow seasons.

Organizations pointed toward emergencies, such as fire departments, attempt to level the need for their services by activities designed to prevent emergencies, and by emphasis on early detection so that demand is not allowed to grow to the point that would overtax the capacity of the organization. Hospitals accomplish some smoothing through the scheduling of nonemergency admissions.

Although action by the organization may thus reduce fluctuations in demand, complete smoothing of demand is seldom possible. But a core technology interrupted by constant fluctuation and change must settle for a low degree of technical rationality. What other devices do organizations employ to protect core technologies?

> *Proposition 5.4:* Under norms of rationality, organizations seek to anticipate and adapt to environmental changes which cannot be buffered or leveled.

If environmental fluctuations penetrate the organization and require the technical core to alter its activities, then environmental fluctuations are exogenous variables within the logic of technical rationality. To the extent that environmental fluctuations can be anticipated, however, they can be treated as *constraints* on the technical core within which a closed system of logic can be employed.

The manufacturing firm which can correctly forecast demand for a particular time period can thereby plan or schedule operations of its technical core at a steady rate during that period. Any changes in technical operations due to changes in the environment can be made at the end of the period on the basis of forecasts for the next period.

Organizations often learn that some environmental fluctuations are patterned, and in these cases forecasting and adjustment appear almost automatic. The post office knows, for example, that in large commercial centers large volumes of business mail are posted at the end of the business day, when secretaries leave offices. Recently the post office has attempted to buffer that load by promising rapid treatment of mail posted in special locations during morning hours. Its success in buffering is not known at this writing, but meanwhile the post office schedules its technical activities to meet known daily fluctuations. It can also anticipate heavy demand during November and December, thus allowing its input components lead time in acquiring additional resources.

Banks likewise learn that local conditions and customs result in peak loads at predictable times during the day and week, and can schedule their operations to meet these shifts (Argyris, 1954).

In cases such as these, organizations have amassed sufficient experience to know that fluctuations are patterned with a high degree of regularity or probability; but when environmental fluctuations are the result of combinations of more dynamic factors, anticipation may require something more than the simple projection of previous experience. It is in these situations that forecasting emerges as a specialized and elaborate activity, for which some of the emerging management-science or statistical-decision theories seem especially appropriate.

To the extent that environmental fluctuations are unanticipated they interfere with the orderly operation of the core technology and thereby reduce its performance. When such influences are anticipated and considered as constraints for a particular period of time, the technical core can operate as if it enjoyed a closed system.

Buffering, leveling, and adaptation to anticipated fluctuations are widely used devices for reducing the influence of the environment on the technological cores of organizations. Often they are effective, but there are occasions when these devices are not sufficient to ward off environmental penetration.

Proposition 5.5: When buffering, leveling, and forecasting do not protect their technical cores from environmental fluctuations, organizations under norms of rationality resort to rationing.

Rationing is most easily seen in organizations pointed toward emergencies, such as hospitals. Even in nonemergency situations hospitals may ration beds to physicians by establishing priority systems for nonemergency admissions. In emergencies, such as community disasters, hospitals may ration pharmaceutical dosages or nursing services by dilution—by assigning a fixed number of nurses to a larger patient population. Mental hospitals, especially state mental hospitals, may ration technical services by employing primarily organic-treatment procedures—electroshock, drugs, insulin—which can be employed more economically than psychoanalytic or *milieu* therapies (Belknap, 1956). Teachers and caseworkers in social welfare organizations may ration effort by accepting only a portion of those seeking service, or if not empowered to exercise such discretion, may concentrate their energies on the more challenging cases or on those which appear most likely to yield satisfactory outcomes (Blau, 1955).

But rationing is not a device reserved for therapeutic organizations. The post office may assign priority to first-class mail, attending to lesser classes only when the priority task is completed. Manufacturers of suddenly popular items may ration allotments to wholesalers or dealers, and if inputs are scarce, may assign priorities to alternative uses of those resources. Libraries may ration book loans, acquisitions, and search efforts (Meier, 1963).

Rationing is an unhappy solution, for its use signifies that the technology is not operating at its maximum. Yet some system of priorities for the allocation of capacity under adverse conditions is essential if a technology is to be instrumentally effective–if action is to be other than random.

The Logic of Organizational Rationality

Core technologies rest on closed systems of logic, but are invariably embedded in a larger organizational rationality which pins the technology to a time and place, and links it with the larger environment through input and output activities. Organizational rationality thus calls for an open-system logic, for when the organization is opened to environmental influences, some of the factors involved in organizational action become *constraints;* for some meaningful period of time they are not variables but fixed conditions to which the organization must adapt. Some of the factors become *contingencies,* which may or may not vary, but are not subject to arbitrary control by the organization.

Organizational rationality therefore is some result of 1. constraints which the organization must face, 2. contingencies which the organization must meet, and 3. variables which the organization can control.

RECAPITULATION

Perfection in technical rationality requires complete knowledge of cause/effect relations plus control over all of the relevant variables, or closure. Therefore, under norms of rationality (Prop. 5.1), organizations seek to seal off their core technologies from environmental influences. Since complete closure is impossible (Prop. 5.2), they seek to buffer environmental influences by surrounding their technical cores with input and output components.

Because buffering does not handle all variations in an unsteady environment, organizations seek to smooth input and output transactions (Prop. 5.3), and to anticipate and adapt to environmental changes which cannot be buffered or smoothed (Prop. 5.4), and finally, when buffering, leveling, and forecasting do not protect their technical cores from environmental fluctuations (Prop. 5.5), organizations resort to rationing.

These are maneuvering devices which provide the organization with some self-control despite interdependence with the environment. But if we are to gain understanding of such maneuvering, we must consider both the direction toward which maneuvering is designed and the nature of the environment in which maneuvering takes place.

A FRAMEWORK FOR THE COMPARATIVE ANALYSIS OF ORGANIZATIONS

CHARLES PERROW

This paper presents a perspective on organizations that hopefully will provide a basis for comparative organizational analysis, and also allow one to utilize selectively the existing theories of organizational behavior.[1] There are four characteristics of this perspective.

First, technology, or the work done in organizations, is considered the defining characteristic of organizations. That is, organizations are seen primarily as systems for getting work done, for applying techniques to the problem of altering raw materials—whether the materials be people, symbols or things. This is in contrast to other perspectives which see organizations as, for example, cooperative systems, institutions, or decision-making systems.

Second, this perspective treats technology as an independent variable, and structure—the arrangements among people for getting work done—as a dependent variable. Goals are conceived of as being in part a dependent variable. What is held to be an independent and dependent variable when one abstracts general variables from a highly interdependent and complex social system is less of an assertion about reality than a strategy of analysis. Thus, no claim is made that for all purposes technology need be an independent variable.

Third, this perspective attempts to conceptualize the organization as a whole, rather than to deal only with specific processes or subparts. Thus, while the importance of technology has often been demonstrated within work groups or for particular organizational processes, here it will be used as a basis for dealing with the organization as an organization.

Finally, and in the long run perhaps most importantly, the perspective holds that technology is a better basis for comparing organizations than the several schemes which now exist (Parsons, 1960; Blau and Scott, 1962; Etzioni, 1961).

None of these points in itself is new, and the last section of this article discusses the uses to which the concept of technology has been put by others. However, the attempt to deal with all four points simultaneously, or, to put it differently, to pay systematic attention to the role of technology in analyzing and comparing organizations as a whole, is believed to be distinctive.

TECHNOLOGY AND RAW MATERIALS

By technology is meant the actions that an individual performs upon an object, with or without the aid of tools or mechanical devices, in order to make some change in that object. The object, or "raw material," may be a living being, human or otherwise, a symbol or an inanimate object. People are raw materials in people-changing or people-processing organizations; symbols are materials in banks, advertising agencies and some research organizations; the interactions of people are raw materials to be manipulated by administrators in organizations; boards of directors, committees and councils are usually involved with the changing or processing of symbols and human interactions, and so on.

In the course of changing this material in an organizational setting, the individual must interact

1. Revision of a paper read at the 1966 Annual Meeting of the American Sociological Association. This paper was prepared during the course of research on industrial corporations supported by Grant No. GS-742, National Science Foundation. Numerous colleagues criticized an earlier version unstintingly, but I would like to single out Ernest Vargas, Geoffrey Guest, and Anthony Kovner, who transcended their graduate student roles at the University of Pittsburgh during the formulation of these ideas in sticky field situations.

with others. The form that this interaction takes we will call the structure of the organization. It involves the arrangements or relationships that permit the coordination and control of work. Some work is actually concerned with changing or maintaining the structure of an organization. Most administrators have this as a key role, and there is a variety of technologies for it. The distinction between technology and structure has its gray areas, but basically it is the difference between an individual acting directly upon a material that is to be changed and an individual interacting with other individuals in the course of trying to change that material. In some cases the material to be changed and the "other individuals" he interacts with are the same objects, but the relationships are different in each case.

There are a number of aspects of technology which are no doubt important to consider in some contexts, such as the environment of the work (noise, dirt, etc.) or the possibilities of seductive or exploitative relationships with clients, patients or customers. For our purposes, however, we are concerned with two aspects of technology that seem to be directly relevant to organizational structure. The first is the number of exceptional cases encountered in the work,[2] that is, the degree to which stimuli are perceived as familiar or unfamiliar. This varies on a scale from low to high.

2. See March and Simon (1958: 141–42), where a related distinction is made on the basis of search behavior. In our view the occurrence of an exceptional case precedes search behavior, and various types of search behavior can be distinguished.

The second is the nature of the search process that is undertaken by the individual when exceptions occur. We distinguish two types of search process. The first type involves a search which can be conducted on a logical, analytical basis. Search processes are always exceptional actions undertaken by the individual. They are nonroutine. No programs exist for them. If a program exists, only a very trivial search is involved in switching from one program to another program when the stimuli change (March and Simon, 1958: 142). But though nonroutine, one type of search may be logical, systematic and analytical. This is exemplified by the mechanical engineering unit of a firm building large machinery, or by programmers writing individual programs for slow readers in a special school. The second type of search process occurs when the problem is so vague and poorly conceptualized as to make it virtually unanalyzable. In this case, no "formal" search is undertaken, but instead one draws upon the residue of unanalyzed experience or intuition, or relies upon chance and guesswork. Examples would be work with exotic metals or nuclear fuels, psychiatric casework, and some kinds of advertising. We can conceive of a scale from analyzable to unanalyzable problems.

If we dichotomize these two continua into the presence or absence of exceptional cases and into the presence or absence of analyzable problems, we have a four-fold table as in Figure 5–2. The upper right-hand quadrant, cell 2, where there are many exceptional cases and a few analytic techniques for analyzing them,

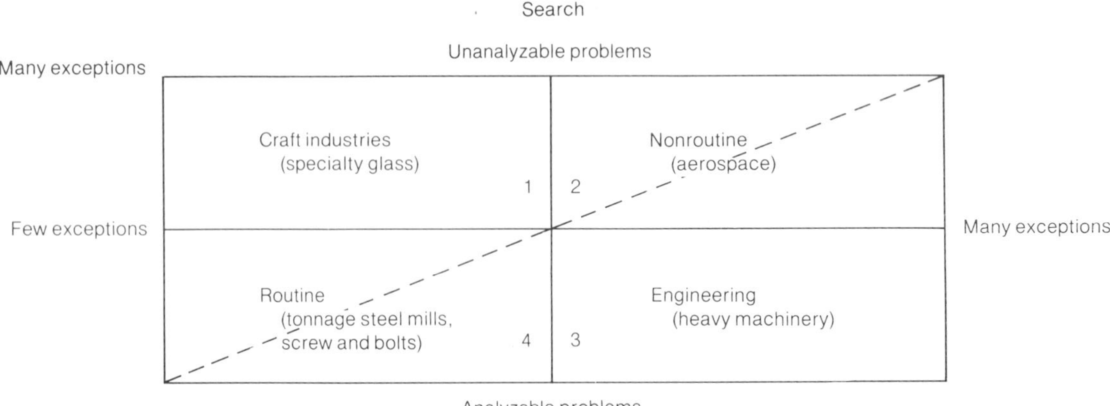

Figure 5-2. Technology variable (industrial example)

is one extreme to which we will refer as nonroutine. In the lower left-hand quadrant, cell 4, we have the routine extreme, where there are few exceptions and there are analytic techniques for handling those that occur. A one-dimensional scheme would follow the dotted line from routine to nonroutine. But note that the other two quadrants may represent viable cases in themselves and they have been labeled with some industrial examples. Few cases would probably fall in the upper left-hand corner of cell 1, or lower right-hand corner of cell 3, but otherwise many organizations are expected to appear in these two cells.

Techniques are performed upon raw materials. The state of the art of analyzing the characteristics of the raw materials is likely to determine what kind of technology will be used. (Tools are also necessary, of course, but by and large, the construction of tools is a simpler problem than the analysis of the nature of the material and generally follows the analysis.) To understand the nature of the material means to be able to control it better and achieve more predictability and efficiency in transformation. We are not referring here to the "essence" of the material, only to the way the organization itself perceives it.

The other relevant characteristic of the raw material, besides the understandability of its nature, is its stability and variability; that is, whether the material can be treated in a standardized fashion or whether continual adjustment to it is necessary. Organizations uniformly seek to standardize their raw material in order to minimize exceptional situations. This is the point of de-individualizing processes found in military academies, monasteries and prisons, or the superiority of the synthetic shoe material Corfam over leather.

These two characteristics interact, of course. On the one hand, increased knowledge of the nature of the material may lead to the perception of more varieties of possible outcomes or products, which in turn increases the need for more intimate knowledge of the nature of the material. Or the organization, with increased knowledge of one type of material, may begin to work with a variety of related materials about which more needs to be known, as when a social service agency or employment agency relaxes its admission criteria as it gains confidence, but in the process sets off more search behavior, or when a manufacturing organization starts producing new but related products. On the other hand, if increased knowledge of the material is gained but no expansion of the variety of output occurs, this permits easier analysis of the sources of problems that may arise in the transformation process. It may also allow one to prevent the rise of such problems by the design of the production process.

A recent analysis of a public defender system by Sudnow highlights the twin characteristics of the material variable (Sudnow, 1965: 255–76). On the one hand, offenders are distributed into uniform categories by means of the conception of the "normal crime," and on the other hand, control over the individual offender is insured because the public defender well understands the offender's "nature"—that is, his low status, limited understanding and intellectual resources, and his impecunious condition. The technology, then, can be routine because there are few exceptions (and these are handled by a different set of personnel) and no search behavior on the public defender's part is required. The lawyer in private practice, of course, is a contrasting case (Street et al., 1966).

It will readily be seen that these two characteristics of the raw material are paralleled in the four-fold table of technology (Figure 5–3). If the technology of an organization is going to move from cell 2 to any of the other cells, it can only do so either by reducing the variability of the material and thus the number of exceptional cases that occur, or by increasing the knowledge of the material and thus allowing more analytic techniques to be used, or both. One may move from cell 2 to cell 1 with increasing production runs, clients served, accounts handled, research projects underway, agency programs administered and so forth, since this allows more experience to be gained and thus reduces the number of stimuli seen as exceptions. If technical knowledge increases, increasing the reliability of search procedures, one may move from cell 2 to cell 3. If both things happen—and this is the aim of most organizations—one may move from cell 2 to cell 4.[3]

3. Some organizations, such as mental hospitals, perceive that their technology is inadequate to their goals, and try to move from cell 4 to cell 2 in the search for a new technology.

Perceived Nature of Raw Material

Not well understood

Variability of Material			
Perceived as uniform and stable	Socializing institutions (e.g., some schools) 1	2 Elite psychiatric agency	Perceived as non-uniform and unstable
	Custodial institutions, vocational training 4	3 Programmed learning school	

Well understood

Figure 5-3. Raw material variables (people-changing examples)

TASK AND SOCIAL STRUCTURE

For our purpose, the task structure of an organization is conceived of as consisting of two dimensions, control and coordination. Control itself can be broken up into two components. They are the degree of discretion an individual or group possesses in carrying out its tasks, and the power of an individual or group to mobilize scarce resources and to control definitions of various situations, such as the definition of the nature of the raw material. Discretion here does not mean freedom from supervision or freedom simply to vary task sequences or pace of work. Both of these are compatible with routine activities, and some nonroutine tasks must be closely supervised or have precise sequences of tasks, once a program is selected, because of their critical nature. Nor does the length of time between performance reviews (Jaques, 1959) necessarily indicate discretion. Rather, discretion involves judgments about whether close supervision is required on one task or another, about changing programs, and about the interdependence of one's task with other tasks.[4] Discretion and power may often be correlated (Perrow, 1961a; Crozier, 1964), but there is an important distinction. Power affects outcomes directly because it involves choices regarding basic goals and strategies. Discretion relates to choices among means and judgments of the critical and interdependent nature of tasks. The consequences of decisions in the case of discretion have no direct influence on goals and strategies; these decisions are formed within the framework of accepted goals and strategies.

Coordination, on the other hand, can be achieved through planning or feedback, to use the terms proposed by March and Simon (1958: 160). Coordination by planning refers to the programmed interaction of tasks, which interaction is clearly defined by rules or by the very tools and machinery or the logic of the transformation process. Coordination by feedback, on the other hand, refers to negotiated alterations in the nature or sequence of tasks performed by two different units.

It is now necessary to distinguish three functional or task areas within management in organizations. Area One, the design and planning function, entails such major decisions as what goods or services are to be produced, who the customers will be, the technology employed, and the source of legitimacy and capital. Area Two, the technical control and support of production and marketing, includes such functions (to use industrial terms) as accounting, product and process research, quality control, scheduling, engineering,

4. This raises serious operationalization problems. In my own work, first-line supervisors were said to have considerable independence in some routine production situations, and to have little in some nonroutine situations, according to a questionnaire, though it was observed that the former had little discretion and the latter a good deal. Kovner found the same kind of responses with a similar question regarding control of job and pace of work among nurses in routine and nonroutine nursing units. See Kovner (1966) and Coser (1958: 56–64).

plant management, purchasing, customer service, advertising, market research, and general sales management. (Not all are important, or even existent, of course, in all industrial organizations.) This is distinguished as a function, though not necessarily in terms of actual persons or positions, from Area Three, the supervision of production and marketing. This area involves the direct supervision of those dealing with the basic raw materials and those doing direct selling (Woodward, 1965). In the subsequent discussion we shall ignore marketing, and, for a time, Area One.

Figure 5–4 shows crudely the kinds of values that might be expected to appear in the task structure, considering only Areas Two and Three—technical control and support of production, and the supervision of production. Some global organizational characterizations of structure are given at the bottom of each cell. Those familiar with Burns and Stalker's work will recognize cell 2 as closest to the organic structure and cell 4 as closest to the mechanistic structure (Burns and Stalker, 1961).

In cell 2, we have nonuniform raw materials in both areas which are not well understood, and thus present many occasions for exceptional handling. However, the search required cannot be logically conducted, but must involve a high degree of experimentation and "feel." In such a technological situation, the discretion of both those who supervise the transformation of the basic raw material, and those who provide technical help for this process, must be high. The supervisors will request help from technical personnel rather than receive orders from them, or there may not even be a clear line of distinction between the two in terms of persons. That is, the clinical psychologist or the quality control engineer will find himself "on the line" so to speak, dealing directly with patients or exotic metals and working side by side with the supervisors who are nominally of lower status. The power of both groups will be high, and not at the expense of each other. The coordination will be through feedback—that is, considerable mutual adjustment must be made. The interdependence of the two groups will be high. The development of product groups and product managers in industry provides an example, as does the somewhat premature attempt of one correctional institution to utilize a cottage system bringing both clinical and line personnel together with joint responsibility for running autonomous cottages (Street, 1966).

In the case of cell 4, uniform stable materials whose relevant nature is perceived as well understood can be handled with few exceptions occurring, and those that do occur can be taken care of with analytical search processes. In such a situation the discretion of both groups is likely to be low. This is a well-programmed production process and there is no need to allow much discretion. Indeed, there is danger in doing so. However, the power of the technical group over the supervisory group is high, for they direct the activities of the supervisors of production on the basis of routine reports generated by the supervisors. Those in Area

	Discretion	Power	Coordination within group	Interdependence of groups	Discretion	Power	Coordination within group	Interdependence of groups
Technical	Low	Low	Plan	Low	High	High	Feed	High
supervision	High	High	Feed		High	High	Feed	
		Decentralized		1	2	Flexible, polycentralized		
				4	3			
Technical	Low	High	Plan	Low	High	High	Feed	Low
supervision	Low	Low	Plan		Low	Low	Plan	
		Formal, centralized				Flexible, centralized		

Figure 5-4. Task structure, task-related interactions

Three are likely to see those in Area Two as hindrances to their work rather than aides. Coordination can be through planning in both groups, and the interdependence of the two groups is low; it is a directive rather than an interdependent relationship.

Cell 3 represents a variation from either of these extremes, for here, in contrast to cell 2, the existence of many exceptions which require search procedures increases both the power and the discretion of the technical group, which handles these exceptions, at the expense of the supervisory group. The supervisors of production respond to the results of these search processes rather than undertake search themselves. In the case of cell 1, the situation is reversed. Because search cannot be logical and analytical, when the infrequent exceptions occur they are handled by those in closest contact with the production process such as teachers and skilled craftsmen, and there is minimal development of administrative services. Of course, in schools that attempt to do little socialization but simply offer instruction and provide custody, technical (administrative) services grow and we move to cell 2.

Having thus related technology to task structure, let us turn to another aspect of structure—the non-task-related but organizationally relevant interactions of people. We call this the social structure.

Figure 5–5 follows our previous four-fold classification and indicates the variety of bases for non-task-related interactions. All are present in all organizations, but the saliency varies. In cell 2, these interactions are likely to revolve more around the mission, long-range goals, and direction of development of the organizations than around the other three bases. This is because of the task structure characteristic of a flexible, polycentric organization, or at least is related to it. The category "social identity" in cell 1 is meant to convey that the non-task-related interactions of personnel that are organizationally relevant revolve around communal or personal satisfactions born of long tenure and close working relationships. This is true especially at the supervisory level, which is a large management group in this type of structure. However, it is very possible, as Blauner and others have shown, for communal relations to develop in cell 4 types of organizations if the organization is located in a rural area where kinship and rural ties are strong (Blauner, 1964). The basis of interaction in cell 3 is instrumental identity and in cell 4, work or task identification. These would also be predicted upon the basis of the technology.

So far we have ignored Area One—design and planning. This area receives more inputs from the environment than the other areas, and thus its tasks and technologies are derived from both internal and external stimuli. If the product environment of the organization—a term meant to cover competitors, customers, suppliers, unions and regulatory agencies—were the same in all four cells of Figure 5–4, we would expect the design and planning areas in cell 4 to have routine tasks and techniques, and nonroutine ones in cell 2. This is because the occasions for design and long-range planning would be few in the one and many in the other. For example, at least until very recently, the

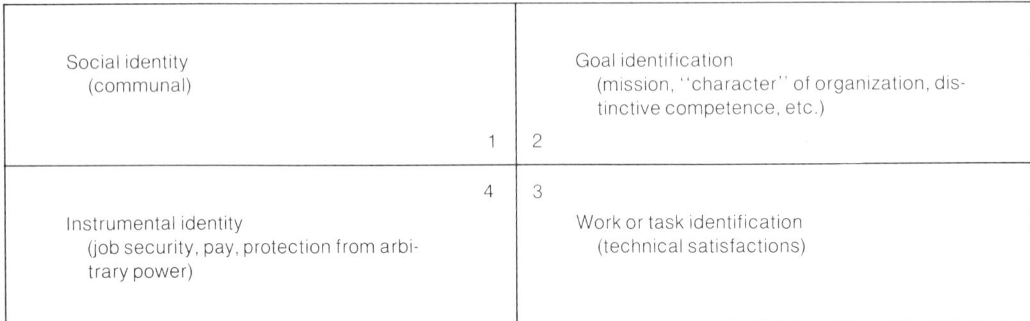

Figure 5-5. Social structure, the bases of non-task-related interaction

decisions that executives in the primary metals industries, railroads and surface mining had to make were probably rather routine, while those of executives in new industries such as electronics and aerospace were probably nonroutine (Chandler, 1962: 329–30; Stinchcombe, 1965: 142–69). One would expect that cell 1 would also be routine, and cell 3 somewhat nonroutine. But the product environment can alter all this. Organizations in cell 4 can be in a rapidly changing market situation even though the technical control and the supervision of production are fairly routine. Consumer goods industries probably deal with many decisions where the search behavior confronts unanalyzable problems such as the hemline of women's clothes, fads in the toy industry, or the length of time that tail fins or the boxy look in autos will last. Generally speaking, however, though the intrinsic characteristics of the product remain the same, rapid changes in the extrinsic characteristics will introduce nonroutine tasks in the design and planning area, even though it hardly alters the routine character of the technical control and the supervision of production (Perrow, 1961b).

These are industrial examples, but it also seems likely that the tasks of Area One in custodial mental hospitals are quite different from those in treatment-oriented hospitals. Relations with the regulatory agencies, supplying agencies, the consumers such as courts and families, and the other agencies that compete for funds or clients, will be rather routine in the first, while they will be quite nonroutine and sensitive in the second. This would not be true, of course, if the latter have the means of isolating themselves from their environment (Street, 1966). Similarly, the market situation of vocational training institutions may change rather quickly as industrial technologies change, requiring changes in the design and planning of the institution, while the market of a public school that attempts to socialize youths will not change as often.

GOALS

Finally, let us turn to the last major variable, goals. Three categories of goals can be distinguished for present purposes (Perrow, 1968). These are system goals, which relate to the characteristics of the system as a whole, independent of its products; product characteristic goals, which relate to the characteristics of the products the organization decides to emphasize; and derived goals, which refer to the uses to which power generated by organizational activities can be put, independent of system or product goals.

We would expect completely routinized organizations to stress those "system" goals of organizational stability, low risk, and perhaps high profits or economical operations rather than growth. (See Figure 5–6.) In terms of "product characteristic" goals, they would be more likely to emphasize quantity than quality, stable lines over unstable or diversified lines, superficial transformations (e.g., instilling discipline in deviant

Cell	System	Product	Derived
1	Stability Few risks Moderate to low profit emphasis	Quality No innovations	Conserv.
2	High growth High risks Low emphasis on profit	High quality Innovative	Liberal
4	Stability Few risks High profit emphasis	Quantity No innovations	Conserv.
3	Moderate growth Some risks Moderate profit emphasis	Reliability Moderate innovations	Liberal

Figure 5-6. Goals

clients) over basic transformation (such as character restructuring), and so forth. Their "derived" goals are likely to emphasize conservative attitudes towards the government, conservative political philosophies, conservative forms of corporate giving. Also, they are perhaps more likely to have individuals who exploit, for their own benefit, relations with suppliers, and who have collusive arrangements with competitors and devious and excessive forms of management compensation. Obviously, these comments upon possible goals are open to serious question. For one thing, we lack such data on goals for a large number of organizations. Furthermore, personalities and the environment may shape goals more than the other variables of technology and structure. Finally, the link between structure and goals is an intuitive one, based upon unproven assumptions regarding attitudes generated by task relations. But the comments are meant to suggest how goals may be shaped or constrained, though hardly specified, through the influence of technology and structure.

SOME CAUTIONS

This truncated perspective ignores the role of the cultural and social environment in making available definitions of raw material, providing technologies, and restricting the range of feasible structures and goals (Perrow, 1961b). It also ignores, for the most part, the role of the product environment—customers, competitors, suppliers, unions and regulatory agencies—and the material and human resources. These will have their independent effect upon the major variables.

In addition, it is not proposed here that there are four types of organizations. The two-dimensional scheme is conceived of as consisting of two continua. Nor are the dimensions and the specifications of the variables necessarily the best. It is argued, however, that the main variables—raw materials, technology, task and social structure, goals, and some differentiation of task areas within organizations, are critical ones. As to the assignment of independent and dependent variables, occasions can be readily cited where changes in goals, for example those brought about by changes in the market place or the personalities of top executives, have brought about changes in the technology utilized. The argument is somewhat more subtle than one of temporal prioritites. Rather, it says that structure and goals must adjust to technology or the organization will be subject to strong strains. For a radical change in goals to be a successful one, it may require a change in technology, and thus in structure, or else there will be a large price paid for the lack of fit between these variables (Perrow, 1961b). Furthermore, as one proceeds, analytically, from technology through the two kinds of structure to goals, increasingly the prior variable only sets limits upon the range of possible variations in the next variable. Thus, technology may predict task structure quite well in a large number of organizations (Woodward, 1965), but these two predict social structure less well, and these three only set broad limits on the range of possible goals.

CONCLUDING STATEMENT

What can we infer about technology as a constraint on organization design? We have already spent a fair amount of time (and space) considering its nature, but how does it affect design decisions? The purpose of this concluding statement is to examine this question. We begin the examination by focusing on coordination. Coordination, after all, is necessary—indeed, critical—to concerted effort and the effective achievement of collective goals. We focus on the impact of technology on coordination by means of Thompson's formulation. We then move on to considering how techology affects the major design variables discussed in this volume: work design, control, decision making, and structure.

TECHNOLOGY AND ORGANIZATIONAL DESIGN: COORDINATION

The types of coordination mechanisms found in organizations appear to be contingent on the nature of the interdependence among the organizational units to be coordinated. Thompson (1967) discusses three types of interdependence: *pooled, sequential,* and *reciprocal.*

Pooled Interdependence

Pooled interdependence is a situation in which units do not rely on each other to a great extent, but the failure of one may endanger the others. When an organization is departmentalized either into a product form or into geographical areas, the units will normally have pooled interdependence. Examples are McDonald's franchises, different Enco gasoline stations, branches of the Bank of America, Sears stores, and the automotive, jet engine, and appliance divisions of General Motors. Schematically, pooled interdependence looks like this:

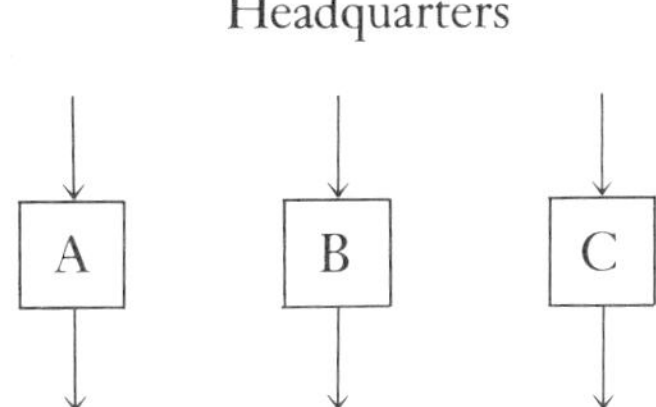

Coordination among units having pooled interdependence is fairly simple: rules, policies, procedures, and other types of formalization are used to standardize activities across the units. Hierarchy (supervision) and committees are used when exceptional problems occur.

Sequential Interdependence

Sequential interdependence is the situation in which unit A must accomplish its task before unit B can start its task, and so forth. Sequential interdependence looks like this:

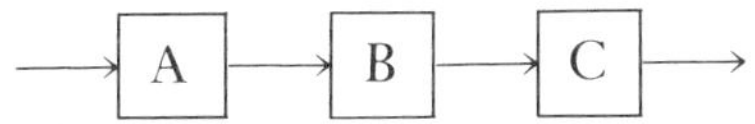

Assembly lines are obvious examples of sequential interdependence. However, sequential courses in a degree program, a university registration procedure, and the preparation of gourmet meals are other examples. Plans and schedules are the dominant coordination mechanisms among units having sequential interdependence. There is also reliance on formalization for the coordination of routine matters and the use of hierarchy (supervision) and committees to handle exceptional problems.

Reciprocal Interdependence

Reciprocal interdependence is the situation in which no single organizational unit is able to accomplish its assigned task until other units have accomplished theirs. Furthermore, the other units cannot act until the first unit has done its part of the task. Schematically, reciprocal interdependence appears as follows:

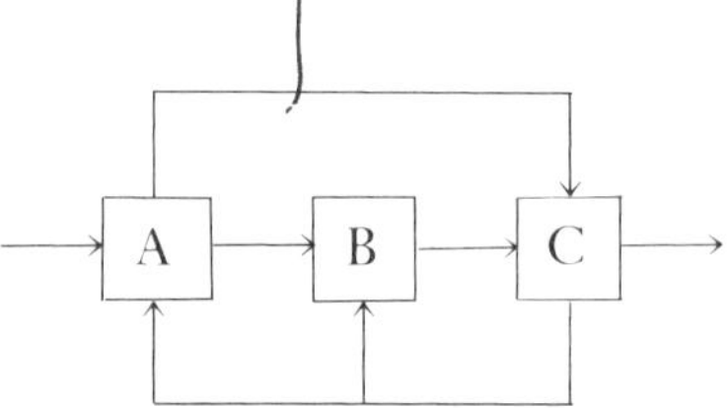

Reciprocal interdependence is a situation in which organizations do not like to find themselves and prefer to avoid, because it is not only messy but expensive. Imagine trying to build a new bomber that will fly at mach six (six times the speed of sound). The engineers designing the fuselage cannot complete their task until much is known about the wing and tail configurations. But the wing cannot be designed without knowledge of the power plant, which depends on the fuselage, wing, and tail configurations and the payload of the plane. Many social programs (such as the War on Poverty) have faced similar problems. Coordination among organizational units having reciprocal interdependence not only uses all of the mechanisms that were mentioned for pooled and sequential interdependence but also relies heavily on individuals called liaison, or integrators, to coordinate the interdependent departments.

RELATING TECHNOLOGY AND COORDINATION

The three typologies of technology that were examined in the introductory remarks have several common features. First, there is very little difference among the mass production, long-linked, and routine concepts of technology. Perrow's idea of craft units and Woodward's unit production are similar, even though Perrow's engineering unit may engage in unit production. Further, both have some aspects of Thompson's mediating and intensive technologies. Additionally, even though the basic concepts are somewhat dissimilar, it is likely that units falling into Perrow's engineering or Woodward's continuous production categories will share many similar characteristics. Finally, Perrow's nonroutine and Thompson's intensive categories share common characteristics. Figure 5–7 is admittedly crude and glosses over many of the distinctions among the various typologies. However, it does serve to illustrate many of their similarities.

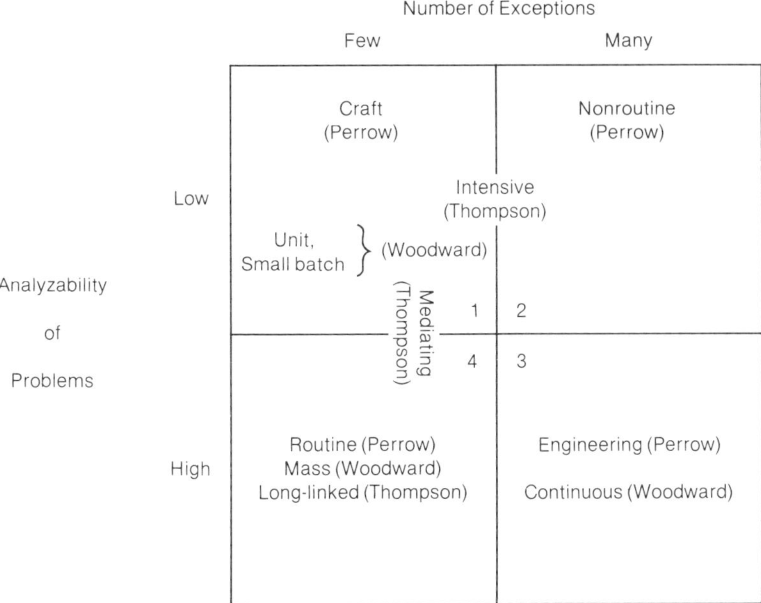

Figure 5-7. Relationships among technology typologies

As mentioned earlier, coordination within cells 1 and 4 of Figure 5–7 will rely heavily on plans and schedules. The primary difference in coordination within each of these cells is that rules, policies, and procedures will be programmed into the sequential production process in cell 4 and clearly written down. In cell 1, these procedures will be programmed into the person performing the craft, rather than the production process, and probably will not be written down.

Coordination within cell 2, on the other hand, will rely heavily on liaison persons providing feedback to the reciprocally interdependent units concerning the effects different activities have on the other units. Coordination used in cell 3 will be mixed. Plans, schedules, and committees will all be used to some extent. While the units in this cell have sequential interdependence, the problems faced by the units will be unique enough to create the need for frequent committee meetings. The primary difference in the coordination within cells 2 and 3 is that in cell 3 there are known and accepted procedures to develop solutions to problems, whereas there are no known or accepted procedures for problem solution in cell 2. Consequently, solutions to problems occurring in cell 3 can be developed within a schedule, whereas problems within cell 2 cannot be confined to a schedule.

TECHNOLOGY AND DESIGN CONSTRAINTS

Ideally there should be no relationships among independent variables. They should stand independently of one another, with each having a separate, distinguishable influence on the set of design variables. But things are not always as we would like them to be in the real world, and in this case, the set of design-conditioning variables—technology, goals, environment, and people—are mutually interdependent. This section will sketch some of these interdependencies.

First, however, a caution. One of the problems with discussing organizational properties one at a time is that they are so interdependent. How can we talk about the impact of technology on structure before we talk about structure? On the other hand, we really cannot meaningfully discuss structural design if we haven't already introduced such design constraints as environment and technology.

So . . . what to do? Our resolution of this dilemma is this. We are assuming that the reader has already been at least *exposed* to such concepts as work design, organizational control-and-decision processes, and organization structure. That exposure will be adequate for this chapter's discussion of technology as a design constraint.

Technology and Goals

The point was made earlier that goals represent constraints on decision makers. In the first part of the discussion concerning technology, it became apparent that technology represents a similar constraint. And as in the case of the chicken and the egg, it is difficult to tell which comes first—technology or goals.

In any event, it appears that certain kinds of technologies are associated with specific goals. The reasons behind this statement can be examined by using Perrow's technology typology. Figure 5–8 illustrates the technologies-goals relationships.

Craft units customize their output to meet customer needs and specifications. The goal emphasis in this type of unit therefore will be quality rather than quantity. Whether the task is to build specialized machinery, a customized Rolls Royce, or provide health and welfare services, the organization will make major efforts to identify and meet customer (client) needs.

Analyzability of Problems	Number of Exceptions: Few	Number of Exceptions: Many
Low	Quality (Craft) Customized	Quality (Nonroutine) Prototypes
High	Quantity (Routine) Standardized	Quality (Engineering) With quantity, cost trade-offs

Figure 5-8. Technology and goals

The purpose of a *nonroutine* unit is to develop new task technologies and products, or at least new applications of old technologies. Prototypes will be developed, and quality will be the primary emphasis. Once a new product or technology is identified and a prototype developed by the nonroutine unit, the new development will be transferred—probably to a unit that uses another type of technology. The clearest example of this sequence of events is the aerospace industry, in which a company will develop an aircraft prototype until it clearly meets the needs and specifications of the Department of Defense. Only after the prototype is accepted will the defense contractor begin actual production of the aircraft.

Organizational units operating in the *engineering* mode will generally attempt to trade off acceptable quality and cost. Whether the organization's output consists of designs for buildings, ships, or bridges, or comes from a hospital surgical ward, a major goal is to provide quality that is both professionally acceptable and acceptable to the customer at a reasonable cost.

It is only when there is an adequate demand and well-understood technologies to produce a product that an organization is able to mass produce it. Therefore the major goal emphasis of any *routine* unit is to produce a large quantity of output with an acceptable quality. Not only will product and output goals vary with the type of technology involved, but other goals will also. We saw in Chapters 1 and 3, for example, that to survive, organizations must simultaneously maintain adequate levels of productivity, efficiency, job satisfaction, and adaptability. We also saw that the more emphasis an organization places on either productivity and efficiency, or job satisfaction and adaptability, the less it will be able to place on the other two.

In other words, just as there are trade-offs between quantity and quality and cost, there are trade-offs among other goals as well. Organizations employing routine technologies will tend to emphasize productivity and efficiency, while organizations using more nonroutine technologies will emphasize adaptability as major goals.

Technology and Environment

The relationship between technology and environment can take one of two forms. First, they may be independent of each other; that is, there is no relationship between the two. This is the case when the environment is conceptualized to consist of culture, values, and the political and economic systems. Second, they may be almost the same thing. This is the case when the environment is defined as the rate of change in the technologies available to the organization. Both Lawrence and Lorsch (1969) and Burns and Stalker (1961) appear to define the environment this way. Our discussion follows this latter view, and is summarized in Figure 5–9.

Craft technologies tend to be stable, changing slowly. Similarly, there is a low, stable demand for the output of the unit, and the output is labor intensive. Consequently, we describe the environment surrounding the unit as stable.

The *nonroutine* organizational unit is designed to develop and implement new organizational technologies. This is usually in response to a rapidly changing and unstable environment.

The environment of the *engineering* unit tends to change more rapidly than in the craft unit but more slowly than in the nonroutine unit. Consequently the task of the engineering unit is to design, apply, and modify known procedures to problems that differ somewhat from one another.

Number of Exceptions

Analyzability of Problems		Few	Many
	Low	(Craft) Stable	(Nonroutine) Unstable
	High	(Routine) Very stable	(Engineering) Moderately stable

Figure 5-9. Technology and environment

Routine technologies are appropriate under very stable environmental conditions. Thus, proven search procedures can be applied to familiar and unchanging problems.

Technology and People

It is clear that different kinds of technologies use different kinds of personnel skills (Delbecq et al., 1969; Grimes and Klein, 1973). These general relationships can be sketched, as in Figure 5–10.

In a *craft*-technology unit, over a period of time the worker will gradually move from unskilled positions to positions requiring greater skills. The traditional apprenticeship model is appropriate, although it may not be formalized. While the basic work force may not have a high degree of formal education, it will nonetheless be highly skilled, because nonstandard outputs are produced.

Employees in *nonroutine*-technology units will be highly educated, trained, and experienced, since new technologies are being developed. They must be able to work with individuals having different backgrounds and also keep up-to-date in their own technical area.

Engineering technologies require a professional education and high expertise. People in these units tend to be task-oriented, and interpersonal skills are not as critical as they are in the nonroutine unit.

Technologies used in *routine*-technology units are capital intensive and call for the use of semiskilled labor inputs. Lengthy training, high skills, and education are all irrelevant to functioning successfully in such units, because the overall task is divided into minute parts that are parceled out to the work force. This machine-paced technology calls for dependent people and bureauciatic management techniques.

Analyzability of Problems		Number of Exceptions: Few	Number of Exceptions: Many
	Low	High skill (Craft) Low education	High expertise (Nonroutine) High education High interpersonal
	High	Low skill (Routine) Low education	High expertise (Engineering) Moderately high education Low interpersonal

Figure 5-10. Technology and people

TECHNOLOGY AND DESIGN VARIABLES

Technology influences the set of organization-design variables according to the basic model: independent variables influence mediating variables: these in turn influence outcome (dependent) variables. Indeed, many of the articles in this book implicitly and explicitly examine this particular relationship.

Technology and Work Design

Since much of this discussion has stated that technologies have a greater influence on the work units employing them than on the organization as a whole, it follows that the technology used by a work unit will have a major impact on the work design of that unit.

The influence of technology on work design can best be seen if we divide "work" into two elements: job scope and job depth. *Job scope* is defined as the number of different tasks or activities a worker undertakes. *Job depth* is defined as the amount of control the worker has over the timing, pace, and methods used to accomplish the task. Technology-work design relationships are summarized in Figure 5–11.

Craft technologies produce made-to-order outputs. This means that each unit is somewhat different from all other units, and that workers in this unit must be capable of adapting their skills to meet the demands of different customers (clients). Since production to customer specification is a major product goal, the worker in the craft unit tends to control the timing, pace, and methods he or she uses to accomplish the task (high depth) as well as perform a variety of activities (high scope).

Organizational units employing nonroutine technology develop and modify methods to accomplish tasks. Consequently, work teams (as opposed to individuals) possess both high

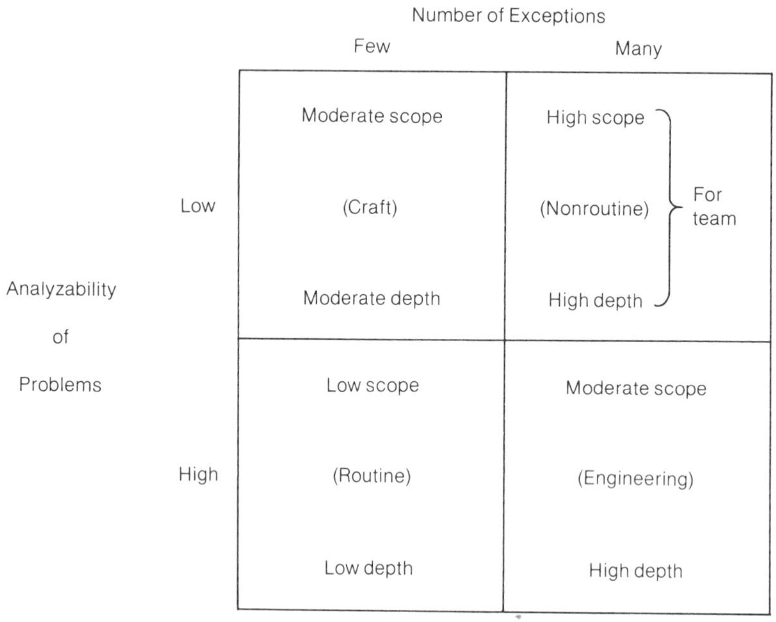

Analyzability of Problems	Number of Exceptions: Few	Number of Exceptions: Many
Low	Moderate scope (Craft) Moderate depth	High scope (Nonroutine) High depth } For team
High	Low scope (Routine) Low depth	Moderate scope (Engineering) High depth

Figure 5-11. Technology and work design

scope and high depth. Because the task has never been accomplished or undertaken by the organization before, a task group with multidisciplinary skills will be assembled to develop a workable prototype. It should be noted that the "prototype" can range from a new program to teach mental retardates or a space shuttle for NASA to an interdisciplinary degree at a university. The fact that teams, or committees, must be used to accomplish the task of the unit, however, places real constraints on any single individual's freedom of action.

Engineering units use professionally trained individuals to accomplish highly technical tasks. The result is that job scope is traded off for job depth. That is, jobs in an engineering unit tend to be low in scope but high in depth. People working in this unit are taught through professional education and training programs to apply a general search procedure to a set of problems that are generally amenable to solution by that search procedure. Consequently, an individual will tend to specialize in some subset of problems in which he or she develops a long-term interest.

Finally, employees in a routine unit perform small pieces of a larger task, with their work being controlled and paced by programmed activities. The result is a job that is both low in scope and depth.

Technology and Organization Control

The technologies an organization chooses to use affect designers' options in designing organizational control strategies. The way such effects occur are shown in Figure 5–12.

Since craft technology uses highly skilled employees to produce nonstandard outputs, it follows that the training program that produces the skilled employees will represent a major control measure. Employees in craft units will tend to be relatively long term and will have entered the "craft" through either a traditional apprenticeship program or through some

Analyzability of Problems	Number of Exceptions: Few	Number of Exceptions: Many
Low	Training (Craft) Schedules	Budgets (Nonroutine) Results
High	Process Schedules Budgets Cost (Routine)	Professional norms and standards (Engineering)

Figure 5-12. Technology and organization control

other type of formal program. Because most training programs socialize the beginner into the "craft," they will have a strong influence on the work norms and values the individual brings to the job. Since the worker has been "programmed" to accomplish the task by the training, it follows that the main task of supervision will be to organize and coordinate task-related activities, rather than to look over (supervise) the workers. Plans, schedules, and budgets will be major aids in the coordination and control process.

Nonroutine units are used to develop and modify technologies. It is difficult, therefore, to use such control mechanisms as supervision, rules, policies, procedures, plans, and schedules to control the unit's activities. Consequently, evaluation in this unit will be based on results. This is so for several reasons. First, it is very difficult to control the process of task accomplishment, because little is known about how to accomplish the task—and the task group must learn as it goes along. (The situation is analogous to NASA trying to put a man on the moon in 1960.) Second, schedules are honored more in the breach than the observance for the same reason: it is difficult to schedule an ill-understood process. Finally, budgets will represent a realistic constraint, if for no other reason than that the project stops when the money runs out.

Professional codes, norms, values, and socialization represent the dominant control mechanism in engineering units. Search procedures taught during the socialization process and positively sanctioned by the professional group will carry greater weight with the employee than will organizational procedures and policy (Scott, 1964). Managers will push for time deadlines to be met and act as consultants in the search process, rather than actually direct the process.

Routine units contain a full range of organization controls. Employee behaviors will be controlled (standardized) through the use of training programs. Rules, policies, and procedures (formalization) will reinforce the control. Because the nature of the task and cause/effect relationships are well understood, management will be able to break the task into small, specialized parts and train unskilled workers to do each of the small parts. Integration (putting together) all the small parts will be accomplished by a standardized process, such as an assembly line or series of standard operating procedures. Indeed, the end product is the result of the combination of the specialization of the unskilled workers and the standardized operating processes. Consequently, control will be embodied in the training program for the specialized workers, where standard operating procedures are taught and supervision designed to make sure that the standard operating procedures are followed.

Technology and Decision Processes

The previous discussion has strongly implied that organizational units using different technologies make decisions in different ways. This section will explicate the relationship between technology and decision making. We will use as our model that developed by Thompson and Tuden (1959).[1] A skeleton of the model is sketched in Figure 5–13.

Briefly, decision makers are not often faced with having to make "inspirational" decisions, since organizations cannot be brought into existence and exist over time without decision makers having a basic agreement concerning ultimate goals. "Judgment" can be exercised in two ways; first, on the basis of the experience of knowledgeable executives, and second, on the basis of groups or committees brought together to solve specific problems. Few organizations use "negotiated" techniques internally, since its frequent use would threaten

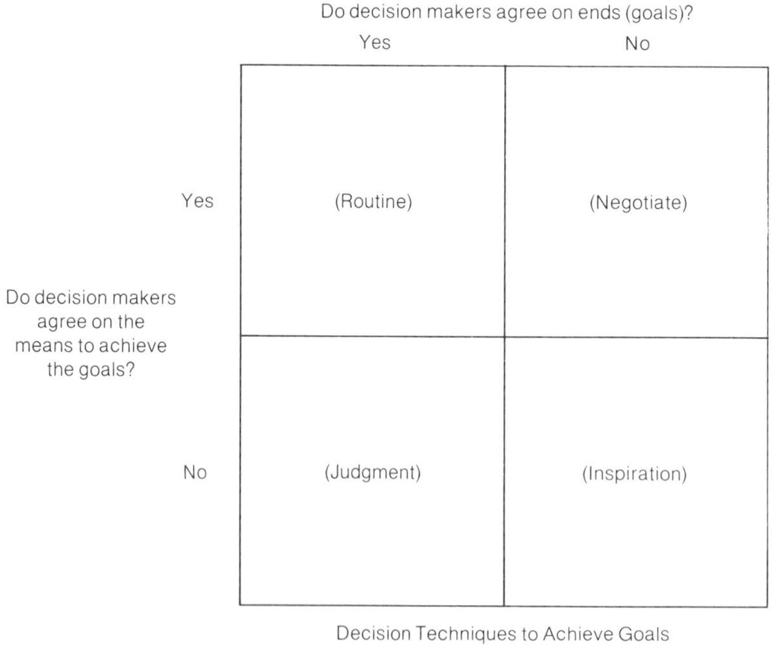

Do decision makers agree on ends (goals)?

Do decision makers agree on the means to achieve the goals?	Yes	No
Yes	(Routine)	(Negotiate)
No	(Judgment)	(Inspiration)

Decision Techniques to Achieve Goals

Figure 5-13. Thompson and Tuden (1959) decision model

1. This model is presented in full in Chapter 9, in the Thompson and Tuden article.

Analyzability of Problems		Number of Exceptions: Few	Number of Exceptions: Many
	Low	Experience, Peer judgment (Craft)	Creative group processes (Nonroutine)
	High	Rules, policy, procedure (Routine) Expert judgment	Individual judgment (Engineering)

Figure 5-14. Technology and decision processes

the status quo and the position of power groups. Therefore different forms of "routine" and "judgment" processes are most germane to the following discussion (summarized in Figure 5–14).

Most problems faced by workers in a craft unit will be of a routine nature, with a solution having been programmed into the worker by past experience. If a unique problem should arise, it would be solved through informal consultation among work unit members (the second type of judgment). This process is in marked contrast to the routine units, where staff specialists are utilized to resolve unique problems.

Nonroutine units handle problems for which there are no known solutions. Therefore their members exercise judgment in reaching their decisions. Decision making in nonroutine departments is characterized by the use of teams or committees using some form of creative decision process (problem solving, nominal groups, or synetics).[2]

Decisions in engineering units fall someplace between routine and nonroutine and have elements of each. In general, the search process is routine and stable. That is, regardless of the nature of the problem, the same general search process is followed. The problems, however, are likely to be highly variable. Finally, judgment is likely to be exercised by a technical expert (an individual) rather than a committee under these conditions.

As we might suspect, unique problems seldom occur when routine technologies are used. Standard solutions are developed to resolve recurring problems. Thus most problems are solved through the use of formalization. When exceptions occur, they are sent up the hierarchy to knowledgeable executive personnel for resolution (management by exception).

2. For a review of each of these types of processes, the reader is referred to the following: problem solving (Maier, 1963); nominal groups (Van de Ven and Delbecq, 1971); synetics (Gordon, 1961).

When the executives have difficulty with the problem, it is likely to be turned over to staff specialists. While problems do get resolved, this is a time-consuming process. It is for this reason that bureaucracies have the reputation of being filled with red tape. The best way to avoid bureaucratic red tape is never to present the bureaucracy with an "exception."

Technology and Organization Structure

Of all the relationships among technology and other variables that have been examined so far, the one between technology and structure has been researched and studied the most often. The heavy emphasis on this particular relationship has occurred because several research studies have indicated that an organization's effectiveness is strongly influenced by its structure (Burns and Stalker, 1961; Woodward, 1965; Lawrence and Lorsch, 1967c).

Definition of Organization Structure

There is broad general agreement that the concept *organization structure* refers to an enduring set of formal role relationships among the people associated with an organization. Unfortunately, there is not such broad agreement concerning how structure should be measured. According to Hall (1977), structure can be represented by the degrees of formalization, centralization, and specialization found in the organization. Hage and Aiken (1969) define structure in substantially the same way, but the Aston group (Pugh, Hickson, et al., 1969) includes other variables, such as standardization and organizational configuration (shape). It should be noted that Hage and Aiken use the term *complexity* to indicate both the degree of specialization and that of professionalization of the work force. Thus a work force that exhibits low complexity will have low specialization, be unskilled, and be unprofessional. A work force exhibiting high complexity will have high specialization and high professionalization. Finally, as was indicated in Table 5–1 (p. 158), Woodward defined structure in terms of spans of control at different levels of the organization (job counts) and configurations.

Technology and Structure

Several of the studies that have examined the relationship between technology and structure have concluded that organizations utilizing stable, routine technologies are most effective when they organize in what is termed a "mechanistic" manner. Conversely, organizations that utilize changing, dynamic technologies are most effective when they organize in an "organic" manner (cf. Burns and Stalker, 1961; Hage and Aiken, 1969). As has been noted, a mechanistic structure is highly centralized, highly formalized, has a low degree of complexity, and a high degree of division of labor. An organic structure is just the opposite, having a low degree of centralization and formalization and a high degree of complexity, with a lower degree of division of labor. These two structures are thought to exist on a continuum, running from mechanistic to organic and upon which all organizations can be placed. These ideas can be modeled as follows:

Routine technologies ⟶ Mechanistic structures ⟶ Effectiveness
Dynamic technologies ⟶ Organic structures ⟶ Effectiveness

The major problem with this rather simplistic approach to the design of organizations has already been pointed out: most organizations operate several different kinds of technologies.

TABLE 5-2 TECHNOLOGY AND ORGANIZATION STRUCTURE

Structure	Craft	Nonroutine	Engineer	Routine
Complexity				
Expertise	Mod.	High	Mod.	Low
Professionalization	Low	High	High	Low
Formalization	Mod.	Low	Mod.	High
Org. centralization	High	Mod.	High	High
Job centralization	Low	Low	Low	High

This means that organizational units operating different technologies should be designed according to the specific technology being used. However, there is a more subtle problem concerning the simple models presented above—a problem that revolves around the issue of centralization.

There are two kinds of decisions that can be centralized or decentralized: those that affect the organization as a whole, and those that are specific to a particular job. These decisions may both be centralized, one or the other may be centralized, or both may be decentralized. The degree of centralization found in any organization depends on the degree to which these two types of decisions are centralized.

Table 5–2 summarizes this discussion and identifies the combination of structural variables that should be utilized with the different kinds of technology.

TECHNOLOGY AND DESIGN OUTCOMES

A point made earlier, in the discussion of goals, needs to be reemphasized at this point. Organizations do not pursue and attempt to maximize single goals. Rather they pursue multiple goals, which may conflict with one another and for which decision makers attempt to develop optimal trade-offs. The same statement should be made concerning the intended and unintended outcomes that result from the organization's design. This section will examine the effects of technology on two types of organizational outcomes: climate and effectiveness.

Technology and Organization Climate

Several points must be made before discussing the relationship between technology and organization climate. First, the term *organization climate* refers to "a set of attributes specific to a particular organization that may be induced from the way that organization deals with its members and its environment" (Campbell et al., 1970: 389).[3] While this definition is much broader than the one given earlier for organization structure, it is similar. Both definitions refer to lasting patterns of relationships among the members of the organization.

Campbell et al. (1970) suggest that climate consists of four factors: individual autonomy, the degree of structure imposed upon the position, reward orientation, and the degree of consideration, warmth, and support. Notice the similarity of these factors and several that have been introduced in other contexts. Individual autonomy and degree of structure are very similar to decentralization and formalization, respectively. Reward orientation includes the general idea of job satisfaction, whereas the consideration-warmth-support factor is very

3. The article by Campbell et al. can be found in Chapter 11 of this book.

reminiscent of the Ohio State leadership dimension of consideration (Stogdill and Coons, 1957). So keeping in mind that "climate" may well be another way of viewing several other constructs, let us look at the relationship among the four types of technology and the four climate factors.

It has been mentioned previously that tasks in a craft unit are moderately high in both scope and depth. Consequently jobs in this unit should have moderate individual autonomy and a moderately low degree of structure. Workers in this unit are likely to be paid by the hour and experience relatively equal pressure from management for both quantity and quality. The job itself is rewarding, as indicated by the relatively high job depth, so job satisfaction should be high. Friendly relationships can be expected to develop both among workers and between workers and supervision, so consideration, warmth, and support should be high (Fullan, 1970).

The nonroutine unit is unusual in terms of individual autonomy, because teams—not individuals—accomplish the task. The result is that although work teams have high autonomy, individuals are highly constrained by the team. Rewards accrue to successful teams more than to individuals. That is, success and failure are shared. Thus successful teams will have high job satisfaction, whereas unsuccessful ones will experience frustration. The team will experience low structure, but the individual will experience more, because the team will impose its own constraints. Successful teams should experience considerably larger amounts of consideration, warmth, and support internally than unsuccessful teams (Blake and Mouton, 1964).

Individuals working in engineering units should experience considerable autonomy in carrying out their tasks because of the pooled interdependence between them. Constraints (structure) will be imposed through general agreement about how to carry out the search process and through organizational control over what problems are accepted to go through the search process. Job satisfaction is high since job depth is high. And friendly relationships can be expected to develop as in the craft unit, although the psychological aspects of the relationships may differ considerably. Therefore consideration, warmth, and support should be high.

The routine unit is very different from those just described. Individuals have little autonomy, because their jobs are controlled by mechanization. This, of course, will be associated with boredom and low job satisfaction for some people and be satisfactory for others.[4] Jobs will be highly structured in order to make them as predictable as possible. Finally, consideration, warmth, and support will be low, because the layout of the assembly line and/or the press for production will allow little opportunity for comradeship on the job.

Technology and Effectiveness

Organizational effectiveness means different things to different people. Price, quality, delivery, and service are important to the customer. The manager emphasizes many of these same items, but is also interested in the internal operation of the organization—job satisfaction, productivity, and so forth. And the IRS is interested in the prompt payment of taxes. To complicate the measurement of effectiveness further, no single set of effectiveness criteria is relevant to all organizations.

4. See Chapter 6 for further discussion of this issue.

As pointed out in Chapter 12, any effort to measure organizational effectiveness must include those outcomes relevant to the organization being studied. These difficulties notwithstanding, organizations must maintain minimum levels of productivity, efficiency, job satisfaction, and adaptability in order to survive over time (Hage, 1965). Thus, effective organizations are those that develop workable trade-offs among productivity, efficiency, job satisfaction, and adaptability. The specific trade-offs developed by organizations using different technologies are as follows.

Unit and small batch production is relatively expensive, demanding both lead time for planning, scheduling, and machine set-up time and a highly skilled labor force. This means that a craft unit will exhibit characteristics of relatively low productivity and high costs (compared with mass-production units) and will be much more adaptable than a mass-production unit. Job satisfaction will be relatively high because of the high job scope and depth.

The nonroutine-technology unit is designed to be adaptable. Its drawbacks are that it is very expensive to have to undertake any task with the use of teams, particularly when each task is unique. Job satisfaction will again be high because of the high scope and depth of the task.

The engineering organization is a design unit, and the professionals working in it generally have pooled interdependence between them. Design work is relatively expensive, because it is labor intensive and because of the search process that must be carried out for each new problem. The work itself is satisfying because of its depth, and the engineering unit is as productive and adaptable as the craft unit.

The major use of mass-production techniques is to produce as many product-units as possible with low unit costs. But the routine-technology organization does this by trading off job satisfaction and adaptability. Job satisfaction is low, relative to the other units, due to the low scope and depth of the individual tasks. Adaptability is low because of the capital intensity of the production process.

SUMMARY AND CONCLUSION

What do we think we know about technology? We began this chapter by discussing several definitions of technology. From there, we summarized typologies of technology that were developed by Perrow (1971), Thompson (1967), and Woodward (1965). It was pointed out that none of the typologies works too well when applied to entire organizations. They are all much more effective, however, when used to analyze organization subunits such as departments or divisions. But when the organization is analyzed using the technology of subunits as the primary tool of analysis, a problem concerning the coordination (integration) of the various subunits occurs. Appropriate coordination mechanisms for subunits having *pooled, sequential,* and *reciprocal* interdependence were then explored. The remainder of this chapter examined the relationships among technology, as developed by Perrow, and the several constraint, design, and outcome variables that are presented in the book. The conclusions reached in these discussions are summarized in Table 5–3

As with any summary effort, Table 5–3 is misleading, because it makes the issues surrounding organization design look fairly simple and straightforward. In reality, of course, they are not. No two organizations or organizational units are alike. Organizations do not

TABLE 5-3 SUMMARY OF THE RELATIONSHIPS AMONG TECHNOLOGY AND OTHER DESIGN VARIABLES

	Craft	Nonroutine	Engineering	Routine
Other Variables				
Goals	Quality	Quality	Quality	Quantity
Environment	Stable	Unstable	Mod. stable	Very stable
People	Skilled	Professional	Professional	Unskilled
Task scope	Mod.	High (team)	Mod.	Low
Design depth	Mod.	High (team)	High	Low
Control	Training, schedules	Budgets, results	Professional norms	Process
Decision strategy	Tradition, judgment	Creative group judgment	Individ. judgment	Routine
Structure				
Complexity	Mod.	High	High	Low
Formalization	Mod.	Low	Mod.	High
Org. central.	High	Mod.	Mod.	High
Job central.	Low	Low	Low	High
Outcomes				
Productivity	Low	Low	Mod.	High
Efficiency	Low	Low	Mod.	High
Job satisf.	High	High	High	Lower
Adaptability	Mod.	High	Mod.	Low
Climate				
Autonomy	Mod.	Team high	High	Low
Structure	Mod.	Team low	Mod.	High
Reward	Mod.	Team high	Mod.	Low
Consideration	Mod.	High	Mod.	Low

use technologies that fit neatly into Perrow's, or any other, typology. The answer to the question of how much centralization, formalization, and complexity are needed to accomplish the organizational task is a continuous tightrope walk of this much formalization, that much complexity, and so forth. Organization design is an art as much as a science.

One of the factors that increases the artlike character of design is the people that make up the organization's membership. Their needs, attitudes, motivation, structures, commitment, personalities, values—their differences and similarities on a wide variety of such characteristics—constrain designers' options. It is to this constraint that we now turn.

Questions for Review

1. Most definitions of technology have several elements in common. What are they?
2. What are the main differences among Thompson's three divisions of technology? Give an illustration of each.
3. Thompson makes five propositions in his article. What are they?
4. What are some examples of rationing?
5. Perrow distinguishes certain types of search processes. Describe these briefly and give examples of each.
6. In his analysis, Perrow specifies functional or task areas within management in organizations. What are they, and what types of areas do they involve?
7. What are the bases of non-task-related interaction for each of the four cells in Perrow's analysis?

8. Thompson discusses different types of interdependence. What are they, and what distinguishes each from the other? What are some examples of each?
9. Certain kinds of technologies are associated with specific goals. Describe two of these technologies and their associated goals.
10. How does organizational control vary among the four technologies: craft, nonroutine, engineering, and routine?

Questions for Discussion

1. Of the several noted in the chapter, which definition of technology do you find most appropriate and most illuminating to your own understanding? Why? If you were to define *technology* yourself, what would you include in your definition?
2. How would you present Perrow's typology of technology to the following audiences:
   a. a group of farm laborers
   b. a conference on business communication
   c. a class of upper-level undergraduate students
   d. a gathering of politicians of varying persuasions?
3. Do you find Thompson's and Perrow's typologies and perspectives to be complementary or in opposition? Are they both complementary and oppositional in different areas? Identify the areas of compatibility and incompatibility.
4. Perrow implicitly assumes that organizations designed congruently with their technologies will be more successful than those not so designed. Do you find validation for this assumption in his article or elsewhere in the text? Why might he suggest such a causal relationship?
5. Has your understanding of and attitude toward technology changed since reading this chapter? How?
6. Perrow contends that technology is a better basis for comparing organizations than other schemes. Do you agree with this contention? Explain your position, specifying why you agree or disagree.
7. Compare and contrast the teaching technology of a small, private vocational school with that of a state university offering professional programs. Using Table 5-3, draw a profile of the relationship between each type of school and its particular design variables.
8. Perrow says that his perspective ignores the role of the cultural and social environment in providing technologies. If these were to be taken into account, what, if anything, do you think would change in Perrow's typology?
9. Organizations are perceived by Perrow as "systems for getting work done, for applying techniques to the problem of altering raw materials." Do you need to accept this premise in order to find Perrow's theory valid? Is is possible to disagree with this premise and still find validity in his theory? Why is this premise needed for Perrow's technology typology?
10. Do you agree with the view that organization design is an art as much as it is a science? Do the articles by Thompson and Perrow influence your viewpoint? If it is an art, where does technology fit in? If it is a science, where does technology fit in with the cultural variable?

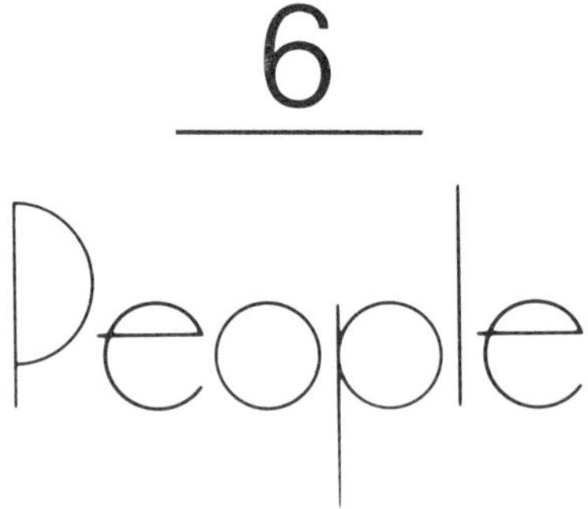

6 People

INTRODUCTORY REMARKS

We have seen that the design of organizations is constrained by environmental and technological circumstances. The intent of this chapter is to point out that organization design must also account for an important internal factor: the membership. *People*—their values, attitudes, beliefs, commitment, behaviors—form an important component of organizational life. Similarly, people's characteristics affect organization designers' options.

In some respects, all people are alike. They are motivated. Their behavior is directed toward satisfaction of personal needs and goals. And yet, people also come to organizations with almost infinite differences. They come with widely varying family, educational, and

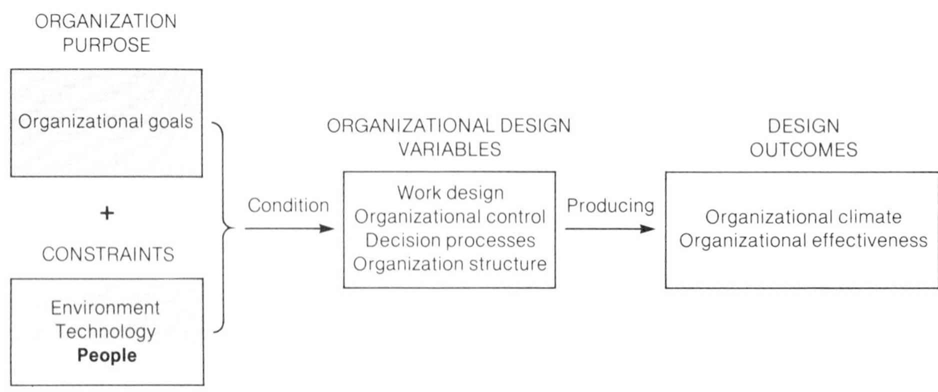

experience backgrounds, exposure to differing previous and current environments, different psychological and biochemical make-ups, different behavioral repertoires, and different perceptual styles (Hamner and Organ, 1978). Organizations often try to limit these natural variations somewhat so that they do not reflect widely differing individual behaviors. Still, individual differences do remain.

The problem of designing organizations, given the widely varying nature of the people in them, becomes a problem of integration—that is, integrating a group of different people so that they can collectively contribute to the accomplishment of organizational objectives. In this chapter we will examine the "people" aspect of design in five stages. First we focus our attention on some particular individual differences. (This focus is the theme of these somewhat lengthy introductory remarks.) Next we elaborate on such differences by presenting three articles, each of which focuses on a different facet of the "people" factor. Third, in the concluding statement we discuss the organizational design implications of people's characteristics. Fourth, this chapter looks at the relationship of these implications to the design outcomes of organizational climate and effectiveness. And lastly, we will try to summarize what we know about the influence of the human factor on the design of organizations.

INDIVIDUAL DIFFERENCES

Much has been written about the relationships among different characteristics of people and work organizations. Here are a few of the most important ones:

1. Biographical variables
2. Work-related values, including sources of satisfaction, dissatisfaction, motivation
3. Life and career stages
4. Organizational commitment
5. Psychological and personality variables

These particular dimensions have been chosen for several reasons. First, they account for a considerable amount of variation in people's behavior. Second, they have immediate relevance to how people behave in organizations. And third, they are currently attracting attention from researchers and teachers in the fields of organization theory and management.

As this discussion develops, keep in mind two factors related to these variables: their average level and their dispersion (Porter, Lawler, and Hackman, 1975). If an organization has employees with a high average level of one of these variables, e.g., strong organizational commitment, then its structural responses should be very different from those that are appropriate when employees have a low level of the variable. Also important is a variable's dispersion:

> Two different organizations may have work forces that average the same degree of experience, abilities, skills, etc., but one of them may have individuals high in these qualities widely scattered throughout the organization while the other may have them concentrated in one unit or section. . . . For both organizations to adopt the same kind of structurally operational features of design would appear to be inappropriate. [Porter, Lawler, Hackman, 1975: 243]

Biographical Variables

Over the last 50 years, attention has focused on numerous demographic characteristics of individuals in organizations. Some of these—age, sex, and race, for example—have been found to be less related to individual behaviors in organizations than the many stereotypes have led us to believe. This is not to say these characteristics have no importance. Because of varying cultural backgrounds and values, age, sex, and race are often related to varying work attitudes and behaviors. But as a basis for most organizational decisions, they are illegal and, objectively, unwise.[1]

The level of skill, abilities, and education of employees is also important. The abilities and educations of an organization's work force need to be adequate for the tasks and technology of that organization. But problems may be created if the employees' abilities and educations are not being fully utilized.

Work Values and Motivation

It is probably trite, yet nonetheless important, to state that employee motivation is a complex subject. As Nadler and Lawler suggest in this chapter's second article:

1. Different environments tend to produce different behavior in similar people, just as dissimilar people tend to behave differently in similar environments.
2. People make conscious decisions about both their willingness to belong to and stay with an organization and their level of effort to direct toward the performance of their jobs.
3. People differ both on the kinds of outcomes they desire from the organizations to which they belong, as well as in terms of the strengths of their needs for different kinds of outcomes.
4. People base their decisions in organizations on their expectations, or their perceptions, of the degree to which given behaviors on their parts will lead to desired outcomes.

This is to say that employees' levels of motivation are largely dependent on the situation they are in and how well that situation fits and satisfies their needs.

Despite various situational differences, however, we can still talk about sources of motivation. In general, we may regard the following as major outcomes—and therefore reasons for behaving—that people seek from their work organizations (Katz, 1964):

1. *Rule compliance or conformity to system norms.* Much behavior in organizations is for the purpose of complying with the rules and norms of those organizations.

2. *Instrumental system rewards.* This refers to rewards such as pension plans or insurance benefits that accrue to everyone for membership in the system.

3. *Instrumental rewards geared to individual effort or performance.* This refers to incentive pay plans, bonus systems, and commission compensation procedures that are tied directly to individual employees' levels of work performance.

4. *Intrinsic satisfaction accruing from specific role performance.* Many employees derive

1. This will be discussed more fully in the concluding statement, when we look at selection of personnel as a design alternative.

feelings of satisfaction, self-esteem, and psychological growth and development from the performance of their jobs.

5. *Internalized values of the individual.* Many individuals—priests and policemen, for example—work for particular organizations because their personal values are consonant with those of their employers. Even when this is not the case, organizations will typically try to "socialize" their employees into internalizing the organizations' values and purposes.

6. *Primary group-based social satisfactions.* The human relations period of management training and organizational focus occurred because of the efficacy of this source of motivation for organizational members. And some of what is now labeled *organizational development* derives from an appreciation of employees' needs for such social satisfactions.

Sources of Motivation: What Is Important?

When we consider this vast array of motivation sources, we must ask the following question: Are certain sources more relevant for today's employees than others? Several years ago Argyris (1964) cited a number of studies to show that workers at the lower end of the organizational ladder suffer from poorer mental health, lower job satisfaction, lower levels of self-esteem, feelings of insecurity, and so forth. Writers about today's college-graduate employees indicate a view that graduates want and expect jobs high in challenge, growth opportunities, and so forth (see Hall, 1971; Ondrack, 1973; Schein, 1964). These kinds of values also seem to be spreading to noncollege youth and women and, slowly, to other sectors of the population (Yankelovich, 1974b).

As Leavitt, Dill, and Eyring (1973) put it, all persons are motivated, even if they are often more motivated to escape work than to do it. Their question is: "How can we motivate people to work harder at jobs that are essentially demotivating?" The job-enrichment literature and efforts are based on just such a question.[2]

Differences in Need Strengths

Large differences in strengths of needs and thus in outcomes desired from work and from one person to another are clearly evident in organizations (Porter, Lawler, and Hackman, 1975). These differences at least partially explain why individuals see different things when they perceive the same jobs and why they perform their jobs differently. A small set of needs have been found to be especially relevant to behavior and motivation in work settings. Need for achievement, need for affiliation, and need for power appear to be particularly important.

Need for Achievement. A strong achievement need (nAch) reflects a strong goal orientation—a desire for challenge and personal accomplishment (McClelland, 1961; Atkinson, 1964). Persons with high nAch are attracted to tasks that challenge their skills and abilities. They will avoid both certain successes and high-risk, potential failures. They prefer to perform tasks whose outcomes depend on their own efforts. And they need quick accurate feedback about how they are doing. Persons with high nAch obviously respond with high motivation in situations of challenge, difficult goals, quick feedback, and contingent rewards.

2. See Chapter 7 for an elaboration of such efforts.

Need for Affiliation. People with a strong need for affiliation (nAff) need to establish and maintain pleasant relationships with others. They need to be liked, to "get along." Obviously group activities are of paramount importance to the employee with high nAff. Even managers need some of it if they are to place importance on supportive organizational climate and facilitative group structures.

Need for Power. This need has to do with the desire to exert control over others. McClelland (1961) has demonstrated the importance of this particular need for managers. Goal setting, decision making, and influencing subordinates are managerial behaviors that require a need for power.

Values Enter the Picture

As is suggested in this chapter's first article, employees also bring values into the organizational situation. These values necessarily affect virtually every aspect of the organization. So it becomes important to look critically at assumptions about the nature of today's employees.

A number of people have questioned whether or not *all* employees are really motivated by enriched, growth-oriented jobs, and by participative, autonomous work environments. Some people may be turned on by job autonomy and challenge and some may not be. For instance, some workers may have been nurtured in urban subcultures that have deeply conditioned them to see work as a simple exchange of time and minimal energy for fair pay and decent conditions. They do not expect to live at work, but rather to get their life's satisfaction away from the job (Lawrence, 1975). Some employees may have strong needs for achievement; others may have strong security needs; still others may have strong affiliation needs.

With regard to the organization, it is apparent that many organization-related values are changing (Yankelovich, 1974a; Viola, 1977). Although the precise details may vary from situation to situation, we can make a general statement: employees are becoming more self-oriented, more concerned with their own relevance and growth. Further, they are more willing to take steps to ensure opportunities for their own psychological successes.

So what should organization designers do? Should they simply throw up their hands and say that since some people want to be taken into account in personally satisfying ways and some do not, other criteria should be used? The answer is "no." The best evidence we have indicates that although some people may be shedding the work ethic, a major problem remains: there are still far too many demotivating jobs for those who need, want, and can handle more challenge and responsibility.[3]

Life and Career Stages

A concept that psychologists have found helpful for understanding changes in people's lives and values over time is the idea of life and career stages. These periods in people's lives occur fairly predictably and are often stressful and trying periods (Hall and Morgan, 1977; Van Maanen and Schein, 1977). Each stage is generally characterized by distinctive developmental needs, concerns, values, and activities, with some form of role transition between stages. That is, one must "master" the developmental tasks of one stage to be able to move on to the next. And as those stages of career change, so also do employees' needs and values.

3. See the review of these and related matters by Pierce and Dunham in Chapter 7.

All the life-stage models start with a similar stage of *Exploration, Identity, Getting into Adult World,* or *Preadulthood* and move through a number of difficult, maturing, often reidentifying, stages to a stage of *Decline, Integrity,* or *Late Adulthood* (Erikson, 1963; Levinson, 1978; Levinson et al., 1974; Super, 1957; Super and Bohn, 1970). Figure 6–1 summarizes and integrates a number of these models.

Other models have been developed and used in recent years either to explain career stages or to show stages of psychological development as they relate to employees' work lives. Again, the models move from levels of low self-reliance, low tolerance for ambiguity, low desire for autonomy, low acceptance of responsibility or goal-oriented behavior, to higher levels of maturity based on these variables. Individual employees differ in terms of the stage of life or career through which they are passing. And they are also likely to be experiencing and trying to cope with problems that vary with the nature of the particular stage through which they are passing.

"Career anchors" have also been used to explain the self-perceived talents, values, and motives that seem to organize and give stability to employees' career-oriented decisions (Schein, 1975; Van Maanen and Schein, 1977). These career anchors provide a key element in an individual's sense of identity. Anchors emerge gradually, as individuals discover what they are good at, what they value, and like to do. In other words, anchors emerge as persons build their career values upon their success experiences.

Following is a short summary of the more common career anchors:

1. *Managerial Competence.* This anchor is held by persons who value opportunities to manage. It includes interpersonal and analytical competencies and emotional stability.

2. *Technical/Functional Competence.* Individuals who hold this set of values prefer to exercise various technical competencies.

3. *Security.* This anchor includes the overriding desire to stabilize one's career situation, either in terms of staying with a particular organization or a particular profession.

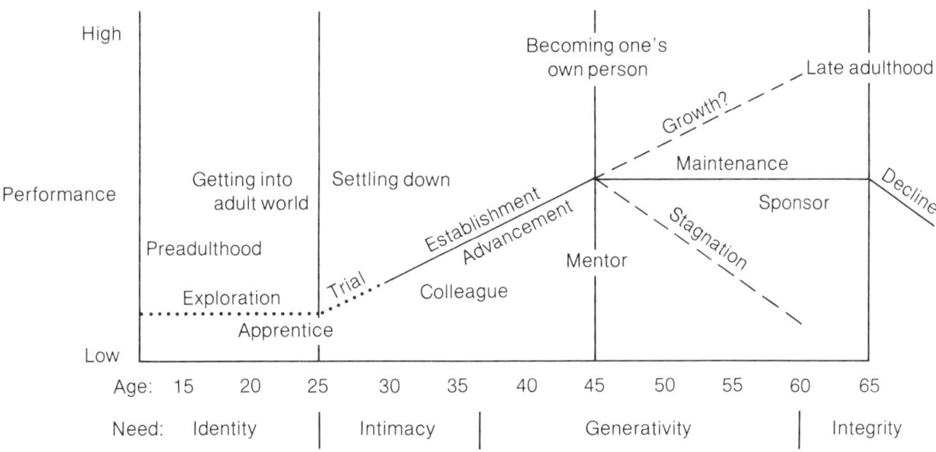

Figure 6-1. An integrative model of life and career stages

Source: Adapted from *Careers in Organizations*, by Douglas T. Hall, (p.57). Copyright © 1976 by Goodyear Publishing Co. Reprinted by permission.

4. *Creativity.* This anchor appears to overlap with a number of the others, including a need for autonomy, managerial competence, and a desire to exercise one's own talents. The overriding value here, though, is the desire to build or create something that the individual can call his or her own, an extension of him- or herself.

5. *Autonomy and Independence.* Persons who hold this career anchor appear to prefer most to be free of organizational constraints (autonomy is more important than the exercising of any type of competence).

The point of all this—the presence of these anchors, as well as the other life and career stages—is that organizations must concern themselves with differing employee career interests and values. In turn this implies the need for varying and flexible types of organizational responses. Thus employees at lower career stages need to be "treated" with more standardized, imposed procedures, while those at higher, more mature levels of psychological existence will perform more effectively with participative, delegative, individualized procedures (Myers and Myers, 1974). Put another way, managers need to alter their supervisory styles between autocratic and delegative, depending on the general maturity level of the subordinates (Hersey and Blanchard, 1977).

Organizational Commitment

The article by Steers in this chapter demonstrates the importance of commitment as a work-oriented value. Commitment involves the following components (Buchanan, 1975):

1. Involvement with one's tasks
2. Identification with the organization's mission (which implies the integration of individual and organizational goals)
3. Loyalty and affection for one's organization (which appears to be a consequence of the other two)

Organization commitment is related to personal and organizational characteristics and experiences (D. Hall, 1976a). This is illustrated in Figure 6–2. As the figure indicates, commitment is a direct result of planning and using one's job as the source of psychological success. Goal setting, frequent performance reviews and feedback, and counseling and support from one's boss are all important to the cycle of events that build commitment. Buchanan (1975) further shows that the following situations have a significant impact on the development of organizational commitment:

1. Feelings of personal importance or indispensability
2. Cohesive and friendly work-group experiences
3. Realization of one's experiences
4. The presence of an organizational norm that values commitment
5. The presence of job challenge in one's first year on the job

In his article, Steers demonstrates the special importance of identification with the task, feedback, interaction, and the level of work to the level of commitment. He suggests that there may be a component to commitment that is more "active" and thus has a stronger influence on individual performance levels than he found. Of course, it may be the achievement of one's job goals that leads to feeling of psychological success and therefore

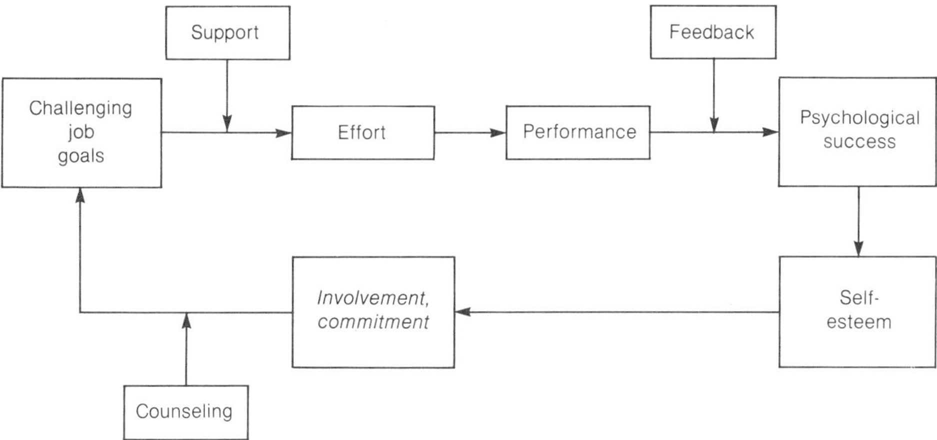

Figure 6-2. Commitment in the career-growth cycle

Source: Adapted from "A Theoretical Model of Career Sub-identity," by Douglas T. Hall, in *Organizational Behavior and Human Performance*, Vol. 6, 1971.

involvement—not the other way around. Nevertheless, there are a number of actions that organizations can take that encourage the development of organizational commitment.

There are many alternative organization designs that deal in small and large ways with the nature of the values and motivation of today's employee. These are detailed in the concluding statement.

Psychological and Personality Variables

As we know, and as the discussion of the nature of the "worker" presented earlier (Chapter 1) demonstrated, behavior in organizations is simply too complex and diverse to assume that all people are motivated solely by economic, social, or self-actualization needs. And yet there is a managerial need to be able to analyze, understand, and predict employee behavior in some realistic way—and still allow for important individual and situational differences.

We have already discussed a number of individual-difference characteristics (biographical variables, different work values, motivation, life and career stages, and commitment). However, the latitude of decision making, flexibility of procedures, or directness of supervision that employees need or want is not based solely on their work values or career stages. Such needs or wants also depend on how people differ in various personality characteristics.

Specifically, personality traits influence the degree to which different types of organization will affect the employee. Let us briefly consider five such characteristics: emotionality, extroversion-introversion, locus of control, authoritarianism, and activation.

Emotionality

A number of researchers have focused on the personality dimension of emotionality (for a review of the literature, see Hamner and Organ, 1978). Emotionality appears to underlie such factors as emotional instability; changeability in mood; sensitivity to stress; tendencies toward guilt, worry, anxiety, and lower self-esteem; feelings of fatigue and concern about physical health; and experience of tension.

Generally, a moderate—but not excessive—amount of emotional arousal has been found to relate to optimal performance (see Figure 6–3). As Hamner and Organ (1978: 169) describe it:

> Persons who score higher on neuroticism will require less externally induced motivation to reach the level of emotional arousal optimal for performance. Along the same line of reasoning, they can withstand less intense external motivational pressure before their performance deteriorates. Persons low in neuroticism may require considerable amounts of external pressure before they "get going" and may not reach their best performance until they are really "under the gun." The difference between the two types is usually most evident when the motivational pressures are of the aversive kind—such as threat or punishment.

Activation

Related to emotionalism is the concept of activation. Activation refers to the general degree of excitation of the brain from external stimulation (Hamner and Organ, 1978; Scott, 1966). Too much or too little activation has dysfunctional relationships to employees' levels of performance (again, refer to Figure 6–3). Maximum performance appears to occur at moderate levels of external arousal. As discussed earlier, employees' internal needs, motivations, and values are important to their levels of performance and other organizationally relevant behaviors. Important also is the degree of external stimulation.

Extroversion-Introversion

Extroversion relates to individual differences in terms of the need for external sensory stimulation (Eysenck, 1967, 1973). Generally, introverts need less stimulation. Extroverts have a greater need for such stimulation.

Extroversion-introversion also relates to behavior at work. On repetitive tasks or in an environment with low levels of stimulation, an introvert will perform better and be more satisfied with the situation. The extrovert gets along better when there is greater variety,

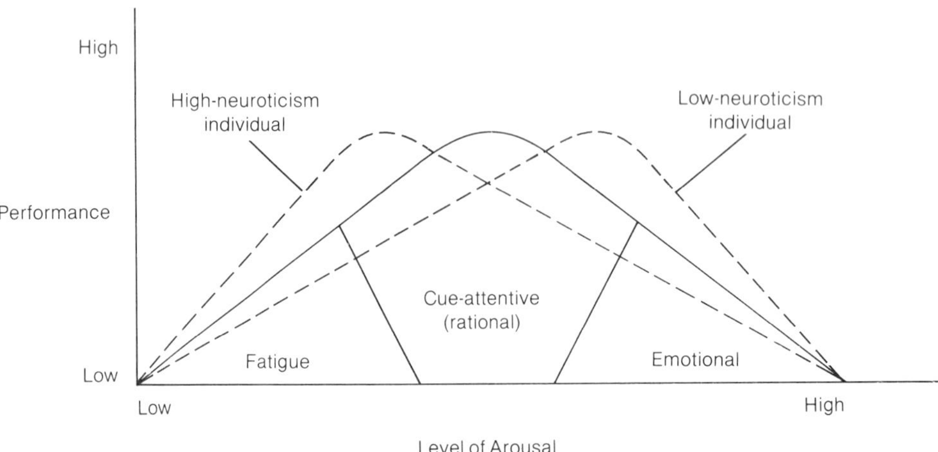

Figure 6-3. Relationship between activation, neuroticism, and employee performance

Source: Adapted from W. Clay Hamner and Dennis W. Organ, *Organizational Behavior: An Applied Psychological Approach* (Dallas, Texas: Business Publications, Inc. © 1978), pp. 170, 323.

distraction, shifts in forces, and generally heavier amounts of environmental sensation (Hamner and Organ, 1978). Research findings have also shown that introverts may be more *conditionable* than extroverts—a critical issue for organizations as they try to shape employee behavior (Cooper and Payne, 1967; Organ, 1975).

Locus of Control

Rotter (1966, 1971a, 1971b) has isolated a belief system—locus of control—which seems to resist change in the short run and also to help predict differences in employee behavior. Locus of control refers to the degree to which a person believes that personal actions can influence outcomes in life. *Internals* believe that most of what happens to them is under their own control. *Externals* believe more in the role of luck, chance, or other influences outside themselves to explain what happens to them. This set of individual differences refers to people's beliefs about whether the outcomes they receive or experience are contingent on their own behavior. That is, these beliefs influence to whom the individual attributes his or her own and others' successes and failures (Bem, 1972).

Internals seem to have better control over their own behavior (probably because they think it is instrumental in determining what happens to them). They are more likely to be political and social activists, successful persuaders but relatively unpersuadable, active searchers for information that will help them achieve their objectives, and likely to be attracted to situations that offer chances for achievement. Externals tend to be on the other end of continuums stretching from these characteristics. Externals also tend to be more easily aroused and more anxious. Obviously, the presence of this personality variable relates to how employees respond to their organizational and task experiences, passively accepting their circumstances or activitely taking personal responsibility for them.

Young people, in particular, appear to be increasing their perceptions of external control and decreasing the degree to which they trust other people (Rotter, 1971a and 1971b; Wrightsman and Baker, 1969). And yet they seem also to be focusing in on their own growth and development in very pragmatic ways—concerned with achievement opportunities, prestige, power, and authority based on expertise, personal style, and participation (Slater, 1970; De Salvia and Gemmill, 1971; Ondrack, 1973).

Authoritarianism

Adorno et al. (1950), Eysenck (1954), and Rokeach (1960) have described the authoritarian person as one who dislikes and fears other people—who feels the world is a dangerous place. The only way to survive in the cruel world is to follow the generally accepted moral values and to unquestioningly obey all persons in positions of power and authority. This person feels that leaders are to be obeyed because they are meant to be in their positions and because of their superior characteristics, such as rationality, practicality, and toughness.

The authoritarian person is the ideal subordinate for the leader who believes that leaders should lead and followers should follow (Rogers, 1975). Authoritarians do not rebel, question the validity of orders, or think for themselves. But Ondrack (1971) and Yankelovich (1974a) have demonstrated that today's young person is less authoritarian than his or her parents or even older brothers and sisters. This is having a strong impact on their work behavior. Because they are less likely to blindly accept orders and rules, new managerial and organizational processes are called for.

Summary of Individual Differences

Employees vary considerably in terms of the many characteristics discussed here. Biographical characteristics, values, motivation needs and drives, career stages, organizational commitment, and psychological and personality variables—all of these make the job of the manager or organizational designer difficult, but not impossible. If a manager knows what his or her employees expect or value, what goals they have, and what rewards they find reinforcing, then that manager has the information necessary to channel the energies of employees in organizationally effective directions.

The Readings

We present, as the first article in this chapter, a discussion by the author and Boris W. Becker on values ("Values and the Organization: Suggestions for Research"). The focus is on ways in which people's values affect—and are affected by—various organizational properties and processes.

In the next article, "Motivation: A Diagnostic Approach," David A. Nadler and Edward E. Lawler III describe a modern approach to examining people and their behavior in organizations. The approach is based on the following assumptions:

1. Behavior is determined by a combination of forces in the individual and forces in the environment.
2. People make decisions about their own behavior in organizations.
3. Different people have different types of needs, desires, and goals.
4. People make decisions among alternative plans of behavior based on their perceptions of the degree to which a given behavior will lead to desired outcomes.

The authors take these assumptions and describe human motivation as being a function of expectations; specifically, expectations about effort required, performance required, and outcomes received. They conclude the discussion by pointing out various actions that managers can take to design organizations that enhance motivation. In short, Nadler and Lawler suggest, organizations need to try to match the rewards their members want to the behaviors the organizations require. In this way, both individual and organizational needs can be met.

A human quality more specific than motivation is commitment. In this chapter's final article, "Antecedents and Outcomes of Organizational Commitment," Richard M. Steers identifies some variables that seem to relate to people's organizational commitment—that is, to their identification with and involvement in their organizations. The author discusses the importance for commitment of such individual and organizational characteristics as enriched tasks, educated and achievement-oriented people, and supportive work groups.

Conclusion

In summary, this chapter is concerned with the impact that an organization's membership has on its design options. In particular, the chapter focuses on the following questions:

1. What characteristics do people bring with them into the organization?
2. What factors underlie human motivation in the organizational setting?
3. What organization-design responses are appropriate for various human characteristics?

VALUES AND THE ORGANIZATION: SUGGESTIONS FOR RESEARCH

PATRICK E. CONNOR
BORIS W. BECKER

Interest in the subject of human values has ranged from abstract contemplation by philosophers and political theorists to empirical scrutiny by quantitative psychologists. With only a few exceptions, however, investigators have not concerned themselves with values and the organization. Specifically, little attention has been paid to the interaction between properties of the organizational setting and values of the actors therein. Employee and managerial attitudes, including their relationship to structural characteristics of the organization (Porter and Lawler, 1965), have been related extensively in the literature. A thorough compendium of such studies is given by Scott and Cummings (1973). Employee and managerial *values*, however, particularly as they relate to organizational performance, have received only scant treatment.

The purpose of this paper is to outline a program of systematic research to fill this theoretical gap.[1] First, values are defined, and their distinction from, yet interrelationship to, attitudes and behavior is specified. Second, the nature of the problem in relating values to organizational properties is discussed. Third, a conceptual framework for viewing the formal organization and various processes within it is provided. Fourth, using this framework, the kinds of relationships among values and organizational characteristics that might reasonably be expected to obtain are specified.

VALUES, ATTITUDES, AND BEHAVIOR

There is a considerable variation in the attention accorded to the general concept of value by scholars in several fields of learning. Despite this variety, some theoretical consensus regarding a definitional posture appears to be developing. Scott (1956) and Kluckholn et al. (1962) define values as a conception of the desirable: "A value is a conception, explicit or implicit . . . of the desirable which influences the selection from available modes, means, and ends of action" (Kluckholn, 1962: 389). Building from this idea, Rokeach (1968: 124) defines values as "abstract ideals, positive or negative, not tied to any specific object or situation, representing a person's beliefs about modes of conduct and ideal terminal modes. . . ." Values thus are global beliefs that "transcendentally guide actions and judgments across specific objects and situations" (Rokeach, 1968: 160).

Attitudes, on the other hand, do focus on specific objects and specific situations. "An attitude is an orientation toward certain objects (including persons—others and oneself) or situations. . . . An attitude results from the application of a general value to concrete objects or situations" (Theodorson and Theodorson, 1969: 19). Indeed, one of the functions of attitudes, being object-specific, is to allow expression of more global underlying values (Katz and Stotland, 1959).

Behavior may be viewed as a manifestation of attitudes and values. In fact, attitudes have been defined by some in terms of the probability of the occurrence of a specified behavior in a specified situation (Campbell, 1950). As Newcomb notes, "such definitions [of attitude], while relatively devoid of conceptual content, serve to remind us that the ultimate referent of attitudes is behaviour" (Gould and Kolb, 1964: 141).

In brief, then, values may be thought of as global beliefs about desirable end-states underlying attitudinal and behavioral processes. Attitudes are seen to constitute cognitive and affective orientations toward specific

1. An earlier version of this paper was presented at the meetings of the Pacific Sociological Association, 1974.

From Patrick E. Connor and Boris W. Becker, "Values and the Organization: Suggestions for Research," *Academy of Management Journal*, vol. 18 (September 1975), pp. 550–61.

objects or situations. Behavior generally is viewed as a manifestation of values and attitudes. It is contended here that behavior in organizations is no exception; indeed, although he develops a conceptual scheme different from that presented here, Churchman has argued (1961) that the *ideal* setting for the study of human values is the complex organization.

STATEMENT OF THE PROBLEM

Although little attention has been paid specifically to the study of values and the organization, the sociological, psychological, and administrative theory literature does contain numerous studies of values as a general human property. Moreover, as noted above, some consensus is developing as to the theoretical conception of "value." There is no agreement, however, as to proper operational characteristics. Although there is a lengthy list of empirical studies in various fields that purport to use values as dependent or independent variables, literature search confirms that what Kluckholn et al. pointed out previously is no less true today, more than a decade later:

> Reading the voluminous, and often vague and diffuse, literature on the subject in the various fields of learning, one finds values considered as attitudes, motivations, objects, measurable quantities, substantive areas of behavior, affect-laden customs or traditions, and relationships such as those between individuals, groups, objects, events (Kluckholn, 1962: 390).

The operational ambivalence of much research is illustrated by a recent report (Locke, 1970). The investigator variously discusses values as being synonymous with emotional reactions, valuation (x is more valuable than y), goals, interests, needs, and outcomes. Even the early work of England (England, 1967) treated managerial values and preference for specified organizational goals as interchangeable quantities; however, England subsequently has focused his attention more narrowly, developing comprehensive profiles of managerial values (England, 1974). For Churchman too, values are the valuations placed by actors on possible outcomes of behavioral acts. Thus, values are seen as inferable from behavior, or predictive of behavior, when the individual is aware of all available alternatives, can freely choose any particular one, and knows the probabilities of outcomes occurring (Churchman, 1961).

Thus the problem facing the organization theorist is two-fold. First, there is a need for researchers to settle upon a commonly accepted operational definition of value. This is not a call for a standardized value-measuring instrument; the creation of such an ultimate instrument is probably not possible, or even desirable, given the variety of research questions and methodologies it would have to serve. Rather, it is a call for acceptance of the fact that values cannot fruitfully be operationalized as attitudes, or goals or objectives, or preferred outcomes. If they are to have any useful meaning apart from these concepts, values must be operationalized as parsimoniously as possible, as desirable end-states of existence underlying attitudes and behaviors. Thus, while such formulations as those by Churchman (1961) and Kluckholn et al. (1962) are equally appealing in their rigor and elegance, the approach advocated by the latter is the more helpful; values have importance beyond the formation and pursuit of goals—they are fundamental to, not identical with, these processes.

The second aspect of the value and organization problem is more pragmatic. A fair amount is known and more is being learned, at an accelerating rate, about relationships among various organizational properties—structural components, for example (Blau and Schoenherr, 1971; Hall, 1972). A fair amount also is known about such organizational processes as power, conflict, leadership, communication, and environment adaptation (Hall, 1972). By contrast, very little is known about the relationships among the various organizational properties and processes and the values of organizational actors.

VALUES AND THE ORGANIZATION

Of the many models of organization, the general systems approach appears to be preferable on a large number of counts. Most comprehensive treatments of organization either embrace the systems approach totally, or at least pay homage to it. See, for example,

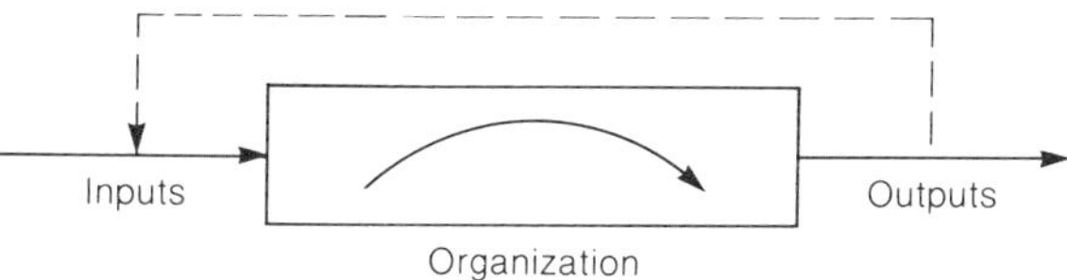

Figure 6-4. Systemic representation of the organization (a)

Hall (1972), Kast and Rosenzweig (1974), Katz and Kahn (1966). Even some critics of systems theory appear to be questioning their earlier views (Peery, 1973).

An Organizational Paradigm

Basically, the systems approach to organizations postulates that organizations acquire resources from the external environment, transform these input resources into output goods and services, and dispose of the outputs in such a way as to facilitate the continual acquisition of additional inputs. This is illustrated in Figure 6–4.

This conceptualization may be elaborated, as by James Thompson (1967), and may be illustrated in greater detail, as demonstrated in Figure 6–5.

Regardless of their precise form (the various feedback loops have been left out of Figure 6–5 for visual clarity), systems models share a conception of the organization as a resource processing entity operating under norms of rationality, which is a subsystem of larger subsystems. Probably the foremost proponent of the systems view for organizational analysis has been Talcott Parsons (1956).

For purposes of this discussion, the systems view has been reformulated, as shown in Figure 6–6, which is an expansion of an earlier formulation (Connor et al., 1973). The concept underlying this view is straightforward. The organization is viewed as a resource processing subsystem. The transformation of input resources into outputs occurs within the formal organizational framework (A). The nature of this transformation is constrained by the contextual components, as well as by various organizational processes (B). The

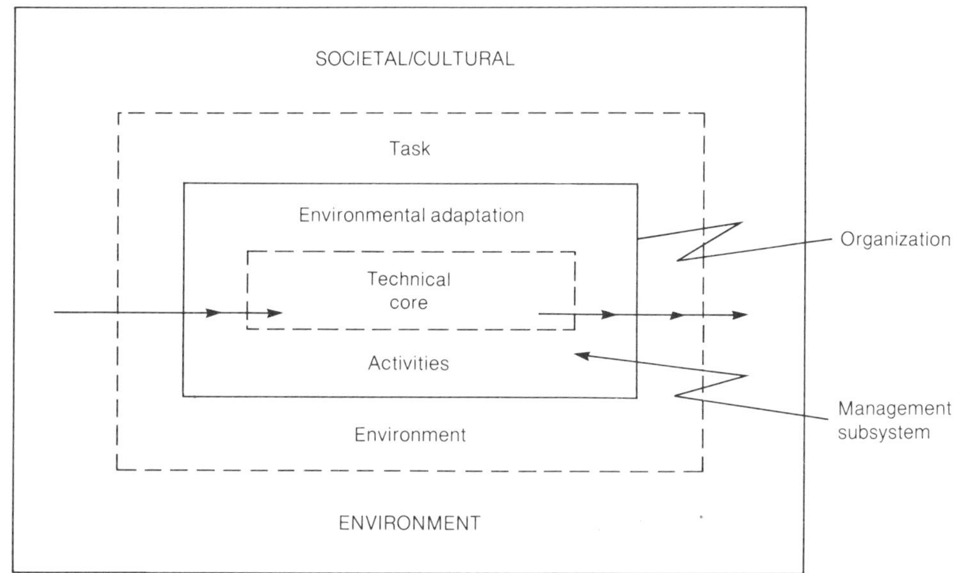

Figure 6-5. Systemic representation of the organization (b)

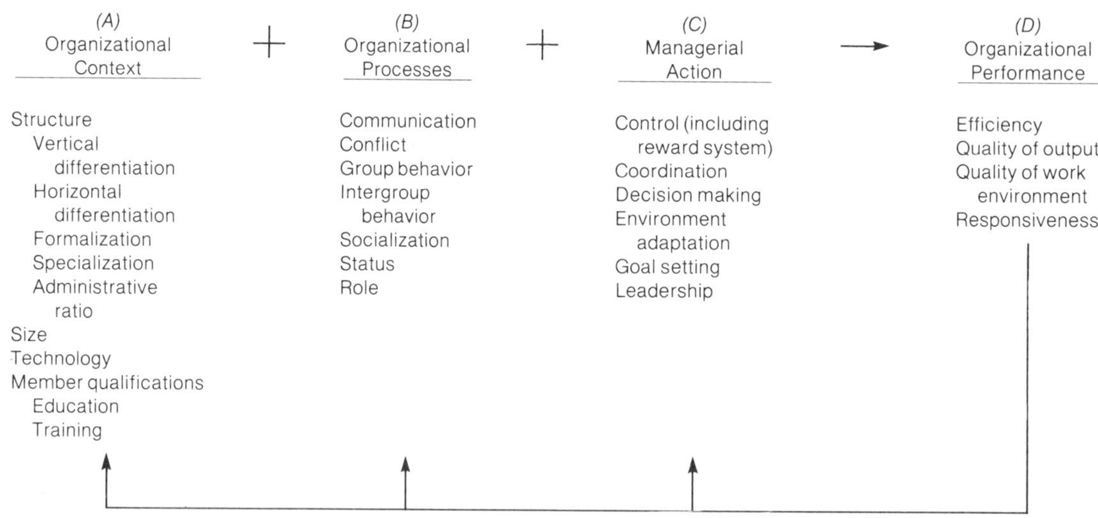

Figure 6-6. An organizational paradigm

transformation is then effected through managerial action (C), and is reflected in ultimate organizational performance (D). The reader is referred to Connor et al. (1973) for an extended description of the variables and processes identified in Figure 6–6.

Values and Organizational Variables

In the literature there have been occasional reports or discussion of values as they relate to the organization. Zald (1963), for example, attempted to determine whose values predict organizational performance. Sikula (1971) related respondents' values to their personal goals. DeSalvia and Gemill (1971) compared values held by students of business administration to those held by practicing managers. Hage and Dewar (1973) compared elite values and organizational structure as predictors of organizational innovation.

In addition to these studies, many investigators have concerned themselves with what Katz and Stotland (1959) call "instrumental" values, as they obtain in organizational settings. The investigations reported by Merton et al. (1957) and Becker et al. (1971) are classics. They demonstrated the effects of medical school socialization on the student. Similar studies have been conducted on other occupational groups in a variety of organizational settings: teachers in public schools (Gross et al., 1958); counselors in juvenile correctional institutions (Perrow, 1966); officers in military schools (Palen, 1972); convicts in prisons (Hefferman, 1972; Thomas and Foster, 1973); patients in mental institutions (Goffman, 1961); scientists and other professionals in various organizations (Moore, 1970; Vollmer and Mills, 1966); and managers in business corporations (Dill et al., 1962).

As a result of such investigations, a great deal is becoming known about how, for example, socialization takes place in complex organizations. Still, little is known of the impact such a process has on the organization or its operations. In particular, it is not known how values of organizational actors interact with organizational properties in effecting socialization, or how such interaction affects other processes or managerial actions. Beyond this specific consideration of socialization, little is understood about the ways in which values affect, are affected by, and interact with a multitude of organizational properties, processes, and managerial actions.

A brief parenthetical observation is in order: Organizational-member values, or value orientations, may be more accurately characterized by the concept "value profile." Probably the best methodological approach to assessing values in organizations is the use of profiles and profile analyses. Thus, the average significance attached to a particular value by a set of organizational members may be viewed and assessed in relation to the significance attached by them to other selected values. Top management, for example, or middle management in small-batch organizations, or some other such member set may be characterized by a profile of value emphases. This profile then may be used in profile analytic tests of hypotheses concerning values.

From the paradigm in Figure 6–6, it can be seen that several classes of questions are seemingly important, yet remain unanswered.

Values and Organizational Context—What is the relationship between values and organizational context? Are member values affected by various contextual components? Are there reciprocal aspects to the relationship? Hodgkinson (1971) found that value orientations differ by hierarchical levels. On the other hand, he found little relationship between values and such biographic data as age, sex, and seniority. Coughlan (1969) also found no relationship between values and biographic variables. In another vein, Woodward (1965) concluded that values of top executives varied by organizational technology. Although these data clearly are insufficient to allow generalizations to be made, as a general testable proposition it is suggested that there *are* stable relationships between values of organizational members and components of organizational context. In particular, the following illustrative hypotheses are proposed:

1. Value orientations vary systematically with hierarchical position.
2. Value orientations vary in accordance with variation in organizational formalization.
3. Value orientations vary in accordance with variations in education and training of members.
4. Value orientations differ in accordance with differences in dominant technology.

Values and Organizational Processes—It cannot be assumed that member values are related only to formal properties of the organization. In fact, it is suspected that values, as a variable, may explain even more of the variance in organizational processes, such as conflict, communication, and group behavior. Hodgkinson (1971), for example, found values of teachers and administrators in elementary schools to be related to their hierarchical status in the school system. He further reports variances in social-interaction perceptions of teachers as a function of value differences.

Unfortunately, little else has been reported on the relationship between values and organizational processes. For purposes of inquiring into the matter, therefore, the following hypotheses are offered:

1. Conflict occurs more frequently and is resolved with greater difficulty, the greater the value differences among parties.
2. Accuracy of communication among organizational members varies directly with value consensus among the members.
3. Group cohesion is directly related to value consensus among group members.
4. Effectiveness of intergroup cooperation is directly related to between-group consensus of member values.

Values and Managerial Action—The implications of values for organizational administration are best identified by considering the ways in which member values relate to specific managerial actions. It is almost certain that decision making, for example, is influenced by the values of those involved in the decision-making process. Thus Drake (1973) reports that the perceived usefulness of group decisions was positively related to similarity of values between the decision makers.

Other managerial actions also are likely to affect and be affected by member values. Pennings (1970) found promotion rates to be directly related to values of subordinates; whether this finding also is reflective of the *superordinates'* values is unknown. Further, Hesel (1971) reports a positive relationship between teachers' values and their pupil-control ideology. Specific hypotheses suggested by these considerations include the following:

1. Perceived decision utility is directly related to degree of value consensus among decision makers.
2. Leadership effectiveness is directly related to degree of value consensus between leader and followers.

3. Emphasis placed on various organizational goals by management (goal profile) is directly related to management's value profile.
4. Effectiveness of administrative coordination is directly related to value consensus among those whose activities are being coordinated.
5. Type of managerial control, as exemplified by criteria used in the organization's reward system, is directly related to management's values.
6. Means by which management performs its environment adaptation functions are directly related to management's values (example: means by which purchasing agent tasks are performed are predictable from management value profiles).

Values and Organizational Performance—As a final aspect, the relationship of member values to ultimate organizational performance is considered. Although many scholars have investigated organizational effectiveness, little consensus exists as to its proper dimensions or how to measure them. A review of the literature suggests the four dimensions indicated in Figure 6–6: efficiency, quality of output, quality of work environment, and responsiveness (Connor et al., 1973). Briefly, *efficiency* includes financial and administrative variables such as labor productivity, profit, waste control, proportion of capacity used, elimination of dysfunctional procedures, improved workflows, and appropriate information systems. *Quality of output* refers both to goods produced and to services rendered by the organization. In the manufacturing sector, a single unit of output may be of superior or inferior quality. This qualitative difference is clearly important to an assessment of organizational effectiveness. In the service sector, the quality of service rendered may be as important as the fact that the service occurred. In the health field, for example, this component may mean utility of the service to the consumer. *Quality of work environment* is reflected in member satisfaction with the organization as a whole, the job being performed, supervision, or interpersonal relationships with organizational colleagues. *Responsiveness* is the ability of the organization to adapt to its external environment and to maintain flexibility to adjust its internal operations to meet changing circumstances. Responsiveness therefore is the coping mechanism which increases the capacity or potential of the organization to survive and prosper over the long range under conditions of uncertainty.

Whether viewed as identical with or underlying the formation and pursuit of organizational goals, values are inherently critical to the organization's performance on these several dimensions. In the latter view, values are seen to lie at the heart of goal setting and strategy choosing processes; in the former view, values *are* the goals. Regardless of which view one holds, there are few data which allow anything except speculation about the relationship between values and organizational effectiveness. What data do exist concern that aspect of organizational effectiveness referred to here as quality of work environment, or elsewhere as organizational climate. Several investigators report findings which show a strong relationship between member values and the character of organizational climate (Coughlan, 1971; Gies and Leonard, 1971; Hodgkinson, 1971).

These studies all were conducted in elementary and secondary schools, however, and they dichotomized organizational climate into "open" and "closed," following the scheme developed by Barnes (1960).

Because of the complexity of the organizational effectiveness construct, and because of the paucity of information regarding it, one is reluctant to offer hypotheses even as imprecise as those presented previously. Some illustrative questions can be posed, however, suggesting the directions that research might take in this area:

1. Is there a direct, stable relationship between organizational performance on various dimensions of efficiency and the management value profile? Worker value profile? Management-worker value consensus?
2. How are worker values related to output quality? Is output quality related to degree of management-worker value consensus?
3. Is value consensus between management and workers related to properties of organizational climate (such as job satisfaction, leadership style, etc.)?

4. Is the organization's ability to be responsive related to top management's value profile? Middle management's? Top-middle consensus? Management-worker consensus? Do the same relationships hold for both external adaptability and internal flexibility?

Questions such as these require investigation if an understanding of the ways in which values relate to the organization's ultimate effectiveness is to be developed.

CONCLUSION

It has been suggested that an important knowledge gap exists in organization theory. This gap concerns the nature of the relationships among values of organizational members and various organizational properties, processes, and activities. The merit of research into this area is relatively clear. First, values may well be more parsimonious predictors of organizational phenomena than are such variables as attitudes, perceptions, and personality traits—all of which are currently used frequently and with little thought of their relationships to underlying value systems (Connor and Becker, 1974). Second, values may supply some critical missing variance. That is, it is not expected that values will always explain 100 percent of the variance of some other variable. To the contrary, the evidence is clear that, even without considering values, there are strong relationships among some variables (Hall, 1972). It is contended, however, that such relationships may be more fully explained by including member values as a distinct variable in the analysis.

Some cautionary remarks are offered. First, the authors have been extremely vague in their operational use of the concept "value," as in the hypotheses and questions presented in the preceding section. This vagueness has been deliberate and it arises out of necessity. As Rokeach states, "Given the present state of development of the social sciences, it is not yet conceptually meaningful or technologically feasible to assess routinely . . . values" (Rokeach, 1969: 547).

This deficiency is reflected in the vast number of value instruments available. A volume published by the University of Michigan's Institute for Social Research contains no less than twelve value instruments, plus several others that could easily be considered value measures (Robinson and Shaver, 1969). Perusal of this volume demonstrates the variety of operational approaches extant, ranging from simple two and three value instruments to complex multivalue arrays. At this stage of research, the authors feel it is unwise to attempt to specify the "universal value set." Rather, different research objectives will call for attention to different kinds of values. For example, research into the relationship between top management values and conflict resolution effectiveness probably would be concerned with value consensus along professional, social harmony, administrative, and rationality dimensions, rather than spiritual and aesthetic .

This paper has emphasized exhortation rather than specifics. However, the current state of knowledge regarding values and the organization is almost nil; thus, exhortation appears to be called for. Organizational researchers have little understanding regarding the function that member values play in organizational processes. Systematic research into such topics as those suggested here may help develop that understanding.

MOTIVATION: A DIAGNOSTIC APPROACH

DAVID A NADLER
EDWARD E. LAWLER III

- What makes some people work hard, while others do as little as possible?
- How can I, as a manager, influence the performance of people who work for me?
- Why do people turn over, show up late to work, and miss work entirely?

These important questions about employees' behavior can only be answered by managers who have a grasp of what motivates people. Specifically, a good understanding of motivation can serve as a valuable tool for *understanding* the causes of behavior in organizations, for *predicting* the effects of any managerial action, and for *directing* behavior so that organizational and individual goals can be achieved.

EXISTING APPROACHES

During the past twenty years, managers have been bombarded with a number of different approaches to motivation. The terms associated with these approaches are well known—"human relations," "scientific management," "job enrichment," "need hierarchy," "self-actualization," etc. Each of these approaches has something to offer. On the other hand, each of these different approaches also has its problems in both theory and practice. Running through almost all of the approaches with which managers are familiar are a series of implicit but clearly erroneous assumptions.

Assumption 1: All Employees Are Alike Different theories present different ways of looking at people, but each of them assumes that all employees are basically similar in their makeup: employees all want economic gains, or all want a pleasant climate, or all aspire to be self-actualizing, etc.

Assumption 2: All Situations Are Alike Most theories assume that all managerial situations are alike, and that the managerial course of action for motivation (for example, participation, job enlargement, etc.) is applicable in all situations.

Assumption 3: One Best Way Out of the other two assumptions there emerges a basic principle that there is "one best way" to motivate employees.

When these "one best way" approaches are tried in the "correct" situation they will work. However, all of them are bound to fail in some situations. They are therefore not adequate managerial tools.

A NEW APPROACH

During the past ten years, a great deal of research has been done on a new approach to looking at motivation. This approach, frequently called "expectancy theory," still needs further testing, refining, and extending. However, enough is known that many behavioral scientists have concluded that it represents the most comprehensive, valid, and useful approach to understanding motivation. Further, it is apparent that it is a very useful tool for understanding motivation in organizations.

The theory is based on a number of specific assumptions about the causes of behavior in organizations.

Assumption 1: Behavior Is Determined by a Combination of Forces in the Individual and Forces in the Environment Neither the individual nor the environment alone determines behavior. Individuals come into organizations with certain "psychological baggage."

David A. Nadler and Edward E. Lawler III, "Motivation: A Diagnostic Approach," in *Perspectives on Behavior in Organizations,* J. Richard Hackman, Edward E. Lawler III, and Lyman W. Porter (eds.) (New York: McGraw-Hill Book Company, 1977), pp. 26-34.

They have past experiences and a developmental history which has given them unique sets of needs, ways of looking at the world, and expectations about how organizations will treat them. These all influence how individuals respond to their work environment. The work environment provides structures (such as a pay system or a supervisor) which influence the behavior of people. Different environments tend to produce different behavior in similar people just as dissimilar people tend to behave differently in similar environments.

Assumption 2: People Make Decisions about Their Own Behavior in Organizations While there are many constraints on the behavior of individuals in organizations, most of the behavior that is observed is the result of individuals' conscious decisions. These decisions usually fall into two categories. First, individuals make decisions about *membership behavior*—coming to work, staying at work, and in other ways being a member of the organization. Second, individuals make decisions about the amount of *effort* they will direct *toward performing their jobs.* This includes decisions about how hard to work, how much to produce, at what quality, etc.

Assumption 3: Different People Have Different Types of Needs, Desires, and Goals Individuals differ on what kinds of outcomes (or rewards) they desire. These differences are not random; they can be examined systematically by an understanding of the differences in the strength of individuals' needs.

Assumption 4: People Make Decisions among Alternative Plans of Behavior Based on Their Perceptions (Expectancies) of the Degree to Which a Given Behavior will Lead to Desired Outcomes In simple terms, people tend to do those things which they see as leading to outcomes (which can also be called "rewards") they desire and avoid doing those things they see as leading to outcomes that are not desired.

In general, the approach used here views people as having their own needs and mental maps of what the world is like. They use these maps to make decisions about how they will behave, behaving in those ways which their mental maps indicate will lead to outcomes that will satisfy their needs. Therefore, they are inherently neither motivated nor unmotivated; motivation depends on the situation they are in, and how it fits their needs.

THE THEORY

Based on these general assumptions, expectancy theory states a number of propositions about the process by which people make decisions about their own behavior in organizational settings. While the theory is complex at first view, it is in fact made of a series of fairly straightforward observations about behavior. Three concepts serve as the key building blocks of the theory:

Performance-Outcome Expectancy Every behavior has associated with it, in an individual's mind, certain outcomes (rewards or punishments). In other words, the individual believes or expects that if he or she behaves in a certain way, he or she will get certain things.

Examples of expectancies can easily be described. An individual may have an expectancy that if he produces ten units he will receive his normal hourly rate while if he produces fifteen units he will receive his hourly pay rate plus a bonus. Similarly an individual may believe that certain levels of performance will lead to approval or disapproval from members of her work group or from her supervisor. Each performance can be seen as leading to a number of different kinds of outcomes and outcomes can differ in their types.

Valence Each outcome has a "valence" (value, worth, attractiveness) to a specific individual. Outcomes have different valences for different individuals. This comes about because valences result from individual needs and perceptions, which differ because they in turn reflect other factors in the individual's life.

For example, some individuals may value an opportunity for promotion or advancement because of their needs for achievement or power, while others may not want to be promoted and leave their current work group because of needs for affiliation with others. Similarly, a fringe benefit such as a pension plan may have great valence for an older worker but little valence for a young employee on his first job.

Effort-Performance Expectancy Each behavior also has associated with it in the individual's mind a certain expectancy or probability of success. This expectancy represents the individual's perception of how hard it will be to achieve such behavior and the probability of his or her successful achievement of that behavior.

For example, you may have a strong expectancy that if you put forth the effort, you can produce ten units an hour, but that you have only a fifty-fifty chance of producing fifteen units an hour if you try.

Putting these concepts together, it is possible to make a basic statement about motivation. In general, the motivation to attempt to behave in a certain way is greatest when:

a. The individual believes that the behavior will lead to outcomes (performance-outcome expectancy)
b. The individual believes that these outcomes have positive value for him or her (valence)
c. The individual believes that he or she is able to perform at the desired level (effort-performance expectancy)

Given a number of alternative levels of behavior (ten, fifteen, and twenty units of production per hour, for example) the individual will choose that level of performance which has the greatest motivational force associated with it, as indicated by the expectancies, outcomes, and valences.

In other words, when faced with choices about behavior, the individual goes through a process of considering questions such as, "Can I perform at that level if I try?" "If I perform at that level, what will happen?" "How do I feel about those things that will happen?" The individual then decides to behave in that way which seems to have the best chance of producing positive, desired outcomes.

A General Model

On the basis of these concepts, it is possible to construct a general model of behavior in organizational settings (see Figure 6–7). Working from left to right in the model, motivation is seen as the force on the individual to expend effort. Motivation leads to an observed level of effort by the individual. Effort, alone, however, is not enough. Performance results from a combination of the effort that an individual puts forth *and* the level of ability which he or she has (reflecting skills, training, information, etc.). Effort thus combines with ability to

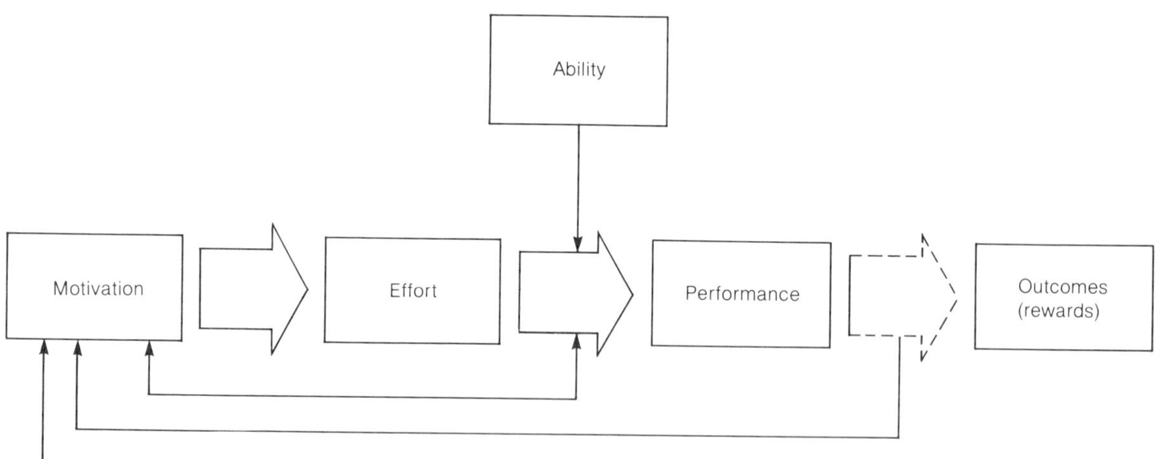

Figure 6-7. The basic motivation-behavior sequence

produce a given level of performance. As a result of performance, the individual attains certain outcomes. The model indicates this relationship in a dotted line, reflecting the fact that sometimes people perform but do not get desired outcomes. As this process of performance-reward occurs, time after time, the actual events serve to provide information which influences the individual's perceptions (particularly expectancies) and thus influences motivation in the future.

Outcomes, or rewards, fall into two major categories. First, the individual obtains outcomes from the environment. When an individual performs at a given level he or she can receive positive or negative outcomes from supervisors, coworkers, the organization's rewards systems, or other sources. These environmental rewards are thus one source of outcomes for the individual. A second source of outcomes is the individual. These include outcomes which occur purely from the performance of the task itself (feelings of accomplishment, personal worth, achievement, etc.). In a sense, the individual gives these rewards to himself or herself. The environment cannot give them or take them away directly; it can only make them possible.[1]

Implications for Managers

The first set of implications is directed toward the individual manager who has a group of people working for him or her and is concerned with how to motivate good performance. Since behavior is a result of forces both in the person and in the environment, you as manager need to look at and diagnose both the person and the environment. Specifically, you need to do the following:

Figure out what outcomes each employee values As a first step, it is important to determine what kinds of outcomes or rewards have valence for your employees. For each employee you need to determine "what turns him or her on." There are various ways of finding this out, including (a) finding out employees' desires through some structured method of data collection, such as a questionnaire, (b) observing the employees' reactions to different situations or rewards, or (c) the fairly simple act of asking them what kinds of rewards they want, what kind of career goals they have, or "what's in it for them." It is important to stress here that it is very difficult to change what people want, but fairly easy to find out what they want. Thus, the skillful manager emphasizes diagnosis of needs, not changing the individuals themselves.

Determine what kinds of behavior you desire Managers frequently talk about "good performance" without really defining what good performance is. An important step in motivating is for you yourself to figure out what kinds of performances are required and what are adequate measures or indicators of performance (quantity, quality, etc.). There is also a need to be able to define those performances in fairly specific terms so that observable and measurable behavior can be defined and subordinates can understand what is desired of them (e.g., produce ten products of a certain quality standard—rather than only produce at a high rate).

Make sure desired levels of performance are reachable The model states that motivation is determined not only by the performance-to-outcome expectancy, but also by the effort-to-performance expectancy. The implication of this is that the levels of performance which are set as the points at which individuals receive desired outcomes must be reachable or attainable by these individuals. If the employees feel that the level of performance required to get a reward is higher than they can reasonably achieve, then their motivation to perform well will be relatively low.

Link desired outcomes to desired performances The next step is to directly, clearly, and explicitly link those outcomes desired by employees to the specific performances desired by you. If your employee values external rewards, then the emphasis should be on the rewards systems concerned with promotion, pay, and approval. While the linking of these rewards can be initiated through your making statements to your employees, it is extremely important that employees see a clear example of the reward process working in a fairly short period of time if the motivating "expectancies" are to be created in the employees' minds. The

1. For reviews of expectancy-theory research, see Mitchell (1974). For a more general discussion of expectancy theory and other approaches to motivation, see Lawler (1973).

linking must be done by some concrete public acts, in addition to statements of intent.

If your employee values internal rewards (e.g., achievement), then you should concentrate on changing the nature of the person's job, for he or she is likely to respond well to such things as increased autonomy, feedback, and challenge, because these things will lead to a situation where good job performance is inherently rewarding. The best way to check on the adequacy of the internal and external reward system is to ask people what their perceptions of the situation are. Remember it is the perceptions of people that determine their motivation, not reality. It doesn't matter for example whether you feel a subordinate's pay is related to his or her motivation. Motivation will be present only if the subordinate sees the relationship. Many managers are misled about the behavior of their subordinates because they rely on their own perceptions of the situation and forget to find out what their subordinates feel. There is only one way to do this: ask. Questionnaires can be used here, as can personal interviews.

Analyze the total situation for conflicting expectancies Having set up positive expectancies for employees, you then need to look at the entire situation to see if other factors (informal work groups, other managers, the organization's reward systems) have set up conflicting expectancies in the minds of the employees. Motivation will only be high when people see a number of rewards associated with good performance and few negative outcomes. Again, you can often gather this kind of information by asking your subordinates. If there are major conflicts, you need to make adjustments, either in your own performance and reward structure, or in the other sources of rewards or punishments in the environment.

Make sure changes in outcomes are large enough In examining the motivational system, it is important to make sure that changes in outcomes or rewards are large enough to motivate significant behavior. Trivial rewards will result in trivial amounts of effort and thus trivial improvements in performance. Rewards must be large enough to motivate individuals to put forth the effort required to bring about significant changes in performance.

Check the system for its equity The model is based on the idea that individuals are different and therefore different rewards will need to be used to motivate different individuals. On the other hand, for a motivational system to work it must be a fair one—one that has equity (not equality). Good performers should see that they get more desired rewards than do poor performers, and others in the system should see that also. Equity should not be confused with a system of equality where all are rewarded equally, with no regard to their performance. A system of equality is guaranteed to produce low motivation.

Implications for Organizations

Expectancy theory has some clear messages for those who run large organizations. It suggests how organizational structures can be designed so that they increase rather than decrease levels of motivation of organization members. While there are many different implications, a few of the major ones are as follows:

Implication 1: The design of pay and reward systems Organizations usually get what they reward, not what they want. This can be seen in many situations, and pay systems are a good example. (Lawler, 1971). Frequently, organizations reward people for membership (through pay tied to seniority, for example) rather than for performance. Little wonder that what the organization gets is behavior oriented toward "safe," secure employment rather than effort directed at performing well. In addition, even where organizations do pay for performance as a motivational device, they frequently negate the motivational value of the system by keeping pay secret, therefore preventing people from observing the pay-to-performance relationship that would serve to create positive, clear, and strong performance-to-reward expectancies. The implication is that organizations should put more effort into rewarding people (through pay, promotion, better job opportunities, etc.) for the performances which are desired, and that to keep these rewards secret is clearly self-defeating. In addition, it underscores the importance of the frequently ignored performance evaluation or appraisal process and the need to evaluate people based on how they perform clearly defined specific behaviors, rather than on how they score on ratings of general traits such as "honesty," "cleanliness," and other, similar terms which frequently appear as part of the performance appraisal form.

Implication 2: The design of tasks, jobs, and roles One source of desired outcomes is the work itself. The expectancy-theory model supports much of the job enrichment literature, in saying that by designing jobs which enable people to get their needs fulfilled, organizations can bring about higher levels of motivation.[2] The major difference between the traditional approaches to job enlargement or enrichment and the expectancy-theory approach is the recognition by the expectancy theory that different people have different needs and, therefore, some people may not want enlarged or enriched jobs. Thus, while the design of tasks that have more autonomy, variety, feedback, meaningfulness, etc., will lead to higher motivation in some, the organization needs to build in the opportunity for individuals to make choices about the kind of work they will do so that not everyone is forced to experience job enrichment.

Implication 3: The importance of group structures Groups, both formal and informal, are powerful and potent sources of desired outcomes for individuals. Groups can provide or withhold acceptance, approval, affection, skill training, needed information, assistance, etc. They are a powerful force in the total motivational environment of individuals. Several implications emerge from the importance of groups. First, organizations should consider the structuring of at least a portion of rewards around group performance rather than individual performance. This is particularly important where group members have to cooperate with each other to produce a group product or service, and where the individual's contribution is often hard to determine. Second, the organization needs to train managers to be aware of how groups can influence individual behavior and to be sensitive to the kinds of expectancies which informal groups set up and their conflict or consistency with the expectancies that the organization attempts to create.

Implication 4: The supervisor's role The immediate supervisor has an important role in creating, monitoring, and maintaining the expectancies and reward structures which will lead to good performance. The supervisor's role in the motivation process becomes one of defining clear goals, setting clear reward expectancies, and providing the right rewards for different people (which could include both organizational rewards and personal rewards such as recognition, approval, or support from the supervisor). Thus, organizations need to provide supervisors with an awareness of the nature of motivation as well as the tools (control over organizational rewards, skill in administering those rewards) to create positive motivation.

Implication 5: Measuring motivation If things like expectancies, the nature of the job, supervisor-controlled outcomes, satisfaction, etc., are important in understanding how well people are being motivated, then organizations need to monitor employee perceptions along these lines. One relatively cheap and reliable method of doing this is through standardized employee questionnaires. A number of organizations already use such techniques, surveying employees' perceptions and attitudes at regular intervals (ranging from once a month to once every year-and-a-half) using either standardized surveys or surveys developed specifically for the organization. Such information is useful both to the individual manager and to top management in assessing the state of human resources and the effectiveness of the organization's motivational systems.[3]

Implicaton 6: Individualizing organizations Expectancy theory leads to a final general implication about a possible future direction for the design of organizations. Because different people have different needs and therefore have different valences, effective motivation must come through the recognition that not all em-

2. A good discussion of job design with an expectancy theory perspective is in Hackman et al. (1975).

3. The use of questionnaires for understanding and changing organizational behavior is discussed in Nadler (1977).

ployees are alike and that organizations need to be flexible in order to accommodate individual differences. This implies the "building in" of choice for employees in many areas, such as reward systems, fringe benefits, job assignments, etc., where employees previously have had little say. A successful example of the building in of such choice can be seen in the experiments at TRW and the Educational Testing Service with "cafeteria fringe-benefits plans" which allow employees to choose the fringe benefits they want, rather than taking the expensive and often unwanted benefits which the company frequently provides to everyone.[4]

SUMMARY

Expectancy theory provides a more complex model of man for managers to work with. At the same time, it is a model which holds promise for the more effective motivation of individuals and the more effective design of organizational systems. It implies, however, the need for more exacting and thorough diagnosis by the manager to determine (a) the relevant forces in the individual, and (b) the relevant forces in the environment, both of which combine to motivate different kinds of behavior. Following diagnosis, the model implies a need to act—to develop a system of pay, promotion, job assignments, group structures, supervision, etc.—to bring about effective motivation by providing different outcomes for different individuals.

Performance of individuals is a critical issue in making organizations work effectively. If a manager is to influence work behavior and performance, he or she must have an understanding of motivation and the factors which influence an individual's motivation to come to work, to work hard, and to work well. While simple models offer easy answers, it is the more complex models which seem to offer more promise. Managers can use models (like expectancy theory) to understand the nature of behavior and build more effective organizations.

4. The whole issue of individualizing organizations is examined in Lawler (1974).

ANTECEDENTS AND OUTCOMES OF ORGANIZATIONAL COMMITMENT

RICHARD M. STEERS

The concept of employee commitment to organizations has received increased attention in the research literature recently as both managers and organizational analysts seek ways to increase employee retention and performance. Employee commitment is important for several reasons. To begin with, recent findings indicate that commitment is often a better predictor of turnover than is job satisfaction (Koch and Steers, 1976; Porter et al., 1974). Moreover, findings by Mowday, Porter, and Dubin (1974) suggest that highly committed employees may perform better than less committed ones. Finally, it has been suggested by some that commitment may represent one useful indicator of the effectiveness of an organization (Schein, 1970; Steers, 1975). These findings have important implications for both organization theory and the practice of management.

Organizational commitment may be defined as the relative strength of an individual's identification with and involvement in a particular organization. It can be characterized by at least three factors: 1. a strong belief in and acceptance of the organization's goals and values; 2. a willingness to exert considerable effort on behalf of the organization; and 3. a strong desire to maintain membership in the organization (Porter et al., 1974). Before such a concept can be operationalized, however, greater understanding is required concerning the process by which commitments are formed and how such commitments influence subsequent behavior in organizational settings.

Although a variety of studies have been reported recently examining certain aspects of commitment, several problems remain. First, few studies have taken a systematic or comprehensive approach to the topic. As a result, we have little information to guide us in model-building attempts. Second, cross-validational studies in which hypotheses or models are tested and then replicated in diverse settings are rare. Thus, the external validity of many of the existing findings must remain in doubt. Third, the majority of existing studies treat commitment as a dependent variable. Consequently, little is known about the behavioral outcomes of commitment. The present study attempted to provide information relevant to all three of these problems by suggesting a preliminary model that incorporates both antecedents and outcomes of organizational commitment and then providing a cross-validational test of the utility of the model.

THE MODEL

The model consists of two parts: 1. antecedents of commitment; and 2. outcomes of commitment. The component dealing with antecedents draws heavily on previous research. When the various studies on determinants of organizational commitment are examined, it becomes clear that major influences can be found throughout the work environment. For the sake of parsimony, these influences can be grouped into three main categories: personal characteristics, job characteristics, and work experiences (see Figure 6–8).

Personal characteristics consist of those variables which define the individual. For instance, commitment has been shown to be related to age (Hrebiniak, 1974; Lee, 1971; Sheldon, 1971), opportunities for achievement (Brown, 1969; Hall, Schneider, and Nygren, 1970; Lee, 1971; Patchen, 1970), education (Koch and Steers, 1976), role tension (Hrebiniak and Alutto, 1972), and central life interest (Dubin, Champoux, and Porter, 1975). Because of the diversity of samples and commitment measures that were used in these studies, they were used in the present investigation as guidelines for the formulation of hypotheses.

The model further suggests that job characteristics

"Antecedents and Outcomes of Organizational Commitment," *Administrative Science Quarterly,* vol. 22, no. 1 (March 1977), pp. 46–56.

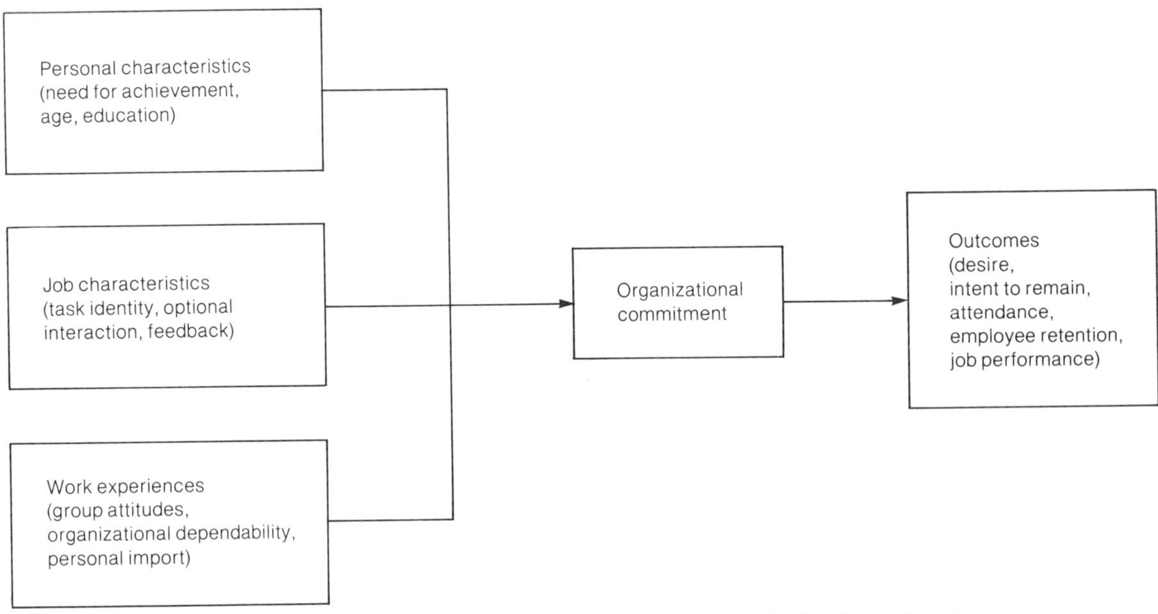

Figure 6-8. Hypothesized antecedents and outcomes of organizational commitment

may also influence commitment to some degree, although the influence is probably more pronounced for other affective responses, like job satisfaction (Stone and Porter, 1975). In particular, we would expect, based on prior research, that commitment would be influenced by job challenge (Buchanan, 1974; Hall and Schneider, 1972), opportunities for social interaction (Sheldon, 1971), and the amount of feedback provided on the job (Ross and Zander, 1957; Porter and Steers, 1973).

Finally, drawing on the work of Buchanan (1974) and others, the model suggests that commitment is influenced by the nature and quality of an employee's work experiences during his or her tenure in an organization. Work experiences are viewed as a major socializing force and as such represent an important influence on the extent to which psychological attachments are formed with the organization. Experiences that have been found to influence commitment include group attitudes toward the organization (Buchanan, 1974; Patchen, 1970), organizational dependability and trust (Buchanan, 1974; Hrebiniak, 1974), perceptions of personal investment and personal importance to an organization (Buchanan, 1974; Patchen, 1970; Sheldon, 1971), and rewards or the realization of expectations (Grusky, 1966).

Thus, the first component of the proposed model suggests that important influences on commitment can be found in three general areas of organizational life. A major advantage of the present study is that it allows for the simultaneous examination of the various antecedents in order to identify the relative strength of relation of each with commitment. Previous studies were more focused and typically did not provide an adequate test of the relative weights of each antecedent.

The second component of the model hypothesizes that commitment leads to several specific behavioral outcomes. First, highly committed employees should have a strong desire and intent to remain with the organization. Such an outcome is implicit in the definition of commitment. Moreover, such behavioral intentions should be manifested in subsequent employee retention or turnover (Porter et al., 1974). In addition, commitment would be expected to be related to attendance. Employees who are highly committed to the goals of an organization and have positive attitudes toward it should be more likely to have a strong desire to come to work and contribute toward goal attainment. Finally, commitment was hypothesized to be related to performance under the assumption that committed employees would expend greater effort on the job. This second part of the model was set forth more on an exploratory level because of the paucity of empirical data available for guidance. Even so, it was felt that knowledge of such possible outcomes was equally important as information concerning antecedents. When taken together, it was hoped that this study would provide for a cross-validated test among divergent samples of the generalizability of the proposed model of organizational commitment.

METHOD

Samples and Research Sites

The study was carried out among two diverse samples of employees in separate organizations. The first sample consisted of employees of a major midwestern hospital. Subjects held a wide variety of technical and nontechnical positions, including administrators, registered nurses, licensed vocational nurses, service workers, and clerical employees. The average age of the subjects was 35, while the average tenure was 8 years. Educational backgrounds ranged from high school degrees through M.S. degrees.

The second sample consisted of research scientists and engineers employed by a major independent research laboratory. Subjects held various technical and administrative positions. The average age of the subjects was 38; the average tenure was 10 years. Educational backgrounds ranged from bachelor's through doctoral degrees. Subjects were engaged in a wide variety of both basic and applied research projects, principally in engineering.

Measures

In order to test the sufficiency of the model, measures were secured on the following sets of variables.

Personal characteristics. Measures of personal characteristics included age, education, and tenure, plus the need strengths of achievement, affiliation, autonomy, and dominance.

Job characteristics. Perceived job characteristics were measured using the scales developed by Hackman and Lawler (1971). The four core dimensions measured were: autonomy, variety, feedback, and task identity. In addition, opportunity for optional interaction (that is, the opportunity to develop close friendships at work) was also measured because of its purported influence on commitment as discussed above.

Work experiences. Work experiences were measured using an instrument developed by Buchanan (1974). In order to remain consistent with the theoretical model outlined above and to avoid problems of multicolinearity between study variables that emerged elsewhere, the following experiences were selected for examination: 1. group attitudes toward the organization; 2. the extent to which subjects' expectations were met by the realities of the job; 3. feelings of personal importance to the organization based upon the actions of the organization over time; and 4. the extent to which the organization was seen as being dependable in carrying out its commitments to employees. Each work experience measure attempts to tap one relatively discreet aspect of organizational life.

Organizational commitment. Commitment was measured using a questionnaire developed by Porter (Porter et al., 1974). Each item of the questionnaire asks the subject to express his or her agreement or disagreement with the item on a seven-point Likert scale, ranging from "strongly agree" to "strongly disagree." Mean commitment levels for the two samples were 5.1 for the hospital sample and 4.4 for the research laboratory (with 7.0 representing the highest possible level of commitment).

Desire and intent to remain. Single item measures of subjects' desire to remain and intent to remain were secured on seven-point scales ranging from strongly disagree to strongly agree.

Behaviors. Job performance was measured in the hospital sample by asking immediate supervisors to rate subjects on four related performance dimensions: overall performance, quality of work, quantity of work, and promotion readiness. In the research laboratory sample, it was only possible to obtain a global measure of overall job performance. Attendance was measured as the number of days absent from work.

Finally, employee turnover data were collected for a period of one year in the hospital sample; it was not possible to obtain this information for the research laboratory.

Data Collection

In both samples, questionnaires were administered on-site by university researchers during regular working hours. Subjects were informed that participation was voluntary and were assured of confidentiality of responses. Of the initial random samples, usable questionnaire data were gather from 382 hospital employees (87 percent of the sample) and 119 scientists and engineers (82 percent of the sample).

RESULTS

Antecedents of Commitment

Initially, attention was focused on testing the first part of the model dealing with the three sets of antecedents of organizational commitment. Toward this end, separate multiple correlations were run between each of the three sets of hypothesized antecedents and commitment. Since interest centered on which set of antecedents was more strongly related to commitment, all the relevant variables in each of the three antecedent categories were used in their respective analyses. To provide for a cross-validation of results, this analysis was performed on both samples. The results are presented in Table 6–1.

The findings provide support for the first part of the model presented in Figure 6–8 by virtue of the fact that all three sets of antecedents were significantly related to commitment. This finding emerged for both samples. It was also found that, for both samples, work experiences were more closely associated with commitment (R = .71 and .64) than the other two sets of variables, thereby providing partial support for Buchanan's (1974) thesis that commitment is largely a function of work experiences. However, these findings extend this thesis by noting the importance of the other two sets of antecedents, thus emphasizing the diverse sources of factors affecting employee commitment in organizations.

TABLE 6–1 MULTIPLE CORRELATIONS BETWEEN ANTECEDENTS AND ORGANIZATIONAL COMMITMENT FOR BOTH SAMPLES

Antecedents	Hospital Employees (N=382)		Scientists and Engineers (N=119)	
	R	F-value	R	F-value
Personal characteristics	.55	24.96**	.42	3.28*
Job characteristics	64	47.86**	.38	3.89*
Work experience	.71	89.26**	.64	20.04**

*Significant at .01 level

**Significant at .001 level

On a more specific level, interest was next focused on an attempt to identify those *specific* variables that most strongly influenced employee commitment. To accomplish this, step-wise multiple regression analyses were run for both samples using all of the independent variables from the three major antecedent categories and treating organizational commitment as the dependent variable (see Table 6–2).

A comparison of the two regression analyses reveals several important findings. To begin with, six antecedent variables were significantly associated with commitment in both samples: need for achievement, group attitudes toward the organization, education (inversely), organizational dependability, personal importance to the organization, and task identity. The ability to replicate these findings across two studies suggests that these variables may represent relatively stable antecedents of organizational commitment.

Second, it also was found that four additional variables were significantly related to commitment in one sample but not the other. These variables were: opportunities for optional interaction, age, met expectations, and feedback.

Finally, an analysis of the findings revealed that specific antecedents that significantly related to commitment could be found in all three general antecedent categories. This finding provides support for the notion that all three categories represent important influences on commitment, as suggested in the model.

Outcomes of Commitment

In order to test the second component of the model, Pearson product-moment correlations were run be-

TABLE 6–2 RESULTS OF MULTIPLE REGRESSION ANALYSES FOR SPECIFIC ANTECEDENT VARIABLES ON COMMITMENT FOR BOTH SAMPLES

Independent Variables	Hospital Employees Beta	Hospital Employees *F*	Scientists and Engineers Beta	Scientists and Engineers *F*
Need for achievement	.19	32.52***	.25	13.46***
Group attitudes	.20	21.75***	.24	6.80***
Education	−.15	19.04***	−.24	11.04***
Task identity	.13	12.61***	.13	3.29*
Optional interaction	.19	25.58***	—	—
Age	.16	19.07***	—	—
Met expectations	.15	10.09***	—	—
Organizational dependability	.12	6.11*	.27	9.79**
Personal importance	.10	4.82*	.22	4.73*
Feedback	—	—	.17	3.90*
	$R=.81$, $R^2_s=.65$		$R=.71$, $R^2_s=.48$	

$N=382$, df=1,373 for hospital employees; $N=119$, df=1,112 for scientists and engineers.

*Significant at .05 level

**Significant at .01 level

***Significant at .001 level

tween commitment and each outcome variable. As shown in Table 6–3, commitment was found to be related to both desire to remain and intent to remain for both samples. Moreover, it was also found to be related to attendance for the scientists and engineers but not for hospital employees. In addition, commitment was found to be inversely related to employee turnover in the hospital sample. (Comparative data on turnover from the other sample were unavailable.) Finally, commitment was marginally related to two of four performance measures for hospital employees, but was not related to the global performance measure for the scientists and engineers.

Thus, while support for part of the second half of the model emerged, particularly with respect to intent and desire to remain and actual turnover, the data appear to be inconclusive with respect to attendance and job performance.

TABLE 6–3 PEARSON PRODUCT-MOMENT CORRELATIONS BETWEEN COMMITMENT AND OUTCOME VARIABLES FOR BOTH SAMPLES

Outcome Variables	Organizational Commitment: Hospital Employees ($N=382$)	Organizational Commitment: Scientists and Engineers ($N=119$)
Desire to remain	.44***	.36***
Intent to remain	.31***	.38***
Attendance	.08	.28**
Turnover	−.17**	NA
Overall performance	.05	.05
Quality of work	.07	NA
Quantity of work	.11*	NA
Promotion readiness	.10*	NA

NA=Not available

*Significant at .05 level

**Significant at .01 level

***Significant at .001 level

DISCUSSION

Several important conclusions emerge from these findings. First, it can be concluded that antecedents of organizational commitment are quite diverse in their nature and origin. In the present study, commitment in both samples was influenced by need for achievement, group attitudes toward the organization, education (inversely), organizational dependability, perceived personal importance to the organization, and task identity. A common theme that runs through many of these variables is the notion of exchange (March and Simon, 1958; Hrebiniak and Alutto, 1972). Individuals come to organizations with certain needs, desires, skills, and so forth, and expect to find a work environment where they can utilize their abilities and satisfy many of their basic needs. When the organization provides such a vehicle (for example, where it makes effective use of its employees, is dependable, and so forth), the likelihood of increasing commitment is apparently enhanced. When the organization is not dependable, however, or where it fails to provide employees with challenging and meaningful tasks, commitment levels tend to diminish. Moreover, when employees have higher levels of education, it may be more difficult for an organization to provide sufficient rewards (as perceived by the individual) to equalize the exchange. Hence, more highly educated people (who also tend to be more cosmopolitan) would be less committed to the organization and perhaps more committed to a profession or trade.

A second important finding of the present study was that major influences on organizational commitment can be found in all three antecedent categories (personal characteristics, job characteristics, and work experiences). Thus, some support is provided for the adequacy of the first component of the model as described in Figure 6–8. Moreover, while all three sets of antecedents appear to be important, work experiences were found to be more closely related to commitment than personal or job characteristics for both samples. Such findings reinforce and enlarge upon the earlier efforts of Buchanan (1974), Hall and Schneider (1972), and Hrebiniak and Alutto (1972) by identifying the more salient features of the commitment process.

The findings of the present study also provide partial support for the second component of the model dealing with the possible outcomes of organizational commitment. Strong support was found for the proposition that commitment is associated with increases in an employee's desire and intent to remain with an organization. In view of the definition of commitment, this finding is not surprising. More importantly, commitment was also significantly and inversely related to employee turnover. This finding supports earlier studies among divergent samples (Koch and Steers, 1976; Porter et al., 1974) and suggests that one of the most significant outcomes of increased commitment is a more stable work force.

In addition, commitment was related to attendance for one sample but not the other. While the present data are not sufficient to explain these mixed results, it is possible that this relationship was contaminated by the pooling of voluntary and involuntary absences in the attendance measure. Even so, the strong positive relationship between these two variables for the one sample cannot be ignored and suggests a fruitful area for future research.

Finally, several comments are in order concerning the rather weak relationship between commitment and performance. While it was hypothesized that these two variables would be related, such an association was found in only two of the five possible situations. Moreover, the magnitude of the two significant relationships was small. Hence, it must be concluded that no direct or consistent association exists between commitment and subsequent job performance for these samples.

Several possible explanations exist for this counterintuitive finding. First, it is conceivable that the two organizations under study, in their efforts to reduce turnover and absenteeism, tended to retain more security-minded "settlers," who were loyal but to whom high performance was not role relevant. In other words, there may be a self-selection process in operation here whereby moderate or low performers feel comfortable (and committed) in a nonthreatening environment, while high performers seek challenge elsewhere. Thus the organization tends to end up with a more stable but less productive or creative work force.

Several lines of evidence may be found in support of this explanation. For instance, neither of the organizations studied were profit-oriented in the conventional sense. Since operating costs were passed along to patients or customers, pressures for efficiency may have been somewhat reduced. Instead, both organizations may have assumed a posture of attempting to retain their highly trained, specialized (and hard to replace) technical personnel at a cost of reduced output. Hence, one explanation may lie in the nature of the organizations studied. In addition, observational data from both organizations suggest that top managers were strongly concerned about employee relations and rather ambivalent about high level performance. In fact, while managers were sensitive to such indices as turnover and absenteeism (both were seen as measures of job satisfaction), they encountered great difficulty in specifying relevant criteria for good employee performance. A recent review of studies of organizational effectiveness suggests that highly effective organizations are generally characterized by an achievement orientation and employee centeredness (Steers, 1977). The two organizations studied tended to ignore the first characteristic (or were unable to assess it accurately) and stress the second. Consequently, it would not be surprising that organizational commitment would not be translated into high levels of performance.

A second possible explanation for the absence of a commitment-performance relationship may lie in the current conceptualization of the commitment construct. Specifically, previous studies of commitment have tended to view commitment simultaneously as an affective response to an employee's environment and as a behavioral intention concerning future performance (Fishbein, 1967). Hence, we tend to think of a highly committed employee as one who strongly identifies with the organization (that is, "I feel good about working here") *and* who is willing to exert high levels of effort on behalf of the organization (that is, "I want to do my best for this company"). Conceptually, however, it may be more meaningful to distinguish between "passive" commitment and "active" commitment. In the present study, it is conceivable that the employees experienced primarily a passive form of commitment and that, for some reason, such affective responses were not translated into behavioral intentions (that is, active commitment). If such a view is correct, it suggests a rethinking of the current approach to the study of organizational commitment, as well as renewed efforts at measuring its various facets.

The third possible explanation for the lack of a commitment-performance relationship follows from existing research on motivation and work behavior (Porter and Lawler, 1968; Steers and Porter, 1975; Vroom, 1964). Specifically, contemporary theories of work motivation suggest that job performance is a function of three variables: motivation level, ability, and role clarity (Porter and Lawler, 1968). Recent research has indicated that all three of these variables are important in the determination of employee performance. Existing definitions of organizational commitment appear to be largely concerned with the motivational aspects of such a model. That is, a highly committed person is thought to exert high levels of effort. However, the notion of organizational commitment as defined in the literature exists independently of human abilities and role clarity. Hence, it seems logical to assume that at least part of the failure to find a strong commitment-performance relationship may have resulted from the failure to control for abilities and role clarity in the present analyses. Again, such a conclusion carries with it recommendations for future investigations.

The three suggested explanations for the lack of a commitment-performance relationship are not mutually exclusive. In fact, they are quite complementary. When taken together, they suggest that highly committed employees will tend to perform well to the extent that: 1. organizations stress high achievement orientations concomitantly with good employee relations; 2. passive commitment (often called loyalty) can be translated into active commitment; and 3. employees possess the requisite skills and abilities and fully understand and accept their particular organizational roles. In other words, it appears that more complex models must be developed and tested in the future concerning the behavioral outcomes of employee commitment to organizations. The present preliminary model is offered as a stimulus to such efforts.

CONCLUDING STATEMENT

What then can we say about people as a factor in the design and operation of organizations? As we have continually emphasized, organizations are social instruments established and designed to perform a task. They are designed, continually redesigned, and operated to best accomplish their purposes under the conditions that prevail. One of the major prevailing conditions is the nature of the "social" part of that instrument.

In the introductory remarks we began our investigation of the ways in which "people" constrain organizational design. There we examined some relevant characteristics that people bring into the organizational situation—characteristics that must be accounted for in design decisions. The three articles that followed then focused on values, motivation, and commitment. The intent of this concluding statement is to see what difference all this makes for organizational design.

DESIGN RESPONSES TO THE HUMAN CONSTRAINT

There are obviously many human characteristics that affect organizations' abilities to accomplish their goals. They cannot afford to presume that their members leave all of these characteristics outside the door when they come to work. These many characteristics are major sources of complexity and uncertainty for organizations. As Thompson (1967), Merton (1957), Katz and Kahn (1966), and others have made clear, reducing this complexity and uncertainty is a fundamental organizational imperative.* In numerous ways, organizations attempt to reduce the variability, instability, and unpredictability of individual human acts.

Generally organizations have been pretty successful at doing so. But the discussion up to now has emphasized that the human constraint is more complex, variable, and uncertain than has been generally assumed. Organizations can accommodate their members' characteristics and behaviors in two broad ways: by changing the people in the organization or by modifying the organization.

Given the need for more careful organizational response to its members, what are organization designers to do? Should they change their organization's personnel or change the organization? Should they change the organization's mix of employee abilities or try to change its members' motivations? Should change efforts be focused on individuals, groups, or the whole organization (Reitz, 1977)? These questions are further confounded by changes in employees brought about by general societal changes, as well as by employees' socialization into the values of the organization. Thus any favorable outcomes from a particular design change may be short-lived, as employees shift into new and unanticipated values, attitudes, and therefore behavior patterns.

The remainder of this statement outlines several alternatives that organizations have for designs recognizing the nature of the human constraint. These alternatives are discussed under the following headings (see Table 6–4):

* Remember that this is also a theme of this book's Chapters 1 and 2.

TABLE 6–4 PEOPLE AND DESIGN VARIABLES AND ORGANIZATIONAL RESPONSES

I. Employee Characteristics	II. People-Related Design Variables	III. Organizational-Design Responses	IV. Organizational Outcomes
1. Biographical 2. Work values and motivation 3. Life and career stages 4. Commitment 5. Personality variables a. Emotionality b. Activation c. Extroversion-Introversion d. Locus of control e. Authoritarianism	1. Personnel systems 2. Work groups 3. Feedback and reward systems 4. Task 5. Organizational structure 6. Physical settings 7. Management systems	1. Change personnel a. Selection b. Training/development c. Socialization d. Performance reviews and feedback e. Contingent rewards f. Individualized reward systems g. Life and career stage-specific assessment and development 2. Change the organization a. Modify goals b. Modify structure 1.) Reduce need for information processing 2.) Increase capacity to process information c. Modify technology and tasks 1.) Job enrichment 2.) Hours of work 3.) Entrepreneurship 4.) Flexible physical setting 3. Change the interface between people and organizations a. OD b. Leadership c. Standing committees d. Institutionalized participation 4. Individualized organizations	1. Effectiveness 2. Climate

1. Changing the people
2. Changing the organization
3. Changing the interface between people and organizations
4. Individualizing organizations

CHANGING THE PEOPLE

When organizations (that is, their managers) recognize the importance and nature of the human factor, one of the broad alternatives for design actions is to try to control the nature of the human element. Different organizational structures require different types of people to function effectively (Davis and Lawrence, 1978; Tosi and Carroll, 1977; Ivancevich and Donnelly, 1975). Organizations attempt many approaches to this. The following is a summary and evaluation of many of them.

Personnel Selection

One of the first options available to the organizational designer is to select personnel to fit the organization, rather than vice versa. The choice as to the fit of individuals with the organization can be made either by the individual or by the organization.

If the person is to be able to make an adequate choice, he or she must be given accurate and complete information about the job and organization. Wanous (1975a, 1975b) has discussed how important the provision of adequate information through realistic job previews is to improving an organization's overall selection procedure.

Beyond this, organizations obviously can try to select, through recruiting and testing procedures, employees who will fit their needs. If this option is to work, though, selection procedures must meet these criteria:

1. People must differ in meaningful ways.
2. Valid data about the characteristics of people must exist or be able to be gathered.
3. Valid descriptions of job requirements must exist.
4. People who are suited for the open jobs must be recruited and apply.
5. A large number of qualified applicants must apply.
6. The selection criteria must be validated by correlating performance data with selection criteria (Lawler, 1974, 1976; Reitz, 1977).

When the "selecting in" process (by the individual) fails, organizations still have the option of "selecting out." Forced turnover of employees, of course, gives organizations the final option for controlling the match between employee and employer.

As Maier (1973), Korman (1977), and the article by Nadler and Lawler point out, though, there are several variables intervening between employees' abilities—presuming they can be measured and matched to job requirements—and their job behaviors. Besides the legal necessities—such as demonstrating the relationship between a firm's ability measurements and later employee performance levels—differences in experience, ability to learn, motivation levels, desired organizational outcomes, etc., confuse the picture. The complexity and interactions of these variables suggest that managers should look for ways to improve existing employee abilities through training and development. This is better than treating them as fixed, immutable properties that can be adequately identified at job-application time and will from that time forward meet the needs of the organization.

Training and Development

Once individuals have been hired, the organization has numerous options for training and developing its employees to meet its requirements. Formal and informal training procedures, such as on-the-job training, coaching, and classroom presentations are frequently used for new employees in entry-level positions at lower levels of organizations. Higher-level employees, particularly managers, are developed with these techniques plus developmental job assignments, study groups, and counseling by superiors.[1]

1. Job assignments are so important to the development of employees, particularly managers, that this issue will be explored fully in the section of this chapter on the interface between people and the organization.

Socialization

Organizational members, of course, come to their jobs with relatively-well established work and occupational attitudes, depending on their degrees of former education and types of experiences (Etzioni, 1975). The training and development processes tend to be for the purposes of increasing job-related skills. But organizations also work at producing attitudes that meet organizational needs. As Perrow (1970) says, ". . . people's attitudes are shaped at least as much by the organization in which they work as by their pre-existing attitudes." Socialization is the name given to this process of the individual taking on the organization's goals as his or her own (Barrett, 1970).

Tosi and Carroll (1976) suggest that employees have one of the following orientations toward their work organizations:

1. *The organizationalist.* This employee is highly committed to the place where he or she works, identifies with the system, and is highly satisfied with job requirements. This person is committed to the organization's goals and is concerned about its success. Clearly this type of employee holds attitudes beneficial to the organization. Attempts to socialize employees are designed to create organizationalists.

2. *Externally oriented persons.* For this group of employees, their jobs are acceptable but not a critical part of their lives. These employees are not psychologically involved with their work organizations. They may perform well, but their personal satisfactions and sources of meaning are sought and found outside their jobs and organizations. These employees are certain targets for organizational socialization attempts.

3. *The professional.* These employees have both an external orientation and are committed to their jobs (and careers). Their self-concept may not be tied up with their organization, but it is with their jobs. The professional orientation is associated with high education, self-control (by standards of the profession and by highly developed standards of ethics and work behavior), long-term commitment to their occupations, recognized authority within specialized areas, and a desire for high autonomy (Pavalko, 1971; Blau and Scott, 1962; Wilson, 1966; Vollmer and Mills, 1966; and Filley, House, and Kerr, 1976).

A growing number of today's employees appear to have this kind of orientation. And their corresponding expectations may be hard to satisfy. But their professional commitment may make them more willing to leave when confronted with conflict by demands for organizational commitment (Filley, House, and Kerr, 1976). The reduction of this conflict is possible, though, through the provision of adequate autonomy, individual recognition, linkages with the outside professional community, collegial rather than bureaucratic authority and control systems, and challenging assignments that lead to organizational rewards, such as promotions (R. Hall, 1976; Filley, House, and Kerr, 1976).

For the employees whom the organization can socialize, there appears to be a number of stages involved. And the organization must apparently vary its approaches according to the needs of the particular stage in which the employee is (Feldman, 1976; Presthus, 1965; Wanous, 1976, 1977).

1. The first stage is one of "getting in." Realistic job previews help the employee to decide to join an organization where attitude and expectation differences are minimized. Flexibility

in job assignments and consideration of the employee's needs and desires also aid in his or her integration into the organization.

2. The second stage involves the "breaking in" of the employee. Orientation and structured training programs, effective performance-feedback systems, and allowance for personalizing of work tasks help build acceptance, competence, and accurate role perceptions.

3. The "settling in" stage involves the employee with the resolution of conflict between work and outside life, as well as the resolution of conflicting work group demands. Counseling, flexibility, and mutual influence of and by co-workers aid in this final stage of socialization.

When successfully socialized, the employee will have internalized work motivation and job involvement. To the extent that an organization can accomplish this, it is a result of obvious benefit to the organization.

Reward and Feedback Systems

One of the more powerful design tools available to managers is influence over the feedback systems of an organization. Defining for employees what the goals of the organization are, what behaviors are required to reach those goals, and which rewards are available (of course, ensuring that those rewards are desirable to the organization's members) for putting forth those behaviors to reach those goals will go a long way toward "producing" the desired behaviors and thus achieving the goals (Hamner, 1977; Hamner and Hamner, 1976). Of course, self-feedback of performance levels, whenever possible, participation in the goal setting, face-to-face and problem-solving performance reviews, rewards contingent on goal achievement matched as closely as possible to individual employee needs and desires improve the efficacy of the overall reward and feedback systems (Carroll and Tosi, 1973).

Assessment and Development of Life and Career Stages

As was discussed in the section on individual differences, the stage of life and/or career in which an individual finds him- or herself influences highly the types of attitudes and needs that person has. Thus it makes sense for organizations to try to work within the constraints of this reality.

The kinds of problems addressed not only vary with the life and career stage but also interact with organizational issues, such as whether the firm is stable or even contracting (Hall and Hall, 1976; Hall and Morgan, 1977). Obviously promotions and career development take on a different look in such situations compared with the growing organization.

Turnover among recently hired employees, who often have high expectations for their new jobs, can be minimized through realistic job previews, challenging first jobs, enriched tasks, and demanding bosses (Berlew and Hall, 1966; Hall and Hall, 1976; Schein, 1964, 1968). High potential employees must first be identified (assessment centers are effective tools for this task). Then they can be quickly developed through planned sequencing of developmental jobs (Hall and Hall, 1976; Jennings, 1971).

The organization must integrate its career development activities with its personnel planning. This means meeting the equal employment opportunity needs of all employees—

majority and minority. It means planning and monitoring internal mobility and career paths. It means providing cross-functional moves, downward transfers, fallback positions, and organizational tenure in stable or contracting organizations. It also means the effective dissemination of career option information, career counseling as a part of the normal performance appraisal, support of educational training activities for all employees, job posting, career development workshops, flexible reward and promotion systems, and accommodation of shifting employee needs through sabbaticals, flexible working hours, and other off-work activities (Hall and Hall, 1976; Van Maanen and Schein, 1977).

More specifically, Hall and Morgan (1977) outline a number of ways that organizations can match design actions to the specific stages in which employees find themselves. Table 6–5 summarizes the varying training needs for different career stages. And Table 6–6 outlines organizational actions for facilitating overall career development.

CHANGING THE ORGANIZATION

If the differences in people can not be eliminated or controlled through the preceding types of personnel actions, the second set of choices open to organization designers concerns changes in the organization itself. If this becomes the direction in which an organization moves, Cherns (1977) suggests that the problems need to be dealt with as near to their point of origin as possible. This means that a wide repertoire of performance to achieve objectives should be allowed, the organization's social support systems need to be consistent with the designed structure, and the ultimate focus probably needs to remain the quality of work life for the organization's members.

TABLE 6–5 TRAINING NEEDS WITHIN CAREER STAGES

Stage	Task Needs	Emotional Needs
Trial	1. Varied job activities 2. Self-exploration	1. Make preliminary job choices 2. Settling down
Establishment advancement	1. Job challenge 2. Develop competence in a specialty area 3. Develop creativity and innovation 4. Rotate into new area after 3–5 years	1. Deal with rivalry and competition; face failures 2. Deal with work-family conflicts 3. Support 4. Autonomy
Mid-career	1. Technical updating 2. Develop skills in training and coaching others (younger employees) 3. Rotation into new job requiring new skills 4. Develop broader view of work and own role in organization	1. Express feelings about mid-life 2. Reorganize thinking about self in relation to work, family, community 3. Reduce self-indulgence and competitiveness
Late career	1. Plan for retirement 2. Shift from power role to one of consultation and guidance 3. Identify and develop successors 4. Begin activities outside the organization	1. Support and counseling to see one's work as a platform for others 2. Develop sense of identity in extraorganizational activities

SOURCE: Douglas T. Hall and M. Morgan, "Career Development & Planning" in *Contemporary Problems in Personnel.* Copyright 1977 by St. Clair Press. Used by permission.

TABLE 6–6 ORGANIZATIONAL ACTIONS FOR FACILITATING CAREER DEVELOPMENT

Entry: Changing Employee Inputs
1. Better links between school and work
2. Training students in job-related skills
3. Realistic job previews in recruiting
4. Better selection for person-job fit

Development through the Job
1. Challenging initial jobs
2. Periodic job rotation
3. Colleague stimulation
4. Frequent feedback and performance review
5. Rewarding good performance

Changing the Boss's Role
1. Make bosses career developers
2. Train managers in job design and career planning
3. Reward managers for employee development

Changing Organizational Structures
1. Matrix organization structures
2. Accounting for human resources
3. Career planning services

Changing Personnel Policies
1. Rotation of managers through "people departments"
2. Life-long job rotation
3. Downward and lateral transfers
4. Tenure
5. Fallback positions for promoted employees
6. Support for dual-career employees

SOURCE: From *Careers in Organizations*, by Douglas T. Hall, p. 57. Copyright © 1976 by Goodyear Publishing Co. Reprinted by permission.

Modification of Goals

The first organizational design action suggested for responding to the human constraint is the modification of the organization's goals. As discussed in Chapter 3, organizational goals reflect the collective objectives of an organization's members. But when the members change, so often do their collective objectives. When this occurs, organizations can take a number of steps (Gamson, 1968; Khandwalla, 1977):

1. Goal displacement and succession—the abandonment of old goals and the introduction of new ones
2. The dissolution of no-longer needed parts of the organization
3. The modification of organizational procedures and rules
4. The modification of informal norms and staff perspectives

Modification of Structure

The second set of actions an organization can take to adapt to its human constraint is to modify its structure. In general the organization can reduce its need for processing information about the complex and volatile people input, or it can increase its capacity to process that information (Galbraith, 1974, 1977; Davis and Lawrence, 1978).[2]

2. Recall the discussion in Chapter 2, especially the article by Galbraith.

To reduce the organization's needs for processing this information, it can try to control its environment (by changing its people, as discussed above). It can also create slack resources to increase lead time and margin for error or create autonomous, self-contained tasks that have less reliance on external resources. This third strategy generally leads to an increased span of control, as well, with its flattened hierarchy, decreased specialization, and often decreased formalization and centralization (Brown, 1966; Gamson, 1968).

To increase its capacity to process this information, the organization can invest in vertical information systems. This generally refers to computerized information systems for handling more of the routine chores and dull and repetitive tasks and thus allowing more opportunity and resources for innovation and planning, better feedback, and the upgrading of jobs—with more control at lower levels. Or the organization can work at creating more effective lateral relations. This involves more direct contact through mechanisms such as liaison roles, task forces, integrating roles, greater use of teams, managerial linking roles, and matrix structures. The greater the degree of complexity and volatility in the human element, the greater the need for an organization to adopt one or more of these strategies.

Modification of Work Design

As discussed in the section on individual differences, many of today's employees seek greater satisfactions directly from the performance of their jobs. Thus, enriching the nature of an organization's jobs is clearly an important design option for many situations. Chapter 7 deals with this design option, so only a brief summary is made here.

For the employee who is high in need for achievement and desires autonomy and greater self-control on the job, an enriched task appears to increase internal work motivation and job involvement. Enriched tasks seem to have the following characteristics:

1. The use of a wide variety of skills on the job
2. A high degree of task identity (requiring the completion of a "whole" piece of work)
3. A job that has a high level of significance (to the job holder, to the organization, to society)
4. A large amount of freedom and discretion in job procedures
5. The capacity in the job itself for feedback about how effectively the job holder is performing (self-feedback) (Hackman and Lawler, 1971; Hackman et al., 1975)

These job characteristics define the traditional provisions for an enriched task. In recent years, though, organizations have used many other, less traditional, approaches to the creation of autonomous, significant, and satisfying jobs. These have included the reinstitution of older patterns of entrepreneurship through structures such as franchises, small research and development groups, and independent work teams (Brown, 1966). We have also seen increasing use of contracts, joint ventures, trade associations, and service firms—all of which often provide opportunities for enriched jobs.

As discussed earlier, there is considerable argument over whether job enrichment is for everyone. The need for organizations to be flexible and to provide alternative work designs varies, depending on the diagnosed needs of the organization's employees. Nevertheless, there is growing consensus among organizational theorists and practitioners that the characteristics as listed by Emery and Thorsrud (1969) are necessary for many, if not most, of today's organizational members to experience meaning in their work:

1. Widened jobs
2. Continuous learning
3. Participation in decision making
4. Social support
5. Meaningful relation between one's job and the outside world
6. Desirable future

Ideally, enriched tasks and meaningful jobs are designed to meet the needs of mature, self-actualizing employees. If not all of an organization's members are of that type, traditional, authoritarian, low responsibility jobs are probably more appropriate and will produce better organizational results.

CHANGING THE INTERFACE BETWEEN PEOPLE AND THE ORGANIZATION

Organizations often make both formal and informal adjustments to pressures from their personnel. But they also work hard at system changes that structure the nature of the interaction between employees and the organization. Again this is only a short summary of these many strategies.

Management Development Through Job Assignments

If job moves are to be used for growth and development (and they can have a strong impact on overall development), care must be taken to use the career-planning process effectively (Berlew and Hall, 1966; Hall and Morgan, 1977; Jennings, 1971; and Van Maanen and Schein, 1977). The following steps are important (Hall and Morgan, 1977).

1. Selection of a target job—with consideration of the individual's career aspirations and values
2. Identification of the skills and experiences necessary to reach the target job
3. Identification of the necessary sequence of jobs to build the required skills and experiences:
   a. Select jobs that provide changes that are large enough to "stretch" the individual's skills and abilities, yet small enough to be manageable.
   b. Consider lateral, developmental, cross-functional moves as well as promotions.
   c. Allow for sufficient time to master the job but not so long that the job becomes routine.
   d. Consider jobs that complement or supplement, not merely duplicate, previous experiences.
   e. Plan alternative moves or sequences (contingency plans), since it is unlikely that all the scheduled moves will take place as planned.

Leadership Styles

Leadership studies invariably conclude that leaders tend to be relationship- or task-oriented. Invariably, they also conclude that a heavy emphasis on both orientations is associated with leadership effectiveness. In line with the focus of this book and this chapter that there is seldom, if ever, one best way, some authors have recently been focusing on the match of leadership style to the situation. Fiedler (1976) suggests the following:

1. Relationship-motivated leaders tend to excel under conditions in which they have moderate influence and control.
2. Task-oriented leaders tend to be most successful under conditions in which they exert a great deal of power and influence (the mechanistic, bureaucratic structure) or under the reverse conditions, in which they have little or no power or influence.

Hersey and Blanchard (1977) have identified the maturity level of subordinates (in terms of their willingness *and* ability to set goals and accept responsibility for goal achievement) as the important element in the environment which determines the appropriate leadership style for the manager to use. Low maturity subordinates are appropriately "led" with autocratic, close supervision. On the other hand, a highly delegative, laissez-faire style is most appropriate for highly mature employees.

Organizational Development

A wide set of procedures and techniques have been developed to essentially open an organization's work climate. This has been collectively labeled Organization Development (OD). Sensitivity training, team building, T-groups, action research, diagnosis and feedback, development of interpersonal skills, mirroring, etc., are all OD techniques and processes. The focus of OD has traditionally been the collective set of work values and attitudes evidenced by work groups and organizations in the way they work together, confront conflict, and cope with change. These procedures are all based on assumptions of the normal, actualizing, self-controlling nature of today's employees.

Management by Objectives

The goal-oriented nature of employee motivation as well as organizations has been a major impetus to the increasing usage of Management by Objectives (MBO). This participative process of identifying managers' operating and developmental objectives, and thus their performance levels, has traditionally been identified with procedures used by effective managers and organizations.

Institutionalized Participation

Since participation in organizational decision making has such pervasive influences on critical employee attitudes such as commitment and motivation, many organizations have developed ways to formalize participation. Worker-management committees, joint study groups, special collective bargaining groups, and many forms of worker management (such as the Scanlon Plan) have evolved to institutionalize the procedures for employee participation and thus to increase motivation, commitment, and goal-oriented performance.

INDIVIDUALIZING ORGANIZATIONS

This chapter has been suggesting that organizations can either try to change the nature of its employees so they will fit the organization or make internal changes to try to fit the organization to its employees. Lawler (1974, 1976) suggests that there isn't much evidence to indicate that organizations adapt very well to either strategy. And even if they are temporarily successful, changes occur so rapidly that the adaptations are by necessity short-lived. The option that is left is to "individualize" the organization, as was shown in the article by Nadler and Lawler.

Basically this is the option being argued for throughout this chapter. Since employees differ in as many ways as they do, it makes sense to try to make the organization as flexible as possible. The more options available to the organization and the more easily these are matched to employee differences, the more likely the organization is to be able to adapt effectively to its environment with an internally acceptable organizational climate.

The following implications are suggested for managers who want to individualize their organizations:

1. Determine what kinds of behavior the organization desires
2. Figure out what outcomes each employee values
3. Make sure the desired behavior is achievable
4. Link the desired outcomes to the desired performances
5. Analyze the total situation to eliminate conflicting expectancies (e.g., between group norms and organizational requirements)
6. Make sure that the outcomes offered are large enough to motivate significant behavior
7. Check the system for equity

If managers in the organization can and will do these things, the pay and reward systems, tasks, and group structures can then be designed to meet the many individual differences faced by the organization. "Only by treating individuals differently is it possible to get them to behave in the same way" (Lawler, 1976: 202).

SUMMARY AND CONCLUSION

This chapter has been concerned with people, as they relate to issues of organization design. We opened the discussion by elaborating the following point: organizations do not hire just part of a person. That is, they do not just hire an individual's mechanical skills or decision-making abilities. They get a whole person—ethnic and family background, level and type of education, political views, culture or lack of it, self-concept, feelings about family, and all the rest.

In the first article, the author and Becker discussed the probable and potential impacts of one additional human variable, people's values. They suggested that little is known about the relations between employees' values and organizational properties. By outlining a number of important questions about the impact of values on organizational contexts, processes, and managerial actions (and vice versa), they made it clear that this is a variable that needs much greater attention.

Employees see themselves as unique individuals. And as Nadler and Lawler indicated in their article, they are. Different people have different needs, desires, and goals. Further, they make decisions about how to act at work based on their expectations that certain behavior will lead to the receipt of outcomes that will satisfy their particular needs, desires, and goals.

On the other hand, organizations see people more as resources—replaceable, trainable, usable for many different purposes. The major human problem for organizations lies at that interface between employees as humans and employees as resources. This is a particularly critical question as people become less willing to accept roles as merely resources. Nadler and Lawler suggested, therefore, that organizations need to try to match the rewards their members want to the behaviors the organizations desire. In this way, both individual and organizational needs can be satisfied. In the third article, Steers identified the variables that seem to relate to employees' degrees of identification with and involvement in their organizations. Enriched tasks, educated and achievement-oriented employees, and personal importance with supportive work groups help improve the level of employee commitment. Even so, commitment does not always seem to relate to job performance, whereas it does seem to improve retention and job attendance.

In short, organizations have traditionally been designed to deal primarily with the skills and abilities of employees—not the whole person. This chapter has emphasized that organizations must deal with all parts of their employees—their memories, motivations, expectations, aspirations, attitudes, and feelings—all of which insist on coming to work with them.

The emerging dilemma, then, as organizations try to meet both their own effectiveness needs and the diverse needs of their members, is one of traditional efficiency versus human needs. As general economic growth has subsided in the 1970s, organizations are putting increasing emphasis on efficiency. At the same time, however, society and employees are moving toward greater mutual acceptance and attention to individual needs. The resolution of this dilemma is obviously a complex affair. Still—the abatement of growth not withstanding—the requirement for organization designs incorporating the human characteristics discussed in this chapter is probably the compelling imperative. Indeed, "it may well be a matter of practical necessity for managers who are interested in organizational survival in a turbulent society" (Viola, 1977: 162–63).

This chapter concludes the discussion of design constraints. In this section we have explored the question, "what affects or constrains designers' options in forming organization designs?" The answer was: environment, technology, and people. We move now to the next logical question: "What is it that designers design?" In the next section, Chapters 7 through 10, we examine four design variables: work design, organizational control, decision processes, and organization structure.

Questions for Review

1. What distinctions do Connor and Becker make between:
   a. values
   b. attitudes
   c. behavior
2. Outline three hypotheses put forward to illustrate that there are stable relationships between the values of organizational members and components of organizational context.

3. Outline four specific hypotheses relating to values and managerial action.
4. When Connor and Becker address the issue of values and organizational performance, what do they mean by the following terms:
   a. efficiency
   b. quality of output
   c. quality of work environment
   d. responsiveness
5. Nadler and Lawler describe some basic assumptions of the new expectancy theory of motivation. Briefly describe two of these assumptions and what they have to offer to a view of motivation.
6. What are the major implications of the expectancy-theory model for the individual manager with a group of people working for him or her?
7. What are the main differences between the implications of expectancy theory for individual managers and its implications for organizations?
8. What are the major conclusions Steers derives from the organizational commitment study outlined in his article, "Antecedents and Outcomes of Organizational Commitment"?
9. What are the main alternatives that organizations have for developing designs that recognize human factors?
10. What are the main career stages in a working individual's life? What task needs characterize each of these stages? What emotional needs characterize each of these stages?
11. Describe three ways that career development may be facilitated through an individual's job.
12. How may personnel policies be changed to facilitate career development?

Questions for Discussion

1. Cooper and Payne maintain that introverts may well be more conditionable than extroverts. What do you understand by the terms *conditionable*, *introvert*, and *extrovert*? Do your definitions agree with Cooper and Payne's? From where did you derive your definitions? Using one of these sets of definitions, how would you classify yourself? Using a past or present work or school environment in which you have participated, evaluate Cooper and Payne's hypothesis.
2. Is there a place for authoritarianism in modern organizations? If so, why, when, where, and how? If not, why not? Define what you mean by *authoritarianism*. Compare your own experiences of authoritarian and nonauthoritarian managers/supervisors/instructors; list positive and negative points for each style wherever possible.
3. To what characteristics would you as a supervisor pay most attention in hiring a potential subordinate? Why would you pay special attention to these particular characteristics? Are these the characteristics on which you would like to be evaluated yourself? If not, why not?
4. How would you define *human motivation?* Do you think that motivation in an organizational setting differs in quantity or quality from motivation in *non*organizational settings? Where possible, draw from your own experiences.

5. List three values that you perceive as being important to you. Then list three specific attitudes that arise from these particular values. How are these values and attitudes manifested in your everyday behavior?
6. Choose one attitude you have had toward people (for instance, at school) that has changed in the last year. Has this change in your attitude reflected itself in your behavior? If so, how?
7. Churchman has argued that the "*ideal* setting for the study of human values is the organization." What do you think is the "ideal setting" for such a study? Do you think there *can* be an ideal setting? What factors would you require for an ideal setting?
8. Connor and Becker ask how worker values relate to output quality. Can you think of some ways in which these might be related and *why* they might be related? If you do not believe that there might be any relation between worker values and output quality, outline your reasons.
9. Write two short career biographies about two people you know. Choose one whose career fits the task-needs sequence outlined in Table 6-4, and one whose career you don't think fits this sequence. In what ways do their personalities differ? How do you personally account for these differences in their careers?
10. The summary states that "organizations do not hire just part of a person." Do you think it is advisable for organizations to hire "the whole person"? Explain.

CASES FOR DISCUSSION

CASE: STATE DRUG COUNCIL

PART I

The State Drug Council had to review, as one of its charges, a variety of proposals dealing with drug abuse in the state. Proposals and programs which the Council might be asked to review included requests for funding on such topics as drug treatment effectiveness, statewide educational programs, level and extent of drug abuse within the state, factors which lead to drug abuse, evaluation of various educational efforts, evaluation and study of law enforcement efforts, support for new treatment facilities, etc. The head of the Drug Council, who readily admitted limited knowledge on the subject, decided to recruit a variety of professionals from the state to provide valid assessment of the proposals submitted.

Several professionals concerned with drug abuse were contacted by the head of the Drug Council and asked to come to a meeting at the capital city headquarters. At the first meeting people involved in drug treatment, law enforcement, drug-related research, and educators from all parts of the state were present. The head of the Drug Council chaired this meeting, which included twenty-two professionals, and after calling the meeting to order told the group he did not want to impose any of his ideas on the group about how it might organize. He was sensitive to the fact that the people involved were donating their time and felt he would let the group decide.

After a few minutes, the meeting degenerated into several people talking at once, each proposing a different approach. The law enforcement people knew each other even though they were from different parts of the state and felt they should form a separate committee. The research methodology people felt it would be difficult to meet regularly as a separate committee because they came from different parts of the state and driving to the capital city took at least one hour each way. The educators, coming from different universities, expressed concern over driving time, while the psychologists and psychiatrists involved in treatment just wanted to be sure that adequate funds went into effective treatment programs. The first meeting was terminated with little resolved except that a second meeting time was set up.

At the second meeting the group continued to flounder as more and more individuals became frustrated and threatened to be absent from such future meetings. At the third meeting the group demanded that the head of the Drug Council provide some direction. He told the group that he had some proposals for them to consider and suggested that they begin by looking at the proposal he had sent to them prior to the meeting, concerning a new treatment clinic. The people involved in treatment suggested they go off by themselves and review the proposal since this was their bailiwick. As the discussion continued, a police chief stated that he perceived real problems with law enforcement officials accepting free and private clinics. He felt that police would see them merely as "crash pads." The educators expressed concern over having the funding sufficient enough to provide adequate publicity in local schools. The research methodology people attacked the lack of effective assessment measures in the proposal and proposed it be sent back for revision. The meeting continued with accusations of "grandstanding" and several people departed early. Most people left this meeting angry and frustrated, and several members told the head of the Drug Council

Source: John F. Veiga and John N. Yanouzas (eds.), *The Dynamics of Organization Theory* (St. Paul: West Publishing Company, 1979), pp. 235–40. This case was written by John F. Veiga and it represents a real situation. All names and places have been disguised. Reproduced by permission from *The Dynamics of Organization Theory* by Veiga and Yanouzas,

The information contained herein has been collected for the sole purpose of providing material for discussion, not to demonstrate correct or incorrect handling of managerial or organizational situations.

that something had to be done or they would not be returning. Prior to the next meeting, the head of the Drug Council sent out a memo detailing what he believed to be the objectives of the group and how he hoped to deal with the problems they had proposed (see Exhibit 1).

> To: Members of Drug Council Advisory Board
> From: Head of Drug Council
> Subject: Council Objectives
>
> The objective of the Advisory Board, as I see it, is to provide recommendations to the State Drug Council concerning various proposals involved with drug abuse. As I see it, some proposals may require specific expertise for evaluation such as those that deal with education. On the other hand, as we discovered last week, most proposals seem to overlap all of our areas of expertise to some extent, and effective recommendations require several inputs. Therefore, it is imperative for all of you to contribute your ideas.
>
> I have asked a management consultant to attend our next meeting and to propose to us how we might organize ourselves. I'd appreciate it if everyone would come and cooperate with her.

EXHIBIT 1 State Memo

Questions

1. As a consultant to the head of the Drug Council, what organizational structure would you propose? What problems can you anticipate with your proposal?
2. What other questions would you like to ask the Advisory Board members and/or the head of the Drug Council? Why?

PART II

After the consultant attended the next meeting of the board, she requested a list of the board members, their areas of expertise, and their geographic locations, shown on page 242.

In addition, after discussing the Board's objectives and past performance with the head of the Drug Council, she met privately with several members and listened to their complaints. The following represents the data she gathered:

Complaint List

1. "A one hour drive each way to a meeting is too much, given the amount of time we waste at the meeting."
2. "You can't do a damn thing with 22 people all talking at once."
3. "Some of the proposals could really benefit from the people in my area (Treatment) getting together separately."
4. "Some of these people don't realize the value of sharing ideas with professionals outside of their own area. They act as if they have the only answer."

Questions

1. Based on the above information, how would you reorganize the Advisory Board? Why?
2. Do you still need additional information? If so, what?

BOARD MEMBER LIST

Member	Area of Expertise	Geographic Location*
1. A. Alfred	Research Methodology	Central
2. T. Brougham	Law Enforcement	Northeast
3. N. Brown	Treatment	Central
4. R. J. Crousee	Research Methodology	Northeast
5. J. F. Donley	Treatment	Southern
6. P. W. Everett	Education	Central
7. J. Francis	Treatment	Northeast
8. T. French	Research Methodology	Southern
9. S. Gant	Education	Southern
10. N. Hughes	Research Methodology	Southern
11. J. L. Hughes	Research Methodology	Central
12. S. Islay	Treatment	Central
13. G. Jones	Treatment	Northeast
14. H. Kronsel	Research Methodology	Northeast
15. M. Listro	Law Enforcement	Central
16. R. Nunes	Research Methodology	Southern
17. L. M. Lacey	Treatment	Southern
18. G. Turner	Research Methodology	Northeast
19. P. Vail	Treatment	Northeast
20. W. Walters	Education	Northeast
21. J. Verna	Law Enforcement	Southern
22. S. Yates	Research Methodology	Central

*Grouped by general location within the state.

PART III

Based on the data gathered, the consultant advised the head of the Drug Council to organize the Advisory Board into a matrix organization. Functional specialities and geographic area were used to form task forces. (Your instructor will provide you with a drawing of the final organization chart.)

According to the design, task forces were set up by geographic location to reduce travel time for each board member. Task forces could then meet near their own state locations. The task force leaders rotated within their teams depending upon the nature of the proposal being evaluated. The functional coordinators (FC) were members of different task forces. These people had the responsibility of meeting regularly with the head of the Drug Council to review the proposals to be examined. After this group reviewed the proposals, one of the task forces would be assigned the evaluation task depending upon current work load with results fed back to the head of the Drug Council through the Functional Coordinators. When a proposal involved just one specialized area, a meeting of all members with that special expertise could be called and they could then make a recommendation. This proposal went into operation immediately after it was presented to the entire group.

Questions

1. Do you think the consultant made a wise recommendation? Why or why not?
2. Do you see any problems for the new organization? If so, what?

CASE: PEOPLE PROBLEMS AT HEALERS HOSPITAL

Michael Flaherty is director of nursing at Healers Hospital. He is talking about problems of staffing and training in the hospital, especially as related to the care of aged patients.

"The primary goal of this hospital is to provide care for the acutely ill and the injured—not of providing care for ill or injured young people or old people. There is no differentiation as to the types of people we care for other than between the ill and the injured. The idea is that our purpose is to care for acute problems, as opposed to chronic illnesses. In this context, the fact that some of our patients are aged, some are chronically ill, and some are both aged and chronically ill—in addition to the acute problem that brought them here—is not reflected in our organization structure.

We have a medical department, an obstetrical department, a surgical department, a pediatric department, and an outpatient department as major divisions. We do not have a geriatric department. The patients are segregated by the general type of problem they have, rather than by age group (except that children are placed in pediatrics).

"Where staff training is concerned, the fact that some of our patients are aged—or more specifically, have one or more of the chronic conditions generally associated with aging, in addition to the ailment or injury that brought them here—does constitute a problem. The problem is actually twofold. One is the technique problem, in which we are concerned with the physical differences related to aging as they affect the acute problem.

"The second training problem is one of attitude. For instance, our nursing personnel are not exposed to a great number of cases of senility. It is difficult for them to accept the fact that although these patients are adults, their behavior is sometimes more like that of small children, and they can't be expected to carry out instructions or remember to use the call button when they need assistance. So when one of them wets or dirties the bed, the tendency is to think of the patient as a "dirty old man," or "dirty old woman," or someone who has done it deliberately—either to aggravate the staff or to make more work for them.

"Many of our people get very impatient with some of the older patients because they are slow and require more time to heal and, consequently, stay longer, or because they require more physical care and assistance, such as care of their dentures and support in walking and having to be lifted in and out of bed, or because they are irritable or have unpleasant dispositions or complain a lot, or because they just 'don't smell good.' Some of the complaints regarding aged patients are real, but it may be the result of medications they are already taking interacting with medications for the current illness. Or maybe it's because of removing some medication they usually need and have, so it won't interact with current medications. Also, some of the people just don't like to touch old people.

"This attitude problem is not insoluble, so far as the professional staff is concerned, because they are with us for an extended period and we have time to work with them and derive some benefit from the training. Our nurses' aides and orderlies, however, are a much more difficult problem. The turnover rate is quite high. Most of them don't stay with us more than a year. And many stay just a few months. It's a continual job, just trying to maintain the minimum level of competence—and an almost impossible job to get above that level. We have to rely mostly on the nurses supervising these people to take care of these attitude and behavioral problems as they become manifest."

Questions

1. How would you describe the people (employees) Mr. Flaherty is discussing? Use the kinds of descriptors presented in Chapter 6.
2. How should the differences among the professional and non-professional staff affect Mr. Flaherty's supervision of them?
3. Design a program of action for Mr. Flaherty to alleviate the problems raised by these differences.

SECTION FOUR

Design Variables

INTRODUCTION TO SECTION FOUR

What is it that designers design? The answer to this question is as complex as the organization itself. As we mentioned in the beginning of the book, organization designers are faced with an almost overwhelming variety of factors, properties, characteristics, forces, and processes that they must mold into a relatively coherent combination—coherent, that is, in terms of meeting goals, given the constraints under which the organization must operate.

Viewing the organization as an open system enables us to identify some specific variables with which designers can work. Resources flowing into the organization require that *work* be designed so as to transform them into output goods and services. Further, that work needs to be *controlled*; different organizational/managerial circumstances call for different control-system designs. Third, the general process by which resources and activities are allocated is called decision making. Thus different *decision processes* must be designed to accomplish organizational goals under various conditions. Finally, all of these factors, processes, and so forth take place within the framework of the organizational *structure*; structural design therefore provides the formal configuration for the organization.

Each of these design variables is treated in the next four chapters:

- Chapter 7: Work Design
- Chapter 8: Organizational Control
- Chapter 9: Decision Processes
- Chapter 10: Organizational Structure

7

Work Design

INTRODUCTORY REMARKS

This chapter begins the discussion of those organizational features, properties, characteristics—in short, variables—that comprise the object of design efforts. As we mentioned in Chapter 2, the view that organizations are open systems underlies our focus on these design variables. Taking this view, we see that the essence of organizational functioning is the transformation of inputs into outputs. Thus we begin our examination of design variables by focusing on work. It is the design of work that sets the stage—that provides the framework—for the flow of resources and activities through the organization.

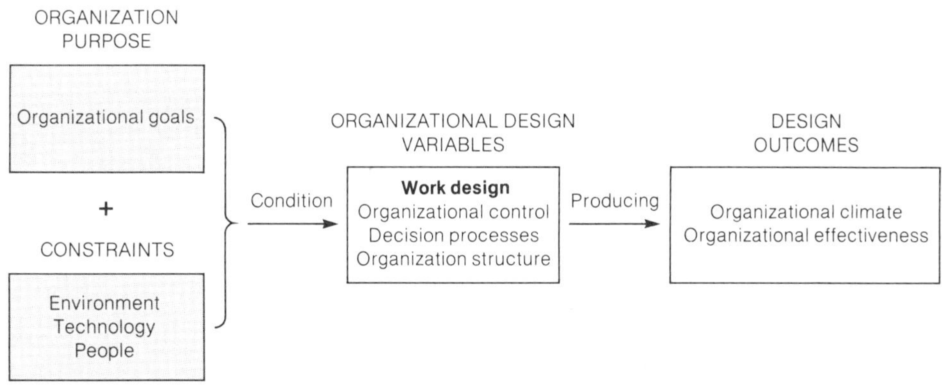

WORK DESIGN: PAST AND PRESENT

What we know (or think we know) about effective work design today depends, of course, on what we thought we knew yesterday. Therefore, let us consider the development of this knowledge.

Past

Since the design of work is fundamental to organizing, it is perhaps surprising that it has received so little attention by managers and scholars over the years. Pierce and Dunham report in this chapter's first reading that work design has for a long time been treated as a simple, straightforward task. The belief was that a short-cycle, simple job can be quickly learned, done by someone with low skill, easily controlled by superiors, and results in high productiveness. This belief, in fact, is still widely held today. A legacy of early industrial engineering is that there is a "one best way" to design any job, and that way should use criteria of standardization, routinization, and an extreme division of labor. That legacy is one of contemporary management's major myths. It certainly is a simplistic way of thinking about work design—ignore everything but the tasks themselves, assume workers are docile and dumb, and forget about the context altogether.

The recent history of work design has taken the situation just sketched and begun to show that it is not all that simple. The two articles in this chapter admirably make the point. In the chapter's first article, Pierce and Dunham describe the situation that early researchers initially attempted to verify: worker responses are directly related to work design. Diagramatically,

Work design→Worker responses

Pierce and Dunham's review notes that this traditional work-design model is simplistic and inaccurate. Instead, there are many factors that apparently moderate the relationship between work design and worker response. Figure 7–1 illustrates the much more complicated and much less certain situation that exists at the present.

This chapter's second article, by Professor Hackman, also eloquently identifies the earlier naiveté regarding the supposed direct relationship between work design and worker response. Hackman differentiates work design into several dimensions (which he terms *core job dimensions*). Workers' psychological and behavioral responses are then differentiated, as well as the person's subjective internal state that translates work design dimensions into these response outcomes. The worker is no longer a simple response organism. On the contrary, several individual differences and other worker-related moderators mentioned by Pierce and Dunham affect the perception of, and experience with, aspects of work design. This all reinforces, of course, our discussion of the "human constraint" in Chapter 6. In addition, Hackman offers another obvious complication for our thinking about work design: the work design of teams. The subject of work design has indeed become rather complicated!

Present

Work design as discussed in this chapter's two articles substantially elaborates the traditional relationship between work design and worker responses. Let us attempt to capture this elaboration by combining Figure 7–1, which summarizes the Pierce and Dunham review,

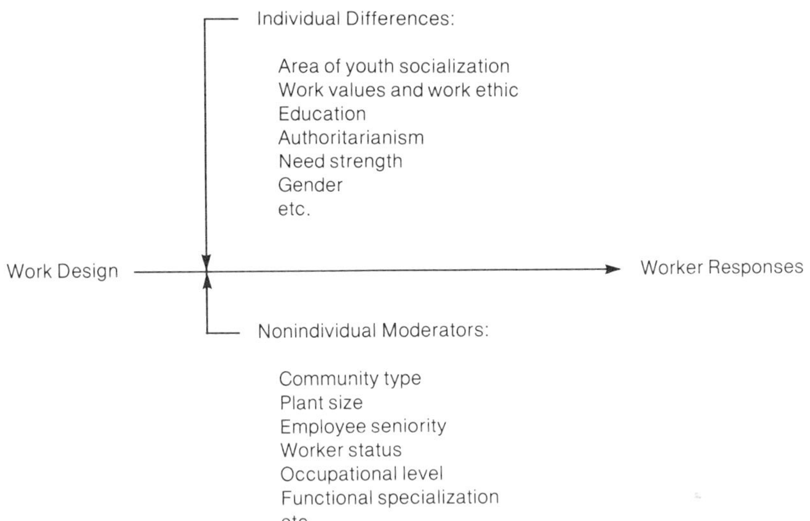

Figure 7-1. Moderating factors on the work-design/worker response relationship (following Pierce and Dunhan, 1976)

with the job characteristics model of work motivation of Hackman. This combined treatment is shown in Figure 7–2.

This combined model begins as did the traditional one with work design (1), that is, the job as defined and specified by someone other than the job incumbent, typically management. What constitutes a job description, however, is seldom what a worker perceives, and the inclusion in this model of core job dimensions (2) reminds us of the characteristics of jobs that workers take to be meaningful to them. Workers are clearly not an undifferentiated class of persons, as the individual (3) and nonindividual (4) differences indicate. The degree to which workers perceive and attribute meaning to the core job

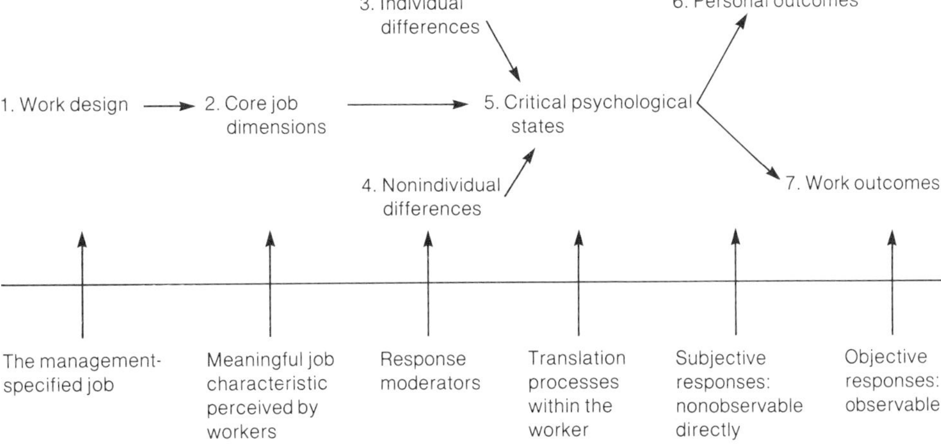

Figure 7-2. Summary work design–work motivation model combining Pierce and Dunham (1976) and Hackman (1977)

dimensions reflects who they are as persons and their social-cultural positions and backgrounds. The model next illustrates that the perceived core job dimensions are moderated by worker differences. The result is three critical psychological states (5) in the worker. These states enable the "translation" of perceived/experienced job characteristics into response outcomes, of which there are two types (6) and (7). One response outcome is personal (6), in the sense that it is the worker's subjective feelings and thoughts about the work—his or her satisfaction with it, motivation to accomplish it, and desire to do quality work or not. The other response outcome is a work (7) one; that is, there are observably objective results in terms of amount of work produced, its quality, its timeliness, and so on.

Summary

The historical evolution of work design has essentially been a story of an ever elaborating way of thinking about it. This has, however, resulted in an interesting mental difficulty: the simplistic and naive earlier way of thinking often left managers with a confident sense of knowing what was what and why. Yet it also led to inaccurate managerial practices and inappropriate organizational designs. Today, in contrast, the empirical evidence available assures us that the topic is a complex one, and at the same time convinces us that we have much to learn so that we can design work in ways that appropriately reflect organizational purposes and constraints and combine with other design variables so as to lead to desired organizational outcomes. Table 7–1 summarizes the main themes in the historical development of work design.

The Readings

The chapter's first selection is a recent review of work design by Pierce and Dunham, "Task Design: A Literature Review." In their article, the authors identify a number of individual and organizational characteristics that affect the ability of task design to produce predictable worker behavior. Values, needs, education, community, organizational size, seniority, occupation—these are but a few such characteristics. Basically, as we mentioned, Pierce and Dunham's review leads them to conclude that a direct cause-and-effect relationship between work design and worker behavior is too simplistic. In fact, a host of factors moderates, or affects, that relationship.

In the second article, "Designing Work for Individuals and for Groups," J. Richard Hackman provides a way of understanding why many people respond positively to "enriched" work. But Hackman continues Pierce and Dunham's theme, pointing out that workers are not simple response organisms. Rather, work design consists of several core job dimensions, whereas worker responses are based on several critical psychological states. The interaction between core job dimensions and these psychological states produces a complex

TABLE 7–1 HISTORICAL THEMES IN THE CONSIDERATION OF WORK DESIGN

From an Early Focus on:	To a Contemporary Focus on:
Job simplification	Increasing job scope
Single jobs	Multiple, related jobs
Job components only	Human and contextual factors too
Managerially designated job features	Perceived and subjectively experienced features as well
Productivity responses	Several types of personal and work outcomes

result, involving both personal and work outcomes. The author provides some specific guidelines for designing work for individuals and for teams. His discussion includes some diagnostic hints as well as some cautionary advice.

Conclusion

In essence, this chapter is concerned with the following questions:

1. What do we mean by "work design"?
2. What is involved—that is, what are the dimensions—in work design?
3. What factors affect the effectiveness of work design?
4. What outcomes result?

TASK DESIGN: A LITERATURE REVIEW

JON L. PIERCE
RANDALL B. DUNHAM

Summary:
The post-Hulin and Blood task design literature is reviewed, and several observations are made: Individual differences (especially growth need strength) and organization variables moderate; affective responses (especially satisfaction with work) are most predictable; objective measures are needed; dimensionality is variable; optimal combinatory models are not widely accepted; and methodological problems are widespread.

Although the history of task design can be traced to the book of Exodus, the recent focus on task simplification can be attributed to Smith (1776), Babbage (1835), Taylor (1911), and Fayol (1916), who discussed improvements in the productive powers of labor derived from the division of labor. During the past three centuries, the forces for task simplification arose out of increasing industrial complexities, goals directed toward greater productivity and efficiency, and a concern for control and standardization of work in organizations. The perceived utility of task simplification was based on experiences of increased labor effectiveness, lower production costs, and greater predictability of system performance.

Tasks designed solely in accord with the prescriptions of classical management theory and industrial engineering may lead to dysfunctional outcomes for both the organization and the individual worker. Scholars of organization behavior have suggested that simplified, low skill level, short-cycle jobs have led to low motivation, job dissatisfaction, low productivity, and other disruptive behaviors (Argyris, 1957; Herzberg et al., 1959; McGregor, 1960).

In hopes of reducing problems attributed to the task design of jobs emerging from the prescriptions of scientific management, practitioners and scholars have focused on job enlargement-job enrichment programs. This relatively new organizational phenomenon is embedded in the belief that enlargement and/or enrichment of task design will enhance the affective, behavioral, and motivational potential of jobs.

Since the early experiments with job enlargement at IBM in 1943 (Walker, 1950), task design has been experimented with by hundreds of organizations in the United States. For example, Ford (Ford, 1973; 1969) reports that a large number of "successful" job enrichment experiments conducted at AT&T led to increased employee motivation, efficiency and productivity, and reduced turnover. In addition, task design has become a major element in the industrial democracy movement in many Western European countries (Herzberg, 1974).

In this review, the term "expanded task design" will be used as a description which encompasses job enlargement and/or job enrichment (i.e., complex tasks). In the past, the terms "enlargement" and "enrichment" have been used interchangeably at some times and differentially at other times. Lawler (1969) has stated that horizontal enlargement increases the number and variety of operations that an individual performs on the job, while vertical enlargement (enrichment) increases the degree to which the job holder controls the planning and execution of the job and participates in the setting of organization policy. These terms have often been confused in the literature. Hopefully use of a single term "task design," to include horizontal and vertical design, and task redesign, will help to integrate the literature.

In this review, research on worker responses to task design will be placed into one of three major categories: a. studies which tested for main effects of task design on worker affective, motivational, and behavioral re-

Abridged from Jon L. Pierce and Randall B. Dunham, "Task Design: A Literature Review," *Academy of Management Review*, vol. 1 (October 1976), pp. 83–97. Reprinted by permission.

sponses; b. studies which tested for interactions between task design and individual differences; and c. studies which tested for interaction between task design and other, non-individual variables (e.g., organizational characteristics). The fourth major section of this review considers research concerned with measurement of the task design construct, dimensionality, and models for combining task design elements.*

MAIN EFFECTS

The main effect investigations reviewed (with a single exception) were based on cross-sectional data. Causality running from task design to employee responses is implied even though it stands as a relatively untested assumption. The issue of assumed causality is not the only problem characterizing the research. For example, failure to measure task design and reliance on the perception of a limited number of job occupants to describe task characteristics were identified. Both procedures run counter to the philosophy underlying the use of perceived task dimensions in the assessment of employee responses.

The experimental studies employed a minimum in terms of desirable research design. Many of the redesign efforts were complex in nature; consequently, it is difficult to discern which employee responses are attributable to task redesign per se, as contrasted with various Hawthorne effects.

The evidence emerging for the main effects investigations suggests that task designs are more frequently associated with positive affective, behavioral, and motivational responses than are narrowly defined tasks. Two of seven survey research investigations suggest that increases in task variety are not necessarily associated with increases in satisfaction and motivation. Affective and motivational responses appear to be more strongly related to task design than are behavioral responses. Satisfaction with work is more strongly related to task design than are other affective, behavioral, or motivational variables.

In the task design manipulation studies, somewhat greater attention was directed toward behavioral outcomes than was the case in the survey investigations. In all but one of the investigations reviewed, evidence suggests improvements in work related behavior associated with expanded task design.

INTERACTIONS WITH INDIVIDUAL DIFFERENCES

The individual studies which tested for individual moderators of the task design-response relationships often produced ambiguous results; but careful examination of these studies as a group reveals a pattern. Conflicting results occurred most often in studies which attempted to index individual differences through sociological level classifications. These studies differed in many ways including their technique for classifying workers into groups which would or would not be expected to respond favorably to expanded task design. The authors argue that the ambiguities observed are to be expected, given the various methods and multiple assumptions employed. The major value of these sociological level studies was that they stimulated further research which led to the direct assessment of personality and psychologically based individual differences.

In later research, individual differences were assessed directly at the individual level rather than through inference from sociological classifications. These individual differences were typically operationalized in terms of work values, Protestant Work Ethic, higher order need strength, or growth need strength. The various individual differences measures appear to index the degree to which workers desire and value intrinsic outcomes derived from expanded task design. Therefore, some workers (e.g., those with strong higher order need strength) respond more favorably to expanded task design than do others.

Research on *non*individual moderators of task design-response relationships should be recognized as exploratory at this point. There is sufficient evidence available to suggest that nontask environmental factors

*Editor's note: This discussion contains only the authors' conclusions regarding the various categories. For details of the specific research studies reviewed, the reader is referred to Pierce and Dunham's original article. The authors' final discussion sections are reproduced here in their entirety.

will influence task design-response relationships. But there is insufficient evidence to isolate which of these environmental variables are the most important moderators, or to identify the process by which these observed moderating effects occur.

The evidence is consistent in showing that additive models always meet or exceed the effectiveness of multiplicative models for combining task design elements. The dimensionality of perceived task design varies greatly across samples, but appears to be multidimensional in nature.

STATE-OF-THE-ART

Most studies of task design-response relationships have categorized task design in one of two ways. Often the design of tasks is discussed in objective terms but without objectively assessing task characteristics. Recently, investigators have begun to obtain perceptual measures of task design. While this allows comparisons between studies, these measures are *perceptual*. The Job Diagnostic Survey (JDS) (Hackman and Oldham, 1975) is currently the most widely used perceptual measure of task design. It produces measures of variety, autonomy, significance, identity, and feedback with reliability estimates typically above .70. The underlying dimensionality of the JDS has been shown to vary across samples. It has been almost universally found that an additive model best describes the relationship between JDS scores and measures of worker responses.

The empirical literature available through the beginning of 1976 is suggestive of a main effect of task design on a number of worker responses. But existing theoretical models fail to completely account for these findings. Workers' affective responses have the strongest and most commonly identified relationships with task design; worker motivational responses are also commonly related to the design of the task, but behavioral responses have not been as strongly or consistently tied to task design.

Clearly some workers respond more favorably to expanded task design than do others. There is currently no single, widely accepted theoretical explanation for this finding. Research which has explored the role of individual characteristics at a sociological level (e.g., urban/rural location) has often, but not consistently, found such variables to moderate task design-response relationships. Most recent research in this area has employed measurement (e.g., Protestant Work Ethic, higher order need strength, growth need strength) at the individual level. These studies typically find that these individual differences moderate the task design-response relationships.

Some research (Dunham, et al., n.d.; Oldham, n.d.) suggests that certain non-task environmental factors may also moderate task design-response relationships. Specific environmental variables which act as moderators have not as yet been well documented or isolated and have not been fitted to a theoretical model. The process by which these variables moderate the task design-response relationship remains unclear.

In summary, the available empirical research suggests that task design often has a positive relationship with various worker responses. Neither the measurement of task design nor the theoretical integration is complete. The boundaries of task design-response relationships have not yet been completely identified.

DISCUSSION

Much of the research to date was prompted by Turner and Lawrence (1965), Blood and Hulin (1967), and Hackman and Lawler (1971). The theoretical foundation for much of this research can be traced to either expectancy theory (Lawler, 1969) or the job characteristic model of work motivation (Hackman and Oldham, n.d.). Post-hoc examination of the existing literature cannot be fully integrated by these theories.

A number of design problems were evident in the research reviewed. Most investigations were one-shot studies. The internal validity of one-shot designs is potentially contaminated and external validity is minimal. In some studies, the unit of analysis did not seem appropriate, given the stated research objectives. For example, many studies discussed individual differences yet made sociological level measures; others discussed individual responses but obtained measures of group responses. Several studies claimed to investigate task design-response relationships but failed to measure a priori task design characteristics. Finally, many studies utilized self-report measures for both dependent and independent variables, thus increasing the probability of artifactual task design-response relationships.

Task design researchers have generally not attempted to differentiate conceptually or empirically the role of the dependent variables in associations with task design. It is not clear if affective, behavioral, and motivational responses are equally affected. These conceptually distinct responses should be treated as such.

Until recently, the task dimensions studied in task design research have generally not been guided by any accepted conceptually and/or empirically developed typology of task design. As a result, a wide variety and range of task charateristics have been explored. Researchers have recently begun to rely on worker generated perceptions for assessing task design, but typically speak in terms of objective task design. Use of perceived measures of task design has been a concern recognized by the authors of the task design measures and many users of this measurement technique. Schwab and Cummings (1976) call attention to the possible confounding of personal preferences and needs with the cognitive measurement of task dimensions.

The attention of some task design researchers has been directed to instruments which measure objective task characteristics such as the Position Analysis Questionnaire (PAQ) (McCormick, et al., 1967). Employing the PQA, Pritchard and Peters (1974) found that intrinsic job satisfaction was more a function of task design than was extrinsic satisfaction, and that task design was also a significant predictor of overall satisfaction. Research is needed to identify which objective task design characteristics are related to perceived task design and in what manner.

The objectives of much of the task design research is to identify "optimal" design to realize improvements in employee responses. Much of the research has been identified as survey research employing one-shot designs. Consequently, employee responses to task design, redesign, and changes per se have not been clearly differentiated. Evidence on the role of Hawthorne effects has accumulated through the years so that a distinction between task re-design and change per se is needed.

The effects of task design on worker responses over time have infrequently been examined (Farris, 1969, Maher and Overbagh, 1971). Research is needed to track the response criteria across extended periods of time so that long term results of task expansion are more fully understood.

Virtually all the research has tested for linear relationships between task design and worker responses. But it is possible that task design which is expanded too much can lead to negative responses. Such a curvilinear relationship may be best understood in terms of a model of individual-task fit. Davis, England, and Lofquist (1968) discussed the importance of an individual-task fit for both satisfaction and satisfactoriness. It has not been adequately determined what specific individual characteristics produce individual differences moderating effects.

Task design research has generally been conducted without considering the contextual, structural, or configurational character of the social system that houses the tasks and role occupants under investigation. Nor have functional limits to task re-design caused by the social system and the differential impact of task design on employee responses due to the organization been adequately examined.

Several nontask environmental variables have been found to moderate task design-response relationships. It has not been determined when or why these variables moderate. Morse and Lorsch (1970) sensitize the researcher to the importance of an organization-task-individual fit for competence motivation.

In summary, a critical review of the literature identified a number of problems and unanswered questions. A careful theoretical integration could allow a more thorough understanding of the effects of task design on worker responses and a resolution of many of the existing ambiguities as research moves toward the development of a science of task design. The study of task design must be framed within complex nomological networks which include relevant individual, technological, and organizational factors.

DESIGNING WORK FOR INDIVIDUALS AND FOR GROUPS

J. RICHARD HACKMAN

As yet there are no simple or generally accepted criteria for a well-designed job, nor is a single technology acknowledged as the proper way to go about redesigning work. Moreover, it often is unclear in specific circumstances whether work should be structured to be performed by individual employees, or whether it should be designed to be carried out by a *group* of employees working together.

The first part of this selection reviews one current model for work design that focuses on the individual performer. In the second part, discussion turns to a number of issues that must be dealt with when work is designed for interacting teams of employees.

DESIGNING WORK FOR INDIVIDUALS

A model specifying how job characteristics and individual differences interact to affect the satisfaction, motivation, and productivity of individuals at work has been proposed by Hackman and Oldham (1976). The model is specifically intended for use in planning and carrying out changes in the design of jobs. It is described below, and then is used as a guide for a discussion of diagnostic procedures and change principles that can be used in redesigning the jobs of individuals.

The Job Characteristics Model

The basic job characteristics model is shown in Figure 7–3. As illustrated in the figure, five core job dimensions are seen as creating three critical psychological states which, in turn, lead to a number of beneficial personal and work outcomes. The links among the job dimensions, the psychological states, and the outcomes are shown to be moderated by the strength of individuals' growth needs. The major classes of variables in the model are reviewed briefly below.

Psychological States The three following psychological states are postulated as critical in affecting a person's motivation and satisfaction on the job:

1. Experienced meaningfulness: The person must experience the work as generally important, valuable, and worthwhile.
2. Experienced responsibility: The individual must feel personally responsible and accountable for the results of the work he or she performs.
3. Knowledge of results: The individual must have understanding, on a fairly regular basis, of how effectively he or she is performing the job.

The more these three conditions are present, the more people will feel good about themselves when they perform well. Or, following Hackman and Lawler (1971), the model postulates that internal rewards are obtained by individuals when they *learn* (knowledge of results) that they *personally* (experienced responsibility) have performed well on a task that they *care about* (experienced meaningfulness). These internal rewards are reinforcing to the individual, and serve as incentives for continued efforts to perform well in the future. When the persons do not perform well, they do not experience a reinforcing state of affairs, and may elect to try harder in the future so as to regain the rewards that good performance brings. The net result is a self-perpetuating cycle of positive work motivation powered by self-generated rewards, that is predicted to continue until one or more of the three psychological states is no longer present—or until the individual no longer values the internal rewards that derive from good performance.

From J. Richard Hackman, Edward E. Lawler III, and Lyman W. Porter (eds.), *Perspectives on Behavior in Organizations* (New York: McGraw-Hill Book Company), pp. 242–56. Adapted from J. R. Hackman, "Work Design," in J. R. Hackman and J. L. Suttle (eds.), "Improving Life at Work: Behavioral Science Approaches to Organizational Change" (Santa Monica, Calif.: Goodyear Publishing Company, 1977). Portions of this material have been adapted from articles by Hackman and Oldham (1975) and Hackman, Oldham, Janson, and Purdy (1975). Reprinted by permission.

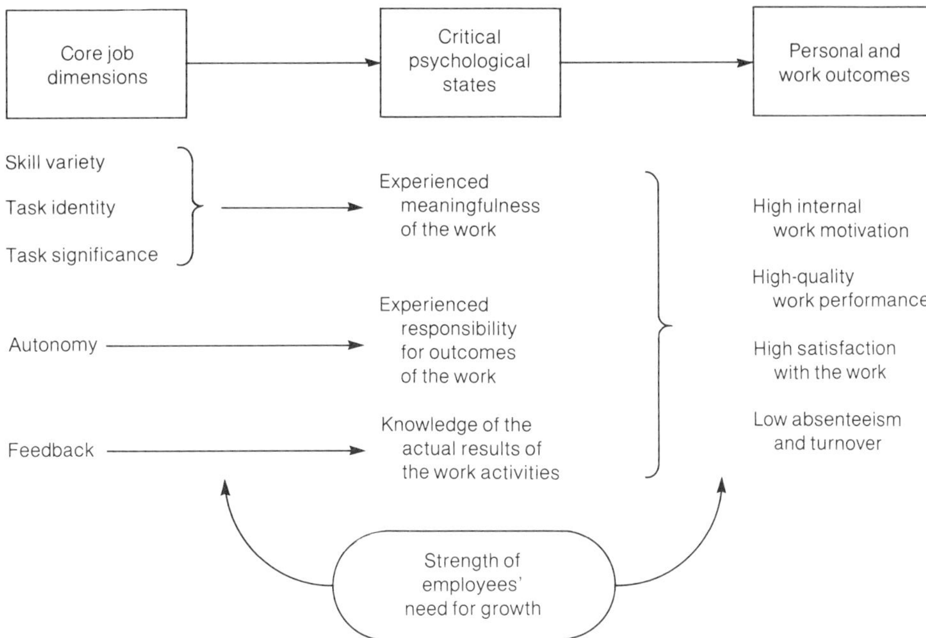

Figure 7-3. The job characteristics model of work motivation

Job Dimensions Of the five job characteristics shown in Figure 7–3 as fostering the emergence of the psychological states, three contribute to the experienced meaningfulness of the work, and one each contributes to experienced responsibility and to knowledge of results.

The three job dimensions that contribute to a job's *meaningfulness* are:

> 1. *Skill variety* The degree to which a job requires a variety of different activities in carrying out the work, which involve the use of a number of different skills and talents of the person.

When a task requires a person to engage in activities that challenge or stretch his or her skills and abilities, that task almost invariably is experienced as meaningful by the individual. Many parlor games, puzzles, and recreational activities, for example, achieve much of their fascination because they tap and test the intellective or motor skills of the people who do them. When a job draws upon several skills of an employee, that individual may find the job to be of very high personal meaning—even if, in any absolute sense, it is not of great significance or importance.

> 2. *Task identity* The degree to which the job requires completion of a "whole" and identifiable piece of work—that is, doing a job from beginning to end with a visible outcome.

If an employee assembles a complete product or provides a complete unit of service he or she should find the work more meaningful than if he or she were responsible for only a small part of the whole job—other things (such as skill variety) being equal.

> 3. *Task significance* The degree to which the job has a substantial impact on the lives or work of other people—whether in the immediate organization or in the external environment.

When individuals understand that the results of their work may have a significant effect on the well-being of other people, the experienced meaningfulness of the work usually is enhanced. Employees who tighten nuts on aircraft brake assemblies, for example, are much more likely to perceive their work as meaningful than are workers who fill small boxes with paper clips—even though the skill levels involved may be comparable.

The job characteristic predicted to prompt feelings of personal *responsibility* for the work outcomes is autonomy. "Autonomy" is defined as the degree to which the job provides substantial freedom, independence, and discretion to the individual in scheduling the work and in determining the procedures to be used in carrying it out.

To the extent that autonomy is high, work outcomes will be viewed by workers as depending substantially on their *own* efforts, initiatives, and decisions, rather than on the adequacy of instructions from the boss or on a manual of job procedures. In such circumstances, individuals should feel a strong personal responsibility for the successes and failures that occur on the job.

The job characteristic that fosters *knowledge of results* is "feedback," which is defined as the degree to which carrying out the work activities required by the job results in the individual's obtaining direct and clear information about the effectiveness of his or her performance.

It often is useful to combine the scores of a job on the five dimensions described above into a single index reflecting the overall potential of the job to prompt self-generated work motivation on the part of job incumbents. Following the model diagrammed in Figure 7–3, a job high in motivating potential must be high on at least one (and hopefully more) of the three dimensions that lead to experienced meaningfulness, *and* high on autonomy and feedback as well—thereby creating conditions for all three of the critical psychological states to be present. Arithmetically, scores of jobs on the five dimensions are combined as follows to meet this criterion:

$$\text{Motivating potential score (MPS)} = \left(\frac{\text{skill variety} + \text{task identity} + \text{task significance}}{3}\right) \times \text{autonomy} \times \text{job feedback}$$

As can be seen from the formula, a near-zero score of a job on either autonomy or feedback will reduce the overall MPS to near-zero; whereas a near-zero score on one of the three job dimensions that contribute to experienced meaningfulness cannot, by itself, do so.

Strength of the Individual's Need for Growth The strength of a person's need for growth is postulated to moderate how people react to complex, challenging work at two points in the model shown in Figure 7–3: first, at the link between the objective job dimensions and the psychological states, and again between the psychological states and the outcome variables. The first link means that persons with a high need for growth are more likely (or better able) to *experience* the psychological states when an objective job is enriched than persons with a low need for growth. The second link means that individuals with a high need for growth will respond more positively to the psychological states, when they are present, than persons with a low need for growth.

Outcome Variables Also shown in Figure 7–3 are several outcomes that are affected by the level of self-generated motivation experienced by people at work. Of special interest as an outcome variable is internal work motivation (Lawler and Hall, 1970; Hackman and Lawler, 1971), because it taps directly the contingency between effective performance and self-administered affective rewards. Typical questionnaire items measuring internal work motivation include: 1. I feel a great sense of personal satisfaction when I do this job well; 2. I feel bad and unhappy when I discover that I have performed poorly on this job; 3. My own feelings are *not* affected much one way or the other by how well I do on this job (reversed scoring).

Other outcomes listed in Figure 7–3 are the quality of work performance, job satisfaction (especially satisfaction with opportunities for personal growth and development on the job), absenteeism, and turnover. All these outcomes are predicted to be affected positively by a job high in motivating potential.

Validity of the Job Characteristics Model

Empirical testing of the job characteristics model of work motivation is reported in detail elsewhere

(Hackman and Oldham, 1976). In general, results are supportive, as suggested by the following overview:

1. People who work on jobs high on the core job characteristics are more motivated, satisfied, and productive than people who work on jobs that score low on these chacteristics. The same is true for absenteeism, although less strongly so.

2. Responses to jobs high in objective motivating potential are more positive for people who have strong needs for growth than for people with weak needs for growth. The moderating effect of an individual's need for growth occurs both at the link between the job dimensions and the psychological states and at the link between the psychological states and the outcome measures, as shown in Figure 7–3. (This moderating effect is not, however, obtained for absenteeism.)

3. The job characteristics operate *through* the psychological states in influencing the outcome variables, as predicted by the model, rather than influencing the outcomes directly. Two anomalies have been identified, however: 1. results involving the feedback dimension are in some cases less strong than for those obtained for the other dimensions (perhaps in part because individuals receive feedback at work from many sources—not just the job), and 2. the linkage between autonomy and experienced responsibility does not operate exactly as specified by the model in affecting the outcome variables (Hackman and Oldham, 1976).

Diagnostic Use of the Model

The job characteristics model was designed so that each major class of variables (objective job characteristics, mediating psychological states, strength of the individual's need for growth, and work motivation and satisfaction) can be directly measured in actual work situations. Such measurements are obtained using the Job Diagnostic Survey (JDS), which is described in detail elsewhere (Hackman and Oldham, 1975). The major intended uses of the JDS are 1. to diagnose existing jobs before planned work redesign, and 2. to evaluate the effects of work redesign—for example, to determine which job dimensions did and did not change, to assess the impact of the changes on the motivation and satisfaction of employees, and to test for any possible alterations after the change in the need for growth of people whose jobs were redesigned.

In the paragraphs to follow, several steps are presented that might be followed by a change agent in carrying out a diagnosis using the JDS.

Step 1: Are Motivation and Satisfaction Really Problems? Sometimes organizations undertake job enrichment or work redesign to improve work motivation and satisfaction when in fact the real problem with work performance lies elsewhere—for example, in the equipment or technology of the job. It is important, therefore, to examine the level of employees' motivation and satisfaction at an early stage in a job diagnosis. If motivation and satisfaction are problems, and are accompanied by documented problems in work performance, absenteeism, or turnover as revealed by independent organizational indices, the change agent would continue to step 2. If not, the agent presumably would look to other aspects of the work situation (e.g., the technology, the workflow) to identify and understand the reasons for the problem which gave rise to the diagnostic activity.

Step 2: Is the Job Low in Motivating Potential? To answer this question, the change agent would examine the Motivating Potential Score of the target job, and compare it with the MPS scores of other jobs to determine whether or not the *job itself* is a probable cause of the motivational problems documented in step 1. If the job turns out to be low on MPS, he would continue to step 3; if it scores high, he would look for other reasons for the motivational difficulties (e.g., the pay plan, the nature of supervision, and so on).

Step 3: What Specific Aspects of the Job are Causing the Difficulty? This step involves examination of the job on each of the five core job dimensions, to pinpoint the specific strengths and weaknesses of the job as it currently exists. It is useful at this stage to construct a profile of the target job, to make visually apparent where improvements need to be made. An illustrative profile for two jobs (one "good" job and one job needing improvement) is shown in Figure 7–4.

Job A is an engineering maintenance job, and is high on all of the core dimensions; the MPS of this job is

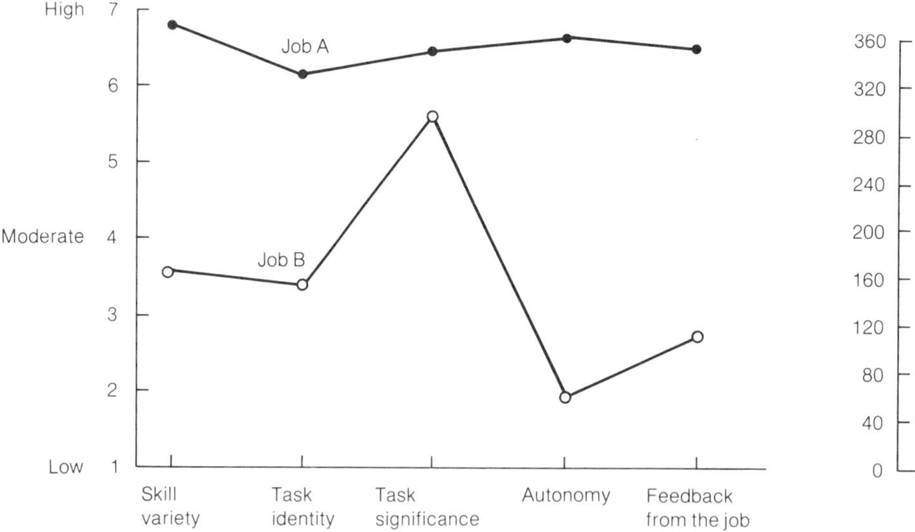

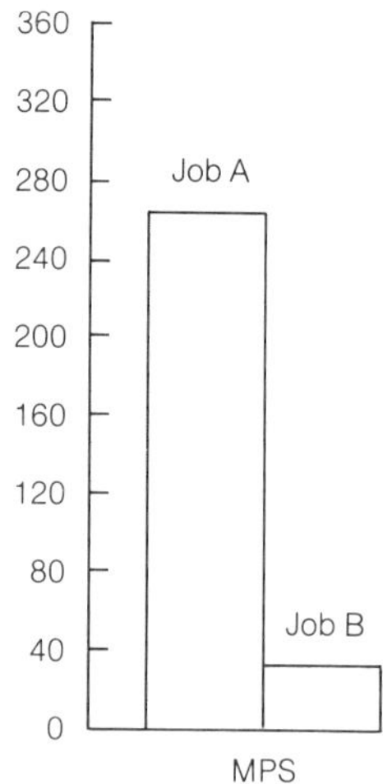

Figure 7-4. JDS profile of a "good" job and a "bad" job

very high: 260.[1] Job enrichment would not be recommended for this job; if employees working on the job are unproductive and unhappy, the reasons probably have little to do with the design of the work itself.

Job B, on the other hand, has many problems. This job involves the routine and repetitive processing of checks in a bank. The MPS of 30—which is quite low—would be even lower if it were not for the moderately high task significance of the job. (Task significance is moderately high because the people are handling large amounts of other people's money, and their efforts potentially have important consequences for the unseen clients.) The job provides the individuals with very little direct feedback about how effectively they are performing; the employees have little autonomy in how they go about doing the job; and the job is moderately low in both skill variety and task identity.

For Job B, then, there is plenty of room for improvement, and many avenues to consider in planning job changes. For still other jobs, the avenues for change may turn out to be considerably more specific: for example, feedback and autonomy may be reasonably high, but one or more of the core dimensions which contribute to the experienced meaningfulness of the work (i.e., skill variety, task identity, and task significance) may be low. In such a case, attention would turn to ways to increase the standing of the job on these latter three dimensions.

Step 4: How Ready Are the Employees for Change? Once it has been documented that there is need for improvement in the focal job, and the particularly troublesome aspects of the job have been identified, then it is appropriate to begin planning the specific action steps which will be taken to enrich the job. An important factor in such planning is determining the strength of the employees' needs for growth, since employees whose needs for growth are strong should respond more readily to job enrichment than employees whose needs are weak. The measure of the need for growth provided by the JDS can be helpful in identifying which employees should be among the first to have jobs changed (i.e., those whose needs for growth are strong), and how such changes should be introduced (e.g., perhaps with more caution for individuals whose needs for growth are weak).

Step 5: What Special Problems and Opportunities Are Present in the Existing Work System? Before undertaking actual job changes, it is always advisable to search for any special roadblocks that may exist in the organizational unit as it currently exists, and for special

1. MPS scores can range from 1 to 343. The average is about 125.

opportunities that may be built upon in the change program.

Frequently of special importance in this regard is the level of *satisfaction* employees currently experience with various aspects of their organizational life. For example, the JDS provides measures of satisfaction with pay, job security, co-workers, and supervision. If the diagnosis reveals high dissatisfaction in one or more of these areas, then it may be very difficult to initiate and maintain a successful job redesign project (Oldham, 1976; Oldham, Hackman, and Pearce, 1976). On the other hand, if satisfaction with supervision is especially high, then it might be wise to build an especially central role for supervisors in the initiation and management of the change process.

Other examples could be given as well. The point is simply that such supplementary measures (especially those having to do with aspects of employee satisfaction) may be helpful in highlighting special problems and opportunities that deserve explicit recognition and attention as part of the diagnosis of an existing work system.

Principles for Enriching Jobs

The core job dimensions specified in the job-characteristics model are tied directly to a set of action principles for redesigning jobs (Hackman, Oldham, Janson, and Purdy, 1975; Walters and Associates, 1975). As shown in Figure 7–5, these principles specify what types of changes in jobs are most likely to lead to improvements in each of the five core job dimensions, and thereby to an increase in the motivating potential of the job as a whole.

Principle 1: Forming Natural Work Units A critical step in the design of any job is the decision about how

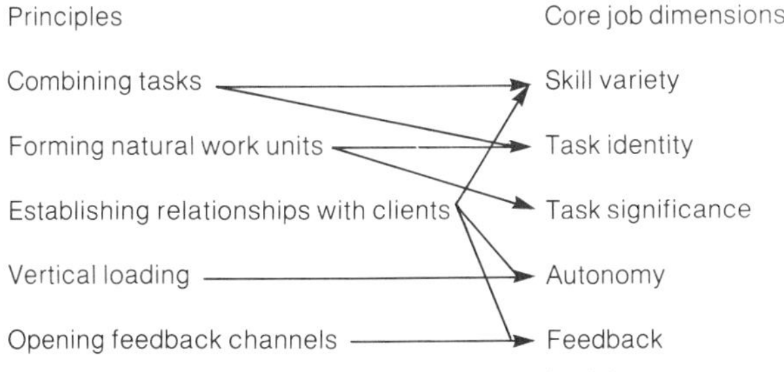

Figure 7-5. Principles for changing jobs

the work is to be distributed among the people who do it. Consider, for example, a typing pool—consisting of one supervisor and ten typists—that does all the typing for one division of an organization. Jobs are delivered in rough draft or dictated form to the supervisor, who distributes them as evenly as possible among the typists. In such circumstances the individual letters, reports, and other tasks performed by a given typist in one day or week are randomly assigned. There is no basis for identifying with the work or the person or department for whom it is performed, or for placing any personal value upon it.

By contrast, creating natural units of work increases employees' "ownership" of the work, and therefore improves the chances that employees will view it as meaningful and important rather than as irrelevant and boring. In creating natural units of work, one must first identify what the basic work items are. In the typing pool example, that might be "pages to be typed." Then these items are grouped into natural and meaningful categories. For example, each typist might be assigned continuing responsibility for all work requested by a single department or by several smaller departments. Instead of typing one section of a large report, the individual will type the entire piece of work, with knowledge of exactly what the total outcome of the work is. Furthermore, over a period of time the typist will develop a growing sense of how the work affects co-workers or customers who receive the completed product. Thus, as shown in Figure 7-5, forming natural units of work increases two of the core job dimensions that contribute to experienced meaningfulness—task identity and task significance.

It is still important that work be distributed so that the system as a whole operates efficiently, of course, and work loads must be arranged so that they are approximately equal among employees. The principle of natural work units simply requires that these traditional criteria be supplemented so that, insofar as possible, the tasks that arrive at an employee's work station form an identifiable and meaningful whole.

Principle 2: Combining Tasks The very existence of a pool, made up entirely of persons whose sole function is typing, reflects a fractionalization of jobs that sometimes can lead to such hidden costs as high absenteeism and turnover, extra supervisory time, and so on. The principle of combining tasks is based on the assumption that such costs often can be reduced by simply taking existing and fractionalized tasks and putting them back together again to form a new and larger module of work. At the Medfield, Massachusetts plant of Corning Glass Works, for example, the job of assembling laboratory hotplates was redesigned by combining a number of previously separate tasks. After the change, each hot plate was assembled from start to finish by one operator, instead of going through several separate operations performed by different people.

Combining tasks (like forming natural work units) contributes in two ways to the experienced meaningfulness of the work. First, task identity is increased. The hotplate assembler, for example, can see and identify with a finished product ready for shipment—rather than a nearly invisible junction of solder. Moreover, as more tasks are combined into a single worker's job, the individual must use a greater variety of skills in performing the job, further increasing the meaningfulness of the work.

Principle 3: Establishing Relationships with Clients By establishing direct relationships between workers and their clients, jobs often can be improved in three ways. First, feedback increases because additional opportunities are created for the employees to receive direct praise or criticism of their work outputs. Second, skill variety may increase, because of the need to develop and exercise one's interpersonal skills in managing and maintaining the relationship with the client. Finally, autonomy will increase to the degree that individuals are given real personal responsibility for deciding how to manage their relationships with the people who receive the outputs of their work.

Creating relationships with clients can be viewed as a three-step process: 1. identification of who the client actually is; 2. establishing the most direct contact possible between the worker and the client; and 3. establishing criteria and procedures so that the client can judge the quality of the product or service received and relay his judgments directly back to the worker. Especially important (and, in many cases, difficult to achieve) is identification of the specific criteria by which the work output is assessed by the client—and ensuring that both the worker and the client understand these criteria and agree with them.

Principle 4: Vertical Loading In vertical loading, the intent is to partially close the gap between the "doing" and the "controlling" aspects of the job. Thus, when a job is vertically loaded, responsibilities and controls that formerly were reserved for management are given to the employee as part of the job. Among ways this might be achieved are the following:

Giving job incumbents responsibility for deciding on work methods, and for advising or helping train less experienced workers.

Providing increased freedom in time management, including decisions about when to start and stop work, when to take a break, and how to assign work priorities.

Encouraging workers to do their own trouble-shooting and manage work crises, rather than calling immediately for a supervisor.

Providing workers with increased knowledge of the financial aspects of the job and the organization, and increased control over budgetary matters that affect their own work.

When a job is vertically loaded, it inevitably increases in *autonomy*. And, as shown in Figure 7-3, this should lead to increased feelings of personal responsibility and accountability for the work outcomes.

Principle 5: Opening Feedback Channels In virtually all jobs there are ways to open channels of feedback to individuals to help them learn not only how well they are performing their jobs, but also whether their performance is improving, deteriorating, or remaining at a constant level. While there are various sources from which information about performance can come, it usually is advantageous for workers to learn about their performance *directly as they do the job*—rather than from management on an occasional basis.

Feedback provided by the job itself is more immediate and private than feedback provided by its supervisor, and can also increase workers' feelings of personal control over their work. Moreover, it avoids many of the potentially disruptive interpersonal problems which can develop when workers can find out how they are doing only by means of direct messages or subtle cues from the boss.

Exactly what should be done to open channels for feedback from the job varies from job to job and organization to organization. In many cases, the changes involve simply removing existing blocks which isolate the individual from naturally occurring data about performance, rather than generating entirely new feedback mechanisms. For example:

Establishing direct relationships with clients (discussed above) often removes blocks between the worker and natural external sources of data about the work.

Quality control in many organizations often eliminates a natural source of feedback, because all quality checks are done by people other than the individuals responsible for the work. In such cases, feedback to the workers, if there is any, may be belated and diluted. By placing most quality-control functions in the hands of workers themselves, the quantity and quality of data available to them about their own performance will dramatically increase.

Tradition and established procedure in many organizations dictate that records about performance be kept by a supervisor and transmitted up (not down) the organizational hierarchy. Sometimes supervisors even check the work and correct any errors themselves. The worker who made the error never knows it occurred and is therefore denied the very information which can enhance both internal work motivation and the technical adequacy of his performance. In many cases, it is possible to provide standard summaries of performance records directly to the workers (and perhaps also to their superiors), thereby giving employees personally and regularly the data they need to improve their effectiveness.

Computers and other automated machines sometimes can be used to provide individuals with data now blocked from them. Many clerical operations, for example, are now performed on computer consoles. These consoles often can be programed to provide the clerk with immediate feedback in the form of a CRT display or a printout indicating that an error has been made. Some systems even have been programed to provide the operator with a positive feedback message when a period of error-free performance has been sustained.

Conclusion The principles for redesigning jobs reviewed above, while illustrative of the kinds of changes that can be made to improve the jobs of individuals in organizations, obviously are not exhaustive. They were selected for attention here because of the links between the principles and the core job dimensions in the motivational model presented earlier. Other principles for enriching jobs (which, although often similar to those presented here, derive from alternative conceptual frameworks) are presented by Ford (1969), Glaser (1975), Herzberg (1974), and Katzell and Yankelovich (1975, Chap. 6).

DESIGNING WORK FOR TEAMS

Often it is easier or more appropriate, given the nature of the work to be done and the organizational circumstances under which it is to be done, to design work for interacting teams rather than for individuals working alone. In such cases, the ultimate aim generally is similar to that sought when individual job enrichment is carried out: that is, to improve the quality of the work experience of the people involved, and simultaneously to increase the quality and quantity of the work produced. The difference is that the work is defined and implemented as a *group* task, rather than as an interconnected set of individual tasks. Because of this a larger chunk of work can be included within the boundaries of the task, thereby increasing the intrinsic meaningfulness of the work. Moreover, the possibility is increased for the development of close, socially satisfying work relationships among team members. Such relationships are highly valued by many people, but difficult or impossible to achieve by means of redesign of individual jobs in such work settings as assembly lines, where individual work stations may be fixed and so widely separated that meaningful social interaction with others is (for all practical purposes) precluded.

Until relatively recently, most work design for teams has been carried out from the perspective of sociotechnical systems theory, and has involved the creation of autonomous or semi-autonomous work groups. Specific arrangements (e.g., how the group task itself is designed, the size and composition of the work group, the nature of the reward system) have varied from project to project, but the following attributes are characteristic of most autonomous work groups:[2]

1. A "whole" task for the group, in which the mission of the group is sufficiently identifiable and significant that members find the work of the group meaningful.
2. Workers who each have a number of the skills required for completion of the group task, thereby increasing the flexibility of the group in carrying out the task. When individuals do not have a robust repertoire of skills initially, procedures are developed to encourage cross-training among members.
3. Autonomy for the group to make decisions about the methods by which the work is carried out, the scheduling of various activities, the assignment of different individuals to different tasks, and (sometimes) the selection of new group members.
4. Compensation based on the performance of the group as a whole, rather than on the contributions of individual group members.

It should be emphasized that these four ingredients are simply summary statements of the kinds of changes that often are made when work is redesigned for interacting teams. They do not represent the only way to design work for groups, nor are these ingredients necessarily the most appropriate ones for any given instance. Therefore, it may be useful to step back from specific change principles and attempt to identify the major *general* criteria for the design of work for teams—and then to explore alternative strategies for attempting to achieve those criteria.

2. See, for example, Bucklow (1966), Davis (1966: 44), Davis and Trist (1974), Gulowsen (1972: 375–78), and Trist, Higgin, Murray, and Pollock (1963, ch. 9).

Design Criteria for Interacting Groups

The two criteria listed below appear to be the minimum requirements for the design of interacting work teams if high productivity by the team and the satisfaction of its members are to be achieved simultaneously.

1. The team itself should be a cohesive group, in which members feel committed to the goals of the group, and in which they can experience significant personal satisfaction through their interactions with teammates.

In a highly cohesive group, members greatly value the rewards (usually interpersonal) that fellow members can provide. This means that the quality of the social experience of members in cohesive groups is likely to be high rather than low. It also means that cohesive groups usually have considerable leverage in enforcing member compliance with group norms. That is, since members of cohesive groups strongly value the rewards controlled by their peers, they are especially likely to engage in behavior that is congruent with group norms. Failure to do so can result in those rewards being made unavailable to them (e.g., being "frozen out") or can lead other group members to negatively sanction their actions (Hackman, 1976).

The problem is that while cohesive groups have been shown to generate a high degree of uniformity of behavior in terms of group norms, the *direction* of those norms is unrelated to the level of cohesiveness of the group (Berkowitz, 1954; Schachter, Ellertson, McBride, and Gregory, 1951; Seashore, 1954). Sometimes highly cohesive groups enforce a norm of low performance; at other times they encourage and support members' efforts toward high performance. Relatively little is known about what factors determine whether group norms will encourage high or low performance (e.g., Lawler and Cammann, 1972; Vroom, 1969: 226–27). It is necessary, therefore, to propose an additional criterion for the design of work teams in organizations.

2. The environment of the work group, including its task, must be such that the group norms that emerge and are enforced are consistent with the two aims of

high productivity and satisfying interpersonal relationships.

Approaches to Work Design for Interacting Groups

Meeting the two design criteria identified above requires, at minimum, attention to 1. the composition and dynamics of the group itself, 2. reward contingencies in the organizational environment, and 3. the structure of the group task. These matters are explored below.

Design and Maintenance of the Group qua Group It is important that members of an interacting work team be able to experience themselves as part of a group that is *psychologically meaningful* to them. Usually this requires that the group be moderately small (usually less than fifteen members, although apparently successful autonomous work groups of larger size have been reported), and that members occupy a single workplace (or at least contiguous workplaces with easy access to one another). Merely calling a set of people a "group" for reasons other than the nature of their relationships with each other (e.g., a set of flight attendants who have the same supervisor but who literally fly all over the country and rarely see one another) does not meet the conditions for creation of an effective work team.

Moreover, while reasonably close and meaningful interpersonal relationships can be important to the success of interacting work teams, group process interventions (e.g., "team building") that focus *exclusively* on relationships among group members—or on the social climate of the group as a whole—should be used with caution. Direct interpersonal interventions can be quite powerful in altering social behavior in a group, and for this reason they may be very useful in increasing the capability and willingness of members to share with one another special skills that are needed for work on the group task. Yet research also shows that when such interventions are used alone, the group's task effectiveness rarely is enhanced (and often suffers) as a result (cf. Hackman and Morris, 1975; Herold, n.d.). Thus while process interventions can be of great use as part of a broader intervention package aimed at creating effective work teams, total reliance on such interventions appears inappropriate if the goal is to work toward simultaneous improvement of the social experience of the members *and* their collective task productivity.

Design of Environmental Contingencies The way the organizational environment of the group is arranged can affect whether or not it is in the best interest of group members to work together effectively and, indeed, whether or not it is *possible* for them to do so. Especially important in this regard are the compensation system and the role of the first-line supervisor.

In almost every case in which autonomous work groups have been successfully created in organizations, pay systems have been arranged so that members were paid on a basis of performance of the group as a whole, rather than in terms of the level of performance of individual employees. Moving to a group-based compensation system increases the chances that internal cooperation and cohesiveness will increase as members work together to obtain the group-level rewards. Moreover, dysfunctional group interaction that grows from the fear (or the fact) of pay inequities among members should diminish when compensation is tied directly to the output of the group as a whole. It should be noted, however, that simply moving to a group-level compensation does *not* eliminate the possibility of less than optimal productivity norms. When group members mistrust management, for example, norms enforcing low productivity may emerge to protect the group against possible changes of performance standards by management. Thus, while group-level compensation plans play an important part in the design of work for interacting teams, they in no way guarantee high group productivity.

Also critical to the design of work for teams is the new role that first-line supervisors play under such arrangements. In many applications, the supervisor moves from having day-to-day (even minute-to-minute) responsibility for the work behavior and productivity of individual employees to a role that primarily involves managing the *boundaries* of the group—not what goes on within those boundaries

(Taylor, 1971). Thus the supervisor assists the group in liaison with other groups, and may serve as the advocate of the group in discussion with higher management, but routine decision making about the work and management of work crises is left to the group. Under such conditions, group members should experience substantially more ownership of their work activities and output, thereby creating the conditions required for members to experience collective responsibility for—and commitment to—their shared task.

Design of the Group Task One of the greatest determinants of whether a group develops a norm of high or low productivity is the design of the group task itself. What task characteristics are likely to prompt high group commitment to effective performance? As a start, the five core dimensions used in the job characteristics model of individual work motivation would seem useful (i.e., skill variety, task identity, task significance, autonomy, and feedback). There is no reason why such dimensions could not be applied to the analysis of group tasks just as they are to individual tasks.

If group tasks were designed to be high on these or similar job dimensions, then an increase in the task-relevant motivation of group members would be expected—and, over time, group norms about productivity should become consistent with the increased motivation of individual group members. Yet, such positive outcomes should come about only 1. if the individual group members identify with and feel commitment to the group as a whole (it is, after all, a *group* task), and 2. if the internal process of the group facilitates and reinforces (rather than impairs) concerted action toward shared group goals.

The core job dimensions have little to offer toward the creation of these two conditions. How, for example, could a group task be designed so that all members see it as providing high autonomy—and therefore experience substantial *personal* responsibility for the outcomes of the *group*? Moreover, given that it is now well documented that how group tasks are designed affects not only the motivation of group members, but also the patterns of social interaction that develop among them (Hackman and Morris, 1975), how can group tasks be structured so that they prompt task-effective rather than dysfunctional interaction among members?

Such questions have no simple answers. And while task design per se potentially can contribute to their solution, the issues raised also are affected by the environmental contingencies that are operative, and by the design and composition of the group itself. Thus, once again, it must be concluded that no single approach can create an effective design for work to be done by interacting teams. Instead, such a goal requires simultaneous use of a number of different handles for change—some of which have to do with the group, some with the task, and some with the broader organizational context.

Group versus Individual Task Design: Which When?

Choices for designing work for individuals or for groups are complex, and in many cases depend on factors idiosyncratic to a given situation. In general, however, a group-based design seems indicated when one or more of the following conditions is present:

1. When the product, service, or technology is such that meaningful individual work is not realistically possible (e.g., when a large piece of heavy equipment is being produced). In such cases it often is possible for a group to take autonomous responsibility for an entire product or service—while the only possible job design for individuals would involve small segments of the work (cf. Walton, 1975).

2. When the technology or physcial work setting is such that high interdependence among workers is required. For example, Susman (1970) has suggested that one effect of increased automation (especially in continuous process production) is to increase interdependence among workers. The creation of autonomous work groups under such circumstances would seem to be a rather natural extension of the imperatives of the technology itself. When, on the other hand, there are no required interdependencies (e.g., telephone installers who operate their own trucks, coordinating only with a foreman or dispatcher), then there would seem to be no real basis on which meaningful

work teams could be formed, and enrichment of individual jobs might be a better alternative.

3. When individuals have strong social needs—and the enrichment of individual jobs would run significant risk of breaking up existing groups of workers that provide social satisfactions to their members. In such cases, designing work for teams would capitalize on the needs of employees, whereas individual-oriented job enrichment might require that individuals give up important social satisfactions to obtain a better job (Reif and Luthans, 1972).

4. When the overall motivating potential of employees' jobs would be expected to be *considerably* higher if the work were arranged as a group task rather than as a set of individual tasks. Probably in most cases the standing of a job on the core dimensions would increase if the job were designed as a group task, simply because a larger piece of work can be done by a group than by an individual. This should not, however, automatically tilt the decision toward group work design—there are numerous interpersonal factors that must be attended to in effectively designing work for interacting groups. Sometimes the risk or effort required to deal with such factors may make it more appropriate to opt for individual task design, even though a group task might be expected to be somewhat better *as a task* than would be any of the individual tasks.

Cautions in Designing Work Groups

In conclusion, three caveats about the design of work for groups are suggested:

1. Existing evidence suggests that the work must provide group members with *substantial* autonomy if they are to experience high responsibility for it. Just as "pseudo-participation" in organizations may be worse than no participation at all, so it is that autonomous work groups should not be formed unless there is reasonable assurance that the result will not be a potentially frustrating state of "pseudo-autonomy." This, of course, requires careful attention to issues of management and supervision, to ensure that managers are both willing and able to provide the group with sufficient real autonomy to carry out the proposed group task (cf. Gulowsen, 1972).

2. The needs of employees who will make up the groups must be carefully attended to, because work in interacting teams on a complex task will not be satisfying or motivating to all people. Optimally, the need of group members for both social interaction and growth should be rather high. If the social needs of group members are high but their needs for growth are low, then there is risk that the group members will use the group solely as a source of social satisfaction. Even if the task were very high in objective motivating potential, members might find the group so much more involving than the task that productivity would suffer. When, on the other hand, members have a high need for growth but low needs for social interaction, then it might be better to consider designing the work for individuals, if technology permits. If employees have both low social needs and low needs for growth, then prospects for creating teams in which members work together effectively and productively on a challenging task would appear very dim indeed.

3. Finally, it should be noted that virtually all of the above discussion has focused on characteristics of groups and of tasks that are likely to generate high *motivation* to perform the task effectively. For some group tasks, the level of motivation (or effort) of group members is not critical to the success of the group; instead, the effectiveness of the performance varies simply with the level of knowledge and skill of the members, or with the performance strategies utilized by the group (cf. Hackman and Morris, 1975). In such circumstances, the attributes of the group, the task, and the environment that would be required for a high degree of group effectiveness would be quite different from those proposed here.

CONCLUDING STATEMENT

What, therefore, can we say about work design as a design variable? As we have seen in the articles by Pierce and Dunham and by Hackman, work design is a basic building block for organization design—the size and nature of jobs will reflect the configuration of the organization. Ways of thinking about work design and how to relate this topic to other features of organizational design are addressed in this concluding statement.

WORK DESIGN AND ORGANIZATIONAL DESIGN

So far this chapter has been concerned with reviewing the emergence of our contemporary understanding of work design. We are now more appreciative that it is a topic of considerable complexity, as well as one about which we have much to learn. Crucial to this book, however, is how the variable of work design relates to the larger subject matter of organization design—and it is to this that we now turn.

In Chapter 1 we saw that certain assumptions held by management about the worker and the organization underlay the evolution of organization and management theory. Let us expand on that point by noting that managers do hold a set of assumptions, whatever their degree of sophistication, which, taken as a set, can be termed a *managerial philosophy* (Miles, 1975). Clearly, managers' assumptions about workers would be a component of such a philosophy. Other components would, for example, state what the manager's basic rights and duties are, the value placed on orderliness and stability, the proper time frame for decision making, and the degree of concern with the organization's external environment.

Managerial philosophies are no doubt held in varying degrees of consciousness by managers. We can immediately see that one's managerial philosophy will affect the organization's purpose and the way organizational constraints are conceived. Classicists, for example, would focus their goals on profits and productivity, give little attention to the environment (with the exception of the organization's market), see the workers in "Theory X" terms, and tend to emphasize strong controls as well as mechanical programs.

The relevant point for our discussion here is that one component of a managerial philosophy is someone's beliefs or value-set about designing. Let us call it a set of *design premises*. Design premises will influence work design, as well as the design variables discussed in the following three chapters. Basically what we are saying is that no design variable will be thought about in a strictly rational way—a point paralleling our discovery that a worker's response to a designated job is moderated by who that particular worker is.

Assumptions and managerial philosophy will indirectly affect organization design in two ways. One is through the effect on purpose and constraints. The other is through the effects of design premises on work design (and the other design variables), which in turn affects the configuration that constitutes the organization's design. This reasoning is shown in Figure 7–6.

WORK DESIGN: ONE MORE TIME

Having discussed the place of work design in the organization design process, it now behooves us to focus on the practice of designing work. This, after all, is the central focus of

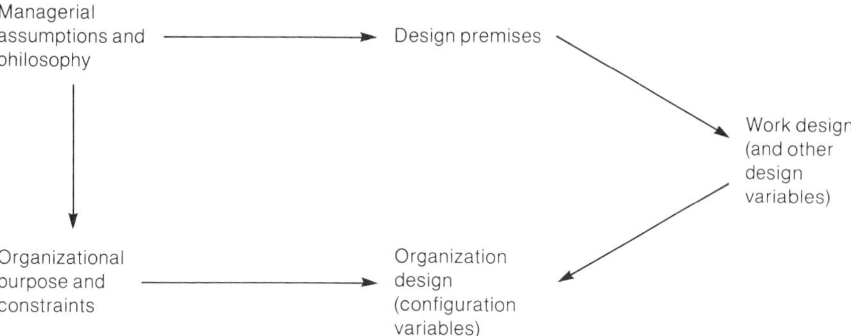

Figure 7-6. How managerial philosophy impacts organization design

this chapter. The following discussion therefore builds from the materials presented in the articles to provide an elaborated and synthesized approach. To do this we will maintain the differentation introduced earlier in Figure 7–2, between those characteristics of a job that are specified by management (1) and those dimensions actually experienced by job holders (2). We keep this differentiation to highlight a simple fact: intentions are not always perceived. Thus careful attention to the actual is necessary in designing work so that desired outcomes—both work and organizational—have a greater probability of occurring.

Job Dimensions

Hackman's five "core job dimensions" clearly are meant to be what we are calling worker perceived job dimensions. That is, they constitute much of a worker's perceived job. To Hackman's list, however, we add an *interaction opportunity* dimension (Turner and Lawrence, 1965; Clark, 1961): jobs provide greater or less opportunity for the job holder to interact with others, not only to get the job done but also to satisfy various human needs. There are therefore six dimensions that together make up the perceived job: skill variety, task identity, interaction opportunity, feedback or information on results, task significance, and autonomy. We note again that each of these dimensions can vary among jobs from zero to quite a lot. The question then becomes, "What characteristics of management-specified jobs contribute to a worker's perceived job?" The answer to this question provides some of the handles on work design available to organization designers.

The characteristics of jobs that are specified for a worker constitute work design. Pierce, Dunham, and Hackman spell out or strongly imply most of these. We list eight management-designated job characteristics. *Skill variety* reflects two job characteristics. These are the actual difficulty of the task (that is, the knowledge and skill necessary to accomplish it) and the variety of the tasks in a job. The more difficult the tasks and the more their variety in a given job, the more the job will be experienced as having a higher skill variety.

The perceived dimension of *task identity* also reflects two job characteristics. These are the degree to which the tasks are parts of larger tasks (task simplification) and the length of time it takes to complete the task (task cycle time). The less tasks are simplified and the longer the cycle time, the more task identity. That is, the more a task is perceived to be a whole task and done from beginning to end, the greater is the task identity.

The job dimension of *interaction opportunity* reflects the task-required interaction. Jobs obviously require written and/or verbal contact with others. Such contact may facilitate coordination with other jobs, processing of supplies or equipment or the transfer of personnel. Jobs obviously can vary greatly in this way. Such required interactions provide the opportunity for a worker to communicate about nonwork-related subjects too. Skill variety, task identity, and interaction opportunity combine to contribute to the experienced meaningfulness of work. Hackman labeled this dimension one of the three "critical psychological states," a state that becomes reflected in outcomes.

A fourth dimension of work design is information on the results of task performance. Jobs do, of course, vary in the amount and importance of information. They also vary as to the regularity with which information is provided to the job holder. Beyond some threshold amount—the minimum necessary to perform the task—such information is perceived as *feedback*—contributions to the worker's "understanding of his or her effectiveness" (another critical psychological state). The greater the task-results information designed into jobs, the greater the feedback, and thus the greater the understanding of effectiveness by a worker.

Another job dimension also contributes to effectiveness understanding, namely, *task significance*. The formal specification of a task's importance—its ranking on a priority of accomplishment, for example—is what task significance reflects. These variables also contribute to a worker's "experienced responsibility," the third critical psychological state. So the greater the designed task importance, the more likely the task will be perceived as significant by a worker.

Responsibility, however, also comes from the perceived job dimension of *autonomy*; that is, the degree to which a job is perceived as providing worker decisions on means for job scheduling and accomplishment. Autonomy reflects the design characteristics of task discretion, since jobs vary in the amount of built-in choice of how and when to be performed. The greater the task discretion, the higher the perceived autonomy and the more the worker's experienced responsibility.

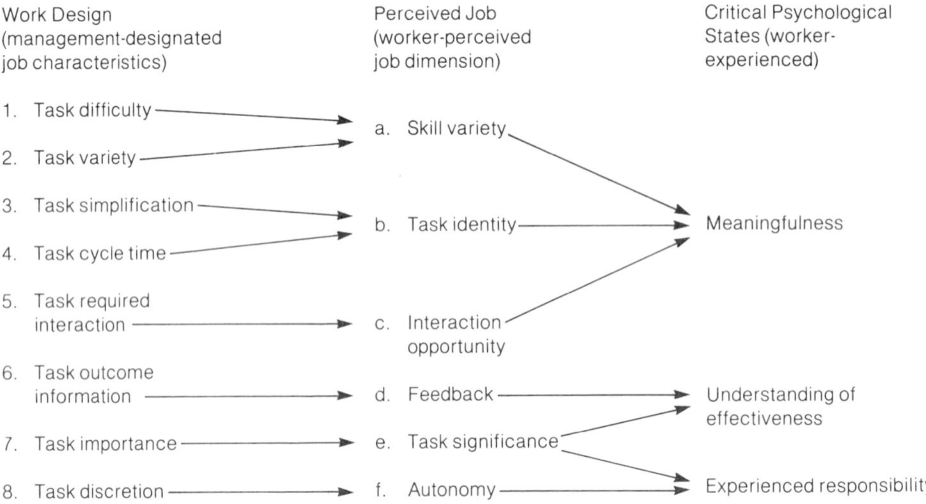

Figure 7-7. An elaborated model of work design: designated and perceived aspects

This somewhat complex discussion of how the eight management-designed job characteristics affect the six dimensions of perceived jobs and the ways these latter contribute to the three critical psychological states specified by Hackman are diagrammed in Figure 7–7.

Work-Design Outcomes

There are at least two ways to view the impact of work design. One was indicated in Figure 7–6. The ways in which jobs are designed at all levels of an organization permits us to describe the configuration of the organization. That is, the ways jobs are designed requires or allows various degrees of formalization, centralization, and so on. The second way to view the impact of work design is to ask what outcomes will occur. The articles by Pierce, Dunham, and Hackman suggested two general categories of outcomes which reflect the critical psychological states discussed earlier.

Those observable, more or less objectively measured outcomes result directly from worker performance or lack of it. We term such results *work outcomes*. The second category consists of those outcomes that concern the subjective internal psychological responses of a worker. These we call *personal outcomes*. In addition, attention is directed to the impact work and personal outcomes have on the outcomes of the organization. (See Figure 2–5. These outcomes are the subject of Chapters 11 and 12.) Let us show these relationships and identify the several types of outcomes by reference to Figure 7–8.[1]

Summary

Look once more at Figures 7–6 and 7–7. The former showed how managerial assumptions about designing organizations encompassed design premises that influence work design. Figure 7–7 illustrates the characteristics of work design that can be manipulated and therefore reflect those design premises. In addition, the immediately preceding section linked those work design variables to workers' psychological states through the dimensions of perceived jobs. Perhaps a short example will illustrate this reasoning. The "classicist" (see Chapter 1, the concluding statement) very likely holds design premises reflecting Theory X assumptions about the worker and "rational-machine" assumptions about the organization. Many of the so-called principles of management (Massie, 1965) reveal what classical-oriented work design premises would be: a high use of the division of labor, coupled with direct supervisory controls, supplemented with formal rules where worker contribution to the work is simple labor. All would lead to the desired outcome—efficiency. This sort of premise would lead work designers to construct jobs where there was high task simplification and low task difficulty, variety, cycle time, required interaction, outcome information, importance, and discretion—very, very routine, repetitive, simple jobs.

It is not difficult to guess what the outcomes of such a design would be. Output would occur at a steady rate of standard quality. On the personal side, the jobs would be experienced as low in all perceived job dimensions. Job holders under such circumstances would, individual differences aside, very likely feel their work is not very meaningful, not

1. Recall that Hackman postulated that outcomes would in part depend on workers' "need for growth." Research on this, however, is at present inconclusive (Brief and Aldag, 1975; Schuler, 1977). Dunham (1977), in fact, suggests that distracting environmental (organizational) factors may confuse this issue.

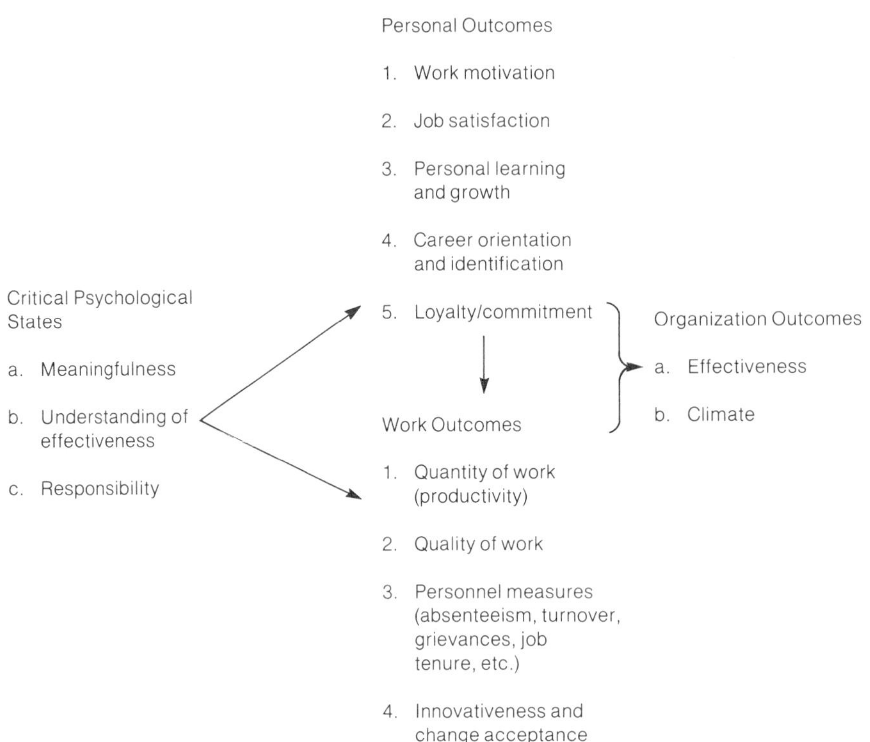

Figure 7-8. Personal, work, and organizational outcomes of work design

understand how effective they are, and tend not to feel very responsible for the results of the tasks they do. (Picture yourself as being eight years into a life-long job as a feather plucker of chicken backs.)

DESIGNING WORK: THE MANAGEMENT OF JOB STRUCTURING

Up to this point we have reviewed and related a host of ideas found to be relevant to work design. The question that is now pertinent is, "How do we do it?" In this section we shall outline and illustrate the process of designing work; that is, what designers might do to structure jobs. As we launch into this, let us recall why work design is so fundamental to organization design.

Work Design and the Organizational System

Organizations are systems with a purpose that exist and function because they have members who do things. That is, members behave in ways that help achieve organizational purposes. Jobs define and directly give direction to member behavior.

Studies in organizational behavior consistently show that prescribed tasks account for the bulk of observed behavior. Work design is therefore an activity under managerial control that offers alternatives which will contribute in a major way to the nature, shape, and functioning of the organization. These two facts—that work design is manageable and that it strongly guides worker behavior—imply the fundamental importance of our topic.

Work Design as a Process

What is the process by which jobs are structured or restructured? What follows will hardly contain any surprises after reading earlier sections. The process can be outlined by a series of questions, which if answered in order will result in work design.

- What is the prevailing managerial philosophy?
  Have any design premises been developed from this philosophy?
- What are the organizational purposes?
  What are the desired organizational outcomes?
  What personal and work outcomes are consistent with organizational outcomes?
- What are the constraints that derive from technology?
- What are the constraints that derive from the people available to be or who already are members?
- What is the nature of the organizational design variables other than work design?
- Given a desired personal and work outcome, what perceived jobs are appropriate?
- What combination of tasks and their characteristics can be constructed so that the perceived jobs desired will occur?

Note that these questions begin by initially focusing on constraining factors, then move backward through Figure 7–2—from outcomes to work design. Note too that each of the above questions actually encompasses several others, those prompted by the ideas found useful for each of the general stages of our reasoning (for example, the several types of work outcomes).

An Example of Work Design

To clarify this process, let us consider an example. What sort of jobs might be appropriate for a fast-food franchise outlet? Profits accrue in this low-profit-margin business as a result of high-volume, standardized food, and quick, efficient service over long hours. The technology of fast-food chains is well known. Large batches of output are continually produced, with holding devices near a multiple-station service counter. Customers trade off a wide menu and personal service for promptness, price, and some self-servicing.

The low-profit margin requires a low labor cost (fixtures, property, equipment, and raw materials are relatively expensive and fixed). The people constraint is in the type of person who will work for minimal wages on a shift basis with little or no expectation of wage increases (we will speak about management in a moment). Students are the obvious labor pool. Labor costs include management too, so keeping the number of these jobs to a minimum is also desirable.

Little in the way of personal outcome is necessary—beyond some minimal work motivation. On the work outcome side, productiveness is very necessary and entails enough quality consciousness so that courteous service results. Other work outcomes, however, are probably irrelevant. Minimal levels of the three critical psychological states can therefore be supported. That is, the six perceived job dimensions can all be allowed to remain low. Thus the structure of all jobs will be toward the simple routine-specialized end of the job structure continuum. So because of student workers (working on shifts for low wages and expected to turn over a lot), the cost of errors, the necessity of learning jobs quickly, and the large span of control to keep administrative wage costs down, the organization will rationally end up with very carefully, tightly designed, small scope jobs for workers.

At the same time, the job of the manager will also be relatively well rationalized, although with considerably more importance, discretion, and variety. Since the manager is the continuing thread in this kind of business, his or her job must be designed to be much more responsible, effective, and meaningful. The technology and organizational control devices are typically well defined, and the size of the firm reduces the importance of structure. Managers are in a position, however, to self-construct many aspects of these work designs so that their perceived jobs result in high degrees of the three critical psychological states. Therefore we predict that those personal and work outcomes that contribute to a successful, surviving business—loyalty, high work motivation, job satisfaction, career identification, innovativeness, tenure, and so forth—will most likely occur also.

What Does the Example Mean?

Our fast-food franchise business example contains two important points for us to consider. First, as we have already said, work design is complex, and it requires a lot of informed judgment to effect (there is no single, simple formula). Second, work design is a process that is highly interdependent on other organizational design variables, constraints, and purposes. While this example was chosen because it would be familiar to most readers, it was also simplified by not speaking to environmental matters. In reality, of course, things change—even in stable industries. People and technologies are never static, and even so-called stable environments are observed to change somewhat over time.

In recent decades, as the interest in work design has increased, there have occurred several changes in the nature of the work force and in other ways—changes that have prompted work designers to invent and experiment. More and more, designers are testing alternatives to the bureaucratically extreme division of labor, and hence small scope jobs. It is to these contemporary developments in work design that we now turn.

CONTEMPORARY EXPERIMENTS IN WORK DESIGN

"It looks like work redesign . . . is to be the darling of the 1970's" (Hackman, 1975: 97). If Hackman is correct, it is probably because work is of central importance both for individuals and for society at large.

> That importance is basically instrumental: work is engaged in primarily for the sake of its product, the goods and services that it generates. But it is no less true that work is often valued for its own sake, that for many people it meets the need for meaningful activity, as defined by others and as experienced by themselves. For many others, however, the work experience is unpleasant and is marked with severe disadvantages. These people persist at work only because they see no alternative way to meet basic needs. If this is both obvious and undesirable, it follows that we should be concerned with ways to make work more meaningful and satisfying, and to do so without paying an unacceptable social price in terms of diminished quantity or quality. [Kahn, 1974: 199]

The reason work design is capturing the fancy of practitioners and scholars alike is simply because it appears to offer the means of rehumanizing the experience of work. The necessity for this has been discussed in Chapter 6, so we will not repeat it here. Rather let us note the several ways in which work design is being experimented with at the present time to make it

TABLE 7–2 STAGES IN WORK-DESIGN DEVELOPMENT

1. Job rotation
   (Task characteristics affected: task variety)*
2. Job enlargement
   (Task characteristics affected: task simplification, task cycle time)
   Job nesting
3. Job enrichment
   (Task characteristics affected: task difficulty, task discretion)
   Flexitime
4. Work modules
   (Task characteristics affected: task importance and task required interaction)
   Social-technical redesign
   Autonomous work groups

*Task characteristics in this table refer to those listed in Figure 7-6. In most cases previously noted characteristics are implied in subsequent stages; that is, task variety from stage 1 is to be added to those of stage 2, and so forth.

more "meaningful" and "satisfying."[2] Table 7–2 outlines the historical appearance of various stages in the development of work design.

Job Rotation

One of the first attempts to provide *job rotation* simply involves two or more workers exchanging jobs on some regular basis. The reasoning is straightforward. Having a chance to perform a set or series of related, simple, and routinized jobs supposedly increases task variety, reduces boredom, and enlarges skill repertoires. Job rotation thus provides a rudimentary on-the-job training. Practical experience with job rotation, however, tends to show little positive results—it is as easy to become bored with several simple, routine jobs as it is with one's own.

Job Enlargement

Another early redesign experiment was termed *job enlargement*. Here the scope of "doing" was increased. That is, more tasks of a similar type were added to the original set of tasks—so-called horizontal job scope. Whereas the purpose of earlier job-enlargement efforts was again primarily to reduce boredom and alienation, note that other work characteristics are affected. While task variety increases, task simplification and task cycle time also tend to be altered by decreasing and lengthening them, respectively. Work experiments in job enlargement sometimes have led to *job nesting* (Ford, 1973). The familiar practice of job pooling—where workers who perform similar tasks are located together, such as a secretarial pool—is the opposite of job nesting, geographically locating together people whose work complements or mutually supports one another.

Job Enrichment

Job enlargement was quickly followed by design experiments in job enrichment. Work is "enriched" by moving control of both work methods and work scheduling to the worker.

2. While we speak of "experiments" here, do not conclude that they are rigorously constructed or executed in a scientific sense. We are speaking, after all, of attempts to effect and assess change under real-world conditions, not in a highly controlled laboratory setting. Still, they are experiments in the sense of being based on good theorizing and careful evaluation. Actually, scores of companies have been involved to some extent, among them such prominent firms as: Texas Instruments; Corning Glass Works; IBM; AT&T; Procter and Gamble; Bankers Trust; Merrill, Lynch, Pierce, Fenner and Smith; Donnelly Corporation; Imperial Chemical Industries, Ltd.; Maytag; Motorola; Gaines Food Company; and Buick.

Job enrichment therefore involves increasing job scope to incorporate what previously were management functions—planning and direction (Paul, Robertson, and Herzberg, 1969). For instance, new task characteristics are tapped through enrichment. Task difficulty and task discretion are both increased. It should be noted too that both job enlargement and job enrichment have the potential of affecting the characteristic of task outcome information too, as more and more "whole" tasks are involved. Job enrichment has led to one particular experiment that is attracting a lot of interest: *flexitime* (Elbing et al., 1975). Flexitime simply involves suspending regular hours of work attendance in favor of individualizing scheduling of worker hours—within various requirements of interaction and cooperation, of course, and as long as the prescribed work output occurs. Obviously not all types of jobs lend themselves to a flexitime approach. For example, jobs tied to customer services or machine-paced work would not.

Work Modules

Most work redesign efforts are concerned with the "goodness-of-fit" between worker characteristics and the properties of the job and work environment (French et al., 1971).[3] Experiments in increasing the scope of jobs vertically and horizontally, together with experiments in varying hours of work, have culminated in the concept of the *work module* (Kahn, 1974). Defining one's own job is central. A work module is built on the task-time unit (the smallest allocation of time to a given task that is sufficient to be economically and psychologically meaningful). When jobs are defined in terms of time-task units and workers provided with their choice, basically self-constructed jobs result. Where the modular allocation of work is applied to sets of jobs, opportunities for work-group experiments exist that dramatically affect at least two task characteristics: task importance and task required interaction.

"Autonomous work groups are work structures where members regulate their behavior around relatively whole tasks" (Cummings and Molloy, 1977:21). Autonomous work groups derive from and are intertwined with sociotechnical systems theory (Cummings and Srivastra, 1976). Task performance requires both a technology—tools, techniques, and methods—and a social system that relates people to the technology and to each other. Structuring these two independent yet correlative elements into an integrated system is the essential issue sociotechnical systems theory addresses. Open systems are self-regulating—hence the autonomous work group. Cummings and Molloy (1977: 25–26) reason thusly,

> . . . Autonomous work groups offer at least two advantages over more traditional task designs at the individual job level. First, many production processes require interdependent tasks that exceed the capacity of single man-machine systems. Designing individual task structures does not account for necessary interactions across separate jobs. Rather, grouping interdependent jobs into relatively whole task groups provides the interaction needed for goal achievement. Second, the traditional method of decomposing production processes into their simplest, elementary parts and then specifying in detail the behavior of these parts results in task designs that are not responsive to

3. The traditional approaches to goodness-of-fit have held jobs inviolate and instead have attempted—through recruitment, selection, and training—to fit persons to jobs. Changes in the work force as well as poor outcome results then forced attention to altering jobs too.

internal control or to workers' needs for autonomy. These task structures, usually at the man-machine level, require an external control apparatus to coordinate the separate parts and to counter variances that arise both within and across parts. This additional control structure requires coordination and produces its own variances, which leads to a next higher-level control system, and so on. An effective method to counter this segregative tendency is to stop the decomposition and task specification process at the group, rather than the individual job level. This allows for the selection and linkage of individual operational units into relatively whole task groups. It also leaves the specification of individual jobs free to vary with the control and task needs of the system. Thus, the group is provided with the necessary freedom to respond to variances from goal achievement, and workers are given sufficient autonomy to master their task environment. Given these advantages, autonomous work groups are a viable alternative to traditional methods of successive decomposition and complete specification task design.

A large number of cases have described sociotechnical reforms and more or less fully autonomous work groups (for example, Walton, 1975; Davis and Trist, 1974; Katzell et al.,1975). While the excitement mounts, the evidence is surely not all in.[4] When we inquire into outcomes of work groups additional factors come into play, not the least of which are the cohesiveness and collaboration of the group (Dailey, 1977).

SUMMARY AND CONCLUSION

This chapter has introduced one of several organizational design variables: work design. As with other aspects of organizational design, work design is a fairly messy topic. The naive and simplistic early approaches have stimulated a host of conceptual and research efforts—efforts intended to provide a greater understanding of, and greater control over, a major level of organizational affairs. This concluding statement has emphasized the differences between perceived job and managerial designated work design, the influence of moderating factors on how work is experienced by job holders, as well as the many types of outcomes that occur.

The two articles included in this chapter have presented up-to-date but quite different discussions of work design. Pierce and Dunham reviewed the historical record of the research on worker responses to work design. They concluded that a direct cause-and-effect relationship is too simple, that in fact a host of individual and nonindividual factors moderated the relationship. We learned that workers, for a variety of reasons, differently perceived the "objective" task (see Figure 7–4). Hackman's article explored the psychological states that moderated work design and both personal and work outcomes. He conceptually speculated that knowledge of results and experienced meaningfulness and responsibility mediated the dimensions of work design and the outcomes that could be expected.

The introductory remarks previewed the articles by Pierce, Dunham, and Hackman and attempted to first show how they may be synthesized (see Figure 7–2). In this statement we have continued to emphasize the distinction between management-designated aspects of work design and those perceived by workers, as well as to carefully complete the lists of each

4. A number of commentators are skeptically critical of work redesign, especially job enrichment (see Fein, 1974; Gomberg, 1973; Hulin and Blood, 1968).

(see Figure 7–7). Further, we have elaborated the outcomes to work design that worker responses result in. We have maintained, following Hackman, that there are both personal, as well as work, outcomes and that these in turn result in organizational outcomes. This statement has also indicated the historical development of work design, noting successive stages of redesign that have increased job scope in vertical and horizontal dimensions and redesigned jobs in relation to time, technology, and work teams.

The story of work design is an unfinished one. To be sure, work design has become more humanized in the last decade, and at present there are energetic efforts to invent and study experiments in job scope and teamwork. For example, work redesign efforts have recently come to be recognized as a significant way to intervene in organizations to change them (Hackman, 1977). Interestingly, the use of work redesign in organizational development efforts was the spark that has furthered our thinking about who should be involved. Whereas experiments have steadily moved in the direction of greater worker control in jobs, the experimentation itself has until recently continued to be viewed as a managerial prerogative. Work modules and organizational change are changing this. Worker representative councils and union leaders are now forcing managers to face the issue of whether a top-down, inherently autocratic approach for achieving more participative, democratically controlled work design is consistent and practical (Calame, 1973; Katzell et al., 1975).

Work design will clearly continue to deserve our attention in years to come. And yet it is only one of several variables we must consider. The concerns noted in the last paragraph in fact direct our attention to the organization design variable discussed in the next chapter: "Organizational Control."

Questions for Review

1. What are some of the moderating factors on the work design-worker response relationship outlined by Pierce and Dunham (1969)?
2. Review the differences between the historical and contemporary views of work design.
3. Review the major discussion points with respect to task-design research made by Pierce and Dunham.
4. Which core job dimensions are associated with which particular psychological states in Hackman's job-characteristics model of work motivation? Define each of these core job dimensions and the associated psychological states.
5. Present an overview of the general results that support the testing of the job-characteristics model of work motivation.
6. Are there any unusual features in the job-characteristics model? If so, what are they?
7. Summarize the general steps that might be followed by a change agent in carrying out a diagnosis, using the JDS.
8. What is the intent of the principle of vertical loading, what are some ways this might be achieved, and what are the potential results?
9. Certain attributes are considered characteristic of most autonomous work groups. What are these? Must they be present in all effective work designs?
10. The choice of designing work for a group seems to be indicated when one or more of a number of conditions is present. Briefly describe these conditions.

11. What general questions would you ask to enable you to describe the process by which jobs are structured and restructured?

Questions for Discussion

1. It was stated that the legacy of early design engineering and its "one best way" to design any job is one of contemporary management's major myths. Is this really a myth? Do you think many managers still consider this view to be a reality?
2. "The historical evolution of work design has essentially been a story of an ever-elaborating way of thinking about it." In your opinion, does this increased elaboration really add to the quality of work design or simply to a high degree of overintellectualized confusion on the part of managers? Would managers be better off using the old classical style? Explain.
3. Do you suppose it would have been possible for the pharaohs of Egypt to build their pyramids if they had paid active attention to such factors as "experienced meaningfulness of the work"? Does this have anything to say about the personal and work outcomes?
4. Have you lived in a group setting in which tasks were assigned to each group member? If so, what were some of the difficulties you encountered in the allocation of, reaction to, and completion of, tasks? How could your new knowledge of task design—and its effects—have helped that situation?
5. Do you think that the basic model of task design, as presented by Hackman, is valid and relevant for all cultural groups? If you were sent to manage a new industrial plant in a basically non-technological nation, how would you apply, adapt, and view these principles?
6. Hackman maintains that "employees who tighten nuts on aircraft brake assemblies . . . are much more likely to perceive their work as meaningful than are workers who fill small boxes with paper clips. . . . " Is this a reasonable assertion? Reasonable or not, is it realistic? Does your personal experience with auto mechanics support or weaken this assertion? Do you think assembly line workers of an auto factory feel responsible for the safety of the eventual owner of the car?
7. How would you handle a situation in which half the potential members of an autonomous work group prefers to remain in their present routinized, simple—and to you, unsatisfying—jobs, rather than join the new group? What would you look for? What questions would you ask yourself and others? Whom would you ask?
8. What other factors can you think of, in addition to those mentioned in this chapter, that might moderate or affect the relationship between task design and worker response? What are your reasons for suggesting these?
9. Pierce and Dunham state that some workers respond more favorably to expanded task design than do others. Although there is currently no single, widely accepted theoretical explanation for this finding, what hypotheses might you offer for it? On what assumption do you make your hypotheses?
10. What cultural/sociological assumptions lie behind the inclusion of "experienced responsibility for outcomes of the work" as a critical psychological state? How have you experienced these assumptions or mores?

8

Organizational Control

INTRODUCTORY REMARKS

Organization designs need to include mechanisms for guiding resources and activities toward organizational goals. Taken together, such mechanisms make up the process of organizational *control*. As we know—and as we shall see in greater detail in this chapter—organizational control can take many forms. Typical forms include the hierarchy, rules and regulations, professional standards, and so forth. As we shall also see, control mechanisms are designed differently, depending on the design constraints.

Organizational control has many meanings and has been interpreted in many ways. In the article by Tannenbaum, who has contributed more to our understanding of the problem than any single other person, control is viewed as the sum of interpersonal influence relations in an organization (also in Tannenbaum, 1968). In a similar vein, Etzioni (1965) finds it

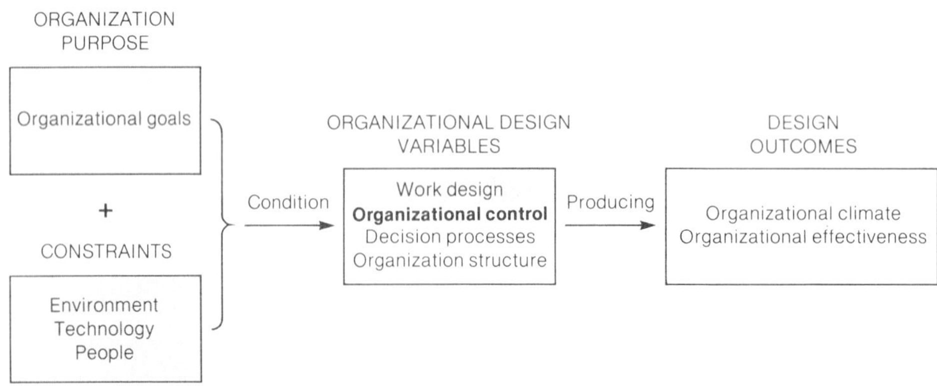

useful to treat control in organizations as equivalent to power. Other than the power-influence approach to control, organization theorists have also treated it as a problem in information flow (Galbraith, 1973; Ouchi and Maguire, 1975), as a problem in creating and monitoring rules through a hierarchical authority system (Weber, 1947; Perrow, 1972; Blau and Scott, 1962), and some have approached organizational control as a cybernetic process of testing, measuring, and providing feedback (Thompson, 1967; Reeves and Woodward, 1970; Sherwin, 1977).

While we will consider questions of power and influence, of information flows, and of bureaucratic structure, we prefer to begin with a more simple-minded view of organizational control. As we will treat it, *organizational control consists of the process of moving an aggregation of people toward a common objective.* We will thus temporarily ignore the real problem, as we saw in Chapter 3, that most organizations do not have a single goal. Further we will assume, for the time being, that a workable form of goal integration has been achieved. We will see that power does not have to be present for control to exist—that there are ways to achieve movement toward a common objective without the use of influence or power. Similarly, we will see that explicit rules combined with a hierarchy of authority constitute only one form of organizational control, and that control can exist without them. All of these points of view, however, deal to some extent with information flows as a part of the process of control. We will therefore find that the informational point of view is a useful one for thinking about organizational control.

The Reading

In this chapter's sole article, Arnold Tannenbaum discusses control in terms of both the individual and the organization. For him, control is defined as a process in which a person, group, or organization determines, or intentionally affects, what another person, group, or organization will do. Tannenbaum proceeds to examine the importance of organizational control for people. In particular, the control process serves a pragmatic function, actually guiding people's behavior. Additionally, however, control has symbolic effects. As Tannenbaum puts it, "the exercise of control is charged emotionally."

The author next examines control as it is exercised—and felt—in a variety of organizational settings. An important aspect of his examination is the idea that the total amount of control in an organization is not fixed. Therefore, says Tannenbaum, if workers increase their level of control (or influence), this does not necessarily mean that managers' control is reduced. His "control curves" are especially helpful in understanding this idea.

Conclusion

In essence, this chapter is concerned with several aspects of organizational control:

1. What is the process called control?
2. Are there different types of control?
3. If so, what organizational circumstances encourage what type of control?
4. In other words, what are the options available in designing a control system?
5. What are the impacts of various control options?

CONTROL IN ORGANIZATIONS: INDIVIDUAL ADJUSTMENT AND ORGANIZATIONAL PERFORMANCE

ARNOLD S. TANNENBAUM

Man's life in contemporary society can be characterized largely as one of organizational memberships. Man commits a major portion of his waking hours to participation in at least one—and more often several—social organizations. His motivation, aspirations, his general way of life, are tied inextricably to the organizations of which he is a part—and even to some of which he is not.

Organizations are of vital interest because one finds within them an important juncture between the individual and the collectivity. That man derives a great deal from organizational membership leaves little to be argued; that he often pays heavily for the benefits of organizational membership seems an argument equally compelling. At the heart of this exchange lies the process of control.

Characterizing an organization in terms of its patterns of control is to describe an essential and universal aspect of organization, an aspect of organizational environment which every member must face and to which he must adjust. Organization implies control. A social organization is an ordered arrangement of individual human interactions. Control processes help circumscribe idiosyncratic behaviors and keep them conformant with the rational plan of the organization. Organizations require a certain amount of conformity as well as the integration of diverse activities. It is the function of control to bring about conformance to organizational requirements and achievement of the ultimate goals of the organization. The coordination and order created out of the diverse interests and potentially diffuse behaviors of members is largely a function of control. It is at this point that many of the problems of organizational functioning and of individual adjustment arise.

Control is an inevitable correlate of organization. But it is more than this. It is concerned with aspects of social life that are of the utmost importance to all persons. It is concerned with the questions of choice and freedom, with individual expression, with problems of the common will and the common weal. It is related not only to what goes on within the organization but also with what the organization does in its external relations. It touches on the questions of democracy and autocracy, centralization and decentralization, "flat" and "tall" organizational structures, close versus general supervision, workers' councils and joint management.

The problems of control and conformity in organizations contribute to a serious dilemma. Organization provides order—a condition necessary for man to produce abundantly and live securely. Abundance and security in turn create opportunities and choice—conditions which form the basis for human freedom. Yet social order itself requires conformity and imposes limitations. Furthermore, the responsibility for creating and sustaining order tends to be distributed unevenly within organizations. Often it is the few who decide about the kind of order to which the many must conform. But regardless of how order is created, it requires the conformity of all or nearly all to organizational norms.

The magnitude of this problem as it applies to our economic institutions has been indicated by Berle and Means (1952):

> To the dozen or so men who are in control there is room for . . . [individual] initiative. For the tens of thousands and even hundreds of thousands of workers and of owners in a single enterprise, [individual] initiative no longer exists. Their activity is group activity on a scale so

Abridged from "Control in Organizations: Individual Adjustment and Organizational Performance," Arnold S. Tannenbaum, *Administrative Science Quarterly*, vol. 7, no. 2 (September 1962), pp. 236–40; 246–57.

> large that the individual, except he be in a position of control, has dropped into relative insignificance.

And the *trend*, according to Barnard, is in the direction of greater concentration of control in the hands of fewer persons:

> There has been a greater and greater acceleration of centralization in this country, not merely in government, and not merely in the organization of great corporations, but also a great concentration on the part of labor unions and other organizations. There has been a social disintegration going along with this material development, and this formulation of organized activities implies payment of a price, the amount of which we are not yet able to assess. [Barnard, 1951]

This, perhaps, is one of the most crucial problems of social morality which we face in the age of massive organization, although the problem is not an entirely new one. We see it in Rousseau's *Social Contract*, Freud's *Civilization and Its Discontents*, Huxley's *Brave New World*, Whyte's *Organization Man*. And social and administrative scientists have become increasingly interested in this question, as indicated by the work by F. Allport, Argyris, Likert, McGregor, and Worthy. As a result, social researchers have applied themselves to the study of the problems of control, individual adjustment, and organizational performance, and a body of facts and hypotheses is growing. We would like to review some of these, drawing heavily upon the work done at the Institute for Social Research at the University of Michigan.[1]

SOME DEFINITIONS

Control has been variously defined, and different terms (e.g., power, authority, influence) are sometimes used synonymously with it. Its original application in business organizations derives from the French usage meaning to check. It is now commonly used in a broader and perhaps looser sense synonymously with the notions of influence, authority, and power. We shall use it here in this broader way to refer to any process in which a person or group of persons or organization of persons determines, i.e., intentionally affects, what another person or group or organization will do.

Control, of course, may operate very specifically, as, for example, a foreman's specifying how a subordinate will do a particular job. Or it may operate more generally, as, for example, the determination of organizational policies or actions. Control may be mutual, individuals in a group each having some control over what others will do; or it may be unilateral, one individual controlling and the others controlled. We ascribe power to an individual to the extent that he is in a position to exercise control. Authority refers to the right to exercise control. If by freedom we mean the extent to which an individual determines his own behavior, being controlled can be seen in general to relate inversely to freedom. The more an individual's behavior is determined by others (i.e., is controlled), the less an individual is free to determine his own course of action.

IMPLICATIONS FOR INDIVIDUAL ADJUSTMENT

The elementary importance of control to people can be seen in the fact that every act of control has two implications: pragmatic and symbolic. Pragmatically, control implies something about *what* an individual must or must not do, the restriction to which he is subject, and the areas of choice or freedom which he has—whether, for example, a worker is transferred to a new machine or stays on the old, whether he is classified into a \$1.75 or a \$2.00 wage category, whether he is free to talk, smoke, rest, slow down, or speed up while on the job. These pragmatic implications are often of vital importance to the controlled individual as well as to the individual exercising power.

Control also has a special psychological meaning or significance to the individuals involved. It may imply

1. This article was made possible by funds granted by the Carnegie Corporation of New York. The statements made and views expressed are the responsibility of the author. I would like to thank Robert Kahn, Rensis Likert, Stanley Seashore, and Clagett Smith for their helpful suggestions.

superiority, inferiority, dominance, submission, guidance, help, criticism, reprimand. It may imply (as some students of control argue) something about the manliness and virility of the individuals involved. The exercise of control, in other words, is charged emotionally.[2]

CONTROL AND PERFORMANCE

Variations in control patterns within organizations have important—and in some cases quite predictable—effects on the reactions, satisfactions and frustrations, feelings of tension, self-actualization, or well-being of members. They also have implications for the performance of the work group and for the organization as a whole.

This can be seen in the plight of the first-line supervisor who sometimes finds himself in the anomalous position of being a leader without power. The first-line supervisor is often referred to as the man in the middle. He is often caught, as an innocent bystander, in a serious cross fire. In effect he may be a messenger transmitting orders from above. On the one hand, he must bear the brunt of resistance and expressed grievances from below and, on the other, must suffer criticism from above for the failure of his subordinates to conform to expectations. The seriousness of this situation is compounded by the fact that orders coming from above are often formed without the advantage of adequate knowledge of conditions at lower levels. The powerless supervisor lacks effective means of gaining the confidence of his men, of understanding their views, and of transmitting this important intelligence up the hierarchy. The orders which he is responsible for relaying, then, are often the least likely to gain full acceptance, thus making his position all the more untenable and that of his subordinates all the more difficult. The powerless leader can do little in the hierarchy on behalf of his subordinates or himself and is relatively helpless in the face of many serious problems which confront him and his work group. This is illustrated by the research of Pelz, who shows that unless the supervisor is influential with his own superiors, "good" supervisory practice on his part is not likely to make much difference to subordinates. Subordinates are more likely to react favorably to "good" and adversely to "bad" supervisory practices *if* the supervisor is influential in the company (Pelz, 1952: 3–11).

2. The criticism which labor groups have sometimes hurled at human relations research in industry is in larger measure a criticism concerning the emphasis which this research has placed on the psychological or symbolic rather than the pragmatic aspect of control. The human relations approach, the argument goes, is not so much concerned with *what* decisions are made by management nor with the implications of these decisions for the welfare of the workers, but rather with *how* these decisions might be conveyed to workers so as to facilitate their acceptance. See, for example, "Deep Therapy on the Assembly Line," *Ammunition*, 7 (1949), pp. 47–51.

TOTAL AMOUNT OF CONTROL IN AN ORGANIZATION

Many administrators seem to face a serious problem in their understanding of supervisory-subordinate relations. They often assume that the amount of control exercised by members of a group or organization is a fixed quantity and that increasing the power of one individual automatically decreases that of others. There is good reason, however, to question this conclusion. The total amount of control exercised in a group or organization can increase, and the various participants can acquire a share of this augmented power. Conversely, the total amount of control may decrease, and all may share the loss. This is illustrated in everyday social situations—friendships, marital relations, as well as supervisory-subordinate interactions. One can easily picture the laissez-faire leader who exercises little control over his subordinates and who may at the same time be indifferent to their wishes. He neither influences nor is influenced by his men. A second supervisor interacts and communicates often, welcomes opinions, and elicits influence attempts. Suggestions which subordinates offer make a difference to him and his subordinates are responsive, in turn, to his requests. To the extent that this may contribute to effective performance—and we have reason to believe that it does if the supervisor also has influence with his manager—the group itself will be more powerful or influential. The manager under these circumstances is more likely to delegate additional areas of decision making to the group, and he, in turn, will respect and be responsive to the group's decisions. To the extent that the organizational hierarchy, from top to bottom, is characterized in these terms, we have a more highly integrated, tightly knit social system. We have, in the terms of Rensis Likert (1961), a more substantial "interaction-influence system."

The importance of the notion of "total amount of control" and of the "interaction-influence system" is illustrated in an analysis by Likert (1960) of data collected in thirty-one geographically separated departments of a large industrial service organization. Each of the departments did essentially the same work, and careful records of department productivity were kept by the company. Nonsupervisory employees were asked the following question in a written questionnaire: "In general, how much say or influence do you feel each of the following groups has on what goes on in your department?" Answers were checked on a five-point scale from "little or no influence" to "a very great deal of influence." Employees answered this question relative to the following groups within their departments: the department manager, the supervisors, the men. Likert then divided the 31 departments into three groups according to their level of productivity. Figure 8–1 shows the average responses of the departments to the question for the third highest in productivity and for the third lowest in productivity.

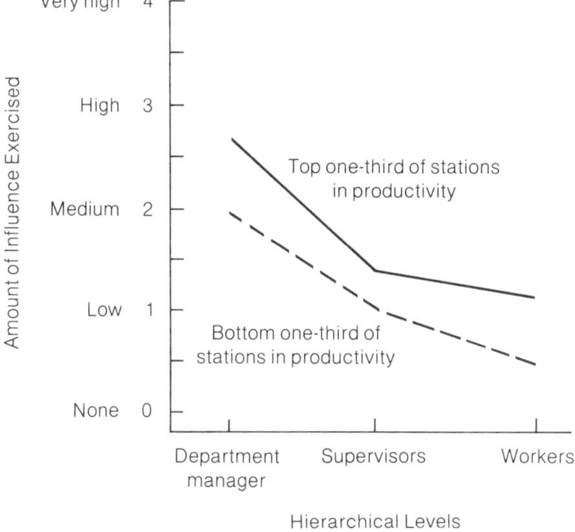

Figure 8-1. Control curves of high- and low-producing departments

According to these employees, not only did they have more influence as a group within the high-producing departments, but so did the supervisors and managers. Likert's (1960) analysis of these departments suggests that the social systems differed in the high- and low-producing departments. The former was characterized by a higher total amount of control, by a greater degree of mutual influence. "The high-performing managers have actually increased the size of the 'influence pie' by means of the leadership processes which they use. They listen more to their men, are more interested in their men's ideas, and have more confidence and trust in their men." There was a greater give-and-take and supportiveness by superiors, a higher level of effective communication upward, downward, and sideward. This all contributed to a greater sensitivity and receptivity on the part of each organization member to the influence of others—superiors relative to subordinates and subordinates relative to superiors. There was in all cases a higher level of mutual influence and control and a more likely integration of the interest of workers, supervisors, and managers. Under these circumstances, the high level of influence among workers was not a threat to managerial personnel. On the contrary, it was part of a process leading to more effective organizational performance (Likert, 1960).

It is interesting to see that similar findings occur in several other types of organizations. In a study of four labor unions, for example, we found that the two more effective, active, and powerful unions had the highest total amount of control exercised by members and officers (Tannenbaum, 1956; Tannenbaum and Kahn, 1958). The most powerful of the four unions had a relatively influential membership—but the leaders (the president, executive board, and bargaining committee) were by no means uninfluential. In this union, members and leaders were relatively more active. They attended more meetings, took part in discussions at meetings, communicated informally about union affairs, and heard and considered the feelings and ideas of others. Members and leaders influenced each other and in the process created effective concerted action. The union "keeps management on its toes" as the personnel manager at the plant philosophically pointed out. In the least effective union, however, the members were relatively uninfluential in union affairs, and so were the leaders. A kind of laissez faire atmosphere prevailed. Members were not integrated and not tied together by bonds of interaction and influence. They were not really part of an organized system. The ineffectiveness of this union was illustrated by the comments of a union field representative: "If the company wanted to take advantage, they could make the people live hard here." An old-timer of the local expressed his disillusionment: "We feel that it is not what it used to be. . . . Nothing happens to grievances. You can't find out what happens to them—they get lost. . . . The [bargaining] committee doesn't fight anymore." The differences between the most powerful and least powerful union in their distributions of control as reported by members is shown in Figure 8–2. Although the wording of the question in this study is somewhat different from that of the industrial service organization study discussed, the implications are very similar.[3]

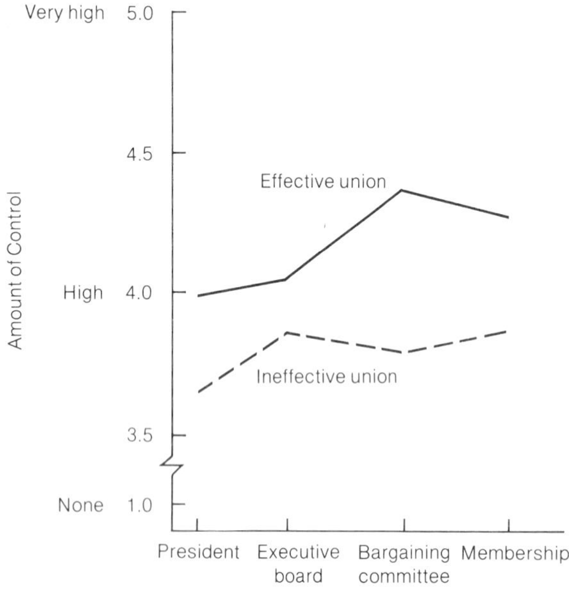

Figure 8-2. Control curves of effective and ineffective unions.

Source: From A. S. Tannenbaum and R. L. Kahn, *Participation in Union Locals* (Evanston, Ill.: Row Peterson, 1958), p. 162.

TABLE 8–1 AMOUNT OF INFLUENCE EXERCISED BY THREE LEVELS AS PERCEIVED BY THE MEN IN TWO PLANTS[a]

Level	Old Plant	New Plant
Men	2.64	3.12*
Foremen	2.42	3.51*
Front office	4.56	4.48

[a]The following questions were employed:
Questions: "In general, how much do you and the other men of your work group have to say about how things are done?"
Responses: 5—"Our foreman gives us a great deal of say in how things are done." . . . 1—"Our foreman gives us hardly any say at all in how things are done."
Question: "In general, how much do you think the foremen have to say about how things are done in this plant?"
Responses: 5—"They have a great deal of say." . . . 1—"They have very little say or no say at all."
Question: "In general, how much say do you think the men in the front office of this plant have in how things are done in this plant?"
Responses: 5—"They have a great deal of say in how things are done in this plant." . . . 1—"They have very little or no say at all in how things are done in this plant."
*Differences significant beyond the .001 level of confidence.
SOURCE: Adapted from *Automation and the Worker: A Study of Social Change in Power Plants* by Floyd C. Mann and L. Richard Hoffman. Copyright © 1960 by Henry Holt and Company, Inc. Reprinted by permission of Holt, Rinehart and Winston.

Mann and Hoffman (1960) applied a similar methodology in studying some of the effects of automation in a power plant. They illustrated, through a comparison of a new, highly automated plant with an older, less automated one, how changes in technology might affect the social structure of a plant, including its patterns of control, worker responsibility, and level of morale. Fewer employees operated the new plant, although the ratio of nonsupervisory to supervisory personnel was about the same. The jobs in the new plant required more knowledge and responsibility of the workers, and, as Table 8–1 illustrates, the patterns of control in the two plants differed too. According to the workers (and supervisors were in essential agreement), the new plant was characterized by more control than the old.

The difference between the plants is particularly interesting at the foreman level. In the new plant, foremen were judged to have more influence than the

3. Question in union study: "In general, how much do you think the president [membership, plant bargaining committee, executive board] has to say about how things are decided in this local?" Responses ranged on a five-point scale from "a great deal of say" to "no say at all."

men; in the old, less. Nor was the more powerful supervisor considered a threat to the workers in the new plant. Despite—or should we say, because of— the greater influence of foremen together with that of the men, the men reported less often that their foremen treated them like inferiors, that he was a "driver" of men, that he was "bossy," or that he said one thing and did another. They reported more often that the foreman tried to get ideas from the work group, that he was a warm and friendly person, that he would "go to bat" for the men, and that he was a "leader" of men. When all the responses are taken into consideration, 66 percent of the men in the new plant and 36 in the old report that they are very satisfied with their immediate supervisor. The new plant is a more tightly integrated social (as well as physical)system. Workers feel more a part of a work group and feel free to call on others in the work group for help with job problems. There is a higher degree of interdependence between foremen and men and to some extent among the men themselves. The foremen in the plant have more influence than their counterparts in the old—and so do the men.

Results from an unpublished study of forty insurance agencies show the same direction. D. Bowers and S. Seashore compared twenty insurance agencies high in sales volume with twenty agencies low in volume. In the high-producing agencies, the general agents, the district agents, and the sales agents as a group were all reported to have more influence in their agencies than were their counterparts in the low-producing agencies.

The clerical experiment discussed previously yielded similar results. The increased control which the clerks reported was not accompanied by a corresponding decrease in the control attributed to supervisory and managerial personnel. The total amount of control reported by clerks increased, accompanied by a more effective social system. Not only did morale increase in this group, but so did motivation and productivity.[4]

Interestingly, the kinds of relationships suggested by these data apply in a voluntary organization too, as indicated by research in over one hundred geographically separate local Leagues of Women Voters (Tannenbaum, 1961: 33–47). The effectiveness of each local league was rated by a group of judges in the national office, and a sample of the members and leaders in each was then asked several questions relating to control within their organizations. The results indicate that members in effective leagues exercised more control than did their counterparts in ineffective leagues, but leaders did not exercise less. A greater total amount of control was ascribed to effective leagues than to ineffective ones.

While these results from a variety of organizations seem to suggest an important hypothesis connecting the total amount of control and organizational performance, our research findings are not completely consistent on this point. A recent study of thirty automobile dealerships, for example, did not reveal any relationship between criteria of effectiveness (including growth in sales during the past year) and the total amount of control within the dealership as reported by salesmen. The automobile sales agency may present a somewhat different social structure in which "individual enterprise" and competitive behavior among salesmen is more at a premium. We do not know what the effect would be if agencies were structured more like the typical business organization with greater emphasis on coordination and cooperative effort. The total amount of control might be greater under these conditions, and this variable might prove, under these circumstances, to have important implications for effective performance.

CONCLUSION

American management is dollar cost conscious. Many managers are also aware of the costs of organized productive effort which cannot be calculated immediately in terms of dollars and cents. These are the human costs of organization, costs paid by members

4. Productivity also increased in a contrasting experimental group within the company under conditions of lowering the amount of control exercised by clerks. Here, however, clerk morale, loyalty, and motivation decreased. Considerable tension was felt in this group, and it gave the appearance of high instability. There is serious doubt that this type of system could sustain itself as well as the other for an extended period under conditions which prevail in American society. See R. Likert, "Measuring Organizational Performance," *Harvard Business Review,* 36 (1958), pp. 41–50, and *New Patterns of Management* (New York, 1961), Ch. 5 and 6.

and ultimately by society as a whole. Nor are they simply in terms of the dissatisfactions which industrial man faces. They may be paid in terms of the shaping of his very personality. The evidence on this is not very clear, but we have reason to believe that adult personality may change as a result of persistent conditions in the environment. The nature of man's experiences in an organization can affect his general mentality and outlook on life. In the clerical experiment described above we saw evidence of slight changes in personality after a year's exposure of clerks to different patterns of control. These changes were in the direction of increasing the "fit" between the worker's personality and the nature of the control structure (Tannenbaum, 1957: 404–6). Notorious "brainwashing" methods represent the ultimate in the process of institutionalized personality change, and we see illustrated in the fiction of Orwell and Huxley the psychological bludgeoning of individual personality into a perfect fit to the institutions of a "hypothetical" society of the future. As Huxley (1953: 16) puts it, "Round pegs in square holes tend to have dangerous thoughts about the social system and to infect others with their discontent." Organizations cannot often tolerate deviants, and there are pressures, sometimes subtle, on deviants to change.

Organizations in a democratic society present a seeming dilemma. As Geoffrey Vickers puts it,

> We are forever oscillating between two alternatives which seem mutually exclusive—on the one hand, collective efficiency won at the price of individual freedom; on the other, individual freedom equally frustrated by collective anarchy. Those who believe in a middle way which is more than a compromise do so in the faith that human beings are capable or can become capable of social organization which is both individually satisfying and collectively effective; and they have plenty of evidence for their faith. On the other hand, our knowledge of the laws involved is still rudimentary. [Vickers, 1957]

Middle ways are sprouting up around the globe today. The work council systems in Yugoslavia, in Germany, France, Belgium, England, though differing radically in character and effectiveness are, within their respective cultures, experiments in the middle way. We have our Scanlon plans, profit-sharing and suggestion schemes, as well as varying degrees of participative management. However, our knowledge of the effects of these systems is, as Vickers says, rudimentary.

If the clues provided by our research so far are substantiated, the middle way will have to take into account the important facts about control: how control is distributed within an organization, and how much it all amounts to. Patterns of control—as they are perceived by organization members, at least—are tied significantly to the performance of the organization and to the adjustments and satisfactions of members. If our research leads are correct, the more significant improvements in the human side of enterprise are going to come through changes in the way organizations are controlled, and particularly through changes in the size of the "influence pie." This middle way leans on the assumption that influential workers do not imply uninfluential supervisors or managers. This is a relatively novel assumption for many managers who have been weaned on the all-or-none law of power: one either leads or is led, is strong or is weak, controls or is controlled. Disraeli was no less influential a leader, however, for having questioned this when he said, "I follow the people. Am I not their leader?" And, managers who in their behavior question the all-or-none principle do not seem less influential for it.

Our middle way assumes further that the worker, or supervisor, or manager, who exercises some influence over matters of interest to him in the work situation, acquires a sense of self-respect which the powerless individual may lack. He can also elicit the respect and high regard of others. This is the key to good human relations. Supervisory training alone cannot achieve this any more than good intentions in bad organization can achieve it. The pattern of control in an organization, however, has a direct and profound effect on the organization's human relations climate. Workers who have some sense of control in the organizations we have studied, are, in general, more, not less, positively disposed toward their supervisors and managers. And their managers are more positively disposed toward them.

We assume further, with some support from research, that increasing and distributing the exercise of control more broadly in an organization helps to distribute an important sense of involvement in the organization. Members become more ego involved. Aspects of personality which ordinarily do not find expression now contribute to the motivation of the members. The organization provides members with a fuller range of experiences. In doing this, however, it creates its own dilemmas, similar in some respects to those described by Vickers.

A first dilemma concerns the increased control to which the influential organization members may become subject. While he controls more, he is not controlled less. The loyalty and identification which he feels for the organization lead him to accept organizational requirements and to conform to organizational norms which he might not otherwise do. We find evidence of this in the behavior of members of the effective union with high total control. Their behaviors were more uniform than were those of members in the ineffective laissez faire union (Tannenbaum and Kahn, 1956: 536–45). Norms and pressures toward conformity existed in the effective union which were lacking in the ineffective one. Members in the effective union pay for the increased control which they exercise (and for the effectiveness of their organization) not only in terms of the greater effort that they put into union activities, but also by their greater sensitivity and accession to controls within the union. An analysis in the thirty-one departments of the industrial service organization described revealed a similar phenomenon. Norms, measured in terms of uniformity in the behavior of workers, were more apparent in the departments having high total control than in those having low control. In these "better" departments, influence by the men as a group was greater, morale was more favorable, productive effort was higher, and so was uniformity (Smith et al., 1962). The exercise of control did not spare the controller from being controlled. The contrary may be true in effective organizations with high total control, where influence tends to be reciprocal.

A second dilemma arises out of the increased involvement and motivation that are likely to accompany the exercise of control. While we see greater opportunity for human satisfaction in the middle way, the result is not simple felicity. Whenever man is highly motivated he may experience the pangs of failure, as well as the joys of success. He will know some of the satisfactions which come from a challenge met and a responsibility fulfilled. He may also feel frustration from the development of goals which are not easily reached.

CONCLUDING STATEMENT

So what can we assume about organizational control as a design variable? Tannenbaum's control curves suggest that the control process is important to overall organizational performance. His discussion concerned degree, or amount, of control. But what about type? That is, do all situations call for the same kind of control? Do we find the same kind of control mechanisms for a canning plant, women's boutique, baseball club, and research laboratory? Obviously the answer is *no*. It is the purpose of the concluding statement to examine the different kinds of control options that are available to designers.

We will first describe three basic "pure" types of organizational control. We call these types *market*, *bureaucracy*, and *clan*. Then we will consider the conditions under which each form is most appropriate. Having laid out the basic framework, we will next consider the implications of each control method for how people are treated in organizations. Finally we will raise the "loose-coupling" point of view, which argues that rational control mechanisms are often not feasible in organizations.

THREE PURE TYPES OF ORGANIZATIONAL CONTROL: MARKET, BUREAUCRACY, AND CLAN

Most of us who study organizations—as well as those of us who work in them—are well aware of hierarchical authority—both of rules and of performance measurements. These are the most highly visible and the most explicit techniques of organizational control. What we sometimes miss, however, is the fact that, in every organization, there are other, almost invisible but equally potent forms of control at work. The forms of control that we see almost all come under the category of *bureaucratic control*, while we miss the *market control* and the *clan control* that exist also. Let us consider a real-life example.

The parts distribution division of a major company has an interesting problem. The purchasing department buys approximately 100,000 different items each year from about 3000 different manufacturers, and it accomplishes this huge volume of work with only 22 employees, of whom 3 are managerial level. On the other hand, the warehousing operation, which stores these items until they are ordered by a customer and then fills the customer orders, has about 1400 employees, of whom about 150 are managers. Now, why is it that the division employs so relatively few people to accomplish the very complex task of evaluating the quality and price of so many items, compared to the number of people required to store and then to distribute them?

An intelligent person might observe that it simply takes more people to lift a box of widgets than it does to buy a box of widgets, and certainly that is so if the box is heavy—but only 22 people to make so many purchasing analyses and decisions? Others might guess that the purchasing officers are "professionalized," with the result that each person can do more work and can do it without very much supervision, thus reducing the costs of control. Again, this is a good point, but probably insufficient to explain the large difference in number of people. Also, someone always points out that of course it takes a lot of supervision to watch over warehouse workers who have relatively dull, physically taxing jobs and who will not work hard without supervision. And of course it never takes much labor to staff a purchasing department, so this division is like any other one. Finally, it might be observed that both activities require about the same level of staffing; the difference is that most of the work involved in purchasing is done by supplier firms, whereas most of the work involved in warehousing and distribution is done within the division. Again, good points, but let us look at them more closely.

Control in the Warehouse

Out in a warehouse, the "pickers" must pick out the proper items to fill an order from a customer, the "packers" must check the items to be sure that the order is as specified and then must pack them properly for shipping. And the foreman must see to it that the work is going along properly. What we are interested in is the control process that the foreman uses to get the work out. The foreman is engaged in an elaborate task. He gathers information concerning the flow of work by watching the actions of the workers, knowing from their behavior which workers are doing their jobs well or poorly. He confirms his observations by checking a record of output for each worker at the end of each day. From time to time, as he observes the pickers and packers at work, the foreman also will stop to inquire of a worker why he or she is doing a job in a particular way, instead of in a way which the foreman prefers. He may also ask someone to stop what he or she is doing and to do a different job instead. In some cases, he will angrily confront a "trouble maker" and demand that he or she behave as he directs. In all of these actions, the supervisor is working within a well-defined set of rules that prescribes both his behavior and that of the pickers and packers. He does so within both the *formal* limits of authority—given by virtue of his rank—and within the *informal* limits of authority—this latter granted to him by the workers as a result of their trust in and respect for him as an individual. Now, these formal limits of authority and of power are not an implicit thing: they are written down in black and white, and each employee, both picker and foreman, knows them by memory. Thus the mechanism of control is explicitly what organization theorists mean when they talk of "bureaucratic control."

Control in the Purchasing Department

In the purchasing department, each purchasing officer does his or her work by sending out a description of the item desired to three or four different manufacturers, asking each one to quote a price for it. After the prices are in, the purchaser adds in any available information concerning the honesty, reliability, and past performance of the supplier. Having processed this information, the purchasing officer then decides to order from one of the suppliers. The supervisor occasionally consults with each purchasing agent to see if they need help. Further, the supervisor strictly reminds the purchasing agents that under no conditions are they ever to accept gifts of any sort from any supplier. Now what is the control mechanism here?

There are indeed some rules concerning how the purchasing agents are to do their jobs—to that extent we could accurately describe the department as being bureaucratic in its control. The more fundamental process of control, however, is exercised in the fact that the purchasing agents are dealing in a very competitive market. There is literally a score of manufacturers competing for each contract that the company signs, and the effect of that competition is to assure that, for any specified item, the price will be as low as possible. To ensure an efficient mechanism of control, the supervisor needs only to guarantee that the agents are not accepting higher-priced contracts in order to take side payments to line their pockets. The agents themselves can each accomplish a great deal of work because of the market. They do not have to go over a bid in detail, attempting to determine whether or not it is a "fair" price for the work required. All they need to do is compare prices, knowing that competitive pressure has guaranteed that the prices are "fair."

In short, much of the work has been performed in a separate firm—that of the supplier—and it is more efficient for the distribution division to "buy" this service than to perform it internally. The market mechanism enables the division to buy these services with a minimum of analysis and of staff work.

Bureaucracies and Markets

Our examination of the control mechanism employed in the purchasing department points up an important fact: the marketplace can serve as an alternative to a bureaucracy as a means of organizational control. It is a limiting case, of course, since a true market is as unattainable as a purely bureaucratic organization. Still, we can identify some important element of control as exercised by either a bureaucracy or a market.

Bureaucracy as Control

A bureaucratic mechanism of control depends fundamentally on the ability of the organization to specify rules concerning how people shall behave or levels of production that they must achieve. It also rests fundamentally upon the acceptance by all employees of the legitimacy of the hierarchy. Such acceptance gives superiors certain rights: first, to specify for subordinates what they shall do; second, to inspect their work closely in order to evaluate performance; third, to redirect their efforts as deemed necessary by the superior; and fourth, to decide on an *ad hoc* basis those questions for which no accepted rule exists. The critical elements of the bureaucratic control mechanism are therefore two: information and authority. The bureaucratic mechanism provides information to managers, to foremen, and to workers in the form of rules of behavior and rules of output to be achieved. These rules provide the capacity to move people toward the organization's objectives, because they are backed up by legitimate authority.

Market as Control

A market also has two critical elements: information and reciprocity. In a market, the information that is transmitted is contained wholly in prices. A price is a single, summary statistic, which—ideally—exactly represents the underlying value of the good or service to which it is attached. In a perfect market, if you know the prices of the alternative goods that you might buy, you need know nothing else. Most specifically, you do not need to know any rules at all (see Arrow, 1974: 20). In our warehouse, for example, if we could attach the correct price to each job, and if the foreman could effortlessly assess the performance of a picker on each job (that is, know that the job has in fact been done as agreed), then he could simply pay each employee for each job done and do away with the whole bureaucratic apparatus. Unfortunately, the conditions necessary for a market to exist are almost never met in reality; prices are very sophisticated, compact pieces of information on the one hand, and on the other hand, we cannot always expect workers (or managers, doctors, or professors) to honestly report their level of performance (Williamson, 1975). Indeed, the effort that would be necessary to run a market mechanism of control in our warehouse example would be so great that it might exceed the cost of running a bureaucracy.

As a pure model, never achieved in any real situation, a market represents a very efficient mechanism of control (Arrow, 1974: 1–29). A market needs only to have prices, reciprocity (Gouldner, 1961), and self-interest. Prices tell people which things they ought to do, self-interest gives them the motivation to do so, and reciprocity provides the minimal level of social control necessary to make exchange feasible. Gouldner (1961) has argued that across time and across societies only two social agreements, or norms, are universally found: these are the incest taboo and the norm of reciprocity. Both, he argues, are absolutely essential to the existence of a social collectivity. The norm of reciprocity, put simply, specifies that when someone does something of value for you, you are obligated to do something of roughly equal value in return. Also, the norm implies that if you fail to meet your obligations, you will suffer punishment from all members of the community, who will act to maintain the norm.

Now, given a norm of reciprocity, you do not have to fear cheating or stealing, and with a price mechanism and a little self-interest, you have a mechanism of control that will guide behavior. Indeed, this market mechanism of control requires no supervisors or managers at all, since people simply choose to do those things that will maximize their profits or wealth. Thus it is vastly more efficient than a bureaucracy, with all of its layers of supervisors, whose job is to manage the rules and carry out the auditing and the redirecting that are necessary in a bureaucracy.

Now we have solved our puzzle. We see why it is that the purchasing department can carry out its apparently immense task with so few people, compared to the number who are employed in warehousing. It participates in a market mechanism, which is a far more efficient mode of control than a bureaucracy. Prices are a much more compact and powerful means of communication than are rules. Yet, it is rare that true prices can be obtained, and for this reason the bureaucratic form is far more common as a technique of control.

Bureaucracies and Clans

Each of us who studies or who works in a large organization knows all about the "informal organization" (Blau, 1955; Blau and Scott, 1962: 89–99) that exists within each "formal organization." The informal network of exchange, of assistance, of friendship that grows up in an organization can be a powerful influence on what actually happens (see, for example, Selznick, 1949; Gouldner, 1954). In a predominantly bureaucratic organization, these informal relationships can be an important secondary form of control. Indeed, this was the major discovery of the Hawthorne Studies (Roethlisberger and Dickson, 1939). This "informal organization" represents something akin to a separate organizational culture, existing apart from the broader culture of the society. In many of the cases cited by sociologists and by organization theorists, this local culture is limited to the immediate work group or department. Typically, the local culture consists of a set of values or objectives and a set of beliefs about what causes what. These values (or ends) and beliefs (about means) are shared by all members of the culture or clan, and they are maintained through a series of rituals and ceremonies.

Sometimes the elements of the culture are so widely shared that they are common to virtually all of the members of an organization. Such cases include the typesetters' union

(Lipset, Trow and Coleman, 1956), the coal mine (Trist and Bamforth, 1951), the forest service (Kaufman, 1967), and the Japanese company (Nakane, 1973; Dore, 1973; Rohlen, 1974). In these cases, the mechanism of control departs radically from the bureaucratic and market forms. The elements of control are basically found in the socialization process through which new members of the organization are molded until their values fit the values of the organization and their beliefs fit the beliefs of the organization (Davis and Lawrence, 1977, note that organizational culture in Japanese companies accomplishes the same control that the elaborate matrix form does in U.S. firms, pp. 55–56). These values and beliefs are reinforced through rituals and ceremonies (Meyer and Rowan, 1977) or through stories and sagas (Clark, 1970).

The result is that each and every member of the organization has firmly implanted in him or her a set of values and beliefs that cause them to behave in a way that will have the effect of moving the organization toward its objectives. Thoroughly unlike the warehouse, where the workers desire to act in ways that are harmful to the organization and thus must be monitored and commanded through an authority structure, the workers in a true clan have been taught to behave so that they desire to do that which the organization wants them to do.

Compared to a bureaucracy, however, a clan is inexplicit about its means of control. Perrow (1972: 32) has noted that one function of rules in a bureaucracy is to serve as the organization's "memory," to pass along learned wisdom to new members. This memory works in a method that is highly explicit compared to the subtle, implicit, and almost invisible social understandings that comprise the mechanism of control in the clan. The advantage of the clan is that it can be far more subtle, more complex, and therefore more complete. In short, clan control can be more pervasive and greater in scope (Etzioni, 1965: 669) in its implicit "rules" of behavior than can the bureaucracy. Because all of its rules must be explicit so that they are easily comprehended by any newcomer, the bureaucracy must limit itself to a relatively small set of rules. As a result, the bureaucracy must be incomplete in its specification of responses to possible problems, and it must be prepared for the top members of its hierarchy to assume the task of ruling on a large volume of "exceptions" to its small and inflexible set of rules.

We have suggested that the bureaucracy is clearly inferior to the clan as a mechanism of control because the clan is so much more complete in its ability to specify responses to a complex world. We have also suggested that the bureaucracy is clearly inferior to the market mechanism because the market employs no managerial resources and is therefore most efficient as a method of achieving exchange. Given all this, however, we are left with an obvious question: why is the bureaucratic form of control so pervasive? The answer, of course, has already been given away, as the attentive reader has noticed. The conditions under which a market or clan can operate effectively are rarely met in reality, whereas the conditions prerequisite to effective bureaucratic control are, by comparison, easily satisfied.

THE SOCIAL AND INFORMATIONAL PREREQUISITES OF CONTROL

It is possible to arrange the three modes of control along each of two dimensions—the informational requirements necessary to operate each control type and the social underpinnings necessary to operate each control type. These are summarized in Table 8–2.

TABLE 8–2 SOCIAL AND INFORMATIONAL PREREQUISITES OF CONTROL

Type of Control	Social Prerequisites	Informational Prerequisites
Market	Norm of reciprocity	Prices
Bureaucracy	Norm of reciprocity; legitimate authority	Rules
Clan	Norm of reciprocity; legitimate authority; shared values, beliefs	Traditions

Social Prerequisites of Control

Let us consider first the social requirements, and then we will consider the informational issues. What we mean by social prerequisites of control is that set of agreements between people that, as a bare minimum, is necessary for a form of control to be employed. Any real organization, of course, will have developed a highly elaborated set of understandings going far beyond this minimum. At the moment, however, our task is to understand the bare minimum without which a social control mechanism cannot function. First, a word about self-interest.

We had noted that a market requires self-interest, in addition to its social and informational needs, in order to function. That is, unless each person seeks to behave in ways that bring him or her pleasure or profit, a market cannot operate. We could say the same of a bureaucaracy and perhaps of a clan, but self-interest, in our terms, is not a social understanding; it is a characteristic of individuals that exists even without social interaction. Certainly, the particular way in which we *express* our self-interest is shaped by social surroundings, but the essential hedonism exists in the individual.

Assuming self-interest, then, we can observe that a market cannot exist without a norm of reciprocity, and that it requires no social agreements beyond that. A norm of reciprocity assures that, should one party in a market transaction be discovered attempting to cheat another, the cheater will be punished by all members of the social system, not just by the victim. The severity of the punishment will typically far exceed the crime, thus effectively deterring potential future opportunists.

Market Control

In a market, the norm of reciprocity is critical because of the costs of running a market mechanism (as opposed to the costs of any other mechanism of control). In a market mechanism, the costs of carrying out transactions between parties have mostly to do with assuring oneself that the other party is dealing honestly, since all information relevant to the substance of the decision is contained in prices and is therefore not problematic (see Williamson, 1975, for a thorough discussion). If honesty cannot be taken for granted, however, then each party must take on the cripplingly high costs of surveillance, complete contracting, and enforcement—in order not to be cheated. These costs can quickly become so high that they will cause a market to fail.

Bureaucratic Control

When a market fails as the mechanism of control, it is most often replaced by a *bureaucratic* form. A bureaucracy is well equipped to deal with opportunism and to take the steps necessary to guard against cheating, because it contains not only a norm of reciprocity, but also the idea of legitimate authority, ordinarily of the rational/legal form (see Blau and Scott, 1962: 27–36, for a discussion). In a bureaucratic control system, the norm of reciprocity is reflected in the notion of "an honest day's work for an honest day's pay," and it particularly contains the idea that, in exchange for pay, people give up autonomy in certain areas, thus permitting their organizational superiors to direct their work activities and to monitor their performance. These steps are possible only if organization members accept the idea that higher office holders have the legitimate right to command and to audit or monitor those in lower positions (within some range, of course as with the "zone of indifference" of Barnard, 1938). Given social support for a norm of reciprocity and for the idea of legitimate authority, a bureaucratic control mechanism can operate successfully.

Clan Control

A *clan* requires not only a norm of reciprocity and the idea of legitimate authority (often of the "traditional" rather than the "rational/legal"form), but also social agreement on a broad range of values and beliefs. Because the clan lacks the explicit price mechanism of the market and the explicit rules of the bureaucracy, it relies for its control upon a deep level of common agreement between members on what constitutes proper behavior. And it requires a high level of commitment on the part of each individual to those socially prescribed behaviors. Clearly, a clan is more demanding than either a market or a bureaucracy, in terms of the social agreements that are prerequisite to its successful operation.

The kinds of social agreements we have been discussing thrive on homogeneity. That is, they are easier to achieve among people who have similar backgrounds than among people whose backgrounds are dissimilar. Thus social agreements are more readily developed in organizations that have low turnover and a relatively homogeneous membership. An organization troubled by high rates of turnover cannot hope to maintain a clan form of control, since it takes very long to acculturate each member in a clan, and turnover becomes devastatingly costly to the organization. A market, however (such as a morning market for poultry and vegetables in Dubrovnik, Yugoslavia), can operate effectively even with a 100 percent turnover of buyers and sellers each day. A bureaucracy cannot survive with 100 percent turnover, but it can withstand rates of turnover far above those which the clan is able to tolerate. Because of its specialization of tasks, its impersonal attitude, and its explicit rules, a bureaucracy is able to take in new employees who have certain specialized skills and quickly integrate them into the organization.

Informational Prerequisities of Control

Bureaucratic Control

While a clan is the most demanding and the market the least demanding with respect to social underpinnings of control, the opposite is true for information. Within *bureaucracies*, each department tends to develop its own peculiar jargon (Galbraith, 1973; Lawrence and Lorsch, 1967c). It does so because the jargon, being suited to particular task needs, provides the department with a very efficient set of symbols with which to communicate complex ideas, thus conserving on the limited information-carrying capacity of an organization. We can also think of the accounting system in an organization as the smallest set of symbols conveying information that is relevant to all organizational subunits. An accounting system is a relatively explicit information system compared, say, to the traditions of the U.S. Senate (Matthews, 1960).

Each of these mechanisms carries information about how to behave, but the accounting system, being explicit, is easily accessed by a newcomer, whereas the traditions of the Senate, being implicit, can be discovered by a freshman senator only over a period of years. On the other hand, the explicit system is far less complete in its ability to convey information. And it has often been noted that there is no accounting measurement that fully captures the underlying performance of a department or corporation, since many of the dimensions of performance defy measurement (Ouchi and Maguire, 1975; Vancil, 1975). Typically, an explicit information system must be created and maintained intentionally and at some cost, while an implicit information system often "grows up" as a natural byproduct of social interaction.

Market Control

In a true *market*, prices are arrived at through a process of competitive bidding, and no administrative apparatus is necessary to produce this information. However, many economists have argued that the conditions necessary for such perfect prices are rarely, if ever, met in reality, with the result that inefficiencies are borne by the parties to the market. Although markets are not organizations in our sense of the word (Arrow, 1974), we can consider as a limit case the profit or investment center in a business as an attempt to control an organization through a price mechanism.

In some large organizations, it is possible, with great effort and a huge accounting staff, to create internal numbers that serve the function of prices. That is, if division managers and department heads attempt simply to maximize their profit by taking the best prices available within the firm, then the firm as a whole will benefit. These "transfer prices" are not the same thing as output, cost, or performance standards—those standards are, in essence, bureaucratic rules. The critical difference is that an internal price does not need a hierarchy of authority to accompany it. If the price mechanism is at work, all that is needed in addition to prices is a norm of reciprocity, accompanied by self-interest.

Only rarely is it possible for an organization to arrive at perfect transfer prices, however, because technological interdependence and uncertainty tremendously complicate the problem for most organizations, to the point that arriving at prices is simply not feasible. Under that condition, the organization can create an explicit set of rules—both rules about behavior and rules about levels of production or output. Although an organization can never create an explicit set of rules that will cover every situation that could possibly confront any of its employees, it can cut the information problem down to size by writing a relatively small set of rules that will cover 90 percent of all events and depend upon hierarchical authority to settle the remaining 10 percent. Thus we see again that acceptance of legitimate authority is critical to a bureaucracy, since it is that property that enables the organization to specify incompletely the duties of an employee, having the employee agree that, within bounds, a superior may specify his or her duties as the need arises (Williamson, 1975: 57–81).

In this manner, the organization deals with the future one step at a time, rather than having to anticipate it completely in advance in a set of explicit rules. In comparison to prices, rules are a rather crude form of information transmisson. Rules are inevitably incomplete in specifying what decision is to be made or what alternative chosen whereas prices are complete in that regard. Rules require appeal to hierarchical authority for exceptional cases; prices do not. And a decision maker can sometimes not be sure that the correct rule is being applied for a given situation. Such uncertainty is never a problem with prices. But rules are always feasible, they are a relatively simple information system to construct—compared to prices—and thus are far more common as a means of control.

Clan Control

In a *clan*, the information system is contained in the rituals, stories, and ceremonies that convey the values and beliefs of the organization. An outsider cannot quickly gain access to information concerning decision rules used in a clan, but the information system does not require an army of accountants, computer experts, and managers. It is just there. Ivan Light (1972), for example, has described the Chinese-American *hui* and the Japanese-American *tanomoshi*; these are revolving credit-lending societies that provide venture capital for starting new businessess. They carry out all of the functions of any Wall Street investment bank, but within their ethnic group, they are able to make loans that would be far too risky for any bank. They are able to make such loans because they enjoy considerable advantages in obtaining, interpreting, and evaluating information about potential borrowers or members.

None of their practices is explicit—even the rate of interest paid by borrowers is left unspecified and implicit. Entry into a *hui* or *tanomoshi* is strictly limited by birthright, a practice which guarantees that each member is part of a social and kinship network that will support the values and beliefs upon which the control mechanism is founded. Clearly, the clan information system cannot cope with heterogeneity or with turnover—characteristics that make it all but infeasible as a central mechanism of control in modern organizations. Like the market, however, the clan is able to operate with great efficiency if the basic conditions necessary to its operation can be met.

Thus we see that in a sense clans and markets represent two "perfect" control mechanisms—each can theoretically make every decision it faces without error. Each, however, requires a condition that is rarely encountered in nature and that can be created or designed only at great cost. The market requires price information, a characteristic rarely found in exchange relations in unadulterated form. However, prices can be designed into the control mechanism of an organization. Further, the cost of doing so may be warranted, especially when the heterogeneity of tasks within the organization or the high rates of turnover make bureaucratic means infeasible.

On the other hand, the clan mode of control requires homogeneous and stable membership and tasks so that all can share common experiences and develop a common set of values and beliefs. Again, this condition is rarely met but can be designed into an organization. The cost of keeping down turnover and of maintaining task homogeneity may be justified if the organization is not capable of utilizing explicit prices or rules for evaluation and control. In a police department, for example, where the behavior of patrol officers cannot be directly observed and audited, cultural forms of control are necessary. In hospitals and in schools, we observe a professional culture operating as a means of maintaining values and beliefs among employees whose true output or production cannot be assessed.

Design Implications

If the price requirements of a market cannot be met and if the social conditions of the clan are impossible to achieve, then the bureaucratic mechanism becomes the preferred method of control. In a sense, the market is like the trout and the clan like the salmon—each a beautiful, highly specialized species that requires uncommon conditions for its survival. In comparison, the bureaucratic method of control is the catfish—clumsy, ugly, but able to live in the widest possible range of environments and, ultimately, the dominant species. The bureaucratic mode of control can withstand high rates of turnover, a high degree of heterogeneity, and it does not have very demanding information needs.

In reality, of course, we will never observe a pure market, a pure bureaucracy, or a pure clan. Real organizations will each contain some features of each of the modes of control. The design problem thus becomes one of assessing the social and informational characteristics of each division, department, or task and determining which of the forms of control ought to be emphasized in each case. Current ideas about the design of organizational control systems are based almost exclusively on the bureaucratic form. The work of March and Simon (1958) deals with decision making in bureaucratic organizations, Parsons (1960) describes problems of vertical control in bureaucracies, Perrow (1972) concentrates on rules as a control mechanism in bureaucracies, and Argyris (1964), Likert (1967), and Tannenbaum (1968) prescribe techniques for reducing some of the undesirable byproducts of what remains an essentially bureaucratic mode of control.

Let us next consider some of the more direct implications of each form of control for the ways in which people are treated in organizations. We will approach this task by looking at each of the stages at which an organization can exercise discretion over people. By doing so, we may discover some additional design variables which can influence the form of organizational control.

PROCESSING PEOPLE THROUGH ORGANIZATIONS

Basically, there are two ways in which an organization can achieve effective people control. Either it can go to the expense of searching for and selecting people who fit its needs exactly, or it can take people who do not exactly fit its needs and go to the expense of installing a managerial system to instruct, monitor, and evaluate them.

Which of these approaches is best depends on the cost of each to the organization. On the one hand, there is a cost of search and of acquisition. Some skills are rare in the labor force, and the organization wanting to hire people with those skills will have to search widely and pay higher wages. Once hired, however, such people will be able to perform their tasks without instruction, and if they have also been selected for values (motivation), they will be inclined to work effectively without close supervision—both of which will save the organization money.

On the other hand, there is the cost of training the unskilled and the indifferent to learn the organization's skills and values. Moreover, there is the cost of developing and running a supervisory system to monitor, evaluate, and correct their behavior. Once in place, however, such a system can typically take in a heterogeneous assortment of people and effectively control them. In addition, its explicit training and monitoring routines enable it to withstand high rates of turnover. High turnover is costly if search and acquisition costs are high. But turnover is relatively harmless to the organization if it hires all comers.

It has also been observed, by people as disparate as sociologists (Etzioni, 1965), social psychologists (Kelman, 1958), and economists (Williamson, 1975), that various forms of evaluation and control will result in differing individual levels of commitment to, or alienation from, the organization and its objectives. In general, a control mode that relies heavily on selecting "appropriate" people can expect high commitment, as a result of internalized values. For example, the U.S. Foreign Service Officer Corps does not hire anyone unless that person already possesses the basic abilities necessary to do the job and also expresses the values deemed central to the foreign service. Such people, in working for the foreign service, are doing things that they have long believed were right and good, and they will be extremely committed to those internalized values. As a consequence, the foreign service does not have to monitor them very closely. That is a good thing, since, not by coincidence, the foreign service would be almost wholly incapable of monitoring and evaluating their performance if it had to do so. Thus control through selection (and, to some extent, by screening out the "mistakes") is the optimal choice.

At the other extreme, a control mode that depends heavily on monitoring, evaluating, and correcting in an explicit manner is likely to offend people's senses of autonomy and of self-control, and as a result will probably result in an unenthusiastic, purely compliant response. In this state, people require even more close supervision, having been alienated from the organization as a result of its control mechanism. Indeed, as is always true of any form of measurement, it is not possible for an organization to measure or otherwise control its employees without somehow affecting them through the very process that it uses to measure them. There is no completely unobtrusive measurement in most organizations. In general, the more obvious and explicit the measurement, the more noxious it is to employees and thus the greater the cost to the organization of using such methods. However, other conditions may demand the use of these more explicit yet offensive techniques of control.

Table 8–3 summarizes the discussion thus far. What we have in Table 8–3 is a set of categories that roughly go together, although we cannot specify exactly where many of the boundaries are between categories.

People Treatment

The *people treatment* alternatives are by now familiar. At one extreme, an organization could be completely *totally unselective* about its members, taking anyone (although we still assume that everyone is to some extent self-interested, hedonistic, or profit maximizing). At the other extreme, an organization could be highly selective, choosing only those individuals who already have both the skills and the values that the organization needs. This practice is most common in the "professional bureaucracies," such as hospitals, public accounting firms, and universities. In an apparent paradox, these most and least selective kinds of organizations will both produce high levels of commitment. That is, members will have internalized the underlying objectives of the organization.

Of course, the paradox is resolved by noting that the completely unselective organization relies on commitment of each individual to self, since it uses a market mechanism of control in which what is desired is that each person simply maximize his or her personal well-being (profit). Since the organization's objective is thus identical to the individual's objective, we can say that internalization of objectives exists, enthusiasm for pursuing the organization's

TABLE 8–3 ORGANIZATIONAL CONTROL: PEOPLE TREATMENT

People Treatment	Form of Commitment (Kelman, 1958)	Corresponding Control type
Totally unselective; take anyone, no further treatment		Market
	Internalization	
Selection / screening		Clan
	Identification	
Training -Skill training -Value training		Bureaucracy
	Compliance	
Monitoring -Monitor behavior -Monitor output		

goals will be high (since they are also the individual's selfish goals), and thus no close supervision will be necessary.

In the other case, where high *selection* is employed, the new organization members will typically have passed through a lengthy period of training that has equipped them with those skills, values, and beliefs that are common to the organization. Having internalized these elements of the organizational culture, they will pursue the organization's goals in an effective manner when left to their own devices, thus requiring no further control.

Most organizations, however, cannot take on all comers (they do not have a price mechanism), and they can rely upon selection and screening only to a limited extent. That is, most organizations can select partially for the skills and values desired but will not be able to find people who exactly fit their needs. In this case, the organizations may rely on *training*, both in the form of formalized training programs and in the form of on-the-job or apprenticeship training to impart the desired skills and values. Typically, training will result in the trainee identifying with either the trainer (who may also be a respected superior) or with the work group or department. In this case, the employee will possess the necessary skills and will pursue the organization's objective. But this is only because he or she identifies with and wants to emulate the respected person or group, not because the underlying objectives have been internalized to the point where the employee believes them to be good and desirable objectives in their own right.

When turnover is particularly high or the work is particularly distasteful, the organization may not be able to achieve its control needs through selection and training. In that case, it relies upon *monitoring* performance, either by measuring behavior or by measuring outputs, comparing these to some explicit standard, and then correcting behavior where necessary. Monitoring produces a purely compliant form of commitment to organizational goals. That is, employees tend to follow directives purely because they have agreed as part of their implied employment contract to submit to higher authority. But this they do without any identification with the organization or internalization of its objectives.

As a result, they will comply only when they are being monitored. However, they are likely also to resent being monitored, so this form of control typically degenerates into one of extreme alienation of workers from management.

Form of Commitment

The link between forms of commitment and types of control is quite direct. *Internalized commitment* is necessary for a market, since a market possesses no monitoring or policing capabilities. Internalization can also support a clan, which has weak monitoring abilities. That is, evaluation is subtle and slow under this form of control, and thus, without high commitment, the mechanism is capable of drifting off course before being corrected.

A clan can also be supported with *identification*, however, and over time, the identification may be converted into internalization of the values of the clan. Identification is also compatible with bureaucratic control, although it exceeds the minimum commitment that is necessary in a bureaucracy.

Compliance is the minimum level of commitment necessary for bureaucratic control, but it is beneath the threshold of commitment necessary for the clan and market forms. The social agreement to suspend judgment about orders from superiors and to simply follow orders (see Blau and Scott, 1962: 29–30) is fundamental to bureaucratic control. Thus we see that because people come with a variety of abilities, values, and beliefs, and because organizations frequently need people packaged in ways that are different from the way they come, people will vary widely in their commitment to organizations.[2]

The more closely the skills and values of a person match the demands of the organization, the more completely the individual will commit himself or herself to the organization. Some organizations, being unable to find enough people who naturally fit them, will take the time necessary to shape new employees in ways that will make them comfortable in the organization. Other organizations, facing different conditions, will find it more advantageous to settle for a lower level of commitment. Perhaps they will even accept some hostility and alienation of lower employees in exchange for the ability to implement mechanisms of control that can function even with individuals who do not share any of the objectives held by the organization.

An Ethical Question

The issue of commitment and control may also pose a moral question of some significance. If organizations achieve internalized control purely through selection, then it would seem that both the individual and the organization are satisfied. If internalization is achieved by training employees in the values and beliefs of the organization, however, then it is possible that some individuals may be subject to economic coercion to modify their values in ways that they dislike. Indeed, this kind of forced socialization is common in certain of our institutions (what Etzioni, 1965, refers to as "coercive" organizations) such as the U.S. Marine Corps and many mental hospitals. In such cases, we accept the abrogation of individual rights as being secondary to a more pressing need. In the case of a company town or a middle-aged employee with few job options, however, we are less likely to approve of this kind of pressure. As long as organizations maintain an essentially democratic power

2. Recall the discussion of such differences, including commitment, in Chapter 6.

structure, this danger remains remote. If the hierarchy of authority becomes relatively autocratic, however, the possibility of loss of individual freedom becomes real.

What are the mechanisms through which an organization can be managed so that it moves toward its objectives? What are the limits of each basic design, and how can the design of these mechanisms be improved? Those are the questions to which we now turn.

LOOSE COUPLING AND THE CLAN AS A FORM OF CONTROL

There is developing a new and somewhat revolutionary view of "organizational rationality" that has direct implications for designing control mechanisms. Basically, this new view —known as *loose coupling* (Weick, 1976)—implies that bureaucratic forms of control are not suitable for many contemporary organizations. Let us briefly consider the underlying "organizational rationality" that dominates the current views of control, and then we will consider the loose-coupling perspective.

An essential element underlying any bureaucratic or market form of control is the assumption that it is feasible to measure, with reasonable precision, the performance that is desired. In order to set a production standard that effectively controls, it is essential that the industrial engineers be able to measure desired output with some precision. In order to control effectively through the use of rules, it is essential that the personnel department know which rules to specify for achieving the desired performance. Indeed, the ability to measure either output or behavior that is relevant to the desired performance is critical to the "rational" application of market and bureaucratic forms of control. Table 8–4 identifies the contingencies that determine whether or not we can safely assume that measurement is possible.

Now, in order to understand Table 8–4, let us agree, for the moment, that if we wanted to control an organization, we would have to monitor or measure something, and that essentially the things we can measure are limited to either the behavior of employees or the results of those behaviors. If (cell 1) we understand the technology (that is, the means-ends relationships involved in the basic production or service activites) perfectly, as in the case of a tin-can plant, for example, we can then achieve effective control simply by having someone watch the behavior of the employees and the workings of the machines. If all behaviors and processes conform to our desired transformation steps, then we can presume that proper tin cans are coming out the other end, without even looking. By specifying the rules of behavior and of process, we could create an effective bureaucratic control mechanism in this case.

TABLE 8–4 CONDITIONS DETERMINING THE MEASUREMENT OF BEHAVIOR AND OF OUTPUT

		Knowledge of the Transformation Process	
		Perfect	*Imperfect*
Ability to Measure Outputs	*High*	1. Behavior or output measurement (tin-can plant)	2. Output measurement (women's boutique)
	Low	3. Behavior measurement (baseball team)	4. Ritual and ceremony, "clan" control (research laboratory)

However, we can also measure unambiguously whether the output meets specifications. Thus we also have the alternative of pure output control with no monitoring of behavior or process at all.

On the other hand (cell 2), suppose that we are designing a control system for a high-fashion women's boutique in San Francisco. What it takes to be a successful buyer or merchandiser is beyond our understanding, so we could not possibly hope to create a set of rules which, if followed by our buyers, would assure success. We can, however, measure the average markdowns that each buyer's leftover dresses must take, the average inventory turnover for each buyer, and the sales volume and profit margin of each buyer. Such measures give us an output-control mechanism. If our output-control mechanism consists of a multiple set of objectives, then it is effectively a bureaucratic mechanism. It is a mechanism that will be managed by having someone in the hierarchy who will monitor the various indicators for each buyer and, using the legitimate authority of office, will enforce not only close monitoring but will also order the necessary corrections in the buyer's decisions.

If, instead, our various indicators can be combined into a single summary statistic or measure of performance—one that captures all aspects of a buyer's performance—then we can simply pay each buyer a fixed amount for each unit of performance. In this way, we will have a price or market mechanism of control, one in which no commanding or use of authority is necessary, since each buyer will be motivated to maximize his or her total income.

In the third case, we could be designing a control mechanism for a baseball team. We can completely specify each step of the transformation process which must occur in order for a player to properly execute double-play combinations, thus giving us the possibility of behavior control. However, the interdependence between players is so great that we cannot use output measures to completely represent the performance of any player. Thus we are limited to behavior control.

Now, suppose that we are running a research laboratory at a multibillon dollar corporation (cell 4). We have little ability to specify rigidly the rules of behavior which, if followed, will lead to desired scientific breakthroughs. We probably can measure the ultimate success of a scientific discovery, but it may take 10, 20, or even 50 years for an apparently arcane discovery to be fully appreciated. Certainly, we would be wary of using a strong form of output control to encourage certain scientists in our lab while discouraging others. Effectively, we are unable to use either behavior or output measurement, thus leaving us with no "rational" form of control.

What happens in such circumstances is that the organization relies heavily on ritualized, ceremonial forms of control. These include the recruitment of only a few selected individuals, each of whom has been through a schooling and professionalization process that has taught him or her to internalize the desired values and to revere the appropriate ceremonies. The most important of those ceremonies, such as "hazing" of new members in seminars, going to professional society meetings, and writing scientific articles for publication in learned journals, will continue to be encouraged within the laboratory.

Now, it is commonly supposed that such rituals, which are common not only in research laboratories but also in hospitals, schools, government agencies, and investment banks, constitute quaint but essentially useless and perhaps even harmful practice. But consider: if it is not possible to measure either behavior or outputs and it is therefore not possible to "rationally" evaluate the work of the organization, what managerial alternative is there but to do the following: 1. carefully select workers so that you can be assured of having an able and committed set of people, and 2. conduct or encourage rituals and ceremonies that serve the purpose of rewarding those who display the underlying attitudes and values that are deemed likely to lead to organizational success. Following such a control strategy thus serves to remind everyone of what they are supposed to be trying to achieve, even if they can't tell whether or not they are achieving it.

Consider the medical profession. In many areas of medical practice, it is not possible to reliably measure the performance of a physician, but we as a society still demand having physicians who try to heal us. We thus are willing to legitimate the medical profession—even though we cannot evaluate its effectiveness—because it has adopted a ritualized form of control. Every physician is carefully selected so that he or she has more ability than necessary for the job; then each one is put through a lengthy socialization process which assures that the finished product is a person who holds the values of helping and of healing. More than that we cannot ask.

Whereas output and behavior control can be implemented through a market or a bureaucracy (Ouchi and Maguire, 1975; Ouchi, 1977), ceremonial forms of control (Meyer and Rowan, 1977) can be implemented through a clan. Because ceremonial forms of control are unable to monitor or evaluate anything but attitudes, values, and beliefs—and because attitudes, values, and beliefs are typically acquired more slowly than are manual or cognitive abilities—ceremonial forms of control require the stability of membership that characterizes the clan.

Loose Coupling

Recently it has been fashionable to argue that relatively few real organizations possess the underlying "rationality" typically assumed in market and bureaucratic forms of control. Parsons (1960), Williamson (1975), and Ouchi (1978) have argued that most hierarchies fail to transmit control with any accuracy from top to bottom. Simon (1962; 1964) has made a convincing case that most organizations have neither a single nor an integrated set of goals and that the subunits of organizations are, as a matter of necessity, only loosely joined to each other. Further, the structure of most organizations seems determined more by their environment than by any purposive, technologically motivated managerial strategy (Evan, 1966; Aldrich, 1972; Pfeffer, 1976). Hannan and Freeman (1977) have argued even more strongly that in fact organizational form may be designed only by nature, through a process of selection. Finally, Cohen, March, and Olsen (1972) have argued that organizational decision processes are far removed from our view of rationality and have chosen instead the metaphor of the "garbage can" to describe them.

If there is any truth in this considerable attack on our notions of the orderliness and rationality with which organizations function, then we must guess that the forms of control that are dominant today may be inappropriate in future organizations. The bureaucratic model of control derives from the first half of the twentieth century, a period during which the great majority of economic organizations was concerned with manufacturing. During that period, it may be that measurement of performance was indeed possible in most cases and that specification of appropriate rules of behavior and of decision making was equally appropriate. It is as a direct result of that era that we saw the development of theories of organization design that emphasized the central importance of technology as the determining factor in designing a rational organization (Woodward, 1965). Organization design theories growing out of that period also advocated the use of techniques such as boundary spanners and buffers for the purpose of "protecting" the core technology of the organization and its essential orderliness and rationality from the messy, uncertain forces in the environment (Udy, 1962; Thompson, 1967).

Since that time, beginning perhaps with the work of Evan (1966) and of Katz and Kahn (1966), we have begun to appreciate the fact that no organization can or should attempt to buffer itself completely from its environment. In the second place, we have recently seen the tremendous growth of service industries and of government as major economic organizations in our society. These organizations have such a low degree of performance measurability and such a high degree of task interdependence that old approaches to control fail in them. We can clearly express the difference in approach as follows: Lawrence and Lorsch (1967a) pioneered the "organization and environment" or "open systems" view of organizations, arguing that in a dynamic environment, organizations must differentiate internally in order to develop specialized expertise at dealing with each element in the environment. However, they must go to great lengths to reintegrate these differentiated parts, in order to achieve a rationalized state of control. In sharp comparison, Meyer and Rowan (1977) have essentially argued that because many contemporary organizations, particularly in the public sector, have an environment consisting of multiple constituencies each with its own, competing objectives (the same point made by Simon, 1964, about all organizations), differentiation is inevitable in both a vertical and horizontal manner, and furthermore integration is not only impossible but undesirable! Any attempt to integrate these diverse sets of objectives will necessarily fail, because objectives are nothing but operationalized values, and value differences are not subject to rational resolution. Thus we can say that the field of the design of organizational control has gone from "differentiation and integration" to "differentiation without integration."

Now, if it is true that many organizations do not easily permit measurement of either behavior or output, and if it is also true that they are loosely coupled internally, then we can hardly imagine that the bureaucratic form can continue to dominate as the mode of control. We see clearly in a recent book on the matrix form of organization (Davis and Lawrence, 1977) that the bureaucratic form is strained almost to the breaking point when it attempts to deal with loosely coupled organizations. Davis and Lawrence also point out that the Japanese company quite easily achieves the control objectives of the matrix form, but in an implicit, nonbureaucratic fashion. Nearly every student of Japanese organizations has made the point that such organizations operate through cultural homogeneity, socialization, and stability of membership. This form is the closest representation that we have seen of the clan model of control.

Under conditions of ambiguity, of loose coupling, and of uncertainty, measurement with reliability and precision is not possible. A control system based on such measurements is likely to systematically reward a narrow range of maladaptive behavior, leading ultimately to organizational decline. It may be that, under such conditions, the clan form of control, which operates by stressing values and objectives as much as behavior, is preferable. An organization that evaluates people on their values and motivation can tolerate wide differences in styles of performance. That is exactly what is desirable under conditions of ambiguity, when means-ends relationships are only poorly understood.

SUMMARY AND CONCLUSION

This chapter has been concerned with organizational control as a design variable. We began the discussion with Tannenbaum's treatment of control as a process in which one person, group, or organization intentionally affects what another person, group, or organization will do. A particularly telling point made by the author was that the total amount of control exercised in an organization is not necessarily fixed. Indeed, increased total organizational control can reflect increased participation and mutual influence—both of which can lead to increased organizational effectiveness.

In this concluding statement we have developed a relatively unified concept for dealing with control as an *organizational* process. Although the conceptual scheme presented here serves as a background for the development of specific design principles and does not itself specify organizational designs, one or two implications are clear. First, it appears that rates of turnover in an organization may be a critical determinant of the control mechanism. Low turnover is conducive to a clan, moderate turnover suggests a bureaucracy, and very high turnover can be tolerated only by a market. Second, we can see that professionalism provides a common alternative to organizational mechanisms of control, and we can see that the clan and market forms, which rely heavily on internalized forms of control, are most compatible with professionalized activities—from public accounting to medicine and plumbing.

Third, we see that the "informal organization," the organizational "climate" or "atmosphere," and the "managerial philosophy" of a firm are more than quaint anachronisms. Indeed, they comprise the culture of an organization. They may even be its principal form of control, and ineffable though they are, they should be taken seriously as mechanisms of control.

Organizations vary in the degree to which they are loosely or tightly coupled. Many organizations, particularly those in relatively stable manufacturing industries, fit the requirements for behavior control or for output control. Control mechanisms of the market or bureaucratic variety can be designed into such organizations. Organizations in the public sector, in service industries, and in fast-growing technologies may not fit these specifications and should have cultural or clan forms of control instead.

A Final Thought

The student of organizational control—and those who wish to design control systems—should take care to understand that clans, which operate on ceremony and on ritual, have forms of control that by their nature are subtle and ordinarily not visible to the inexperienced eye. Many is the eager young manager who has taken a quick look around, observed that no control mechanisms exist, and then begun a campaign to install a bureaucratic or market mechanism of some sort, only to trip over elaborate ceremonial forms that are in place and working quite effectively.

It is a fact of contemporary organizational life that such inexplicit forms of control, being by their nature nonquantifiable, are held by most of us to be somehow of doubtful pedigree and are therefore frequently not defended with much enthusiasm when questioned by outsiders. How many of us would feel comfortable explaining to a new division chief, or to a Senator Proxmire, or to an outside auditing team that, "Our control mechanisms are here, it's just that you can't see them until you've been around a few years. Be patient." Perhaps more to the point, how many of us would feel comfortable presenting to top management a control-system design that rests primarily on the idea of the formal organization as myth, ceremony, and ritual?

Questions for Review

1. How does Tannenbaum define *control,* and how does he see it operating?
2. What was one of the most interesting differences noted by Mann and Hoffman in their study of some of the effects of automation in a power plant?
3. Tannenbaum comments that increasing and distributing the exercise of control more broadly in an organization creates dilemmas. What are they?
4. Consider the idea, "total amount of control." How is the importance of this notion illustrated in Likert's analysis?
5. What are basic "pure" types of organizational control, and how do they function?
6. Which one of these types of organizational control is the most subtle and most pervasive? Why does it have these characteristics?
7. Summarize the social and informational prerequisites of control outlined in the concluding statement.
8. Describe the more important information prerequisites of bureaucratic control. How do these compare with the information prerequisites of clan control?
9. What are the relative merits of the "search and acquisition" method of people control as compared with those of the "training the unskilled" approach?
10. What are the design implications of dealing with control as an organizational process?

Questions for Discussion

1. Tannenbaum comments that a person's life in contemporary society can be largely characterized as one of organizational membership. What formal and informal organizations are part of your daily life? What proportion of your time do you spend in completely non-organizational settings? What does this say about you and the society in which you move?
2. Tannenbaum asserts that "control is an inevitable correlate of organization." Do you agree? Support your position.
3. *Control* connotes different meanings to every individual. What does it mean to you personally? What does it mean to you professionally? Is there a difference? If so, why? How have you derived these meanings? How do you think they might influence your actions and reactions to "control situations" within organizations?
4. Tannenbaum observes in his article that "organizations cannot often tolerate deviants, and there are pressures, sometimes subtle, on deviants to change." How would you define *deviant?* Would your definition differ from organization to organization? In what organizational situations do you consider or have you considered yourself to be deviant?

Did you experience subtle pressure to change? In what ways have you yourself exerted pressure on others in an attempt to pressure them to change from their "deviant" position?

5. What is your reaction to the analogy of the bureaucratic method of control being a catfish: . . ."clumsy, ugly, but able to live in the widest possible range of environments and, ultimately, the dominant species"? Why should it be the dominant species? Is it really able to live in the widest range of environments? Are there other methods of control that might equal the survival potential of the bureaucracy?
6. "The more closely the skills and values of a person match the demands of the organization, the more completely the individual will commit himself or herself to the organization." Do you agree with this assertion? Is it always true? What, if any, might be possible exceptions? Might the converse be true? Under what circumstances?
7. In referring to many mental hospitals, the comment is often made to the effect that:
   a. forced socialization is common, and
   b. we accept "the abrogation of individual rights as being secondary to a more pressing need."

   What is your reaction to these comments? What needs might be more pressing than individual rights in a mental hospital? Who is the "we" who accepts this abrogation? Under what other circumstances might these conditions be accepted?
8. The argument was made that most hierarchies fail to transmit control from top to bottom with any accuracy. What theoretical or on-the-job exposure have you had to this phenomenon? In which type of organization would you surmise that accuracy might be the highest?
9. This chapter concludes with the question, "How many of us would feel comfortable presenting to top management a control-system design that rests primarily on the idea of the formal organization as myth, ceremony, and ritual?" How comfortable would you feel doing this? What would you anticipate to be the typical objections?
10. What is your overall reaction to the idea that there are three pure types of organizational control—market, bureaucracy, and clan? What are the strengths and weaknesses of such an idea and its application?

9

Decision Processes

INTRODUCTORY REMARKS

Human and nonhuman resources are employed for the purpose of achieving organizational goals. *Decision making is the process of allocating resources in pursuit of those goals.* Further, as we have seen, organizations operate under different circumstances; that is, organizations are faced with different constraints. Different constraints necessitate different goals—or rather, using the terminology of Chapter 3, different goal mixes. Decision making is treated as a design variable, therefore, because different constraints and different goal mixes call for different decision processes.

The purpose of this chapter is to examine the nature of organizational decision processes, focusing on the ways that goals, environment, technology, and people must be taken into account in their design. The two articles that are included present such an examination, and we will have more to say about the matter in the concluding statement.

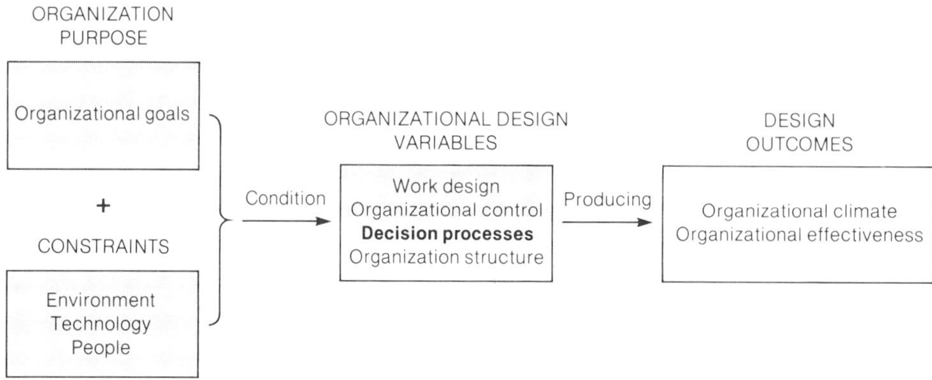

DECISION CONDITIONS

Traditionally decisions have been viewed as occurring under three distinct sets of conditions. These conditions are typically labelled *certainty*, *risk*, and *uncertainty*. Although you have doubtlessly run into these conditions in introductory books or courses (see, for example, Haimann et al., 1978: 503–8), a brief review is in order.

Decision Making under Certainty

The classical condition for decision making is one in which alternatives are perfectly known, as are outcomes. That is, the decision maker has perfect information about the complete set of alternatives available. Further, the decision maker knows that each alternative will lead to one—and only one—outcome, which is also known.

Operating under a condition of certainty would seem to be an attractive position for a decision maker. The fly in the ointment, of course, is that it is an unattainable state. It is safe to say that there never has been, and probably never will be, a decision for which all the alternatives and outcomes are known with perfect certainty. Ours is not that kind of world. Even the most extreme circumstance will have some—however small—degree of uncertainty. The following story, traditionally attributed to the Greek historian Herodotus (c. 484–425 B.C.), illustrates the point:[1]

> A thief had been sentenced to be executed. As he was being led away, he made a bargain with the king: in one year he would teach the king's favorite horse to sing hymns.
>
> The other prisoners watched the thief singing to the horse and laughed. "You will not succeed," they told him. "No one can."
>
> The thief replied: "I have a year, and who knows what might happen in that time? The king might die. The horse might die. I might die. And perhaps the horse will learn to sing."

Decision Making under Risk

By and large, the lot of organizational decision makers is a repetitive one. That is, most managers, regardless of their function or hierarchical level, make roughly the same basic decision over and over. Whether it is a small ordering decision made each morning by a supervisor or a substantial financial decision made every two years by a university president, managerial decisions tend to repeat themselves.

An element of risk enters the picture, of course, as a result of this repetitiveness. If a given alternative is frequently best for a particular decision, and if that decision gets made frequently, then that given alternative will be selected on a frequent basis. If, further, that alternative has two outcomes, one desirable and one undesirable, the decision maker runs a *risk* each time that the undesirable outcome will occur. This is what Simon means in this chapter's first article, when he tells about the importance of intelligence activities for each decision occurrence. Gathering relevant data for each occurrence should not be perfunctory, because at some time the undesirable outcome is bound to occur. The decision maker has to do all that is possible to guard against that eventuality.

1. We are grateful to Jennifer Bailes, who reminded us of this story—described in Niven and Pournelle (1974: 467).

Decision Making under Uncertainty

At the opposite end of the decision-condition spectrum is that known as uncertainty. Under uncertainty, the decision maker knows nothing. The total set of alternatives is only incompletely understood, the various outcomes that may or may not occur are unclear, and even their probabilities are not known.

The reason decision making under uncertainty is interesting, of course, is that this is the condition that characterizes virtually all organizational decisions. For all the amount of familiar, unsurprising, routine, and repetitive decisions that they encounter, organizational decision makers can never be quite certain that they have examined every possible alternative, foreseen every potential outcome, or even correctly assessed the attendant probabilities. Of course, this is what makes the real world of managerial decision making adventuresome.

Figures 9–1, 9–2, and 9–3 (adapted from Haimann et al., 1978: 504, 505, 507) illustrate the three conditions. Referring to these figures, and following Simon (1976), we can describe each condition as follows:

- *Certainty*: All alternatives are known. Each alternative has one outcome, which is known.
- *Risk*: All alternatives are known. At least one alternative has at least two possible outcomes. All outcomes are known. The probability that for a given alternative a specific outcome will occur is known.
- *Uncertainty*: The complete set of alternatives is unknown. The set of outcomes for any alternative is unknown. The probability that for a given alternative a specific outcome will occur is unknown.

The Readings

We open the chapter with Herbert A. Simon's article, "Decision Making and Organizational Design." In this piece the author discusses his well-known distinction between programmed and nonprogrammed decisions and their respective implications for organizational design. There are four elements to Simon's discussion. First, decision making is a process, rather than a single event—a process consisting of three phases: data gathering ("intelligence" activities), identifying and assessing alternatives ("design" activities), and selecting an alternative ("choice" acitivity). Second, decisions tend to vary from those that call for highly routinized techniques in making them ("programmed" decisions), to those for which the organization has no specific procedures ("nonprogrammed" decisions).

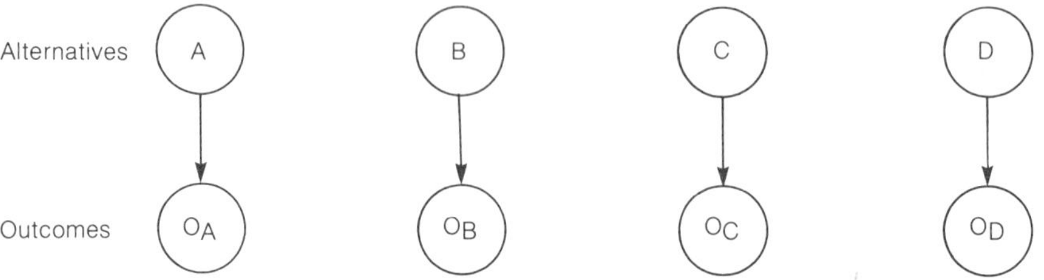

Figure 9-1. Condition of certainty (alternatives and outcomes known)

Source: Theo Haiman, William C. Scott, and Patrick E. Connor, *Managing the Modern Organization,* 3d. ed. (Boston: Houghton Mifflin Co., 1978).

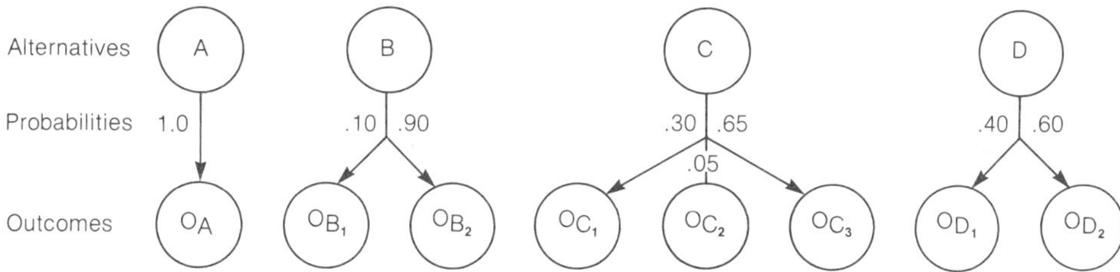

Figure 9-2. Condition of risk (alternatives known, outcome probabilities known)

Source: Theo Haiman, William C. Scott, and Patrick E. Connor, *Managing the Modern Organization,* 3d. ed. (Boston: Houghton Mifflin Co., 1978).

Third, Simon identifies traditional and modern techniques for dealing with both types of decisions. Fourth, the author examines organizational characteristics that are beginning to emerge in response to the changing character of decision making. Simon concludes by offering what he calls a sketch of the new organization, identifying the critical dimensions of the emerging modern organization.

James D. Thompson and Arthur Tuden continue the discussion in the second article, "Strategies, Structures, and Processes of Organizational Decisions." For them, the question is, "what kinds of methods or strategies are used in making what kinds of decisions?" The authors describe four strategies commonly used: these they label *computation, judgment, compromise,* and *inspiration.* Thompson and Tuden then describe an organization design appropriate to each strategy. The article concludes with the emphasis that decision making is, as Simon said earlier, a process and not a single event. The authors then discuss some managerial implications of this point.

Conclusion

In summary, this chapter deals with the single most important of all the organizational processes: the allocation of resources. We are concerned here with the following questions:

1. What do we mean by the term *decision process*?
2. What alternatives do organizations have in conducting their decision processes?
3. Which decision-process designs are most compatible with what design-constraint conditions?

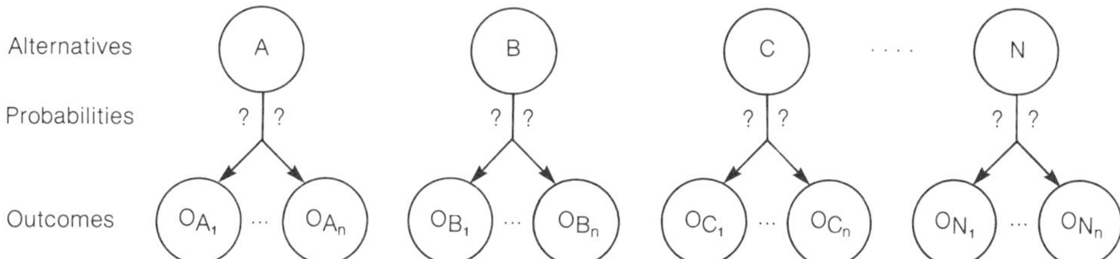

Figure 9-3. Condition of uncertainty (alternatives not known, outcomes not known, probabilities not known)

Source: Theo Haiman, William C. Scott, and Patrick E. Connor, *Managing the Modern Organization,* 3d. ed. (Boston: Houghton Mifflin Co., 1978).

DECISION MAKING AND ORGANIZATIONAL DESIGN

HERBERT A. SIMON

THE EXECUTIVE AS DECISION MAKER

What part does decision making play in managing? I shall find it convenient to take mild liberties with the English language by using *decision making* as though it were synonymous with *managing*.

What is our mental image of a decision maker? Is he a brooding man on horseback who suddenly rouses himself from thought and issues an order to a subordinate? Is he a happy-go-lucky fellow, a coin poised on his thumbnail, ready to risk his action on the toss? Is he an alert, gray-haired businessman, sitting at the board of directors' table with his associates, caught at the moment of saying 'aye' or 'nay'? Is he a bespectacled gentleman, bent over a docket of papers, his pen hovering over the line marked (X)?

All of these images have a significant point in common. In them, the decision maker is a man at the moment of choice, ready to plant his foot on one or another of the routes that lead from the crossroads. All the images falsify decision by focusing on its final moment. All of them ignore the whole lengthy, complex process of alerting, exploring, and analysing that precede that final moment.

Intelligence, Design and Choice in Decision Making

In treating decision making as synonymous with managing, I shall be referring not merely to the final act of choice among alternatives, but rather to the whole process of decision. Decision making comprises three principal phases: finding occasions for making a decision; finding possible courses of action; and choosing among courses of action. These three activities account for quite different fractions of the time budgets of executives. The fractions vary greatly from one organization level to another and from one executive to another, but we can make some generalizations about them even from casual observation. Executives spend a large fraction of their time surveying the economic, technical, political, and social environment to identify new conditions that call for new actions. They probably spend an even larger fraction of their time, individually or with their associates, seeking to invent, design, and develop possible courses of action for handling situations where a decision is needed. They spend a small fraction of their time in choosing among alternative actions already developed to meet an identified problem and already analysed for their consequences. The three fractions, added together, account for most of what executives do.[1]

The first phase of the decision-making process—searching the environment for conditions calling for decision—I shall call *intelligence* activity (borrowing the military meaning of intelligence). The second phase—inventing, developing, and analysing possible courses of action—I shall call *design* activity. The third phase—selecting a particular course of action from those available—I shall call *choice* activity.

Let me illustrate these three phases of decision. In the past five years, many companies have reorganized their accounting and other data-processing activities in order to make use of large electronic computers. How has this come about? Computers first became available commercially in the early 1950s. Although, in some vague and general sense, company managements were aware that computers existed, few managements had investigated their possible applications with any thoroughness before about 1955. For most companies, the use of computers required no decision before that time because it hadn't been placed on the agenda. (Cyert, Simon, and Trow, 1956.)

1. The way in which these activities take shape within an organization is described in some detail in March and Simon (1958), chapters 6 and 7.

Abridged from Herbert A. Simon, *The New Science of Management Decision,* © 1960, pp. 1–8, 35–50. Reprinted by permission of Prentice-Hall, Inc., Englewood Cliffs, New Jersey.

The intelligence activity preceding the introduction of computers tended to come about in one of two ways. Some companies—for example, in the aircraft and atomic energy industries—were burdened with enormously complex computations for engineering design. Because efficiency in computation was a constant problem, and because the design departments were staffed with engineers who could understand, at least in general, the technology of computers, awareness of computers and their potentialities came early to these companies. After computers were already in extensive use for design calculations, businesses with a large number-processing load—insurance companies, accounting departments in large firms, banks—discovered these new devices and began to consider seriously their introduction.

Once it was recognized that computers might have a place in modern business, a major design task had to be carried out in each company before they could be introduced. It is now a commonplace that payrolls can be prepared by computers. Programs in both the general and computer senses for doing this are relatively easy to design in any given situation.[2] To develop the first computer programs for preparing payroll, however, was a major research and development project. Few companies having carried their investigations of computers to the point where they had definite plans for their use, failed to install them. Commitment to the new course of action took place gradually as the intelligence and design phases of the decision were going on. The final choice was, in many instances, almost *pro forma*.

Generally speaking, intelligence activity precedes design, and design activity precedes choice. The cycle of phases is, however, far more complex than this sequence suggests. Each phase in making a particular decision is itself a complex decision-making process. The design phase, for example, may call for new intelligence activities; problems at any given level generate subproblems that, in turn, have their intelligence, design, and choice phases, and so on. There are wheels within wheels within wheels. Nevertheless, the three large phases are often clearly discernible as the organizational decision process unfolds. They are closely related to the stages in problem solving first described by John Dewey (1910):

- What is the problem?
- What are the alternatives?
- Which alternative is best?

It may be objected that I have ignored the task of carrying out decisions. I shall merely observe by the way that seeing that decisions are executed is again decision-making activity. A broad policy decision creates a new condition for the organization's executives that calls for the design and choice of a course of action for executing the policy. Executing policy, then, is indistinguishable from making more detailed policy. For this reason, I shall feel justified in taking my pattern for decision making as a paradigm for most executive activity.

Developing Decision-Making Skills

It is an obvious step from the premise that managing is decision making to the conclusion that the important skills for an executive are decision-making skills. It is generally believed that good decision makers, like good athletes, are born, not made. The belief is about as true in the one case as it is in the other.

That human beings come into the world endowed unequally with biological potential for athletic prowess is undeniable. They also come endowed unequally with intelligence, cheerfulness, and many other characteristics and potentialities. To a limited extent, we can measure some aspects of that endowment—height, weight, perhaps intelligence. Whenever we make such measurements and compare them with adult performance, we obtain significant, but low, correlations. A man who is not a natural athlete is unlikely to run the four-minute mile; but many men who are natural athletes have never come close to that goal. A man who is not 'naturally' intelligent is unlikely to star in science; but many intelligent scientists are not stars.

A good athlete is born when a man with some natural endowment, by dint of practice, learning, and experience develops that natural endowment into a mature skill. A good executive is born when a man with

2. For a good discussion on the use of the computer for such purposes, see Gregory and Van Horn (1960).

some natural endowment (intelligence and some capacity for interacting with his fellow men) by dint of practice, learning, and experience develops his endowment into a mature skill. The skills involved in intelligence, design, and choosing activities are as learnable and trainable as the skills involved in driving, recovering, and putting a golf ball. I hope to indicate some of the things a modern executive needs to learn about decision making.

Executive Responsibility for Organizational Decision Making

The executive's job involves not only making decisions himself, but also seeing that the organization, or part of an organization, that he directs makes decisions effectively. The vast bulk of the decision-making activity for which he is responsible is not his personal activity, but the activity of his subordinates.

Nowadays, with the advent of computers, we can think of information as something almost tangible; strings of symbols which, like strips of steel or plastic ribbons, can be processed—changed from one form to another. We can think of white-collar organizations as factories for processing information. The executive is the factory manager, with all the usual responsibilities for maintaining the factory operation, getting it back into operation when it breaks down, and proposing and carrying though improvements in its design.

There is no reason to expect that a man who has acquired a fairly high level of personal skill in decision-making activity will have a correspondingly high skill in designing efficient decision-making systems. To imagine that there is such a connection is like supposing that a man who is a good weight lifter can therefore design cranes. The skill of designing and maintaining the modern decision-making systems we call organizations are less intuitive skills. Hence, they are even more susceptible to training than the skills of personal decision making.

Programmed and Nonprogrammed Decisions

In discussing how executives now make decisions, and how they will make them in the future, let us distinguish two polar types of decisions. I shall call them *programmed decisions* and *nonprogrammed decisions*, respectively. Having christened them, I hasten to add that they are not really distinct types, but a whole continuum, with highly programmed decisions at one end of that continuum and highly unprogrammed decisions at the other end. We can find decisions of all shades of gray along the continuum, and I use the terms programmed and nonprogrammed simply as labels for the black and white of the range.[3]

Decisions are programmed to the extent that they are repetitive and routine, to the extent that a definite procedure has been worked out for handling them so that they don't have to be treated *de novo* each time they occur. The obvious reason why programmed decisions tend to be repetitive, and vice versa, is that if a particular problem recurs often enough, a routine procedure will usually be worked out for solving it. Numerous examples of programmed decisions in organizations will occur to you: pricing ordinary customers' orders; determining salary payments to employees who have been ill; reordering office supplies.

Decisions are nonprogrammed to the extent that they are novel, unstructured, and consequential. There is no cut-and-dried method for handling the problem because it hasn't arisen before, or because it is so important that it deserves a custom-tailored treatment. General Eisenhower's D-Day decision is a good example of a nonprogrammed decision. Remember, we are considering not merely the final act of ordering the attack, but the whole complex of intelligence and design activities that preceded it. Many of the components of the decisions were programmed—by standard techniques for military planning—but before these components could be designed they had to be provided with a broader framework of military and political policy.

I have borrowed the term *program* from the computer trade, and intend it in the sense in which it is used there. A *program* is a detailed prescription or strategy that governs the sequence of responses of a system to a complex task environment. Most of the programs that govern organizational response are not as detailed or as precise as computer programs. However, they all have

3 See March and Simon (1958), pp. 139–42 and 177–80 for further discussion of these types of decisions. The labels used there are slightly different.

the same intent: to permit an adaptive response of the system to the situation.

In what sense, then, can we say that the response of a system to a situation is nonprogrammed? Surely something determines the response. That something, that collection of rules of procedure, is by definition a program. By nonprogrammed I mean a response where the system has no specific procedures to deal with situations like the one at hand, but must fall back on whatever *general* capacity it has for intelligent, adaptive, problem-oriented action. In addition to his specific skills and specific knowledge, man has some general problem-solving capacities. Given almost any kind of situation, no matter how novel or perplexing, he can begin to reason about it in terms of ends and means.

This general problem-solving equipment is not always effective. Men often fail to solve problems, or they reach unsatisfactory solutions. But man is seldom completely helpless in a new situation. He possesses general problem-solving equipment which, however inefficient, fills some of the gaps in his special problem-solving skills. And organizations, as collections of men, have some of this same general adaptive capacity.

The cost of using general-purpose programs to solve problems is usually high. It is advantageous to reserve these programs for situations that are truly novel, where no alternative programs are available. If any particular class of situations recurs often enough, a special-purpose program can be developed which gives better solutions and gives them more cheaply than the general problem-solving apparatus.

My reason for distinguishing between programmed and nonprogrammed decisions is that different techniques are used for handling the programmed and the nonprogrammed aspects of our decision making. The distinction, then, will be a convenient one for classifying these techniques. I shall use it for that purpose, hoping that the reader will remind himself from time to time that the world is mostly gray with only a few spots of pure black or white.

[Table 9–1] will provide a map of the territory I propose to cover. In the northern half of the map are some techniques related to programmed decision making, in the southern half, some techniques related to nonprogrammed decision making. In the western half of the map I placed the classical techniques used in decision making—the kit of tools that has been used by executives and organizations from the time of the earliest recorded history up to the present generation. In the eastern half of the map I placed the new techniques of decision making—tools that have been forged largely since the Second World War, and that are only now coming into extensive use in management in this country. I shall proceed across the map from west to east, and from north to south, taking up, in order, the north-west and the south-west quadrants, the north-east quadrant, and the south-east quadrant.

I can warn you now to what conclusion this journey is going to lead. We are in the midst of a major revolution in the art or science—whichever you prefer to call it—of management and organization.

Some Fundamentals of Organizational Design

An organization can be pictured as a three-layered cake. In the bottom layer, we have the basic work

TABLE 9–1 TRADITIONAL AND MODERN TECHNIQUES OF DECISION MAKING

Types of Decisions	Decision-Making Techniques	
	Traditional	Modern
Programmed: Routine, repetitive decisions Organization develops specific processes for handling them	1. Habit 2. Clerical routine: standard operating procedures 3. Organization structure: common expectations; a system of subgoals; well-defined informational channels	1. Operations research: mathematical analysis; models; computer simulation 2. Electronic data processing
Nonprogrammed: One-shot, ill-structured, novel policy decisions Handled by general problem-solving processes	1. Judgment, intuition, and creativity 2. Rules of thumb 3. Selection and training of executives	Heuristic problem-solving techniques applied to: a. training human decision makers b. constructing heuristic computer programs

processes—in the case of a manufacturing organization, the processes that procure raw materials, manufacture the physical product, warehouse it and ship it. In the middle layer, we have the programmed decision-making processes, the processes that govern the day-to-day operation of the manufacturing and distribution system. In the top layer, we have the nonprogrammed decision-making processes, the processes that are required to design and redesign the entire system, to provide it with its basic goals and objectives, and to monitor its performance.

Automation of data processing and decision making will not change this fundamental three-part structure. It may, by bringing about a more explicit description of the entire system, make the relations among the parts clear and more explicit.

The organizations of the future, then, will be hierarchies, no matter what the exact division of labor between men and computers. This is not to say that there will be no important differences between present and future organizations. Two points, in particular, will have to be re-examined at each stage of automation:

1. What are the optimal sizes of the building blocks in the hierarchy? This is the question of centralization and decentralization.
2. What will be the relations among the building blocks? In particular, how far will traditional authority and accountability relations persist, and how far will they be modified? What will be the effect of automation upon subgoal formation and subgoal identification?

Size of the Building Blocks: Centralization and Decentralization. One of the major contemporary issues in organization design is the question of how centralized or decentralized the decision-making process will be—how much of the decision making should be done by the executives of the larger units, and how much should be delegated to lower levels. But centralizing and decentralizing are not genuine alternatives for organizing. The question is not whether we shall decentralize, but how far we shall decentralize. What we seek, again, is a golden mean: we want to find the proper level in the organization hierarchy—neither too high nor too low—for each important class of decisions.

Over the past twenty or more years there has been a movement toward decentralization in large American business organizations. This movement has probably been a sound development, but it does *not* signify that more decentralization is at all times and under all circumstances a good thing. It signifies that at a particular time in history, many American firms, which had experienced almost continuous long-term growth and diversification, discovered that they could operate more effectively if they brought together all the activities relating to individual products or groups of similar products and decentralized a great deal of decision making to the departments handling these products or product groups. At the very time this process was taking place there were many cross-currents of centralization in the same companies—centralization, for example, of industrial relations activities. There is no contradiction here. Different decisions need to be made in different organizational locations, and the best location for a class of decisions may change as circumstances change.

There are usually two pressures toward greater decentralization in a business organization. First, it may help bring the profit motive to bear on a larger group of executives by allowing profit goals to be established for individual subdivisions of the company. Second, it may simplify the decision-making process by separating out groups of related activities—production, engineering, marketing, and finance for particular products—and allowing decisions to be taken on these matters within the relevant organizational subdivisions. Advantages can be realized in either of these ways only if the units to which decision is delegated are natural subdivisions—if, in fact, the actions taken in one of them do not affect in too much detail or too strongly what happens in the others. Hierarchy always implies intrinsically some measure of decentralization. It always involves a balancing of the cost savings through direct local action against the losses through ignoring indirect consequences for the whole organization.

Organizational form, I said earlier, must be a joint function of the characteristics of humans and their tools and the nature of the task environment. When one or the other of these changes significantly, we may expect concurrent modifications to be required in organizational structure—for example, in the amount of centralization or decentralization that is desirable.

When the cable and the wireless were added to the world's techniques of communication, the organization of every nation's foreign office changed. The ambassador and minister who had exercised broad, discretionary decision-making functions in the previous decentralized system, were now brought under much closer central control. The balance between the costs in time and money of communication with the center had been radically altered.

The automation of important parts of business data-processing and decision-making activity, and the trend toward a much higher degree of structure and programming of even the nonautomated part will radically alter the balance of advantage between centralization and decentralization. The main issue is not the economics of scale—not the question of whether a given data-processing job can better be done by one large computer at a central location or a number of smaller ones, geographically or departmentally decentralized. Rather, the main issue is how we shall take advantage of the greater analytic capacity, the larger ability to take into account the interrelations of things, that the new developments in decision making give us. A second issue is how we shall deal with the technological fact that the processing of information within a coordinated computing system is orders of magnitude faster than the input-output rates at which we can communicate from one such system to another, particularly where human links are involved.

Let us consider the first issue: the capacity of the decision-making system to handle intricate interrelations in a complex system. In many factories today, the extent to which the schedules of one department are coordinated in detail with the schedules of a second department, consuming, say, part of the output of the first, is limited by the computational complexity of the scheduling problem. Often the best we can do is to set up a reasonable scheduling scheme for each department and put a sizeable buffer inventory of semi-finished product between them to prevent fluctuations in the operation of the first from interfering with the operation of the second. We accept the cost of holding the inventory to avoid the cost of taking account of detailed scheduling interactions.

We pay large inventory costs, also, to permit factory and sales managements to make decisions in semi-independence of each other. The factory often stocks finished products so that it can deliver on demand to sales warehouses; the warehouses stock the same product so that the factory will have time to manufacture a new batch after an order is placed. Often, too, manufacturing and sales departments make their decisions on the basis of independent forecasts of orders.

With the development of operations research techniques for determining optimal production rates and inventory levels, and with the development of the technical means to maintain and adjust the data that are required, large savings are attainable through inventory reductions and the smoothing of production operations, but at the cost of centralizing to a greater extent than in the past the factory scheduling and warehouse ordering decisions. Since the source of the savings is in the coordination of the decisions, centralization is unavoidable if the savings are to be secured.

The mismatch— unlikely to be removed in the near future—between the kinds of records that humans produce readily and read readily and the kinds that automatic devices produce and read readily is a second technological factor pushing in the direction of centralization. Since processing steps in an automated data-processing system are executed in a thousandth or even millionth of a second, the whole system must be organized on a flow basis with infrequent intervention from outside. Intervention will take more and more the form of designing the system itself—programming—and less and less the form of participating in its minute-by-minute operation. Moreover, the parts of the system must mesh. Hence, the design of decision-making and data-processing systems will tend to be a relatively centralized function. It will be a little like ship design. There is no use in one group of experts producing the design for the hull, another the design for the power plant, a third the plans for the passenger quarters, and so on, unless great pains are taken at each step to see that all these parts will fit into a seaworthy ship.

It may be objected that the question of motivation has been overlooked in this whole discussion. If decision making is centralized how can the middle-level executive be induced to work hard and effectively? First, we should observe that the principle of decentralized profit-and-loss accounting has never been carried much below the level of product-group departments and cannot, in fact, be applied successfully to fragmented segments of highly interdependent activities. Second, we may question whether the conditions under which middle-management has in the past exercised its decision-making prerogatives were actually good conditions from a motivational standpoint.

Most existing decentralized organization structures have at least three weaknesses in motivating middle-management executives effectively. First, they encourage the formation of and loyalty to subgoals that are only partly parallel with the goals of the organization. Second, they require so much nonprogrammed problem solving in a setting of confusion that they do not provide the satisfactions which, we argued earlier, are valued by the true professional. Third, they realize none of the advantages, which by hindsight we find we have often gained in factory automation, of substituting machine-paced (or better, system-paced) for man-paced operation of the system.[4]

The question of motivation we have just raised has a broader relevance than the issue of decentralization and I will discuss it later, in the section on authority and responsibility relations. Meanwhile, we can summarize the present discussion by saying that the new developments in decision making will tend to induce more centralization in decision-making activities at middle-management levels.

Authority and Responsibility. Let me draw a sketch of the factory manager's job today. How far it is a caricature, and how far a reasonably accurate portrait, I shall let you decide. What is the factory manager's authority? He can hire and fire. He can determine what shall be produced in his factory and how much. He can make minor improvements in equipment and recommend major ones. In doing all of these things, he is subject to all kinds of constraints and evaluations imposed by the rest of the organization. Moreover, the connection between what he decides and what actually happens in the factory is often highly tenuous. He proposes, and a complex administrative system disposes.

For what is the factory manager held accountable? He must keep his costs within the standards of the budget. He must not run out of items that are ordered. If he does, he must produce them in great haste. He must keep his inventory down. His men must not have accidents. And so on.

Subject to this whole range of conflicting pressures, controlling a complex system whose responses to instruction is often erratic and unpredictable, the environment of the typical middle-management executive—of which the factory manager is just one example—is not the kind of environment a psychologist would design to produce high motivation. The manager responds in understandable ways. He transmits to his subordinates the pressures imposed by his superiors—he becomes a work pusher, seeking to motivate by creating for his subordinates the same environment of pressure and constraint that he experiences. He and his subordinates become expediters, dealing with the pressure that is felt at the moment by getting out a particular order, fixing a particular disabled machine, following up a particular tardy supplier.

I do not want to elaborate the picture further. The important point is that the task of middle managers today is very much taken up with pace setting, with work pushing, and with expediting. As the automation and rationalization of the decision-making process progress, these aspects of the managerial job are likely to recede in importance.

If a couple of terms are desired to characterize the direction of change we may expect in the manager's job, I would propose rationalization and impersonalization. In terms of subjective feel the manager will find

4. The general decline in the use of piece-rates is associated with the gradual spread of machine-paced operations through the factory with the advance of automation. In evaluating the human consequences of this development, we should not accept uncritically the common stereotypes that were incorporated so effectively in Charlie Chaplin's *Modern Times*. Frederick Taylor's sophisticated understanding of the relations between incentives and pace, expressed, for example, in his story of the pig-iron handler, is worth pondering.

himself dealing more than in the past with a well-structured system whose problems have to be diagnosed and corrected objectively and analytically, and less with unpredictable and sometimes recalcitrant people who have to be persuaded, prodded, rewarded, and cajoled. For some managers, important satisfactions derived in the past from interpersonal relations with others will be lost. For other managers, important satisfactions from a feeling of the adequacy of professional skills will be gained.

My guess, and it is only a guess, is that the gains in satisfaction from the change will overbalance the losses. I have two reasons for making this guess: first, because this seems to be the general experience in factory automation as it affects supervisors and managers; second, because the kinds of interpersonal relations called for in the new environment seem to me generally less frustrating and more wholesome than many of those we encounter in present-day supervisory relations. Man does not generally work well with his fellow man in relations saturated with authority and dependence, with control and subordination, even though these have been the predominant human relations in the past. He works much better when he is teamed with his fellow man in coping with an objective, understandable, external environment. That will be more and more his situation as the new techniques of decision making come into wide use.

A Final Sketch of the New Organization

Perhaps in the preceding paragraphs I have yielded to the temptation to paint a Utopian picture of the organization that the new decision-making techniques will create. If so, I have done so from an urge to calm the anxieties that are so often and so unnecessarily aroused by the stereotype of the robot. The anxieties are unnecessary because the existence in the world today of machines that think, and of theories that explain the processes of human thinking, subtracts not an inch, not a hair, from the stature of man. Man is always vulnerable when he rests his case for his worth and dignity on how he differs from the rest of the world, or on the special place he has in God's scheme or nature's. Man must rest his case on what he is. This is in no way changed when electronic systems can duplicate some of his functions or when some of the mystery of his processes of thought is taken away.

The changes I am predicting for the decision-making processes in organizations do not mean that workers and executives will find the organizations they will work in strange and unfamiliar. In concluding, I should like to emphasize the aspects in which the new organizations will much resemble those we know now.

1. Organizations will still be constructed in three layers; an underlying system of physical production and distribution processes, a layer of programmed (and probably largely automated) decision processes for governing the routine day-to-day operation of the physical system, and a layer of nonprogrammed decision processes (carried out in a man-machine system) for monitoring the first-level processes, redesigning them, and changing parameter values.

2. Organizations will still be hierarchical in form. The organization will be divided into major subparts, each of these into parts, and so on, in familiar forms of departmentalization. The exact bases for drawing departmental lines may change somewhat. Product divisions may become even more important than they are today, while the sharp lines of demarcation among purchasing, manufacturing, engineering, and sales are likely to fade.

But there is a more fundamental way in which the organizations of the future will appear to those in them very much like the organizations of today. Man is a problem-solving, skill-using, social animal. Once he has satisfied his hunger, two main kinds of experiences are significant to him. One of his deepest needs is to apply his skills, whatever they be, to challenging tasks—to feel the exhilaration of the well-struck ball or the well-solved problem. The other need is to find meaningful and warm relations with a few other human beings—to love and be loved, to share experience, to respect and be respected, to work in common tasks.

Particular characteristics of the physical environment and the task environment are significant to man only as they affect these needs. The scientist satisfies them in one environment, the artist in another; but they are the same needs. A good business novel or business biography is not about business. It is about love, hate, pride, craftsmanship, jealousy, comradeship, ambition, pleasure. These have been, and will continue to be man's central concerns.

The automation and rationalization of decision making will, to be sure, alter the climate of organizations in ways important to these human concerns. I have indicated what some of the changes may be. On balance, they seem to me changes that will make it easier rather than harder for the executive's daily work to be a significant and satisfying part of his life.

STRATEGIES, STRUCTURES, AND PROCESSES OF ORGANIZATIONAL DECISIONS

JAMES D. THOMPSON
ARTHUR TUDEN

Despite the apparent importance of decision making for theories of administration and the considerable attention recently devoted to the topic, present models and knowledge of decision making have generated few hypotheses about administration, and they have not been adequately linked with organizational models.

A major deficiency of most decision models has been that they are economically logical models seeking to describe maximization processes. These *econo-logical* models have utility as criteria against which to reflect behavior, but they have contributed little toward the explanation or prediction of behavior.

Simon (1955) has achieved a major breakthrough with his "satisficing" model. This is much more than the mere substitution of one word of one concept for another, for Simon's model is a *psycho-logical* model designed to describe and predict behavior. Its full significance seems not yet to be widely recognized.

This psychological model of decision making is essentially one dealing with individual human beings. It applies equally to purposive choices of a personal or an organizational nature. Its generalizability is, however, both a source of power and of limitation, for it does not deal explicitly with the particular phenomena which surround the making of decisions in organizational contexts.

As a companion to the psychological model, therefore, we wish to develop *sociological* models. We believe they will point to important decision-making behavior which has been observed in organizations but which is neither described nor predicted by econological or psychological models.

We will attempt to show 1. that there are several types of decisions to be made in and on behalf of collective enterprises, 2. that each type of decision calls for a different strategy or approach, 3. that there are several varieties of organizational structures which facilitate these several strategies, and 4. that the resulting behavior defines variations in decision processes. It has been our purpose to construct models which are neither culture-bound nor discipline-bound, containing no evaluative or normative elements.

WORKING DEFINITIONS

"Choice" from among alternatives seems to be the end-point of decision making, but the term *decision* will not be confined simply to ultimate choice. Rather, *decision* will refer to those activities which contribute to choice, including recognizing or delimiting and evaluating alternatives as well as the final selection. Thus an individual may have responsibility for making a final choice on behalf of an organization, but if others help him delimit or evaluate alternatives we will not describe that individual as *the* decider.[1]

The term *decision* in this paper should also be understood to refer to organizational decisions. Personal decisions, i.e., choices presumed by an individual to have consequences only for himself, are excluded (Barnard, 1936). Likewise, unconscious choices or habits are not within the scope of this paper.

The term *decision unit* will be used to refer to that individual or group within an organization which has power, responsibility, or authority to choose, on a particular issue, for the organization. To illustrate, in American jurisprudence, "the court" may be the appropriate organization, but the power to decide

1. For the notion of "composite decisions" see Herbert A. Simon, (1957a). See also R. Tannenbaum and F. Massarik (1950).

Reprinted from *Comparative Studies in Administration* by James D. Thompson. Edited by the Staff of the Administrative Science Center, by permission of the University of Pittsburgh Press.

certain issues is assigned to a single presiding judge as the decision unit; other issues are assigned to a jury as the decision unit; still others are assigned to a panel of justices as the decision unit.

TYPES OF DECISION ISSUES

The notion of differing types of issues calling for decisions is not new. More than a decade ago Simon (1945) distinguished ethical from factual decisions but no one seems to have extended his analysis. More recently there has been considerable discussion of decision making under the differential conditions of certainty, risk, and uncertainty.[2] Dorwin Cartwright has suggested distinguishing among judgment, preference-ranking, and "actual decision making" (which he defines as commitment to action).[3] There have, however, been few attempts to build typologies of issues or decisions.

A typology of issues will enable the sorting out of a. those aspects of decision situations which *confront* decision units from b. those actions which decision units may take in such situations.

The main elements of decision—found both in the econological and psychological models available—seem to be three: 1. alternative courses of action, 2. differential consequences of the several alternatives (means), and 3. evaluation of the potential outcomes on some scale of desirability (ends).[4]

We will work with two of those three variables, dropping "alternative courses of action," since by definition a unit called upon to decide is aware of at least one pair of alternatives. Before working with the remaining two variables, however, we wish to redefine them slightly in order to achieve greater generalizability.

The notion of "consequences of alternative courses of action" assumes only a concern with present and future, not with past actions. Yet it seems reasonable, for example, to conceive of the trial jury as a decision unit which works backward from one present fact, e.g., a corpus delicti, to choose one of several possible past actions which may account for the present fact. This sequence may also characterize certain decisions in scientific research and in audits or inspections. The notion of *causation*, as applied to several alternatives, seems to us to subsume both questions of present and future states and questions of past actions which may explain present states.

We would also like to avoid some of the implications of such terms as desirability scale, which is inanimate, and to substitute for them some term with more explicit behavioral overtones. For this purpose we will speak of *preferences about outcomes*. In conceiving of our major variables as *causation* and *preferences*, we have gained a certain flexibility without losing the value of previous work on economic models. The means-ends approach falls within our scheme, but we have the added advantage of being able to include other approaches too.

Since we are dealing with organizations—social systems—it cannot be taken for granted that causation will be "known" as soon as a decision issue appears, nor can it be assumed that the organization is certain of its preferences regarding the several alternatives apparent. Often the organization's decision unit cannot simply choose, but must act to determine what its knowledge or beliefs are regarding cause-and-effect relationships, and what its preferences are about the postulated effects.

Now, if the two variables *causation* and *preferences* are reflected against the additional question of whether there is *agreement or consensus within the decision unit* about these two matters, it is possible to construct a fourfold typology of decision issues.

		Preferences about Possible Outcomes	
		Agreement	Disagreement
Beliefs about Causation	Agreement	Computation	Compromise
	Disagreement	Judgment	Inspiration

2. For example, see the collection of papers edited by M. J. Bowman, *Expectations, Uncertainty and Business Behavior* (New York: Social Science Research Council, 1958); and R. D. Luce and H. Raiffa, *Games and Decisions* (New York: John Wiley & Sons, 1957).

3. In Bowman, *op. cit.*

4. We believe this is not inconsistent with the statements of such diverse writers as Simon (1953), Richard C. Snyder (1958), and Jacob Marschak (1954).

The labels in the four cells—computation, judgment, compromise, and inspiration—are descriptive of four *strategies* which we believe are approriate for the four types of decision issues. In the following section we will elaborate on those strategies, and connect them with certain types of social structures. For the time being we will deal only with "pure" cases.

PURE STRATEGIES AND STRUCTURES

Decision by Computation

Where there is agreement regarding both causation and preference, i.e., where a preference hierarchy is understood and where knowledge is available or believed to be available, decision making is a technical or mechanical matter. In its extreme form, this situation requires no genuine choice, since the problem-solution appears as common sense.

But in many instances, the appropriate techniques for equating cause-effect knowledge with known preferences are quite complicated. The data may be so voluminous for example, that only an electronic calculator can make sense of them. Likewise, the particular sequences of action involved in the techniques may be hard to master and difficult to carry out, so that only the highly trained specialist can arrive at an appropriate choice. In either event, the strategy for decision is straightforward analysis, and we term this decision by computation.

A Structure for Computation

Assuming for the moment complete freedom to build an organization which will face *only* computation issues, and that our guiding norms are economy of effort and efficiency of performance, what kind of organization shall we build?

This will be an organization of specialists, one for each kind of computation problem we can anticipate, and we want to introduce four constraints or rules to: 1. prohibit our specialists from making decisions in issues lying outside their spheres of expert competence, 2. blind each specialist to the organization's preference scale, 3. route all pertinent information to each specialist, and 4. route every issue to the appropriate specialist.

The organization which we have just built contains the heart of what Max Weber described as the "pure type" of bureaucracy. This bureaucratic model is clearly expressed in the "formal" or "official" structure of the great majority of business firms, governmental agencies, and military units. For each of these, presumably, preferences can be stated with some clarity. Members are appointed to positions only so long as they embrace those preferences. Moreover, bureaucracy is formulated on the assumption that rules or procedures can be established for classes of cases or problems, and that the events which will call for organizational decisions are repetitive or serial events for which expert competence can be developed. Candidates for these positions are expected to hold licenses or degrees indicating successful completion of training for the specialized positions, or to pass tests.

It is in these organizations that the concept and practice of "delegation" seems most widespread, and that decision units officially are comprised of single individuals. Expert specialization means that the organization can enjoy the economy of assigning problems to individuals or their electronic counterparts.

Decision by Majority Judgment

Where causation is uncertain or disputed, although preferences are clearly known and shared, decision making takes on new difficulties. Lacking in acceptable "proof" of the merits of alternatives, the organization must rely on judgment.[5] Triangulation illustrates this simply and clearly. Each member of the three-man team is presumed competent by virtue of his training and his equipment to make a judgment, but because none has indisputable and complete evidence, none is permitted to make the decision alone, and no member may outvote or override the judgment made by other members. But triangulation is a special case of the more general problem—special because each judge focuses on the same empirical phenomenon from his own special vantage point. More frequent, perhaps, is the case where there is not only differential perception but

5. See Leon Festinger's (1950) important distinction between "social reality" and "external reality" as bases for the validation of opinions of group members.

also differential interpretation, and this is most clearly illustrated by the voting situation in which the collective judgment determines the decision. We will refer to this strategy of organizational decision as one of majority judgment.

A Structure for Majority Judgment

What kind of organization shall we build as an ideal one to handle only judgmental problems? This is to be an organization of wise and knowing men, operating according to constraints or rules which: 1. require fidelity to the group's preference hierarchy, 2. require all members to participate in each decision, 3. route pertinent information about causation to each member, 4. give each member equal influence over the final choice, and 5. designate as ultimate choice that alternative favored by the largest group of judges—the majority.

What we have just described may be labeled, for lack of a better term, a *collegium*. This concept has been used in ecclesiastical literature to refer to a self-governing voluntary group, with authority vested in the members. Whatever this type of organization is labeled, the social science literature does not seem to contain formal models of it, as it does for bureaucracy.

Nevertheless, this type of organization is described in case studies of "voluntary associations" and in the constitutions and bylaws of many organizations, including many American universities and trade unions. All of these not only take steps to "get out the vote," but incorporate into their bylaws provisions requiring a quorum for the transaction of official business. Direct elections of government officials approximate the collegial situation, with each literate citizen-of-age presumed to have equal competence and influence at the polls.

Governing boards of directors or trustees are also established on the collegial principle, with the requirement of a quorum in order for judgments to be binding.[6]

6. The typical conception of the corporation as pyramidal in form, with ultimate authority peaking in the office of the president, is thus misleading. It would be more descriptive to think of the corporation as a wigwam, with a group at the top.

Decision by Compromise

On occasion there may be agreement by all parties as to the expected consequences or causes of available alternatives, but lack of consensus over preferences toward such "facts." Neither computation nor collective judgment is "appropriate" for this type of issue, for the blunt fact is that if one preference is satisfied, another is denied. An organization facing this situation may fall apart through schism, civil war, or disinterest, unless some common item or point can be found on the several extant preference scales. It can be illustrated by imagining an organization composed of two factions. For faction A, the preference scale runs 1, 2, and 3, while for faction B, the scale is 4, 5, and 6. In this case, in order for either faction to obtain at least an acceptable solution the other must be denied all satisfaction, and this presages the end of the organization. If the preference scales run 1, 2, and 3, in that order, and 3, 4, and 5, both factions can attain a modicum of satisfaction by choosing 3. The appropriate strategy where causation is conceded but preferences are in dispute thus appears to be one which will arrive at the common preference. We will refer to this strategy as decision by compromise.

A Structure for Compromise

Now the task is to construct an ideal organization to handle compromise types of issues economically and efficiently.

Whereas computation problems call for the smallest possible decision unit, and collective judgment for the widest possible participation, compromise seems to require a decision unit of intermediate size. What we want is a structure to facilitate bargaining, and since this involves detailed and subtle exploration of the several factional preference scales, the decision unit must be small enough to permit sustained and often delicate interchange. On the other hand, there is the requirement that all factions—or certainly all important factions—be involved in the decision. This leads, we think, to the *representative body* as the appropriate structure.

For this purpose, we will build rules or constraints into our organization to: 1. require that each faction hold as its *top* priority preference the desire to reach agreement, i.e., to continue the association, 2. ensure that each faction be represented in the decision unit, 3. give each faction veto power, and 4. give each faction all pertinent, available information about causation.

The United Nations Security Council approximates this type of decision unit, if we assume that the member nations represent all important blocs. Federations often provide the representative structure for boards of directors. The American Congress appears to fit this pattern, with the "veto" requirement relaxed because of the size of the body. It is possible to conceive of the Congress as an arena for bargaining and compromise, rather than judgment, with the vote considered merely a mechanical device for measuring at any point in time the current state of negotiations.

The representative decision unit, operating toward compromise, is also seen, though less formally, in many loosely organized societies in the form of "consensus decision making" by councils of tribal chiefs or elders.[7] In these instances power is relatively diffused, so that a "veto" of an alternative by any one member of the decision unit prevents the choice of that alternative. While not necessarily elected, members of the decision unit have to maintain followings and thus may be considered representatives. This is clearly brought out in the studies cited.

The American trial jury for capital cases can also be seen as an attempt to ensure bargaining or weighing of the evidence against the conflicting preferences of freeing the innocent and punishing the guilty. The jury situation differs from many other compromise situations in that each member of the unit is presumed to be an advocate of *both* of the competing values (rather than an advocate of one factional position) who "bargains with himself." The requirement of unanimity for the jury seeks to remove the decision from the area of majority judgment to one of arriving at a choice endorsable by all members of the decision unit.

Decision by Inspiration

The fourth and in our typology the final type of issue is one in which there is disagreement both as to causation and as to preferences. This is, of course, a most dangerous situation for any group to be in; certainly by definition and probably in fact the group in this situation is nearing disintegration. While this situation seems to be far removed from the usual discussions of decision making, we believe it has empirical as well as theoretical relevance.

The most likely action in this situation, we suspect, is the decision not to face the issue. Organizations which appear to be slow to seize opportunities or to respond to environmental events may, on close inspection, be organizations which contain disagreement as to both preferences and causation. To the extent that the organization in this predicament can avoid an issue, it may at least maintain itself as an organization. If it is forced to choose, however, the organization is likely to dissolve—unless some innovation can be introduced.

Anthropologists have recorded on numerous occasions institutionalized means of gaining inspiration by referring "insoluble" problems to supernatural forces, and it is no secret that responsible public officials in "less superstitious" nations call on Divine Guidance when they must make momentous decisions for which there is no precedent and the consequences are highly uncertain. A related device is for the group to rely on a *charismatic* leader.

As Weber (1958) pointed out, the charismatic leader is thought by his followers to have solutions or at least the wisdom to find them. Frequently he offers a new set of ideals or preferences which rally unity out of diversity, by shifting attention. Pointing to a real or fancied threat from outside is one ancient device for this.

The 1958 election of De Gaulle and adoption of the new French communante seems to reflect the charismatic or inspirational type of situation.[8] But it also seems possible for individuals in nominal positions of leadership to attain and articulate enough imagination to create a new vision or image and thereby pull together a distintegrating organization. This seems consistent with the conclusion of Karl Deutsch and his

7. F. M. and M. M. Keesing, *Elite Communication in Samoa* (Stanford: Stanford University Press, 1956); W. B. Miller, "Two Concepts of Authority," *American Anthropologist* (April 1955); and M. Nash, "Machine Age Maya: The Industrialization of a Guatemalan Community," *American Anthropologist,* Part 2 (April 1958).

8. Although nominally a choice by vote, the majority approached unanimity, and it seems that voters were not asked to judge his ability to solve such specific problems as the war in Africa, but rather were asked to impute to him and endorse qualities of omnipotence.

colleagues (1957) as to the importance of innovation and invention in bringing about political integration. Whatever the particular form of leadership exercised, we believe that decisions of this type—where there has been dissensus about both causation and preferences—are *decisions by inspiration*.

A Structure for Inspiration

It is difficult to conceive of an ideal structure for decision by inspiration, for the thinking of the social scientist is oriented toward pattern and organization, while the situation we face here is one of randomness and disorganization. If these situations occur it probably is seldom by design. Nevertheless, an attempt to deliberately construct such a situation might be instructive for the student of organization.

What we are trying to build now has been labeled by Durkheim (1951) as a state of *anomie*, normlessness, or deregulation. As a rough approximation, anomie occurs when former goals or values have lost their meaning or significance or when such goals appear unobtainable with the means available. Thus, our problem is to create a situation of chaos, but to do so with an aggregation of persons who in some sense can be considered to constitute a group or collectivity. We will therefore call for the following constraints: 1. the individuals or groups must be interdependent and thus have some incentive for collective problem solving,[9] 2. there must be a multiplicity of preference scales and therefore of factions, with each faction of approximately equal strength, 3. more information must be introduced than can be processed, and it must be routed through mulitple communication channels,[10] and 4. each member must have access to the major communication networks, in case inspiration strikes.

9. This does not guarantee, of course, that the various factions will remain members of the organization, for we have not ruled out the possibility that they will exploit other resources as substitutes for those provided by the organizations.

10. Dissensus over causation might be achieved by *withholding* pertinent information about cause and effect, but this is not foolproof because organization members can invent *fictions* to fill in the missing gaps. Dubin describes organization fictions as ways of dealing with the unknown, and suggests that fictions can provide the ideological goals and purposes necessary to an organization, as well as beliefs regarding the efficacy of available means. See Dubin (1951).

While it is doubtful if empirical cases of organizational anomie are deliberately created, there seems to be evidence that the more carefully structured organizations do sometimes find themselves in a state of anomie. The routed military organization, for example, is characterized by de-emphasis of military values and an abundance of rumors, contradictory information, and loss of contact or faith in nominal leaders.

Anomie and inspiration probably appear in less stark form in formal organizations, for the most part. Befuddled administrators of organizations caught up in forces which are not understood may and sometimes do rely on decision by inspiration in one of two forms: a. imitation of more prestigeful and successful organizations, or b. importation of prestigeful and authoritative management consultants to tell them what they should want and how to go after it.

In each of these illustrations the effect is to convert the *anomic* situation into something resembling a computational situation, and to rely upon a decision unit composed of one individual, as in the case of bureaucracy. The basis for designating the "expert" differs, of course. But the production of a new vision, image, or belief is basically a creative kind of activity and it is doubtful if either voting or bargaining structures are likely to produce it.

Designation of Decision Units

Our argument to this point, regarding types of pure issues, pure strategies, and pure structures, can be diagrammed thus:

		Preferences about Possible Outcomes	
		Agreement	Nonagreement
Beliefs about Causation	Agreement	Computation in bureaucratic structure	Bargaining in representative structure
	Nonagreement	Majority judgment in collegial structure	Inspiration in "anomic structure"

Note what this suggests about differences in composition of decision units. For a computation issue, the "ideal" decision unit consists of an individual, acting on behalf of the entire organization. For the voting type of issue, the decision unit is made up of the entire membership. In the compromise situation, a group of representatives or delegates constitute the ideal decision unit. In the inspiration situation, the individual again becomes the most appropriate decision unit.

MIXED SITUATIONS

There are a variety of reasons why the purity of our illustrations may be relatively infrequent.[11] A major proposition of this essay is that usually an organization adopts one of the four strategies—computation, collective judgment, compromise, or inspiration—as its dominant strategy, and bases its structure on that strategy.

To the extent that this is true, we can expect or predict several kinds of organizational difficulties which will be presented to administrators when the organization faces issues or problems which do not fit the formal neatness of our pure types. We can also expect difficulties if the appropriate constraints are not present within the particular decision unit. Finally, we can predict that problems will arise if an issue calling for one strategy is presented to a decision unit built to exercise a different kind of strategy.

Confusion of Issues

The difficulties of means-ends distinctions are as real for operating organizations as for scientific observers. Psychological time perspectives have much to do with whether a particular issue is seen as one of means or ends. Despite the fact that social systems of various kinds generally are expected by members to persist through time, their members may attach different valences to varying periods of the future. The holder of the short-run viewpoint may see an issue as one of preferences, while the long-run adherent sees the issue as one of causation.

In a dynamic and complex organization, moreover, the range of possible outcomes widens rapidly as the time span is extended.[12] If this is true, then members of an organization probably are less inclined to grant the competence of experts for long-run decisions, even when they would grant the ability of the same experts for short-run matters.

Thus different members of an organization or of its decision unit may respond to the same stimulus in varying ways, some seeing it as a matter for computation, others as a judgment matter, and still others as requiring bargaining.

Absence of Structural Constraints

One constraint common to all of the pure structures described earlier, except for the case where the decision unit is an individual, was that each judge, each bargainer, each faction, had equal power to influence the choice. While this usually is a formal specification for such units as trial juries, legislatures, or boards, we know that such units in fact exhibit inequality of membership. Strodtbeck et al. (1957), for example, reports that sex and social status affect the amount of participation of jury members in the decision process, the perceptions that fellow jurors have of their competence as jurors, and the degree to which they influence the outcome.[13] Such factors as party loyalty and party discipline, seniority, political skills, and the endorsement of pressure groups may affect the legislator's ability to make his voice heard as loudly as the next one. Within bureaucracies there are well-known inequalities between offices and divisions which formally are equal, and such scholars as Dalton (1950) have documented some of the reasons why computational experts may temper their computations with other considerations.

Another constraint common to all but the anomic structure was that each participant in the decision unit

11. On the other hand we have no proof that the pure examples are rare. Millions of organizational decisions of a computational nature, for example, probably are made every day in bureaucracies. The mixed situations may be more noticeable and memorable because of the difficulties they pose rather than because they are more frequent.

12. This is suggested by the decision trees of decision theorists. See Luce and Raiffa, *Games and Decisions, op. cit.*

13. Similar observations have been made in the hospital setting by A. H. Stanton and M. S. Schwartz, *The Mental Hospital* (New York: Basic Books, 1954).

have access to all available, pertinent information about causation. In fact, despite all of the attention given to communication in modern organizations, the condition called for by this constraint is at best approximated but seldom achieved. Colleagues of the expert in a bureaucracy, then, may grant the competence and good intentions of an official, but refuse to honor his decision on grounds that he did not know the local or "real" situation. Well informed minorities may control the collegial body whose other members are ill-informed, and "private information" obtained by one faction may make a mockery of the compromise situation.

Inappropriate Decision Units

If organizations were completely pliable, it would be a relatively simple thing to assign each problem to a decision unit designed especially for it. But, of course, organizations would cease to be organizations if they were completely pliable. Regularity, pattern, and structure are inescapable.

Another important source of structural rigidity is the shifting nature of human knowledge. Types of problems which at one time are identified by members of a group as appropriate for judgment may at another time be defined as computational problems, as the group changes its beliefs about cause-and-effect relations.

Thus problems which once called for voting or inspirational strategies have become problems for computation or bargaining, and traditional structures are threatened. The city manager movement threatens both the party organization and the council by redefining certain types of problems as no longer subject to bargaining or voting but as appropriate for expert computation. The increasing scope of required expertise forces the American Congress to establish bureaucratic agencies to make decisions which once were prerogatives of the legislature—and Congress then becomes jealous of its own creations.

Expansion Tendencies in Decision Issues

Decision issues appear to be broader, more complex, and more time-consuming as we move from computation issues to voting to bargaining issues. There is reason to believe that, left to their own devices, members of social systems tend to expand decision issues. In a revealing summary of community issues and the course of their disposition, Coleman (1957) notes a tendency for transformation of issues from specific to general, and from disagreement to antagonism. Bales (1953) also notes in small problem-solving groups, that interpersonal tensions mount as the decision process moves from orientation to evaluation to control.[14]

As knowledge becomes increasingly pluralistic, in the sense that new specialized logics are developed, the bureaucracy encompasses not one but several sets of beliefs about appropriate means to organizational ends. Thus the competence of the single expert becomes doubted and members define issues as calling for judgment rather than computation. If, for example, the expert can be forced to admit that his is but a professional opinion—a tactic in jury trials—the way is cleared to insist that others be consulted and a balance of judgments obtained. This has also been a common practice in communities where public health experts have decided to introduce fluoride into the public water supply (Coleman, 1957).

It is clear that in the past several decades, American corporations have shown a proliferation of specialized staff agencies, each with its own logic for maximizing a particular function or procedure. As the beliefs about causation have thus become increasingly pluralistic, there has been a plea for the development of "generalists," but also there seems to have been a corresponding increase in the use of decision units appropriate to judgmental issues. Committees, conferences, staff meetings, and "clearance" procedures have not only proliferated but have been dignified on wall charts—at least to the extent of dotted lines.

With problems which appear to call for judgment, the heat of debate can lead proponents of the several alternatives to overstate their cases and discount missing information; often it also leads them to refer to more general but extraneous organization preferences as a means of finding moral justification for the selection of the alternative they endorse. When this

14. For a report on the increasing use of committees for key decisions on new products, on personnel policy, production volume, and long-range planning, see "Committees: Their Role in Management Today," *Management Review* (October 1957).

occurs, the issue is no longer one of judgment regarding causation, but becomes one of dispute over (relevant) ends and thus subject to compromise.

ADMINISTRATION AND DECISION MAKING

We can now offer the general proposition that an important role for administration is to *manage* the decision *process,* as distinct from *making the decision.* We are not suggesting that administrators do one to the exclusion of the other, but if issues are not automatically crystallized, the ideal structural constraints are not automatically present, or appropriate decision units are not automatically selected, it may fall to administrators to take action which will facilitate decisions.

The following discussion is not offered as exhaustive, but as illustrative of the potential utility of considering administrative roles with respect to the decision process.[15]

Where a time dimension is not clearly implied by the nature of the issue, one role of administration is to delineate by fiction or otherwise such a time dimension. This facilitates the sorting out of means from ends, by the decision unit, and thus tends to contain the issue from expanding into a more complex one.

When there are many alternatives available, a role of administration is to provide machinery for elimination of all but a few. This can be particularly important when an issue is assigned to a voting unit, which seems to be able to operate effectively only on binary problems. At one level of generality this is an important role for Congressional committees (Lathan, 1952). At a more general level of analysis this is the function of political parties in the two party system; the necessary compromises of platform and candidates are achieved before the issue is put to the electorate. By way of contrast, in multi-party France the function of compromising a plurality of interests devolved on the legislature more than on intraparty processes, and was an important factor in the lack of effectiveness of the Fourth Republic (MacRae, 1958).

In the bargaining situation the important role of administration may be to obtain initial mutual commitment to reaching agreement, and to maintain this commitment as taking priority over factional preferences. This approach may guard the issue from expanding into one of anomie, for as Dubin (1957) points out, mutual commitment to the necessity for reaching agreement in effect moves the issue in the direction of judgment and voting.[16] One method of handling the bargaining issue, and seemingly an indispensable one when the preference scales do not contain common items, is to place the particular issue in a larger context. This can be done by "horse-trading," thus assuring the losing faction on the present issue of priority treatment on a future issue.[17]

Another role of administration which seems to be important under certain conditions is that of crystallizing consensus about preferences. Ambiguity in a decision situation may result in lack of knowledge, on the part of members of a decision unit, of the similarities of their preferences. When this is the case, an administrator who can sense the agreement and articulate it may play a vital part in organizational decision. In this connection it appears that timing may be as important as sensitivity to cues. Keesing and Keesing (1956), observing formal group deliberation in Samoa, note that a senior elite person may choose to speak early if he wants to give guidance to the discussion *or knows that prior informal consultations have made clear a unanimous stand*, but that usually he will let others carry the active roles, making his pronouncements after the debate has pretty well run its course.

A final suggestion regarding possible roles of administrators in facilitating organizational decision-making concerns the extremely complicated kinds of issues that frequently face administrators of "loose"

15. For a similar conclusion, though approached differently, see Philip Selznick, *Leadership in Administration* (Evanston, Ill.: Row Peterson and Co., 1957).

N. W. Chamberlain (1950), in a study of the corporate decision-making process as applied to the transfer of employees, notes the distinction between deciding and managing the decision process, and offers a number of stimulating hypotheses.

16. See Berelson in Eulau et al. (1956: 110).

17. The important role of the larger context in facilitating decisions was suggested to us by Professor Bela Gold, School of Business Administration, University of Pittsburgh.

organizations. We have in mind such social systems as the community (as viewed by a mayor, council, or manager); the school district (as viewed by the superintendent or board), or the bloc of nations (as viewed by their diplomats and officials). We refer to these as "loose" organizations because only a portion of the relevant "members" are directly subject to the hierarchy of authority. In the legal sense, that is, some of the groups are not "members," although in the behavioral sense they are.[18]

When such organizations face important and complicated issues, we believe, it may become necessary for administrators to redefine the issue into a series of issues, each assigned to an appropriate decision unit. It may also be that there are patterns in the sequence in which the series is handled. For example, in order to achieve a "community decision" on a fluoridation or school bond issue, it may be necessary to *first* get agreement and commitment of the powerful elements on preferences. This might be done "informally" in the smokefilled room, by compromise, and it might include the important choice as to whether to tackle the issue at all. After that decision is made, the *second* step might be to frame a judgmental issue for presentation to an electorate. Finally, within the limits of the majority decision, specialists can be presented with such issues as the proper equipment for fluoridation or the most appropriate timing for bond issues.

We feel rather safe in predicting that there is a cumulative effect in this sequence. Weakness in the first step probably forecasts trouble in succeeding steps, and so on.

Administrative Tendencies to Narrow Issues

It seems apparent that in terms of time and effort, issues increase in "cost" in the same order in which they increase in breadth; computation is the quickest and simplest and involves the fewest members; judgment by voting membership is slower and diverts the energies of many; and bargaining usually is a drawn-out, energy-consuming process.

18. Such "loose" organizations are found in industry, too. For an instructive analysis of this, see Ridgway (1957).

Organizations operate in environmental contexts and hence cannot always take a leisurely approach in making decisions. The actions of competitors or of potential collaborators and clientele frequently place time deadlines on issues. Moreover, the interrelatedness of the parts of large organizations may mean that delay at one point suspends activities at others, and when costs must be reckoned closely this fact exerts serious pressures to have issues settled promptly.[19]

Thus if an issue can be defined in more than one way, reponsible officials may be tempted to define it in an easier, faster, and less frustrating way, i.e., as calling for computation rather than judgment, or as appropriate for voting rather than bargaining.[20] In some cases the pressures of time, or habit, may lead administrators to force issues into molds which are patently inappropriate.

Timing of Choice and Consensus

Except in situations where force can be brought to bear on members, it appears that consensus or acceptance of both means and ends is necessary for effective organizational action.

The four types of issues posited above are successively "broader" in the sense that they incorporate into the issue itself the necessity of finding or building

19. Rose Laub Coser (1958), comparing medical and surgical wards in a hospital, finds that the emergency nature of the surgical setting results in decision making by fiat, whereas the more tentative, diagnostic atmosphere in the medical ward results in decision making by deliberation and consensus.

20. March, Simon, and Guetzkow see this tendency. They write: "Because of these consequences of bargaining, we predict that the organizational hierarchy will perceive (and react to) all conflict as though it were in fact individual rather than intergroup conflict. More specifically, we predict that almost all disputes in the organization will be defined as problems in analysis, that the initial reaction to conflict will be problem-solving and persuasion, that such reaction will persist even when they appear to be inappropriate, that there will be a greater explicit emphasis on common goals where they do not exist than where they do, and that bargaining (when it occurs) will frequently be concealed within an analytic framework." In March and Simon (1958: 131).

Lipset, surveying political sociology, writes: "Inherent in bureaucratic structures is a tendency to reduce conflicts to administrative decisions by experts; and thus over time bureaucratization facilitates the removing of issues from the political arena." In Merton et. al. (1958: 102).

consensus. It is only in the simplest type—computation—that consensus on means and ends exists prior to the decision. The judgment issue involves finding a cause and effect hypothesis about which a majority can agree. The bargaining issue involves finding a preference on which consensus can be established. The anomic situation requires the creation of both preferences and causation-beliefs acceptable to a majority.

If the fact or the fiction of consensus is not present at the time a choice is made—and this may frequently be the case when rapid decisions are necessary—the required consensus must be achieved following choice. The hypothesis here is that for organizational decisions to be implemented effectively both consensus and choice are necessary. If for reasons of expediency, choice is made *before* consensus is achieved, the burden of achieving consensus *following* choice remains.

This hypothesis, if accurate, has important implications not only for decision making but for the larger administrative process of which decision is a part.

CONCLUSION

We have attempted to develop a format for studying decision processes in organizations, by identifying four major types of decision issues and pairing them with four major strategies for arriving at decisions. For each strategy, we have suggested, there is an appropriate structure. Obviously there are many combinations and permutations of issues, strategies, and structures, but we believe that the format suggested points to a limited number of such arrangements, and that patterns can be found in them. We hope we have shown that this approach to organizational decision processes has important implications for theory and application.

What has been presented here can be considered no more than a first approximation. The empirical evidence along these lines has not been collected systematically, and further conceptual development undoubtedly will be necessary. It is possible, for example, that added leverage can be gained by distinguishing between "lack of agreement" and "disagreement," and thus developing a nine-fold typology of issues.[21] This format could also be extended into an analysis of how decisions are blocked or prevented. Such an extension should tell us something about the important area of belligerent behavior in or between organizations, and it should also provide a useful test of the models presented here.

Whatever the eventual results, we hope we have made the case for development of sociological models of decision processes, which can be joined with the psychological "satisficing" model to their mutual advantage.

21. Suggested by Professor Frederick L. Bates, Department of Sociology, Louisiana State University, in private communication.

CONCLUDING STATEMENT

What can we say about the decision process as a design variable? We begin our wrap-up by examining the nature of decision making, recalling that Simon as well as Thompson and Tuden emphasized that it is a process, not a single event. Our examination focuses on decision making as both an individual (cognitive) process and an administrative/organizational one. Finally, we explore decision making as a process that is designed in keeping with organizational goals and the now familiar constraints of environment, technology, and people.

DECISION MAKING AS PROCESS

We can describe decision making as constituting two different, though similar, processes. The first process describes the cognitive stages through which the individual decision maker progresses. The second process has more obvious managerial implications. Both processes acknowledge certain realities about decision making, especially as it occurs in organizations: bounded rationality and satisficing. This dual reality has been identified by Simon (1976).

The Limits of Rationality

Completely objective rationality suggests a pattern of thinking and acting in which the decision maker 1. assesses all potential alternatives in a comprehensive fashion, 2. considers the whole complex of outcomes that would follow from each choice and combination of choices, and 3. using clear and consistent criteria, singles out the one alternative that best solves the problem.

Actual behavior, however, falls short of objective rationality. It does so in at least three ways (Simon, 1976: 81):

1. Rationality requires a complete knowledge and anticipation of the consequences that will follow on each choice. In fact, knowledge of consequences is always fragmentary.
2. Since these consequences lie in the future, imagination must supply the lack of experience in attaching value to them.
3. Rationality requires a choice among all possible alternative behaviors. In actual behavior, only a few of all these possible alternatives even come to mind.

In short, rationality is not—cannot be—either objective or complete. It is subjective and limited. That is, real rationality employed by real decision makers is bounded. It is bounded by the decision maker's subjective faculties and by the incompleteness of the decision maker's knowledge.

Satisficing

So, what is the decision maker to do? Again, Simon (1976: xxiii–xxx) tells us: instead of viewing decisions as being made under the imperatives of objective rationality, we should recognize that they occur according to the reality of *administrative* rationality. Objective rationality calls for decisions that maximize—that produce the very best choice among all those available. Administrative rationality, on the other hand, dictates a course of action that is satisfactory, or "good enough."[1] Simon points to some examples of satisficing criteria, examples familiar to the business executive, if not to the classical economist: "share of market," "adequate profit," "fair price."

As we mentioned, you should keep both of these aspects of decision reality in mind when considering the following processes. They apply to the decision maker whether viewed as a socio-psychological individual or an organizational-role incumbent.

Decision Making as a Personal Process

Social psychologists have learned a great deal about the mental (cognitive) and psychological processes that the decision maker undergoes.[2] While the specifics may vary, depending on which researcher is describing them, the consensus seems to be that the decision maker goes through such stages as the following:

Stage 1: Awareness. Just about the first thing that happens is that the decision maker becomes aware of some problem, threat, or challenge—some change in the status quo. A phone call, letter, memorandum, computer-printout—any of these can occur and result in the decision maker's becoming cognizant of some difficulty. If, after preliminary exploration, the decision maker thinks the problem should be pursued, Stage 2 is entered.

Stage 2: Alternatives. At this point the decision maker sets out to identify the alternatives that may be helpful in solving the problem or generally overcoming the difficulty. This alternatives-identification stage may involve activities that range from armchair contemplation to a full-scale, formal, departmental investigation. Regardless of the specific tasks performed, the decision maker embarks at this stage on a journey to a decision.

Stage 3: Choice. At this point the reality of bounded rationality comes into full view, producing a choice that "satisfices," rather than maximizes the problem. That is, having identified the various alternatives available, the decision maker now selects the one that most satisfactorily resolves the difficulty

Stage 4: Commitment. Now that a solution has been identified, it remains for the decision maker to act. Specifically, it is at this point that organizational resources are committed. And it is this stage at which we can say a decision is made. That is, to select an alternative intellectually and then do nothing about it is not making a decision. For the administrative decision maker, the test is the commitment of organizational resources. Thus we also refer to this as the decision stage.

Stage 5: Recommitment. Most people think of the stage following the commitment of resources as an evaluation stage: the decision is set in motion (Stage 4), and then its results or effects are assessed. While this view is correct, of course, we use the label *recommitment* to emphasize that organizational decision making is a process in which the flow of scarce resources is critical. Thus the decision maker assesses the results of the decision and either continues the resource commitment or cycles back to an earlier stage—in extreme cases, all the way back to Stage 1.

---

1. A common story is that the word *satisfice* combines the terms, *satisfy* and *suffice*.
2. Refer, for example, to Jones and Garard (1967: 186–226).

Decision Making as an Administrative Process

We can describe the organizational decision process in many of the same terms as those for the individual. Basically, the steps taken in organizational decision making follow those outlined earlier in the chapter by Simon (intelligence, design, choice). Expanding on suggestions by Knudson et. al. (1973: 252), we are able to identify eight relatively distinct steps that comprise an organizational decision process.

Step 1: Determine the problem. Frequently the initial perception of a problem differs from the actuality of that problem. Thus the first step in the organizational decision-making process is to determine—accurately—the difficulty, challenge, or whatever that may require some decision.

Step 2: Identify decision criteria. Before organizational resources can be rationally committed to a particular alternative, there needs to be some understanding of what a good decision should be. That is, there needs to be a set of criteria identified that when met will allow decision makers to conclude that a good decision has been made.

Step 3: Prioritize criteria. Not all criteria are equally important. Thus the third step in conducting organizational decision making is to rank order the decision criteria according to their relative importances.

Step 4: Weight criteria. Not only are some criteria more important than others, their *degree* of relative importance varies. That is, criterion number 1 may be twice as important as the criterion ranked number 2. In turn, that second most important criterion may be only slightly more important than criterion number 3. Thus the next step is to assign, as realistically as possible, relative weights to the decision criteria.

Step 5: Communicate criteria. Recall that most organizational decisions tend to repeat themselves. Further, many involve or affect a variety of people. If a given problem—a problem that crops up again and again—tends to have a relatively stable set of criteria for its solution, then the people involved or affected should be aware of what those criteria are.

Consider an example: a common decision faced by executives concerns whom to promote to a new, higher level, managerial position. Let us say that a given choice is between two lower level managers, Charles and Susan. Let us say further that Susan is given the promotion for the following reason: On balance, Charles and Susan are equally qualified, except Susan has systematically trained two of her subordinates to take over her job. On the basis of this desirable managerial behavior, Susan gets the job. Charles, on the other hand, protests that in his several years with the organization, involving a number of favorable performance evaluations, no one has ever indicated to him that he should be training his subordinates for higher positions.

Now, in our position as observers, we might say that Charles should know that he should be training his subordinates. Still, the point is that subordinate development is apparently important to organizational management. Accordingly, those managers should *communicate* that desire—that criterion—to the membership. To put it bluntly: if you want people to meet a set of criteria, let them know what those criteria are.

Step 6: Collect data. This step involves developing a set of alternatives from which a satisfactory decision may be recalled. At this stage decision makers gather information regarding the appropriateness of each alternative—information regarding both the alternative as a workable possibility and its potential outcomes. *Appropriateness* is defined, of course, in terms of the criteria (weighted) previously established. The several decision-process steps we have described thus far are pointedly illustrated by the following dialogue (abridged from Carlisle, 1976: 52–54):

> Then I asked Johnson whether he had ever tried to get MacGregor (Johnson's boss) to make a decision, and his response was:
>
> "Only once. I had been on the job for only about a week when I ran into an operating problem I couldn't solve, so I phoned MacGregor. He answered the phone with that sleepy 'Hello' of his. I told him who I was and that I had a problem. His response was instantaneous: 'Good, that's what you're being paid to do, solve problems,' and then he hung up.
>
> "I was dumbfounded. I didn't really know any of the people I was working with, so because I didn't think I had any other alternative, I called him back, got the same sleepy 'Hello,' and again identified myself. He replied sharply, 'I thought I told you that you were paid to solve problems. Do you think that I should do your job as well as my own?' When I insisted on seeing him about my problem, he answered, 'I don't know how you expect me to help you. You have a technical problem, and I don't go into the refinery any more; I used to, but my shirts kept getting dirty from the visits, and my wife doesn't like washing all the grime out of them, so I pretty much stuck in my office. Ask one of the other men. They're all in touch with what goes on out there.'
>
> "I didn't know which one to consult, so I insisted again on seeing him. He finally agreed—grudgingly— to see me right away, so I went over to his office, and there he was in his characteristic looking-out-the-window posture. When I sat down, he started the dirty-shirt routine—but when he saw that I was determined to involve him in my problems, he sat down on the sofa in front of his coffee table and, pen in hand, prepared to write on a pad of paper. He asked me to state precisely what the problem was, and he wrote down exactly what I said. Then he asked what the conditions for its solution were. I replied that I didn't know what he meant by that question. His response was, 'If you don't know what conditions have to be satisfied for a solution to be reached, how do you know when you've solved the problem?' I told him I'd never thought of approaching a problem that way, and he replied, 'Then you'd better start. I'll work through this one with you this time, but don't expect me to do your problem solving for you because that's your job, not mine.'
>
> "I stumbled through the conditions that would have to be satisfied by the solution. Then he asked me what alternative approaches I could think of. I gave him the first one I could think of—let's call it X—and he wrote it down and asked me what would happen if I did X. I replied with my answer—let's call it A. Then he asked me how A compared with the conditions I had established for the solution of the problem. I replied that it did not meet them. MacGregor told me that I'd have to think of another. I came up with Y, which I said would yield result B, and this still fell short of the solution conditions. After more prodding from MacGregor, I came up with Z, which I said would have C as a result. Although this clearly came a lot closer to the conditions I had established for the solution than any of the others I'd suggested, it still did not satisfy all of them. MacGregor then asked me if I could combine any of the approaches I'd suggested. I replied I could do X and Y and then saw that the resultant A plus C would indeed satisfy all the solution conditions I had set up previously. When I thanked MacGregor, he replied 'What for? You could have done that bit of problem solving perfectly well without wasting my time.' "

Step 7: Make the decision. By now, the problem has been determined, criteria specified, and alternatives identified. It now remains to select that alternative which most satisfactorily meets the criteria. As in our earlier discussion of the cognitive stages of decision making, "make the decision" means putting organizational resources into action.

Step 8: Follow through. Once an alternative has been selected, and corresponding resources committed, decision makers need to follow through. That is, they need to communicate the decision to the people who are affected and assess the impact of the decision on the original problem.

We mention communicating the decision because of its importance to its eventual success. Consider the earlier example, in which the decision was made to promote Susan instead of Charles. A key step that has to be made is to communicate the decision to Charles in such a way that he learns what he can do to develop his managerial skills. If he reacts to the decision by withdrawing, or even resigning, then the decision *process* has been bungled.

Similarly, it is important that decision makers monitor the results generated when the decision is put into operation. The familiar organizational process of control comes into play here. Results are compared against the criteria. If found wanting, decision makers cycle the process back up a few steps.

To repeat: as pointed out earlier by Simon and by Thompson and Tuden, decision making is not a solitary event to be executed. It is a multistep process to be designed and managed. Thus in a particular case the decision itself (step 7) may be sound—but if the follow through is mishandled, then the *process* has not been successful. And what is critical is the effective design and management of that process.

DESIGNING THE PROCESS

Traditional bureaucratic theory established the hierarchy as the framework for decision making. The locus of decisions—who makes what decisions—was pretty well concentrated (centralized) in the upper echelons.

As you are aware, modern administrative theory developed with the consensus that centralized decision making is not effective under all circumstances. Employee participation in the decision process was proposed as an alternative. The idea is that "participative decision making" improves employee commitment to organizational processes (Vroom, 1964). This commitment is seen to result from perceived individual influence on decisions.

Implicitly, this train of thought uses the term *participation* as a unimodal concept, related to the practice of democratic decision making in an organization. Tannenbaum and Schmidt's (1958) classic discussion, for example, treated participation as a general organizational characteristic, ranging on a single dimension from one *boss-centered* extreme ("manager makes decision and announces it") to another, *employee-centered* extreme ("manager and nonmanagers jointly make decision within limits defined by organizational constraints").

Designing Decision Patterns

This view is overly simplistic for two reasons. First, *participation* takes on different meanings, depending on the type of decision and the circumstances under which it is being made. Second, the issue is not how much, on average, do employees participate in organizational decisions. Rather, the issue is who participates to what degree in what decisions (Connor et al., 1973).

To put the issue in other words, different organization-structural conditions, different situation-specific circumstances, such as the nature of the decision, and different functional characteristics of individual decisions (e.g., production, personnel) also may influence the nature of participation and its value to the organization. As Vroom (1973: 80) has suggested, "the critics and proponents of participative management would do well to direct their efforts toward identifying the properties of situations in which different decision-making approaches are effective. . . ."

We will now attempt to follow Vroom's advice. First we consider some factors that affect the utility of using various decision rules in participative-decision situations. We then examine the process of designing appropriate decision patterns.

Decision Rules in Participative Decision Making

When a group of people makes a joint decision, it is necessary to have some standard or principle for recognizing when a decision has been reached. These standards are called decision rules. Some common rules are (Klopfer, 1975):

- *Consensus rule.* All group members must agree with the proposed decision.
- *Majority rule.* At least one-half (sometimes two-thirds) of the group members must agree with the proposed decision.
- *Plurality rule.* More group members must agree with the proposed decision than do support any of the alternative decisions.

Which decision rule is best to use? The answer depends on the type of decision being made.[3] For example, if the alternatives contain, or are believed to contain, a single correct decision, then groups using a consensus rule are more likely to be accurate (although more conservative) than majority-rule groups.

Unfortunately, most decisions made by groups do not have one clearly correct alternative. Several choices are available, but it is not possible to verify the decision objectively. Policy decisions are a case in point. Which decision rule should be used in this type of situation? Consider some evidence.

In one experimental study (Davis et al., 1975) 647 undergraduates served as members of mock juries, which deliberated to reach a verdict in a rape case. The students were separated into 72 juries; 36 juries used a consensus rule, and 36 required a two-thirds majority. None of the juries convicted the defendant. When jury members later were asked for their individual opinions anonymously, it turned out that those people who were members of consensus-rule juries continued to accept the verdicts of their group more than did the members of the two-thirds majority juries.

Now, the students in this study knew they were participating as subjects in an experiment. They had little reason to believe their decisions were consequential. Consensus rule yielded more stable decisions. What about the case in which the matter being decided is important to the decision maker? Klopfer (1975) used a decision topic previously rated by subjects as important. Subjects were assigned to one of 16 consensus-rule groups, or one of the same number of majority-rule groups. Subjects in half the groups were led to believe their decision making might have real impact (high consequence), while subjects in the other groups were not (low consequence). Several days after their participation, group members were asked to make an individual decision and to rate their satisfaction with the

3. This decision is taken from Haimann et al. (1978: 514–15).

group decision making. Subjects in consensus-rule groups making high-consequence decisions showed a tendency to reject their group's decision and revert to their own original points of view.

Regarding decisions that have no clear best solution, the conclusion to be drawn is this: consensus rule may be a difficult criterion to achieve with important or high-consequence decisions. However, the evidence suggests that consensus rule is preferable with less important issues for producing stable decisions. Several studies also suggest that consensus rule takes more time but is more satisfying in both cases.

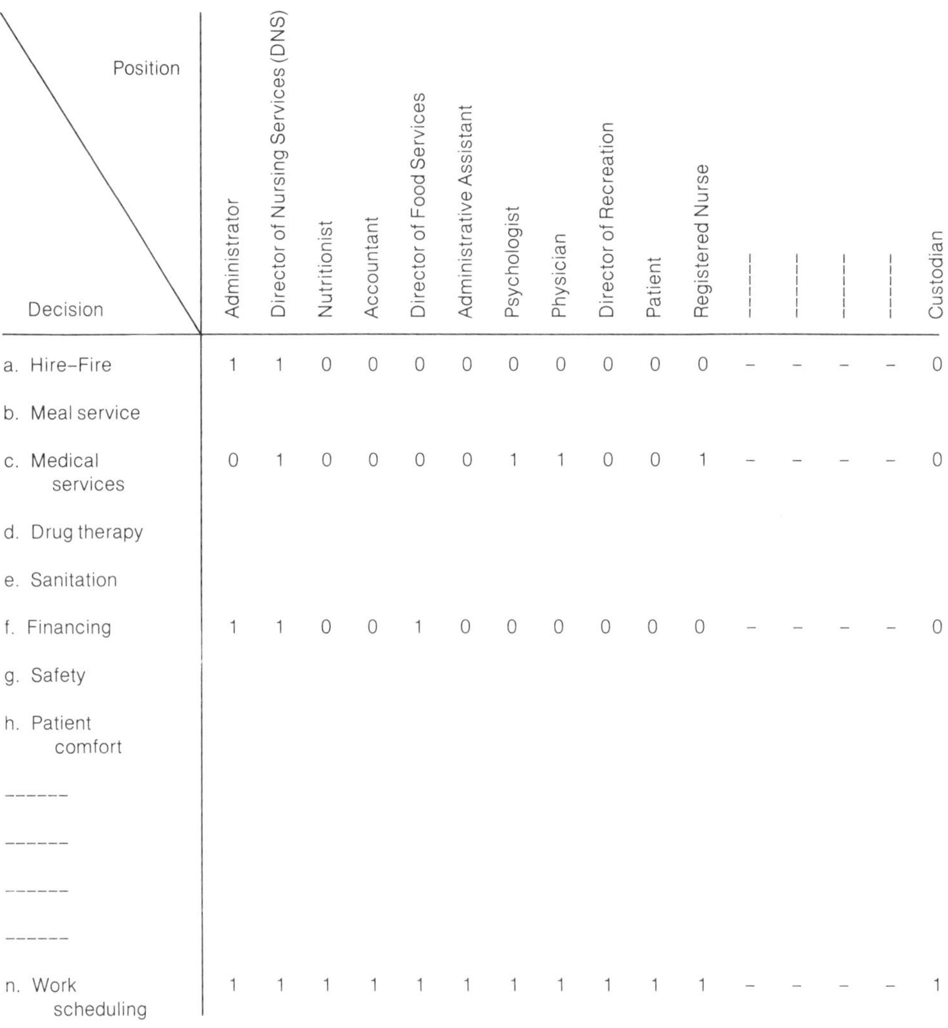

Decision \ Position	Administrator	Director of Nursing Services (DNS)	Nutritionist	Accountant	Director of Food Services	Administrative Assistant	Psychologist	Physician	Director of Recreation	Patient	Registered Nurse	------	------	------	------	Custodian
a. Hire–Fire	1	1	0	0	0	0	0	0	0	0	0	–	–	–	–	0
b. Meal service																
c. Medical services	0	1	0	0	0	0	1	1	0	0	1	–	–	–	–	0
d. Drug therapy																
e. Sanitation																
f. Financing	1	1	0	0	1	0	0	0	0	0	0	–	–	–	–	0
g. Safety																
h. Patient comfort																

------																
n. Work scheduling	1	1	1	1	1	1	1	1	1	1	1	–	–	–	–	1

1 = Participation
0 = No participation

Figure 9-4. Illustrated decision matrix for a medical setting

Designing Decision Patterns

The above considerations suggest the importance of the character of participation in decisions; that is, the importance of designing different decision-making patterns, depending on the participation circumstances. Do systematic variations in decision patterns exist among organizations in an industry where technology and workflow are common, but where social-structural properties vary?

As an illustration of decision patterns, a simple matrix model to represent participation in decision making in a medical setting is shown in Figure 9–4. The rows of this matrix represent organizational decisions. The columns denote organizational positions. The most common view of participative decision making is a continuum, ranging from high autocratic at one end to high democratic at the other (Tannenbaum and Schmidt, 1958). The first participation pattern in Figure 9–4 (row *a*—Hire-Fire) is high autocratic, showing senior administrators participating in this decision (represented by a 1) and no other organizational member participating (represented by a 0). A pattern reflecting high democratic participation is seen on row *n* (Work Scheduling), in which all organizational positions take part. However, rows *c* and *f* each represent additional patterns. Only some positions participate in each of these decisions. Row *c* involves only the Director of Nursing Services, the Psychologist, the Physician, and the Registered Nurse. Row *f* involves only the Chief Administrator, the Director of Nursing Services, and the Director of Food Services.

To extend the notion of decision pattern further, we can identify two different, but related, decision-pattern "profiles." A *decision profile* reflects the level of participation in a specific decision area for each position. Figure 9–5 illustrates such a profile. The

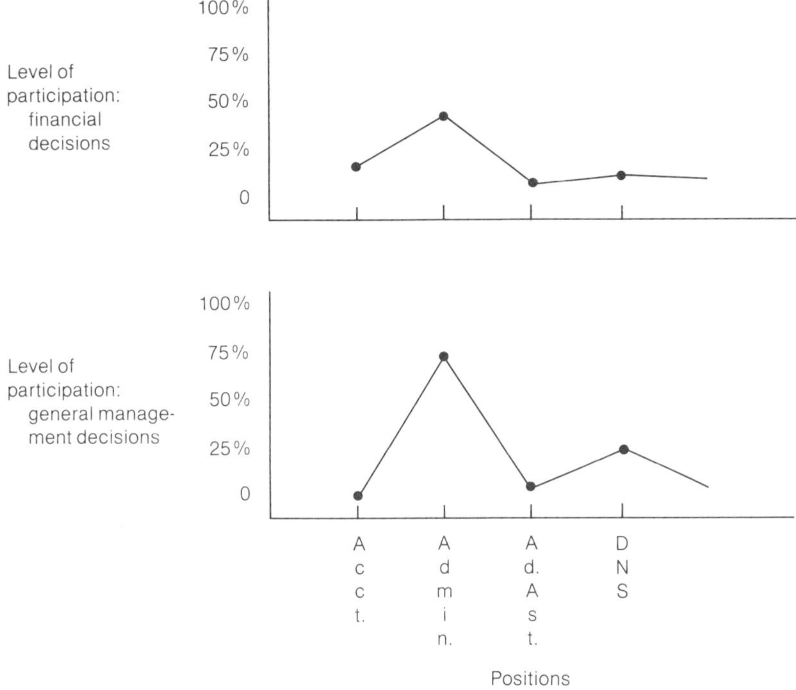

Figure 9-5. Illustration of partial decision-profiles

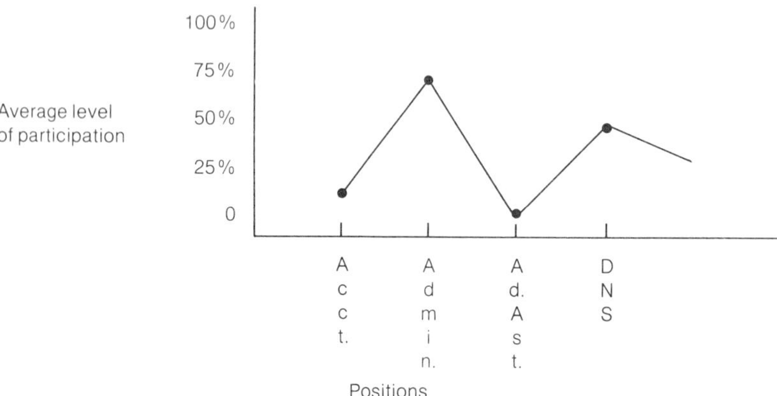

Figure 9-6. Illustration of a partial participation-profile

participation profile is the level of participation for each position, averaged over all decisions. This type of profile is illustrated in Figure 9–6.

As an interesting sidelight, the reader might note that Figure 9–6 is an indirect—actually, a fairly direct—indication of the distribution of power in the organization. People who tend to have a relatively large impact (high participation) on decisions can be said to wield a concomitantly large amount of power.

When we consider the latter two participation patterns in Figure 9–4 (rows *c* and *f*), plus the profiles depicted in Figures 9–5 and 9–6, we see that the concept of shared decisions is extended. Participation is not simply a matter of the average degree to which all employees participate in organizational design. Rather, organizational designers need to think in terms of decision patterns—patterns that may vary from decision to decision; but that remain relatively stable for a given set of organizational circumstances, such as environmental uncertainty and technological complexity.

SUMMARY AND CONCLUSION

This chapter has been concerned with decision processes. We began our discussion by considering an overall framework that guides organizational decision making (Simon). Specifically, programmed and unprogrammed decisions were compared, and a three-phase process was identified: intelligence, design, and choice; certain organization-design implications were then noted.

Thompson and Tuden extended the discussion by examining four specific decision strategies; these they labeled *computation, majority judgment, compromise,* and *inspiration.* The authors then identified four structural designs that corresponded to the decision strategies: bureaucratic, collegial, representative, and anomic, respectively. Of course, these decision strategies and structural designs are ideal types. The article therefore concluded with a discussion of the more common variations that are actually found in organizations.

We wrapped up the discussion by examining decision making as a dual process. The first process described the cognitive stages through which the decision maker progresses. The second process identified a series of eight steps—distinct, yet connected—of which organizational decisions are composed. We then concluded with a discussion of decision patterns. It is these patterns that designers must develop in accordance with the requirements of the decision and organizational circumstances.

Questions for Review

1. Compare the traditional and modern techniques of decision making for programmed types of decisions as outlined by Simon.
2. Compare the traditional and modern techniques of decision making for nonprogrammed types of decisions as outlined by Simon.
3. What conclusions regarding the occupational profile 20 years in the future does Simon reach?
4. On what foundation does Simon base his assertion that complex systems are generally hierarchical?
5. What are the two points that Simon thinks will need to be re-examined at each stage of automation? What are some of the implications he sees for these?
6. In what ways does Simon see new organizations with more automation still closely resembling present organizations?
7. Review the typology of decision issues developed by Thompson and Tuden. Summarize the nature of each type of decision within it.
8. Thompson and Tuden suggest a number of possible roles for administrators in facilitating organizational decision making. Briefly describe these.
9. In what ways does Simon see actual behavior falling short of objective reality?
10. Depending on which researcher is describing them, the consensus seems to be that the decision maker goes through certain stages, or steps, in the decision-making process. What are they?

Questions for Discussion

1. "Most managers, regardless of their function or hierarchical level, make roughly the same decision over and over." What do you think about this statement? How is it true or untrue, accurate or inaccurate? What might characterize decisions as being "the same"?
2. "It is generally believed that good decision makers, like good athletes, are born, not made. The belief is about as true in the one case as it is in the other." From your reading in this chapter and your own observation, discuss the accuracy and validity of such an assertion.
3. Simon asserts that "Any society can . . . devise means for eliminating most of the inequity associated with the displacement of skills." While he also says that any society *should* devise such means, do you think that any means for eliminating displacement inequity can really be devised successfully? Explain.
4. "Implicit in discussions of routine work is the assumption that any increase in routinization of work decreases work satisfaction and impairs the growth and self-realization of the worker." Do you agree that this assumption is implicit in discussions of routine? *Does* routinization decrease work satisfaction in all workers?

How does your view agree with or differ from Simon's? Give reasons for your position.

5. "Hierarchy is the adaptive form for finite intelligence to assume in the face of complexity." Discuss the implications of this statement for religious and political systems. How would this reflect on the clan and bureaucratic forms of control outlined earlier, in Chapter 8?
6. In drawing a structure for compromise, Thompson and Tuden comment that "the jury situation differs from many other compromise situations in that each member of the unit is presumed to be an advocate of *both* of the competing values (rather than an advocate of one factional position) who bargains with himself." Discuss this statement. Do you agree or disagree with this analysis? Why?
7. Thompson and Tuden observe that "organizations would cease to be organizations if they were completely pliable. Regularity, pattern, and structure are inescapable." In view of your reading in the text to this point and in view of your past reading on the subject, what is your reaction to this statement?
8. What do you understand by the term *participative decision making?"* Under what circumstances have you seen participative decision making applied? In what situations have you thought it to be—or do you think it might be—useful?
9. ". . . Evidence suggests that consensus rule is preferable with less important issues for producing stable decisions." Why should consensus rule be preferable with less important issues? Should it not be preferable with more important issues?
10. Do you agree that different decision-making approaches are effective for different situations? Is one approach universally preferable to another? What is your own experience of decision-making processes? How does this support or refute your position?

10

Organization Structure

INTRODUCTORY REMARKS

Probably no organizational property has been more studied, researched, and manipulated than organization structure. As we have seen, early writers—especially Weber (1946), Gulick and Urwick (1947), and Michels (1949)—described organization structure as a formal setting, a framework, within which various human phenomena occurred. Interestingly, the focus of such writers' attention was on those human phenomena, not on the structure per se. Several path-breaking case studies—of the Tennessee Valley Authority (Selznick, 1949), a gypsum mine and factory (Gouldner, 1954), government employment and regulatory agencies (Blau, 1955), and a union (Lipset, et al., 1956)—are well-known instances of this attention. Many of the early writers couched their descriptions in prescriptive terms (Weber's ideal-type bureaucracy is a case in point), and proceeded to deal with other matters, such as worker satisfaction and informal communication patterns.

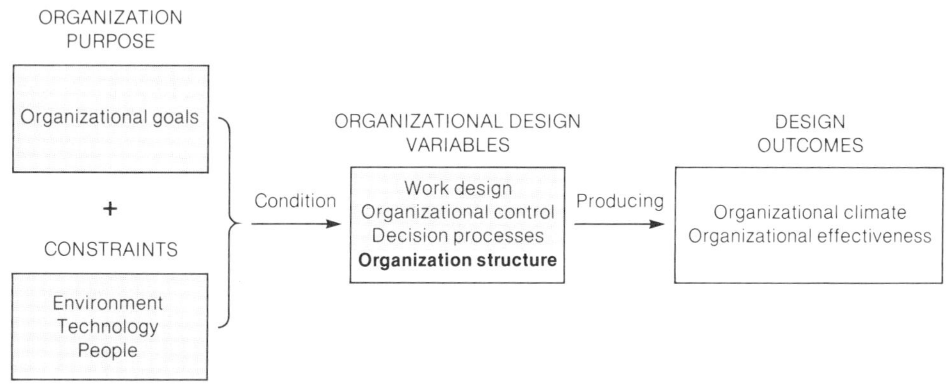

MAJOR TRENDS

Following the work of the early analysts, there developed two major trends in the conceptual and empirical treatment of structure (Scott, 1975: 2–3). First, structure became viewed as a dependent variable, a property that varies from situation to situation. That is, instead of seeing structure as an independent variable—a given, as it were—scholars and researchers started treating it as an outcome, one whose variation needs explaining. This trend was catalyzed in large part by the work of Udy (1959; 1962).

The second trend in the study of structure reflected a larger shift in organizational analysis. Specifically, general systems theory began finding its way into the study of organizations. Building on the work of von Bertalanffy (1951), Boulding (1956), and others, organization analysts began developing a systems-theoretic model of the organization. Katz and Kahn (1966) and Thompson (1967) are probably as responsible as anyone for making such a model an explicit part of organizational analysis.

The importance of this latter trend cannot be overemphasized. Indeed, there is probably no modern work on organization that is not based, at least implicitly, on a systems view. The point for our concern, of course, is that the move to a general systems viewpoint allows us to see "organizational structures as selected and shaped by the actions of and transactions with salient environmental units" (Scott, 1975: 3). It is this systems-based idea that has led to our treating structure as an organization design variable.

Structure and Design

How is organization structure a design variable? To answer this question, we revert to the idea that organizations are social instruments—instruments designed to perform some function. How that instrument is shaped—how it is structured—depends on the function, as well as where, how, and with whom it is to be performed. In short, it depends on goals, environment, technology, and people.

In a sense, this chapter is a review of some ideas that have gone before. We found it necessary, for example, in investigating the nature and importance of organizational environment and technology, to show how they affect structure. The focus here, however, is specifically—rather than incidentally—on structural design. We begin, in these introductory remarks, by identifying the key elements involved in the construct.

In all of this chapter's discussion, you should remember two important aspects of structure: *differentiation* and *integration*. Put simply, organization designers must decide how best to divide labor—activities and resources; that is, how best to differentiate. They must also design organizational mechanisms for ensuring that the results of that divided-up labor come together in some common goal accomplishment. In other words, they must design mechanisms that integrate, thus facilitating a unity of effort among the different subunits.

ORGANIZATION STRUCTURE: WHAT IS IT?

Historically, structure has referred to the pattern of relationships among organizational members, tasks, and activities. In *A Modern Dictionary of Sociology*, Theodorson and Theodorson (1969: 287) define structure as "the rationally ordered systems of norms and roles governing the relationships of persons in groups or in specified social situations." More specifically, we can say this:

> *Organization structure is the organization's official arrangement of roles, authority relationships, and communication patterns.*

This arrangement is usually conceived as consisting of several dimensions—dimensions that are interdependent yet distinct.

Dimensions of Structure: Review

One of the earliest attempts to specify structural dimensions was that of Max Weber (1946). In describing his ideal organization form, "bureaucracy," he identified several characteristics (1946: 196–98):

1. *Hierarchy of authority.* This is the vertical chain of command, through which orders and information flow.
2. *Specified jurisdictions.* Each position-holder has an administrative "territory" to which his or her legitimate influence is limited.
3. *Formal rules.* The performance of both technical and administrative tasks is governed not by personal whim or caprice but by rules that apply impartially.
4. *Written records.* "The files" form a rational and consistent basis for performing both technical and administrative tasks.

Weber's sociological ideas about the ideal form of organization would have been found acceptable to the early writers on management and administrative theory. Lyndall Urwick, for instance, identified several managerial processes that depend on the following characteristics of organization structure:

1. *Scalar relationships.* This dimension is similar to Weber's hierarchy of authority.
2. *Specialization.* Technical tasks are divided into various functions, while administration specializes in "planning," rather than technical performance.
3. *Span of control.* This dimension governs the "shape" of the organization, referring to the number of subordinates one manager can oversee (Urwick comments, p. 52, "no human brain should attempt to supervise directly more than five, or at the worst, six other individuals whose work is interrelated").
4. *Line-staff.* This distinction was actually an attempt to design a structural vehicle ("staff") to assist managers in their work, particularly in acquiring and analyzing information.

Incidentally, it should be noted that the classicists were as much interested in the problem of coordination as they were in dividing up labor in a rational manner. Urwick (1937), just cited, spends a goodly portion—in fact, the majority—of his paper on coordination. Furthermore, Urwick's paper is contained in a book that is a basic source of classical thinking: *Papers on the Science of Administration* (Gulick and Urwick, 1937). That book, taking all eleven articles together, is devoted at least as much to examining ways of achieving unity of effort as it is to ways of dividing labor and responsibility. Thus the dual theme of differentiation and integration made explicit by Lawrence and Lorsch (1967a) has a long history.

A later systematic effort to identify basic structural dimensions was that of Derek Pugh and his colleagues at the University of Aston, in Birmingham, England. The Aston group began their research by identifying six characteristics of structure: specialization, standardization, formalization, centralization, configuration, and traditionalism (Pugh et al., 1968). After gathering data on these and other organizational properties, the researchers concluded that the structure of an organization can be described using the following four dimensions:

1. *Structuring of activities.* This dimension reflects the degree to which organizational activities are prescribed, or patterned.
2. *Concentration of authority.* One aspect of structure concerns the degree to which decision-making authority is distributed ("dispersed") throughout the organization.
3. *Line control of workflow.* This dimension reflects the degree to which control of the flow of work depends and rests not on impersonal means, such as rules or schedules, but in the hands of the operating personnel themselves and their immediate supervisors.
4. *Supportive component.* The final Aston dimension concerns the amount of organizational activities that support the primary production process. Clerical, transportation, and catering activities are typical examples.

Taken together, the four Aston dimensions convey more about the organization than previous attempts did. In particular, they suggest a dynamic quality—one missing in earlier descriptions. The dimensions reflect some critical aspects of organizational functioning. Authority relationships and the flow of work are especially notable.

The other recent major attempt to identify and specify structural dimensions has been that of Peter Blau and his Comparative Organization Research Program at the University of Chicago (now at Columbia University). That work produced an important book, *The Structure of Organizations* (Blau and Schoenherr, 1971), in which four distinct dimensions of structure are identified:

1. *Size.* Strictly speaking, of course, this is not a typical dimension of structure. Still, Blau and Schoenherr found that organization size is a social-structural characteristic that has great impact on other properties.
2. *Differentiation.* This dimension reflects the degree to which organizational labor, both technical and administrative, is divided.
3. *Standardization and formalization.* This dimension refers to the degree to which decision making is based on a detailed system of formalized procedures.
4. *Administrative component.* Blau and Schoenherr's dimension is conceptually (if not operationally) similar to the Aston group's "supportive component."

DIVISION OF LABOR: DIMENSIONS FOR DESIGN

There are two likely ways to react to the above discussion. One way is to throw up our hands (figuratively speaking, of course) and say "it's the same story—ask four organization/management theorists a question (like what are the dimensions of organization structure) and you get four different answers." The other reaction is to conclude that although the vocabulary of the four approaches above varies somewhat, the messages are similar.

Frankly, we like the second interpretation. Even though many of the labels differ, all of the analysts are treating structure similarly, as a pattern of relationships governing the performance of organizational roles. They all see structure as involving the degree to which tasks are divided into specialized activities, the degree to which formal rules govern the performance of those tasks, the degree to which authority is concentrated or distributed in the organization, and the shape or configuration of the enterprise. Accordingly, for our purposes we will identify the following structural-design dimensions: complexity, specialization, formalization/standardization, and centralization. Each is described as follows.

Complexity

Complexity is referred to by many authors as meaning internal segmentation of jobs within an organization. Hage (1965), for instance, defines complexity as the number of occupational specialties and the amount of training required by each. However, this view looks at only one aspect of complexity—specialization (more about this in a moment). A broader approach is taken by the Aston group (Pugh et al., 1968). They use the term *configuration* in their discussion of complexity. Components of configuration are vertical levels of management and lateral spans of control.

While Pugh et al. discuss complexity in terms of shape, it must be kept in mind that "shape" explains neither the degree of authority a manager has over a subordinate nor the interactions between people in different parts of the organization.[1] At best, configuration will show some indication of the hierarchical nature of positions and indicate the major activities performed.

In the following discussion, therefore, we will examine three aspects of structural complexity.

a. Horizontal differentiation
b. Vertical differentiation
c. Span of control

Horizontal Differentiation

Horizontal differentiation refers to the degree to which technical labor—labor involved in the production of the organization's output—is divided. The usual index of horizontal differentiation is the number of major divisions or departments within the organization. Following this approach, there are basically two ways such labor is divided:

> The first way is to give highly trained specialists a rather comprehensive range of activities to perform, and the second is to minutely subdivide the tasks so that nonspecialists can perform them. The first approach is exemplified by the professional. . . . He is given the responsibility and the authority to carry out the task to its completion. The second form . . . is most plainly seen on the assembly line, where each worker performs only one or a few repetitive tasks. The nature of the task itself is important here, since it is the routine and uniform task that is most amenable to the second type of differentiation; nonroutine and quite varied tasks are more commonly subdivided according to the first type. [Hall, 1977: 132–33]

1. On this subject, see Landsberger (1961), Strauss (1962), and Sayles (1964). For a review, see Hall and Leidecker (1978).

Vertical Differentiation

Most organizations are designed in such a way that a hierarchy of positions is created; one position is defined as having the authority to control another. Supervisory position, for example, is defined as having more authority than that of a worker, and, accordingly, sanctioning powers are attached to the position. Supervisors may be allowed to evaluate the work of their subordinates, determining by these evaluations who receives what rate of pay and who is to be recommended for promotion. An organizational hierarchy presumes a graded distribution of authority from lower to higher officials, with authority increasing as scope of responsibility is enlarged.

In essence, vertical differentiation indicates the above. Thus we see Pugh et al. (1968: 78) suggest that vertical differentiation can be measured by a "count of the number of job positions between the chief executive and the employees working on the output." In short, vertical differentiation refers to the degree to which administrative labor—labor involved in the management of the enterprise—is divided. The usual index of this division is the number of managerial levels the organization contains. Thus most measures of this dimension describe the depth of the organizational hierarchy.

Span of Control

Span of control is a basic building block of hierarchy (Haimann et al., 1978: 130–31). The concept relates to the number of subordinates a manager can effectively supervise.

The span concept directs attention to the complexity of human and functional interrelationships in an organization. The number of interrelationships among individuals grows at a rapid pace when people are added to a department. Thus there are obviously limitations to the number of subordinates one person can effectively control (Graicunas, 1937).[2] Furthermore, span of control also has significance in terms of shape of the organization that evolves through growth. If each manager controls few people (low horizontal differentiation), there will be many levels (high vertical differentiation) in the organization. If the span is narrow, there will be few levels.

Specialization

Specialization has been described in various ways. However, instead of clarifying, these attempts have often confused the issue. Let us resolve the confusion by presenting two typical attempts, and then a unifying third.

The Aston group (Pugh et al., 1963) defines specialization as the manner in which labor and duties are divided and dispersed within the organization. Specialization is thus seen as a result of the division of labor. In this definition, specialization is divided into specialization of *tasks* and specialization of *roles*. Specialization of tasks occurs if a specific person is assigned a particular task to perform on a full-time basis. Role specialization implies the narrowness with which the role is defined. Specialization, in this view, involves increasingly simplified and subdivided tasks and roles.

A different view of specialization is also popular (Hage, 1965). Hage maintains that specialization increases as the number of specialties within the organization increases. This

2. Recall Graicunas' formula $R = n(\frac{2^n}{2} + n - 1)$, where R equals all types of relationships that might concern a manager, and n is the number of that manager's subordinates.

would agree with the Aston definition. Hage, however, goes on to state that the degree of specialization is also dependent on the amount of training required to perform the tasks of the specialties. By this definition specialization implies professional skills, a view dissimilar from that of the Aston group.

The dissimilarity in these two approaches arises from the failure to distinguish between the two means of division of labor. Organizational tasks may be divided into increasingly simplified subtasks. These subtasks may be performed by unskilled labor. This form of division of labor is consistent with a routine technology. If the tasks are complex, they may be divided among members with professional skills. The former case is consistent with the Aston approach; the latter with Hage's.

Tyler (1973) addresses this discrepancy and proposes a unifying definition. He refers to two forms of specialization: task specialization and personal specialization. These two forms of specialization are seen as independent variables, illustrated in Figure 10–1. Tyler combines the two forms into a single dimension, which he terms *role variety*. Role variety is defined as "the number of completely dissimilar occupational categories in the organization" (Tyler, 1973: 385), where high dissimilarity means roles are not very interchangeable. An organization composed of many noninterchangeable roles, such as engineering project teams (cell 1), would be said to exhibit a high degree of specialization. On the other hand, organizations whose members perform relatively routine tasks (cell 3) may well have a high degree of task specialization, owing to the work's narrow scope. Personal specialization—that based on education, training, and experience—will be low: tasks (roles) are relatively interchangeable.

In short, the dimension of organization structure called *specialization* is really a dual dimension. It concerns both the task itself and the individual performing it. Conveniently, however, Tyler (1973) has shown that the degree of role variety captures the essence of this dimension.

Formalization/Standardization

The repetition of routine tasks is a frequent occurrence in many organizations. As we saw in Chapter 9, the organizational response is to design programmed behavior (Simon, 1960b). This process is known as *formalization*, or *standardization*.

In its essence, formalization is the means by which an organization determines the conditions (how, when, and by whom) under which tasks are to be performed. As such,

Personal Specialization	Task Specialization: High	Task Specialization: Low
High	1. Project teams	2. Professional agencies
Low	3. Routine organizations	4. Amorphous organizations

Figure 10-1. Classification of organizations by types of specialization

formalization involves two things: 1. the degree to which rules and regulations governing people's behavior exist; and 2. the degree to which they are enforced. Such rules and regulations can, of course, be in written or unwritten form.

Centralization

Put simply, centralization is the degree to which members participate in decision making; the concept refers to "the loci of authority to make decisions affecting the organization" (Pugh et al., 1963: 289). For simplicity, let us use two factors that are involved in centralization:

a. The location of the actual decision-making function at particular points in the authority structure
b. The promulgation of rules for decisions, which limit the discretion of subordinates

Location of Decision Making

Complete centralization of an organization consists of having a single member make and carry out all decisions and determine all coordination. Any departure from this constitutes some degree of decentralization. Rule by members of a committee is not as centralized as rule by a single individual. Again, however, we must remember that centralization/decentralization are ideal states. They are conditions that are not attained—indeed they are unattainable. As Levy (1966: 16–17) puts it:

> No organization ever reaches the point at which the action of its members is completely centralized or completely decentralized. A completely decentralized organization would lack all structure of organization or coordination.

On the other hand, as we discussed in Chapter 9, the limits of rationality are such that a completely centralized organization would be operationally—if not theoretically—impossible.

A structural view of centralization may be taken from Meyer (1968: 215), who measured the dimension by degree of horizontal and vertical differentiation. The implication is that the greater the number of subunits (horizontal differentiation of tasks) in an organization, the greater the extent to which authority is centralized in the head of the organization. By the other scale, increasing the "vertical division of labor . . . necessitates decentralization of authority and its distribution throughout an organization" (Meyer, 1968: 214). The thought behind this view is : when administrative authority is centralized in few positions, managing is carried out largely by a central headquarters that issues directives to the operating staff. Otherwise, in a structure with a large proportion of authority positions, managing entails more reciprocal adjustments because of the greater opportunity—and requirement—for communication between managerial and operating personnel. In short, "few managers imply a centralized authority structure, which encourages management through one-sided directives with little feedback from operating levels, thus reducing the autonomy of subordinates" (Blau, 1968: 458).

Therefore, horizontal differentiation tends to centralize decisions in the head of the department. By contrast, vertical differentiation is associated with delegation of authority to lower levels. The two differentiation dimensions thus have opposite consequences for the centralization of decision-making authority.

Promulgation of Rules

In their functional essence, rules comprise a substitute for direct, personally given orders. Like personal orders, rules specify workers' obligations by directing them to do particular things in definite ways. Usually, rules are given more deliberation than personal orders and thus tend to be more carefully expressed. Obligations that they impose therefore tend to be less ambiguous than a hastily worded personal command. Considered in this light, rules are a form of communication that first, make explicit workers' tasks and second, shape and specify subordinate-manager relationships.

A rule that concentrates authority in a manager might state that "promotions are made solely by the manager." On the other hand, a rule that removes authority from the supervisory structure might state that "promotions are based on examination scores." In short, regulations can serve to centralize authority in the managerial hierarchy, or they can remove decisions from the hierarchy.

Summary

Several researchers have attempted to identify and specify properties that comprise the structure of organizations. These attempts have ranged from the early works of the classicists, represented by Weber (1946) and Urwick (1937), to more recent efforts, specifically those of the Aston group (Pugh et al., 1968) and Blau (Blau and Schoenherr, 1971; also see Blau, 1970). Table 10–1 summarizes the dimensions identified by each. We have combined these attempts into four dimensions: complexity, specialization, formalization, and centralization.

The Readings

This chapter contains two articles that discuss the design of organization structure. In the first, "Matrix Organization Designs: How to Combine Functional and Project Forms," Jay Galbraith discusses structural changes undergone by a hypothetical firm, "The Standard Products Co." As the company experienced various changes, especially in the marketplace, it became obvious to its managers that the firm would require new procedures, coordinating devices, communication channels, and so forth. In short, Standard Products would require a new structural form to deal with its changed situation. Galbraith traces these structural changes, explaining the bases for them. A matrix structure emerges as the culmination of the evolution process.

TABLE 10–1 DIMENSIONS OF ORGANIZATION STRUCTURE IDENTIFIED BY FOUR ANALYSES

Max Weber *Bureaucracy* (1946)	Lyndall Urwick *Organization as a Technical Problem* (1937)	Aston group (Pugh et al., 1968)	Peter Blau (1970; Blau and Schoenherr, 1971)
1. Hierarchy of authority	1. Scalar relationships	1. Structuring of activities	1. Size
2. Specified jurisdictions	2. Specialization of labor	2. Concentration of authority	2. Differentiation of labor (horizontal and vertical)
3. Written records	3. Span of control	3. Line control of workflow	3. Standardization and formalization
4. Formal rules	4. Line-staff distinctions	4. Supportive components	4. Administrative component

In the second article, "New Management Job: The Integrator," Paul Lawrence and Jay Lorsch report some design implications of their well-known research (Lawrence and Lorsch, 1967b). They put the matter simply:

> Because of the rapid rate of market and technological change, with the accompanying strains and stresses on existing organizational forms, managers are becoming increasingly concerned with the difficulty of reconciling the need for specialization with the need for integration of effort.

The authors suggest that the solution to this problem is to create specific managerial roles whose primary focus is "integration." The form of such roles would vary, of course, depending on the various environmental and technological factors that a particular organization faces. The integrator role may be filled by a single individual, or it may require a whole department. Lawrence and Lorsch discuss the criteria for deciding the form of such a role, plus the characteristics integration activities should have.

Conclusion

Taken together, the articles in this chapter explore two main questions:

1. How, given the state of the several design constraints, should organizational activities and resources be differentiated; that is, divided up?
2. What kinds of mechanisms should be designed so as to integrate, or coordinate, those differentiated activities and resources?

MATRIX ORGANIZATION DESIGNS: HOW TO COMBINE FUNCTIONAL AND PROJECT FORMS

JAY R. GALBRAITH

Each era of management evolves new forms of organization as new problems are encountered. Earlier generations of managers invented the centralized functional form, the line-staff form, and the decentralized product division structure as a response to increasing size and complexity of tasks. The current generation of management has developed two new forms as a response to high technology. The first is the free-form conglomerate; the other is the matrix organization, which was developed primarily in the aerospace industry.

The matrix organization grows out of the organizational choice between project and functional forms, although it is not limited to those bases of the authority structure (Mee, 1964). Research in the behavioral sciences now permits a detailing of the choices among the alternate intermediate forms between the project and functional extremes. Detailing such a choice is necessary since many businessmen see their organizations facing situations in the 1970s that are similar to those faced by the aerospace firms in the 1960s. As a result, a great many unanswered questions arise concerning the use of the matrix organization. For example, what are the various kinds of matrix designs, what is the difference between the designs, how do they work, and how do I choose a design that is appropriate for my organization?

The problem of designing organizations arises from the choices available among alternative bases of the authority structure. The most common alternatives are to group together activities which bear on a common product, common customer, common geographic area, common business function (marketing, engineering, manufacturing, and so on), or common process (forging, stamping, machining, and so on). Each of these bases has various costs and economies associated with it. For example, the functional structure facilitates the acquisition of specialized inputs. It permits the hiring of an electromechanical and an electronics engineer rather than two electrical engineers. It minimizes the number necessary by pooling specialized resources and time sharing them across products or projects. It provides career paths for specialists. Therefore, the organization can hire, utilize, and retain specialists.

These capabilities are neccessary if the organization is going to develop high technology products. However, the tasks that the organization must perform require varying amounts of the specialized resources applied in varying sequences. The problem of simultaneously completing all tasks on time, with appropriate quality and while fully utilizing all specialist resources, is all but impossible in the functional structure. It requires either fantastic amounts of information or long lead times for task completion.

The product or project form of organization has exactly the opposite set of benefits and costs. It facilitates coordination among specialties to achieve on-time completion and to meet budget targets. It allows a quick reaction capability to tackle problems that develop in one specialty, thereby reducing the impact on other specialties. However, if the organization has two projects, each requiring one half-time electronics engineer and one half-time electromechanical engineer, the pure project organization must either hire two electrical engineers—and reduce specialization—or hire four engineers (two electronics and two electromechanical)—and incur duplication costs. In addition, no one is responsible for long-run technical development of the specialties. Thus, each form of organization has its own set of advantages and disadvantages. A similar analysis could be applied to geographically or client-based structures.

The problem is that when one basis of organization is chosen, the benefits of the others are surrendered. If

Jay R. Galbraith, "Matrix Organization Designs: How to Combine Functional and Project Forms," *Business Horizons,* 14, no.1 (February 1971) pp. 29–40.

the functional structure is adopted, the technologies are developed but the projects fall behind schedule. If the project organization is chosen, there is better cost and schedule performance but the technologies are not developed as well. In the past, managers made a judgment as to whether technical development or schedule completion was more important and chose the appropriate form.

However, in the 1960s with a space race and missile gap, the aerospace firms were faced with a situation where both technical performance and coordination were important. The result was the matrix design, which attempts to achieve the benefits of both forms. However, the matrix carries some costs of its own. A study of the development of a matrix design is contained in the history of The Standard Products Co., a hypothetical company that has changed its form of organization from a functional structure to a matrix.

A COMPANY CHANGES FORMS

The Standard Products Co. has competed effectively for a number of years by offering a varied line of products that were sold to other organizations. Standard produced and sold its products through a functional organization like the one represented in Figure 10–2. A moderate number of changes in the product line and production processes were made each year. Therefore, a major management problem was to coordinate the flow of work from engineering through marketing. The coordination was achieved through several integrating mechanisms:

Rules and procedures—One of the ways to constrain behavior in order to achieve an integrated pattern is to specify rules and procedures. If all personnel follow the rules, the resultant behavior is integrated without having to maintain on-going communication. Rules are used for the most predictable and repetitive activities.

Planning processes—For less repetitive activities, Standard does not specify the procedure to be used but specifies a goal or target to be achieved, and lets the individual choose the procedure appropriate to the goal. Therefore, processes are undertaken to elaborate schedules and budgets. The usefulness of plans and rules is that they reduce the need for on-going communication between specialized subunits.

Hierarchical referral—When situations are encountered for which there are no rules or when problems cause the goals to be exceeded, these situations are referred upward in the hierarchy for resolution. This is the standard management-by-exception principle. This resolves the nonroutine and unpredictable events that all organizations encounter.

Direct contact—In order to prevent top executives from becoming overloaded with problems, as many

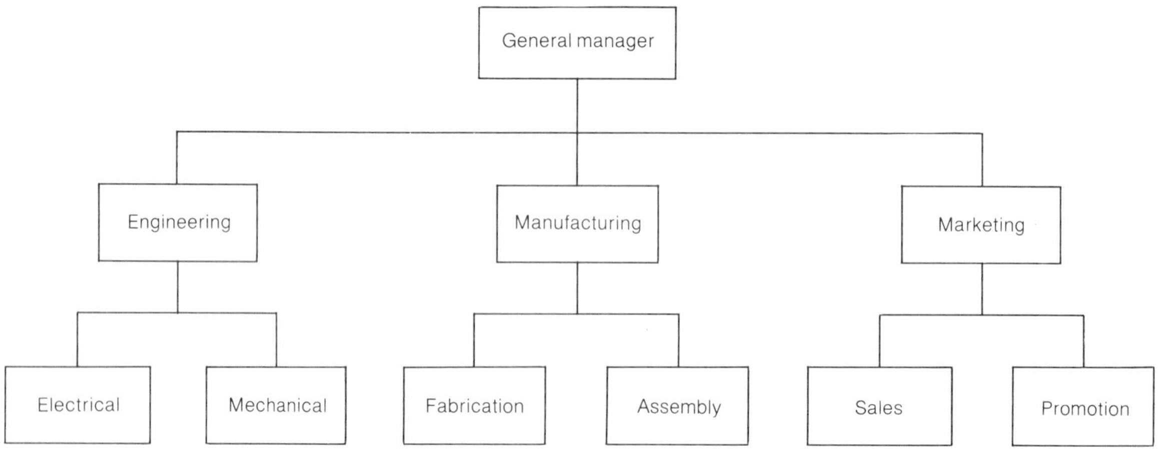

Figure 10-2. Standard's functional organization

problems as possible are resolved by the affected managers at low levels by informal contacts. These remove small problems from the upward referral process.

Liaison departments—In some cases, where there is a large volume of contacts between two departments, a liaison department evolves to handle the transactions. This typically occurs between engineering and manufacturing in order to handle engineering changes and design problems.[1]

The Standard Products Co. utilized these mechanisms to integrate the functionally organized specialties. They were effective in the sense that Standard could respond to changes in the market with new products on a timely basis, the new products were completed on schedule and within budget, and the executives had sufficient time to devote to long-range planning.

Matrix Begins Evolution

A few years ago, a significant change occurred in the market for one of Standard's major product lines. A competitor came out with a new design utilizing an entirely new raw material. The initial success caused Standard to react by developing one of their own incorporating the new material. They hired some specialists in the area and began their normal new product introduction activities. However, this time the product began to fall behind schedule, and it appeared that the product would arrive on the market at a time later than planned. In response, the general manager called a meeting to analyze the situation.

Task Force. After a briefing, it was obvious to the general manager and the directors of the three functions what was happening. Standard's lack of experience with the new material had caused them to underestimate the number and kinds of problems. The uncertainty led to a deterioration in usefulness of plans and schedules. The problems affected all functions, which meant that informal contacts and liaison processes were cumbersome; therefore, the majority of the problems were referred upward. This led to overloads on the directors of the functions and the general manager, which in turn added to the delays. Thus, the new situation required more decision making and more information processing than the current organization could provide.

The directors of engineering and manufacturing suggested that the cause of the problem was an overly ambitious schedule. More time should have been allowed for the new product; if realistic schedules were set, the current coordination processes would be adequate. They proposed that the schedules be adjusted by adding three to six months to the current due dates, which would allow more time to make the necessary decisions.

The director of marketing objected, reporting that the company would lose a good percentage of the market if the introduction was delayed. A number of big customers were waiting for Standard's version of the new product, and a delay would cost the company some of these customers. The general manager agreed with the marketing director. He proposed that they should not change the schedule to fit their current coordination processes, but that they could introduce some new coordination mechanisms to meet the scheduled due dates.

The group agreed with the general manager's position and began to search for alternative solutions. One of the solution requirements suggested was to reduce the distance between the sources of information and the points of decision. At this point the manufacturing director cautioned them about decentralizing decisions. He reminded them of previous experiences when decisions were made at low levels of the engineering organization. The data the decision makers had were current but they were also local in scope; severe problems in the manufacturing process resulted. When these decisions were centralized, the global perspective prevented these problems from developing. Therefore, they had to increase decision-making power at lower levels without losing the inputs of all affected units. The alternative that met both requirements was a group with representation from all the major departments to enter into joint decisions.

1. For a more detailed explanation, see Jay R. Galbraith, *Organization Design* (Reading, Mass.: Addison-Wesley Publishing Co., Inc., 1971).

The group was appointed and named the "new product task force." It was to last as long as cross-functional problems occurred on the new product introduction. The group was to meet and solve joint problems within the budget limits set by the general manager and the directors; problems requiring more budget went to the top management group. The purpose was to make as many decisions as possible at low levels with the people most knowledgeable. This should reduce the delays and yet ensure that all the information inputs were considered.

The task force consisted of nine people; three, one from each function, were full-time and the others were part-time. They met at least every other day to discuss and resolve joint problems. Several difficulties caused them to shift membership. First, the engineering representatives were too high in the organization and, therefore, not knowledgeable about the technical alternatives and consequences. They were replaced with lower level people. The opposite occurred with respect to the manufacturing representatives. Quite often they did not have either information or the authority to commit the production organization to joint decisions made by the task force. They were replaced by higher level people. Eventually, the group had both the information and the authority to make good group decisions. The result was effective coordination: coordination = f (authority × information).

Creation of the task force was the correct solution. Decision delays were reduced, and collective action was achieved by the joint decisions. The product arrived on time, and the task force members returned to their regular duties.

Teams. No sooner had the product been introduced than salesmen began to bring back stories about new competitors. One was introducing a second-generation design based on improvements in the raw material. Since the customers were excited by its potential and the technical people thought it was feasible, Standard started a second-generation redesign across all its product lines. This time, they set up the task force structure in advance and committed themselves to an ambitious schedule.

Again the general manager became concerned. This time the product was not falling behind schedule, but in order to meet target dates the top management was drawn into day-to-day decisions on a continual basis. This was leaving very little time to think about the third-generation product line. Already Standard had to respond twice to changes initiated by others. It was time for a thorough strategy formulation. Indeed, the more rapid the change in technology and markets, the greater the amount of strategic decision making that is necessary. However, these are the same changes that pull top management into day-to-day decisions. The general manager again called a meeting to discuss and resolve the problem.

The solution requirements to the problem were the same as before. They had to find a way to push a greater number of decisions down to lower levels. At the same time, they had to guarantee that all interdependent subunits would be considered in the decision so that coordination would be maintained. The result was a more extensive use of joint decision making and shared responsibility.

The joint decision making was to take place through a team structure. The teams consisted of representatives of all functions and were formed around major product lines. There were two levels of teams, one at lower levels and another at the middle-management level. Each level had defined discretionary limits; problems that the lower level could not solve were referred to the middle-level team. If the middle level could not solve the problem, it went to top management. A greater number of day-to-day operating problems were thereby solved at lower levels of the hierarchy, freeing top management for long-range decisions.

The teams, unlike the task force, were permanent. New products were regarded as a fact of life, and the teams met on a continual basis to solve recurring interfunctional problems. Task forces were still used to solve temporary problems. In fact, all the coordination mechanisms of rules, plans, upward referrral, direct contact, liaison men, and task forces were used, in addition to the teams.

Product Managers. The team structure achieved interfunctional coordination and permitted top management to step out of day-to-day decision making. However, the teams were not uniformly effective. Standard's strategy required the addition of highly skilled, highly educated technical people to continue to innovate and compete in the high technology industry. Sometimes these specialists would dominate a team because of their superior technical knowledge. That is, the team could not distinguish between providing technical information and supplying managerial judgment after all the facts were identified. In addition, the specialists' personalities were different from the personalities of the other team members, which made the problem of conflict resolution much more difficult (Lawrence and Lorsch, 1967a).

Reports of these problems began to reach the general manager, who realized that a great number of decisions of consequence were being made at lower and middle levels of management. He also knew that they should be made with a general manager's perspective. This depends on having the necessary information and a reasonable balance of power among the joint decision makers. Now the technical people were upsetting the power balance because others could not challenge them on technical matters. As a result, the general manager chose three technically qualified men and made them product managers in charge of the three major product lines (Lawrence and Lorsch, 1967b). They were to act as chairmen of the product team meetings and generally facilitate the interfunctional decision making.

Since these men had no formal authority, they had to resort to their technical competence and their interpersonal skills in order to be effective. The fact that they reported to the general manager gave them some additional power. These men were successful in bringing the global, general manager perspective lower in the organization to improve the joint decision-making process.

The need for this role was necessitated by the increasing differences in attitudes and goals among the technical, production, and marketing team participants. These differences are necessary for successful subtask performance but interfere with team collaboration. The product manager allows collaboration without reducing these necessary differences. The cost is the additional overhead for the product management salaries.

Product Management Departments. Standard Products was now successfully following a strategy of new product innovation and introduction. It was leading the industry in changes in technology and products. As the number of new products increased, so did the amount of decision making around product considerations. The frequent needs for trade-offs across engineering, production, and marketing lines increased the influence of the product managers. It was not that the functional managers lost influence; rather, it was the increase in decisions relating to products.

The increase in the influence of the product managers was revealed in several ways. First, their salaries became substantial. Second, they began to have a greater voice in the budgeting process, starting with approval of functional budgets relating to their products. The next change was an accumulation of staff around the products, which became product departments with considerable influence.

At Standard this came about with the increase in new product introductions. A lack of information developed concerning product costs and revenues for addition, deletion, modification, and pricing decisions. The general manager instituted a new information system that reported costs and revenues by product as well as by function. This gave product managers the need for a staff and a basis for more effective interfunctional collaboration.

In establishing the product departments, the general manager resisted requests from the product managers to reorganize around product divisions. While he agreed with their analysis that better coordination was needed across functions and for more effective product decision making, he was unwilling to take the chance that this move might reduce specialization in the technical areas or perhaps lose the economies of scale in production. He felt that a modification of the information system to report on a product and a functional basis along with a product staff group would provide the means for more coordination. He still needed the effective technical group to drive the innovative process. The general manager also maintained a climate where collaboration across product lines and functions was encouraged and rewarded.

The Matrix Completed

By now Standard Products was a high technology company; its products were undergoing constant change. The uncertainty brought about by the new technology and the new products required an enormous amount of decision making to plan-replan all the schedules, budgets, designs, and so on. As a result, the number of decisions and the number of consequential decisions made at low levels increased considerably. This brought on two concerns for the general manager and top management.

The first was the old concern for the quality of decisions made at low levels of the organization. The product managers helped solve this at middle and top levels, but their influence did not reach low into the organization where a considerable number of decisions were made jointly. They were not always made in the best interest of the firm as a whole. The product managers again recommended a move to product divisions to give these low-level decisions the proper product orientation.

The director of engineering objected, using the second problem to back up his objection. He said the move to product divisions would reduce the influence of the technical people at a time when they were having morale and turnover problems with these employees. The increase in joint decisions at low levels meant that these technical people were spending a lot of time in meetings. Their technical input was not always needed, and they preferred to work on technical problems, not product problems. Their dissatisfaction would only be aggravated by a change to product divisions.

The top management group recognized both of these problems. They needed more product orientation at low levels, and they needed to improve the morale of the technical people whose inputs were needed for product innovations. Their solution involved the creation of a new role—that of subproduct manager (Lorsch, 1971). The subproduct manager would be chosen from the functional organization and would represent the product line within the function. He would report to both the functional manager and the product manager, thereby creating a dual authority structure. The addition of a reporting relation on the product side increases the amount of product influence at lower levels.

The addition of the subproduct manager was intended to solve the morale problem also. Because he would participate in the product team meetings, the technical people did not need to be present. The subproduct manager would participate on the teams but would call on the technical experts within his department as they were needed. This permitted the functional department to be represented by the subproduct manager, and the technical people to concentrate on strictly technical matters.

Standard Products has now moved to a pure matrix organization as indicated in Figure 10–3. The pure matrix organization is distinguished from the previous cross-functional forms by two features. *First*, the pure matrix has a dual authority relationship somewhere in the organization. *Second*, there is a power balance between the product management and functional sides. While equal power is an unachievable razor's edge, a reasonable balance can be obtained through enforced collaboration on budgets, salaries, dual information and reporting systems, and dual authority relations. Such a balance is required because the problems that the organization faces are uncertain and must be solved on their own merits—not on any predetermined power structure.

Thus over a period of time, the Standard Products Co. has changed from a functional organization to a pure matrix organization using dual authority relationships, product management departments, product teams at several levels, and temporary task forces. These additional decision-making mechanisms were added to cope with the change in products and technologies. The changes caused a good deal of uncertainty concerning resource allocations, budgets, and schedules. In the process of task execution, more was learned about the problem causing a need for rescheduling and rebudgeting. This required the processing of information and the making of decisions.

In order to increase its capacity to make product relevant decisions, Standard lowered the level at which decisions were made. Coordination was achieved by making joint decisions across functions. Product managers and subproduct managers were added to bring a general manager's perspective to bear on the joint decision-making processes. In addition, the information and reporting system was changed in order to provide reports by function and by product. Combined, these measures allowed Standard to achieve the

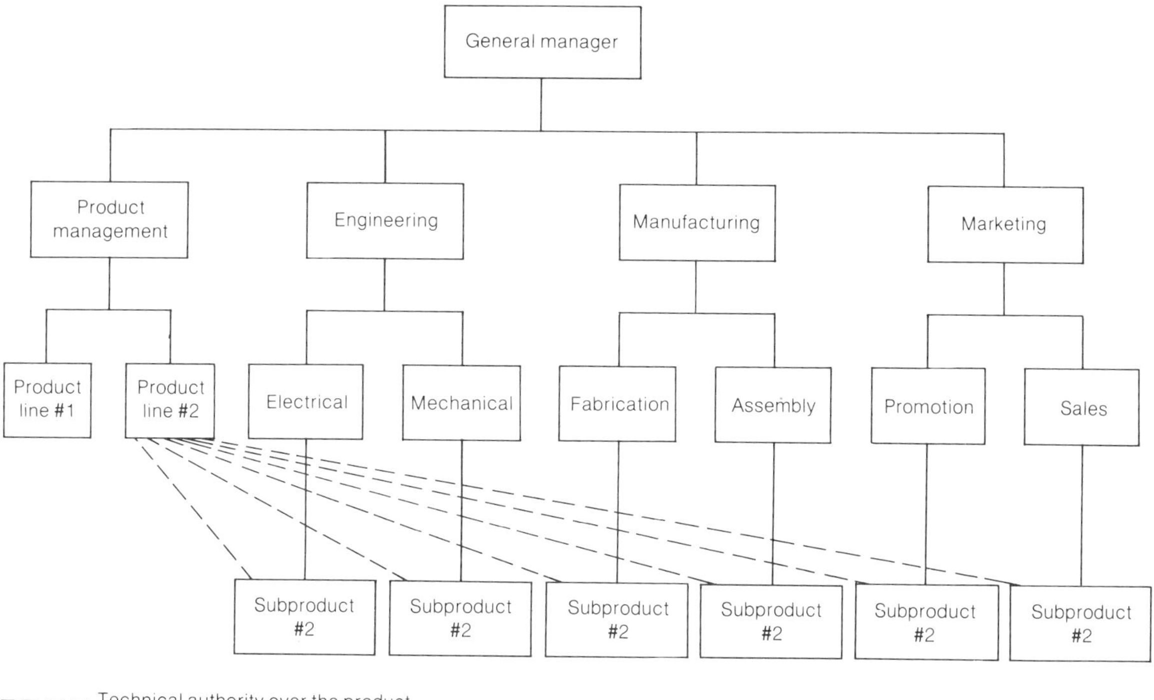

Figure 10-3. Standard's pure matrix organization

high levels of technical sophistication necessary to innovate products and simultaneously to get these products to the market quickly to maintain competitive position.

HOW DO I CHOOSE A DESIGN?

Not all organizations need a pure matrix organization with a dual authority relationship. Many, however, can benefit from some cross-functional forms to relieve top decision makers from day-to-day operations. If this is so, how does one choose the degree to which his organization should pursue lateral forms? To begin to answer this question, let us first lay out the alternatives, then list the choice determining factors.

The choice, shown in Figure 10–4, is indicated by the wide range of alternatives between a pure functional organization and a pure product organization with the matrix being half-way between. The Standard Products Co. could have evolved into a matrix from a product organization by adding functional teams and managers. Thus there is a continuum of organization designs between the functional and product forms. The design is specified by the choice among the authority structure; integrating mechanisms such as task forces, teams and so on; and by the formal information system. The way these are combined is illustrated in Figure 10–4. These design variables help regulate the relative distribution of influence between the product and functional considerations in the firm's operations.

The remaining factors determining influence are such things as roles in budget approvals, design changes, location and size of offices, salary, and so on. Thus there is a choice of integrating devices, authority structure, information system, and influence distribution. The factors that determine choice are diversity of the product line, the rate of change of the product line,

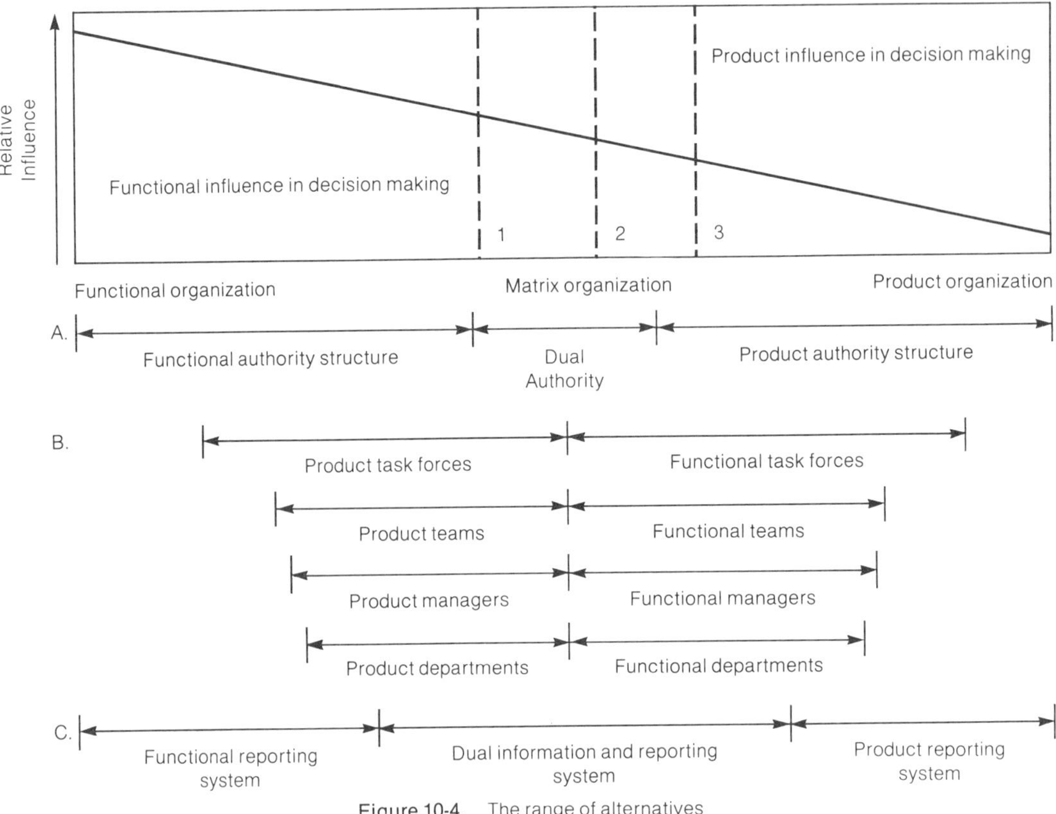

Figure 10-4. The range of alternatives

interdependencies among subunits, level of technology, presence of economies of scale, and organization size.

Product Lines

The greater the diversity among product lines and the greater the rate of change of products in the line the greater the pressure to move toward product structures.[2] When product lines become diverse, it becomes difficult for general managers and functional managers to maintain knowledge in all areas; the amount of information they must handle exceeds their capacity to absorb it. Similarly, the faster the rate of new product introduction, the more unfamiliar are the tasks being performed.

2. For product line diversity, see Alfred Chandler, *Strategy and Structure* (Cambridge, Mass.: The M.I.T. Press, 1962). For product change rate, see Tom Burns and G. M. Stalker, *Management and Innovation* (London: Tavistock Publications, 1958).

Managers are, therefore, less able to make precise estimates concerning resource allocations, schedules, and priorities. During the process of new product introduction, these same decisions are made repeatedly. The decisions concern trade-offs among engineering, manufacturing, and marketing. This means there must be greater product influence in the decision process. The effect of diversity and change is to create a force to locate the organization farther to the right in Figure 10–4.

Interdependence

The functional division of labor in organizations creates interdependencies among the specialized subunits. That is, a problem of action in one unit has a direct impact on the goal accomplishment of the other units. Organizations usually devise mechanisms that uncouple the subunits, such as in-process-inventory and order backlogs. The degree to which inventories and backlogs develop is a function of how tight the schedule is. If there is a little slack in the schedule, then the functional departments can resolve their own problems. However, if rapid response to market changes is a basis of competition, then schedules are squeezed and activities run in parallel rather than series (Galbraith, 1970). This means that problems in one unit directly affect another. The effect is a greater number of joint decisions involving engineering, manufacturing, and production. A greater need for product influence in these decisions arises due to the tight schedule. Thus the tighter the schedule, the greater the force to move to the right in Figure 10–4.

Although the tightness of the schedule is the most obvious source of interdependence, tight couplings can arise from reliability requirements and other design specifications. If the specifications require a more precise fit and operation of parts, then the groups designing and manufacturing the parts must also "fit and operate" more closely. This requires more coordination in the form of communication and decision making.

Level of Technology

If tight schedules and new products were the only forces operating, every organization would be organized around product lines. The level of technology or degree to which new technology is being used is a counteracting force. The use of new technologies requires expertise in the technical specialties in engineering, in production engineering, in manufacturing, and market research in marketing. Some of the expertise may be purchased outside the organization.

However, if the expertise is critical to competitive effectiveness, the organization must acquire it internally. If the organization is to make effective use of the expertise, the functional form of organization is superior, as described earlier in the article. Therefore the greater the need for expertise, the greater the force to move to the left in Figure 10–4.

Economies of Scale and Size

The other factor favoring a functional form is the degree to which expensive equipment in manufacturing, test facilities in engineering, warehousing facilities in marketing are used in producing and selling the product. (Warehousing introduces another dimension of organization structure, for example, geographical divisions. For our purposes, we will be concerned only with product and function dimensions.) It is usually more expensive to buy small facilities for product divisions than a few large ones for functional departments. The greater the economies of scale, the greater the force to move to the left in Figure 10–4. Mixed structures are always possible. That is, the capital intensive fabrication operation can organize along functional process lines, and the labor intensive assembly operation can organize along product lines.

The size of the organization is important in that it modifies the effect of expertise and economies of scale. That is, the greater the size of the organization the smaller the costs of lost specialization and lost economies of scale when the product form is adopted. Thus while size by itself has little effect on organization structure, it does moderate the effects of the previously mentioned factors.

The Choice

While research on organizations has not achieved a sophistication that would allow us to compute the results of the above factors and locate a point in Figure 10–4, we can still make our subjective weightings. In addition, we can locate our present position and make changes in the appropriate directions as product lines, schedules, technologies, and size change during the normal course of business. The framework provides some basis for planning the organization along with planning the strategy and resource allocations.

If the organization's present structure is on the left side of the figure, many of the symptoms occurring in the Standard Products example signal a need for a change. To what degree are communication overloads occurring? Are top executives being drawn into day-to-day decisions to the detriment of strategy development? How long does it take to get top level decisions made in order to continue work on new products? If the answers to these questions indicate an overload, then some movement toward a matrix is appropriate. Probably a sequence of moves until the bottlenecks disappear is the best strategy; this will allow for the proper attitudinal and behavioral changes to keep pace.

If the organization is product organized, then movements to the left toward a matrix are more subtle. They must be triggered by monitoring the respective technological environments.

An example from the aerospace industry may help. In the late fifties and early sixties the environment was characterized by the space race and missile gap. In this environment, technical performance and technology development were primary, and most firms adopted organizations characterized by the dotted line at "1" in Figure 10–4. The functional departments had the greatest influence on the decision-making process. During the McNamara era, they moved to point "2." The environment shifted to incentive contracts, PERT-cost systems, and increased importance of cost and schedule considerations.

Currently, the shift has continued toward point "3." Now the environment is characterized by tight budgets, a cost overrun on the C-5 project, and Proxmire hearings in the Senate. The result is greater influence by the project managers. All these have taken place in response to the changing character of the market. A few firms recently moved back toward point "2" in response to the decreasing size of some firms. The reduction in defense spending has resulted in cutbacks in projects and employment. In order to maintain technical capabilities with reduced size, these firms have formed functional departments under functional managers with line responsibility. These changes show how changes in need for expertise, goals, and size affect the organization design choice.

Many organizations are experiencing pressures that force them to consider various forms of matrix designs. The most common pressure is increased volume of new products. Organizations facing this situation must either adopt some form of matrix organization, change to product forms of organization, or increase the time between start and introduction of the new products process.

For most organizations, the matrix design is the most effective alternative. Managers must be aware of the different kinds of matrix designs and develop some basis for choosing among them.

NEW MANAGEMENT JOB: THE INTEGRATOR

PAUL R. LAWRENCE
AND JAY W. LORSCH

What will be new and unique about organizational structures and management practices of business enterprises that are their industries' competitive leaders a decade from now? Because of the rapid rate of market and technological change, with the accompanying strains and stresses on existing organizational forms, managers are becoming increasingly concerned with the difficulty of reconciling the need for specialization with the need for integration of effort.

Consequently, the purpose here is to explore this problem and to suggest that one of the critical organizational innovations will be the establishment of management positions, and even formal departments, charged with the task of achieving integration. Moreover, the integrative function will be on a par with such traditional functions as production, sales, research, and others.

That may seem to be a startling statement, particularly since we know of no organziation which has yet established a department—even a small one—formally labeled "integration."

However, before we can evaluate our prediction, we first need to define what we mean by the term *integration*. As used in this article, integration is the achievement of unity of effort among the major functional specialists in a business. The integrator's role involves handling the nonroutine, unprogrammed problems that arise among the traditional functions as each strives to do its own job. It involves resolving interdepartmental conflicts and facilitating decisions, including not only such major decisions as large capital investment but also the thousands of smaller ones regarding product features, quality standards, output, cost targets, schedules, and so on. Our definition reads much like the customary job description of any company general manager or divisional manager who has "line" authority over all the major functional departments.

Although the need for organizational integration is not new, the traditional method of using the "shared boss" as the integrator is rapidly breaking down, and a radically new approach is becoming necessary. The increasingly dynamic nature of many organizational environments is making the integrating job so important and so complex that it cannot be handled by a single general manager, no matter how capable he may be.

Substance can be added to our definition of integration by identifying some of the diverse titles under which this activity is currently being performed. In recent years there has been a rapid proliferation of such roles as product manager, brand manager, program coordinator, project leader, business manager, planning director, systems designer, task force chairman, and so forth. The fine print in the descriptions of these various management positions almost invariably describes the core function as that of integration, as we define it.

These new integrative assignments are joining some older ones, such as those carried on by production control people in resolving schedule conflicts between production and sales, and by budget officers in addressing interdepartmental conflicts around the allocation of capital and operating funds.

The emergence of these integrating jobs in considerable numbers now makes it practical to turn the spotlight of systematic research on them to learn how to manage them effectively. This article largely reports on the findings from our recent study, which answer four key questions about the management of the integrating function:

Paul R. Lawrence and Jay W. Lorsch, "New Management Job: The Integrator," *Harvard Business Review*, November–December 1967,

1. How should integrators be oriented and motivated?
2. What patterns of conflict resolution and influence should they employ?
3. What authority should they have, and how do they get it?
4. Who are the most qualified people for these positions?

To find answers to these questions, we have identified the characteristics of both the organizations and the people who are performing the integration task more effectively than others (1967c). But before turning directly to these questions, we first want to shed more light on the reasons for the present emergence of the integrative function.

EMERGING NEED

When modern large-scale corporations appeared in considerable numbers in the first two decades of this century, they developed around such basic production technologies as oil-refining, iron-steel conversion, and automobile assembly. At first, engineers and other production specialists played a dominant role. Since the very productivity of these firms generated a need for a predictable and controllable distribution system, in the 1920s and 1930s marketing experts came to the fore. Channels of distribution were built up in each industry, and the entire mix of product design, promotion, advertising, pricing, and so on, was elaborated. The boundaries between industries were still relatively clear, and the markets were reasonably predictable.

However, once the effects of the depression abated, the very success of the marketers helped provide consumers with an abundance of standard products that led to a demand for product differentiation. This demand, combined with the stimulus of the post-World War II period, force-fed the widespread emergence in the late 1940s and 1950s of research and development as a major industrial function.

Crucial Activity

Industrial R&D technology has already broken down the existing boundaries between industries. Once-stable markets and distribution channels are now in a state of flux. Product differentiation has parlayed into a welter of choices at every stage of the sequence from basic raw materials to ultimate consumer items. The industrial environment is turbulent and increasingly difficult to predict. Many complex facts about markets, production methods and costs, and scientific potentials for product and process improvement are relevant to investment decisions about these myriad product varieties.

All of these factors have combined to produce a king-size managerial headache: there are just too many crucial decisions to have them all processed and resolved through the regular line hierarchy at the top of the organization; they must be integrated in some other way.

The current importance of R&D groups in modern organizations is making the integrator's role crucial for another reason. Research has introduced into the corporation an entirely new set of people—namely, the scientists—who have their own unique way of being productive. They are specialists who work by a different clock and in a different style from hard-nosed production managers or outward-oriented sales managers. Management has learned, by and large, that these differences are necessary if each type of specialist is to do his job well. But, as these specialists diverge in their working styles, it becomes increasingly difficult to achieve the necessary integration. New roles have to be introduced to get the integration job done. Company after company is committing more and more managerial manpower, under any guise or rubric, to achieve collaboration between highly specialized people spread throughout all organizational functions and levels.

SURVEY FINDINGS

To this point in the discussion, we have demonstrated that integrative roles are needed and are being developed in many companies. In fact, our study of ten organizations in three distinctly different industries—plastics, consumer foods, and containers—provides dramatic evidence of the importance of effective integration in any industry. This is because our research reveals a close correlation between the effectiveness of integration among functional departments and company growth and profits. However, separate integrating roles or departments are not the solution for all organizations. While formal integrative roles are highly important in R&D-intensive industries, such as plastics and consumer food products, in a comparatively stable industry, such as containers, integration can often be achieved through the management hierarchy.

The important point is that in the future more organizations will be operating in rapidly changing environments, and the problem for managers will be to make certain that this integrative function is effectively carried out. In order to do this, they will need to learn how to select, train, organize, supervise, and control these new integrators.

Organization Structure

Two questions arise when we think of designing the structure of the organization to facilitate the work of integrators:

1. Is it better to establish a formal integration department, or simply to set up integrating positions independent of one another?
2. If individual integrating positions are set up, how should they be related to the larger structure?

In considering these issues it should first be pointed out that if an organization needs integrators at all, it is preferable to legitimize these roles by formal titles and missions rather than to leave them in an informal status. We derive the primary evidence on this point from an intensive study of an electronics company, where the limitations of using informal integrators are clearly revealed.[1] This research demonstrates that the effectiveness of the informal integrators is severely circumscribed when it comes to dealing with difficult interdepartmental relationships. Consider:

In this organization the boundaries between the production and engineering departments were not well established, and there was intense competition and conflict between these two groups. The informal integrators were unable to achieve effective collaboration, at least in part because their roles were not clearly defined. Therefore, their integrative attempts were often seen as inappropriate infringements on the domains of other departments.

For example, an engineering supervisor, whose own inclinations and interests led him to play a coordinating role between the two departments, was frequently rebuffed by the production personnel because he was seen as intruding into their activities. Without a clearly defined role, his integration efforts were limited to exchanging information across the interface of the two departments.

These data indicate that the more intense the problem of interdepartmental collaboration is, the more need there is for the integrative roles to be formally identified so that such activities are seen as legitimate.

The question of whether to establish independent integrative roles or to create a formal department is illuminated to a considerable extent by our data. Consider:

- In the plastics industry, which has the fastest rate of technical change of the three industries we studied, the basic departments (production, sales, and research) are the most highly specialized and differentiated. Five of the six plastics companies studied, including the one with the best integration record, have what could be called "full-scale integrating departments," although they are not formally labeled as such. (See Figure 10–5 for suggested structural solutions to the integration problem.)
- In the consumer foods industry, which has both a medium rate of technical change and a medium degree of difference between basic departments, one of the two companies studied uses a full-scale "integrating department"; the other—with the better integration record—simply utilizes a set of scattered integration roles.
- The container industry has the most stable technology; and thus only slight differences are perceptible between basic departments. In this industry the company with the best integration record has no formal integrators of any kind; it relies entirely on its regular line organization to do the coordinating. By contrast, a second container company, employing a full-fledged integrating department, has experienced considerable integrating difficulties. This suggests not only that the department is redundant, but that it actually impedes the coordination process.

1. Unpublished study conducted by John Seiler and Robert Katz for the Division of Research, Harvard Business School.

Stable and Homogeneous Environment

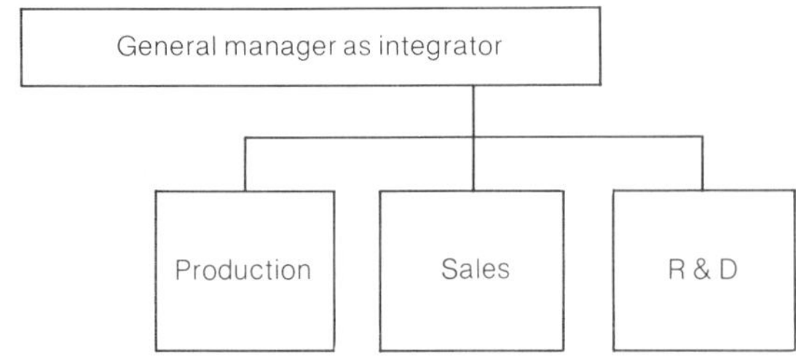

Semidynamic and Heterogeneous Environment

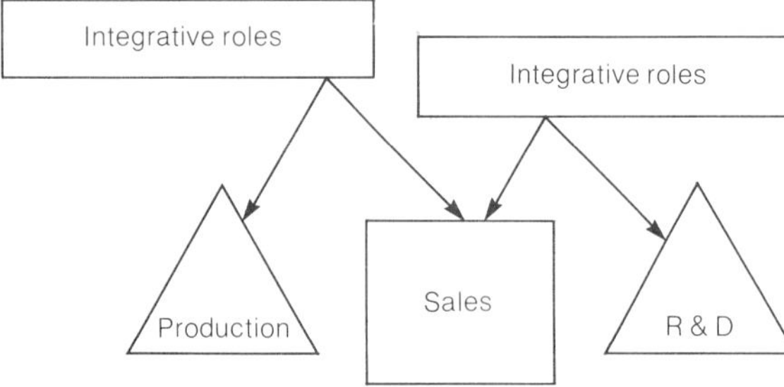

Highly Dynamic and Heterogeneous Environment

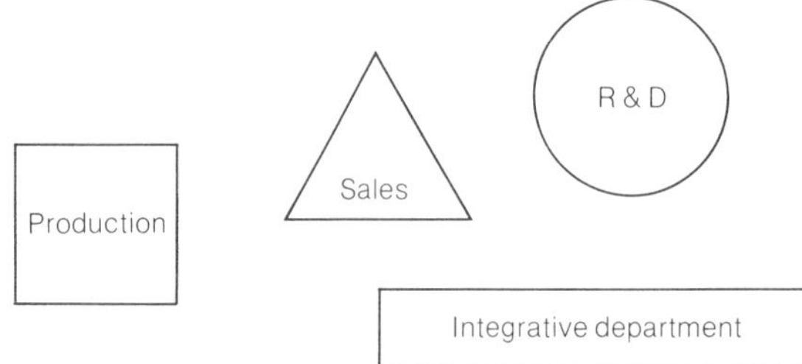

Figure 10-5. Structural solutions to the organizational integration problem

All of this evidence indicates that the elaborateness of the integrating function should vary both with the complexity of the problems and with the size of the gap that specialization creates between the basic departments. Moreover, management should keep in mind that it is possible to get too many integrators into the act as well as too few.

BEHAVIOR CHARACTERISTICS

Our research enables us to identify four important characteristics about the behavior of effective integrators, as well as the organizational practices that contribute to their effectiveness:

1. Integrators need to be seen as contributing to important decisions on the basis of their competence and knowledge, rather than on their positional authority.
2. Integrators must have balanced orientations and behavior patterns.
3. Integrators need to feel they are being rewarded for their total product responsibility, not solely on the basis of their performance as individuals.
4. Integrators must have a capacity for resolving interdepartmental conflicts and disputes.

Since these findings offer some important prescriptions about the behavior of effective integrators, let us examine each of these characteristics more closely.

Decision Contribution

One of the major and most frequently expressed dilemmas facing managers in integrating positions is whether they are able to contribute to important decisions. An integrator interviewed in our study expressed this common concern:

> My key frustration is that I do not have the authority over the people I must deal with. I cannot yell at the research guy. I have to try to influence him by being persuasive. My major tool is strictly my personality.

Although this integrator, like many of his colleagues, complains that he does not have formal authority over the other groups with whom he works, our measures of actual influence on decisions in the organizations studied indicate that all integrators, except for those in the less well-integrated container company, have a larger voice in interdepartmental decisions than their peers in functional departments. And their influence is essential in industries requiring highly specialized and well-integrated organizations, where the integrator must often initiate activities for managers in other departments.

Personal Competence. There is another important factor related to influence that distinguishes the integrators in effective organizations from those in less effective ones. In the more effective, the integrators are influential because of their knowledge and expertise, while in less effective organizations they are influential only because of the formal authority of their positions.

In the well-integrated organizations, the functional managers described the influence of the integrators (although, again, they did not always call them integrators) in comments such as these:

> He [the integrator] has a powerful job if he can get the people to work for him. A good man in that job has everybody's ear open to him. A good coordinator has to be thoroughly oriented to his market or to his process. Whichever area he is working in, he has to be able to make good value judgments.

> They [the integrators] are the kingpins. They have a good feel for our [research] ability, and they know the needs of the market. They will work back and forth with us and the others.

> They [the integrators] are on the border of research, so we work closely together. They are just a step away from the customer, so when I make a change in a material, I let them know, because they may have a customer who can use it. The good thing about our situation is that they are close enough to sales to know what they are doing and close enough to research to know what we are doing.

These and similar comments indicate that the managers in effectively integrated organizations view the integrators as persons who have knowledge of and expertise in solving organizational problems. This personal competence appears to be the foundation on which their large voice in interdepartmental decisions rests.

Positional Power. In the organizations that were having difficulty in achieving integration, the tone of the functional managers' commentaries on the influence of the integrators was quite different:

> We [in research] have to go by what they [the integrators] say. They have the upper hand. And if we can't get their approval, we have to shut up.

> Nobody wants to pull the wool over his [the integrator's] eyes, since he reports to the general manager. That would be disastrous . . . I don't think anybody could be in that role and have many friends. You have to be too aggressive.

> He [the integrator] is supposed to know the field, and he may think our product isn't any good. This is fine if you have confidence in him, but we have had bad experiences with some of them. As the knowledge of chemistry grows, his [the integrator's] knowledge of the market must grow. I guess I would appraise the situation this way: just because they [the integrators] have had twenty years' experience doesn't mean they have twenty years of knowledge.

Comments like these suggest that the integrators in organizations having integration problems were influential only because of the formal authority given to them by the top management and because of their proximity to top management. Other responses stressed that generally the integrators in these companies were considered less knowledgeable about industry conditions. Moreover, the specialist managers frequently volunteered disparaging remarks about the integrators' abilities and knowledge.

Other Factors. In planning for these integrating positions, attention must be given to placing them at levels in the organization where the incumbents will have ready access to the knowledge and information relevant to decisions. In the well-integrated organizations we studied, for example, this level was usually at the middle of the management hierarchy. Since these organizations were in dynamic, rapidly changing industries where knowledge was complex and uncertain, only those middle managers with specific problem experience had been able to master the required knowledge.

If the integrator selected has had prior work experience in two or more of the several functional departments, the specialist managers will regard him as competent because of the knowledge that his experience has provided. While persons with these ideal qualifications may be extremely scarce, it is important to recognize the necessity of finding integrators with broad knowledge to fill these crucial positions. One common failing of the less well-integrated organizations is their tendency to assign young managers lacking sufficient experience in all facets of the business to these positions. Although this may provide a useful learning experience for the young managers, our evidence suggests that it really does not lead to effective integration.

Balanced Orientation

The second important characteristic of effective integrators is that their orientations and ways of thinking strike a good balance between the extremes of the members of the specialized departments whose efforts they are integrating. For instance, our study shows that:

- Research scientists think about long-term projects and issues and about solutions to scientific and technical problems.
- Production managers and engineers, on the other hand, are concerned with shorter term problems, especially those that relate to an efficient and timely plant operation.
- Sales personnel are also concerned with shorter term issues, but for them the important problems are those that deal with the market—that is, how to meet sales objectives, what to do about competitors' product changes, what characteristics a new product must have to meet the needs of customers, and so forth.

These differences in ways of thinking are, of course, part of what makes it difficult for these groups to collaborate effectively.

The fact that the effective integrators have balanced orientations means that they share more ways of thinking and more behavior patterns with the functional managers than those managers normally do with each other. In a sense, effective integrators speak the language of each of the specialist groups, and thus they are able to work at resolving interdepartmental conflicts. When integrators do not have balanced orientations, their ability to facilitate joint decision making between functional managers suffers. For example:

In several of the organizations studied the integrators did not have a balanced time orientation. Typically, because they were overly concerned with immediate, short-term problems, it was difficult for them to work effectively with the more long-term-oriented scientists. Several comments from the scientists illustrate this difficulty:

> I am no coordinator, but I can see that one of our troubles is that the [integrative] people are so tied up in day-to-day matters they can't look to the future. They are still concerned with 1967 materials when they should be concerned with 1968 markets.
>
> We get lots of reports from them [the integrators] and we talk to them frequently. The trouble is that all they present to us [in research] are the short-term needs. These aren't the long-range things we are interested in.
>
> They [the integrators] only find out about problems when they learn that somebody has quit buying our material and is buying somebody else's, and this keeps you on the defense. A lot of our work is catch-up. We would like more future-oriented work from them.

Similarly, there were complaints from the production and research personnel when the integrators were so preoccupied with marketing problems that they did not seem to understand technical or production issues:

> Our relations with them [the integrators] are good, but not as good as with research. They are not as cost-conscious as the laboratory men. They are concerned with the customer.
>
> He [the integrator] is under a lot of pressure to work with the salesmen on existing products. What he should be, and often tries to act like, is a liaison person, but in reality he is not. He is too concerned with sales problems.

Our research also reveals that effective integrators tend to use an interpersonal style of behavior that falls between the two characteristic behavior orientations of specialized departments. At one extreme, sales personnel are most concerned with maintaining sound personal relationships with their colleagues in other departments. At the other extreme, production managers (and research scientists to a lesser extent) are primarily concerned with getting on with the job, even if this causes the disruption of some established relationships. Our evidence indicates that, to be effective, an integrator needs to think and act in ways which evenly balance the highly social and the highly task-oriented behavior patterns of the units he is attempting to link.

Our research further reveals that entire integrating departments are much more effective when they are intermediate in their degree of structure in relation to the specialized departments they are linking. To analyze the formalization of structure, we examined the degree to which formal rules are utilized, the average span of control, the frequency and specificity of both departmental and individual performance reviews, and the number of levels in the hierarchy.

We found, for example, that most of the formally integrated companies were in an industry where specialized departments had to develop distinctly different organizational practices to perform their respective tasks. Thus, at one extreme, the production units needed highly formalized organizational practices to perform their more routinized tasks. At the other extreme, researchers with problem-solving tasks were more effective in units that had less formalized structures. Between these extremes, the sales personnel operated most effectively with intermediate organizational practices.

When the integrators worked within an intermediate structure, they developed behavior patterns not too unlike those of the different specialists they were linking, and thus they were able to work effectively with all of them.

While our data on the need for intermediate orientations and structures are drawn from a study of integrators attempting to link research, sales, and production units, the same conclusions would seem to hold for integrators linking other functional units.

Performance Recognition

The third important characteristic of effective integrators is the basis on which they see themselves being evaluated and rewarded. For example, in organizations where the integrators were highly effective, they reported that the most important basis for their superior's evaluation was the overall performance of the products on which they were working. Where the integrators were less effective, the superior's evaluation was more on the basis of their individual performance.

This indicates that if integrators are to perform effectively in coordinating the many facets of complex decisions, they need to feel they are being evaluated and rewarded for the total results of their efforts. When they feel they are judged only on the basis of their performance as individuals, they may become so concerned with making decisions to please their superiors or to avoid rocking the boat that they will easily overlook what is desirable from the point of view of their total product responsibility.

Conflict Resolution

The final characteristic of effective integrators is the mode of behavior they utilize to resolve interdepartmental conflict. It seems inevitable that such conflicts will arise in any complex organization from time to time. So, rather than being concerned with the essentially impossible goal of preventing conflict, we are more interested in finding ways for integrators and their colleagues to handle it. Our analysis identifies three modes of behavior for resolving conflict.

Confrontation Technique. The first method, *confrontation,* involves placing all relevant facts before the disputants and then discussing the basis of disagreement until some alternative is found that provides the best solution for the total organization. Confrontation often involves extended discussion. Consider this typical comment from a manager who utilizes this technique:

> Our problems get thrashed out in our committee, at our level. We work them over until everybody agrees this is the best effort we can make. We may decide to ask for more plant, more people, or something else. We all have to be realistic and take a modification sometimes, and say this is the best we can do.

Smoothing Approach. The second technique for dealing with conflict, *smoothing,* emphasizes the maintenance of friendly relations and avoids conflict as a danger that could disrupt these relations. Managers using this approach are, in effect, indicating anxiety about facing the consequences of their conflicting points of view. Such action, they feel, might not only threaten their continuing friendly relations, but even their jobs. So they smooth over their differences, perhaps by using superficial banter and kidding, and thus sidestep conflict. One manager described this method as follows:

> I said what I thought in the meeting, but it didn't bother anybody. Perhaps I should have been harsher. I could have said, 'I won't do it unless you do it my way.' If I had said this, they couldn't have backed off. I guess I didn't have the guts to push it that far because our relations are wonderful. We are friendly and happy as larks. We kid one another and go about our business. I've never run into more cooperative people. I think they think I am cooperative too, but nothing happens.

Forcing Method. The final approach, *forcing*, entails the straight-forward use of power in resolving conflict. The disputing parties bring to bear whatever power or influence they have to achieve a resolution favoring their own point of view. This mode of behavior often results in a "win-lose" struggle. Unfortunately, it is often the objectives of the total organization that suffer the greatest loss. One manager described how he and his colleagues sometimes force the decisions they desire:

> We have lots of meetings that consist of only two members of our four-man team. They get together and discuss things because they think the other two members won't agree. Then, they try to force their decision on the others. Well, this obviously isn't acting as a team. It's our weak spot.

Our data indicate that there is a close relationship between the effectiveness of integration in an organization and the reliance of its members on confrontation as a way to resolve interdepartmental conflict.

While confrontation showed up as a common mode of resolving conflict in all of the ten organizations we studied, the integrators and functional managers in the six most effectively integrated organizations did significantly more confronting of conflict than their counterparts in the four less well-integrated organizations. Similarly, the managers and integrators in the two organizations that had achieved a medium degree of integration were confronting conflict more often than the managers in the least effectively integrated organizations.

There is one other point worth considering: in the highly integrated organizations, we also found that the functional managers were using more forcing, and/or less smoothing, behavior than their counterparts in the less effective organizations. This suggests that, while confrontation of conflict must be the primary basis for resolving interdepartmental issues, it is also important to have a backup mode of some forcing behavior to ensure that the issue will at least be addressed and discussed, and not avoided.

PERSONALITY TRAITS

The foregoing findings offer some significant clues about the behavior of effective integrators, but they leave unanswered one important question: What type of person makes an effective integrator? It is important, as we suggested earlier, that effective integrators have a combination of broad work experience and education. But it is also important that they have certain personality traits.

Underlying Motives

To learn about these predispositions, an exploratory study was made of nearly 20 integrators in one company, half of whom were highly effective in the judgment of their superiors and half of whom were less so.[2] Specifically, we were interested in measuring their underlying motives and preferred behavioral styles.

Affiliation Need. Looking first at underlying motives, we find that the only significant difference between the highly effective integrators and their less effective colleagues is in the *need for affiliation.* The effective integrators are higher in this need than their less effective associates—that is, they pay more attention to others and to their feelings; they try harder to establish friendly relationships in meetings; and they take on more assignments that offer opportunities for interaction.

Achievement Need. There is no statistically significant difference between effective and less effective integrators, or between effective integrators and functional managers, in the *need for achievement* motive. However, there is a tendency for effective integrators to be slightly lower in this motive than less effective integrators. This is worth pointing out, even though the difference is not large, because it seems to run counter to the findings of several managerial studies, which report that managers with a higher need for achievement generally tend to be more successful. (McClelland, 1961)

Our exploratory research suggests that to be effective, integrators must have achievement needs that are near the norm of managers in general, but are not especially high. On the one hand, integrators should set high personal goals, do well in competitive situations, have an entrepreneurial view of work, and seek managerial positions of high responsibility. But, on the other

2. The data were collected and analyzed in collaboration with Professor George Litwin of the Harvard Business School.

hand, they should not be any higher in their need for achievement than the average manager in the organization. In fact, if integrators are too high in this motive, it may reduce their effectiveness in achieving collaboration and resolving conflict, perhaps because they will see interdepartmental conflict as a competitive rather than a collaborative challenge.

Power Need. Both effective and less effective integrators are very similar in their *need for power* and are also close to the norm of managers in general. While we cannot distinguish between the two sets of integrators on this dimension, we can at least conclude that effective integrators *should* try to influence others by persuasive arguments or by taking leadership roles in group activities. In addition, they *should* aspire to managerial positions that allow exercise of power, influence, and control.

Preferred Styles

In addition to measuring the integrators' motives, their preferred behavioral styles were investigated, with certain interesting results:

- Effective integrators prefer to take significantly more initiative and leadership; they are aggressive, confident, persuasive, and verbally fluent. In contrast, less effective integrators are retiring, inhibited, and silent, and they avoid situations that involve tension and decisions.
- Effective integrators seek status to a greater extent; they are ambitious, active, forceful, effective in communication, and have personal scope and breadth of interests. Less effective integrators are restricted in outlook and interest, and are uneasy and awkward in new or unfamiliar social situations.
- Effective integrators have significantly more social poise; they are more clever, enthusiastic, imaginative, spontaneous, and talkative. Less effective integrators are more deliberate, moderate, and patient.
- Effective integrators prefer more flexible ways of acting; they are adventurous, humorous, and assertive. Less effective integrators are more industrious, guarded, methodical, and rigid.

We should stress one point about these personality traits of effective integrators compared with managers in general. In other managerial studies, as indicated earlier, high need for achievement has been associated with success. Furthermore, this drive for achievement has led to the behavioral styles of initiative leadership, capacity for status, and social poise. But while effective integrators prefer these same styles, their underlying drive is only a moderately high achievement need and—most importantly—a high affiliation need. If these motives in turn lead to relatively high initiative, capacity for status, social poise, and flexibility, then the integrators can be effective in meeting the requirements and demands of their jobs.

The reader probably has already recognized the connection between these personality traits and the behavior characteristics described earlier. Since effective integrators are predisposed to take the initiative, it is not surprising that they have high influence in their organizations. Similarly, it is to be expected that these individuals who prefer to take the initiative, who have special poise, and who are relatively flexible, are effective in helping to resolve conflicts.

This description of the effective integrator's behavior and personality perhaps dispels one widespread managerial myth—namely, that the word "integrator" is somehow associated with a passive, unassertive role, rather than with the role of an active "leader."

CONCLUSION

While American industry still needs many types of organizations, as the trend continues for more and more industries to be characterized by rapid rates of technological and market change, more organizations will be like the R&D-intensive firms described here. These firms will require both high differentiation between specialist managers in functional units and tight integration among these units. Although differentiation and integration are essentially antagonistic, effective integrators can help organizations obtain both and thus contribute to economic success. This article has described the characteristics of effective integrators—how they should be rewarded, and where they should be placed in the organization. Organizations in dynamic industries that want to achieve a competitive advantage will have to give careful attention to the planning of their integrating jobs and to the selection and development of the people who fill them.

CONCLUDING STATEMENT

So what can be said about organization structure as a design variable? We began this chapter by exploring the essence of the thing; that is, its dimensions. Next we were exposed to two specific aspects of structure: differentiation (Galbraith's functional versus project versus matrix forms) and integration (Lawrence and Lorsch's integrator role).

Let us use this concluding statement to wrap up the discussion and offer some ideas regarding structure and organization design. We begin by examining interrelationships that exist among the various structural dimensions. Next we consider four principal ways that these dimensions are combined (integrated). Finally, we offer some guidelines for designing a structure, given the constraints under which the organization must operate.

Before we begin, however, a note of explanation is in order: In a sense, "organization structure" could be viewed as an outcome variable, rather than as an independent design variable. After all, structure is essentially a social framework, composed of roles and relationships that arise out of humans interacting with one another. Still, we prefer to treat organization structure as an independent variable: it is something that managers have some opportunity to vary. Structural dimensions can—to an extent, at least—be manipulated, altered, and fine-tuned. To what extent, of course, is a question of design constraints. We will turn to that issue at the end of this chapter.

DESIGN DIMENSIONS: INTERRELATIONSHIPS

As we have mentioned, the dimensions identified for structural design are distinct. They are not, however, independent of each other. Indeed, we recall that the essence of design is compatability—in this case, compatability between the dimensions and other organizational constraints and properties, as well as compatability among the dimensions themselves. Let us consider some of the more common interrelationships.

Specialization

Specialization tends to be related to organization shape (Hall, 1977). This relationship depends, of course, on the nature of the organization's tasks and the manner in which they

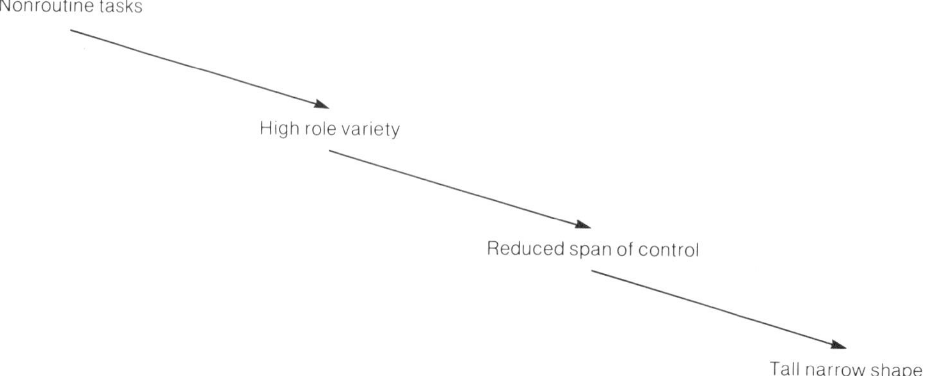

Figure 10-6. Specialization and organizational shape (a)

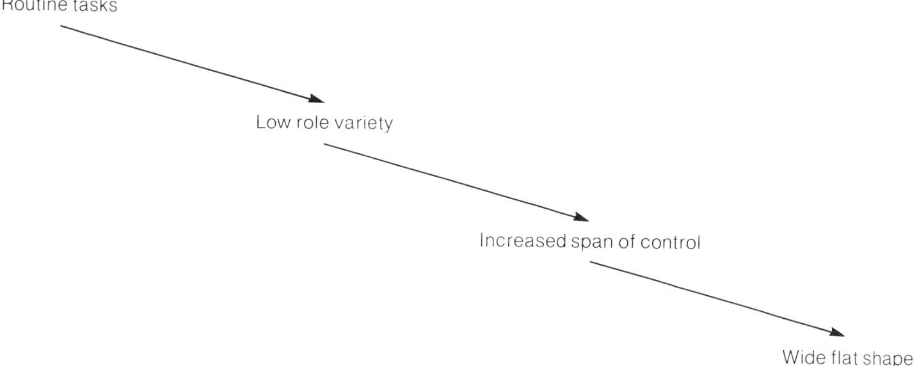

Figure 10-7. Specialization and organizational shape (b)

are allocated. If nonroutine tasks are divided among professionals, a tall narrow shape tends to evolve. If the tasks are routine and assigned to nonprofessionals, the tendency is toward a wide flat configuration.

Communication provides the key to the relationship between shape and specialization. In situations requiring high-skill employees—employees who need to use their expert judgment—managers attempt to maintain a high degree of personal contact (Blau and Scott, 1962). As a result, a high degree of role variety reduces the administrative span of control. With a reduced span of control, the organization tends to become tall and narrow, as illustrated in Figure 10–6. It is important to note that in this case the narrow span of control is the result of a desire to facilitate communication, rather than a direct attempt to control the personal behavior of the professional.

If organizational tasks are routine, allowing low role variety, managers can supervise a greater number of people. Because of the routine and repetitive nature of the technology, the manager requires less immediate feedback from the workers. The need for close personal contact is thereby reduced. The resulting organization shape is wide and flat (shown in Figure 10–7).

Formalization

Hage (1965) has developed 21 corollaries from seven major propositions. Five of these relationships are concerned with formalization. A high degree of formalization was seen to result in: 1. high production, 2. low job satisfaction, and 3. low adaptability to change. High task complexity resulted in low formalization. Finally, a high degree of centralization leads to formalization.

Hall (1977) describes three relationships concerning formalization. The first states that organizations dealing with routine technologies tend to develop more formalization as their size increases. The relationship between size and formalization does not hold with nonroutine organizations. Next, power concentration tends to lead to formalization.

Formalization appears to be most prevalent in routine organizations with a centralized power structure. Under these conditions, managers attempt to specify the behavior of their subordinates. Consistency and high production are sought with little variation desired or allowed.

If the organization utilizes a highly complex technology, it must remain flexible and adaptable to change. Organizations of this sort tend to employ members with professional skills. Since formalization reduces adaptability and professionals desire less defined tasks, managers will be less inclined to institute formalization in nonroutine organizations.

Centralization

The degree to which decision making is concentrated—organizational centralization—is related to the other structural dimensions. In a relatively centralized organization, for example, we would expect an emphasis on rules (formalization), thus reducing the real discretion that members could exercise.

This suggestion is supported by Hage and Aiken (1967) in their study of social welfare agencies. They found that organizations in which decisions were made by only a few people at the top relied on rules and close supervision as a means of ensuring consistent performance from workers. These organizations were also characterized by a less professional staff. Conversely, therefore, the presence of a well-trained staff is related to a reduced need for extensive rules and policies.

Additional evidence comes from Blau et al. (1966). In their analysis of 254 government finance departments, they found that in those organizations with highly formalized personnel procedures and rigid conformity to these procedures, there was a decentralization of authority. As for the relation between expertise and the degree of decentralization, Blau (1968: 453) comments:

> Responsibilities of various kinds tend to be delegated by management to lower levels in agencies where the staff has relatively high qualifications. . . . Parallel relationships with expertness, though they are somewhat less pronounced, are revealed by other indications of decentralization of responsibilities, such as the top executive's policy to let his decision heads make most decisions, and the fact that first-line supervisors, not higher officials, formally evaluate the performance of nonsupervisory employees. In sum, managerial authority over decision making appears indeed to be more decentralized in organizations with large proportions of trained experts than in others.

In cases where the work force does not, or is assumed not to have this decision-making ability, formalized personnel procedures would probably be associated with a more centralized decision-making system with formalization level more consistent throughout all phases of the operation.

Various organizational implications of centralization/decentralization are illustrated in Table 10–2. Each cell describes a type of organization—a type dictated by the interaction of decision location and organizational policies. Reduced to basics, there are several factors that combine to determine how centralized an organization should be (Meyer, 1968: 211–28):

a. Degree to which the task is routinized or nonroutinized.
b. Difference in expertise between the manager and the subordinate.
c. Amount of flexibility and rapid response necessary to the organization.

Based on these factors, we can conclude that there are two different structures available to organizations:

1. control through a centralized authority using a wide span of control, which renders a bureaucracy very responsive to the wishes of its leader and very flexible in its operations,

TABLE 10–2 CENTRALIZATION AND ORGANIZATION TYPES

Level for Referring	Policies, Procedures, and Rules	
Decisions *not* Covered by Policies	*Few Policies / Broadly Defined*	*Many Policies / Narrowly Defined*
TOP Headquarters personnel	1. *Autocracy*/highly centralized. Few decisions are made by lower level personnel, and these are governed by broad policies. Most decisions must be referred to higher level management.	2. *Bureaucracy*/centralized. Decisions are made by operating personnel within the framework of restrictive policies, procedures, and rules; problems not covered must be referred to higher levels for decisions or policy clarification.
BOTTOM Operating personnel	3. *Collegial*/highly decentralized. Most decisions are made at lower levels without policy restrictions; other decisions made at lower levels within the framework of policies.	4. *Bureaucracy*/decentralized. Most decisions are made at lower levels within the framework of the policies; personnel have discretion on problems not covered by policies.

SOURCE: Arlyn J. Melcher, *Structure and Process of Organizations: A Systems Approach*, © 1976. (Englewood Cliffs, New Jersey: Prentice-Hall, Inc.), p. 150. Reprinted by permission.

due to increases in the importance of rules and practices that allow authority to accure to top managers; and

2. control by increasing the importance of rules that remove decisions from the managerial hierarchy by increasing the delegation of decisions to lower levels in organization, relying on competent specialists to receive policies from above and transmit them to their subordinates.

This discussion leads us to conclude that if an organization performs tasks that can be accomplished by subdividing into extremely small units, it will do so and have a low, wide structure. Tasks requiring specialists will result in a taller, narrower organization, since using specialists to perform routine work would obviously result in higher managerial costs.

Structural-Design Dimensions: Summary

The structural dimension of *complexity* takes two forms: 1. horizontal differentiation through an intense division of labor or through the performance of tasks by specialists, and 2. vertical differentiation through distribution of authority and responsibility to aid decision-making processes. In terms of structure, organizations with an intense subdivision of labor tend to have less vertical differentiation. Those with horizontal differentiation by specialists usually have rather tall hierarchies. These differences are largely attributable to the nature of the technology being employed in the organization.

Two conflicting definitions of *specialization* were described. The source of this difference was suggested to be a failure to distinguish between the two means by which tasks are allocated in organizations. A third definition, incorporating "role variety," was introduced as a more satisfactory means of describing specialization. Specialization was seen to be related to the nature of organization tasks, the shape of the organization, and the degree of professionalization of organization members.

Formalization/standardization was defined as the degree to which the organization specifies the manner in which members behave. This dimension was seen to be related to organizational technology, centralization of authority, job satisfaction, productivity, and professionalism.

We found *centralization* to be associated with the degree to which members participate in decision making. The conclusions by Blau and Meyer suggest that the higher the degree of hierarchy, the greater the decentralized control. The characteristics that both Blau and Meyer ascribe to tall, narrow, and decentralized organizations are: expertise, written rules and regulations, clear ordering of positions, and hierarchy. Characteristics of a short, broad, and centralized organization are personal rules, personal evaluations, and low expertise.

Having discussed one basic element of structure, the division of labor, by describing some basic structural dimensions and their interrelationships, we turn now to the second element, integration.

DESIGNING ORGANIZATIONAL INTEGRATION

There is one unbreakable rule of organizations: labor that is subdivided (differentiated) must be integrated if unity of effort is to be achieved. Since achieving unity of effort is the *raison d'etre* of organizations, designing effective integration mechanisms is as important as designing structural dimensions. And the more tasks and resources are interdependent, the even more important all this becomes.

Organizations use a variety of integration mechanisms. Traditionally such mechanisms have been identified as falling into three categories: *hierarchical, administrative processes,* and *voluntary* (Litterer, 1973: 459–67). There is, however, a fourth category: *structural.*

Hierarchical Coordination

One of the basic reasons for developing a hierarchy is to afford some coordination of subdivided labor. Thus, as we pointed out in Chapter 4, a most basic way to improve the chances that the metal-shop and paint-shop activities will ultimately result in the accomplishment of common goals is to create a position called "Manager of Manufacturing" (Figure 10–8). The essence of this managerial role, as we said, is to integrate the activities that have been differentiated into metal-shop and paint-shop tasks.

Hierarchical relationships are also used to coordinate when things go awry. In this chapter's first article, Galbraith terms this situation integrating by hierarchical referral: "When situations are encountered for which there are no rules or when problems cause the goals to be exceeded, these situations are referred upward in the hierarchy for resolution. This is the standard management-by-exception principle. This resolves the nonroutine and unpredictable events that all organizations encounter."

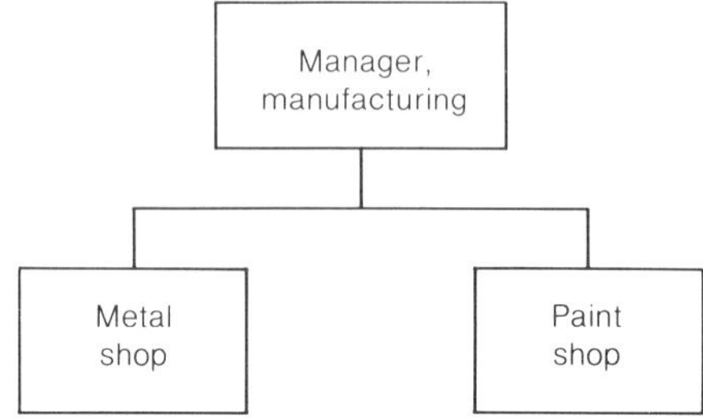

Figure 10-8. Integrating with the hierarchy

Administrative Processes

As basic as the hierarchy is, organizations also design a variety of administrative processes to effect coordination. In essence, administrative processes consist of formal procedures—rules, schedules, plans, and so forth—that are designed to coordinate resources and activities automatically. Using routing slips, for example, memoranda can be routed from department to department, thereby sharing information and plans among units whose work interact.

Again, as we saw in Galbraith's article, there are two basic administrative methods for accomplishing the integration that organizations require: 1. rules and procedures, and 2. planning processes:

> *Rules and procedures*—One of the ways to constrain behavior to achieve an integrated pattern is to specify rules and procedures. If all personnel follow the rules, the resultant behavior is integrated without having to maintain ongoing communication. Rules are used for the most predictable and repetitive activities.
>
> *Planning processes*—For less repetitive activities, organizations do not specify the procedure to be used but specify a goal or target to be achieved, and let the individual choose the procedure appropriate to the goal. Therefore, processes are undertaken to elaborate schedules and budgets. The usefulness of plans and rules is that they reduce the need for ongoing communication among specialized subunits.

Galbraith's discussion of administrative processes indicates that elements of technology, especially in the form of routineness, are important in determining the appropriate design of integrating processes. More about this in the next section.

Voluntary Coordination

Voluntary coordination comes about as a result of the following: "the group or individual sees a need, finds a program, and applies it" (Litterer, 1973: 455). For an individual or group to behave in such a manner, of course, they need to have some knowledge of departmental goals, as well as the conditions prevailing at the time. This is the sort of knowledge that many people do not have. Voluntary activities are therefore difficult to use as a basis of organizational coordination.

Still, some form of voluntary coordination occurs in most organizations at one time or another—it may even be a regular part of organizational life. As Galbraith said in the first article, organizations use *direct contact* as one integrating mechanism: "In order to prevent top executives from becoming overloaded with problems, as many problems as possible are resolved by the affected managers at low levels by informal contacts. These remove small problems from the upward referral process."

Organization designers recognize that voluntary coordination depends on and is affected by at least four factors (Litterer, 1973: 459–65):

Individual Commitment. In Chapter 6 we saw the importance that commitment to the organization can play in determining an individual's behavior. The more that people identify with the organization and its goals, the more likely they are to initiate or participate in ad hoc relationships that are formed to get some problem solved or task accomplished. As Litterer (1973: 460) puts it, "when people have a strong commitment to an organization, share a concept of organization tasks, and there is an easy flow of information, rapid and effective voluntary coordination is possible."

Role perception. Obviously an important factor in affecting an individual's participation in voluntary coordination is how that person perceives his or her organizational role. An individual whose role is self-perceived in a narrow fashion ("I am a mason") will be less likely to engage in voluntary coordination than the person whose role is self-perceived as much wider ("I am helping construct a cathedral").

Organization practices. Organization designers can formulate a number of organizational practices that will affect voluntary coordination. Employee selection and training practices are particularly critical. Management development programs, job rotations, regular meetings—all such activities can contribute to a climate that encourages voluntary coordination. In addition, organizational policies that define and delimit decision-making roles affect such coordination. A manager whose decision making is constrained by an upper dollar limit, for example, will obviously need to coordinate with other levels and units on a decision which exceeds that limit.

Group behavior. As we know, most people—managers as well as non-managers—are members of a variety of organizational groups. The shared values, attitudes, and norms of those groups can encourage or discourage voluntary coordination.

Structural Mechanisms

Organizations frequently use integrating mechanisms that can best be described as structural in character. The hierarchy is a case in point. In addition to this common approach (so common we separated it out for emphasis) are such devices as committees, task forces, project groups, single individuals, and liaison departments. We saw in this chapter's second article (Lawrence and Lorsch) that organizations frequently use a combination of these "integrators." Whatever the form such structural units may take, Lawrence and Lorsch pointed out that their effectiveness depends on four characteristics:

1. Integrators need to be seen as contributing to important decisions on the basis of their competence and knowledge, rather than on their positional authority.
2. Integrators must have balanced orientations and behavior patterns.
3. Integrators need to feel they are being rewarded for their total product responsibility, not solely on the basis of their performance as individuals.
4. Integrators must have a capacity for resolving interdepartmental conflicts and disputes. If integration is to be an effective component of organizational design, these requirements must be met.

Organizational Integration: Summary

Just as the subdivision of labor is crucial to effective organizational design, so too is integration. We have seen that organizations typically employ types of integrating strategies: hierarchy, administrative processes, voluntary coordination, and structural mechanisms. These strategies are summarized in Table 10–3.

Considering the last category, structural mechanisms, allows us to conclude this statement with a review of that form of organization described earlier by Galbraith, the matrix design. This design, after all, is a deliberate attempt to accomplish, under certain conditions, both structural imperatives, differentiation and integration.

TABLE 10–3 INTEGRATING MECHANISMS USED BY ORGANIZATIONS

Hierarchy	Administrative Processes	Voluntary Coordination	Structural Mechanisms
Employs managerial position, chain of command, authority relationship between subordinates and boss to coordinate resources and activities in two or more subordinate positions.	Rules and procedures; planning processes. Such process provides for "automatic" coordination among organizational elements.	Affected by: individual's commitment, role perception, organization practices, and group behavior	Individual roles, departments, teams, committees, task forces. Such "integrators" are effective when they are allowed to coordinate —and are rewarded accordingly.

ORGANIZATION STRUCTURE: THE MATRIX DESIGN

Galbraith's article described the basic characteristics of three main forms of organization structure—functional, product, and matrix. There is no need to repeat that discussion. Another point made in Galbraith's article does bear repeating, however. The pure matrix structure is not the best organizational form for every enterprise. Rather, the most appropriate form depends on the circumstances under which the organization is operating.

Organizational Circumstances: For and Against Matrix

Matrix structures are designed to facilitate the coordination of resources and activities that cannot be effectively coordinated either by purely functional or purely product forms. Circumstances that determine the appropriateness of this coordinating vehicle are three:

a. Similarity of resources utilized across product lines
b. The degree of routineness of the production technology
c. The dynamic nature of the task environment

We will consider, for the sake of this discussion, that each circumstance can be described as a bi-polar dimension: thus we discuss resources as being either similar or diverse, technology as routine or nonroutine, and task environment as static or dynamic. These dimensions can be pictured, as in Figure 10–9, with each cell representing a unique condition, or set of circumstances. The issue then is which cell is appropriate for which of the three types of structure (functional, matrix, product)? Let us look at each of these combinations in order.

Cell 1. Organizations falling into the first cell in Figure 10–9 have the following characteristics: resources are similar across product lines, their technology is basically routine, and the environment is static. This combination seems ideal for a pure *functional* form of organization. Since products use common (similar) resources, the organization can enjoy economies of scale in pooling those resources. Thus it can effectively organize by functional grouping of activities. The routine technology, especially in light of a relatively stable environment, allows management to coordinate across functional lines through planning and schedules (Thompson, 1967).

Cell 2. Organizations in this cell differ from the former in that their technology is nonroutine. Still, resource similarity and a static environment invite the use of a *functional* design.

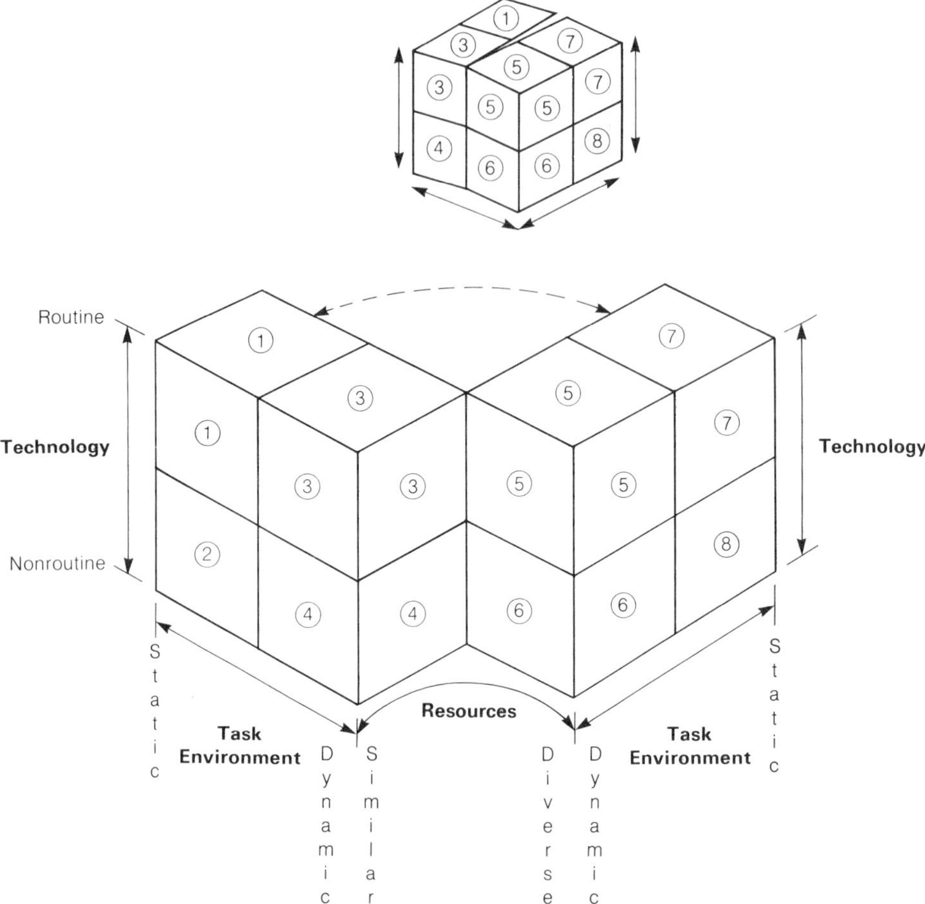

Figure 10-9. Dimensions for functional/matrix/project designs

Cell 3. In this situation, the organization still employs a routine technology, and utilizes resources that are relatively similar across product lines. However, the introduction of dynamic environmental conditions changes the picture somewhat.[3] With environmental demands or opportunities changing, perhaps unpredictably, a purely functional form of organization will be too rigid. Such a design might be hard-pressed to take advantage of new product demands, for example. Thus as Galbraith suggested, structural modifications will have to be introduced: product task forces, committees, teams—these are all typical examples. Such organizations will possess structures that are much closer to a matrix design.

Cell 4. As an organization's technology becomes less routine, designers are forced to amplify their product emphases. Product groups will become more formalized, even taking on departmental identities. Organizations with cell 4 characteristics will start to take on a *matrix* design.

3. Refer to Chapter 4 for an elaboration of the term *dynamic environment.*

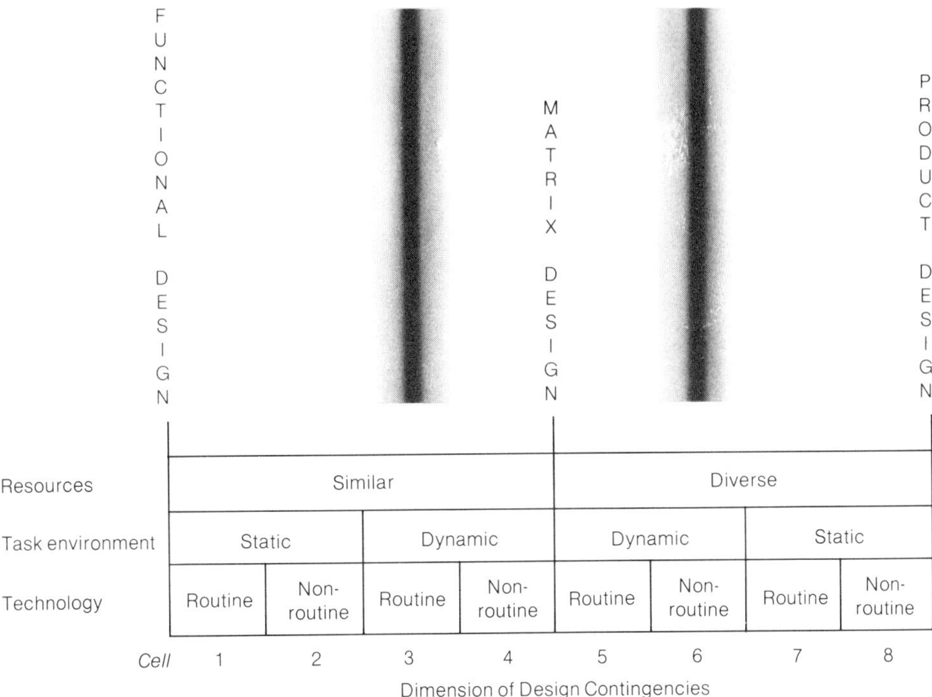

Figure 10-10. Dimensions/design match-ups

Cells 5 and 6. Even though they employ diverse resources, organizations with these characteristics are still faced with a task environment that is unstable. Therefore they cannot afford to rigidify their structure into a pure product form. A matrix-type design will still prevail—especially to take advantage of new product demands that are important, but insufficient to create a formal product department.

Cells 7 and 8. As we have said, organizations operating under a stable environment will be able to take on a fairly stable structure. However, if they are unable to share resources across product lines, as in cells 7 and 8, their structure will be designed in a *product* format.

Functional/Matrix/Product Designs: Summary

We have examined three dimensions that are important to designers in deciding what kind of structure is most appropriate. These dimensions were identified as the following: resources (similar-diverse), technology (routine-nonroutine), and task environment (static-dynamic). Figure 10–10 illustrates the dimension/structure match-ups.

SUMMARY AND CONCLUSION

This chapter has been concerned with the design variable, organization structure. We began the discussion by reviewing two historical trends in its analysis and treatment. First, structure became viewed as an independent variable, a property that varies from situation to situation. Second, the general trend toward viewing organizations as open systems paved the way to examining structure as an organizational property influenced by environmental and technological factors. Next we identified those dimensions that comprise the organization-structure design variable: complexity, specialization, formalization/standardization, and centralization.

We then examined a major structural form, the matrix organization. In that discussion Galbraith traced the development of a hypothetical organization, as it moved from a functional to a matrix structure. This development was seen to result from changes in the environment, especially the marketplace.

In the second article, Lawrence and Lorsch discussed a variety of structural methods for accomplishing the integration of diverse activities and resources. These methods go by the name *integrator.* They may reside in an individual's role or take the form of a complete departmental unit. Together, the Galbraith and Lawrence and Lorsch articles explore two themes critical to organizational success: differentiation and integration.

This dual theme is continued in the concluding statement. Here we have examined the various ways in which the dimensions are interdependent. Next we presented a brief review of integration. We concluded by examining the conditions—resources, technology, and environment—that are important to deciding what overall form an organization's structure should take: functional, matrix, or product. Figures 10-9 and 10-10 illustrate this analysis.

This chapter concludes the discussion of design variables. In this section we have examined the question, "what is it that designers design?" The answer was work design, organizational control processes, decision processes, and organization structure. We move now to the "so what?" question—that is, what is it that results from organization designing? In the next section, Chapters 11 and 12, we examine two design outcomes, organizational climate and organizational effectiveness.

Questions for Review

1. The Aston group concluded that the structure of an organization can be described using certain dimensions. Briefly describe these dimensions.
2. In contrast to the Aston group, Peter Blau and his Comparative Organization Research Program identified other distinct dimensions. What were these? Which of these is conceptually similar to one of the Aston group's?
3. Galbraith mentions certain factors that influence choice of integrating devices, authority structure, information system, and influence distribution. What are these factors, and how are they described?
4. In what ways do Lawrence and Lorsch see the integrative functions emerging historically?
5. Research by Lawrence and Lorsch led them to identify four important characteristics about the behavior of effective integrators, as well as the organizational practices that contribute to their effectiveness. What are these?
6. What are the modes of behavior by effective integrators for resolving conflict? How do they differ from each other?
7. What were two of the results obtained from Lawrence and Lorsch's investigation of preferred behavioral styles?

8. What are two of the factors that combine to determine how centralized an organization should be?
9. What are two basic administrative methods for accomplishing the integration that organizations require?
10. Briefly review the "cell" design and its application to the three types of structure.

Questions for Discussion

1. "No organization ever reaches the point at which the action of its members is completely centralized or completely decentralized. A completely decentralized operation would lack all structure of organization or coordination." How valid an assertion do you consider this to be? What are the implications of this assertion?
2. Galbraith concludes by commenting that "for most organizations, the matrix design is the most effective alternative." Do you agree with this conclusion, based on his example of Standard Products? Would you agree with his conclusion, based on your own reading and experience?
3. Lawrence and Lorsch recommend that "if an organization needs integrators at all, it is preferable to legitimatize these roles by formal titles and missions rather than to leave them in an informal status." What is your opinion of this recommendation? Is there a need for "informal integrators" in addition to formal ones in order to ensure success? Where might informal integrators be more successful than formal? Where might formal integrators be more successful than informal?
4. The concluding statement to this chapter asserts that "achieving unity of effort is the *raison d'être* of organizations . . . ." How does this statement compare with other *raisons d'être* already mentioned in this text? Do they conflict? In what ways are they aligned? Do you agree that this is the main reason for being for an organization? Why?
6. Evaluate the usefulness to an organization of the cell design—dimensions for functional/matrix/project designs. On what basis do you make this evaluation?
7. What are the three most useful concepts you have learned from your study of this chapter on organizational design? Why did you choose these three? Do they relate to each other?
8. " 'Span of control' is a basic building block of hierarchy." Evaluate the validity of this assertion. What other building blocks are required for the existence of a hierarchy?
9. "Each era of management evolves new forms of organization as new problems are encountered." Is this the only reason why new forms of management are evolved? Does the evolution of new forms of management parallel the evolution of any other area?
10. Galbraith reflects that "when one basis of organization is chosen, the benefits of the others are surrendered." Is this necessarily always true? If it is, then is there any way to overcome this? Is there any way to reap all of the benefits? Why?

CASES FOR DISCUSSION

CASE: CONTROLLING EMPLOYEE BEHAVIOR IN FERNWOOD NURSING HOME

Ruth Newman, R.N., the charge nurse for the graveyard shift (11:00 P.M. to 7:30 A.M.) at the Fernwood Nursing Home facility, is responding to a question about what problems she has with employees, and how she handles them.

"I don't have a great number of problems. I find that most of the people who come to work here really want to work. If they're not willing to work, they probably won't last through the first couple of weeks on the job. The job of aide or orderly in this type of facility is a very physically demanding one and is carried out in aesthetically unpleasant conditions. I would say that my biggest problems are in the attitudes of the workers toward the patients. No matter how tired the aide or orderly is, I cannot allow, and will not tolerate, any display of impatience or ill temper toward a patient.

"Most of this is taken care of during the initial training period, which is conducted by our chief of nursing. While they are learning the basic job skills needed in caring for patients, they're also learning how it feels to be in the patient's place. They have to use the bedpan, have their teeth brushed by someone else, and be fed. We hope that this will give them some insight into the patients' feelings toward having these intimate functions being taken care of by a stranger. Hopefully, it may help the aide to be patient when one of her charges spends 10 minutes to do a less efficient job of teeth cleaning than the aide could have done in one minute—or to watch a patient spilling food when the resulting mess could be avoided by the aide taking over the feeding task. The whole point is to avoid degrading the patient if it is in any way possible to do so. This makes the difference between good nursing care and the simple mechanical process of providing for physical requirements of the patients.

"I try to encourage the aides and orderlies to help each other. Part of this, I think, is accomplished by having them take breaks at scheduled times, regardless of what they are doing at the time. It gets them away from their patients for a while, and it also keeps them from having their breaks with the same people all of the time. I control the break schedule, and I arrange it so that different people are taking breaks together each night. This kind of helps to ensure that they all know each other. It gets new people into the group faster and helps keep small cliques from forming. I try to encourage some of the informal social activities, such as birthday and farewell parties—so long as everyone is included.

"I also make each aide responsible for her own section. If she needs help from others, she is in charge of their activities while they are in her section. This applies regardless of the relative seniority of the people involved and even if I am the one who is helping. Of course, if there is a medical problem, I take charge, because I do not delegate any of my responsibility in that area. I also assign the sections to the aides on a rotating basis so that everyone works on every section. The only exception to this is in the case of the one orderly we have assigned to the shift at present. He is the backup man. He helps when needed as a source of extra muscle for the aides, fills in when someone is sick and doesn't come in or leaves early, and answers calls while the nurses are making rounds. We didn't have an orderly on the shift for quite some time, and when this young man was assigned, I asked the aides how they

---

The information contained herein has been collected for the sole purpose of providing material for discussion, not to demonstrate correct or incorrect handling of managerial or organizational situations.

thought would be the best way to use him. This is what they wanted, and I went along with it, even though he probably does fewer of the dirty jobs than the others.

"Most of the disciplinary problems are taken care of by the aides themselves. Sometimes I talk to one of the workers when I feel that he or she is not doing their part, but mostly, if I talk to them, it's about their attitude toward the patients."

Questions

1. What type of control does Ms. Newman employ? Refer especially to the discussion in Chapter 8.
2. Design a formal control system that takes advantage of Ms. Newman's tactics.

CASE: PLANT A—A PROBLEM CONCERNING ORGANIZATION STRUCTURE

One portion of a major manufacturing company produces television sets. The vice-president of manufacturing hires you, a management consultant specializing in human relationship systems, to offer your recommendations on the organization structure of plant A. (Note: not all parts of the organization are shown—only those relevant to the case are depicted; see Exhibit 1.)

He tells you that some of the problems include the following:

- Too much is being spent for supervisory salaries.
- The foremen are extremely dissatisfied. Their biggest complaints are that it takes too long to get decisions made when things have to be referred upstairs—which is often; also that there is poor cooperation among departments. Main assembly foremen say that when sub-assemblies are not made right or are not coming through on schedule that it takes a big meeting involving six or seven people to get things straightened out. The foremen of packing and shipping are always having arguments with the main assemblyline foremen over such things as the packers not working fast enough to take sets off the line as fast as the line workers produce them.
- Foremen complain that it takes too much time to get a maintenance man when something goes wrong on the line. The foreman calls the maintenance department by phone but usually the maintenance men are all busy so the foreman has to get his general foreman to put some pressure on. Foremen complain that with everybody competing for the maintenance men, the guys who are friends of the maintenance foremen get helped first.
- Foremen complain that they are not allowed to make enough decisions and that they have to refer too many to their bosses for answers. They think they can make more themselves. Foremen say that they don't receive enough information from "upstairs," and that they don't have much of an idea of what is going on in other parts of the organization. Yet the superintendents say that the foremen are not capable of making decisions because they do not have enough of the "whole picture."
- Foremen, particularly those in the packing and shipping department complain that they are supervised too closely. General foremen say the same thing—that they are constantly being checked up on by the superintendents and assistant superintendents.

We have reason to believe this case was prepared by a Ms. J. R. Abbott. Despite our best efforts to locate the author, we were not able to do so.

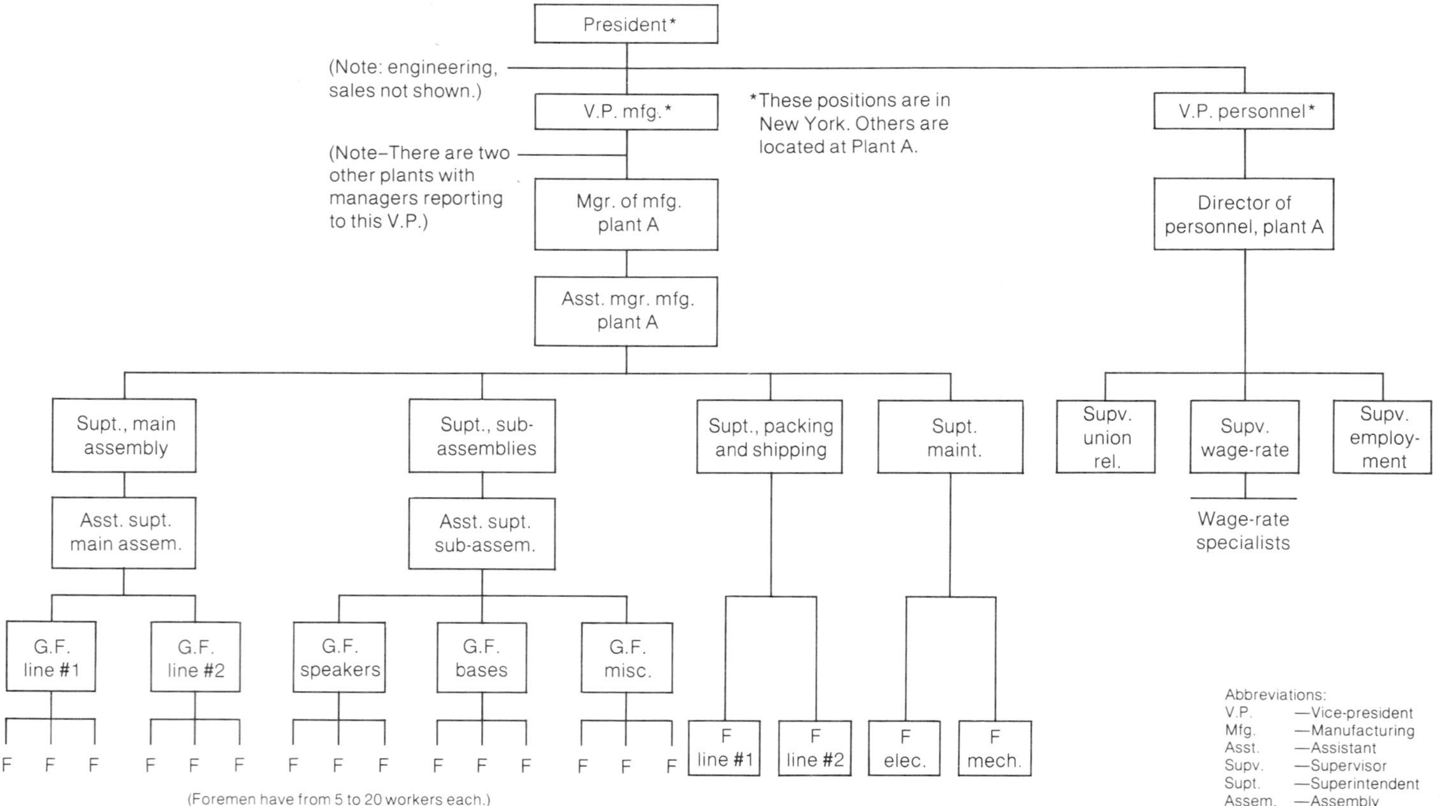

Exhibit 1. Organization structure for Plant A

- The personnel manager complains that the line managers don't seem to pay much attention to him and constantly fight the suggestions he makes or the programs he wants to get done. He says that his wage rate men get only resistance from the foremen and that in disputes—which are many—the manager of manufacturing is always siding with the foremen and against him.

Questions

1. What would you say is wrong with this organization structure?
2. What changes would you suggest to improve it? (Obviously one cannot make a complete diagnosis and recommendation from the limited information given, but at least several needed changes in the structure should be apparent.)
3. State how each change will improve upon the problems given above. (Remember, you are dealing here only with change of structure—not with education or training or getting people to pass more information down the line.)

CASE: A DESIGN PROBLEM AT RIDGEMONT

The administrator of the Ridgemont Convalescent Center describes her organization as being a rather wide, flat structure. There are ten departments and each department head reports directly to the administrator. The administrator does the necessary coordinating between departments. Exhibit 1 is a copy of the organization chart as extracted from the *Organization Policies and Procedures Manual.* The chart is consistent with the administrator's description.

The actual organization structure is illustrated in Exhibit 2. It is at considerable variance with the above view. The administrative assistant functions more as head of all the administrative staff services. The relationship between the nursing and dietary departments is more of a line-staff type than of co-equal departments. The volunteer services coordinator and the bookkeeper maintain most of their contracts with the other departments—including routine business with the administrator—through the administrative assistant. In fact, the administrative assistant controls and coordinates all of the administrative functions such as personnel, advertising, sales, payroll, collections, and financial record keeping.

The housekeeper heads a department equal in organizational status to that of the director of nursing services (DNS). In fact, however, she receives her day-to-day work assignments from the DNS and must get permission from the latter to deviate from these work assignments.

The recreation director is in a similar situation. Any recreation activities, since they involve the patients, require the cooperation of the nursing staff. The recreation director found that any projects suggested directly to the administrator were votoed by the DNS on the grounds that they interfered with proper patient care. The recreation director found that the only workable solution was to present the idea to the director of nursing services, allow her to make the decision, and then allow her to present the idea to the administrator as required. In effect, the only real contact between the recreation director and the administrator is through the DNS.

The physical therapist's relationship with the DNS is based more on convenience than anything else. The therapist prefers to be represented in intraorganizational matters by the

The information contained herein has been collected for the sole purpose of providing material for discussion, not to demonstrate correct or incorrect handling of managerial or organizational situations.

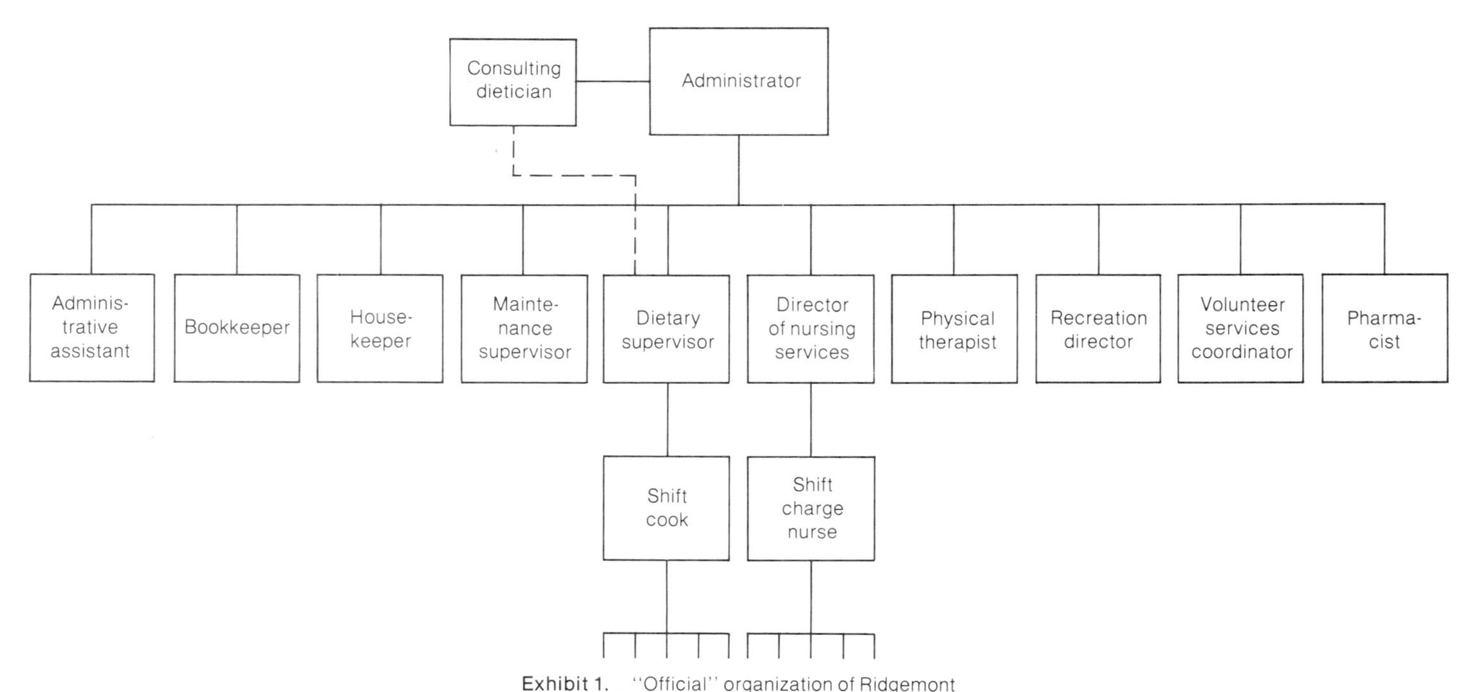

Exhibit 1. "Official" organization of Ridgemont

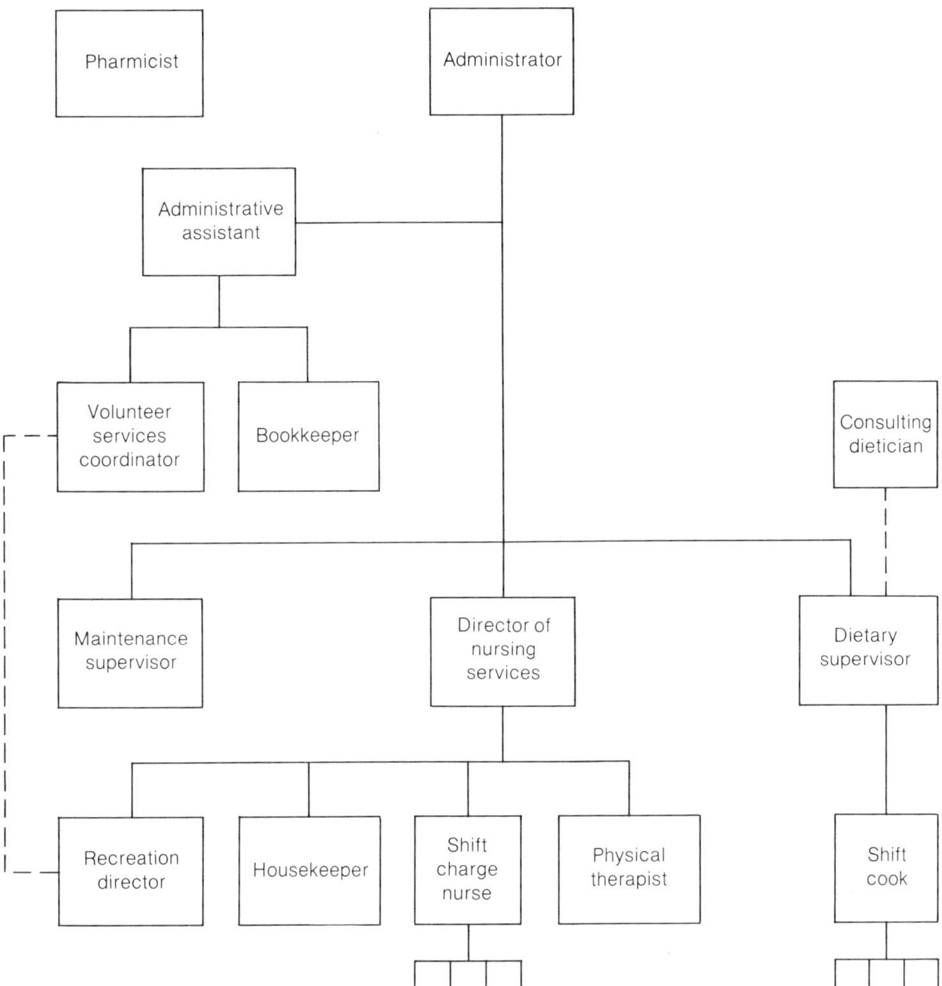

Exhibit 2. "Actual" organization of Ridgemont

nursing director and to rely on the professionally prescribed responsibilities of a registered physical therapist and a registered nurse to govern other relationships.

The director of nursing services actually sees herself as occupying a position immediately below the administrator and superior to all the others in the hierarchy of the organization. When the administrator is absent, she expects the administrative assistant, who is also designated as deputy administrator, to defer to her judgment in all matters. This view by the DNS is strongly disputed by the dietary supervisor and the maintenance supervisor.

The maintenance supervisor refuses to accept from the director of nursing services any communication regarding any aspect of his job, which he construes to be in any way directive in nature. He insists that all decisions as to what maintenance is to be done, or the relative priority of various jobs, are to be made by himself or the administrator only. He further insists, in conferences concerning maintenance, that the nursing department's requests do not receive any higher priority than those of any other department.

The dietary supervisor and the director of nursing services have a considerable degree of personality conflict. The departments are the two largest and involve the greatest commitment of resources to operate. Each is completely convinced that hers is the most important of all the departments. The nursing department has direct charge of the patients and of most of the facility except the kitchen, while the operations of the dietary department have the greatest impact on the day-to-day profitability of the overall operation and therefore get the greatest amount of attention from the administrator. Both supervisors are very strong-willed and each is particularly unwilling to yield anything to the other.

The one remaining department, the pharmacy, does not really appear to be a part of the organization at all. Its operations are more analagous to those of an independent contractor than those of an integral part of the organization. The pharmacist and his assistants work in a room to which they have sole access and communicate with other departments, primarily nursing and bookkeeping, by written communications only. There is practically no interpersonal contact with members of the pharmacy by members of any other department. Pharmacy-based charges to patients are billed separately on a statement originating in the pharmacy. The pharmacist rarely attends staff conferences and appears to independently establish the hours of operation and working conditions for the pharmacy personnel.

The consulting dietician, although not a part of the organization in the formal sense, is shown in Exhibit 1 as reporting directly to the administrator. In fact, this relationship does not exist. The dietician works directly with the dietary supervisor and normally communicates with the administrator, either through the dietary supervisor or jointly with her.

QUESTION: Why do you suppose the actual organization structure is so different from the prescribed (official) one?

DESIGN TASK: Develop Exhibit 3, an ''ideal'' organization structure. Prepare a narrative, describing your reasoning.

CONSTRAINTS:

1. You may not hire or fire anyone.
2. You may not do something totally facetious, such as assign the Director of Nursing Services to a dishwashing task, in the hope she will resign.
3. You may eliminate and/or create new positions or roles.

SECTION FIVE

Design Outcomes

INTRODUCTION TO SECTION FIVE

We said at the beginning of this book that organizations are designed for the purpose of accomplishing goals. Is goal accomplishment—more or less successfully—therefore the only outcome of organization design? The answer is a ringing yes . . . and no. Yes, if the concept "organizational goal" is sufficiently broad; no, if "organizational goal" is narrowly defined.

In essence, as we mentioned in Chapter 2, there are two principal organization-design outcomes. First, the way in which an organization is designed will produce a working *climate*—a climate that affects the organization's members, their psychoemotional states, and, of course, their behavior. This outcome provides the focus for the first part of this section, Chapter 11, "Organizational Climate."

The second major organization-design outcome is overall organizational effectiveness. We shall see in Chapter 12 that even though we regard organizational effectiveness as a design outcome, it is an organizational *process.* As a process, organizational effectiveness concerns the means by which resources are transformed into outputs and the side effects of that transformation, as well as the end result. As a concept, organizational effectiveness is multidimensional. As we saw for other variables, the so-called "bottom line" of overall organizational effectiveness is not a line at all so much as a profile.

11

Organizational Climate

INTRODUCTORY REMARKS

Taken as a whole, an organization's design produces inside the enterprise a situation, or set of conditions, that is referred to as the organization's climate. Some people think of climate as reflecting an organization's "personality." Thus an organization takes on a character—a psycho-social-emotional environment—that affects people's task and nontask behavior.

What about organizational climate as a design outcome? The conditions under which the organization operates, plus the structural and process characteristics of the organization itself, serve to produce a climate, or atmosphere, within which members function. The purpose of this chapter is to discuss what we know about this aspect of the organization. Specifically, we define the term *organizational climate* in these introductory remarks. Next we describe its dimensions, both in the article by Campbell et al. and in the concluding statement. Finally, we examine its relationship to organization design.

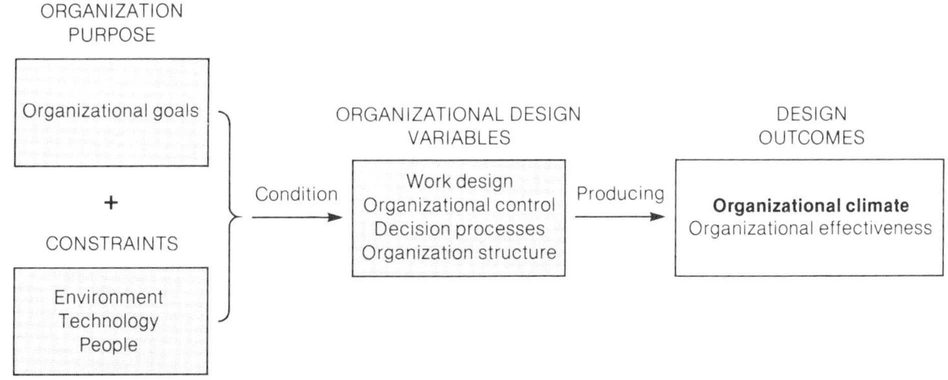

ORGANIZATIONAL CLIMATE: WHAT IS IT?

Traditionally, there are three principal ways of thinking about organizational climate. The first treats climate as a set of organizational characteristics that can be described with reasonable objectivity. The second views climate as a set of organizational characteristics that are real insofar as they are perceived by the organizational membership. And the third describes climate in terms of individual, rather than shared, perceptions (James and Jones, 1974).[1] Let us examine each of these approaches in order.

Climate as Objective Organizational Characteristics

One of the earlier attempts to make sense of the construct was that by Forehand and Gilmer (1964). They defined organizational climate as:

> a set of characteristics that describe an organization and that (a.) distinguish the organization from other organizations, (b.) are relatively enduring over time, and (c.) influence the behavior of people in the organization. [1964: 362]

The difficulty with this definition is relatively clear: there are several organizational characteristics that meet the definition's criteria (a., b., and c.). Size, basis of departmentalization, primary goals, and reward policies are just a few that come immediately to mind. In fact, a recent text on organizational behavior (Hamner and Organ, 1978: 279), describes organizational climate as consisting of such properties as "the size, structure, leadership patterns, interpersonal relationships, systems complexity, goal direction, and communication patterns of the organization."

To make sense as a unique construct, climate must be thought of in terms of people. That is, organizational climate intuitively connotes a set of characteristics/properties/attributes that have to do with the psycho-social-emotional atmosphere of an organization. Two recent definitions of organizational climate capture this important idea:

> Climate describes the characteristc behavioral processes in a social system at one particular point in time. These processes reflect the members' values, attitudes, and beliefs, which thus have become part of the construct. [Payne and Pugh, 1975: 1126–28]

> Organizational climate refers to a set of attributes that can be perceived about an organization and/or its units and may be described by the practices, processes, and ways of dealing with members of the unit and its environment. [Hellriegel and Slocum, 1976: 351]

Taken together, these two definitions serve to remind us that the importance of organizational climate lies in its perceptual nature. This idea leads us to the second common approach to the subject.

Climate as Perceived Organizational Characteristic

In this chapter's article on organizational climate, Campbell et al. offer the following definition:

1. This section is based on James' and Jones' (1974) excellent review of the organizational-climate literature.

> Climate is a set of attributes specific to a particular organization that may be induced from the way that organization deals with its members and its environment. For the individual member within the organization, climate takes the form of a set of attitudes and expectancies which describe the organization in terms of both static characteristics (such as degree of autonomy) and behavior-outcome and outcome-outcome contingencies.

This definition suggests that climate is an organizational characteristic, and at the same time one that is important, because it is perceived by the organizational membership. Climate thus becomes a concept:

> reflecting the content and strength of the prevalent values, norms, attitudes, behaviors, and feelings of the members of a social system which can be operationally measured through the perceptions of system members or . . . other objective means. [Payne and Pugh, 1975: 1141]

The two preceding definitions lead us to conclude that climate is composed of two distinct, yet interrelated sets of characteristics: *organizational characteristics,* such as type of communication and task specialization, and *psychological characteristics*, such as felt attraction and satisfaction with performance (Indik, 1965). Thus the climate of an organization can be thought of in both "objective" and "perceptual" terms. However, some analysts believe that these terms are important because they relate to individuals, not to an indistinct collection of people. "What is psychologically important to the individual must be how he perceives his work environment, not how others might choose to describe it" (Schneider and Bartlett, 1970: 510). This idea suggests the third common way of thinking about the concept.

Climate as Individual Perception

Several researchers have approached the study of organizational climate by treating it as an individually perceived phenomenon.[2] That is, the working atmosphere of an organization has meaning only to an individual, because it is the individual who does or does not participate in decisions, is or is not treated with warmth and affection, has or does not have autonomy, and so forth. If climate is related to people's behavior, it is because people perceive climate, interpret it, and respond to the stimuli that comprise it. And, say the analysts, these are all individual actions.

The difficulty with such an approach is that it is self-contradictory. It is true, of course, that it is individuals—rather than groups, for instance—who perceive. Perceptions are interpretations of objects, persons, and events. That is, perceptions involve the selection and decoding of external stimuli, forming an internal representation of the object, person, or event. And as we said, it is individuals who select and decode.

However, in the organizational context, there must be some set of objects, persons, and events that are relatively common to members; otherwise there is no "organization." Thus while individuals may differ as to their perception or interpretation, it is those common stimuli that make up what we call the organization's climate. For a particular individual, his or her interpretation of the stimuli produce—for that individual—a *psychological* climate (James and Jones, 1974: 1108). And while individual-specific psychological climates are important, it is organizational climate that is germane to our study of organization design.

2. For reviews, see James and Jones (1974) and Payne and Pugh (1975).

Therefore, for us organizational climate is a macro concept reflecting:

> . . . the character of the organization as the public, customers, politicians, employees, and prospective employees see it. This is the general tenor of the organization; the impressions it gives to those who come into contact with it. [Connor and Bloomfield, 1977: 104]

Slightly more specifically, our focus here is on organizational climate as a set of organizational characteristics reflected in members' beliefs, feelings, and behavior with respect to themselves and one another. What these characteristics are—and what their relationships are to organization design—constitute the focus of the rest of this chapter.

The Reading

What makes one organization's climate different from another's? Although there is no firm agreement among scholars, researchers, and managers, the set of factors described by Campbell et al. in this chapter's article is a good place to start:

1. *Individual autonomy*—the freedom of the individual to be his or her own boss, without being continually accountable to higher management.
2. *Degree of structure*—the degree to which an individual's supervisor establishes his or her objectives and methods of work.
3. *Reward orientation*—the degree to which a profit or sales orientation is encouraged.
4. *Consideration, warmth, and support*—the harmony and supportiveness that management and workers express toward themselves and each other.

The authors review a number of attempts to describe organizational climate. They then provide a synthesis of those attempts; points 1–4, above, reflect that synthesis. Next, Campbell et al. describe and analyze some recent attempts to do research on organizational climate. The authors conclude that (a.) consistence in climate is beneficial to organizational performance, and (b.) individual differences (as we discussed in Chapter 6) are important in determining organizational climate.

Conclusion

In essence, this chapter is concerned with climate as an outcome of organizational design. As Steers and Porter (1975: 298–99) note, organizational climate results from several forces. Past experiences, formal organization properties and relationships, the nature of the tasks that organizational members perform, the organizational members themselves (that is, their needs, expectations, values, and so forth), and management's leadership style are several of the forces that contribute to an organization's climate.

Our discussion of climate focuses on the following questions:

1. What is meant by organization climate?
2. How do various design variables contribute to the development of an organization's climate?
3. What sort of climate is preferable under what conditions, or design constraints?

ENVIRONMENTAL VARIATION AND MANAGERIAL EFFECTIVENESS

JOHN P. CAMPBELL, MARVIN D. DUNNETTE
EDWARD E. LAWLER, III and KARL E. WEICK, JR.

SITUATIONAL DETERMINANTS OF MANAGERIAL PERFORMANCE

It is difficult to specify what is meant by a "situational variable." Being realistic about the matter, defining such a characteristic as any variable which has relevance for management performance but which has not yet been discussed in this volume would probably be more descriptive than any other specification. Beyond this, perhaps a few additional points can be made.

The class of determinants we have in mind includes such things as the structural properties of organizations (e.g., organization size or number of levels of supervision), the psychological "climate" (e.g., pressure for production, perceived reward system, individual autonomy), industry characteristics (e.g., growth industry, competitive, tight labor market), and the specified role characteristics of the management job (e.g., formal power, procedural rules, constraints). They are properties not of individuals but of environments. Specific individuals will perceive these properties differently; however, a significant environmental effect must remain if it is to be labeled a situational variable. In analysis of variance terms, the total variability in behavior must not be explained entirely by 1. differences between individuals and 2. error. Some variability in management performance must be attributable to differences in the environmental variable, to the interaction between the environmental characteristic and individual differences, or to both. Perhaps an analogy to the weather is appropriate. Differences in temperature, precipitation, and wind velocity are general characteristics of the environment which exert an effect on an individual's behavior (e.g., he adds antifreeze to the radiator). Significant differences attributable to weather persist, even though particular individuals interpret the same conditions differently. For example, heavy snow means more indoor activity for most people but increased outdoor activity for some, and what is a "warm" day for one person may be a "comfortable" day for another. Even if there were no "average" effects on behavior due to differences in weather, it would still be an environmental variable in our terminology if there was an interaction effect. For example, some people may become less active and some more active as the temperature changes, but the average activity level of the population stays the same.

Given the existence of a situational effect, a number of methodological and conceptual problems arise. These include such things as the form of the relationships, the processes involved, the loci of the situational variables, and the means used to measure them.

Predictors versus Moderators

It is very easy to speak of situational or environmental "determinants" of managerial performance as if the linkage of environmental differences to behavior was easily understood and the causal nature of the relationships was known or could be assumed. Obviously, at the present time it is more proper to speak of correlates than determinants, even though a few experimental studies do exist. What is perhaps not so obvious is a corresponding ambiguity in the form of the correlational relationship between a situational variable and a measure of performance.

Can an environmental variable be used as a predictor of behavior or should a direct relationship with performance be ruled out? Would it make better sense to conceive of environmental characteristics as a moderator of the relationship between characteristics of individuals and their performance on the job? Another way of phrasing the question is to ask whether situational variables combine additively or interactively with the previously discussed correlates (e.g., individual differences) of performance. For example, does an autonomous environment enhance or detract from everyone's performance in similar fashion, and are differences in autonomy thereby correlated with performance, or is there an interactive relationship, with particular individual differences correlated with performance only for certain levels of autonomy? The distinction is crucial in terms of how research on situational variables should be pursued and the kinds of data that should be collected. Further, successful a priori specification of the nature and magnitudes of the relationships would add considerably to the theoretical understanding of environmental characteristics. To date, the nature of the linkage between situational variables and job behavior has not been very well conceptualized.

How the Environment Influences the Individual

Forehand and Gilmer (1964) discuss the problem of specifying how organizational environment differences are translated to differences in behavior. They mention three mechanisms:

1. *Definition of stimuli.* Environmental characteristics such as the structure of an organization, the implicit theories held by its management, or the economic condition of the industry have considerable influence on the relevant stimuli which impinge on an individual in his work role. For example, a shrinking market may elicit managerial skills associated with holding cost down, preventing waste, and increasing market share rather than those concerned with increasing production and developing new products.
2. *Constraints upon freedom.* Certain attributes of the situation may actually prevent certain behaviors from occurring. The structure of the organization may place a number of restraints on management communication or the degree of autonomy. Such structurally imposed constraints may be either deleterious or facilitative, relative to performance effectiveness.
3. *Reward and punishment.* Besides influencing what sorts of stimuli will be perceived and what types of responses are permitted, the environment can also specify the reinforcement contingencies for various managerial behaviors. It seems intuitively obvious that the situation should help determine the behavior-reward contingencies in an organization. For example, a manager in a very autonomous organization would make much broader decisions without consulting his superior than a comparable manager in a very nonautonomous organization. The situation is one in which a great deal of independent action is rewarded. Supposedly, a lack of independent action would be punished in some fashion.

The situation a manager is in should also affect his behavior by arousing various motives. If we consider the theory of need achievement, people have a certain "amount" of different needs (e.g., *n* Ach, *n* Aff, *n* Pow) which are relatively permanent characteristics. However, for these motives or needs to have a significant effect on behavior, they must be aroused. In this formulation scores on need for achievement will not predict performance unless the situation arouses this need by inducing cognitions of competition with a standard of excellence. The essential point is whether different situations elicit or arouse different needs. It would seem quite likely that this is the case. For example, the need for power might be elicited more in one organization than in another.

These effects on behavior must also be considered in relation to individual differences. People have different needs and see various outcomes as more or less desirable, and these differences must be considered. As Litwin and Stringer (1966) point out, different individuals may expect different rewards and punishments for various kinds of behavior. Climate, for example, should not act in the same way for all individuals as an arouser of needs or motives. . . .

DIMENSIONAL ANALYSES OF SITUATIONAL VARIABLES

Perhaps the most frustrating feature of an attempt to deal with situational variables in a model of management performance is the enormous complexity of the environment itself (Sells, 1963). It makes the definition and measurement of situational characteristics very difficult, and a fruitful taxonomy of environments is the key to unraveling this portion of our model. Although it is here that a certain amount of empirical work has been done, the surface has barely been scratched.

Researchers concerned with a taxonomy of situational characteristics have borrowed heavily from the methodology of differential psychology and have made considerable use of the factor analytic approach. In so doing they have tended to use the term "organizational climate" in place of "environment" or "situation."

Climate Factors

One way to get a firmer grasp on the concept of organizational climate is to consider some potential properties of climate. Forehand and Gilmer (1964) feel that climate consists of a set of characteristics that describe an organization, distinguish it from other organizations, are relatively enduring over time, and influence the behavior of the people in it. Georgopoulos (1965) speaks of a normative structure of attitudes and behavioral standards which provide a basis for interpreting the situation and act as a source of pressure for directing activity. Litwin and Stringer (1966) add the notion that these properties must be perceivable by the people in the organization and that an important aspect of climate is the "patterns of expectations and incentive values that impinge on and are created by a group of people that live and work together." H. H. Meyer (1967) expands on one aspect of the Litwin and Stringer definition by suggesting that climate arises as the result of the style of management, the organization's policies, and its general operating procedures. Gellerman (1959) feels the goals and tactics of men whose attitudes "count" are a significant determiner of climate.

From this collection of properties, components, and determiners that various authors feel contribute to climate, we might define climate as a set of attributes specific to a particular organization that may be induced from the way that organization deals with its members and its environment. For the individual member within the organization, climate takes the form of a set of attitudes and expectancies which describe the organization in terms of both static characteristics (such as degree of autonomy) and behavior-outcome and outcome-outcome contingencies.

When organizational climate is defined in this way, it can be seen that many kinds of organizational factors are potentially relevant contributors to it. The crucial elements are the individual's perceptions of the relevant stimuli, constraints, and reinforcement contingencies that govern his job behavior. For this reason, the basic data used by a number of investigators to organize a taxonomy of "climate" factors are individual perceptions of organizational properties.

For example, Litwin and Stringer (1966) report a questionnaire developed to measure organizational members' perception in six different areas:

1. *Structure.* Perception of the extent of organizational constraints, rules, regulations and "red tape"
2. *Individual responsibility.* Feelings of autonomy, of "being one's own boss"
3. *Rewards.* Feelings related to being confident of adequate and appropriate rewards—pay, praise, special dispensations—for doing the job well
4. *Risk and risk taking.* Perceptions of the challenge and risk in the work situation
5. *Warmth and support.* Feelings of general good fellowship and helpfulness prevailing the work settings
6. *Tolerance and conflict.* Degree of confidence that the climate can tolerate differing opinions

These dimensions proved to distinguish various organizational subunits and have been incorporated into some experimental studies to be reviewed in a later section.

A broader and somewhat more systematic study of climate dimensions is described by B. Schneider and Bartlett (1968). The research sites were a group of sales agencies making up two different insurance companies. An item pool of 299 items describing various characteristics of the agencies was administered to 143 management personnel, and the responses were factor analyzed. Among other things, the respondents were asked to indicate what managers did in the agencies, what agents did, how people were treated, and what kinds of people were in the agencies. Thus, the 143 managers were not describing their own climate (i.e., the organization above them), but what they perceived the climate of the organization below them to be. Schneider and Bartlett admit the possible biasing effect of having managers describe their own agencies.

Six factors emerged. Their labels and descriptions are given below:

1. *Managerial support.* Similar to the factor of consideration found in the Ohio State studies. It refers to managers taking an active interest in the progress of their agents, backing them up with the home office, and maintaining a spirit of friendly cooperation.
2. *Managerial structure.* Refers to the manager requiring agents to adhere to budgets, be knowledgeable regarding sales material, and produce new customers. It tends to be a "sales-or-else" factor.
3. *Concern for new employees.* Most of the items are typified by a concern for the selection, orientation, and training of a new agent.
4. *Intra-agency conflict.* Refers to the presence of ingroups or outgroups within an agency and the undercutting of managerial authority by the agents.
5. *Agent independence.* These items describe agents who tend to run their own business and do not pay much attention to management.
6. *General satisfaction.* Refers to the degree to which the agency sponsors periodic social get-togethers and the agents express satisfaction with various management and agency activities.

The final form of the questionnaire contains 80 items for the six factors. At a conceptual level Schneider and Bartlett view the agency climate factors both as possible predictors of later performance and as potential moderators of the relationship between selection information and performance measures. In the predictor instance an individual would be asked to respond with his preferences for climate characteristics and/or his expectancies, and they could then be correlated with later performance.

The climate factors derived in the above two efforts are meant to generalize across the perceptions of all individuals in the organization. In contrast, the two studies described below were specifically aimed at specifying climate dimensions as perceived by managers.

Taguiri (1966) asked a small sample of managers participating in a Harvard management course to name the things that mattered most to them in their organizations. From their replies, he developed a standardized questionnaire which he administered to a larger sample of managers and then factor analyzed their responses. Five factors resulted:

1. Practices related to providing a sense of direction or purpose to their jobs—setting of objectives, planning, and feedback
2. Opportunities for exercising individual initiative
3. Working with a superior who is highly competitive and competent
4. Working with cooperative and pleasant people
5. Being with a profit-minded and sales-oriented company

One phase of a large study on role conflict reported by Kahn, Wolfe, Quinn, Snoek, and Rosenthal (1964) also bears on the dimensional analysis of climate. During the course of the study, 53 "focal" supervisory and management positions were selected to represent the full spectrum of the managerial hierarchy. Next, an average of seven "role senders" (usually superiors and subordinated) were chosen for each focal position on the basis of the closeness of their interaction. The role senders were then asked to respond to 36 questionnaire items indicating the degree to which they advocated compliance or noncompliance with normative or expected *role* behaviors on the part of the focal individuals. The responses were factor analyzed, and five factors seemed to emerge: 1. rules orientation, or the degree to which company-oriented rules are followed; 2. the nurturance of subordinates, or communicating and consulting with subordinates, taking an interest in them, and taking responsibility for their training morale; 3. closeness of supervision, or supervising the work pace and work methods of subordinates; 4. universalism, or the degree to which the individual should identify with the organization as a whole rather than with his particular work group; and 5. promotion-achievement orientation, or the degree to which an individual should try to take advantage of every opportunity for promotion, try to make himself look good in the eyes of his superiors, and come up with original ideas for handling work.

It is extremely difficult to draw generalizations from and integration of the results of these four studies. The individual perceptions which make up the data were obtained from vastly different orientations, or "sets." Taguiri asked managers to rate the importance, or valence, of various organizational characteristics in terms of their motivating properties. Kahn et al. asked individuals (not necessarily managers) to indicate what a particular manager should do relative to a specific set of role behaviors. The implication is that respondents felt such role characteristics were necessary for the effective operation of the organization. In contrast, the Schneider and Bartlett items asked managers to describe their work groups.

A Synthesis

Even though these are very different sets relative to what was required of the respondents, a good deal of communality seemed to result, at least in the outward appearance of the factors. All the studies yielded either five or six factors, and at least four seem to be common across all the investigations. Our composite view of these recurring factors is as follows:

1. *Individual autonomy.* This is perhaps the clearest composite and includes the *individual responsibility, agent independence,* and *rules orientation* factors found by Litwin and Stringer, Schneider and Bartlett, and Kahn et al., respectively, and Taguiri's factor dealing with opportunities for exercising individual initiative. The keystone of this dimension is the freedom of the individual to be his own boss and reserve considerable decision-making power for himself. He does not have to be constantly accountable to higher management.
2. *The degree of structure imposed upon the position.* Litwin and Stringer's *structure;* Schneider and Bartlett's *managerial structure;* Taguiri's first factor dealing with direction, objectives, etc.; and Kahn et al.'s *closeness of supervision* seem similar enough to be lumped under this label. The principal element is the degree to which the objectives of, and methods for, the job are established and communicated to the individual by superiors.
3. *Reward orientation.* Another meaningful grouping includes Litwin and Stringer's *reward* factor; Schneider and Bartlett's *general satisfaction* factor, which seems to convey reward overtones; Kahn et al.'s *promotion-achievement orientation,* and Taguiri's being with a profit-minded and sales-oriented company. These factors do not hang together quite as well as the previous two groups and seem to vary a great deal in breadth. However, the reward element appears to be present in all.
4. *Consideration, warmth, and support.* This dimension lacks the clarity of the previous three. Managerial support from the Schneider and Bartlett study and nurturance of subordinates from Kahn et al. seem quite similar. Litwin and Stringer's *warmth* and *support* also seems to belong here since apparently this is a characteristic attributable to supervisory practices. Taguiri's mention of working with a superior who is highly competitive and competent does not fit quite so easily, but nevertheless seems to refer to the support and stimulation received from one's superior. However, the human relations referent is not as clear as in the factors derived from the other studies.

SUMMARY

In this article we have attempted to identify some of the conceptual difficulties inherent in investigating situational effects, review research dealing with taxonomic efforts, and review the empirical evidence on situational effects. On a conceptual level there is a polyglot of variables that can be subsumed under the rubric the "situation." We grouped these under the following four headings: 1. structural properties, 2. environmental characteristics, 3. organizational climate, and 4. formal role characteristics. The relationship of a situational variable to managerial performance may be conceptualized as an experimental main effect, a predictor (in the correlational sense), a moderator, or some combination of these. Research studies have tended to focus on only one of the three at any one time. There are also serious problems regarding the "level of explanation" associated with the relationship between a situational variable and managerial performance. If the independent variable is a structural property such as organization size, the connecting chain is certainly much longer than in the case of a climate variable which is assessed by means of the individual's *perceptions* of what the organization is like.

Most research has centered around dimensions of organizational climate. Even though there have been relatively few studies and they varied widely in their approach, four factors appear common to them. These we have labeled 1. autonomy, 2. structure, 3. general reward level, and 4. warmth and support. Further research should build on these efforts and attempt to determine the nature of the factor structure in different settings and how it interacts with individual differences. Unfortunately, no such beginning taxonomic work exists with regard to other types of situational variables.

At the empirical level things have not progressed very far, but perhaps a few inferences can be made. The simulation studies by Frederiksen (1966, 1968) and Litwin and Stringer (1966) strongly suggest a number of beneficial effects for organizations which maintain a consistent climate. They further suggest that if individual differences are not taken into account, there is little reason to expect *mean* differences in performance under different climate conditions. One thing these studies do not do is suggest how the influence of climate differs for different tasks. Studies of climate should take a cue from a laboratory experiment by Roby, Nicol, and Farrell (1963) which showed that a decentralized structure was best if the task required cooperative effort but that a centralized structure was best if individuals (students in this case) worked independently toward a common goal.

Perhaps one of the most important findings to emerge from the empirical research is the importance of the initial job assigned to an individual. His expectations and aspirations regarding his career in an organization seem to be very much a function of the skill requirements and difficulty level of his first few jobs. It should be the aim of every organization to "stretch" its personnel by offering them appropriate challenges. If it does not, a self-defeating circle could be created, for the analyses by Berlew and Hall (1964) suggest that over time an individual's expectations for himself tend to approximate those the organization has for him.

In sum, the "situation" has been shown to encompass an exceedingly complex set of variables, especially when their dynamic and interactive properties are considered. Again, not much research has been forthcoming, but there is considerable promise for the future.

CONCLUDING STATEMENT

Therefore what can we say about organizational climate, particularly with regard to its being an outcome of organizational design? We began this chapter by defining it as a macro concept that reflects a shared perceptual character of the organization. Next, the article by Campbell et al. proposed a set of dimensions that make up the variable, *climate*.

The purpose of this concluding statement is to relate climate to organization design. We approach this task in two stages. First, we examine some sets of dimensions that may be more appropriate than those of Campbell et al. The purpose, incidentally, of that examination is twofold: (a.) to emphasize the dimensional character of the construct, because it is through climate's dimensionality that organization design implications become clear, and (b.) to look at more than just four or five dimensions.[1]

The second purpose of this concluding statement is actually to tie climate, through its dimensions, to organization design. We show how different climates get produced by different circumstances and different designs. With this second purpose in mind, we now turn to the question of which dimensions can logically be thought of as comprising organizational climate.

DIMENSIONS OF ORGANIZATIONAL CLIMATE

It would be fruitless to attempt to review every attempt made in the past two or three decades to specify the properties or attributes that characterize organizational climate. But we can report a few of the major ones. The principal attempts are summarized in Table 11–1. The reason for this exercise is to acquire as clear a grasp as possible on the construct. That is, one of the things that happens when people design organizations is that the working atmosphere is affected. Designers therefore need to understand the nature and character of those effects.

Campbell et al.

In this chapter's article, Campbell and his associates summarized several analysts' attempts to describe organizational climate.[2] It would, of course, be wasteful to reproduce those

TABLE 11–1 THREE ANALYSES OF ORGANIZATIONAL CLIMATE

Campbell et al. (1970)	Likert (1967)	Payne and Pugh (1975)
1. Individual autonomy	1. Leadership processes	1. Progressiveness and development
2. Position structure	2. Motivational forces	2. Risk taking
3. Reward orientation	3. Communication processes	3. Warmth
4. Consideration-warmth support	4. Character of interaction and influence	4. Support
	5. Character of goal setting or ordering	5. Control
	6. Character of control processes	

1. Thanks are extended to Nancy M. Muska for her helpful comments on this discussion.

2. The authors specifically examined the analyses by Litwin and Stringer (1966), Taguiri (1966), and Schneider and Bartlett (1968).

descriptions. You may either review the article or examine Table 11–1. We do want to emphasize, however, the *conclusion* drawn by the authors—namely, organizational climate consistently is described by the following dimensions:

1. *Individual autonomy:* the freedom of the individual to be his or her own boss, having considerable decision-making power, and not being continually accountable to higher management.
2. *Position structure:* the degree to which the objectives of, and methods for, the job are established and communicated to the individual by higher management.
3. *Reward orientation:* the degree of reward/profit/achievement orientation fostered and reflected by managerial and nonmanagerial personnel.
4. *Consideration-warmth-support:* the degree to which psycho-socio-emotional needs are met and nourished by other organizational members, managers and nonmanagers alike.

Likert

The work by Rensis Likert is not usually reviewed as part of the traditional climate literature. Nonetheless, his attempt to distinguish among four distinct "management systems" (1967) is a contribution to our understanding of climate. An organization that can be described as having System 1 characteristics, for example, will clearly have a working environment different from an organization with System 4 characteristics. Table 11–2 summarizes some of these differences.

As we can see from Table 11–2, the "character" of an organization for Likert is determined by several factors, ranging from the style of leadership exercised by management to the ways in which cost, productivity, and other control information is used. Examination of Likert's "Management Systems" (and remember that Table 11–2 depicts only the two extreme systems) suggests that organizational climates differ as a function of such features as general degree of participation in organizational matters and the level of trust, mutual esteem, and confidence shared by the membership—managers and nonmanagers alike.

Payne and Pugh

Writing in Dunnette's *Handbook of Industrial and Organizational Psychology,* Roy Payne and Derek S. Pugh (1975) examined the relationships between organizational structure and climate. The authors recognize the difficulty discussed in the introductory remarks: climate is an organizational attribute, but its importance is determined by the way people perceive it. Payne and Pugh thus identify two major variables that impinge directly on climate: organizational structure and the individual.

For Payne and Pugh, "the Individual" refers to people's personalities, needs, abilities, satisfactions, and goals. The authors suggest that structure is a relatively objective

TABLE 11–2 LIKERT'S (1967) "MANAGEMENT SYSTEMS" AS ORGANIZATONAL CLIMATES

Organizational Variable	System 1	System 4
1. Leadership processes		
a. Mangers' trust and confidence in subordinate	No confidence or trust	Complete confidence and trust
b. Subordinates feel comfortable discussing important aspects of their jobs with immediate superiors.	Subordinates do not feel at all comfortable	Subordinates feel completely comfortable
2. Character of motivational forces		
a. Manner of motivational forces	Fear, threats, punishment and occasional rewards	Rewards based on compensation system developed through participation
b. Responsibility felt by members for achieving organizational goals	Top management feels responsibility; lower levels feel less; rank and file feel little and even may behave in ways to defeat organizational goals	Personnel at all levels feel real responsibility for organization's goals and behave in ways to implement them
3. Character of communication process		
a. Direction of information flow	Downward	Down, up, and with peers
b. Extent to which downward communications are accepted by subordinates	Viewed with suspicion	Generally accepted, but if not, openly and candidly questioned
4. Character of interaction and influence		
a. Amount and character of interaction	Little interaction, and always with fear and mistrust	Extensive, friendly interaction with high degree of confidence and trust
b. Amount of cooperative teamwork present	None	Substantial amount throughout the organization
5. Character of goal setting or ordering		
a. Manner in which usually done	Orders issued	Except in emergencies, goals are usually established by means of group participation
6. Character of control processes		
a. Purpose for which control data (e.g., accounting, productivity, cost, etc.) are used	Used by top management for policing and in a punitive manner	Used for self-guidance and for coordinated problem solving and guidance, not used punitively

SOURCE: Abridged and modified from Rensis Likert, *The Human Organization* (New York: McGraw-Hill Book Company, 1967), pp. 4–10. Used by permission.

organizational property, whereas individual and climate characteristics are more subjective (hence the solid- and dotted-line boxes). The following summarizes Payne and Pugh's conception of organizational climate:

1. *Progressiveness and development:* the degree to which organizational conditions foster people's development and encourage the growth and application of new ideas and methods.
2. *Risk taking:* the degree to which people feel free to experiment, innovate, and otherwise take risks without fear of ridicule and reprisal.

3. *Warmth:* this dimension reflects the level of positive feelings that organizational members express for one another.
4. *Support:* the degree to which organizational members show trust and support for each other.
5. *Control:* the degree to which control of people's behavior is formalized ("bureaucratic"), as opposed to internal (interpersonal).

Summary

So far in this chapter we have seen that the idea of organizational climate is imperfectly formed, to say the least. In the first place, not everyone agrees as to the proper way even to define the thing, much less describe it. Still, we were able to identify a variety of dimensions that comprise what most people seem to mean by the term. The specific dimensions used by a particular individual, whether researcher, student, manager, or designer, depend on what aspects of the organization—what attributes, what nuances—the individual wishes to tap.

The question still remains, however: what does all this have to do with organizational design? It is to this issue that we now turn.

CLIMATE AND ORGANIZATION DESIGN

What kinds of conditions produce what kinds of organizational climates? That is, viewing climate as an outcome variable, what sorts of climate characteristics are engendered by an organization's design? Let us address these questions by focusing on the organizational properties we have already examined: organizational goals; design constraints of environment, technology, and people; design variables of work design, organizational control, decision processes, and organization structure. Further, to keep the discussion manageable, let us consider those properties in terms of two extremes, closed/stable/mechanistic and open/adaptive/organic. Finally, we will describe organizational climate with the dimensions identified earlier by Campbell et al.: *individual autonomy, position structure, reward orientation,* and *consideration-warmth-support.* Our examination is brief, since all of these properties, characteristics, dimensions, and so forth have already been discussed at some length in previous chapters and sections of this volume. The examination is summarized in Table 11–3.[3]

Closed/Stable/Mechanistic Designs

We have seen that organizations can be characterized according to the conditions they face and the designs they take on. Specifically, conditions and designs can be thought of as varying between stable/mechanistic conditions on the one hand, and dynamic/organic conditions on the other (Burns and Stalker, 1961; Lawrence and Lorsch, 1967). For the former, *organizational goals* center around efficiency, stability, and security. In essence, the organization's goal mix tends to be simplex.

Constraints on organizational designs—environment, technology, and people—are similarly closed and stable. *Environmental* conditions are placid, uncertainty is low, and there are

3 Some of the terminology employed in Table 11–3 is adapted from Kast and Rosenzweig (1973, 315–18) and Nemiroff and Ford (1976).

TABLE 11–3 ORGANIZATIONAL CLIMATE AS A FUNCTION OF ORGANIZATION DESIGN CHARACTERISTICS

	Characteristics of Organization Design	
Organizational Properties	*Closed / Stable / Mechanistic*	*Open / Adaptive / Organic*
Organizational goals	Efficiency, stability, security, risk aversion, maintenance: simplex goal mix	Effective problem-solving, innovation, growth, adaptability, risk taking: complex goal mix
Constraints on design		
Environment	Placid, certain, determinate, few elements	Turbulent, uncertain, indeterminate, many elements, diverse
Technology	Repetitive, routine, standardized, programmed, unchanging: simplex	Varied, nonroutine, nonstandardized, heuristic, changing: complex
People	Low need strengths, bureaucratic orientation, "local," low commitment	High need strengths, low bureaucratic orientation, "cosmopolitan," high commitment
Design variables		
Work	Easy, homogeneous, short-run, narrow scope, low discretion	Difficult, varied, long-run, broad scope, high discretion
Organizational control	Specific—rules, procedures, hierarchy: "bureaucratic"	Generalized—norms, internalized values, peers: "clan"
Decision process	Programmed, computational, autocratic: centralized	Nonprogrammed, judgmental, participation
Organization structure	Simplex, low role-variety, high formalization/standardization, centralized	Complex, high role-variety, low formalization/standardization, decentralized
Organizational Climate	*Closed / Stable / Mechanistic*	*Open / Adaptive / Organic*
Individual autonomy	Low	High
Position structure	High	Low
Reward orientation	Low	High
Consideration-warmth-support	Low	High

few, relatively similar, elements impinging on the organization. The organization's *technology* tends to be routine, standardized, relatively unvarying—in short, simplex. *People* who comprise the organizational membership have correspondingly low skills, low higher-need strengths, and low commitment (to their repetitive, routine jobs).

Design variables—work design, organizational control, decision processes, and organization structure—have traditionally bureaucratic/mechanistic properties. *Tasks* are narrow in scope, of short-run duration, and relatively homogeneous in nature. *Control processes* are task- or activity-specific. That is, control is exercised by means of rules, procedures, hierarchical relationships, and so forth. Organizational *decision making* is conducted in an autocratic, programmed, computational way. Centralization is a hallmark in this type of organization. Finally, such organizations' structural patterns are simplex, characterized by low role variety and high formalization/standardization.

Organizational Climate

What kind of organizational climate is fostered by such an organizational situation? It is apparent that *individual autonomy* will tend to be relatively low. Well-understood and simplex goals, repetitive, routine technology, centralized, autocratic, and bureaucratic control- and decision-structures—all this works against the individual's having much discretion over his or her activities.

On the other hand, *position structure*—the degree to which a position's objectives and tasks are set by higher management—will be relatively high in this sort of organization. Indeed the whole idea of a mechanistic form is to minimize deviations from a narrowly prescribed standard.

What about *reward orientation*? At first glance, it is not obvious that closed/stable/mechanistic designs will necessarily foster climates that are low on reward orientation. But when we think about it, we realize that such organizations tend to emphasize means, rather than ends—after all, "ends" are standardized, simplex, and well understood. Thus the rules, procedures, schedules, and so forth that guide the production of those ends take on added significance. Further, what little empirical evidence there is (for example, Dieterly and Schneider, 1974) suggests that the level of reward orientation is lower in an organization possessing a closed/stable/mechanistic design.

The final climate dimension is that labeled *consideration-warmth-support.* It is apparent that such a design as we have been discussing is likely to foster a climate that is low on this dimension. A mechanistic, procedure-oriented, autocratic organization will hardly be expected to have a working atmosphere in which employees' psycho-socio-emotional needs are met and nourished.

In short, a closed/stable/mechanistic organization—the traditional bureaucratic form—is suggestive of a machine (March and Simon, 1958). And as we might expect with a machine, the working ambience leaves much—by our modern, somewhat humanistic values—to be desired. The issue was put tellingly by the 19th century French novelist, Honoré de Balzac (in Blau and Meyer, 1971: 100):

> The clerks of departments find themselves sooner or later in the condition of a wheel screwed on to a machine; the only variation of their lot is to be more or less oiled.

Open/Adaptive/Organic Designs

As noted earlier, the open/adaptive/organic label signifies a set of conditions and design characteristics rather opposite to those described in the preceding section. *Organizational goals* focus on adaptability, innovation, growth, and risk taking; the organization's goal mix tends to be relatively complex.

Design constraints tend to be characterized by uncertainty and complexity. The organization's environment, for instance, will be turbulent and uncertain, containing a large number of dissimilar elements with which the organization must deal. *Technology* is correspondingly complex. It is varied, nonroutine, with relatively little standardization. Problem solutions are reached judgmentally, rather than with preprogrammed and rigid decision rules. Accordingly, the *people* in such an organization will tend to have high skill levels, be working on higher-order needs, and have a relatively high level of commitment to their work.

The *design variables* that describe open/adaptive/organic organizations have properties rather different from those identified in the preceding section. *Tasks* are broad in scope, varied in their demands, and afford the worker a measure of discretion. *Control processes* are, accordingly, generalized. That is, organizational control is interpersonal (as opposed to impersonal), relying on norms, standards set by peers, internalized values, and the like. Similarly, *decision processes* are fairly participative in nature. The decisions themselves are complex, requiring judgment, skill, expertise, and so forth. Since such virtues do not reside solely in those who are in top management positions, decision patterns tend to be dispersed, reflecting a relatively decentralized format. Finally, as we know, the *structure* of an organic organization is complex and informal, with high role variety.

Organizational Climate

As we might expect, this type of organizational design tends to foster a climate rather different from that described previously.[4] It seems hardly necessary to go through the argument in the same detail as before: *individual autonomy*—the opportunity/necessity to exercise individual judgment and discretion—will obviously be higher in this sort of organization than in the former.

It is difficult for top management (or anyone, for that matter) to prescribe goals and tasks very precisely when conditions are uncertain or complex. Therefore, *position structure* will be low. An organic-type organization must, of necessity, be less concerned with ill-defined means, and more concerned with effective ends. Accordingly, *reward orientation* tends to be relatively high in such organizations (see Dieterly and Schneider, 1974).

Finally, open/adaptive/organic designs encourage people to develop, grow, and otherwise increase their own capabilities. Such encouragement tends to engender a climate that is high on *consideration-warmth-support*. Indeed, this is the prototypic characteristic of "self-renewing" organizations (Golembiewski, 1972).

The metaphor used to describe the closed/stable/mechanistic organization was that of the machine. A metaphor for the second type of design is the biological organism—actually, a cybernetic-growth organism (Mills, 1967:19–23). The idea is that open/adaptive/organic organizations have two critical properties: they seek self-determination and they seek growth (although not necessarily growth in a strictly physical or financial sense). Cybernetics comes into the metaphor because self-determination and growth require that the organization learn—about its goal-accomplishing effectiveness and its own identity and form. Such learning requires a climate much different from that described by Balzac.

SUMMARY AND CONCLUSION

This chapter has been concerned with an important result, or outcome, of the design process: organizational climate. We began the discussion with an article by Campbell et al. ("Environmental Variation and Managerial Effectiveness"). The authors reviewed a variety of organizational-climate research, both theoretical and empirical. They concluded that the construct, organizational climate, is "a set of attributes specific to a particular

4. Note we say the climate is *different from*—not *better than*. Different conditions call for different responses. Different organizational conditions call for different organizational climates. And as Hellriegel and Slocum (1974: 277) concluded, "an effective climate in a simple and static environment may prove to be dysfunctional in a dynamic and complex environment."

organization that may be induced from the way that organization deals with its members and its environment."

After examining many attempts to modify the construct, Campbell et al. provided a synthesis; namely, that climate is composed of the following dimensions:

- individual autonomy
- position structure
- reward orientation
- consideration-warmth-support

In this concluding statement we have examined the relationship of organization design to organizational climate. Specifically, we reviewed several descriptions of the construct. We then asked, "what sorts of designs seem to produce what climate characteristics?" To address this question, we first recalled the organizational properties that are relevant to organizational design: goals, environment, technology, people, task design, organizational control, decision processes, and organization structure. Next, we characterized each of these properties in terms of two extreme cases: closed/stable/mechanistic versus open/adaptive/organic. We then described organizational-climate characteristics that can reasonably be expected to derive out of the two extreme designs. Table 11–3 summarized the various properties/characteristics so identified. If we think about it, we can see that the two extremes describe those two imaginary organizations we have mentioned several times—Alpha and Beta. In essence, Alpha is a closed/stable/mechanistic sort of enterprise. Beta is more open/adaptive/organic. Design-climate profiles can thus be illustrated for Alpha and Beta as in Figure 11–1.

In essence, a closed/stable/mechanistic design tends to produce a climate that is also closed and mechanistic. A design that is open/adaptive/organic, on the other hand, has the potential of fostering a climate that is equally open, innovative, and growing—for the members as well as the organization. Organizational climate is not, however, the same as organizational effectiveness. What impacts do different design characteristics have on overall organizational performance? We turn to this question in the following chapter.

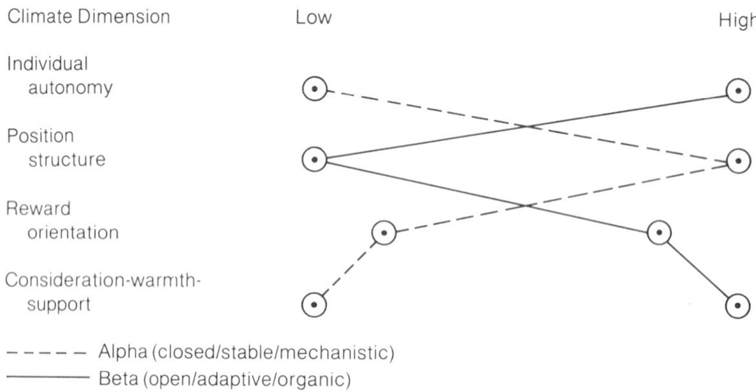

Figure 11-1. Two design-climate profiles

Questions for Review

1. What are some of the definitions of *organizational climate?* By whom are they made? How do they differ from each other?
2. Forehand and Gilmer mention three mechanisms that relate to how organizational environment differences are translated to differences in behavior. What are these three mechanisms? Discuss them briefly.
3. Litwin and Stringer developed a questionnaire to measure organizational members' perception in different areas. What were these areas? What were the informal descriptions of these areas?
4. What are the labels and descriptions given to the six factors that emerged from Schneider and Bartlett's study of climate dimensions?
5. Campbell et al. develop a synthesis of the recurring factors in the studies they mention. What are these recurring factors, and what factors do they embrace in other studies?
6. The "character" of an organization is determined, in Likert's findings, by several factors. What are these, and what are their subdivisions?
7. What is Payne and Pugh's conception of organizational climate?
8. Compare the organizational climate in a closed/stable/mechanistic organization with that in an open/adaptive/organic organization.
9. What are the organizational properties of an open/adaptive/organic organization?
10. What are the organizational properties of a closed/stable/mechanistic organization?

Questions for Discussion

1. "It should be the aim of every organization to 'stretch' its personnel by offering them appropriate challenges." Do you agree with this assertion by Campbell et al.? Are there some personnel who might not, necessarily, be stretched? What do you consider to be an appropriate challenge?
2. What did the article by Campbell et al. contribute to your understanding of organizational climate?
3. After reading the article by Campbell et al., what particular aspect of organizational climate would you be most interested in pursuing on an investigatory/research basis?
4. "What is psychologically important to the individual must be how he perceives his work environment, not how others might choose to describe it." What are the implications of this statement made by Schneider and Bartlett? Should organizations cater to the individual's perception of his or her work environment?
5. "In the organizational context, there must be some set of objects, persons, and events that are relatively common to members; otherwise there is no 'organization.' " Does this statement apply only to organizations? Does it apply at all to organizations?

12

Organizational Effectiveness

INTRODUCTORY REMARKS

This chapter is essentially the "punch line" of the book. When all is said and done, the test of an organization's design is whether the organization is effective—that is, whether the organization is doing the job (usually jobs) it was set up to do. However, determining an organization's effectiveness is as difficult as it is critical. The bottom line on a profit-and-loss statement is probably important to profit-making enterprises. Likewise, such measures as price:earnings ratios, dividends paid out to stockholders, and net return on investment are also useful in assessing effectiveness.

But are these the only indexes of effectiveness? And what about not-for-profit organizations? Price:earnings ratios make little sense for government agencies (from federal bureaucracies to local family-counseling centers), voluntary associations, and "third-sector"

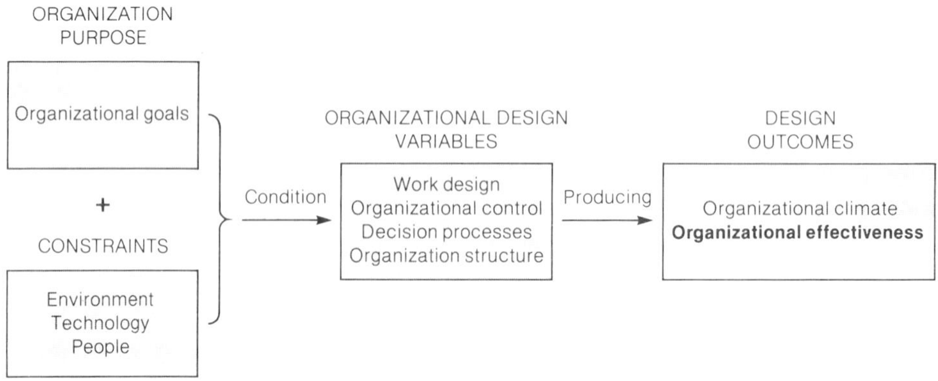

organizations (Etzioni, 1973). The essential purpose of this chapter is to examine questions about what does make sense for them.

We will conduct this examination in the following stages. First, we will briefly review in these introductory remarks two useful, although different ways to get at "effectiveness." Next, we present two important articles on the subject, one by Child, the other by Steers. In the concluding statement we summarize various criteria that are used in measuring organizational effectiveness. Finally, we relate effectiveness to organizational design.

ORGANIZATIONAL EFFECTIVENESS: WHAT IS IT?

One of the reasons the subject of effectiveness is so popular among organization writers and practitioners is that most people have some idea as to what it means. Campbell (1976:30–31)[1] puts it this way:

> Strictly speaking, it is not possible for anyone concerned with the effectiveness of organizations to avoid using it as a construct or to avoid operating via some kind of theory. Without a theory of some sort—even if it has never been made public—it is not possible to say that variable X is a measure of organizational effectiveness and variable Y is not.

What kinds of ideas do people have about effectiveness? That is, how do people decide which factors, characteristics, and properties are X variables, and which are Y? There are two general schemes that people use: the *goal-centered* view and the *natural systems* view.[2]

Goal-Centered View

A view of effectiveness that centers around organizational goals provides a relatively explicit means of defining and assessing organizational performance. The idea is this: the organization is assumed to be managed by people who are rational decision makers. Further, decisions are made with respect to a relatively few reasonably well-understood goals. Managerial strategies that will foster optimal goal attainment can therefore be developed. As a consequence, according to this view, the way to assess organizational effectiveness is to identify criteria for evaluating how well the goals are being achieved.

A goal-centered view of organizational effectiveness is not without its dangers, however (Etzioni, 1960b). Indeed, as reasonable as it is to use goals to judge how well an organization is doing, there are some problems:

1. Whose goals should be used? Those of top management? Owners? Middle management?
2. Which goals should be used? Long range? Short range? Technical? Administrative?
3. What about public versus private goals? Should public goals be ignored? If so, does that mean that they are really meaningless? Are private goals therefore the only ones that have meaning? And if so, whose private goals? . . . . which brings us back to the first point.

---

1. This section follows the discussion in Campbell's (1976) article.
2. Gouldner (1959) distinguishes between a rational model and a natural-system model of organizational analysis. Etzioni (1960b) refers to these two schemes as a *goal model* and a *systems model*. These distinctions are essentially similar for our purposes.

These questions reflect the multiple nature of goals. As we saw in Chapter 3, some goals are set to accommodate the organization's requirement for long-term survival. Some are set to help guide day-to-day actions. Thus different goals reflect different time spans (Gibson et al., 1976). In the short run, production-related goals are important. But the organization must also pursue adaptivity and developmental goals if it is to survive and prosper. These goals are more middle or long run.

Despite the difficulty of focusing on such a messy concept, organizational goals must, by the supposed rational nature of the enterprise, be taken into account in assessing organizational effectiveness. Probably the best way to do so is in conjunction with the second general approach: the natural-systems view.

Natural-Systems View

The natural-systems view rests on the assumption that the essence of organizational effectiveness is not contained in a large set of goals that has varying importance (and even meanings) to different groups of people. Rather, the ultimate object of decisions and activities is the continuing viability of the enterprise. Thus:

> To assess an organization's effectiveness, one should try to find out if the organization is internally consistent within itself, whether its resources are being distributed judiciously over a wide variety of coping mechanisms, whether it is using up resources faster than it should, and so forth. [Campbell, 1976:31]

Such an assessment moves the analysis away from goals, per se, and onto the system's functioning as a social unit. Moreover, such an assessment means that an organization is effective to the degree that resources and activities are used to fulfill total system viability. In other words, such an assessment means that an organization must realize its goals insofar as the conditions under which it operates allows it to do so. In developing this approach, Etzioni (1960b: 262) said it well:

> A measure of effectiveness establishes the degree to which an organization realizes its goals under a given set of conditions. But the central question in the study of effectiveness is not, "How devoted is the organization to its goals?" But rather, "Under the given conditions, how close does the organizational allocation of resources approach an optimum distribution?" *Optimum* is the key word: what counts is a balanced distribution of resources among the various organizational needs, not maximal satisfaction of any one activity.

Goals and Systems

Optimum is indeed the key word. By speaking about an optimum distribution of activities and resources, we begin to realize that the key to effectiveness lies in recognizing an important organizational reality: *an organization is effective to the degree that it accomplishes systemic goals.*

Reconciling the two effectiveness schemes discussed above is therefore a straightforward matter. Recall from Chapter 3 that organizations pursue a variety of goals. That is, resources and activities are utilized in many ways for many purposes. As we saw, however, only a few *types* of activities and resource-utilization patterns occur. We examined seven different sets of types (refer back to Table 3-1 for a description of those seven typologies). Although each typology is useful, we recommended that by Edward Gross (1969) as especially germane to organization design. Gross discovered that organizations pursue five types of goals. He labeled these *output, adaptation, management, motivation,* and *position.*

Now the point of thinking about organizations as pursuing several types of goals is that it allows us to recognize that organizations do not give the same relative emphasis to accomplishing goals in each of the different categories. That is, organizations differ in the degree to which they direct activities and resources toward the pursuit of goals within each category. In short, as we discussed in Chapter 3, organizations do not pursue a particular goal. Rather they pursue a *goal mix.*

The concept of goal mix allows us to reconcile the two effectiveness views. Specifically, the organization must produce a good or service that is attractive to consumers and clients. Hence, the organization is effective to the degree that it can achieve its output goals. But it is also obvious that the organization must be concerned with its viability and functioning. Hence, it must achieve goals of adaptation, management ("organizational maintenance"), and the like. Such goals call to mind the simple open-systems diagram we have sketched before. That is, an organization's goal mix involves more than just output. It also involves goals relating to input and output processes, as well as transformation processes within the technical core.

Thus we realize that the very definition of goal mix suggests a marriage of the goal-centered and the natural-systems views: organizations pursue goals with varying intensities, depending on the nature of their environmental, technological, and human circumstances. In short, *an organization is effective to the degree that it achieves its goal mix on a continuing basis.*

COMPONENTS OF ORGANIZATIONAL EFFECTIVENESS

As we have seen, it is necessary to recognize that organizational effectiveness revolves around the achievement of systemic goals—of the organization's goal mix. It is not enough, however, to restrict our focus to five or six goal types. To relate effectiveness to organization design, we need to elaborate our description of the construct.

Several writers have attempted to provide such an elaboration. In fact, a rather large number of writers have done so—too many to review here. In this chapter's second article, Steers examines 17 separate studies and their 15 distinct criteria for evaluating organizational effectiveness. Child, on the other hand, reviews in the first article some 10 propositions that describe for him effective organizations.

In addition to Child and Steers, three other writers have attempted to synthesize what we understand organizational effectiveness to be. These analysts are Richard Beckhard (1969), John P. Campbell (1976), and William M. Evan (1976). Let us review their ideas in order.

Beckhard

Richard Beckhard (1969) speaks primarily from an organizational-development (OD) perspective. For Beckhard, there is reasonable consensus among OD people about the nature of organizational effectiveness. Or to put it more actively, Beckhard says there is reasonable consensus among OD people as to what a healthy organization is. This consensus is described by 10 characteristics that define a healthy—that is, effective—organization. These characteristics are the following:[3]

1. The total organization, the significant subparts, and individuals, manage their work against *goals* and *plans* for achievement of these goals.
2. Form follows function (the problem, or task, or project, determines how the human resources are organized).
3. Decisions are made by and near the sources of information regardless of where these sources are located on the organization chart.
4. The reward system is such that managers and supervisors are rewarded (and punished) comparably for:
   short-term profit or production performance,
   growth and development of their subordinates,
   creating a viable working group.
5. Communication laterally and vertically is *relatively* undistorted. People are generally open and confronting. They share all the relevant facts including feelings.
6. There is a minimum amount of inappropriate win/lose activities between individuals and groups. Constant effort exists at all levels to treat conflict and conflict-situations as *problems* subject to problem-solving methods.
7. There is high "conflict" (clash of ideas) about tasks and projects, and relatively little energy spent in clashing over *interpersonal* difficulties because they have been generally worked through.
8. The organization and its parts see themselves as interacting with each other *and* with a *larger* environment. The organization is an "open system."
9. There is a shared value, and management strategy to support it, of trying to help each person (or unit) in the organization maintain his (or its) integrity and uniqueness in an interdependent environment.
10. The organization and its members operate in an "action-research" way. General practice is to build in *feedback mechanisms* so that individuals and groups can learn from their own experience.

Campbell

Another writer who has attempted to provide an elaboration of the organizational-effectiveness construct is John P. Campbell (1976). His contribution stems from having examined the empirical literature dealing with measures of effectiveness criteria. His conclusion is that there are some 30 distinct criteria that people employ in assessing organizational performance.

Campbell's list is so illustrative of the subject's complexities that it is reproduced in full here. As Campbell readily admits, the criteria are not completely independent of one another; they therefore overlap. Still, organizational effectiveness is a construct that does in fact have different meanings to different people; it may therefore be useful to maintain the overlaps. The alternative may be to reduce the list to so few variables that only one or two concepts about effectiveness are satisfied.

3. Richard Beckhard, *Organization Development: Strategies and Models.* Addison-Wesley, Reading, Massachusetts 1969, pp. 10–11. Used by permission.

For example, is job satisfaction the continuum on which the real payoffs are made, or is it a means to an end? In other words, is satisfaction important because it is related to some more distal variable that is the organization's real concern? Which of these are means and which are ends is a value judgment on somebody's part. It is made implicitly or explicitly in organizations every day and cannot be avoided. [Campbell, 1976: 36]

It is not new, of course, to say that value judgments play a part in specifying what one means by organizational effectiveness. Moreover, it is not trivial to say so. In fact, values come into the organization-design/organization-effectiveness relationship quite strongly, as we shall see in the concluding statement.

Synthesized List of Possible Indicators of Organizational Effectiveness

1. *Overall Effectiveness:* A general evaluation that takes in as many single criteria as possible and results in a single judgment about the effectiveness of the organization. It has been measured primarily by two methods: archival performance records, either single or in some combined form, and overall ratings or judgments obtained from persons thought to be knowledgeable about the organization.
2. *Productivity:* Usually defined as the quantity or volume of the major product or service that the organization provides and can be measured at three levels: individual, group, and total organization. Both archival records and ratings have been used, and in at least one case, independent observation of ongoing work was used to obtain a measure of production.
3. *Efficiency:* Usually thought of in terms of a ratio that reflects a comparison of some aspect of unit performance to the costs incurred for that performance. There have been relatively few attempts to operationalize this concept, and all but one of these is a measure taken directly from organization records or a factor derived from such records.
4. *Profit:* The amount of revenue from sales left after all costs and obligations are met. Percent return on investment or percent return on total sales are sometimes used as alternative definitions.
5. *Quality:* The quality of the primary service or product provided by the organization may take many operational forms, which are largely determined by the kind of product or service provided by the organization. They are too numerous to mention here.
6. *Accidents:* or the frequency of on-the-job accidents resulting in lost time. We found only two examples of accident rates being used as a measure of organizational effectiveness.
7. *Growth:* or an increase in such variables as total manpower, plant capacity, assets, sales, profits, market share, and number of innovations. It implies a comparison of an organization's present state with its own past state. Only four studies attempted to use measures of growth.
8. *Absenteeism:* or the relative frequency with which people are absent from work. The

SOURCE: John P. Campbell, "Contributions Research Can Make in Understanding Organizational Effectiveness," *Organization and Administrative Sciences,* vol. 7 (Spring/Summer 1976):36–38. Used by permission.

usual definition stipulates unexcused absences but even within this constraint there are a number of alternative definitions.

9. *Turnover:* This is usually some measure of the frequency and amount of voluntary terminations and refers to a change in actual personnel within the organization, however that change occurs. All but one of the turnover measures we reviewed are archival, but even with this constraint there are a surprising number of variations and a few studies used directly comparable measures.

10. *Satisfaction:* Satisfaction has been defined many ways but perhaps the modal view references satisfaction to the achievement or possession of certain outcomes provided by the organization and defines it as an individual's perception of the degree to which he or she has received an equitable amount of the outcome. That is, satisfaction is the degree to which individuals perceive they are equitably rewarded by various aspects of their job situation and the organization to which they belong.

11. *Motivation:* In our present context this is the strength of the predisposition of an individual to engage in goal-directed actions or activity on the job. It is not a feeling of relative contentment with various job outcomes as is satisfaction, but more akin to a feeling of readiness or willingness to work at accomplishing the job's goals. As an organizational index, it must be "summed" across people.

12. *Morale:* This is an often used variable that is difficult to define or even to understand how organizational theorists and researchers are using it. The modal definition seems to view morale as a predisposition in organization members to put forth extra effort in achieving organizational goals and objectives. It includes feelings of commitment and is a group phenomena involving extra effort, goal communality, and feelings of belonging. Groups have some degree of morale while individuals have some degree of motivation (and satisfaction). By implication, morale is inferred from group phenomena.

13. *Control:* Refers to the degree of, and distribution of management control that exists within an organization for influencing and directing the behavior of organization members.

14. *Conflict/Cohesion:* A bipolar dimension defined at the cohesion end by an organization in which the members like one another, work well together, communicate fully and openly, and coordinate their work efforts. At the other end lies the organization with verbal and physical clashes, poor coordination, and ineffective communication.

15. *Flexibility/Adaptation* (Adaptation/Innovation): Refers to the ability of an organization to change its standard operating procedures in response to environmental changes. Many people have written about this dimension, but relatively few have made attempts to measure it.

16. *Planning and Goal Setting:* or the degree to which the organization systematically plans its future steps and engages in explicitly goal setting behavior.

17. *Goal Consensus:* Refers to the degree to which all individuals perceive the same goals for the organization, which is distinct from actual commitment to those goals.

18. *Role and Norm Congruence:* The degree to which the members of an organization are in agreement on such things as what kinds of supervisory attitudes are best, performance expectations, morale, role requirements, etc.

19. *Managerial Interpersonal Skills:* or the level of skill and efficiency with which the management deals with superiors, subordinates, and peers and includes the extent to which managers give support, facilitate constructive interaction, and generate enthusiasm for meeting goals and achieving excellent performance. It is meant to include such things as consideration, employee centeredness, etc. We realize that this variable is often used as a "predictor" of other variables. However, within some models of organizational effectiveness it has the character of a systemic variable which is indicative of an organization's health.
20. *Managerial Task Skills:* or the overall level of skills the organization's managers, Commanding Officers, or group leaders possess for performing tasks centered on work to be done, and not the skills employed when interacting with other organizational members.
21. *Information Management and Communication:* Refers to the collection, analysis, and distribution of information critical to organizational effectiveness.
22. *Readiness:* The usual definition of this variable is in terms of an overall judgment concerning the probability that the organization could successfully perform some specified task if asked to do so. Work on measuring this variable has been largely confined to military settings.
23. *Utilization of Environment:* The extent to which the organization successfully interacts with its environment and acquires scarce, valued resources necessary to its effective operation. For example, it includes the degree to which it acquires a steady supply of manpower and financial resources.
24. *Evaluations by External Entities:* Such evaluations refer to evaluations of the organization or organizational unit by those individuals and organizations in its environment with which it interacts. Loyalty to, confidence in, and support given the organization by such groups as suppliers, customers, stockholders, enforcement agencies, and the general public would fall under this label.
25. *Stability:* Stability refers to the maintenance of structure, function, and resources through time, and more particularly through periods of stress.
26. *Internalization of Organizational Goals:* or the acceptance or internalization of organizational goals within that organization. It includes their belief that the organization's goals are right and proper. This is *not* the extent to which goals are clear or agreed upon by the organization members (goal clarity and goal consensus, respectively). Thus, it refers to the acceptance not the understanding of the organization's goals.
27. *Value of Human Resources:* A composite criterion, where the components refer to measures of individuals. It refers to the total value or total worth of the individual members of an organization, in an accounting or balance sheet sense, to the organization. It is another way of combining many of the variables discussed so far but it deals only with the role of human resources, not other kinds of assets, in organizational effectiveness.
28. *Participation and Shared Influence:* or the degree to which individuals in the organization participate in making the decisions which directly affect them.

29. *Training and Development Emphasis:* or the amount of effort the organization devotes to developing its human resources.
30. *Achievement Emphasis:* Almost an analog to the individual need for achievement, this refers to the degree to which the organization appears to place a high *value* on achieving major new goals.

Evan

A third analyst who has examined organizational effectiveness is William M. Evan (1976). His analysis is especially pertinent to our interests because he has used an explicitly open-systems approach. In fact, his treatment follows our simple input-output diagram sketched earlier. Evan identifies four "systemic processes" (1976: 19):

1. *Inputs* (I) of various types of resources
2. *Transformations* (T) of resources with the aid of social and/or technical mechanisms
3. *Outputs* (O) which are transmitted to other systems
4. Feedback effects (F), whether positive or negative

We hardly need to elaborate on the first three items. Input, transformation, and output processes have already been discussed at length, both in this volume and elsewhere (Katz and Kahn, 1966; Thompson, 1967; Kast and Rosenzweig, 1974). Feedback effects, however, do require some further mention.

As we have seen (Chapter 3), organizational systems seek to achieve a set of goals. More dynamically, though, organizational systems engage in goal-setting, goal-seeking, and goal-changing processes. Increases in deviations from predetermined goals result from *positive-feedback* effects. Decreases in such deviations result from *negative-feedback* effects.

For Evan, organizational effectiveness is described by the relationships among the four processes listed above (input, transformation, output, and feedback). Conventional representations of organizational effectiveness involve the first three processes. Feedback effects, on the other hand, are represented by changes. Specifically, feedback is reflected in the following ratios: $\Delta I/I$, $\Delta T/T$, $\Delta O/O$, $\Delta T/I$, $\Delta T/O$, and $\Delta O/I$. In short, organizational effectiveness is composed of several systemic interrelationships, reflected in at least nine ratios:

1. $\frac{O}{I}$	4. $\frac{\Delta I}{I}$	7. $\frac{\Delta T}{I}$
2. $\frac{T}{I}$	5. $\frac{\Delta T}{T}$	8. $\frac{\Delta T}{O}$
3. $\frac{T}{O}$	6. $\frac{\Delta O}{O}$	9. $\frac{\Delta O}{I}$

One attractive feature of Evan's approach is that the nine organizational-effectiveness ratios suggest different operational criteria for assessing organizational performance. Business firms, for example, commonly use return on investment as an O/I criterion. Colleges and universities might use number of students graduated. Change in working capital, on the other hand, is a conventional $\Delta I/I$ criterion for business firms. Change in student enrollment is such a criterion for colleges and universities. Table 12–1 illustrates some criteria for each ratio and for six different types of organizations: business organizations, administrative agencies, hospitals, courts, prisons, colleges, and universities.

Table 12–1 suggests another attractive feature of Evan's approach: an organization's goals (public or otherwise) do not overwhelm the assessment of organizational effectiveness. That is, as Evan (1976: 24) says:

> It is possible to develop organizational effectiveness measures for different organizations, as well as suborganizations, without *directly* and explicitly identifying their goal or goals, but *indirectly* by measuring dimensions of inputs, transformations, and outputs.

Still, a goal orientation does marry well with Evan's systems approach. The point, as we have emphasized several times, is that organizations pursue a variety of goals. Evan's ratios provide us with a useful means of identifying that variety: return on investment, inventory turnover, volume of sales, change in product quality—these all represent different goals, goals that relate to both the output and the continual functioning of the organizational system. In short, Evan's ideas combine the best of both the goal-centered and the natural-systems approaches discussed earlier.

The Readings

For as important a subject as organizational effectiveness is, surprisingly little research has been done on it. This chapter contains two articles, however, that reflect the state of knowledge about organizational effectiveness. In the first article, "What Determines Organizational Performance? The Universals versus the It-All-Depends," John Child contrasts two schools of management thought. The first school, says the author, maintains that whatever the situation or circumstances, certain factors universally determine the performance of any organization. The opposing school holds that so-called universals are not realistic; the effect of any factor on organizational effectiveness varies, depending on the organization's goals, size, technology, markets, and so forth.

Which school is correct? Child admits that he is not certain but does offer some tentative conclusions. In particular, the author advances 10 propositions about the factors that determine organizational performance. Half of his propositions refer to universals, the other half to contingencies. Child concludes, therefore, that effective organizational performance does depend on some factors that remain relatively stable across many situations. It also depends on some factors that managers need to design to fit a particular circumstance.

In the second article, "When is an Organization Effective?," Richard M. Steers argues that effectiveness is not a "thing"—a thing that can be captured in a single data point, ratio, or even index. Rather, says Steers, organizational effectiveness must reflect the *processes* that make up an organization's functioning.

Steers begins his discussion by noting a variety of problems in assessing organizational performance. He identifies eight such problems, characterized by the following questions:

1. Is there any such thing as organizational effectiveness?
2. How stable are the assessment criteria?
3. Which time perspective is most appropriate in assessment?

TABLE 12–1 ILLUSTRATIVE INDICATORS OF SYSTEMIC PROCESS VARIABLES OF ORGANIZATIONAL EFFECTIVENESS FOR DIFFERENT TYPES OF ORGANIZATIONS

Some Systemic Process Variables

Type of Organization	$\frac{O}{I}$	$\frac{T}{I}$	$\frac{T}{O}$	$\frac{\Delta I}{I}$	$\frac{\Delta T}{T}$	$\frac{\Delta O}{O}$	$\frac{\Delta T}{I}$	$\frac{\Delta T}{O}$	$\frac{\Delta O}{I}$
Business organizations	Return on investment	Inventory turnover; kilowatts of energy per direct employee	R and D / Volume of sales	Change in working capital	Change in administrative personnel to total personnel (A/P); change in labor unit cost; change in automation	Change in volume of sales; change in quality of products	Change in inventory turnover; change in kilowatts of energy per direct employee	Change in R and D; / Volume of sales	Change in return on investment
Administrative agencies (*e.g.*, FTC)	Total number of cases processed and decided / Annual budget	Cost of information system / Annual budget	Cost of information system / Total number of cases processed and decided	Change in workload; change in annual budget	Change in A/P	Change in number of cases processed and decided	Change in cost of information system / Annual budget	Change in cost of information system / Total number of cases processed and decided	Change in rate of compliance with administrative regulations
Hospitals	Total number of patients treated / Annual budget	Capital investment in medical technology / Annual budget	Capital investment in medical technology / Total number of patients treated	Change in number of patients treated	Change in A/P	Change in patient recovery rate by type of cases	Change in capital investment in medical technology / Annual budget	Change in capital investment in medical technology / Total number of patients treated	Change in incidence of illness among discharged patients by type of case
Courts	Total number of cases disposed and adjudicated / Annual budget	Cost of information system / Annual budget	Cost of information system / Total number of cases disposed and adjudicated	Change in backlog of cases	Change in A/P	Change in number of cases decided	Change in cost of information system / Annual budget	Change in cost of information system / Total number of cases disposed and adjudicated	Change in number of cases decided / Number of cases on calendar, by type of case
Prisons	Number of inmates / Annual budget	Cost of information system / Annual budget	Cost of information system / Number of inmates	Change in number of new inmates	Change in A/P	Change in number of discharged inmates	Change in cost of information system / Annual budget	Change in cost of information system / Number of inmates	Change in rate of recidivism among inmates
Colleges and universities	Number of students graduated / Annual budget	Cost of information system / Annual budget	Cost of information system / Number of students graduated	Change in student enrollment	Change in A/P	Change in number of students graduated; change in number of publications of faculty	Change in cost of information system / Annual budget	Change in cost of information system / Number of students graduated	Change in rate of admission of students whose parents are alumni; change in rate of alumni contributors

4. Are the various assessment criteria related to each other?
5. How accurate are the assessment criteria?
6. How widely can the criteria be applied?
7. How do such criteria help us understand organizational dynamics?
8. At what level should effectiveness be assessed?

The author then proceeds to describe three examples of *in*effective organizations, all of which leads to his "process model" for analyzing effectiveness. The process model focuses on goal optimization, organizations as systems, and human behavior.

Conclusion

In summary, this chapter ties together much of the book's previous material by addressing the following questions:

1. What is the concept, *organizational effectiveness*?
2. What are the dimensions of organizational performance that comprise overall effectiveness?
3. How does effectiveness relate to organization design?
4. What sorts of effectiveness criteria are relevant for what circumstances or combinations of design constraints?

WHAT DETERMINES ORGANIZATION PERFORMANCE?
The Universals vs. the It-All-Depends

JOHN CHILD

One school of management thought maintains that, irrespective of the circumstances, certain factors, attributes—call them what you will—universally determine the performance of any organization. The opposing school (newer, and perhaps for that reason just as doctrinaire) argues that universals are not reflections of reality, that the effect of any factor on organizational performance varies with the objectives, size, markets, and other characteristics of the particular organization. This is the contingency school.

Which school is correct? Research, including our own investigations, discourages dogmatism, permits tentative generalizations, and indicates strongly the need for further research. Based on the research to date, however, ten propositions are advanced here about the factors that determine organizational performance; half of these propositions refer to universal attributes, while the other half lend themselves to a contingency approach to organizational performance.

But first, a few caveats that qualify what follows. The question of what determines the levels of performance achieved by organizations still defies a sure answer. The problem is extremely complex because, as Jonathan Boswell said in his *The Rise and Fall of Small Firms*, "A vast number of influences on performance are at work. Some of these are quantifiable, others aren't; some are external to the firm, others are internal and managerial, and of the latter many are subtly interwoven."

Both universalistic and contingency perspectives assume that it is possible to identify factors that will to some degree determine levels of performance. A major difficulty, however, lies in the fact that performance is not simply a dependent variable. The performance levels achieved by an organization constitute a vital input of information to its managers that is likely to stimulate them to make adjustments in policies and modes of operation. These adjustments may be an attempt to correct a poor level of performance or to accommodate the consequences of good performance, such as a growth in scale, and so to sustain the favorable trend. In other words, it is unrealistic to regard performance *only* as a variable dependent on other factors.

These introductory remarks contain the elements of a simple framework that will be used to bring together the more salient research findings on the performance of organizations. This framework is sketched out in Figure 12–1 in terminology that applies particularly to business organizations. Briefly, the strategy and plans that are formulated are regarded as major determinants of an organization's activities, and hence a critical influence on its eventual performance. Strategic decisions are responses to pressures imposed on managers by the various participants within the organization and its environment, with managers' own stakes in ownership being a strongly influencing factor. The design of organization structure in the light of situational contingencies is included as a potential determinant of how effectively the tasks of the organization are carried out. The quality of management is regarded as a pervasive element that can affect all aspects of organizational behavior.

The managerial, strategic, and organizational factors that have emerged as correlates of performance will now be discussed separately, with research findings organized around the ten major propositions mentioned earlier.

MANAGERIAL CORRELATES OF PERFORMANCE

"The good manager" is the keynote of one of the most popular universalistic theories about performance. This

Excerpted, by permission of the publisher, from *Organizational Dynamics*, Summer 1974, ©1974 by AMACOM, a division of American Management Associations.

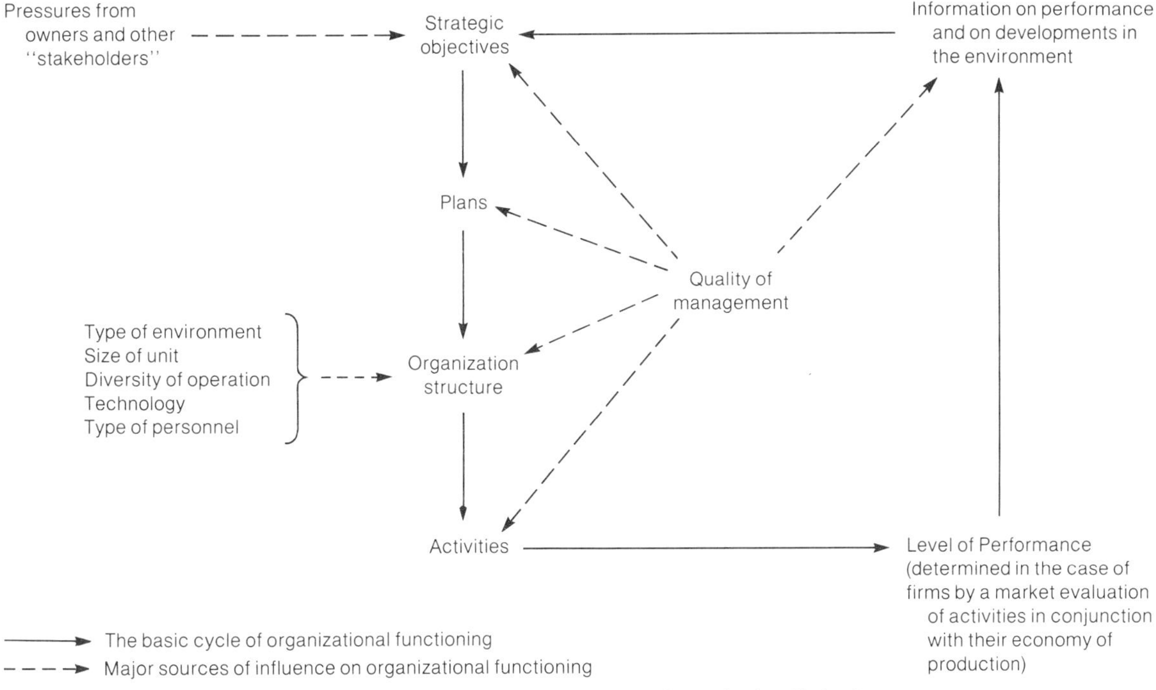

Figure 12-1. Performance in the context of organizational behavior

theory holds that the successful leadership of any organization will depend on the presence of certain qualities of character, drive, competence, and dedication among its managers. Thus, a British survey carried out in the early 1960s concluded that "thrusting" managerial attitudes "are considerably more likely to lead to high and profitable growth than are the sleepy attitudes and practices with which they are contrasted."

Youth, technical qualification, and a stake in the ownership of the organization are among the factors often thought of as promoting more effective management. For example, in recruiting, the relative merits of youth, with its supposed adaptability and energy, as against the experience of more mature applicants, have often occasioned debate. What are the facts?

Proposition 1: Organizations run by younger teams of top managers will tend to achieve higher levels of performance.

The journal *Management Today* found in its 1973 survey of the boards of the 200 largest British companies that those having the oldest boards showed lower profitability and growth than companies with the youngest directors. As the journal put it, there was no refutation here of "the common-sense view that companies dominated by conservatively reared older men are less likely to produce dynamic performance."

Our research at the Aston Management Centre did not find that the age of senior managers correlated systematically with company profits, but it did relate to growth in sales, income, and assets measured over a five-year period. In each one of six industries sampled, younger managements typically achieved higher rates of company growth. At their best, the "young Turks" achieved quite outstanding growth performances. Although there was a lot of variation in the levels attained, the least successful young teams did no worse than the least successful older managements. Two economists, Peter Hart and John Mellors, have also independently looked at the age of company chairmen and the growth of net assets in four British industries and reached the same conclusion: The growth of companies controlled by older men tends to be slower, although less volatile.

So a fairly general link seems to exist between youthful management and more rapid growth. But how should we interpret this observation? After all, it may signify little more than that faster-growing companies recruit and promote younger people more rapidly into senior vacancies. Is youth among managers just a consequence of growth already achieved?

Favoring this argument is the fact that managers in faster-growing companies tended to have had shorter periods of service with the company and to have reached their present posts via fewer intermediate positions. On the other hand, they had not on the whole been in their present jobs for any less time than had managers in slow-growing companies.

The personal qualities that we found to characterize younger managers support the view that age is, indeed, an operative influence. Younger managers were more likely to press actively for change and innovation within their companies. They questioned prevailing systems of formal rules and authority more keenly. They also had greater confidence in their own abilities to succeed in the high positions they held than did older managers. The confident attitudes and behavior found among younger managers are just the kind likely to promote a striving for innovation and rapid growth.

I have devoted some space to the question of youthful management because it may be an influence on performance that applies in most types of organization and upon which managers can act. Research findings to date point to the need for career systems that allow young people of proven ability and appropriate experience to advance rapidly to senior positions. The other side of this coin is the justification of the practice found in some American corporations where, after the age of 50 or so, senior executives may be transferred into less demanding positions.

In British industry, the rapid promotion of able men and women who are still in their prime is slowly becoming more usual, but a planned transfer of older people to less responsible positions, as opposed to more brutal methods like dismissal or compulsory early retirement, is not. This always tends to be resisted by the older executives who hold power in company managements, and it is important for transfers of this kind not to entail a loss of remuneration and privilege. The question remains, nevertheless, whether holding down top management positions is to be primarily a reward of age and long service or a recognition of who is best able to meet the requirements of the job—quite possibly a relatively young man.

Proposition 2: Organizations run by formally better-qualified teams of top managers will tend to achieve higher levels of performance.

The reasoning behind this proposition is the straightforward notion that the possession of formal qualifications is likely to indicate that managers have a certain level of attested expertise and ability. This potential influence on levels of performance cannot, of course, be entirely separated from the age factor, since younger managers tend more often to possess these formal qualifications than do older managers.

Some evidence emerges from British studies that the financial success of companies is generally greater when a relatively high proportion of their directors have formal professional qualifications. D. P. Barritt found this to be the case after studying the profits of larger British companies in the 1950s. More recently, in the mid-1960s, a study by Roger Betts of 23 companies, chiefly in construction and plastics, found that those achieving a higher rate of growth in profits had a greater average number of formal qualifications held per director. In both industries, the successful companies had a significantly high proportion of directors concerned with research and development and (it appeared) possessing scientific qualifications.

There is some support, then, for the proposition that formally qualified management teams will achieve superior performance. And the balance within top executive or directorial teams of types of qualifications may also relate to success. For example, in the study by Betts just cited, there was evidence that poor-performing companies had a heavy weighting of men with production and engineering backgrounds. Another study of 93 major British companies achieving the highest and lowest rates of return on capital during the period 1966–72 found that the high performers had more directors with accounting qualifications, while the low performers had more directors with engineering qualifications. This proportionate relationship of directors' qualifications appeared to be more closely associated with organizational performance than the total number of qualifications within the board.

Proposition 3: Organizations run by managers with a substantial personal stake in their ownership will tend to achieve higher levels of performance.

A number of studies have been made in the United States and Britain of the relation between the control of companies and their levels of performance. Overall, the results suggest that companies with a concentration of ownership control (rather than dispersed ownership) tend to have higher rates of profit *and* higher rates of growth, but differences in levels of performance have often not been significant, and the measures of ownership influence have been formalistic and indirect.

In our studies, we have found that where there was a greater concentration of ownership control, chief executives attached particularly great importance to maximizing profits and growth: There were, however, no significant links between the ownership control factor and rates of profit actually achieved, and the only significant link with growth was found in the tendency for owner-controlled companies to have a more rapid growth in net assets over a five-year period.

Rather fewer studies have looked at managers' stockholdings in relation to company performance, but the results that emerge are more clear-cut, indicating that when managers have greater personal stake in ownership, the performance of companies tends to be superior. For example, a study by Steve Nyman of the 100 largest British commercial and industrial companies found that higher levels of stockholding by directors were significantly associated with higher rates of growth. A larger stake in ownership was also associated with the achievement of higher rates of profit, although this result was only just statistically significant. Given higher growth and higher profitability, it is not surprising that a greater stake in ownership was also associated with a higher stock market rating and a higher price-earnings ratio.

In short, there is a clear tendency for the company in which control is linked with a stake in ownership to be a superior performer. The motivational implications of this relationship for all types of organizations are significant, since they suggest that whenever managers have a direct personal stake in the success of an undertaking, its performance will be enhanced. There is also a suggestion here that the objectives held by managers may influence the performance of their organizations, which leads us to a consideration of strategic factors.

Proposition 4: The performance standards set by an organization's management will be influenced by the norms of performance among other organizations of a similar type.

Strategy deals with the objectives established for an organization and the effort to attain them. For example, if we establish the objective of sustaining a given annual rate of growth, this may mean diversification into a faster-growing industry in order to achieve the objective. There is ample evidence that normal rates of profit and growth vary among industries and that these variations can have an important influence on the performance of firms, especially smaller ones whose activities are usually confined to a single industry. In addition to reflecting certain shared economic circumstances having to do with size of markets, growth of overall demand, structure of the industry, and so forth, the differentiation of company performance levels by industry also reflects the presence of shared standards by which many firms are content to judge themselves. This phenomenon—of managements' assessing performance against localized, rather than general, standards—is likely to be even more widespread outside the business sphere, where mechanisms to enforce universal economic standards such as stock market ratings are absent. It is this consideration that underlies the proposition made above.

Proposition 5: The less dispersed top-management objectives are and the more agreement there is among senior managers as to which objectives have priority, the more successful the organization will be in attaining them.

Chief executives in our study of British firms were asked to rate the importance to their companies of ten possible objectives, scoring each of them separately along five-point scales. Nearly all of the respondents gave very high priority to maximizing net profit over the long term (five years) and to achieving a high rate of growth. Because of this strong measure of agreement, the rating of these objectives did not discriminate between successful companies and others.

The evaluation of certain other objectives did differentiate. In the more profitable companies, with above-average rates of return for their industries on sales and on net assets, chief executives attached lower importance to a high level of distributed dividends, but greater importance to a high level of rewards and benefits for employees. In more profitable firms they also showed less concern for the company's prestige. In the faster-growing companies, chief executives attached low importance to maximizing short-term profits over a 12-month period, to paying out a high level of dividends, and to "service to the wider community."

A comparison of three sugar confectionary companies with contrasting performance profiles illustrates these points in greater detail. Company X was a poor performer by any criterion. Company Y had an outstanding growth record and had maintained an average level of profitability. Company Z was highly profitable and had achieved an average level of growth. As Table 12–2 shows, the chief executive of all three companies attached considerable importance to major objectives such as maximizing long-term profitability, growth, and market share. In Company X, however, the chief executive hardly discriminated in his assessment among these objectives and others in the list we gave him. In the two better-performing companies, less importance was attached to objectives like prestige, a high dividend payout, and service to the community. In growth-Company Y, innovation was given a high rating. In Company Z, which was securing high margins on high-quality traditional lines, less emphasis was given to growth and market share than in Company Y, and somewhat more stress was placed on maximizing profits in the short term.

Findings like these, even though they concern chief executives' views alone, suggest that the mix of strategic objectives selected for a business may influence its performance. In the sample as a whole, the companies achieving greater commercial success were those whose top managements were more singleminded in pursuing longer-term profit and growth objectives. Chief executives in these companies also paid considerable attention to the building up of internal strengths, such as providing favorable conditions for employees and retaining surpluses within the business to finance further profitable expansion.

In companies where chief executives attach more importance to external points of reference, such as prestige, serving the community, and paying higher

TABLE 12–2 RATING OF OBJECTIVES IN THREE CONFECTIONERY COMPANIES*

Objective	Ratings of Importance**		
To maximize:	*Company X*	*Company Y*	*Company Z*
1. Net profit over five years	5	5	5
2. Rate of growth	5	5	4
3. Market share	4	5	4
4. Employee rewards	4	5	5
5. Net profit over one year	5	3	4
6. Prestige	5	3	2
7. Innovation	4	5	2
8. Assets and reserves	4	2	1
9. Dividends distributed	4	2	1
10. Service to the wider community	4	1	1

*Company X was a small family firm with low profitability and low growth, old product and old technology. Company Y was an American-owned firm of small to medium size, with average profitability and rapid growth, some new products and advanced technology. Company Z was a medium-size subsidiary, with high profitability and average growth, traditional high-quality products, enjoying high margins on low-cost technology.

**5—Extremely important
**4—Very important
**3—Moderately important
**2—Not very important
**1—Not at all important

dividends, financial performance tends to be poorer. Whether this association between a lower concern for external interests and superior performance can continue through the 1970s, with the present growing insistence on company social responsibility, remains to be seen. On the whole, though, the message of these findings seems clear: If you want to manage a successful business, concentrate on a few key objectives and avoid distractions. This also implies, of course, that careful thought should be given to the selection of key objectives in the first place.

ORGANIZATION STRUCTURE AND PERFORMANCE

Managerial attributes and the quality of strategy appear to have some relation to levels of performance in most organizations, even though the organizations differ in their environment, diversity, size, technology, and personnel. When we turn to a third possible influence on performance, the design of organization structure, we find most authorities taking the view that the type of situation is vital. This is the contingency approach mentioned earlier, which states that the design of organization most appropriate for high performance can be formulated only with contingent circumstances in mind. According to this theory, there are no general principles of organization.

The argument goes as follows: Contingent factors such as the type of environment or the size of the organization have some direct influence on levels of success. There may, for example, be economies of scale open to the larger organization. Certain environments, such as particular industries, may be more beneficent and provide greater opportunity. Second, it is assumed that a set of structured administrative arrangements consciously adapted to the tasks that are to be done, to the expectations and needs of people performing the tasks, to the scale of the total operation, to its overall complexity, and to the pressures of change being encountered will themselves act to promote a higher level of effectiveness than will a structure ill-suited to these contingencies. Organization structure is seen in this way to modify the effects of contingencies upon performance. Last, the all-pervasive quality of management affects both strategic decisions as to the type of conditions under which the organization will seek to operate and the design of its internal structure.

Environment. According to contingency theory, different approaches to organizational design are conducive to high performance, depending on whether or not the environment in which the organization is operating is variable and complex in nature, or stable and simple. Variability in the environment refers to the presence of changes that are relatively difficult to predict, involve important departures from previous conditions, and are likely, therefore, to generate considerable uncertainty.

Complexity of the environment is said to be greater the more extensive and diversified the range of an organization's activities, which correspondingly take it into more diverse sectors of the environment. These diverse sectors are all relevant areas of external information that it should monitor. There is evidence that the degree of environmental variability is a more important contributor to uncertainty among managerial decision makers than is complexity. I shall discuss variability now and return to complexity in a later section on diversity of operations.

Proposition 6: In conditions of environmental variability, successful organizations will tend to have structures with the following characteristics: 1. arrangements to reduce and to structure uncertainty; 2. a relatively high level of internal differentiation; and 3. a relatively high level of integration achieved through flexible, rather than formalized, processes.

This mouthful of a proposition attempts to distill the essence of what we know so far about a highly complex issue. Among possible arrangements to reduce and structure the uncertainty generated by a changing environment are a closer liaison with the separate independent organizations upon which one's own organization is highly dependent as supplier or customer (even to the extent of vertical or horizontal integration), and attempts to secure a better quality of intelligence from outside the organization.

The critical nature of a variable environment and the need for liaison with outside organizations and for a significant intelligence activity all mean that an organization is under pressure to employ specialist staff in boundary or interface roles—that is, in positions where they form a link with the outside world, scooping in and evaluating relevant information. This may well take the form of setting up more specialist departments and thereby increasing the internal differentiation of the organization.

If there are many new significant external changes to which an organization has to adapt, and if it has become fairly differentiated to cope with these, then there will be all the more need to achieve a degree of integration among its personnel that not only offsets their specializations from one another but, over and above this, permits them to react swiftly to new developments in a coordinated manner. Flexible, rather than highly formalized, methods of coordination and information-sharing will be required. This generally means a greater amount of face-to-face participation in discussions and decision making, with an emphasis on close lateral relations among members of different departments instead of formal links up and down hierarchies or via periodic formal meetings. This mode of working also implies a higher degree of delegation, particularly when it comes to operational decisions.

Various studies that have examined organizational performance in relation to structure and variable environments have produced sufficiently consistent findings to support the conclusions we have just made. Each study, of course, examines the structural elements I have mentioned in more detail. In the United States there is the well-known work of Paul Lawrence and Jay Lorsch, as well as studies by Robert Duncan, Pradip Khandwalla, Anant Negandhi, and Bernard Reiman, among others. Of British studies, Tom Burns' and G. M. Stalker's is the best known.

Our own research at Aston indicated that companies in the variable science-based environment characterizing electronics and pharmaceuticals that were achieving above-average levels of growth tended to rely less on formal procedures and documentation than did slow-growing companies. Among firms in more stable environments, high-growth companies relied more (but only marginally so) on formalized methods of integration than did less successful firms.

These organizational differences between high- and low-growth companies located in contrasting environments were most marked in certain areas of management. Within the stable sector, faster-growing companies had significantly more formalization in the production area, especially in matters like defining operator tasks, training operators, and recording their performance. The faster-growing companies in variable environments particularly made little use of formal training procedures, standardized routine personnel practices, and formal hierarchical channels for communication or seeking and conveying decisions.

Size of unit. Here the major proposition is this:

Proposition 7: Organizations that increase their degree of formalization to parallel their growth in size will tend to achieve higher levels of performance.

Critics contend that the problem of the large organization is the dead weight of bureaucratic administration that it takes on. In an attempt to hold together its many divisions and departments, the large organization emphasizes conformity to the rules, a trait that has prompted the observation that "a new idea has never come out of a large corporation." Many studies of organization have confirmed that large scale does indeed breed bureaucracy in the form of highly compartmentalized jobs and areas of work, elaborate procedural and paperwork systems, long hierarchies, and delegation of routine decisions to lower-level managers within precise discretionary limits.

Much as critics may decry bureaucracy, we found that in each industry the more profitable and faster-growing companies were those that had developed this type of organization in fuller measure with their growth in size above the 2,000-or-so employee mark. At the other end of the scale, among small firms of about 100 employees, the better performers generally managed with very little formal organization. The larger the company, the higher the correlation between more bureaucracy and superior performance.

Poorly performing large companies tend to specialize their staff less, to have less developed systems and procedures, and to delegate decision making less extensively. It is also worth noting that among the poorly performing companies the strength of the relation between changes in size and changes in structure is noticeably reduced, compared with that among high performers.

When the nature of each organization's environment is taken into account, as well as its size, the association between organization and performance becomes more complicated. The need for companies operating in a more variable environment to keep a check on the formality in their organization, especially its routine-enforcing elements, probably explains why it is the successful companies in a more stable environment that most rapidly take on a formal bureaucratic type of structure as they grow larger. The rate at which companies tend to develop bureaucratic structures as their size increases varies according to the environment and performance in the following sequence from low to high: below-average performers in stable environments; below-average performers in variable environments; above-average performers in variable environments; above-average performers in stable environments.

Managers, it appears from our research, have to take note of multiple contingencies, such as environment plus size, when planning the design of their organization. When there is not much variability in the environment, the need to develop organization to suit size becomes relatively more dominant. In this environment, the better-performing companies tend to develop formalized structures at a faster rate as they grow than do poor performers. When the environment is a variable one, however, these differences in structural development are reduced, because the contingency of coping with uncertainty tends to offset the contingency of coping with large scale. We found that in a variable environment, the rate of increase in formalization accompanying growth in scale is higher for good performers, but the absolute level of their formalization only reaches that of poor-performing companies at a size approaching 10,000 employees. The picture is complex indeed, as most practical managers are well aware!

Diversity of Operations. Now comes the eighth proposition:

Proposition 8: Organizations that group their basic activities into divisions once these activities become diversified will tend to achieve higher levels of performance.

This proposition expresses the fundamental argument for the divisionalized organizational structure that has become the dominant form among large business firms today and that can also be seen in some large public undertakings. Organizations having a spread of different products or services, and having outlets in a number of regions, operate in a complex total environment. Such organizations are also likely to be large. Because of both their size and their diversity, they will almost certainly experience communications difficulties.

To overcome these problems, it is logical to create decentralized, semiautonomous operating units or divisions, for these can group formal relationships in a way that reflects the necessities of exchanging information and coordination around common problems. These commonalities may center around product groups, favoring a product division type of organization, or they may center on geographical regions, favoring an area division structure. If both product and regional coordination are equally vital, then a mixed, or "grid," structure may be logical.

Technology. This brings us to the ninth proposition:

Proposition 9: Organizations that design their workflow control and support structures to suit their technologies will tend to achieve higher levels of performance.

The research we conducted indicated that the pattern of specialization in production and ancillary areas such as production control and maintenance was predictable in terms of the technology employed. In addition, the proportion of total employment allocated to some of the ancillary functions varied along with differences in technology. For example, more rigid technologies, such as those of a process type, tend to have relatively few production control specialists and internally specialized production control departments. Most control is actually built into the technology itself.

These associations between technology and the structure of employment lead one to ask whether, along with environment, size, and diversity, there is some logic of adjustment to contingencies here. If there is, does the extent to which organizations adapt to the logic predict differences in their performance?

The closeness of fit between technology and the pattern in which roles were specialized did not vary significantly between good- and poor-performing companies. What did distinguish the more successful firms was that they tended to vary their investment in manpower devoted to production support activities according to differences in their technology. For instance, among companies using heavy plant and more rigid production systems, the more profitable and faster-growing ones had significantly larger percentages of their total employment given over to maintenance activities. In other words, allocation of manpower in relation to technological requirements appears to improve performance.

Type of Personnel. Now let's consider the last proposition:

Proposition 10: Organizations that adopt forms of administrative structure consistent with the expectations and perceived needs of their personnel will tend to achieve higher levels of performance.

This proposition is a cornerstone of the behavioral study of organizations. Readers of *Organizational Dynamics* will already be familiar with the work of Chris Argyris, Frederick Herzberg, Rensis Likert, Douglas McGregor, and others who have argued for structures and styles of management that secure a higher degree of commitment to the organization from employees by more adequately meeting their expectations and their needs as mature adults. In a broader context, moves to enrich jobs and the developments in industrial codetermination now under way in Europe also reflect an implicit faith in Proposition 10, since they start from the premise that employees' expectations and perceived needs are not being fulfilled adequately by existing organization forms.

The results of many research studies indicate that the proposition is valid. Indeed, some would call it a truism. While it is unnecessary to review familiar ground, some qualifications are in order. The proposition refers to the expectations and perceived needs of personnel. This reference to the perceptual level is important, for whatever the order of man's universal psychological needs, it is clear that different types of people do not have the same requirements of their work at the conscious perceptual level. One has only to compare the professional employee with the manual worker to realize that sociocultural factors are crucial in shaping different expectations as to what constitute legitimate conditions of work. Similarly, research of a cross-cultural nature has indicated that different supervisory styles are effective with employees located in different cultural milieux where different attitudes toward work and authority are evident. In short, Proposition 10 indicates that managements need to spend time ascertaining the expectations of different groups among their employees if they want to have a reliable idea of which arrangements will secure the willing commitment of those employees.

CONCLUSION

I have discussed ten propositions, of which half support the universalistic argument on organizational performance and half support the contingency argument. These two arguments have sometimes been regarded as completely opposed, but the findings of research indicate several ways in which they are compatible.

In essence, the contingency approach stresses that managers should secure and evaluate information on their operating situation and that they should adapt the design of their organizational structure when necessary. It will quite possibly prove to be a general rule that managerial qualities such as the personal flexibility and drive associated with youth or the thrust for performance spurred on by a personal stake in stock appreciation enhance a company's ability to adjust to new contingencies. This is a universalistic type of statement, which includes two of the propositions I have advanced; it is nevertheless quite compatible with a contingency view of organizational design.

A further example of compatibility between the two arguments can be provided. The priority top managements give to different objectives is probably a factor that always influences the performance profiles that they attain. At the same time, the performance of any two companies having identical sets of objectives is unlikely to be the same, because this will also be determined by how they decide to adjust to prevailing contingencies.

The practical implications of the first five universalistic propositions have already been discussed. The first two draw attention to the desirability of selecting and developing managers who possess a combination of relative youth and relevant qualifications. Proposition 3 supports the general thrust of research on motivation and reward by indicating that the performance of organizations is enhanced when they grant their managers a sizable personal stake in their development. The fourth and fifth propositions indicate how the objectives management selects can shape performance, and how a greater degree of boardroom consensus over objectives will increase the chances of achieving good performance. These last two propositions speak for the practical importance of good communication, information sharing, and other hallmarks of effective integration among top executives.

The thrust of the last five propositions, and supporting research, is that the design of organization is likely to influence a company's performance. The problem has to be worked out in the context of each company's own circumstances. Several evaluations have to be made before deciding on the form of organization that is most appropriate. First, we must assess the nature of present and future contingencies. In other words, just what kind of institution are we, and what do we want to be in terms of markets, size, type of production, and so on? Second, what are the organizational requirements imposed by relevant contingencies? For example, a large unit will have particular problems of coordination and communication. What alternative organizational designs might satisfy these requirements?

Third, if different contingencies pose the dilemma of conflicting requirements, what policies could we formulate to modify the contingencies themselves? Some companies, for example, that seek to enter a faster-growing but more variable market or that seek to combine successful new product development with economies of large-scale, standardized "bread and butter" operations are finding that they can circumvent the size contingency by setting up small, internally flexible, venture-management units or similar companies-within-companies.

The important point is that there are usually several ways of securing an effective match between a company's internal organization and the contingencies it faces. This fact tends to be overlooked by those who share the present-day public concern about large bureaucratic firms and other institutions. A bureaucracy can be operated in different ways, and not necessarily with the proverbial "dead hand." And even if large scale brings too much bureaucracy to permit desirable levels of participation and sensitivity to change, there are in most areas of activity various possibilities for developing units into smaller ones without incurring any loss in their efficiency.

In conclusion, it is already possible to identify certain managerial and organizational factors that are related to company performance, but in the future it will be necessary to go further and initiate experiments and changes in these variables that, it is hoped, will demonstrate how far they actively determine performance. It is, however, abundantly clear that company performance is not the prey of random and uncontrollable forces.

WHEN IS AN ORGANIZATION EFFECTIVE? A Process Approach to Understanding Effectiveness

RICHARD M. STEERS

While most organizational analysts agree that the pursuit of effectiveness is a basic managerial responsibility, there is a notable lack of consensus on what the concept itself means. The economist or financial analyst usually equates organizational effectiveness with high profits or return on investment. For a line manager, however, effectiveness is often measured by the amount and quality of goods or services generated. The R&D scientist may define effectiveness in terms of the number of patents, new inventions, or new products developed by an organization. And last, many labor union leaders conceive of effectiveness in terms of job security, wage levels, job satisfaction, and the quality of working life. In short, while there is general agreement that effectiveness is something all organizations should strive for, the criteria for assessment remain unclear.

In view of the many different ways in which managers and researchers conceptualize organizational effectiveness, it comes as no surprise that there is equal disagreement over the best strategy for attaining effectiveness. A principal reason for this lack of agreement stems from the parochial views that many people harbor about the effectiveness construct. As mentioned, many define effectiveness in terms of a single evaluation criterion (profit or productivity, for example). But it is difficult to conceive of an organization that would survive for long if it pursued profits to the exclusion of its employees' needs and goals or those of society at large. Organizations typically pursue multiple (and often conflicting) goals—and these goals tend to differ from organization to organization according to the nature of the enterprise and its environment.

Another explanation for the general absence of agreement on the nature of effectiveness arises from the ambiguity of the concept itself. Organizational analysts often assume, incorrectly, that it's relatively easy to identify the various criteria for evaluating effectiveness. In point of fact, such criteria tend to be somewhat intangible; indeed, they depend largely on who is doing the evaluating and within what specific frame of reference.

A number of organizational analysts have tried to identify relevant facets of effectiveness that could serve as useful evaluating criteria. I recently reviewed 17 different approaches to assessing organizational effectiveness and found a general absence of agreement among them. Table 12–3 summarizes the criteria used in the 17 models and notes the frequency with which each is mentioned. As this table reveals, only one criterion (adaptability-flexibility) was mentioned in more than half of the models. This criterion was followed rather distantly by productivity, job satisfaction, profitability, and acquisition of scarce and valued resources. Thus there is little agreement among analysts concerning what criteria should be used to assess current levels of effectiveness.

PROBLEMS IN ASSESSMENT

This absence of convergence among competing assessment techniques poses a serious problem for both managers and organizational analysts. If appropriate assessment criteria cannot be agreed upon, it would be manifestly impossible to agree completely on an evaluation of an organization's success or failure. This inability to identify meaningful criteria to be used across organizations results in part from ignoring several questions (or problems) that must be resolved if

An earlier version of this article was presented at the 1976 annual meeting of the American Psychological Association. The author wishes to express his appreciation to the Office of Naval Research for support of the initial study.

TABLE 12–3 FREQUENCY OF OCCURRENCE OF EVALUATION CRITERIA IN 17 MODELS OF ORGANIZATIONAL EFFECTIVENESS

Evaluation Criteria	No. of Times Mentioned ($N = 17$)
Adaptability-flexibility	10
Productivity	6
Job satisfaction	5
Profitability	3
Acquisition of scarce and valued resources	3
Absence of organizational strain	2
Control over external environment	2
Employee development	2
Efficiency	2
Employee retention	2
Growth	2
Integration of individual goals with organizational goals	2
Open communication	2
Survival	2
All other criteria	1

SOURCE: Richard M. Steers, "Problems in the Measurement of Organizational Effectiveness," *Administrative Science Quarterly*, vol. 20, #4 (December), 1975, p. 549.

we are to derive more meaningful approaches to assessing organizational effectiveness. Eight such issues are:

1. *Is there any such thing as organizational effectiveness?* It is only logical to ask whether there is indeed empirical justification for any such construct. In the absence of any tangible evidence, it may be that organizational effectiveness exists only on an abstract level, with little applicability to the workplace and its problems. But if effectiveness is indeed a viable concept from a managerial standpoint, its definition and characteristics must be made more explicit.

2. *How stable—consistently valid—are the assessment criteria?* A second problem encountered in attempts to assess effectiveness is that many of the assessment criteria change over time. In a growth economy, for example, the effectiveness of a business firm may be related to level of capital investment; during a recession or depression, however, capital liquidity may emerge as a more useful criterion, and high fixed investment may shift from being an asset to being a liability. Clearly, such criteria do not represent permanent indicators of organizational success. In fact, it is probably this transitory nature of many effectiveness criteria that has led some investigators to suggest that adaptabilty or flexibility represents the key variable in any model of effectiveness.

3. *Which time perspective is most appropriate in assessment?* Contributing to the problem of criterion instability is the question of which time perspective to take in assessing effectiveness. For example, if current production (a short-run criterion) consumes so much of an organization's resources that little is left over for investment in R&D, the organization may ultimately find itself with its products outmoded and its very survival (a long-term criterion) threatened. Thus the problem for the manager is how best to allocate available resources between short- and long-term considerations so that both receive sufficient support for their respective purposes.

4. *Are the assessment criteria related positively to each other?* Most approaches to assessing effectiveness rely on a series of relatively discrete criteria (for example, productivity, job satisfaction, profitability). The use of such multiple measures, however, often leads to situations in which these criteria are in conflict. Consider, for instance, an organization that uses productivity and job satisfaction as two of its criteria. Productivity can often be increased (at least in the short run) by pressuring employees to exert greater energy and turn out more goods in the same period of time. Such managerial efforts are likely, however, to result in reduced job satisfaction. On the other hand, it's possible to increase job satisfaction by yielding to employee demands for increased leisure time and reduced production pressures—but at the price of lower productivity. Thus, while the use of multiple evaluation criteria adds breadth to any assessment attempt, it simultaneously opens the door to conflicting demands that management may not be able to satisfy.

5. *How accurate are the assessment criteria?* A further problem in assessing organizational effectiveness is how to secure accurate measures for assessment purposes. How does an organization accurately measure managerial performance or job satisfaction, if these are to be used as effectiveness criteria? And how consistent are such measures over time? In point of fact, we tend to measure the performance of the individual manager

loosely in terms of an overall rating by his superior and to measure job satisfaction frequently in terms of turnover and absenteeism rates. Such operational definitions have their obvious limitations. Performance ratings, for example, may be skewed by personality factors, and a low turnover rate may indicate low performance standards born of a complacent or indifferent management.

6. *How widely can the criteria be applied?* A major problem with many of the criteria suggested for assessing effectiveness is the belief that they apply equally in a variety of organizations. Such is often not the case. While profitability and market share may be relevant criteria for most business firms, they have little applicability for organizations like a library or a police department. Thus, when considering appropriate criteria for purposes of assessment, we should take care to ensure that the criteria are consistent with the goals and purposes of a particular organization.

7. *How do such criteria help us understand organizational dynamics?* The organizational analyst of necessity is concerned with the utility of the effectiveness construct. What purposes are served by the existence of evaluation criteria for assessing effectiveness? Do they provide insight into the dynamics of ongoing organizations? Do they help us to make predictions concerning the future actions of organizations? Unless such models facilitate a better understanding of organizational structures, processes, or behavior, they are of little value from an analytical or operational standpoint.

8. *At which level should effectiveness be assessed?* Finally, managers face the problem of the level at which to assess effectiveness. Logic suggests evaluating organizational effectiveness on an organizationwide basis. Such an approach, however, ignores the dynamic relationships between an organization and its various parts. We must bear in mind that the individual employee ultimately determines the degree of organizational success. If we are to increase our understanding of organizational processes, we must develop models of effectiveness that enable us, to the greatest extent possible, to identify the nature of the relationships between individual processes and organizational behavior. Moreover, a comparison of the relative effectiveness of various departments or divisions is also useful. It is highly likely that certain of these subunits (for example, sales) may be more successful than others within the same organization. The existence of such differences complicates even further any attempts to draw firm conclusions concerning the effectiveness of a given organization.

Even a cursory examination of these problems reveals the magnitude and complexity of the subject. If managers are to reduce their dependence on simplistic criteria for evaluating effectiveness, we must provide them with a framework for analysis that surmounts these problems.

One solution that at least minimizes many of the obstacles to assessing effectiveness is to view effectiveness in terms of a process instead of an end state. Most of the earlier models of effectiveness place a heavy emphasis on identifying the criteria themselves (that is, the end state). Although such criteria may be useful, they tell us little about the ingredients that facilitate effectiveness. Nor do they help the manager better understand how effectiveness results. Hence, it appears that we need to re-examine our notions about the concept of organizational effectiveness and about the kinds of analytical models managers require to help them make their own organizations effective.

EFFECTIVE AND INEFFECTIVE ORGANIZATIONS

Perhaps one of the best ways to understand the notion of organizational effectiveness is to examine several instances of *in*effectiveness. Consider the following three examples:

1. *Farm tractors.* There are many examples of organizations that correctly identify the nature of the problem and set relevant goals but then select a less than optimal strategy for attaining those goals.

One such example can be seen in the activities of the first Henry Ford as he tried to maintain the profitability of Ford Motor Company during the depression of the 1930s—when, of course, the demand for new cars had declined. Alfred Chandler reports in his book *Strategy and Structure* that Ford decided to enter the farm tractor market in order to employ some of his unused plant capacity. Within a relatively short period of time, his engineers had designed and built a versatile yet inexpensive tractor. Unfortunately, however, Ford selected an inappropriate marketing and distribution strategy for the new product. He tried to market the tractors through his existing automobile distribution system, which was largely concentrated in major cities and was not attuned to the needs of farms. Hence his product (however good it may have been) never really reached its intended market. The venture failed commercially until Ford realized his mistake and created a supplementary distribution system that reflected market realities and communicated with the farming audience in its own terms.

2. *Slide rules.* Whereas Example 1 represents an attempt to apply the wrong strategy to the right goal, Example 2 we may describe as an attempt to apply the right strategy to the wrong goal—a goal that became wrong because of a technological advance that created a shift in market demand.

Ths example involves a company that manufactures slide rules. For many years, the organization had a reputation for producing and selling high-quality slide rules for a variety of applications. With the advent of relatively inexpensive electronic pocket calculators, however, sophisticated computations could be completed quickly and accurately. Almost overnight, demand shifted from slide rules to calculators. Within two years, sales dropped by 75 percent. The company either failed to predict environmental changes accurately or was unable to adapt to them in order to achieve its profit goal.

3. *Regulatory agencies.* A third type of problem exists when an organization chooses an inappropriate strategy to achieve a suboptimal goal. Typically, we find examples of this type of situation in public bureaucracies (perhaps because of a lack of competitive pressure).

Consider the example of the Interstate Commerce Commission, an agency of the U.S. Government charged with facilitating and regulating commerce between the states. Purportedly, its primary goal is to achieve an effective level of operation in such commerce. In actual practice, however, many complain that its operative (or real) goals are just the opposite. For example, in order to ensure "equity" between the various trucking lines, the ICC for many years required certain firms to drive from point *A* to point *B* not directly, but through some out-of-the-way point *C*. The rationale for such a policy was based in part on the belief that smaller firms, which often had less efficient routes, needed to be protected from the larger firms, which had more resources at their disposal. As a result, costs increased for both trucking firms and the customer, and delivery times lengthened for all concerned.

In each of these cases, we have a clear example of ineffectiveness. The nature of the problem in each case, however, is quite different. Moreover, the strategies chosen by the organizations to achieve their stated objectives are also quite different. It is this lack of convergence in most approaches to organizational effectiveness that has led to so much confusion—not only over how organizations achieve effectiveness, but indeed over what we mean by the notion of effectiveness itself.

What Is Organizational Effectiveness?

The term *organizational effectiveness* has been used (and misused) in a variety of contexts. As noted above, some equate the term with profit or productivity, while others view it in terms of job satisfaction. While many analysts view these criteria as definitions of organizational effectiveness, a few investigators suggest that such variables actually constitute intervening variables that enhance the likelihood that effectiveness will result.

If we accept the notion that organizations are unique and pursue divergent goals (as the three examples suggest), then such definitions are too situation-specific and value-laden to be of much use. Instead, it appears more useful initially to follow the lead to Talcott Parsons and Amitai Etzioni and define organizational effectiveness in terms of an organization's ability to acquire and efficiently use available resources to achieve their goals. Viewed from this perspective, all three examples cited previously represent a case of goal failure.

Such a definition requires elaboration. First, we are focusing on operative goals as opposed to official goals. It seems more appropriate to assess the relative level of effectiveness against the real intended objectives of an organization rather than a static list of objectives meant principally for public consumption. For example, we often see public advertisements by corporations claiming that "progress is our most important product" or "the things we do improve the way we live." Such statements (or official goals) often give the impression that the company's primary objective is progress, while in fact other goals (for example, profit, growth, or an acceptable rate of return on investment) probably represent more accurate statements of intent (that is, operative goals). Thus whatever objectives the organization truly intends pursuing, it is against these criteria that effectiveness is best judged. Such an approach has the added advantage of minimizing the influence of the analyst's value judgments in the assessment process. While many would argue, for example, that job satisfaction is a desirable end, it remains for the organization, not an outside analyst, to set such a goal.

Inherent in such a definition, moreover, is the notion that effectiveness is best judged against an organization's ability to compete in a turbulent environment and successfully acquire and use its resources. This suggests that managers must deal effectively with their external environments to secure needed resources. Finally, this approach recognizes the concept of efficiency as a necessary yet insufficient ingredient (or facilitator) of effectiveness.

A Note on Efficiency

People often discuss efficiency and effectiveness as being interchangeable. Our approach is to clearly separate the two notions yet to recognize the importance of and interrelation between them. While we define effectiveness as the extent to which operative goals can be attained, we define efficiency as the cost/benefit ratio involved in the pursuit of those goals. An example should clarify this distinction. Shortly after World War II, a ranking German officer observed that the Allies had not "beaten" Germany but had instead "smothered" her. In other words, the officer was suggesting that while the Allies had been effective in the pursuit of their objectives, they had not been particularly efficient.

At some point, however, we would expect that increased inefficiency would have a detrimental effect on subsequent effectiveness. When this notion is applied to a business environment, it appears that the more costly goal effort becomes, the less likely the business is to be effective. As an example of this efficiency-effectiveness relationship, consider some of the current experiments in job redesigning, such as the Volvo and Saab-Scania experiments in Sweden. Several prominent investigators have noted recently that, while job enrichment may have desirable social consequences, the costs associated with such efforts may be so high that they increase the price of the product beyond what customers are willing to pay. Hence the notion of efficiency emerges as an important element of organizational effectiveness.

A PROCESS MODEL FOR ANALYZING EFFECTIVENESS

From a static viewpoint, it may be enough to define effectiveness in terms of attaining operative goals. However, if we are to understand more fully the processes involved in bringing about an effective level of operations, it is necessary to take a more dynamic approach to the topic. The approach suggested here is essentially a "process model" of effectiveness. Its aim is to provide managers with a framework for analysis of the major *process* involved in effectiveness. This approach contrasts sharply with earlier models that merely listed the requisite criteria for assessing organizational success.

The process model that is proposed here consists of three related components: 1. the notion of goal optimization; 2. a systems perspective; and 3. an emphasis on human behavior in organizational settings.

Goal Optimization

If we examine the various approaches currently used to assess organizational effectiveness, it becomes apparent that most ultimately rest on the notion of goal attainment. A primary advantage of using the operative goal concept for assessing levels of effectiveness is that organizational success is evaluated in the light of an organization's behavioral intentions. In view of the fact that different organizations pursue widely divergent goals, it is only logical to recognize this uniqueness in any assessment technique.

While many variations on the goal approach to

evaluating effectiveness exist, the most fruitful approach is to view effectiveness in terms of goal *optimization.* Instead of evaluating success in terms of the extent to which "desired" goals have been maximized, we recognize a series of identifiable and irreducible constraints (for example, money, technology, personnel, other goals, and so on) that serve to inhibit goal maximization. Managers are seen as setting and pursuing "optimized" goals (that is, desired goals within the constraints dictated by the resources available). A company may, for example, feel that a 10 percent return on investment is a realistic goal in view of resource availability, the existing market environment, and so forth. We would argue that it is against this *feasible* goal set, not against an ultimate goal set, that effectiveness be judged.

The goal optimization approach has several advantages over conventional approaches: First, it suggests that goal maximization is probably not possible and that, even if it were, it might be detrimental to an organization's well-being and survival. In most situations, for example, there appears to be little chance for a company to maximize productivity and job satisfaction at the same time. Instead, compromises must be made—compromises that provide for an optimal level of attainment of both objectives.

Second, goal optimization models recognize the existence of differential weights that managers place on the various goals in the feasible set. For instance, a company may place on the pursuit of its profit goal five times the weight, and resources, that it puts on its affirmative-action employment goal or its job satisfaction goal. While real-life examples would obviously be far more complex, this simple example emphasizes the differential weighting aspect inherent in any assessment of organizational effectiveness.

Third, the model also recognizes the existence of a series of constraints that can impede progress toward goal attainment. Many of these constraints (for example, limited finances, people, technology, and so on) may be impossible to alleviate, at least in the short run. Consider the case of the slide rule manufacturer. The production of slide rules requires a radically different technology than that required by the production of electronic calculators. Thus this firm, which had a competitive advantage using one technology, lost its edge when market demand shifted. Of course, if this company had anticipated environmental changes, accurately and far enough in advance, it might have developed new applications for existing technology—assuming the infeasibility of changing it. The firm might, for instance, have devoted its energies to developing new precision-measurement instruments not based on electronics. Thus it is important to recognize such constraints—and how a company reacts to them—in any final assessment of success or failure.

Fourth, this approach has the added advantage of allowing for increased flexibility of evaluation critieria. As the goals pursued by an organization change, or as the constraints associated with them change, a new optimal solution will emerge that could represent new evaluation criteria. Hence the means of assessment would remain current and would reflect the changing needs and goals of the organization.

Last, from the standpoint of long-range planning, weighted goals and their relevant constraints could be modeled by using computer simulations to derive optimal solutions for purposes of allocating future resources and effort.

The use of computer-simulation models in long-range planning has become commonplace among larger organizations. The same technique could be applied to examining organizational effectiveness. Major organizational and environmental variables could be systematically manipulated to analyze the impact of such changes on resulting facets of effectiveness (for example, profits, market share, adaptation, and productivity). From such manipulations, optimal solutions could be derived that would help managers direct the future of the enterprise.

Systems Perspective

The second important aspect of a process model of organizational effectiveness is the employment of an open-systems perspective for purposes of analysis. Such a perspective emphasizes interrelationships between the various parts of an organization and its environment as they jointly influence effectiveness.

If we take a systems perspective, we can identify the four major categories of influences on effectiveness (see Figure 12–2): 1. organizational characteristics, such as structure and technology; 2. environmental charac-

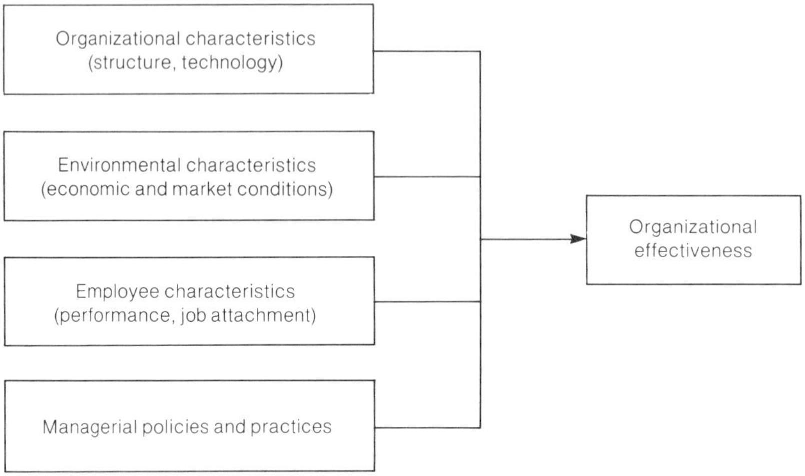

Organizational characteristics (structure, technology)

Environmental characteristics (economic and market conditions)

Employee characteristics (performance, job attachment)

Managerial policies and practices

→ Organizational effectiveness

Figure 12-2. Major influences on organizational effectiveness

teristics, such as economic and market conditions; 3. employee characteristics, such as level of job performance and job attachment; and 4. managerial policies and practices. While the precise manner in which these variables influence effectiveness goes beyond the scope of this article, it is suggested that these four sets of variables must be relatively consonant if effectiveness is to be achieved. The negative outcomes that result when these characteristics do not fit we saw in the example of the Ford tractor. While the product itself was good, the failure to recognize environmental variations and to adapt the marketing structure accordingly led to ineffectiveness.

Thus managers have a reponsibility to understand the nature of their environment and to set realistic goals that accommodate and/or exploit that environment. Given these goals, the more effective organizations will tend to be those that successfully adapt structure, technology, work effort, policies, and so on to facilitate goal attainment.

Behavioral Emphasis

A final aspect of the process approach to understanding and analyzing effectiveness is the emphasis on the role of individual behavior as it affects organizational success or failure. The position taken here is in opposition to the stand taken by many that effectiveness is best examined exclusively on a "macro" (or organization-wide) basis. Instead, it appears that greater insight can result if analyses include consideration of how the behavior of individual employees impacts upon organizational goal attainment. If an organization's employees largely agree with the objectives of their employer, we would expect them to exert a relatively high level of effort toward achieving those goals. If, on the other hand, organizational goals largely conflict with employees' personal goals, there is little reason to believe that employees would exert their maximum effort.

As an interesting example of the importance of individuals in goal attainment, consider the controversy over automobile seat belts. In an effort to improve traffic safety, the federal government initially passed a law that required auto manufacturers to install seat belts in all new cars. When this action failed to have the desired consequences (many people simply did not use them), additional laws were passed requiring manufacturers to install warning lights, buzzers, and so forth to remind drivers to use seat belts. Finally, when these measures also proved ineffective, laws were passed requiring manufacturers to install devices that made it mandatory to use seat belts before the ignition could be activated—although even these devices could be circumvented with a degree of ingenuity. While the initial goal was laudatory, the processes (means) used to achieve this goal were largely ineffective because they ignored the predispositions and behavior patterns of most drivers. Perhaps a more effective strategy (certainly in terms of time and cost) would have been simply to pass a law nullifying accident insurance claims for drivers injured while not wearing seat belts.

Hence when we examine organizational effectiveness, it is important to recognize and account for the people who ultimately determine the quality and quantity of an organization's response to environmental demands.

CONCLUSION

Most contemporary organizations exist in turbulent environments in which threats to survival and growth are relatively commonplace. Within such environments, managers must try to secure and properly utilize resources in an effort to attain the operative goals set forth by the organization. The process by which they do so—or fail to do so—is at the heart of the concept of organizational effectiveness.

In the above discussion, I have tried to review the various approaches that have been taken to evaluating organizational effectiveness. Little homogeneity exists between the various approaches. This lack of consensus, in turn, results from the existence of at least eight problems inherent in the existing models. In an effort to overcome many of these problems, I have proposed a process model of organizational effectiveness.

The model described differs from the earlier models. Instead of specifying the criteria for effectiveness (for example, when is an organization effective?), this model focuses on the process of becoming effective (for example, what conditions are most conducive to effectiveness?). It is argued that the actual criteria for evaluation vary depending on the particular operative goals of the organization. Because of this, it appears appropriate to place greater emphasis on understanding the dynamics associated with effectiveness oriented behavior.

It is further recommended that one way to conceptualize organizational effectiveness *as a process* is to examine three related factors. First, optimized goals (that is, what an organization is capable of attaining) can provide realistic parameters for the assessment process. Given an organization's operative goals, we can ask intelligent questions about the appropriateness of managerial resource-allocation decisions. In other words, is there a better way for managers to expend their limited resources?

Important questions to consider in connection with this first factor include the following:

- *To what extent are we applying our limited resources toward the attainment of our various goals?* In point of fact, organizations often make resource-allocation decisions independent of goal decisions, resulting in "unfunded" goals and "funded" nongoals. This behavior is perhaps most clearly exemplified in the practice by various state and federal legislatures of passing authorization bills and appropriation bills separately. Thus it is possible (and, in fact, it often happens) that a bill (goal) becomes law without the appropriation of resources to implement it.

- *Is there a clear relationship between the amount of resources we spend on the various goals and the importance of each goal?* If, for example, an organization truly believes it places equal weight on making a profit and on improving quality of working life, are such beliefs reflected in the allocation of resources? This does not suggest that equivalent amounts of resources must be spent on each goal. Instead, it implies that sufficient resources be spent to bring about the attainment of both goals.

- *What kind of return on investment, per goal, are we getting on our resources?* If organizations pursue multiple goals, it would seem logical to examine the efficiency of effort invested in each goal. It may be that an organization is highly efficient in realizing its less important goals and relatively inefficient in realizing its more important goals. Where such inefficiencies are noted, decisions must be made concerning the desirability of continuing the pursuit of a goal. Where a goal is viewed as worthwhile (for example, hiring the hard-core unemployed), companies may pursue the goal despite a low return on investment.

- *Is the entire organization working together for goal attainment?* As shown in the Ford tractor example, there are instances in which an organization's existing marketing channels are not suited to newer products—a "bad fit" that leads to suboptimal results. Moreover, a fairly common complaint against research and development departments is that scientists stress basic research projects at the expense of applied projects that generally have more immediate and more certain payoffs.

• *Is the "fit" between the organization and its environment changing?* Organizations should continually raise questions concerning their place in the external environment. We saw in the example of the slide rule manufacturer how a company can lose a major share of its market by failing to adjust to changes in market demand. Under such circumstances, and without the necessary technology to compete with manufacturers of electronic calculators, this firm may find it desirable to establish its niche in the market by specializing in drafting equipment or other instruments not based on electronics. A relatively successful example of such organization-environment fit can be seen in American Motors Corporation (AMC), which for many years has specialized in small cars and jeeps while the "Big Three" stressed medium- and large-sized cars. As the other auto makers shift their focus toward small cars, however, AMC (with fewer resources) may find it necessary to adjust its efforts toward newer markets. Hence flexibility in the face of environmental change remains an important area of concern for effective organizations.

Second, it has been stressed throughout our discussion that the use of a systems perspective allows for the explicit recognition of the ways in which various organizational factors blend together to facilitate or inhibit effectiveness-related activities. This approach forces managers to employ more comprehensive analytical models when they ask questions about why the organization achieved or failed to achieve a particular goal. It facilitates a broader perspective both on the nature of the problem and on its possible solutions.

Third, it is highly desirable to recognize the important link between individual behavior and organizationwide performance. That is, any consideration of how organizations become effective (or more effective) must account for the primary determinant of ultimate organizational performance: the employees of the organization. Recent efforts to institute management-by-objectives programs in organizations represent one such attempt to coordinate the efforts of various employees toward specific organizational objectives. Taken together, these three related factors should help managers and organizational analysts understand the various ways in which organizations move toward or away from goal attainment and organizational effectiveness.

Two general conclusions (with important implications for managers) emerge from our analysis of organizational effectiveness. First, the concept of organizational effectiveness is best understood in terms of a continuous process rather than an end state. Marshaling resources for goal-directed effort is an unceasing task for most managers. In view of the changing nature of the goals pursued in most organizations, managers have a continuing responsibility to recognize environmental changes, to restructure available resources, to modify technologies, to develop employees, and so forth in order to use the talents at their disposal to attain goals that are themselves in perpetual flux.

Second, our analysis also has emphasized the central role of contingencies in any discussion of effectiveness. Thus it is incumbent upon managers to recognize the unique qualities that define their own organization—its goals, structures, technologies, people, environments, and so on—and to respond in a manner consistent with this uniqueness. Our conclusion cautions against the arbitrary use of "rules" or "principles" for achieving success. Such rules and principles are of little use viewed against the background of organizational diversity. Instead, responsibility must fall to the organization and its management to develop employees so that they can better recognize and understand the nature of a particular situation and respond appropriately. When viewed in this manner, organizational effectiveness becomes largely a function of the extent to which managers and employees can pool their efforts and overcome the obstacles that inhibit goal attainment.

CONCLUDING STATEMENT

What can we conclude about organizational effectiveness? More specifically, what can we say about organizational effectiveness as a design outcome? As we have seen in Child's and Steers' articles, there are many difficult problems in trying to define and measure organizational effectiveness. Nonetheless, effective organizational performance—however defined and measured—is a necessary object of any rational design process. Therefore we have little choice except to cope with those problems as well as possible.

ORGANIZATIONAL EFFECTIVENESS AND DESIGN

How does one—whether student, consultant, analyst, or designer—select proper (or at least useful) criteria for assessing organizational effectiveness? The answer to this question is not easy. For one thing, as we mentioned earlier, the selection will inevitably be colored by one's values or perspective. We can see this phenomenon operating when we observe differences in criteria selected by those within an organization and those outside (Hrebiniak, 1978: 307–10). Insiders' perspectives, desires, and goals are frequently different from those outside. Table 12–4 illustrates some differences that might develop.

Values and Criteria: An Example

People differ in their selection of performance criteria more than simply on the basis of whether they are fulfilling an internal or external role, however. Fundamental *values* also play a part.[1] Consider the following example: Recently the author and a colleague measured values of a group of nursing-home administrators—that is, of the chief managerial officer of each of some 40 nursing-home organizations. A relatively standard measure of values developed by Carlson and Levy (1970), was employed.[2]

Carlson and Levy's measure distinguishes two principal value orientations: individualistic and interpersonal. That is, people are scored as to whether they are mainly oriented toward

TABLE 12–4 PERFORMANCE CRITERIA AS A FUNCTION OF PERSPECTIVE

Organization	Internal	External
Business organization	Profit (ROI) Efficiency Market share Sales increases	Pollution control Quality products Ethical behavior Social awareness
Competitive	Fun	Winning
Sports team	Character formation Group cohesion	
Hospital	Quality Cost (efficiency)	Cost efficiency Quality

SOURCE: Reproduced by permission from *Complex Organizations*, by Lawrence G. Hrebiniak,

1. For a discussion of this idea, refer to Chapter 6—especially the article by Connor and Becker, "Values and the Organization: Suggestions for Research."
2. Actually, we modified the measure somewhat. See Becker and Connor (1977) for the rationale.

individualistic kinds of values or interpersonal ones. Our nursing-home administrators followed normal trends and tended to separate into the two value camps. Some scored as highly individualistic in their value orientations, some as highly interpersonal.

We also asked the subjects—and here is the crux of this example—to describe what, for them, is "an ideal nursing home organization." The restrictions were modest. They were told to assume they did *not* have an infinite amount of human and material resources they could squander. On the other hand, they were to assume that miserliness was not necessary either. In other words, these experienced managers were told to be realistically idealistic!

The results were fascinating. Top managers with markedly different value orientations described the "ideal nursing home" quite differently. Here are two sample descriptions. The first was penned by a person who scored extremely high on the individualistic-value scale. The second scored equally high on the interpersonal-value scale.

"IDEAL NURSING HOME"

Individualistic-Value Orientation

> The ideal nursing home is a 90-bed facility located 30 miles from a metropolitan city. The community would have a university, three hospitals and would be at least 50 percent agribusiness-oriented. There would be at least two other good quality homes located there. This home would be of recent construction (2–4 years old) and would be a for-profit facility.

"IDEAL NURSING HOME"

Interpersonal-Value Orientation

> The ideal nursing home is intensely warm in the radiance of human love and warmth toward the members of the home and to all of those who come into contact in the home. Joy fills the air. It is a place where human needs and companionship are truly met. It is a large home, which seems as a very knitted family. There is a personal relationship between staff and residents. There is a true beauty and love for the elderly.

It is obvious from these descriptions that the two managers differed markedly in their conception of what an ideal nursing-home organization is. It is equally apparent that they would tend to select different criteria for assessing organizational performance. We emphasized in Chapter 6 that values play a role in people's behavior in organizations. Values play an equally important role in decisions about designing and evaluating organizational effectiveness.

Effectiveness Dimensions for Design

With all the criteria for assessing organizational effectiveness, how are organization designers to decide which ones should be used? If only a bottom-line sort of criterion is used, such as net return on investment, much of the ongoing dynamics that makes an organization "healthy" is lost. In fact, as Steers pointed out earlier, this is the problem with using any single criterion. On the other hand, organization designers who attempt to use a large number of criteria, such as Campbell's 30 items, or Likert's factors, run the risk of being overwhelmed by more criteria than they can realistically handle. The problem begins to resemble that described by Simon in Chapter 9: in the first place, complete information is not available—and even if it were, designers' cognitive abilities would not be up to the job of processing it.

So, what is a designer to do? We suggest a set of dimensions that recognize the systemic-goal approach discussed earlier in this concluding statement. The set is that identified in the Connor and Becker article contained in Chapter 6, "Values and the Organization: Suggestions for Research." Figure 6–8 identifies the dimensions: *Efficiency, Quality of Output, Quality of Work Environment,* and *Responsiveness* (Connor, Egan, and Karmel, 1973: 8–9).

Efficiency

The classic definition of efficiency, as we noted earlier in our discussion of Evan's (1976) analysis, is the ratio of output to input: O/I. Frequently this ratio is translated into a cost-minimization measure. That is, there are two ways to increase efficiency: increase the quantity of output, holding input constant, or decrease the input necessary to produce a given quantity of output.

However, efficiency means more than cost minimization. It also includes such financial and administrative factors as labor productivity, profit, waste control, proportion of capacity used, accuracy of communication, elimination of dysfunctional procedures, improved work flow, and appropriate information systems.

Quality of Output

The ongoing effectiveness of an organization is also reflected in the quality of its goods or services. For health-care organizations, for example, two facilities may have relatively comparable efficiency data, yet one provides better patient care than the other. Nursing homes frequently are distinguished on just such a basis. On a comparable note, government agencies may differ in terms of how good or useful their service is to the client. Manufacturing organizations may be distinguished on the basis of the overall quality of their product. While cost data may be comparable, one firm's product may be more durable, more dependable, and more attractive to the consumer.

Quality of Work Environment

This dimension captures the essence of what we mean be organizational climate. Quality of work environment is the employee's perception of the "goodness" of the organization as a place to work. This perception is reflected in satisfaction with the organization as a whole, the job being performed, supervision, and interpersonal relationships with organizational colleagues. Satisfaction with these factors is manifested in employees' attitudes and behaviors.

Responsiveness

Responsiveness refers to two related, although distinct, aspects of organizational effectiveness. Basically this dimension concerns the ability of the organization to respond to changes that take place either in the long- or short-run.

Adaptability refers to the organization's ability to respond to external trends—in legal, technological, financial, and social conditions. How well the organization adapts to such long-run changes will naturally influence its ongoing effectiveness.

Internal changes or trends must be met as well. Employee re-education, design of new management structures, and new information and operating systems need to be developed over time. Organizational effectiveness also reflects the enterprise's ability to meet these challenges.

Flexibility involves the requirement that the organization respond to emergency or crisis situations. Flexibility therefore concerns the ability of the organization to cope with short-term changes. Sudden changes in the marketplace, prime interest rates, suppliers' delivery of needed resources—the organization's overall effectiveness will depend in part on its ability to be flexible enough to meet such challenges as these.

Designing to Effectiveness Dimensions

As stated above, organizational effectiveness is for us a multidimensional, goal-systemic construct. It is multidimensional in that it involves "numbers" (efficiency-type criteria), qualitative factors (of output and work environment), and ability to change (responsiveness). Further, the effectiveness dimensions relate back to the idea of organizational goal mix. Let us see how this latter point works.

Recall from earlier discussions our hypothetical organizations Alpha and Beta. Alpha is basically a mechanistic-type enterprise, operating under relatively static conditions. Beta, on the other hand, is a relatively organic organization experiencing fairly dynamic conditions. In Chapter 3 we described these conditions in terms of environmental, technological, and employee characteristics. Figure 3–8 summarized our discussion of the relevance of Alpha and Beta's circumstances for their goals. Basically we found that Alpha organizations tend to put some emphasis on output-type goals, whereas Beta organizations have to emphasize support goals (adaptation, management, motivation, and position). Their respective goal-mix profiles are reproduced in Figure 12–3.

Figure 12–3 suggests the interrelationships among goals, design, and effectiveness. Organizations such as Beta have to pursue support-type goals, owing to the turbulent/uncertain/complex nature of their circumstances. Accordingly, as we saw in Chapters 7–10, they tend to develop designs that are essentially dynamic/organic/adaptable in character. On the other hand, Alpha-like organizations operate under conditions that are relatively

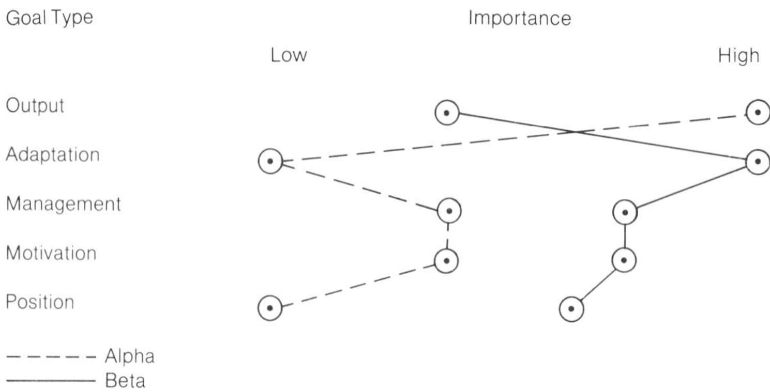

Figure 12-3. Organizational goal mix: Alpha and Beta

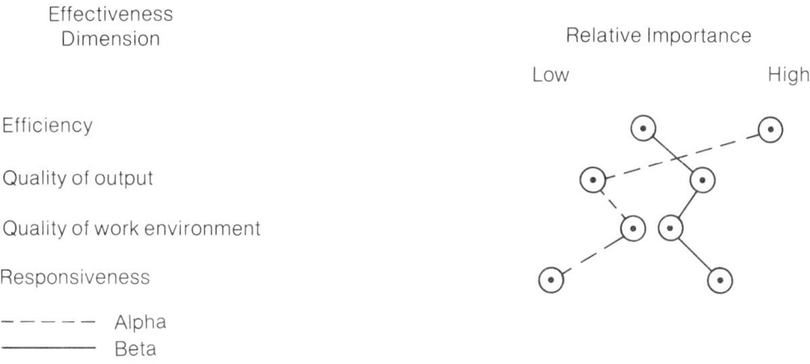

Figure 12-4. Effectiveness profiles for organizations Alpha and Beta

static/predictable/simplex. These circumstances enable them to de-emphasize support-type goals. The straightforward, placid, simplex nature of their industry makes it unnecessary to emphasize (compared to Beta organizations) adaptation and the other support goals. Instead, Alpha organizations can, in the tradition of the machine model (March and Simon, 1958) place their emphasis on maximizing output. Mechanistic designs are, of course, classically suited for just such circumstances.

Whatever its form, whether organic or mechanistic, an organization's design affects its performance. Thus—and this is the key to this discussion—the *criteria* by which that performance is assessed are emphasized, or weighted, in accordance with the goal mix the organization is trying to achieve. For Beta-like organizations, effectiveness criteria will be relatively weighted toward the dimensions of quality of output and responsiveness. Alpha organizations, on the other hand, will emphasize efficiency-type criteria. Figure 12–4 illustrates the *effectiveness profiles* one would expect to find for our two organizations, Alpha and Beta.

Summary

The goals-designs-effectiveness relationship may be summarized in three sentences. Organizations that emphasize output goals and de-emphasize support-type goals develop mechanistic designs. In turn, such designs lead to organizational performance that is most appropriately assessed in efficiency terms. Conversely, organizations that emphasize support-type goals develop organic designs which in turn lead to performance whose evaluation must include qualitative and responsiveness factors.

We are not suggesting that these latter organizations (Beta-type enterprises) ignore output goals or efficiency criteria. Obviously they cannot, especially in a world of scarce (and growing scarcer) resources. Rather we are suggesting some relative emphases—we are comparing two extreme types. And the result of this comparison is persuasive: *consistency is critical to an effective goals-constraints-design-outcome relationship.* It is this consistency that allows Alpha-type organizations to be distinguished, as we have done, from Beta types.

These ideas are all represented in Figure 12–5. The figure performs two functions. First, it summarizes a great deal of earlier discussion, some of which was captured in Figures 3–6, 3–7, 3–8, 4–3, 4–4, 11–1, 12–3, and 12–4. Second, it illustrates the consistency we have

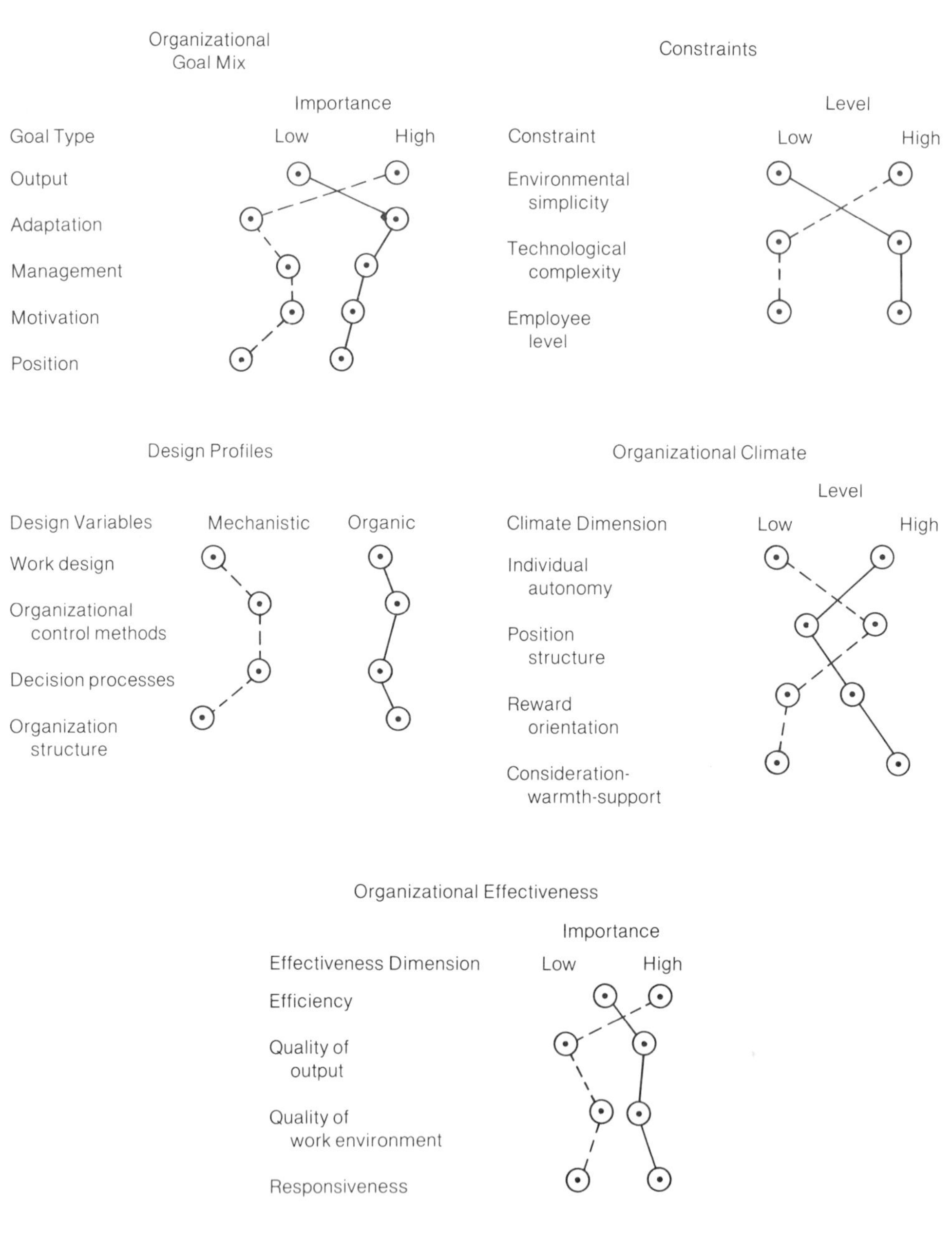

Figure 12-5. Relationships among goals, constraints, designs, and outcomes: organizations Alpha and Beta

been describing. As we move from left to right and down Figure 12–5, we cannot help but realize that organization design is a mediating process. That is, bearing in mind that an outcome is desired in terms of what was wanted (goals), we cannot help but realize that organization design is indeed what we said it was in Chapter 2: *the process of specifying optimal combinations of organizational characteristics to achieve desired organizational outcomes.*

SUMMARY AND CONCLUSION

This chapter has dealt with the "punch line" of organization design: overall organizational effectiveness. We began our examination with a discussion (in the introductory remarks) of the essential nature of the construct. We examined two main views: the goal-centered and the natural-systems views. We concluded that the most fruitful approach is a combination of the two. Next we considered several sets of effectiveness criteria. We specifically reviewed criteria described by Beckhard (1969), Campbell (1976), and Evan (1976). We observed again the utility of marrying the goal-centered and natural-systems approaches for understanding organizational effectiveness. Thus organizational effectiveness means that an organization is achieving its systems goal mix on a continuing basis.

Next we considered the thoughts of Child ("What Determines Organization Performance/The Universals vs. the It-All-Depends"). Essentially the author asked what factors are important to determining organizational effectiveness. As he pointed out, one school of thought maintains that certain factors always (universally) determine organizational performance. An opposing school argues that such factors vary considerably from situation to situation.

After discussing the pros and cons of each argument, Child concluded that the answer is "both of the above." He detailed that answer by offering the following propositions:

- Proposition 1: Organizations run by younger teams of top managers will tend to achieve higher levels of performance.
- Proposition 2: Organizations run by formally better qualified teams of top managers will tend to achieve higher levels of performance.
- Proposition 3: Organizations run by managers with a substantial personal stake in their ownership will tend to achieve higher levels of performance.
- Proposition 4: The performance standards set by an organization's management will be influenced by the norms of performance among other organizations of a similar type.
- Proposition 5: The less dispersed top-management objectives are, and the more agreement there is among senior managers as to which objectives have priority, the more successful the organization will be in attaining them.
- Proposition 6: In conditions of environmental variability, successful organizations will tend to have structures with the following characteristics: 1. arrangements to reduce and to structure uncertainty; 2. a relatively high level of internal differentiation; and 3. a relatively high level of integration achieved through flexible, rather than formalized, processes.
- Proposition 7: Organizations that increase their degree of formalization to parallel their growth in size will tend to achieve higher levels of performance.

- Proposition 8: Organizations that group their basic activities into divisions—once these activities become diversified—will tend to achieve higher levels of performance.
- Proposition 9: Organizations that design their workflow control and support structures to suit their technologies will tend to achieve higher levels of performance.
- Proposition 10: Organizations that adopt forms of administrative structure consistent with the expectations and perceived needs of their personnel will tend to achieve higher levels of performance.

As the propositions imply, Child concluded that certain factors, such as managerial qualifications and employee incentives, can be counted on to be important under virtually all conditions. Other factors, associated with organization-design characteristics, should be varied, so as to coincide with the organization's market, size, type of production, and so forth.

In the second article, ("When Is an Organization Effective? A Process Approach to Understanding Effectiveness"), Steers analyzed several alternative methods for assessing organizational performance. These methods range from those using a single criterion to those using multiple criteria. He concluded that the most fruitful approach to getting a handle on organization effectiveness consists of three related components: 1. organizations attempt to achieve an optimal combination of goals (rather than maximize one goal), 2. organizations are open systems, and 3. people's behavior, especially as individuals, is critical to organizational performance.

Steers emphasized that the best way to think about organizational effectiveness is as a process: "Instead of specifying the criteria for effectiveness (for example, when is an organization effective?), this model focuses on the process of becoming effective (for example, what conditions are most conducive to effectiveness?)." The author concluded with a suggestion. If we are to understand organizational effectiveness, we need to place greater emphasis on understanding the *dynamics* associated with effectiveness oriented behaviors and processes.

We wrapped up the chapter with our concluding statement, where we did two things. First, we specified a set of four dimensions on which organizational effectiveness can be assessed.

Second, we examined the relationship between effectiveness and organization design. In particular, we identified four effectiveness dimensions: efficiency, quality of output, quality of work environment, and responsiveness. We explored these dimensions as they relate to design characteristics of two hypothetical organizations: Alpha, a static/mechanistic organization, and Beta, a dynamic/organic type of enterprise. We concluded by noting that the successful pursuit of organizational effectiveness turns on maintaining a consistency among the variables that have been the focus of this book: goal mix, design constraints, design characteristics, and the design outcomes of organizational climate and effectiveness.

This chapter brings to a close our examination of specific variables that are involved in organization design. We conclude this book with the following section. Chapter 13 contains a couple of specific illustrations of organization design. Chapter 14 provides a final look at concepts of organization theory and organization design, especially those that are emerging and are likely to take on an increasing importance in the next few years.

Questions for Review

1. What characteristics as outlined by Beckhard define a healthy, or effective organization?
2. What are the criteria for, or possible indicators of, organizational effectiveness as synthesized by Campbell? How are they defined?
3. Evan identifies four processes in his open-systems approach to organizational effectiveness. What are these?
4. Give examples in the business organization setting for the following indicators/ratios:

$$\frac{\Delta T}{T}, \frac{\Delta O}{I}, \frac{T}{O}, \text{ and } \frac{\Delta O}{O}.$$

5. Child offers caveats about levels of performance in an organization. What are these?
6. What are Child's 10 major propositions about the factors that determine organizational performance?
7. How does Child defend his proposition, "organizations that group their basic activities into divisions, once these activities become diversified will tend to achieve higher levels of performance."? How does he defend his proposition, "organizations that design their work-flow control and support structures to suit their technologies will tend to achieve higher levels of performance."?
8. What are some of the questions Steers believes need to be answered if more meaningful approaches to assessing organizational effectiveness are to be developed?
9. What are the advantages Steers sees to a goal-optimization approach to effectiveness evaluation?
10. Steers considers that certain questions should be considered in connection with managers looking for better ways to expend their limited resources. What are they?

Questions for Discussion

1. "An organization is effective to the degree that it accomplishes systemic goals." Examine the implications of this statement for the interrelationship of the two effectiveness schemes—goal-centered and natural systems. How does this differ from the following statement: "An organization is effective to the degree that it achieves its goal mix on a continuing basis."
2. Which three or four of Campbell's criteria for possible indicators of organizational effectiveness do you consider the most important? How do they relate to each other?
3. Which three of Beckhard's characteristics of a healthy organization do you consider most important and relevant? How do they relate to each other?
4. How well do you see Evan's systemic process variables of organizational effectiveness applying in colleges and universities?
5. "Evan's ideas combine the best of both the goal-centered and the natural-systems approaches. . . ." Do you agree with this conclusion? Give reasons, based on your study of Beckhard's and Campbell's approaches.
6. Child brings up the question of "whether holding down top management positions is to be primarily a reward of age and long service or a recognition of who is best able to meet the requirements of the job—quite possibly a relatively young man." As a bright middle manager in your early thirties, how would you answer this question? As a long-term

experienced manager in your late fifties, how would you answer the same question? Is it possible to offer any solution to this question that would satisfy both kinds of managers? Is it ever possible to separate the subjective components of such responses from the objective?

8. Which of Child's propositions do you find most realistic, persuasive, and valid? Why? What personal experiences have you had that might influence your choice of proposition(s)?
9. Steers comments that "it is difficult to conceive of an organization that would survive for long if it pursued profits to the exclusion of its employees' needs and goals or those of society at large." Can you think of organizations that have done just this and survived? In what circumstances might such an organization be able to survive?
10. Choose three of the questions posed by Steers and apply them to one or two of the effectiveness-evaluation theories presented earlier in the chapter. Do these theories hold up under the scrutiny of Steers' questions? In what ways do they pass muster, and in what ways are they deficient?

CASES FOR DISCUSSION

SAVEMORE FOOD STORE 5116

The Savemore Corporation is a chain of four hundred retail supermarkets located primarily in the Northeastern section of the United States. Store 5116 employs over 50 persons, all of whom live within suburban Portage, New York, where the store is located.[1]

Wally Shultz served as general manager of store 5116 for six years. Last April he was transferred to another store in the chain. At that time the employees were told by the district manager, Mr. Finnie, that Wally Shultz was being promoted to manage a larger store in another township.

Most of the employees seemed unhappy to lose their old manager. Nearly everyone agreed with the opinion that Shultz was a "good guy to work for." As examples of his desirability as a boss, the employees told how Wally had frequently helped the arthritic porter with his floor mopping, how he had shut the store five minutes early each night so that certain employees might catch their buses, of a Christmas party held each year for employees at his own expense, and his general willingness to pitch in. All employees had been on a first-name basis with the manager. About half of them had begun work with the Savemore Corporation when the Portage store was opened.

Wally Shultz was replaced by Clark Raymond. Raymond, about 25 years old, was a graduate of an Ivy League college and had been with Savemore a little over one year. After completion of his six-month training program, he served as manager of one of the chain's smaller stores before being advanced to store 5116. In introducing Raymond to the employees, Mr. Finnie stressed his rapid advancement and the profit increase that occurred while Raymond had charge of his last store.

I began my employment in store 5116 early in June. Mr. Raymond was the first person I met in the store, and he impressed me as being more intelligent and efficient than the managers I had worked for in previous summers at other stores. After a brief conversation concerning our respective colleges, he assigned me to a cash register, and I began my duties as a checker and bagger.

In the course of the next month I began to sense that relationships between Raymond and his employees were somewhat strained. This attitude was particularly evident among the older employees of the store, who had worked in store 5116 since its opening. As we all ate our sandwiches together in the cage (an area about 20 feet square in the cellar fenced in by chicken wire, to be used during coffee breaks and lunch hours), I began to question some of the older employees as to why they disliked Mr. Raymond. Laura Morgan, a fellow checker about 40 years of age and the mother of two grade-school boys, gave the most specific answers. Her complaints were:

Questions

1. Raymond had fired the arthritic porter on the grounds that "a porter who can't mop is no good to the company."
2. Raymond had not employed new help to make up for normal attrition. Because of this, everybody's work load was much heavier than it ever had been before.
3. The new manager made everyone call him "*Mister* . . . he's unfriendly."

1. At the time of this case, the author, a college student, was employed for the summer as a checker and stockboy in store 5116.

This case was prepared by Professor John W. Hennessey, Jr., Amos Tuck School of Business Administration, Dartmouth College.

4. Raymond didn't pitch in. Wally Shultz had, according to Laura, helped people when they were behind in their work. She said that Shultz had helped her bag on rushed Friday nights when a long line waited at her checkout booth, but "Raymond wouldn't lift a finger if you were dying."
5. Employees were no longer let out early to catch buses. Because of the relative infrequency of this means of transportation, some employees now arrive home up to an hour later.
6. "Young Mr. Know-it-all with his fancy degree . . . takes all the fun out of this place."

Other employees had similar complaints. Gloria, another checker, claimed that ". . . He sends the company nurse to your home every time you call in sick." Margo, a meat wrapper, remarked "Everyone knows how he's having an affair with that new bookkeeper he hired to replace Carol when she quit." Pops Devery, head checker who had been with the chain for over 10 years, was perhaps the most vehement of the group. He expressed his views in the following manner: "That new guy's a real louse . . . got a mean streak a mile long. Always trying to cut corners. First it's not enough help, then no overtime, and now, come Saturday mornings, we have to use boxes[2] for the orders 'til the truck arrives. If it wasn't just a year 'til retirement, I'd leave. Things just aren't what they used to be when Wally was around." The last statement was repeated in different forms by many of the other employees. Hearing all this praise of Wally, I was rather surprised when Mr. Finnie dropped the comment to me one morning that Wally had been demoted for inefficiency, and that no one at store 5116 had been told this. It was important that Mr. Shultz save face, Mr. Finnie told me.

A few days later, on Saturday of the busy weekend preceding the July 4 holiday, store 5116 again ran out of paper bags. However, the delivery truck did not arrive at 10 o'clock, and by 10:30 the supply of cardboard cartons was also low. Mr. Raymond put in a hurried call to the warehouse. The men there did not know the whereabouts of the truck but promised to get an emergency supply of bags to us around noon. By 11 o'clock, there were no more containers of any type available, and Mr. Raymond reluctantly locked the doors to all further customers. The 20 checkers and packers remained in their respective booths, chatting among themselves. After a few minutes, Mr. Raymond requested that they all retire to the cellar cage because he had a few words for them. As soon as the group was seated on the wooden benches in the chicken wire enclosed area, Mr. Raymond began to speak, his back to the cellar stairs. In what appeared to be an angered tone, he began, "I'm out for myself first, Savemore second, the customer third, and you last. The inefficiency in this store has amazed me from the moment I arrived here. . . ."

At about this time I noticed Mr. Finnie, the district manager, standing at the head of the cellar stairs. It was not surprising to see him at this time, because he usually made three or four unannounced visits to the store each week as part of his regular supervisory procedure. Mr. Raymond, his back turned, had not observed Finnie's entrance.

Mr. Raymond continued, "Contrary to what seems to be the opinion of many of you, the Savemore Corporation is not running a social club here. We're in business for just one thing . . . to make money. One way that we lose money is by closing the store on Saturday morning at eleven o'clock. Another way that we lose money is by using a 60-pound paper bag to do the job of a 20-pound bag. A 60-pound bag costs us over 2 cents apiece; a 20-pound bag costs less than a penny. So when you sell a couple of quarts of milk or a loaf of bread, don't use the big bags. Why do you think we have four different sizes anyway? There's no great intelligence or effort required to pick the right size. So do it. This store wouldn't be

2. The truck from the company warehouse bringing merchandise for sale and store supplies normally arrived at 10 o'clock Saturday mornings. Frequently, the stock of large paper bags would be temporarily depleted. It was then necessary to pack orders in cartons until the truck was unloaded

closed right now if you'd used your common sense. We started out this week with enough bags to last 'til Monday . . . and they would have lasted 'til Monday if only you'd used your brains. This kind of thing doesn't look good for the store, and it doesn't look good for me. Some of you have been bagging for over five years . . . and you ought'a be able to do it right by now . . . ." Mr. Raymond paused and then said, "I trust I've made myself clear on this point."

The cage was silent for a moment, and then Pops Devery, the head checker, spoke up: "Just one thing, Mis-tuh Raymond. Things were running pretty well before you came around. When Wally was here we never ran outta bags. The customers never complained about overloaded bags or the bottoms falling out before you got here. What're you gonna tell somebody when they ask for a couple of extra bags to use in garbage cans? What're you gonna tell somebody when they want their groceries in a bag, and not a box? You gonna tell them the manager's too damn cheap to give 'em bags? Is that what you're gonna tell 'em? No sir, things were never like this when Wally Shultz was around. We never had to apologize for a cheap manager who didn't order enough then. Whatta you got to say to that, Mis-tuh Raymond?"

Mr. Raymond, his tone more emphatic, began again. "I've got just one thing to say to that, Mr. Devery, and that's this: store 5116 never did much better than break even when Shultz was in charge here. I've shown a profit better than the best he ever hit in six years every week since I've been here. You can check that fact in the book upstairs any time you want. If you don't like the way I'm running things around here, there's nobody begging you to stay. . . ."

At this point, Pops Devery interrupted and, looking up the stairs at the district manager, asked, "What about that, Mr. Finnie? You've been around here as long as I have. You told us how Wally got promoted 'cause he was such a good boss. Supposin' you tell this young fellar here what a good manager is really like? How about that, Mr. Finnie?"

A rather surprised Mr. Raymond turned around to look up the stairs at Mr. Finnie. The manager of store 5116 and his checkers and packers waited for Mr. Finnie's answer.

Questions

1. Given the discussion in Chapter 11, how would you describe the organizational climate of Savemore 5116 when Wally Shultz was manager? How about now, under Clark Raymond?
2. What are some likely causes of these differences?
3. Assume you take over as Mr. Raymond's replacement. What steps would you take to correct the problems you see?

OCEAN ELECTRONICS, INC.

In June of 1967, Ralph Roberts graduated from Florida Atlantic University with a master's degree in ocean engineering. Ralph was not the typical June graduate; at age 36 he had spent 12 years in the United States Navy. During those 12 years Ralph had learned a great deal about naval electronics. The more he studied electronics the more ideas he had about ways to improve existing equipment. With little opportunity to have his ideas studied, Ralph made an important decision; he left the Navy and, with the aid of his G.I. benefits, entered the University of California at Santa Barbara to major in ocean engineering. His academic record was spotty. His science, engineering, and math courses all showed outstanding performance, yet his studies in the social sciences and humanities were never more than average, and often below average.

This case was prepared by Professor Thomas W. Zimmerer, Department of Industrial Management, Clemson University.

Upon graduation from the University of California at Santa Barbara, Roberts looked to continue his education and came to the newly founded Florida Atlantic University in Boca Raton, Florida. The location had been responsible for the formation of an excellent department of ocean engineering. Ralph's record in his major allowed him to be accepted, and his record at Florida Atlantic University was much above average. His faculty viewed Ralph as an outstanding student. His knowledge of practical ocean engineering, gained through his years in the Navy, lent much to his research projects. It was during his research for his master's thesis that Ralph made some interesting findings. The result of these findings were the basis of a series of ocean electronics sounding instruments whose rate of accuracy was three times better than existing equipment. Encouraged by his professors, upon graduation Ralph sought financial assistance to establish a production facility to gain the rewards of his research. He believed that much of the profits could be diverted into the development of an ocean research company to allow Ralph to continue his work.

Jim Stanton was contacted in May of 1967 by the chairman of the Ocean engineering department about forming a corporation to support the work of Ralph Roberts. Stanton talked to Roberts, asking him what he wanted in terms of selling the new electronics process. Roberts commented that, "I want freedom to do research and a company which will encourage my research by plowing back profits into the firm." Stanton and two Miami associates formed Ocean Electronics, Inc., giving Ralph Roberts 20 percent ownership for his patents and put up a total of $1,400,000.

Stanton stated that, "We thought we saw a good investment, and we put up the needed money. It will be financially rewarding to all involved."

Jim Stanton:
to interviewer My associates, David Rubin and Tim O'Leary, and I wanted to invest in a company which could take advantage of the rising market for specialized electronics. Ralph has some patents which we felt provided the nucleus for forming a mutually profitable business venture. We gave Ralph 20 percent ownership in the company which, in 1969, netted him $15,000 in dividends, plus his salary of $10,000 a year. Our prediction for 1970 indicated that his share of distributed earnings will be in the neighborhood of $26,000. That's not a bad neighborhood, is it?

Interviewer: No, I guess not. What was your role in the early formation of the company and its management?

Jim: When Ike Lawson, the chairman of the Ocean engineering department at Florida Atlantic University, called me and told me of Ralph, I made an appointment to visit the campus and meet with both Ike and Ralph. At the meeting I was impressed with the capabilities Ralph had shown in his work and told him that I would see if capital could be raised. I subsequently met with David Rubin and Tim O'Leary, and they agreed to join in the venture.

Now, as far as management, I am chairman of the board and in the early stages was active in its management.

Interviewer: What do you mean, *active*?

Jim: Well, Ralph was busy making operational the new inventions, so I hired both Ron Able, the manager of sales, and Herb Schultz, the production manager.

Interviewer: Was Ralph ever involved with these decisions?

Jim: Yes, he concurred on all decisions. He was president of the company but, as I said, involved at that time with our technical problems.

THE OTHER EXECUTIVES (See Exhibit 1).

Manager of Production, Herb Schultz, Age 47

Herb had been hired in December of 1967 by Jim Stanton. Herb had been the assistant manager of production of a medium-sized electronics firm located in the southwest United States.

Interviewer: Why did you come with a new firm? Ocean was just being established and its future was not secured.

Herb: Well, I like this business. Production is a real challenge. Before, I was the assistant manager; I want to be the top man.

Interviewer: Are you happy you made the change?

Herb: You bet, I came here and started from scratch. I have ordered all our production equipment, installed it, designed the work layout, hired and trained the men; in general, I feel it's my area.

Interviewer: What is the work force in your production area?

Herb: At present we have two other engineers and 15 technicians. We have grown from just myself and no one has ever been laid off. In fact, only two men have left the shop, and both had offers we just couldn't match. They left with our best wishes for success.

I think we have a very compatible work group. We have never failed to meet a production schedule. Each technician respects his fellow workers and this respect breeds cooperation.

Interviewer: Does Ralph ever interfere with your operation?

Herb: In the past six months Ralph has been causing us a few headaches. He [Ralph] never really cared how we assembled the instruments. He did worry

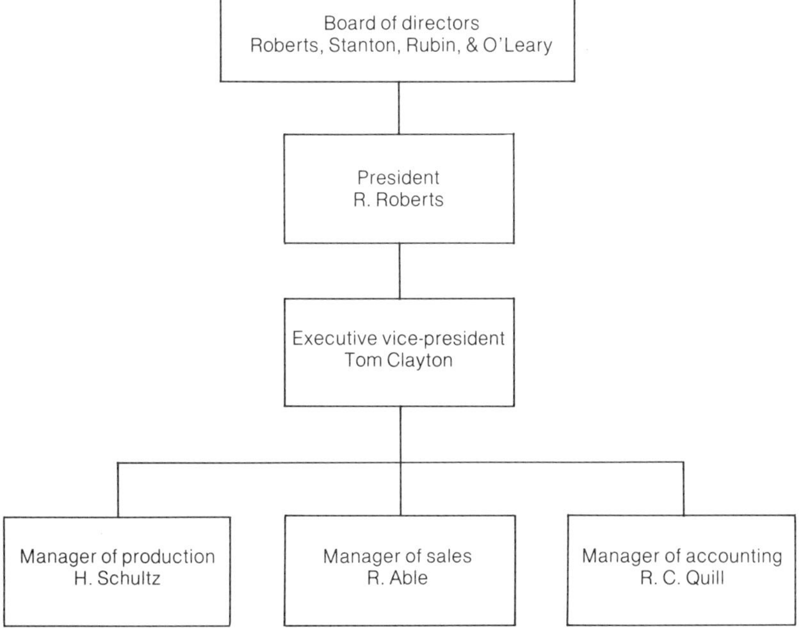

Ocean Electronics, Inc. organizational chart

about quality—he always has—and so have I. My men are proud of our quality. Because of the nature of electronic instruments of this type, we inspect each before shipment. Lately he has been making all sorts of ridiculous requests. Two months ago he wanted us to stop assembly of one line so that he could alter the model to include some new improvement he had just developed. Well, it took all Ron Able and I could do to convince him that it would be better to include the changes on next year's line. The cost to redesign our assembly processes in mid-production seemed to have no impact on his opinion.

Interviewer: Can you still work with Ralph?

Herb: If Ralph would only go back to the way it was; he does the research, and I assemble the instruments.

Manager of Sales, Ron Able, Age 37

Ron also came to the company when it was being formed. Ron had been in the ocean instruments industry with a major producer and was hired because of his proven selling ability. He had many major Washington contacts, which had given him the reputation of being the top man in the field when it came to government contracts.

Interviewer: What brought you to Ocean Electronics, Inc.?

Ron: Money. I thought that Ocean Electronics was going to be a winner. The new technology that Ralph was developing was going to set the pace in the future. It is easy to sell the best, and Ralph Roberts had the patents for the next generation of ocean instruments.

Interviewer: How successful has Ocean Electronics, Inc., been?

Ron: Very successful, I believe; and what's more, this is only the beginning. From what I see around the industry, we have the finest electronic ocean instruments in the world. The established firms are really sitting up and taking notice of our products. In fact, I will predict that the 1970 sales will be at $1,400,000, and that 1971 will approach $3,000,000.

Interviewer: How would you describe the customer relations of Ocean Electronics, Inc.?

Ron: To be truthful, spotty.

Interviewer: Can you explain further?

Ron: Many of the sales we make are to governmental agencies, primarily the Department of Defense. They have very exacting standards, and if you wish to compete for a contract, you had better have a product which matches their specs. To this point we are great; the technical specialists of the Department of Defense evaluate our product and make a recommendation that it be purchased over its competitors; then, since we are still small and new, we are investigated as to ability to comply with the contract. In other words, will we be able to do what we said we could? These personnel are not technical types in general. On occasion, Ralph has given these men a tough time. Not by design, but Ralph is just not too aware of how to handle these visitors.

Interviewer: What specifically did he do?

Ron: On a number of occasions while we were entertaining visitors, Ralph would begin on his favorite conversation: his research and his electronic in-

	struments. When most of the visitors showed no technical knowledge of the workings of the product or the nature of his research, Ralph would put them down and just leave, seldom even a good-bye.
Interviewer:	Has this happened with civilian clients as well?
Ron:	Yes, it has. Most people don't mind eccentrics, but they prefer polite ones.

By June of 1970, Ocean Electronics, Inc., was 2½ years old and was a financial success. (See Exhibit 2.)

Company facilities had been expanding and in 1970 the physical plant comprised two buildings located in an industrial park in Pompano Beach, Florida. One building, the largest, was now used exclusively for production. It had originally served as the entire facility until the recent completion of the office building and research laboratory. The research laboratory had been designed by Ralph and included the finest in modern electronic equipment. The company also owned two boats, which were used as test beds for new equipment and for the personal use of the executives.

Tom Clayton, the executive vice-president, had been hired in 1969 by the board of directors to oversee the general operations of the company. Ralph had not really been opposed to Tom's being hired because he felt that this would take a lot of troublesome problems off his back.

Ralph: *to interviewer*	I just didn't realize that business had so many time-consuming problems. In research, you work at one problem until it's solved. This day-to-day business stuff was really getting to me. Last year Jim Stanton brought up to the Board of Directors the idea of hiring an executive vice-president. Jim said he knew of someone with excellent qualifications who would administer the day-to-day business problems and coordinate with the functional area (sales and production).
Interviewer:	What was your reaction to his suggestion?
Ralph:	Well, in 1967 when we started, everything was great. I worked on perfecting my inventions and packaging them in a size that fits the needs of boat and ship owners. Each product, though identical in theory, differed in its application, depending on the size of the ship. For instance, an ocean-going freighter is not as limited as to size and weight as a 30-foot pleasure boat. The 30-foot boat, on the other hand, won't need the range and accuracy of the ocean-going freighter. Then there are military uses that completely differ again. Anyway, while I was getting all

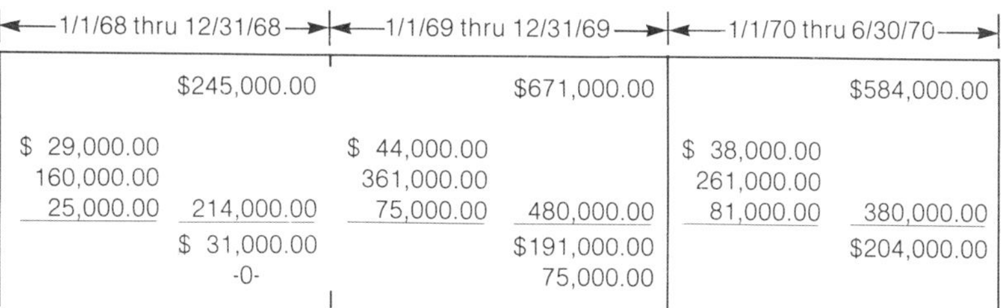

	1/1/68 thru 12/31/68		1/1/69 thru 12/31/69		1/1/70 thru 6/30/70	
Sales (net)		$245,000.00		$671,000.00		$584,000.00
Less expenses						
Administrative	$ 29,000.00		$ 44,000.00		$ 38,000.00	
Operating	160,000.00		361,000.00		261,000.00	
Research	25,000.00	214,000.00	75,000.00	480,000.00	81,000.00	380,000.00
Net profit		$ 31,000.00		$191,000.00		$204,000.00
Dividends		-0-		75,000.00		

Exhibit 2. Ocean Electronics, Inc. income statement

those technical problems solved, Jim Stanton brought together Ron Able and Herb Schultz. He knows about business, and if he said they were qualified it was all right with me; besides, I was really busy.

Interviewer: What happened after you perfected the product?

Ralph: When I was satisfied with the product, we began production and started our sales campaign. About this time Jim Stanton let me take over the reins. By mid-1968 we were showing a profit and the outlook was very promising. Ron and Herb were in almost every day about one thing or another. Delivery schedules, production runs, pricing polices, discounts; it was all new to me. What worried me most was our lack of research. I didn't have the time to get any research done. From the middle of 1968 until we hired Tom Clayton was a miserable time for me. I felt a little lost sometimes. I guess Ron and Herb saw this, and they tried to help. When Tom came, it got me back where I wanted to be.

On a warm July afternoon, Ralph was speaking to Tom Clayton about the proposed cut in the research budget.

Ralph: I don't understand the stockholders; we must do research to prosper. It was my research that got this whole thing started.

Tom: Ralph, look at their side. They put up over a million dollars to get this company going and they want to get a return on their investment.

Ralph: [Interrupts] Return, hell, they want to milk it dry.

Tom: Now that's not so. You own 20 percent of the company yourself. And, besides, the proposed budget for research for 1970 was $110,000 and all of it is yours. That was more than a 45 percent increase over last year.

Ralph: But I'm on to something, and we need to buy the equipment now. You don't turn research ideas on and off like water from a faucet.

Tom: We understand that, but there are other things to consider.

Ralph: [Interrupting] You and your bastard costs. I'm going back to the lab. (Ralph leaves.)

Questions

1. Are different parties (people, groups) using different definitions of "organizational effectiveness" for Ocean Electronics, Inc.?
2. How would you help Tom Clayton resolve this difficulty?

SECTION SIX

Organization Design: Present and Future

INTRODUCTION TO SECTION SIX

We have covered a fair amount of territory since the beginning of this book. Back in Section One we asked this question: what ideas, concepts, and practices underlie processes of organization design? We dealt with that question by discussing two subjects. First, we examined a variety of organization-theory concepts (Chapter 1). The purpose of the examination was to provide a basis for dealing with the essence of this book, organizational design. Just as engineers require a knowledge of physics, organization designers require a knowledge of organization theory.

Our examination of organizational concepts began by tracing the development of organization theory. Next we reviewed the currently most useful concept, the open-systems approach, exploring the relationships we might reasonably expect to obtain among a selected set of critical organizational variables. We also explored the importance of uncertainty for organizational functioning. Finally we detailed some important assumptions about the human nature of workers that underlay various organizational approaches.

Second, we focused our attention on organization design (Chapter 2). Organization design was defined as the process of specifying optimal combinations of organizational characteristics to achieve desired organizational outcomes. We began the examination with the reminder that dealing with organizational properties, rather than being restricted to dealing with people, is a legitimate and often fruitful approach. Next we took an overview of the subject, focusing on two important distinctions: mechanistic-organic organizational forms and differentiation-interaction processes. Third, we examined the critical role that uncertainty plays in organization design. Finally we developed an organization-design framework to be used to structure the remainder of the text (goals-constraints-design-outcomes). Using that framework, we used the succeeding chapters to address these questions: Why Design? (Chapter 3) What constrains our options? (Chapter 4–6) What do we design? (Chapters 7–10) What results? (Chapters 11 and 12)

In this section, we wrap up our examination of organizational design with two chapters. Chapter 13 offers a discussion of a somewhat applied nature, presenting a couple of illustrative design processes. Chapter 14, in contrast, is more conceptual, and we return to our initial considerations: organization theory and organization design. Here, however, we note some changes and some trends. It is fitting that the title of the book's final article is "Designing Organizations to Match Tomorrow." It is to accomplish such an endeavor that this effort has been aimed.

13

Some Design Applications

INTRODUCTORY REMARKS

In this chapter we depart somewhat from the discussion carried throughout the previous chapters. We have progressed from the question, "Why design?" to "What results from designing?" We now ask, "How do these ideas work?" To answer this question, we consider the problem of design applications. Specifically we investigate the processes that designers can use to create and implement their design.

The Readings

We open the investigation with an article by Jay W. Lorsch, "Contingency Theory and Organization Design: A Personal Odyssey." In his discussion, Lorsch focuses on four issues of organization design—issues that he is convinced are critical to effective designing:

1. What are the advantages and costs of encouraging variations in organization design among the units of large organization?
2. How do designers choose among various bases of organization: product, function, matrix, and so forth?
3. When should a design incorporate a variety of design options?
4. How can designers choose between centralization and decentralization?

The author addresses these issues by applying contingency analysis. As Lorsch puts it, "Contingency theory focuses on finding a situationally relevant solution to a given design problem." He discusses each of these issues in terms of situational circumstances, much as we have been doing throughout this book.

In the second article, "A Goal Approach to Organizational Design," Stefan D. Bloomfield and the author describe an attempt to redesign a large public-agency organization. Using a set of goal statements elaborated from Gross' (1969) goal typology (discussed in Chapters 3 and 12), the organization's design team specified a set of organizational properties. The design team first rank-ordered the goal types:

1. Output
2. Adaptability/flexibility
3. Motivation
4. Positional
5. Management

Next, specific objectives that corresponded with the goal types were identified. Various organizational properties were then specified—those that would contribute to the accomplishment of the previously identified goals. Specification of such properties was the essence of the design effort.

Conclusion

In summary, the purpose of this chapter is to present a couple of organization-design examples. That is, we are concerned here with the application of organization-design concepts and ideas to specific design problems. The article by Lorsch examines some broad issues, and that by Connor and Bloomfield describes a specific attempt at organizational design. In the concluding statement we do two things. First, we describe some objectives that organization designing serves. Second, we consider several strategies for conducting the organization-design process.

CONTINGENCY THEORY AND ORGANIZATION DESIGN: A PERSONAL ODYSSEY

JAY W. LORSCH

This paper is a personal odyssey in that it attempts to consolidate my experiences over the past decade in applying the contingency theory of organization to organization design problems. Since becoming a certified professional in 1964, my involvement with these issues has been three-fold: first, I have worked as a researcher conducting investigations contributing to the contingency theory of organizations. The principal studies in which I have been involved either as a collaborator, dissertation supervisor, or both are, in chronological order: *Organization and Environment,* with Paul R. Lawrence; "Organizational Choice: Product vs. Function," *Harvard Business Review,* with Arthur Walker; *Managing Diversity and Interdependence,* with Stephen Allen III; and *Organizations and Their Members,* with John J. Morse. Second, as a teacher, I have instructed graduate students and executives in using theoretical concepts to solve organization design problems. Finally, as a consultant to various management groups, I have worked with them in applying theoretical concepts to reach decisions about organization design for their companies. In these application efforts I have been fortunate to deal at several levels of organization; at the level of basic functional units (a production plant, a marketing department, or a research laboratory), at the level of a product division, where the principal issues are relationships among functional units, and at the corporate level, where the issues concern relations among product divisions and between them and the corporate headquarters.

From these experiences I have encountered four major issues, which I shall explore in this paper:

1. The question of uniformity versus differentiation of organization design. What are the advantages and costs of encouraging variations in organization design among the units of a large organization?
2. The appropriate basis of organization; by product, by function, etc. What are the issues managers should consider in thinking about such bases of dividing up the work of their organizations?
3. The choice of simultaneous versus stratified structure. With the increasing trend to matrix or grid structures which incorporate two or more bases of organizations simultaneously there is a need to understand what costs and benefits these forms have relative to structures where the various bases of organizations are stratified (contained at only one level).
4. The long-standing issue of centralization versus decentralization. What do these terms mean in practice and what guidelines can organization theory offer the practitioner to think about choices along this dimension?

These issues have several common characteristics, which lead me to focus on them. They are examples of the tough trade-off decisions which managers face in organization design choices. While contingency theory specifically and organization theory in general do provide concepts and propositions for dealing with these issues, there are currently important questions raised by managers which suggest opportunities for further research around each of these issues. In discussing my experience with these issues from the perspective of researcher, teacher, and consultant, I not only shall summarize what I have learned, but also will point to major opportunities for more research. In this way I hope this paper will not only serve as a summary of my experience, but also as a stimulus to future knowledge building.

DEFINITIONS

Before turning to the discussion of these four issues, it probably is important to be sure that the reader and I are on the same semantic ground by defining what I understand both contingency theory and organization design to mean. Since this paper is a personal trip, the starting point for defining contingency theory is as it was originally defined by Lawrence and Lorsch (1967). Basically, they argue that in effective organizations there will be a contingent relationship between the organization's environment and the organization's internal functioning. Such a perspective has not only been developed in our own work, but also in the work of Thompson (1967), Woodward (1965), Burns and Stalker (1961), and more recently Duncan (1972), among others. Many of these authors have focused on the uncertainty or complexity of the external environment as the important contingent variable.

My own view is that the important variables to which organization functioning is contingently related are more complex. The first of these variables is how homogeneous the major segments of the organization's environment are not only along the dimension of uncertainty, but also in terms of the time required to get feedback about results and the dominant strategic goals which each sector of the environment poses for the organization. Environmental homogeneity is important because it is clearly related to the state of differentiation inside the organization, which is one of the major organization variables I find to be important. Differentiation is defined as the extent to which organization units are different in terms of members' behavior and orientations and the unit's formal practices. The more heterogeneous the parts of the environment are the more internal differentiation the organization will have to achieve to be effective.

More recent work (Lorsch and Morse, 1974) suggests that the state of differentiation in organizations is not only contingent upon the homogeneity of parts of the environment, but also may be contingent upon certain predispositions of the members of each unit. For example, research units not only are faced with an environment with high uncertainty, long-term feedback about results, and goals emphasizing the importance of scientific discovery, but they also have scientists as their members who prefer autonomy from authority, ambiguity, and a chance to work alone. The challenge for managers and organization designers is to create an organization which will fit not only the external environment, but also these predispositions of its members. Such an organization would have a loose structure, few rules, infrequent evaluations, procedures emphasizing long-term and scientific orientations. In contrast, if we have a manufacturing unit in the same organization, such a unit would likely be faced with a more certain and short-term environment where the goals emphasize cost and efficiency. The members of such units, according to Lorsch and Morse, prefer more management control, less ambiguity, and closer peer working relationships. Thus the organization which fits these conditions would have higher formality of structure, tighter controls and procedures, and a short time frame for members with emphasis on cost and efficiency issues. This would be quite different from that appropriate to the research unit (Table 13–1). Thus, the degree of internal differentiation seems to be contingently related to not just environment factors, but also members' predispositions.

There is, however, another environmental factor upon which organization functioning seems to be contingent—the pattern of interdependence the environment imposes upon the organization. This is important because of its impact on a second major organization state, integration (the quality of collaboration among organization units). For example, Thompson (1967) identified three types of interdependence—pooled, sequential, reciprocal (Figure 13–1). Lorsch and Allen (1972) have demonstrated how sequential interdependence in a vertically integrated multibusiness firm required more effort devoted to achieving internal integration than in a conglomerate firm with only pooled interdependence.

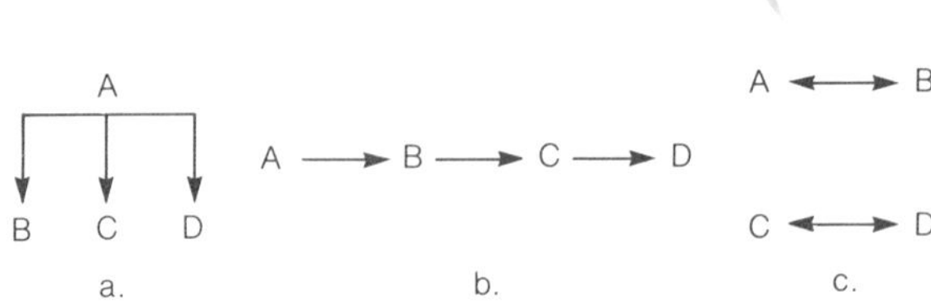

Figure 13-1. Thompson's three types of interdependence: (a) pooled, (b) sequential, (c) reciprocal

TABLE 13–1

	External Environment	Members' Predispositions	Organization Characteristics
Research Unit	Uncertain Long range Science goals	High tolerance for ambiguity Autonomous of authority Working independently	Low structure Few procedures Long-term timeframe Scientific goals
Manufacturing Unit	Certain Short range Cost/efficiency goals	Low tolerance for ambiguity Direction from authority Working independently	Tighter structure More procedures Short-term timeframe Scientific goals, etc.

In essence, then, contingency theory argues that effective organizations will achieve a congruence between the environmental characteristics outlined above and the internal states of differentiation and integration among its units. Further, it argues that the state of differentiation is also contingent upon the predispositions of members of the various organization units. But this organization perspective also suggests that the states of differentiation and integration are essentially antagonistic. The more different organization units are the more difficult it is (and the more effort is required) to achieve integration (Lawrence and Lorsch, 1967a; Lorsch and Allen, 1972). To achieve both the required differentiation and integration, organizations must find ways to resolve the conflicts which emerge among differentiated units, so as to work together in an intergrated fashion. Thus, the day-to-day behavior of organization members involves two kinds of activities and interactions. First are those aimed at achieving the differentiated goals of a particular subunit; for example, reaching decisions and implementing them about how to operate a production facility on the most efficient basis. Second are the activities and interactions which involve integrating one unit with another.

If we bear these two broad categories of behavior in mind, we can then turn to what I understand the term "organization design" to mean. Fundamentally for me, organization design is concerned with planning and formal organization variables, which are one important way administrators attempt to shape and influence the behavior of organization members. These formal variables include the structure of the organization (as represented in organization charts and job descriptions), measurements schemes (accounting systems, management information systems, performance appraisal schemes), and reward practices (compensation, career paths, benefits, etc.).

UNIFORMITY VERSUS HETEROGENEITY OF ORGANIZATION DESIGN

This issue has had its genesis for me in one of the fundamental tenets of contingency theory—that each unit should have an organization design and hence members' behavior which fits its particular external environment and its members' predispositions (Lawrence and Lorsch, 1967c; Lorsch and Morse, 1974). While the underlying reasons for this position were outlined briefly above, an elaboration may now be useful. First, however, we need to accept the notion that there is at least a rough connection between the shape of organization design variables and how members behave.

Accepting this connection between organization design variables and behavior, let me state the arguments from contingency theory for differentiating organization design among various organization units. First, to the extent that units are dealing with heterogeneous parts of the environment, such differentiation encourages members' behavior within each unit which is consistent with the unit's task of dealing with its particular external environment. If we conceive of an organization as an information-processing system, then we basically are arguing that one reason for differentiation of organization design is that it creates within each unit a pattern of information flows which is consistent with the information-processing requirements of the external environment (Galbraith, 1973;

Kotter, 1974). A second reason for differentiation is related to the motivation of organization members (Lorsch and Morse, 1974). The evidence gathered by Lorsch and Morse indicates that organization members will not only be more effective, but also will gain feelings of competence, which are powerful psychological rewards, if the design fits members' predispositions as well as the nature of the external environment. It is important to stress that in thinking about differentiation of organization design, I am centrally concerned with the issue in relation to the design of functional units (e.g., production, sales, research, engineering—to use the example of an industrial enterprise). The reason for this is that such functional units are usually the building blocks of larger product and territorial divisions of activity. Therefore, it is within these basic units that the issue of the employees' transaction with the organization is generally arranged, and differentiation in design among them will ultimately lead to differentiation among the larger units of which they are a part.

The two reasons for differentiation in organization design among functional units (facilitating information processing and motivation) are drawn from empirical research in which I have been involved. However, a reason for differentiation along a quite different organization axis has been suggested to me by both my teaching and consulting experience. Here I am thinking about the necessity to design organizations which fit the predispositions of the organization members at various stages of their lives and careers. Recent work in human development has suggested that we all pass through several stages or crises in our lives (Erikson, 1960)*. Each of these stages raises different psychological issues. For example, in their twenties and thirties people are more absorbed in their own careers and accomplishments. However, in their forties and fifties, as they reassess their accomplishments and potential and come to grips more fully with their own mortality, people are more apt to be less concerned with their own careers and to be more interested in bringing along the next generation. At these various stages different psychological rewards are more or less salient to the individual. Thus, even within one function such as manufacturing, the rewards which a manager in his thirties with a young family seeks (money, career advancement) may be quite different from those desired by a manager in his fifties with a grown family (helping to develop the next generation; retirement benefits). What is important to motivate employees is to create a situation where they are able to maximize the rewards they expect from their work (Porter and Lawler, 1968). While I would be the first to argue for the need for more research about the importance of differentiation by career stages, I currently view it as an added and useful wrinkle to the notion of differentiation of organization design, because it should improve the fit between employee expectations and organization requirements. Further, it is an idea which is entirely consistent with the contingency view of designing organizations to fit situational realities, including individual predispositions.

So far I have outlined the principal arguments for differentiating organization design. Yet since I raised this as a major issue, there is clearly another side to the argument. It comes from practicing managers when I teach or consult with them about these ideas. While they accept the requirements for differentiation among functional units (or by career stages) as a theoretical proposition, when they come down to making choices about design, their natural tendency is to opt for uniformity rather than differentiation. One reason is that they prefer the simplicity of a single compensation scheme or measurement procedure. "It is less trouble to develop one scheme and less complex to administer," is a common theme. Frankly, this is an area where I believe some systematic research could be important. Is there a way to assess the psychological and economic benefits and costs of designing and administrating a simpler, more uniform organization design as opposed to a more differentiated one? A part of such a study would clearly have to focus upon the issue of equity, which is also a major reason managers argue for uniformity. Their concern is that treating one group of employees differently from another will lead to feelings of injustice and unnecessary competition. Lawler's recent work suggests that this is a valid consideration (Lawler, 1971).

*Ed. note: Recall the discussion of such stages in Chapter 6.

Paradoxically, the prescriptions which occur to me as a result of my experience with this issue are quite different depending upon which of my three hats I am wearing. As a researcher (or in the context of this paper a stimulator of research) I would argue for more research attention to the cost and benefits of uniformity of organization design. Does it affect people's feelings of equity? Is it easier to administer? How does it compare with the advantages of differentiation that emerge from contingency theory? As a teacher or consultant, however, in the absence of hard research evidence to the contrary, I shall continue to push for more differentiation. This direction makes sense because the natural proclivity of my managerially oriented students and clients is to opt for uniformity. As a practical matter I feel it is important for them to be fully exposed to the other side of the issue, because ultimately, as in most administrative issues, I suspect we shall conclude that somewhere between the extremes is the richest pay dirt.

PRODUCT VERSUS FUNCTION

While the issue of differentiation versus uniformity is a real concern to practicing managers, the second issue which I shall discuss turns out, in my opinion, to be more illusory than real. My interest in the question of when it is appropriate to choose a functional basis of organization or a product basis was first stimulated by Arthur Walker, a doctoral candidate at the time, who had already had considerable industrial experience. Walker felt, and my contacts with managers verified, that this was a matter that worried managers as they thought about organization design.

Walker and I agreed that he should examine this issue in two production plants for his doctoral research. One had a traditional functional organization with manufacturing, quality control, scheduling, and various engineering groups reporting to the plant manager. The other plant had product organization with several organization units, each responsible for one product, reporting to the plant manager. Reporting to each unit manager were the functional specialists involved in manufacturing that product (foreman, engineers, schedulers, etc.). Using the concepts from contingency theory Walker was able to draw some interesting conclusions from this comparison, which we summarized (Walker and Lorsch, 1968). For routine predictable tasks a functional basis of organization seemed more appropriate, while when the organization was faced with a task of a problem-solving nature, the product base of organization was more appropriate. While there has apparently been a favorable response to this article (it has been reprinted in more books than anything else on which I have collaborated) I have been increasingly uneasy with it.

My concern is not with the findings per se, although they are clearly tentative and based on limited data. Rather my uneasiness is with the premise underlying the study and our article that managers faced a mutually exclusive choice between a functional and product base of organization. This I now feel is a false dichotomy, even though many managers talk as if it existed. My teaching and especially my subsequent consulting work suggest to me that the real issue managers face is a question of when, as organizations grow, to add a product level of organization to coordinate the functional organization around various products (Figure 13–2).

When an organization grows by proliferating products, the functional structure becomes unworkable, because the single management hierarchy is not an adequate mechanism to handle all the information which needs to be processed to reach integrated decisions across several functions. Therefore the organization designers decided to insert a new level of management—Product Division General Managers, whose function is to facilitate integration among the functional specialists working on their products. True, this means the original functions get split into several smaller entities, but the members of the units seem to maintain their functional identities, the necessary differentiation, and the sense of competence this allows.

A second issue, which this discussion suggests could be worthy of more explanation, is the question of how and why managers use other organization bases (time, territory) than function and product. Since Miller's intriguing paper on this subject, I have seen no attention devoted to this topic (Miller, 1959). Certainly the contributions to organization theory since then should enable us to improve our understanding of how and why managers combine the financial, prod-

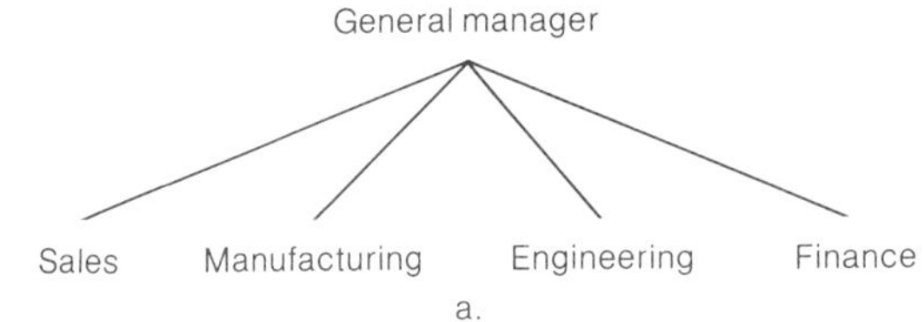

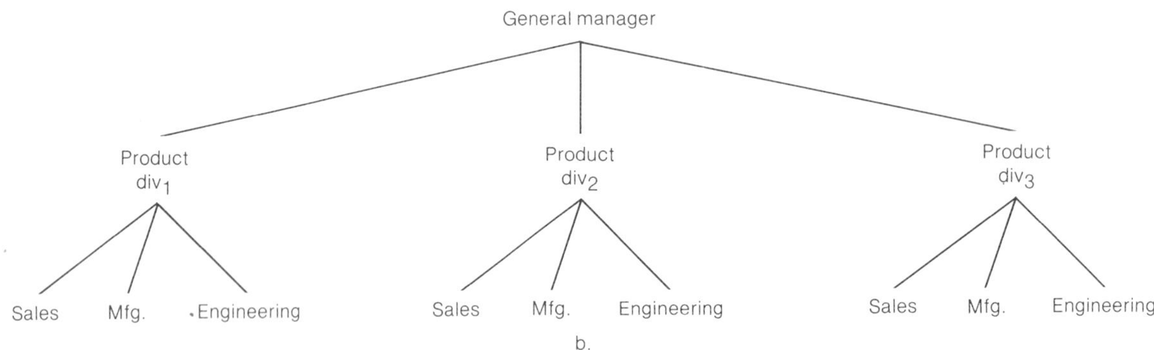

Figure 13-2. Product and function basis of organizations: (a) functional organization, (b) product organization.

uct, territorial, and temporal bases of organization. Recognizing that there are really at least four bases of organization that can be used in organization design, and that these are frequently used in complex combinations at various levels of organization structure, is a useful lead into the next issue with which I want to deal, the question of what I shall call stratified and simultaneous structures.

STRATIFIED AND SIMULTANEOUS STRUCTURES

During the past decade my contact with business firms has revealed an increasing reliance on structural forms, which have been labeled matrix, grid, and more recently, multidimensional (Goggin, 1974). While I generally do not enjoy the terminological debates that occupy some social scientists, I did want to find a set of terms that was more apt to capture what I see as the essential difference between this new form of organization and the more conventional structural patterns considered above. At first, describing the distinction as being between multidimensional and undimensional structures appealed to me. But I then recognized (as we have just discussed) that most large organizations contain more than one basis or dimension of organization. Rather, what is truly distinctive about matrix structures is that they combine two or three dimensions of organizations *simultaneously* at the same hierarchical level. In contrast, more conventional structures may be territorial at one level, functional at the next, and be divided by products at the highest level. In this sense they are *stratified* structures.

To speculate about why simultaneous structures are becoming a more common design pattern, it is useful first to consider their history. The most widely held opinion seems to be that these structures first emerged in the aerospace and defense industries particularly during the 1950s and 1960s (Goggin, 1974). While there is no question that there has been a proliferation of these structures in these government-dominated industries, I believe these structures, like so many human inventions, were discovered and developed in several places without any clear originator. Specifically, the product manager concept, which emerged in consumer product companies as well as some industrial firms perhaps a decade earlier, is an example of a simultaneous structure. Similarly, the account management form of organization, which has been traditional in advertising agencies, is also an example of simultaneous structures. My reason for mentioning the multiple origins of these simultaneous structures is that these examples provide important clues as to what organization designers have tried to achieve through these structural inventions.

From a contingency perspective, this simultaneous structure seems to be appropriate when the external environment and the organization's size create a requirement for a complex pattern of differentiation and integration simultaneously at the same organization levels. This is true whether we look at the wide array of scientists and engineers who must collaborate to build a rocket to put a man on the moon; or artists, copywriters, consumer researchers, and marketers developing an advertising campaign; or research, engineering, manufacturing, financial, sales, and marketing personnel promoting and selling soap. In all these instances there are several groups of functional specialists whose different points of view must be maintained for effective results as well as to assure their motivations. Further, it is critical to focus the efforts of some of these specialists on one set of products, while others work on another. Thus there is a need for differentiation not only by function but also by product. At the same time integration is required among the several groups of specialists working on each product to achieve unity of effort, while integration also must be achieved within each function to allocate resources and effort and to standardize approaches and methods where this is necessary.

The external environment creates these requirements in the sense that the information that must be processed requires several sets of specialists and also because it requires a simultaneous set of interdependent decisions. The uncertainty and rate of change of information also is important because the more uncertain and more dynamic the information in the environment, the more organization members have to rely on face-to-face communications to explore options and reach decisions. Prearranged procedures, schedules, and plans are simply not adequate integrative mechanisms under such conditions.

Another aspect of the external environment, which can create the need for such complex patterns of differentiation and integration, is the life span of products or projects. Where there is relatively short life span, it is desirable in both human and economic terms to be able to move personnel from one project to another. The integration this requires over time can be well managed by the functional and product sides of the organization working together. This latter point is closely connected to the issue of organization size. Not only do simultaneous structures facilitate the allocation of human (as well as financial and technical) resources from one project or product over time; it enables several products or programs to share the same resources at a given point in time. Thus an engineer may work on more than one aerospace project simultaneously, a copywriter may write for several advertising campaigns, or one plant can produce several products concurrently. When the organization is of a small enough size in relationship to the number of relatively independent activities to be performed, a simultaneous structure will facilitate such resource allocation decisions by providing functional and product managers who can consider the issues from their differential viewpoints, resolve conflicts, and reach integrated decisions.

So far, in considering the contingencies that I believe make a simultaneous structure appropriate, I have focused on two diverse structures: product (or project) versus function. The points which I have been making are even more apparent in three-dimensional situations. The most obvious example is the multinational firm, where differentiation and integration by function, product, and *territory* are frequently required simultaneously. The complex multinational environment requires managers who have functional expertise and knowledge to collaborate with other managers who are specialists in product know-how and who focus their effort on the health of their products. Both of these groups must also coordinate their efforts with another set of managers who know about conditions in various parts of the world and who are interested in results in their respective geographic spheres. It is, therefore, not surprising that simultaneous structures have become a prevalent and apparently workable solution to deal with such complex requirements for differentiation and integration.

In summary, I am suggesting that simultaneous structures have clear advantages over stratified ones where the organization is of a size or faces environmental conditions such that a set of tradeoff decisions must be made among several differentiated points of view to achieve integration concurrently along at least two dimensions of organization. Managers with whom I have worked either as a teacher or consultant have little difficulty understanding the logic of this argument. Therefore, while I am not suggesting that we should not have more systematic research to nail down the conditions under which simultaneous structures are appropriate, this is not the primary area in which I think more investigation is needed. Rather, like the other two major issues discussed above, my concern stems from my experience in watching managers deciding whether such structures will work for them and how to make them function effectively.

These managerial concerns stem from two sources. First is the intrinsic complexity of simultaneous structures. Such structures frequently mean one individual finds himself working for at least two supervisors. There can be a great deal of ambiguity about one's legitimate individual responsibility. This can mean conflict within the person and/or between his bosses about what he or she should be doing. These conflicts are in addition to those which naturally emerge from the differentiated points of view existing at the same level. The second point of managerial concern, which is clearly connected to the first, is a belief many managers seem to have in the sanctity of the unity of command (Davis, 1974). The idea that a structure in which many individuals have more than one boss can be workable is difficult for many managers to accept. There is also the concern expressed that only individuals can be held accountable. The idea of holding a group of individuals jointly responsible for results is anathema to many managers. Yet in a simultaneous structure this is often required. For example, the profitability of product A in country B may be the result of actions and decisions taken jointly by functional, product, and area managers, and they must be held accountable collectively. Even when confronted with numerous examples that illustrate that it can work, and by first-hand reports from experienced managers who have seen this sort of structure work, many managers find it hard to accept.

Another closely related issue with which I have observed managers struggling in building simultaneous structures, is how to determine measurement and reward schemes that fit. In mentioning this issue I am reemphasizing my assumption that to have a maximum impact on behavior an organization design must be developed so that all the elements are internally consistent with each other. Structure, measurement, and rewards must fit together to encourage behavior that is consistent with the external environment and rewarding to individual members.

CENTRALIZATION AND DECENTRALIZATION

The final major issue which I wish to discuss is another example of the sort of faddism that concerns me. As I have observed the organization scene during the past decade I have been fascinated by the frequent pendulum swings as managers shift their organization approaches from what they label a "centralized" approach to a "decentralized" one or vice versa. Much of this actually takes the form of changes in organization structure, rewards, and measurement and is usually accompanied by public relations announcements revealing the dawning of a new era in the management of the corporation. Let me be clear—some of this activity is well thought out and has even been well documented (e.g., Cordiner's account of the organization change at General Electric and Sloane's even more comprehensive statement of his experience at General Motors.) (Cordiner, 1956; Sloane, 1964.) But in many companies there has been a tendency to follow the trend by such major companies without any careful thought to whether what a General Motors or Dupont does is appropriate for that company

If I have seemed vague to this point about defining the terms centralization and decentralization, this is intentional. As Allen and I (Lorsch and Allen, 1972) began to write about all the data we had analyzed and the pattern of differentiation, integration, and conflict resolution we had found in the companies studied, we asked ourselves, how do mangers talk about these issues, how can we communicate with them? It was then we recognized how unclear both managers and organization theorists were about what decentralization and centralization really meant. The most widely accepted definition was that what distinguished a centralized organization from a decentralized organization was the distribution of authority to make decisions. But as we reviewed our own findings this definition seemed highly inadequate, since we could clearly see that the distribution of decision-making authority was only one piece of a complex pattern of factors which were descriptive of the multibusiness organizations we were studying.

It was at this point that we happened to reread Drucker's account of decentralization at General Motors (Drucker, 1946). He concluded that the term decentralization really referred to a whole new social order which had two functions: to allow each product division to be effective and to weld the whole corporation together. This way of thinking about these issues was highly consistent with our own emerging view. In both his description and our own data the parameters which indicate how centralized or decentralized a multibusiness organization is include:

1. The degree of differentiation in terms not only of power but also time perspective, goals, and unit structure
2. The formal integrative mechanism (structure, reward, measurement) used to tie the parts together
3. The flow of information throughout the organization
4. The pattern of decision making and conflict resolution

Where we found ourselves in disagreement with Drucker was in regard to the emphasis he seemed to put on decentralization as a panacea to the organization problems of many large firms. Our own approach, as the reader will appreciate, was to attempt to understand the contingent relationship between these organization characteristics and the firms' total environment.

Basically, what we have found is that the pattern of these internal characteristics appropriate for effective functioning depends upon two environmental factors. First is the diversity of businesses in which the company is involved. Here our concern is with the same sort of informational properties that Lawrence and Lorsch focused upon, only now our concern was with the total pattern of information facing each business as well as the headquarters. The more diverse these parts of the environment are the more internal differentiation required in orientations and organization practices. The second environmental factor found to be of critical importance was the interdependence required by the environment among divisions and/or with the headquarters. Using Thompson's typology of interdependence we found that highly diversified firms operated in environments where only pooled interdependence was required between the divisions and the headquarters (Thompson, 1967). Effective firms of this type were able to achieve this simple form of integration even in the face of high differentiation with relatively little effort on the part of managers and with quite simple integrative devices. The only integrative device was the group vice president's position, which was a new level in the hierarchy as the firm grew and added product divisions. Such other integrative mechanisms as the corporate staff and planning systems could be kept relatively simple.

In contrast, in the vertically integrated firms the interdependence required was more complex, with a sequential pattern among divisions and a pooled pattern between the divisions and the headquarters. Here the effective firm required more integrative effort and more complex integrative mechanisms. For example, a large corporate staff was in order because the divisions all shared certain technical and/or market problems and also because the flow of materials among them had to be managed. Similarly, a more complex planning system was in order. Also, in these situations more influence over major decisions at the corporate level was appropriate to manage the interdependence among divisions.

In summary, our findings suggested that the question of choosing a design along the decentralized or centralized continuum was more complex than just changing the delegation of authority. It also involved creating formal devices to achieve the pattern of differentiation and integration required by the environment at the corporate-divisional level. This clearly involves not only the design elements mentioned above (corporate staff, planning systems, and group vice president positions) but also the type of measurement scheme and reward practices.

Again, my concern in raising these issues is not with what Allen and I have learned so far, although again I would urge more studies to confirm, elaborate, and modify our findings. Rather the issues go beyond what we learned. One important issue is why there is this pendulum tendency in so many companies. Why the oscillation between a centralized mode and a decentralized mode? Several explanations suggest themselves. One is that choices about corporate strategy modify the environmental requirements facing the company. As managers make strategic decisions, they add a new subsidiary, create new interdependencies, etc.; such occurrences, in effect, redefine the environment in which the company operates. Under this view the shifts in organization emphasis would be an appropriate response to changing environmental requirements. Another explanation is that exogenous economic conditions create pressures for change. For example, I have observed several companies in the past two years make decisions to "centralize" certain functions. Basically what they are doing is changing the organization so that certain activities previously carried out in the product divisions are done in a corporate unit. Again, such changes affect the pattern of differentiation, integration, and decision making. For example, when purchasing is centralized, the need for interdependence between the corporate headquarters and divisions is greater. Such changes seem to be made because external conditions dictate them. The rising cost of raw materials means purchasing should be centralized to share central expertise. The increased regulations and problems with employee relations suggest centralizing the personnel activity. Finally, of course, the general concern with profits can lead to a decision to reduce duplication in certain functions at the division level where economics of scale seem possible. Again, all these possibilities suggest potentially valid reasons for the shift from one organization mode to the other. The final explanation of this pendulum effect is simply that managers shift to follow the prevailing management fashion. What we need, it seems to me, is a more thorough understanding of why these changes are made. Do any of these explanations make sense? To what extent do managers understand and have a valid rationale for such shifts in design? With such knowledge we can more intelligently guide managers in making design choices.

A second research opportunity that suggests itself in this area is to enhance our understanding of how measurement and reward schemes can be designed to reduce unnecessary conflict and competition. One of the clear advantages of a decentralized design, which permits divisional autonomy and differentiation, is the psychological satisfaction it gives division managers. They feel and act as if they were operating their own enterprises and this is intrinsically rewarding. A principal design tool used to gain this result is the profit center concept. Each division's top managerment is measured upon and rewarded for divisional profits. The difficulty arises when upper management, for any number of legitimate reasons, decides to change signals and create a more interdependent and centralized design with more control at the top. Ideally, they would like to achieve this without sacrificing the values of divisional autonomy. The design tools used to do this are usually some form of transfer pricing, which has the unfortunate consequence of producing much unnecessary game playing and nonproductive conflict (Dearden, 1967).

Whether those of us interested in organization design can find more adequate solutions to this problem than managers is the question I would raise, in the hope it would stimulate some to try. Whether the answer comes from empirical research studies, better conceptualization, or just plain old-fashioned invention, it seems to me it is a most important issue. From my observation, management's inability to find a more adequate solution has created many situations where acquisitions have not lived up to their full potential and where new opportunities cutting across divisions have not been realized. To solve many of the complex system-wide problems our society faces, such as mass transit and housing, gaining such crossdivisional cooperation in large companies is necessary. In this sense I think the stakes are large not just for individual firms, but for the whole society.

A GOAL APPROACH TO ORGANIZATIONAL DESIGN

PATRICK E. CONNOR and STEFAN D. BLOOMFIELD

Using organizational goals as a starting point in an organizational design study is suggested by the concept of organizational rationality. The predominant view in the literature on organizations—from the classicists (Gulick and Urwick, 1937; Weber, 1958), to the open-systems advocates (Katz and Kahn, 1966; Thompson, 1967), to the empiricists (Blau and Schoenherr, 1971; Hall, 1972; Pugh et al., 1969: 115–26)—has been that the "organization is conceived as an 'instrument'—that is, as a rationally conceived means to the realization of . . . goals" (Gouldner, 1959: 404). Indeed, the essential purpose of formal organizations is "the pursuit of relatively specific objectives on a more or less continuous basis" (Scott, 1964: 488). Thus, as Gross (1969: 277) observed, "The central concept in the study of organizations is that of the organizational goal. . . . It is the presence of a goal and a consequent organization of effort so as to maximize the probability of attaining the goal which characterizes modern organizations."

This viewpoint establishes a rationale for organizational structure: "The specific goals pursued will determine in important respects the characteristics of the structure" (Scott, 1964: 290). That is, within the framework of rationality, organizational structures are the tools for effectively pursuing organizational goals (Gouldner, 1959). The resurgence of contingency theories of organization reflects this idea; organizations are designed, continually redesigned, and managed to best accomplish their purposes under prevailing conditions. Borrowing from engineering terminology, goals are the specifications to which organizations are designed.

When goals serve as the basis for organizational design, the set of goal specifications must be comprehensive, yet analytically and operationally tractable. Unfortunately, the process of specifying goals is usually arduous and frustrating. Organizations have multiple goals (Hall, 1972; Perrow, 1970), of which many are difficult to define and often seemingly contradictory (Wildavsky, 1972: 509–20). Although goals such as production quotas, profit levels, and product parameters are relatively easily stated, goals relating to quality of service, internal morale, external image, and organizational flexibility are usually difficult to specify quantitatively. The familiar dependence on proxy variables in such cases may yield precise results only at the expense of significant distortion in later evaluation and analysis (Etzioni, 1960: 275–78).

As a consequence, an attempt to elicit a comprehensive list of organizational goals usually produces a lengthy and awkward compilation of statements—some relating directly to specific structural properties, and others phrased in lofty generalities with heavy political overtones. Procedures must then be developed to reduce such sets of goal statements to a form more amenable to analysis. In particular, the goals must be arrayed in a way that facilitates assigning priorities among goals, and allows for their operational restatement.

STRUCTURING ORGANIZATIONAL GOALS

The need suitably to structure sets of organizational goal statements is addressed by developing a body of evidence which finds that there exists only a limited number of distinct goal types (Hall, 1972). Perrow (1970), for example, observed that organizations are subject to many influences, and as a result pursue five major goal categories. While differing in some respects from Perrow's formulation, the findings of Edward Gross (1969: 277–94; 1968: 518–44; 1974) support the categorization of organizational goals into five goal types. The work of Bertram Gross (1965: 195–216)

From Patrick E. Connor and Stefan D. Bloomfield, "A Goal Approach to Organizational Design"; from Paul C. Nystrom and William H. Starbuck (eds), *Prescriptive Models of Organizations,* North Holland/TIMS Studies in the Management Sciences (Amsterdam: North Holland Publishing Company), 5 (1977): 99–110. Used by permission.

on organizational effectiveness led him to identify seven different goal types for organizations.

These typological approaches to defining organizational goals share two important properties. First, each recognizes that organizations are characterized by a variety of goals; as on-going social systems, organizations maintain activities and resources directed to many purposes. But, significantly, these purposes can be conceptually grouped into a small number of well-defined categories. Second, output goals constitute only one goal type in each of the formulations, although these goals are usually distinguished by their importance to organizational survival and prosperity. In comparison, other types may be most properly viewed as support goals (Gross, 1969: 277–94; 1974).

A typological approach to organizational goals provides a helpful mechanism for dealing with "complex sets of . . . attributes by identifying a more parsimonious set of constructs" (McKelvey, 1975: 509–25). Of course, organizations vary in the relative emphases given to different categories of organizational goals, particularly the support goals. Identifying the set of relative emphases, the organization's goal mix, establishes a ranking of individual goals corresponding to the ranking of their goal category. For goals that suggest specific structural properties (Lawrence and Lorsch, 1969; McKelvey and Kilman, 1975: 24–36; Scott, 1964), this ranking may be extended to the subsequent selection of design characteristics, providing a mechanism for resolving conflicts among such characteristics. Finally, the structure imposed on the goal identification process through use of a typology serves an auditing function by pointing out duplication within the list of goal statements, and by revealing areas in which important organizational goals may have been inadvertently omitted.

SPECIFYING ORGANIZATIONAL CORRELATES

A goal approach to organizational design requires specifying structural properties which will facilitate the accomplishment of these goals. That such a specification is possible follows from Etzioni's (1960: 257–78) concept of a real goal (or what Perrow [1970] terms an operative goal): one that is actively being pursued by a substantial part of the organization. This pursuit is reflected in members' activities and resource utilization patterns. Directing resources toward goal accomplishment, however, requires a variety of organizational design characteristics—control mechanisms, departments, communication links, and so on. These characteristics comprise what may be termed the goals' organizational correlates. Conflicts between different organizational correlates may be resolved by reference to the priorities previously assigned to the goals themselves through use of the typology.

The specific methods used to categorize goals, assign priority rankings, identify organizational correlates, and specify a final organizational design probably will vary considerably among different types of organizations and between differently constituted organizational study teams. The following case study illustrates these methods.

AN APPLICATION

A unit of a large federal agency used a goal approach for their organizational redesign. The agency maintains its principal offices in Washington, D.C., with subordinate units at regional, local, and field office levels. A formal line and staff structure exists at the Washington offices, creating a clearly defined hierarchy for both staff specialists and line officers. Staff positions correspond to the agency's traditional missions, called functions. Staff personnel obstensibly act as technical specialists in their respective functional areas, reporting to and advising line officers. The line officers are delegated the sole authority to issue directions and orders within their specified areas of responsibility.

Two principal factors prompted the agency's decision to explore possible organizational redesign. The first was the gradual expansion of the agency's roster of functional specialists, paralleling the emergence of specialized technical disciplines within universities. The attempt to incorporate these disciplines into the prevailing organizational structure revealed basic incompatibilities between the traditional functional areas and the new technical specialties. These difficulties were compounded by the need to accommodate new interdisciplinary, and consequently interfunctional, specialties. Agency management believed that the resulting structural arrangements blurred the established functional roles, promoting interfunctional rivalry and reduced organizational effectiveness.

The second factor was a growing tendency for functional staff personnel to bypass designated line authority and to issue orders directly This was most noticeable in the functional areas central to the agency's primary missions. The tendency of staff personnel to oversee directly operations within the central areas was extremely frustrating to the line officials whose managerial prerogatives were being usurped, especially since these line officers—in contrast to many other federal agencies—were career officials rather than political appointees.

These developments led agency management to believe that the formal organizational structure was no longer adequate to administer effectively the agency's missions. Therefore, selected regional and local offices were directed to develop new structures more appropriate to their individual needs. One such unit was a local office, of about 550 employees, that had played a flagship role in several aspects of the agency's missions.

Rather than unilaterally developing and imposing a new organizational design, local management appointed a study team of employees to propose a new organizational structure. The team was composed of six employees representing several different hierarchical levels and functional areas. These members were selected on the basis of their observed interest and commitment to the organization, without regard to their overall knowledge of the organization or their previous managerial experience. The resulting lack of managerial expertise within the team, coupled with a restrictive time constraint, precluded the use of many sophisticated procedures otherwise appropriate in such a redesign study. The authors participated in the study as technical resource personnel, charged with providing occasional guidance to the study process and monitoring its validity. In order that the final recommendations be credible as an in-house product, the authors were cautioned that all value judgments, decision criteria, and ultimate design specifications should be those of the study team members solely.

To augment its limited knowledge of the local office's missions, the design team initially compiled a comprehensive list of goal statements for the organization. This list was generated by soliciting inputs from employees at all levels of the local office, as well as obtaining official guidelines issued from the Washington and regional offices. This produced a set of forty-six goal statements, ranging from quite specific to extremely general. Several goals related directly to structural properties of the organization, and others had no apparent organizational correlates. The length and extreme diversity of this set of goal statements suggested the need for a goal typology to facilitate the analysis.

THE GOAL TYPOLOGY

Selection of an appropriate goal typology was governed by three criteria: the typology must be scientifically supported, directly applicable to the organization, and meaningful to the design team. The authors suggested the classification scheme developed by Edward Gross (1969: 277–94; 1968: 518–44; 1974) categorizing organizational goals into five principal classes as follows:

1. Output Goals. Those goals that are reflected in products or services intended to affect society.
2. Support Goals. *a.* Adaptation Goals—Those goals reflecting the need for the organization to cope effectively with its environment; these concern the need to attract clients and staff, to finance the enterprise, to secure needed resources, and so on.
   b. Management Goals—Those goals reflecting the need to administer the organization, to handle conflict, and to establish priorities for attending to output goals.
   c. Motivation Goals—Those goals directed toward developing a high level of satisfaction on the part of staff and clients.
   d. Positional Goals—Those goals aimed toward maintaining the organization's position and image in comparison to other organizations in the same industry, and in the face of attempts or trends to change its position.

The authors considered the validity of this typology to compare most favorably with those of Perrow (1970), Bertram Gross (1965: 195–216), and others

(Lawrence and Lorsch, 1969; Parsons, 1960; Thompson and McEwen, 1958: 23–31). Edward Gross's categorization appeared to be the result of more systematic examination than the others, having been derived as part of an extensive empirical research program (Gross, 1968: 518–44; 1974).

The design team agreed that Gross's typology was pertinent and would be useful. Team members endorsed the notion that output goals form a superordinate class of their own—the raison d'etre of the organization. Other goals, by contrast, were seen as ends intended to better facilitate achievement of the output goals. The support-goal subcategories, moreover, seemed well-suited to the organization. Being employees of an agency subject to extensive and often sensitive dealings with the public, team members readily acknowledged the existence and importance of adaptation goals. Although lacking formal managerial training, team members appreciated the need for well-coordinated organizational maintenance activities, and thus endorsed the necessity of management goals. Finally, as representatives of different constituencies within the organization, team members expressed strong concern that the organization maintain as favorable a working climate as possible, and strive to retain the unique character distinguishing it from its sister agencies. This concern led the team to support identification of motivational and positional goals.

ESTABLISHING THE GOAL MIX

Realizing that the original list of goal statements might yield conflicting prescriptions for organizational structure, the study team thought it prudent to identify the agency's goal mix early in the redesign process. The team recognized, moreover, that assigning priorities to the categories of the goal typology would serve not only to establish corresponding rankings for individual goals, but also would encourage team members to adopt a total-organization viewpoint emphasizing large-scale, overall goals.

The process used to assign goals to the five categories of the typology was tedious but straightforward. Each goal was thoroughly discussed and assigned—by consensus—to one or more categories. Many goals addressed several classes of organizational goals. For example, the goal statement, "Decision making . . . must de-emphasize intuitive reliance in favor of the increased capability and options offered by sophisticated analytical and computer systems," clearly pertained to the class of management goals, but was also thought to reflect adaptation and positional goals; it was therefore assigned to all three categories.

The subsequent process of assigning priorities to the typology was conditioned strongly by the context of the redesign study. Although many mechanisms exist for formally gathering and incorporating wide-scale organizational input into such a ranking task, the study team rejected such efforts as impractical within their time constraints. Instead, since the team was formed to represent several employee constituencies, team members decided to rely on their own perceptions of the agency's role, as reinforced or modified by the now-categorized goals. The goal typology, therefore, was extensively discussed within the group until a consensus was achieved for the assignment of priorities. Table 13–2 presents the goal typology as rewritten by the study team, and as ranked to display the agency's goal mix.

DEVELOPING ORGANIZATIONAL CORRELATES

Developing structural properties corresponding to the set of goal statements was also a relatively straightforward, albeit judgmental, process. The design team examined each goal statement to identify one or more organizational correlates. For example, one goal statement was: "Increase public confidence in the organization's competence and credibility in long-range planning, especially by providing that decision making be open and visible to the public." The design team decided that pursuit of this goal would be facilitated by creating "a formal long-range planning unit whose charge includes acquiring input from the public." This organizational correlate was then designed into the emerging structure.

Through these activities, decision-making units were formed, linking pins were established, formal communication paths were identified, and job descrip-

TABLE 13–2 GOAL TYPOLOGY ADOPTED BY THE ORGANIZATION

Priority	Goal Type	Organizational Description
1	Output	The organization exists for the purpose of producing output. Normally output is tangible, although some may be intangible and feature lack of organizational activity, such as pleasant experiences on the part of the public served.
2	Adaptability/flexibility	This class of goals deals with the ability of the organization to respond to external stimuli whether they come from out-of-agency or from other and/or higher units in-agency. Examples: severe budget cut, increase in delegation to units, changing program needs, public concerns, emergencies.
3	Motivation	Synonym is *morale*. This class of goals involves maintenance and improvement of those forces which cause employees to want to perform tasks for the organization. A normal organization cannot function in the absence of employee motivation.
4	Positional	This class of goals speaks to the character of the organization as the public, customers, politicians, employees, and prospective employees see it. This is the general tenor of the organization; the impressions it gives to those that come into contact with it. This is what makes one organizational unit appear somewhat different from another. These goals are closely allied to motivational goals.
5	Management	Organizations have goals as to how they wish to administer organization resources in terms of such organizational properties as structure, communication processes, lines of authority, decision-making processes, and control processes.

tions were modified. In short, a variety of organizational correlates were specified by the team and were then assigned priorities corresponding to those of the goal statements from which they derived.

It should be noted that the process of developing organizational correlates was actually less tidy than is suggested here. Each goal statement was exhaustively discussed and analyzed to isolate any content relevant to structural properties of the organization. Some goal statements had no implications for structure—for example, "Utilize available local-unit personnel skills and training to meet program requirements." It was also discovered that many of the organizational correlates were implied by more than one goal statement; in such cases, the correlate was assigned a priority equal to that of the highest ranked statement. In all, the forty-six goal statements produced twenty-six distinct organizational correlates. Finally, many goal statements concerned factors not necessarily appearing on an organizational chart, but rather relating to tasks for managers or their departments. These tasks were described in a narrative forming an integral part of the redesign proposal.

Table 13–3 presents an illustrative sample of some goals and their organizational correlates.

DEVELOPING THE ORGANIZATIONAL DESIGN

The final task facing the study team was to develop a new organizational design incorporating the organizational correlates. First, each member independently developed a broadbrush design comprised solely of organizational elements implied by the correlates. This demonstrated the degree to which the correlates were perceived to specify an organizational structure. With these initial designs displayed before them, the team members developed their recommendations after extensively discussing the strengths and weaknesses of their individual designs.

Specification of the final design was considerably simplified by the substantial overlap among the broadbrush designs, due in large measure to the high priority assigned to minimizing distinct organizational subunits. The extensive consolidation of tasks and functions implied by this organizational correlate was a clear distinguishing feature of each individual's design. Thus, the final design task was reduced primarily to rearranging five or six major organizational subunits to facilitate the communication needs addressed by other correlates. That being accomplished, equitable distribution of resources and power among the primary line officers was the criterion for final design selection.

The final design differed substantially from the existing organizational structure, shown in Figure 13–3. The existing structure had emphasized differentiation by function—that is, mission—with staff specialists ostensibly serving in an advisory capacity to line

TABLE 13–3 SELECTED GOAL STATEMENTS AND THEIR CORRESPONDING ORGANIZATIONAL CORRELATES

Goal Statement	Goal Type	Organizational Correlate
1. (a) Provide for an organization which can adjust to the imposition of additional work loads, changes in direction, and the addition of new skills. (b) Develop an organization which can respond to nonrecurring goals by adjusting current goals and subunit resource allocations as imposed goals are received. (c) Provide an organization having flexibility in program execution to respond quickly to emergency situations.	Adaptation	Provide as few distinct organizational units as possible consistent with smooth organizational functioning (Priority 2).
2. Decision making . . . must deemphasize intuitive reliance in favor of the increased capability and options offered by sophisticated analytical and computer systems.	Adaptation Positional Management	Provide a unit charged with computer and systems development, capable of analytical work to furnish technical assistance to all levels of the organization (Priority 2).
3. Increase public confidence in the organization's competence and credibility in long-range planning, especially by providing that decision making be open and visible to the public.	Positional Management	Identify a formal long-range planning unit whose charge includes acquiring input from the public (Priority 4).
4. Provide for the minimum number of necessary reviews and review levels consistent with the costs, the risks of unsatisfactory performance, and the evaluation skills available.	Motivation Positional Management	Maintain absence of identifiable "review" units in the local office (Priority 3).
5. Provide for program execution based upon short-range planning and programming.	Management	Provide short organizational links between short-range planning and the program execution level (Priority 5).
6. A more precise control device needs to replace present accountability procedures as a means to effect accountability among agency subunits.	Management	Maintain in the local office an identifiable group with capability to audit or inspect against goals and standards (Priority 5).

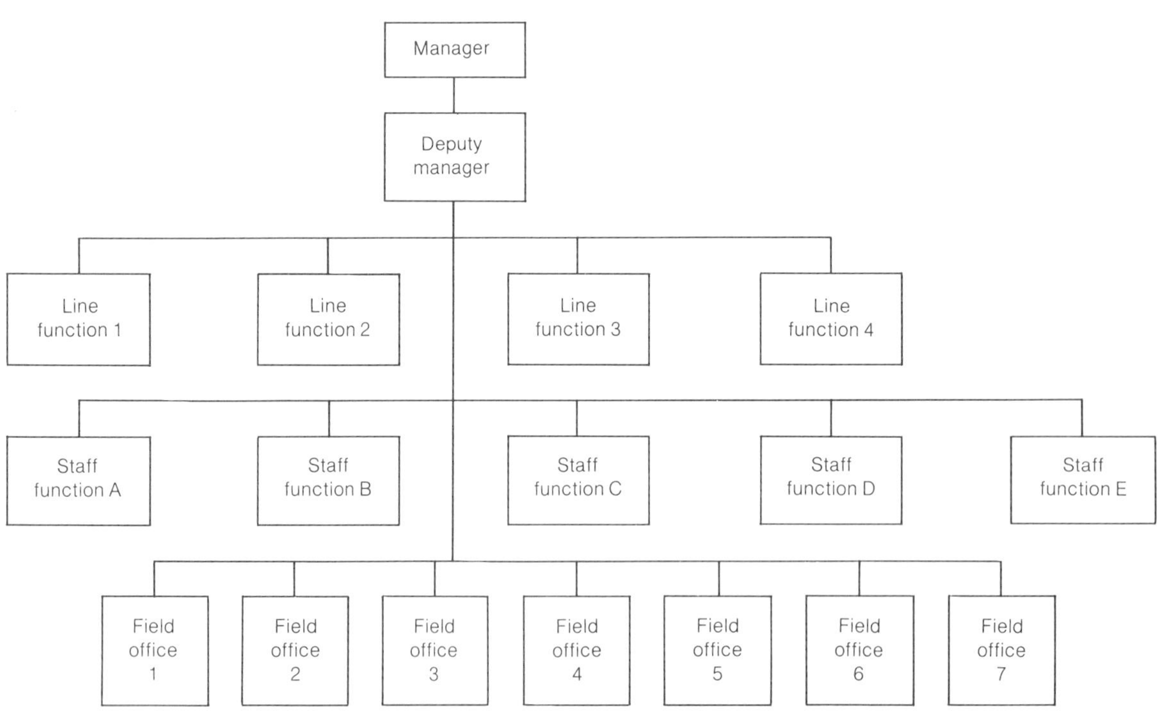

Figure 13-3. The original organizational design

officials. As may be inferred from the organizational chart, this distinction between line and staff was often unclear, particularly to the line officials at the field office level. The new design, Figure 13–4, produced an organizational structure relatively free of functional emphasis. Instead, the design emphasized fundamental organizational processes, such as long-range planning and resource planning, through integration of the functional areas into these major processes.

OUTCOMES OF THE REDESIGN

To integrate functional tasks into the organizational process units—support, operations, planning—the staff specialist's role was redefined explicitly as support to the decision makers. To emphasize this distinction, staff members were no longer invited to formal discussions among line officers except when specifically needed, and then were dismissed after their contribution had been made. The results of this change were threefold: line officers, especially at field office levels, became considerably more confident of their role as decision makers; staff officers went through a period of disorientation and anxiety with regard to their reduced role in the decision-making process; and lines of decision responsibility and accountability were significantly clarified, to the relief of top management and their line officers.

Because local-unit management could not be persuaded to conduct a formal evaluation, no systematic assessment of the new design's effectiveness can be presented. However, a series of interviews with top and middle managers revealed general agreement on two significant outcomes of the redesign. First, local-unit flexibility was improved. The new design allowed, even encouraged, an increased level of collaborative activity when unexpected events required a rapid organizational response. Officers directing the major organizational-process units report that they were able to quickly shift their personnel and resources to meet changing functional demands. Although increased flexibility within these large units was achieved at the

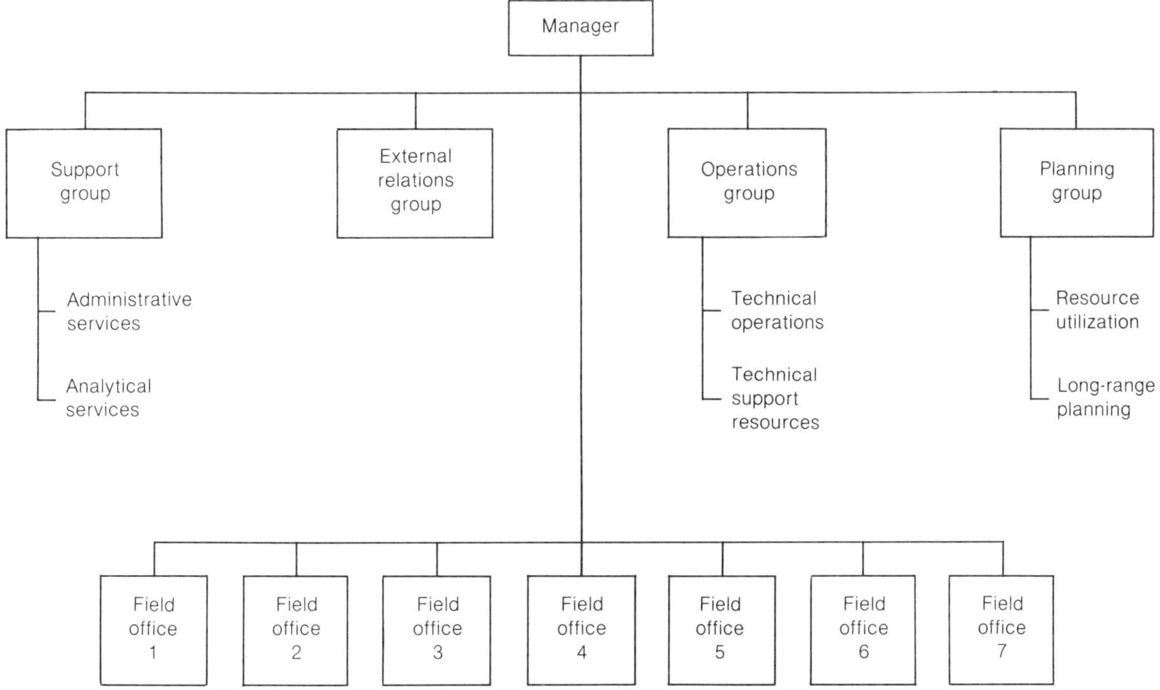

Figure 13-4. The new organizational design

expense of more formal communication needs between units, the trade-off was perceived to be greatly to the organization's advantage.

Second, the new design appeared after two years of operation to have been wholly accepted by the organizational membership. Local-unit management reported little tendency by organizational members to revert to previous modes of operation. The discomfort and disorientation initially experienced by many staff personnel appreciably eased, aided by the traditionally high personnel transfer rates within the agency and by personal counseling services made available during the reorganization. On balance, management concurred that the new design enabled a more effective pursuit of organizational goals.

CONCLUDING STATEMENT

What can we now say about the applied side of organization design? The problem, as we see from the preceding articles, is that the subject is long on ideas and concepts but short on operating rules. As with most behavioral science topics, there is more information on how to think about it than how to do it. Despite the slight engineering-type knowledge available, however, we can draw some useful operating conclusions from the growing organization-design literature. We first review the objectives to be served by designing. Then we consider some organizational strategies for developing designs.

OBJECTIVES OF DESIGNING

We said earlier that the purpose of designing is to enhance the organization's continuing ability to achieve its goals under the conditions in which it operates. We used the term *continuing ability* to signify that organizations pursue their goals as an ongoing endeavor. This pursuit is not a one-time event. Similarly, organization designing is not a one-time event. It also is a continuing process. As McKelvey (1976:28) says:

> Organization design [is] a dynamic incremental process pursuing stated design objectives, using methods of implementation compatible with them.

McKelvey's comment suggests that effective designing requires specific, stated design objectives—preferably operational ones. The organization-theory/organization-design literature provides us with at least four operational objectives. The objectives concern four central problems faced by all organization design efforts. These are the problems of interdependence, differentiation/integration, uncertainty, and participative norms.[1] The four objectives are summarized in Table 13–4.

Interdependence

The first objective is that identified by Thompson (1967). He saw the main design problem to be that of departmentalizing into coherent task units, while minimizing costs of

TABLE 13-4 OBJECTIVES OF DESIGNING

Design Problem	Design Objective
Interdependence	Form subunits so as to maximize the similarity of resources and activities within the subunits and minimize transactions across subunit boundaries.
Differentiation/integration	Develop internal characteristics (leadership style, decision process, personality styles, and so forth) of each subunit so as to make it compatible with its particular task environment, and then develop integrative mechanisms as needed to coordinate all subunits.
Uncertainty	Develop mechanisms (procedures, subunits, roles) to improve the organization's information-processing ability in the face of increasing task uncertainty.
Participative norms	Form subunits that maximize member homogeneity with regard to values and attitudes about decision-making norms and that minimize task-related interdependencies among subunits.

1. This discussion is based in part on that by McKelvey and Kilmann (1975) and McKelvey (1976).

coordinating goals, plans, activities, and resources across units. The fact that such units are not independent of each other—indeed, says Thompson, subunits have *pooled, sequential*, or *reciprocal* interdependence—makes the design problem even more difficult. For Thompson, then, a key design objective was:

> . . . form subunits so as to maximize the similarity of resources and activities within the subunits and minimize transactions across subunit boundaries.

Differentiation/Integration

The second design objective is that offered by Lawrence and Lorsch (1967a). As we have seen throughout this book, Lawrence and Lorsch discovered that effective organizations had two major features in common. First, they formed subunits that were compatible with the various task-environment elements the units faced. Second, the effective organizations had well-developed mechanisms for coordinating goals, plans, activities, and resources across those subunits. For Lawrence and Lorsch, therefore, differentiation and integration provide the key to successful designing. Accordingly, the second design objective is:

> . . . develop internal characteristics (leadership style, decision process, personality styles, and so forth) of each subunit so as to make it compatible with its particular task environment, and then develop integrative mechanisms as needed to coordinate all subunits.

Uncertainty

The third design objective has been offered by Galbraith (1973; 1974; 1977). As we saw in Chapter 2, Galbraith sees task uncertainty as a continual obstacle to rational organizational functioning. The greater the task uncertainty, says Galbraith, the greater the amount of information that must be processed by decision makers in order to achieve a given level of performance.

For Galbraith, then, developing organizational forms to cope with uncertainty—to process the necessary information—becomes a key design requirement. Recall from Chapter 2 that he develops four design strategies for such coping: create slack resources, create self-contained tasks, invest in vertical information systems, and create lateral relationships. These strategies are all aimed at meeting the following design objective:

> . . . develop mechanisms (procedures, subunits, roles) to improve the organization's information-processing ability in the face of increasing task uncertainty.

Participative Norms

The fourth design objective that can be gleaned from the literature concerns the process, as well as the ends, of design. Specifically, McKelvey and Kilmann (1975) start with the idea that organizations are "purposeful" systems. That is, say the authors, organizations attempt to exercise will or conscious choice. The following properties characterize organizations: 1. they attempt to pursue specified objectives; 2. they constrain the autonomy of their subunits to varying degrees; and 3. their subunits attempt to act purposefully.

Given this view of organizations, McKelvey and Kilmann argue that designing should serve to link individual effectiveness to subunit effectiveness to organizational effectiveness. For the authors, the main way to establish these links is by having individuals participate in the design process. Further, these links are strengthened by developing subunits that contain people who share values and attitudes about decision-making modes. The design objective thus becomes:

> . . . form subunits that maximize member homogeneity with regard to values and attitudes about decision-making norms and that minimize task-related interdependencies among subunits.

There are several advantages to pursuing this design objective. Doing so: "1. increases the ability of an organization to respond to uncertain and changing environments by forming subunits better able to make changes in their objective and structure; 2. makes it possible for managers to condition the autonomy of their subunits through negotiation about objectives, rather than through the use of rules and regulations; 3. allows subunits to make decisions about forming their own internal and external integrative devices; and 4. increases the ability of an organization to provide an internal environment where the motivation of individuals and groups is improved by encouraging their purposefulness" (1975:33).

IMPLEMENTATION STRATEGIES

McKelvey and Kilmann (1975) point out that maximizing agreement about decision making is facilitated by the use of a process that involves a wide variety of employees in determining the design configuration. This raises the logical question: What alternatives do organizations have for involving members in design? There are at leave five strategies; they are summarized in Table 13–5.[2]

From Table 13–5 we see that involving organizational members in developing and implementing designs can result from an *autocratic-direction*, *passive-influence*, *guidance*, *active-participation*, or *composite* strategy. These five strategies represent an increasing degree of active participation by organization members, with autocratic direction consisting of no shared involvement.

Autocratic-direction is the classic method used by organizations to modify their designs. In this case, top management decides for one reason or another that the enterprise needs reorganizing. Executives examine reorganization goals, problems, and alternatives; select a set of new design characteristics; and announce the changes. Organizational members and

TABLE 13–5 STRATEGIES FOR DEVELOPING AND IMPLEMENTING DESIGNS

Strategy	Characteristics
Autocratic direction	Autocratic decision making about designing; top-down; no organization member participation.
Passive influence	Organization members' design ideas, desires, etc. surveyed; results may or may not influence design decision.
Guidance	Organization members belong to a steering committee; committee's guidance may or may not be followed by design team.
Active participation	Organization members hold positions on design team; members' design ideas, desires, etc. thus affect eventual result.
Composite	Combination of two or more strategies; basic purpose is to include a wide variety of organization members—those who will be directly affected and those only indirectly affected by the design.

2. This discussion is guided by that of Bjørn-Andersen and Hedberg (1977).

subunits at various levels then proceed to arrange themselves—their titles, their tasks, and their roles—accordingly. The degree of participation and thus ownership in this process by the member is, of course, minimal.

Passive-influence is the weakest form of participation by organization members. In this process, designers use some method of acquiring information from the membership. This information usually concerns members' desires, opinions, attitudes, and feelings about possible redesign alternatives. The redesigning project reported by McKelvey and Kilmann (1975) is a case in point. Members were queried as to their preferences for redesign. Those preferences were recorded, tabulated, and submitted to the units' chief executive officer, who then oversaw the reorganization.

Guidance is the term given to the strategy of using members' representatives on steering committees. The function of such committees is to provide guidance to design teams in the line organization. This is clearly a compromise strategy—it is neither nonparticipation nor is it active participation. And, as with many neither-fish-nor-fowl compromises, this one is beset by problems. Bjørn-Andersen and Hedberg (1977) describe a company that used this method of creating and implementing an important design. The result: neither the steering-committee members nor the larger membership felt there was any real influence over the design.

"Guidance" runs a definite risk of becoming "advice"—to be taken or rejected as the design team pleases. And to add insult to injury, co-optation may occur: "Representatives in these arrangements may become captive participants who formally share responsibilities for decisions which they cannot actually influence" (Bjørn-Andersen and Hedberg, 1977:135).

Active participation in designing is made possible when members take positions on the design teams. Such people probably will not bring sophisticated organizational or managerial training to their role. Still, their knowledge of the organization and the problems that no doubt have led to the redesign effort is likely to enable them to make real contributions. The example reported by Connor and Bloomfield in this chapter is a case in point. Members from several departments and levels comprised the design team. These members had been chosen almost at random, and they attempted to reflect their constituents' views as faithfully as possible. As a result, the organization's membership had a strong voice in the design that eventually resulted.

Finally, a *composite strategy* can be used in creating and implementing designs. Composite strategies consist of two or more strategies, such as those we have been discussing. Consider the case of Norwegian industry. There has been extensive experimenting with organizational designs in Norwegian firms. One result of this experimenting is that many firms have structures characterized by high worker involvement in decision making. Based on these experiences, Bjørn-Andersen and Hedberg (1977:135–136) report a useful recommendation: extensive organizational redesign may be facilitated by an approach that progresses simultaneously on three levels. First, form a team of people who will be directly and critically affected by the redesign. The purpose of this team will be to create the design, guided by defined objectives.

Second, form a team of people who will be less directly affected by the new design. This team shall be charged with setting overall design objectives, taking charge of organizational development activities, and preparing adequate information, training, and instructions for implementing the new design.

TABLE 13–6 CONSIDERATIONS FOR GUIDING DESIGN ACTIVITIES

Managerial System

Control system processes

Planning. Making rules and regulations clearer and more specific when controlling; forming new goals when adapting.

Deciding. Making relatively programmed computational choices among known alternatives when controlling; making unprogrammed new appreciations of the environment and the organization's role in it and new appreciations of the organization's changing internal environment when adapting.

Initiating change. A reactive initiation of change in employee behavior to get the organization back on track toward its intended goals when controlling; a proactive initiation of changes to alter the objectives and form of the organization to be more compatible with changing environments when adapting.

Communicating with other members. Making sure that communications flow through the known channels as necessary when controlling.

Vitalizing. Minimizing the devitalizing, demotivating effects of running the control system when controlling; finding ways of linking up organizational and individual purposes and interest and establishing an organizational sense of identity when adapting.

Staffing. Maintaining the competence of employees filling the various positions in the organization when controlling; anticipating new kinds of competence and making sure these competencies are available to the organization when adapting.

Relational processes

Budgeting. Allocating financial resources among subunits.

Differentiating. Dividing and distributing responsibility and authority among members and subunits.

Coordinating. Coordinating activities of the members once they have been differentiated into subunits.

Conflict handling. Reducing conflicts inherent in any complex design composed of people with different knowledge, opinions, and perceptions.

Technical System

Work processes

Maintaining. Keeping in operating condition or repairing the physical facilities of the unit operation.

Transferring. Changing location or orientation of materials or information between other unit operations.

Transforming. Changing characteristics or state of materials or information.

Inspecting. Identifying quality or quantity characteristics of materials, information, or operation.

Storing. Placing materials or information so as to be available for future use.

Logistics flow processes

Locating. Finding optimal location of supplies, customers, and plants.

Transporting. Finding optimal transportation of inputs and outputs with respect to delivery time and cost.

Staffing. Finding an optimal mix of different technical specialities at a given time and finding an optimal flow rate of personnel up through the hierarchy and through careers.

Scheduling and balancing. Scheduling jobs and balancing flows through assembly lines.

Grouping. Finding optimal groupings of functions and products to take advantage of similarities in supplies, functions, products, or customers.

Social systems

Acting. Taking and acting out of roles.

Interacting. Communicating with other people in one way or another.

Forming sentiments. Forming values and attitudes as a result of activities and interactions.

Norm building. Developing social rules, regulations, folkways, and standards of behavior.

Sanctioning. Giving of positive or negative sanctions to control behavior.

Influencing. Exerting power, influence, leadership, and maintaining status.

Maintaining. Enhancing cohesion, meeting social needs, keeping system or group together.

SOURCE: Bill McKelvey, "Toward More Comprehensive Organization Design Objectives," in Ralph H. Kilmann, Louis R. Pondy, and Dennis P. Slevin (eds.), *The Management of Organization Design—I.* (New York: Elsevier North Holland Publishing Company 1976) pp. 44–46.

Finally, form a third group, representing everyone else who has a legitimate interest in the new design. This group will meet occasionally and act as a sounding board for basic design ideas. It is important, of course, that these teams share some common considerations as they go about the design process. Several illustrative considerations, based on an open-systems view of the organization, are presented in Table 13–6.

In short, organizations have several strategies for developing and implementing designs available to them. The strategies vary according to the degree of participation by organizational members, ranging from virtually none to considerable. It is clear that organizations that already have a relatively high level of participation in decision making—organizations having, as discussed in Chapter 11, organizational climates that are open, supportive, and participative—are well advised to employ a comparably high-participation designing strategy.

SUMMARY AND CONCLUSION

This chapter has been somewhat of a departure from preceding ones. We have been interested in seeing if we could identify some operational guides for designing. We began with an article by Jay Lorsch, "Contingency Theory and Organization Design: A Personal Odyssey." The author applied contingency analysis to answer such questions as, "How do designers choose among various bases of organization such as product, function, and matrix?" and, "How can designers choose between centralization and decentralization?" He found that first, these and other questions are much more complicated that they appear. And second, differentiation/integration analysis is useful—indeed, necessary—in answering them.

In the second article, "A Goal Approach to Organizational Design," Connor and Bloomfield described an actual redesigning project. A design team was formed, organizational goals identified, and appropriate organizational properties specified. The redesign resulted from a weighted combining of those properties. The weighting stemmed from goal priorities. In short, organizational goals were used to generate a new design.

Finally, we used the concluding statement to do two things. First, we identified some objectives that designing processes serve. These objectives involved such design problems as interdependence, differentiation/integration, uncertainty, and participative norms. Next we examined a variety of strategies organizations can use to develop and implement designs. The strategies were distinguished in part on the basis of participation. That is, the strategies varied from one in which organizational members make virtually no contribution to design decisions to one in which many different members contribute.

Questions for Review

1. What issues of organization design does Lorsch see as critical to effective designing?
2. Lorsch views the day-to-day behavior of organization members as involving two kinds of activities and interractions. What are they in each case?
3. Drucker, Allen, and Lorsch see parameters that indicate how centralized or decentralized a multibusiness organization is. What are these parameters?
4. According to Connor and Bloomfield, Perrow's and Gross' typological approaches to defining organizational goals share two important properties. What are these shared properties?
5. What, according to the text, are the main design problems and objectives provided by organization/theory/design literature?
6. Galbraith develops a number of strategies aimed at meeting uncertainty. What are they?

7. One design objective identified by the author is the following: "form subunits that maximize member homogeneity with regard to values and attitudes about decision-making norms and that minimize task-related interdependencies among subunits." What are the advantages of pursuing this objective?
8. What are the strategies suggested in this chapter for developing and implementing designs? What are the characteristics of each?
9. What are the considerations for guiding design activities in the managerial system? Under what two sets of processes do these fall?
10. What are the considerations for guiding design activities in the technical system, and under what processes do these fall?

Questions for Discussion

1. Lorsch quotes recent psychological studies in human development that suggest people go through a number of different stages or crises in their lives. Review the work by Erikson quoted in Chapter 6 and other material you may have recently read on this. Do you think that this identification of stages has a strong experiential foundation? Is it possible that overemphasis of "stages" in organization theory may actually create more conscious difficulties for employers and employees than it may identify or solve? Why?
2. How does the "stage" theory of human development relate to promotion by seniority (if at all)?
3. Lorsch mentions that "the idea of holding a group of individuals jointly responsible for results is anathema to many managers." Is this idea anathema to you? Why? Is it anathema to other professionals you currently know? Why?
4. Is there any real foundation to the difficulty many managers have in accepting that a workable structure can exist in which many individuals have more than one boss? On what do you base your opinions?
5. Which of the design applications mentioned in this chapter appeared most enlightening to you? Why? Does the soundness of the application justify the theoretical framework on which it was built?

14

Theory and Design: A Final Look

INTRODUCTORY REMARKS

We began this book by examining two sets of ideas that are important to designing: organization theory and organization design concepts. It is fitting, presumably, to conclude the effort by taking a last look at these ideas. As Lorsch pointed out in the previous chapter, it appears increasingly important to connect theory and practice—to connect organization-theoretical ideas and organization-design requirements.

Usually, the purpose of concluding chapters is to bring together much—if not all—of the material that preceded it. This is not, however, the purpose of this chapter. That bringing-together function was performed by Chapter 12, "Organizational Effectiveness." Rather, our intent here is to bring to your attention some ideas that are currently making the rounds of organization/management theory.

There are at least three such ideas that are important for both theory and design. The first idea is that our society is currently moving into a limited-growth situation. If such an idea is correct (and many people believe it is), just how useful is our present knowledge of theory and design—knowledge developed in years of growth, growth, and more growth?

The second idea is that organizations are not clear and distinct entities, even in the open-systems sense. Rather, some analysts see organizations to be loosely connected assemblages of people, groups, interests, resources, and so forth. If this idea is correct, do we then need to revise our theory and design practices?

Finally, many believe that however environmental, technological, and human conditions progress, organizations will have to develop the capability for self-design. Indeed, it has been the intent of this book all along to contribute to that capability.

The Readings

William G. Scott critically examines in the first article, "Organization Theory: A Reassessment," the conventional open-systems view of organizations. He suggests that there are several assumptions that underlie the "paradigm" of contemporary management—assumptions that may or may not be valid in our changing world. Basically, Scott asks, does our view of organizations hold in a society characterized by increasingly scarce resources and limited—or even negative—growth?

In this chapter's second article, "Designing Organizations to Match Tomorrow," Hedberg et al. argue that organization design is a continuing process. Therefore, say the authors, organizations must develop the capability to continually "self-design." In particular, policymakers and managers need to modify the ways organizations evaluate their performances, and they should try to stimulate experiments in organizations' strategies and in people's careers. The authors admonish today's designers to experiment, support each other, and generally avoid isolation.

Conclusion

In drawing this book to a close, we examine two basic questions in this chapter:

1. What organization-theoretic concepts can help us design organizations under modern conditions?
2. How can designers stay on top of their jobs—that is, how can organizations develop the capacity for self-design?

ORGANIZATION THEORY: A REASSESSMENT

WILLIAM G. SCOTT

This author's first organization theory paptcr (Scott, 1961: 7–26), which appeared in the *Academy of Management Journal* in 1961, had a certain immediate acceptance and remained remarkedly durable in the following years. One reason for the popularity of this article was the emphasis which it placed on systems theory. However, another more important reason for its continued success was that it demonstrated that systems theory was an elaboration of the management "paradigm." *The term paradigm is used throughout this essay to refer to a composite of values, premises, models, and techniques in management.* The paradigm represents the core of the field as it has developed through the refinement of theory, research, and practice over 75 years. The usefulness of paradigmatic analysis has been shown by Thomas S. Kuhn (1962) and by Petro Georgiou (1973: 291–310).

Presently, systems theory provides the field of management with concepts imputed to every single important movement to appear since 1960, including organizational development, contingency theory, organization behavior, sociotechnical systems, industrial dynamics, operations research, management information systems, and human resource systems. Even the venerable fields of business policy and management principles are yielding to a systems approach. A distinction must be made between systems theory and systems analysis, however. Systems analysis provides a mathematical, computer-based technology that, like a taxicab, can take you almost anywhere without regard to ends. Systems theory, following the traditions of Ludwig von Bertalanffy (1952), is paradigmatic in nature and embodies a world view of values, methodology, and technique.

During simpler times, the classical model of bureaucracy had served management theory and practice well. However, due to the need to respond to the military and the consumer, to the demands of national policy, and to internal imperatives, some organizations were becoming not only complex, but of gigantic size as well during the 1950s. These organizations contained highly trained people devoted to the development, financing, production, and distribution of advanced products and processes. Such organizations were theoretical anomalies—they fell outside limits of the classical model and required a new model which projected different types of organization stuctures and styles of management practice. The systems model seemed to fill this need, and as a result the age of systems thinking began for management in the late 1950s.

The 1960s began with a certitude that national achievement would follow trends of the previous decade, although at an accelerated pace. Many people believed that the pace would be set by an elite of enlightened politicians, managers, and technologists. This belief was fed by the typical American optimism regarding the future. While the sources of this optimism remain murky, they appear to lie in our social, political, and economic institutions; in our science and technology; in our abundance of resources; in the instrumental and pragmatic powers of our educational institutions; and in the rectitude of our cause in world affairs (Heilbroner, 1959).

The author's original paper was written against this background of national events and conventional optimism. For its time (more than 10 years ago) the article was a reasonable statement of the *technical* elements of organization theory in the management paradigm. But what was its strength proved also to be its weakness, *the emphasis on the technical aspects of organization theory shrouded the values upon which the theory itself rested*. Failure to discern these values caused two related errors in the analysis: a. ignoring the ambience in which organization theory existed, and b. treating classical and systems theory as essentially

Abridged from William G. Scott "Organization Theory: A Reassessment," *Academy of Management Journal,* 1974, 17: 242–54.

different models of organization. Actually, the two models are not different in their ultimate values; rather, differences lie in their operational premises, nothing more.

THE CONSERVATISM OF CLASSICAL AND SYSTEMS MODELS

Classical and systems models are conservative because they belong to the dominant paradigm of management thought and practice. Rationality is the common medium shared by both models within this paradigm. Management rationality has been defined in other places as being indistinguishable from the notion of efficiency, the ratio of $E = O/I$ (Scott and Mitchell, 1972). The purpose of management, and hence the purpose of organization theory, is to increase the value of E by adjusting the relative values of outputs over inputs.

While one can quibble about definitions and become confused by pseudohumanistic rhetoric, the major implications of this proposition must be accepted, because otherwise it would not be possible to explain management's role in organizations. The role of management has been socially and legally defined as the stewardship of resources: if the stewardship function is executed successfully, the wealth of an organization is protected and increased; the welfare of the clients and constituents is improved; and the fortunes of the management are advanced.

Organization theory contributes to the science and art of the managerial process that is implicit in the concept of stewardship. An organization theory that works counter to the stewardship notion is simply inconceivable within the value framework of management thought that has developed over the last 75 years.

Values of the Conservative Models

The values of conservative theory correspond to American utilitarian beliefs that hold material *growth* to be efficacious, material *abundance* to be limitless, and *consensus* to be the natural manner of human relationships. Heilbroner discusses American optimism as rooted in the faith in economic growth, which in turn is based on a bountiful natural environment (Heilbroner, 1959). Dahrendorf discusses consensus as it is woven into the fabric of management theory (Dahrendorf, 1959). Both the classical and systems models assume these beliefs because they are the ultimate *a priori* values of conservative organization theory.

These values supply the criteria for acceptable social, economic, and technological policies. They define the nature of the problems to be solved by management theory and practice and establish the parameters of research in management and allied fields. They influence the curricula to be studied in courses of learning in management. They determine the content of communication between managers of organizations and the people served by them; and they control the expectations that people have of the managers of organizations. As such, these *a priori* values are the ruling forces of the paradigm.

Operational Premises in Classical and Systems Models

Operational premises reflect the implied governance mode of the model and provide the foundations upon which managerial techniques are built. When classical and systems models are compared, such as in Kast's and Rosenzweig's (1973: 315–18) treatment of contingency theory, differences are drawn between their operational premises. The shorthand for categorizing these differences often is expressed in terms of autocratic or democratic modes of organizational governance.

For example, the classical model is considered to be deterministic, closed, mechanistic, inflexible, narrowly adaptable to change, and oriented toward hierarchy as the means of coordination and control. Alternatively, the systems model is considered to be probabilistic, open, organic, flexible, broadly adaptable to change, and oriented toward lateral and diagonal organizational interfaces as the source of coordination and control.

THE EROSION OF OLD VALUES

The attention that management gives to operational premises results in the disappearance of *a priori* values. When we debate the relative merits of operational premises, we think we are discussing values. In reality we are doing no such thing. But why this concern with the values of growth, abundance, and consensus? They have served admirably in the past. Indeed, the belief in them has been justified.

A single nation never had such a friendly environment, such abundant resources, and such a vital, innovative people. These factors, coupled with a strong work ethic and an insatiable desire for material well-being, made growth appear as a limitless possibility. These are the factors that Heilbroner (1959) attributes to the "special circumstances" of American history.

American management had a large part in reinforcing these beliefs. "Faith without good works is hollow." Management supplied the good works through an enviable record of achievement. So impressive is the evidence in the form of goods and services that growth has become the basis of public and private policy for economic development, technological change, and social uplift both domestically and internationally.

What politician, public administrator, or business executive in practice supports overtly to his constituents policies of economic contraction, reduction of agency services, or stabilization of sales volume and corporate earnings? How many university courses are offered in "How to Shrink a Business"? How frequently do articles appear in the professional literature about management strategies of organizational stability or decay? These things seldom happen because they reflect values that are foreign to American expectations and, thereby, are foreign to the mainstream of management thought and practice. However, lately there is some doubt—but more, there is cynicism—about these values and the management practices that achieve them.

Many factors have contributed to the erosion of old values in our society, with Watergate and the Vietnam war among the most prominent. However, there are more proximate sources of strain on the management paradigm—for example, the declining reserves of natural resources, growing resistance to environmental contamination, changes in work expectations, and crises in confidence.

Declining Reserves of Natural Resources

The Club of Rome studies of world resources are well known (Meadows et al., 1972). They conclude that world resources will not sustain present levels of population growth and consumption. These studies project resource crises by 1990. Similar projections are also made by the English study, *Blueprint for Survival.* Recently the U.S. Geological Survey added the weight of its authority to the impending crises by identifying American deficiencies in its natural resource base (Brobst and Pratt, 1973).

As of this writing, America is in the midst of a shortage atmosphere that includes many basic commodities such as gasoline, oil, natural gas, lumber, and agricultural feed grains. In addition, embargoes on several commodities have been either imposed or contemplated. The present crises in these commodities may be the result of short term dislocations brought on by government economic and foreign policy; nevertheless, they have focused public attention on shortage. The consequences, although unforeseeable, may be to create a national "scarcity mentality." Shortages, coupled with inflation, could well force the American public to scale down consumption expectations.

Agriculture, energy, and mineral resources are the foundation of an industrial society. Thus, shortages of any of these can influence the state of mind of citizens, causing a reevaluation of priorities and a shifting of values. Indeed, if consumption patterns do change, management in the basic institutions of our society will have to respond with organizational strategies that rest on nongrowth assumptions.

Resistance to Environmental Contamination

That we have gone through some significant cultural changes in our thinking about the environment is indisputable. For example, there was rejoicing during the depression on the southside of Chicago when smoke poured from the stacks of the steel mills. At that time, the smoke meant people were at work. Now that same smoke is accepted at best as a mixed blessing. As another example, not too long ago an industrialist said, "We always believed God gave us Puget Sound to dump waste into." Such an observation now sounds as curious as a defense of the Divine Right of Kings.

It is obvious that the preservation and nonabuse of our environment is of great concern and of urgent importance. The environment is a resource, and how this resource is used depends upon present-day values.

Historically, we have leaned toward exploitation of the environment, but now attitudes are moving toward conservation. If this is more than a passing trend (and who can say now?), then attitudes governing the use of those resources which are essential to the technology of society will change toward a vision of scarcity that is consistent with the conservationist mentality.

Changes in Work Expectations

Attitudes about the environment are not the only facet of value change. A theme of some persistence is that man should rediscover humanism, which in contemporary argot is translated as a quest for innerpersonal and interpersonal satisfaction—Consciousness III, so to speak. There is no point in reviewing here the enormous amount of literature from Maslow (1964) to Reich (1970) pertaining to this subject, except to examine one subtlety of the modern humanistic movement as it bears on management.

Whether deservedly or not, humanism adapted to the management process has the taint of manipulation. It is difficult to imagine management using techniques like organizational development, sensitivity training, or job enrichment out of a pure "milk of human kindness." Certainly management expects the goal of rationality to be promoted if people find their work more rewarding in humanistic terms. This must be one reason for paying humanist-type change agents consulting fees. They create and apply behavioral technologies that management thinks are valuable for raising the efficiency of human resources—humanist technologies and technologists serve materialistic ends.

The difficulty of applying humanism in this manner is that personal satisfaction and organizational efficiency are compatible only at a most superficial level. The kinds of satisfaction sought for man by true humanists are nonmateralistic. Hence, any attempt to mold humanism to the goals of organizations (as we know them) either will pervert the humanistic values or erode organizational rationality. We cannot have it both ways.

Declining Confidences

Public opinion polls for the last six years show continuously declining faith in the time-honored institutions and their representatives in American society. Currently, the process of deterioration has reached an all-time low. It includes not only government, church, business, and labor, but also the professions which have been insulated in the past—law, medicine, and education.

There are two reasons for taking note of this: (a) old confidences are intimately related to values of the established management paradigm, and (b) old confidences are being replaced with new confidences. What effect the new confidences will have on the paradigm is indeterminate, other than that they are contributing to the destruction of the old value base. The shift from old to new confidences seems to be occurring along these dimensions:

1. Declining confidence in individuality, rising confidence in group processes
2. As a corollary, declining confidence in the individual's inherent value to a community or to an organization, and a rising confidence in the individual's dispensability
3. Declining confidence in some absolute, unassailable moral nature of man and a rising nihilism which expresses a confidence in the malleability of man and the contingency approach to organizations
4. Declining confidence in the spontaneity of behavior and a rising confidence in the efficacy of planning
5. As a corollary, declining confidence that somehow the future will yield to individual strivings and a rising confidence in the goodwill and kindly ministrations of organizational leadership to provide for the individual's future

Obviously this shifting of confidences will strain the management paradigm because the values of growth, abundance, and consensus ultimately have to do with the more conventional norms of individual welfare. Paradoxes probably will appear that cannot be resolved by traditional management wisdom as regards individual autonomy, freedom, creativity, and organizational stewardship. These changing confidences, along with dwindling resources, changing work expectations, and environmental use attitudes, are eroding the paradigmatic structure of contemporary management. A fair question to ask now is, "What might be the shape of the future?"

THE RADICAL MODEL

Paradigmatic thinking restricts us to those models and values that are already sanctioned. However, thoughtful people must explore alternatives for management that lie outside the boundaries of the paradigm if for no other reasons than:

1. There are limits to growth, and
2. Other than the restricted usefulness of utilitarian economic models, we do not understand the implications for management should the belief and the reality of growth, abundance, and consensus diminish in our world view.

But where can a discussion that will move further than the limits of conventional management thinking be introduced? As a *beginning*, it is possible to start with values that are opposite to those of the conservative models and see where they lead in terms of organizational governance and operational premises. The model may be called "radical" because it does affect vital principles.

A small disclaimer is necessary. One should not be so naive as to imagine that the radical model, whatever its final form, will be fulfilled completely any more than the conservative models have reached full realization. These models—the conservative and the radical—are analytical types that represent present, and perhaps future, directions in management theory and practice.

Values

The values of the radical model are stability or decay, scarcity, and conflict. Analysis of the interrelationships among these values has substantially different results as they are polar to the conservative models' values. Thus, organizations in mature industrial societies confronting a nongrowth future might expect that their sources of surplus may disappear. If so, one of the chief means for securing consensus will vanish or become attenuated. As a result, instead of expecting to participate in an ever-expanding largess, people will find it necessary to compete for the *relative size* of their share of fixed organizational resources. These conditions can do nothing but emphasize the conflictual nature of relationships among organizational interest groups.

The values of scarcity, stability, and conflict are alien to the traditionally optimistic American world view. Therefore, few people would disagree that associating these values with models of management is paradigmatic treason. Yet, if there is any truth in what was said previously about the erosion of old values, it may be that a vision of new values is coming into focus. Why not the values of the radical model? Perhaps, but we should not leave this subject without raising one important objection.

The form in which the radical values are presented depicts a static future. Such a future is not foreseeable within 5, 10, or even 15 years. Organizations are in fluid, turbulent states; therefore, one would need considerable hubris to disregard the arguments of those who speak of "future shock," changing organizations, and contingency theory. Knowledgeable observers of the contemporary management scene such as Bennis and Slater (1968), Kast and Rosenzweig (1973), and Toffler (1970) try to show a moving picture of organizations. The change and dynamism inherent therein probably is the best current representation of the organizational condition with which management must contend.

Another form of radical values is needed to account for organizational turbulence during this period of rapid change. One possibility is to represent the value structure of the radical model as movement either forward or backward along three continua:

1. Growth↔Stability or decay
2. Abundance↔Scarcity
3. Consensus↔Conflict

In certain ways, this form of the radical model is a closer approximation to what contemporary economic models of development or stability attempt to portray for emerging nations and mature nations. Such a general framework of analysis may not be inappropriate for organizations. The difficulty with this interpretation of radical values is that it leaves management grappling with the problems of randomness, indeterminacy, and ambiguity. However, these conditions, which arise from value oscillations, may be precisely what are responsible for throwing the present management paradigm out of gear.

Operational Premises

Various government modes are implicit in the radical model. The first form of the model suggests two alternatives—federalism and totalitarianism. If we look to a future of *federalism* we might expect premises to emerge that will legitimatize politicization of structure and behavior, competing class interests, confrontation of interest groups, pluralism of instrumental ends, and functional decentralization. If the future holds *totalitarianism* for organizations, then such premises may appear to legitimatize elitism, mass homogenization, medicobehavioral technology, elaboration of control technique, and the propaganda of integration.

Traces of totalitarian and federal operational premises are found presently in organization theory. For example, the matrix structure requires the politicization of structure and behavior in order to work. The use of techniques to acquire greater power of predictability and control of process is as old as organization theory itself. This is not a surprising discovery since totalitarianism and federalism are in direct lineage from the traditional autocratic and democratic governance modes. However, the former two differ from the latter two in several crucial ways. Totalitarianism and federalism pertain to more complex organizational environments, rest upon much more advanced technology and, of course, are derived from different values.

Finding a word to label the governmental mode of the second version of the radical values is difficult because there are no equivalents in political science. Burnham (1941) realized that the locus of sovereignty has shifted away from traditional forms of government and property. The result is to create a managerial society in which primary modules of government and economic management are administrative in nature. Therefore, we have to offer as a label the graceless word "managementocracy."

The indeterminate nature of the second form of the radical model is likely to cause a progressive enhancement of this equally graceless occupation for the next decade or two. Management in this period of value oscillation should take comfort governing organizations with operational premises that will legitimatize contingency, planning, group decision making, scientism, and uncertainty. Whatever premises emerge in support of these concepts and processes will be useful for management regardless of where the organization is on the value continua and in spite of the direction the organization is moving on the continua.

CONCLUSION

The changing circumstances in America relating to resources, environment, expectations, and confidences may cause significant value shifts. If these shifts occur, they will alter the management paradigm by bringing into serious question the pertinence of its cherished values—growth, abundance, consensus. With different values, like no-growth, either the operational premises of theory and practice will change or new connotations will be given to old premises. This reasoning explains the contention that the extant management paradigm is loaded with anomalies and why it is necessary to start thinking about alternative values, models, and premises.

Some will say that a chic form of pessimism has been adopted by this author in order to establish a brief in behalf of the case. True, it is currently fashionable to make gloomy predictions about the future. Therefore, if this whim was succumbed to, it was in part to provide a foil for contrasting the simple-minded optimism that is so much the essence of management theory and practice. But, beyond this, the present pessimism rests on a much more substantial foundation than mere journalistic artifice.

It is also possible, as others may argue, that technology will be able to solve the problems that man and technology combined have produced. For example, the energy crisis, caused by diminishing availability of crude petroleum, may be overcome by converting the vast Montana coal reserves into oil or by developing an economical means for hydrogen or lithium fusion.

However, these technological solutions to the energy crisis must first face environmental objections. These objections notwithstanding, the process of continuously seeking technical solutions to technical problems drops us into the Ellulian trap of *La Technique* (Ellul, 1964). This trap threatening human dignity creates even greater dilemmas in the metaphysical domain.

The real challenge to the management paradigm lies, perhaps, between the fashionably pessimistic and the simple-minded optimistic forecasts of the shape of the future. Even if this compromise is accepted as a reasonable assessment of the future, it still means that the extant paradigm will change. No doubt this experience will be excruciating for many, because it will be the first time that such a change has occurred in the management field. The test of our maturity as scholars and practitioners will come from our ability to rethink our values, reorder our priorities, relinquish our models, and reconsider our premises.

DESIGNING ORGANIZATIONS TO MATCH TOMORROW

BO L. T. HEDBERG,
PAUL C. NYSTROM, AND WILLIAM H. STARBUCK

Organizations might be matched to tomorrow's world on the basis of accurate forecasts. But who knows which forecasts, if any, will turn out to have been accurate? Some forecasts have said that energy shortages, famines, and ecological decay will occur unless limits are placed on resource consumption (Forrester, 1971; Meadows et al., 1972; Oltmans, 1974); these limits would require that nonindustrialized societies consume more resources while industrialized societies consume less. Other forecasts have stated that different societies will grow at different rates, with the important constraints on consumption arising from social and political decisions rather than from ecology (Mesarovic and Pestel, 1974). Still other forecasts have asserted that consumption can rise indefinitely because vast potentials remain for using solar energy, new agricultural methods, pollution controls, and innovations that are still to be discovered (Cole et al., 1973; Kahn et al., 1976). The diverse forecasts even outnumber the forecasters.

However, the most effective designs for tomorrow's organizations vary little from forecast to forecast, because all of the forecasts imply that there will be rapid social and technological change. Equilibrium in resource consumption would not eliminate change. Quite the contrary. A fixed resource pool means some activities must be deleted whenever new activities are undertaken, and hence means an increased proportion of activities that are in decline. Since most forms of social and technological change are insuppressible, equilibrium in resource consumption would bring more rapid change between and within societies. Moreover, if organizations continue to behave inertially, consumption in the industrialized societies would exceed the long-run equilibrium levels; cutting back consumption would cause distress that might be avoided through gradual transitions.

Organizational inertia also impedes the creation and use of technological innovations. If technological innovations escalate consumption per capita while allowing populations to multiply, the world's saturating ecology would likely impose more and more constraints. Ecologically destructive or inefficient methods would have to be nonbenevolently forced out of use as soon as better methods appear. Either organizations would have to be made less inertial or traditionally inertial organizations would have to be replaced more frequently.

Because social and technological change appear likely to accelerate, social institutions ought to be designed to accommodate rapid change and to extract the benefits from it. Today's institutions find rapid change stressful largely because of networks of private and public organizations that lack adaptiveness. This article discusses ways to increase organizations' adaptiveness so that societies can respond creatively to ecological constraints and technological innovations. The next section explains how organizations in benevolent environments accumulate inertia and become less capable of handling transitions into new, perhaps nonbenevolent, environments. Then follows a statement of the basic alternatives open to policy makers who want to steer populations of organizations. It is advocated that top managers and policy makers stimulate the evolution of self-designing organizations—organizations that continuously diagnose their important problems, explore their future options, and invent new solutions as they develop. Some key properties of self-designing organizations are spelled out in the final sections: participatory information systems that trans-

Bo L. T. Hedberg, Paul C. Nystrom, and William H. Starbuck, "Designing Organizations to Match Tomorrow," from Paul Nystrom and William H. Starbuck (Eds), *Prescriptive Models of Organizations*, North-Holland/TIMS Studies in the Management Sciences, 1977, 5: 171–81. Used by permission.

mit diverse messages, strategic experiments that disrupt complacency and stimulate curiosity, and jobs and careers that provide satisfying lives despite rapidly changing work environments.

GROWING INFLEXIBLE BECAUSE OF BENEVOLENCE

The mental characteristics of people are important determinants of how organizations act. Human brains can analyze the implications of only a few simultaneous influences, and they bog down in the difficulties of weighing numerous future uncertainties. Therefore, organizations have to keep acitivities simple—by breaking big tasks down into small ones, by ignoring contingencies and potential options, by grouping stimuli and responding to them with standardized routines. For example, accountants and internal revenue agents compare tax returns with various rules of thumb: careful investigations are not wasted on returns that conform to ordinary patterns.

Whether standardized routines produce good solutions depends on an environment's constancy and benevolence. Environments that change slowly provide time in which to create new methods and to refine old ones. However, organizations are unlikely to try to improve methods that appear to work, and familiar results are usually assumed to be nearly optimal. Benevolent environments rarely make enough threats to keep organizations alert: lost opportunities are less visible than are customers' complaints, law suits, or financial losses.

Decades of almost continuous economic growth have encouraged the organizations in industrialized societies to depend on standardized routines. Signals that routines are failing are rare; resource margins are adequate to absorb the errors from slightly inappropriate responses to slightly misperceived stimuli; responses can be invented gradually. Organizational failures are typically attributed to managerial inexperience and to deviations from conventional practices rather than to stresses originating in environments.

Furthermore, standardized routines have been tailored to gradually expanding economies. Budgets are thought of as minimum aspirations rather than as upper limits to expansion; financial plans focus on maximizing growth while retaining small buffers against temporary setbacks. Long-term commitments, such as purchase contracts, assume that productivities will rise through learning and through returns to scale as well as through technological innovations. Forecasts of demands for products or services reflect managers' ambitions more than external realities (Crecine, 1969; Pondy, 1969: 47–60; Schumacher, 1973).

Consistently benevolent environments undermine organizations' readiness to act and their sensitivity to environmental events. Fewer resources are expended monitoring environmental happenings. Plans replace messages as the media for intra-organizational coordination. Redundancies and irrationalities are shifted out of job assignments and authority domains. Organizational ideologies grow up about standardized routines, and conformity to tradition becomes a primary criterion for accomplishment (Clark, 1972: 178–84; Hedberg, 1973; Mitroff and Kilmann, 1976: 189–207; Nystrom et al., 1976: 209–30).

STEERING THE POPULATION OF ORGANIZATIONS

If the future is going to expose organizations to rapid change and possibly to less benevolent environments, policy makers will have two basic options. Substantial increases in organizational death rates can be accepted, with resources being transferred from dying to newly born organizations. Alternatively, organizations can be made more adaptive so that they can survive to explore and to develop in altered environments.

These two options are not mutually exclusive, and policy makers are likely to use both. However, improving organizations' adaptiveness wastes fewer resources and promises more benefits than does stimulating higher turnovers in the population of organizations. Small, incremental changes cause less difficulties for organizations and their members than do abrupt, revolutionary shifts. Organizational death nearly always causes psychological stress and consumes human and material resources. Policies to increase organizations' deaths and births require effective systems for transferring resources from dying to newborn organizations. At present, efficient transfer systems exist mainly for financial resources: transfers of people, knowledge, and equipment are handled poorly. Unless the new organizations are more congruent with long-term environmental constraints than were the former organizations, replacing one organization with another brings only the temporary benefits of change as such. It is doubtful that anyone knows enough about the future to say reliably which organizations are the most appropriate ones to die or what kinds of organizations ought to be created.

Traditional strategies for designing organizations start with forecasts of what stresses tomorrow's organizations will face, and then attempt to design organizations that meet the envisioned needs. Although these forecast-oriented designs are common, both their realism and effectiveness must be questioned.

Some liabilities of forecast-oriented designs derive from the difficulty of taking the future into account. To the extent that the future can be predicted, it is easier to specify some of its constraints than to imagine opportunities that might be realized within these constraints. Consequently, forecast-oriented designs tend to be conservative solutions that fail to reap full advantage from their environments.

Forecast-oriented designs readily become self-fulfilling prophesies: they can create the situations they were designed to meet. For example, if forecasts predict considerable technological innovation, organizations will incorporate large research departments that generate technological innovations. Similarly, if public agencies expect aggressive animosity from their clients, they will use physical barriers and rigid rules to protect employees from clients and will use esoteric jargon and impersonal procedures to keep clients at a disadvantage; frustration and bewilderment then breed ill will and noncompliance. In many instances, the major contribution of forecasts is to foster social change in one direction instead of another.

If policy makers are going to facilitate particular kinds of social change, they certainly ought to acknowledge the value premises underlying their social policies, and they should choose their social policies overtly after comparing alternative futures. But it is far from clear that top managers and policy makers ought to control social change directly.

The alternative way to design organizations to match the future is to adopt a metastrategy in which the top managers and policy makers define their role as similar to that of arithmetic teachers, whose effectiveness is measured by their student's ability to solve arithmetic problems rather than by their own ability to solve such problems. Within this metastrategy, the goal shifts from solutions invented by policy makers to combinations of hardware, software, and people which continually invent, revise, adapt, generate, and modify their own solutions (Hedberg et al., 1976: 41–65).

Self-designing organizations are more promising vehicles for approaching the uncertain future than are organizations that rely on forecasts. Self-designing organizations would evaluate their own defects and strong points; they would develop opportunities instead of defending past actions; they would adapt to surprises; and they would resist the accumulating of inertia.

The main prerequisite for self-designing organizations is probably an ideological commitment to impermanence. Organizations should be seen as means, not ends. Members should avoid basing their personal satisfactions on the roles and methods that characterize the present, and they should seek satisfactions in the activities and skills that are creating the future. Current methods and policies should be questioned continuously, and strategies should be chains of experiments; even apparently adequate methods should be discarded in order to make way for new trials (Landau, 1973: 533–42; White, 1969: 32–42; Wildavsky, 1972: 509–20).

Self-designing organizations will encounter at least three groups of technical problems. Firstly, self-designing organizations need timely information about changes in their environments and their performances, so that they will have enough time to invent appropriate methods. Secondly, means are needed to counteract organizational inertia and to keep organizations exploring alternative futures. Thirdly, self-designing organizations have implications for their members' jobs and reward systems; they are likely to require new attitudes toward work and new job systems. The ensuing sections of this article discuss these problem areas in sequence and point out actions that policy makers and managers can take in order to foster self-designing organizations.

TRANSMITTING CHANGE SIGNALS

Self-designing organizations depend on efficient information systems that can trigger timely adjustments to changing internal and external conditions. The important characteristics of information systems include input signals from diverse sources and rapid perceptions of change. For example, one study found that hospitals with information systems that highlight both expenses and medical performances can better achieve high-quality treatments at low cost and better match their internal structures to environmental requirements than can hospitals with information systems that focus primarily on monetary measures (Gordon et al., 1974). Another study found that the more profitable business firms are those that use diverse criteria to evaluate themselves (Grinyer and Norburn, 1975: 70–97).

Although new computer technologies can improve information processing, crucial improvements are needed in the information being processed. Most organizations currently rely on accounting systems and formal reports to measure their performances, but these measures are at best partial. Organizations that suddenly find themselves in trouble evidently are ones that have relied on routine, formal reports too heavily (Nystrom et al., 1976: 209–30). Because accounting systems reflect material and financial resources—neglecting such resources as skilled personnel, know-how, or investments in future markets—organizations can accumulate hidden resources and dissipate them without recognizing these trends or measuring most of the trends' effects (Hopwood, 1973: 83–98).

When there are no generally accepted performance measures, organizations can respond to observed deficiencies by shifting to new performance measures that portray their activities favorably (Nystrom, 1975: 104–13). Even when performance measures are generally accepted ones, evaluation and adaptation suffer from insufficient upward communication; messages are often distorted or blocked while traveling from lower organizational levels toward decision centers.

Participation in organizational governance can improve organizational self-evaluations by bringing in outside expertise and by making better use of inside expertise. Representatives of workers, customers, clients, suppliers, patients, governments, interest groups, and citizens can supply additional information about opportunities and threats in organizations' environments or expose obscure difficulties within organizations, thereby improving organizations' reaction times and their decision bases. Participation in organizational governance may also reinforce members' loyalty and increase organizations' cohesion in the face of rapid change. Organizations with informal, nonhierarchical communication links react faster and more easily to changes in their environments.

Widespread participation in organizational governance will require information systems that keep each participant adequately informed. Although, so far, electronic information technology has been used mainly to increase control by top-level personnel, it could help to decentralize decisions and to distribute decision aids and accurate information to lower-level personnel, customers, clients, or community members (Mumford and Sackman, 1975; Simon, 1973: 268–78).

How should managers and policy makers improve performance measurements? Rather than allocating resources to elaborate performance evaluations, policy makers should foster informal communications and should encourage managers to elicit brief performance appraisals from diverse groups. Policy makers and managers also should combat reliance on formal accounting systems, and they should reject misleading precision in statements about past performances and future expectations. Top managers ought to monitor environments more and internal methods less. Time and effort ought to be invested searching for new measures of organizational success that include ecological consequences.

STIMULATING ORGANIZATIONAL CURIOSITY

Management theories have long prescribed skill specialization, systematic coordination, clear objectives, and unambiguous authority structures. These widely accepted prescriptions say an organization should be internally differentiated and yet haromonious, should use explicit communication channels and explicit decision criteria, and should act decisively and consistently. Such properties can enhance the performances of organizations that inhabit slowly changing environments: ad hoc analyses can be replaced by standardized routines; routines can be multiplied, reduced to their essential elements, and then preserved in capital equipment and training programs; communications can be compressed with efficient codes; and responsibilities can be delineated precisely (Galbraith, 1973; Khandwalla, 1974: 74–97; Starbuck and Dutton, 1973: 21–28). Because they are designed for benevolent and relatively slowly changing environments, today's organizations avoid debates and conflicts, and they impose rationality on activities.

Rapid change will require increased risk-taking and experimentation by organizations that seek to survive. Competition in a stabilized population of organizations or pressures from technological innovations will favor organizations that can seize opportunities and create unique niches of competence. Increased risk-taking will raise organizational death rates, but will also improve the adaptiveness of the surviving organizations.

Self-designing organizations will need planning systems that expect the unexpected and that stimulate curiosity; such systems will differ from the systems currently advocated for long-range planning. In fact, a study of British firms found no evidence that consensus about objectives, clearly defined roles, or formal planning correlated positively with financial performance or innovativeness. Instead, financial performance correlated positively with reliance on informal, unofficial communication channels and with the number of different kinds of information used during reviews of company policies. Organizations with elaborate long-range planning systems seemed less able to explore their futures than organizations with less programmatic ways of forming strategies (Grinver and Norburn, 1975: 70–97).

Organizations' searches for new modes of behavior are motivated by dissatisfaction and triggered by signs of failure, and intervals of doubt and reappraisal precede genuine efforts to reorient strategies. Reappraisals are not fostered by the organizational practices that clarify goals and that allocate tasks logically and unambiguously. Consequently, self-designing organizations ought to use logical contradictions, ambiguities, and overlaps to counteract complacency and to stimulate innovations.

The essence of all efforts to reduce organizational inertia is to induce organizations to act as if optimal is an impossible state. Links between current methods and current goals should be seen as transient. Behaviors should be planned as sequences of experiments to test the stability of environmental phenomena and to discover better ways of behaving in the future, and the experiments should continue even after optimal behaviors appear to have been found. Because shifting environments and uncertain futures give organizations the task of optimizing unknown criteria, continuous experimenting along a trial-and-error trajectory makes better sense than does attempting once-and-for-all solutions to problems that will change (Box and Draper, 1969; Campbell, 1969: 409–29; Lindblom, 1959: 79–88; Starbuck, 1974: 67–76).

Experiments can be stimulated by making organizations pursue different goals at different times, by letting separate departments pursue incompatible goals simultaneously, and by undertaking iterative improvements instead of attempting to find overall optima immediately (Wildavsky, 1972: 509–20). All of these strategies remind organizations' members that goals and criteria are erroneous approximations that can be corrected and improved.

The key design challenge is to balance the levels of discretionary, uncommitted resources. Discretionary resources must be available if organizations are to try experiments, to develop new capabilities, to take risks, and to survive transitions to new environments. But when discretionary resources grow too large, there are not enough warnings of change, and so adaptive capabilities wither.

If policy makers and managers want to encourage adaptiveness, they should think thrice before punishing entrepreneurial ventures. Promotions and incentives ought to reward people who deviate from familiar methods, who take risks, and who ask imaginative questions. Occasional failure ought to be every manager's right, and policies and educational programs ought to foster ideological commitments to exploring unknowns rather than to mastering the known. Instead of criticizing organizational subunits for having unclear and contradictory goals or for duplicating the activities of other subunits, policy makers and top managers should interpret conflict and ambiguity as generators of healthy changes. Investment policies and tax incentives ought to favor flexible assets that convert to diverse uses and ought to nurture efforts to recycle existing assets. Hiring criteria should place high values on people's versatility and their preparedness to learn, and organizations ought to set up programs to help their personnel unlearn outdated traditions and standardized routines. Contracts and commitments should shrink the long term and focus on the short term.

LIVING IN SELF-DESIGNING ORGANIZATIONS

An orientation toward flexibility will mean that most interpersonal relationships are temporary ones, that job assignments will change frequently, and that hierarchical statuses and prerogatives will shift. There may be high job turnover as people depart who dislike newly adoped task arrangements, and as people arrive who possess needed abilities. Departments, work groups, and individuals require latitude in which to evaluate and to reorient themselves, and this in turn means latitude in which to err and to harm themselves.

There are real reasons for wondering how satisfying such jobs can be. How much pride can people take in rapidly vanishing accomplishments and in solutions which are automatically assumed to be faulty? Can the people who prefer clear, stable assignments learn to be happy with endless sequences of experiments and reorientations? Will inconsistencies and ambiguities induce apathy and alienation in people, as they did in Pavlov's dogs? Little is known about such issues. Unstable, experimental situations may make today's people uncomfortable mainly because today's organizations promote stability, consistency, and permanence. Perhaps people can draw as much satisfaction from the activities that keep organizations viable as they now draw from repreated routines and familiar structures (Wildavsky, 1972: 509–20). Perhaps people can take pride in creating new methods rather than in reusing elegant methods, and people can enjoy partially answering important questions instead of precisely answering inaccurate questions (Mitroff and Featheringham, 1974: 383–93). Perhaps careers that aggregate similar jobs in different organizations can be more satisfying than careers that aggregate different jobs in the same organizations.

What actions should policy makers and managers take to improve jobs and employment systems? People should be encouraged to try our alternative jobs, and transfer systems should be developed that reduce the difficulties and expenses of discovering new employment opportunities, of moving into new organizations, or of changing occupations. A person's long-term financial security should not depend on continued employment with the same organization. Information about job openings and available people should be widely disseminated, perhaps through publicly supported information systems. Educational curricula ought to deemphasize narrow specialization, and educational policies ought to treat learning as a lifetime activity. Opportunities should be created for people to distribute through time the cost of mid-career reorientations. There should be as much freedom for individual people—to innovate, to experiment, and to adapt—as there is for the organizations people can and will create.

STARTING TO BEGIN

Because no one can accurately forecast the future, no one can design organizations that match tomorrow's challenges. However, self-designing organizations would reduce the costs of forecast errors by rapidly adapting to what really occurs. Self-designing organizations redesign themselves to match tomorrow.

Individual organizations can strive to become self-designing and to remain so, and some organizations may succeed. But today's social environments seriously impede the redesign efforts of isolated, individual organizations, and self-designing organizations will not grow prevalent unless they receive support from compatible social institutions and appreciative ideologies. People will have to face up to the deficiencies in systematic methods, rational analyses, and consistent behaviors; and people will have to acknowledge the virtues of impermanence, dissension, bare adequacy, uncertainty, and ambiguity. Societies will have to follow new policies and put new social technologies into operation—technologies that encourage flows of people and of information, and policies that foster continuous experiments and strategic versatility by people and by organizations. Policy makers and mangers as well as everyone else will have to honor the complementarities among actions by individuals, by organizations, and by societies, because the social institutions needed to support self-designing organizations must themselves be supported from below.

It is far from obvious what steps can take the world from where it is to where it ought to be. Yet this ignorance is itself an informative guide to action: it implies that steps will have to be discovered progressively through incremental experiments in pursuit of ambiguous, shifting goals. Ignorance of what steps to take is also reassuring, for it means that experiments still lie ahead. The excitement and fun come from designing, not from having designed.

CONCLUDING STATEMENT

Finally, what can we say about contemporary organization theory and design? What developments can we anticipate in the near future? And, therefore, what recommendations to organizational designers can we offer? The articles in this chapter have addressed themselves nicely to these questions. We will therefore keep this concluding statement relatively brief, using it to review some important ideas. We consider the ideas of growth versus no-growth, loose coupling, and self-designing organizations.

ORGANIZATIONS: GROWTH, STABILITY, OR DECLINE?

The first idea in developing organizational thought that needs to be pursued is that raised by Scott in the first article, "Organizational Theory: A Reassessment." Specifically our ideas/concepts/theories about organizations have served us well during periods of growth and expansion. Will they serve us equally well during periods of contraction? As the author pointed out, organization theory and practice have rested on the assumption that growth and expansion are inevitable. Further, managers have felt duty bound to make sure that that inevitability is met.

But what about a society operating with a no-growth mentality? For such a society, organizations will be constrained to make do with what they have, rather than encouraged to go out and get more. Will our current ideas/concepts/theories even be relevant to—much less helpful for—such a condition?

Scott sounded a pessimistic note in answering this question. He suggested that the "classical values" are simply too conservative. Scholars, researchers, and practitioners will be unable to change their conceptions of appropriate processes and outcomes. Instead, argued the author, people will have to abandon those values. They will have to replace them with those of the "radical model." These latter values are stability or decay, scarcity, and conflict.

The other pessimistic note sounded by Scott concerns turbulence. He predicted that in the next few years organizations will fluctuate along three continua:

Growth ↔ Stability or Decay
Abundance ↔ Scarcity
Consensus ↔ Conflict

In other words, he argued that organizations will move from left to right along these continua, although the movement will be back and forth. Some years will see relative growth and abundance. Some will see the opposite. The *trend*, however, will be toward stability (or decay) and scarcity. As a result, organizations will move from relatively open and adaptive organisms, in which consensus is a dominant operating mode, to closed and static mechanisms, in which conflict prevails.

Frankly, we both agree and disagree with Scott's conclusions. We do agree with his view of changing organizational circumstances. There is persuasive evidence, as he pointed out, that we are embarked on an era of limited (or no) growth; an era in which scarce resources are even scarcer.

Granting this view, however, why is our conventional view of organizations therefore inappropriate? Basically we have said that the organization is a system, a system that is open to its surroundings. It acquires resources, processes them, generates output, disposes of the outputs in such a way as to continue acquiring more input, and so on. The thrust of this conception is threefold: 1. resources flow through the organization; 2. organizational properties and processes get designed and redesigned to deal with this flow and the attendant uncertainties; and 3. the organization's success at all this is assessed in terms of multiple criteria. These criteria relate to internal matters, external matters, and the relationships among them.

Does a changing circumstance alter the essential sensibility of this view? No doubt, as resources become scarcer, such environment-engaging activities as noted in Chapter 4 will change. Moreover, conflict management will become more usual—and consensus management less usual—than in times of abundance. Still, the open-system/contingency-design paradigm encompasses these eventualities. Changing circumstances—even those predicted by Scott—will probably have little direct effect on that paradigm.

LOOSELY COUPLED ORGANIZATIONS

There is a second idea that is influencing developing organizational thought. This idea, mentioned earlier in Chapter 8, was first articulated by Glassman (1973). Its popularization began with an article by Karl Weick (1976).[1] The essence of the idea is that organizations are *not* tidy, efficient structures, rationally performing according to plans that are designed to maximize goal achievement. Instead, organizations are loose assemblages of people, resources, activities—assemblages that may or may not contact each other in some form or fashion.

The following passage by James March illustrates the idea (in Weick, 1976:1):

> Imagine that you're either the referee, coach, player or spectator at an unconventional soccer match: the field for the game is round; there are several goals scattered haphazardly around the circular field; people can enter and leave the game whenever they want to; they can throw balls in whenever they want to, as many times as they want to, and for as many goals as they want to; the entire game takes place on a sloped field; and the game is played as if it makes sense.

The author points out that this description, as bizarre as it seems, could serve to describe a real organization. Consider schools, for instance: substitute principals for referees, teachers for coaches, students for players, parents for spectators—and schooling for soccer. Doesn't the example make sense? To be sure, it makes a different kind of sense from conventional descriptions of school organizations. But it does make a kind of sense nonetheless. Most of us reading the passage and thinking about a grade school or high school can see the resemblances. The point, of course, is that those resemblances no doubt differ from what we see when conventional descriptions are used. In short, the idea of loose coupling suggests nonconventional images of organizational actions.

The question remains, however: What are these nonconventional images that we see, and are they useful? Basically they describe organizations in which activities are not tightly and

1. This section follows Weick's (1976) discussion.

unambiguously connected. Conventional systems thinking can lead the unwary to believe that once an event occurs, there is an effect that ripples inexorably throughout the organization. After all, the organization is seen to be a system of variables that are extensively interconnected. Recall our own discussion back in Chapter 1, in which we used Henderson's (1935:14) diagram of systems interdependencies (reproduced here as Figure 14–1).

We noted that Henderson explains his diagram as follows (1935: 86):

> The four rigid bodies A, B, C, and D are fastened to a framework a, b, c, d by the elastic bands 1, 2, 3, 4, and 5. A, B, C, and D are joined one to another by the elastic bands 6, 7, 8, 9, and 10. Here the conditions of statical equilibrium can be worked out mathematically, or determined empirically by introducing spring-balances into the bonds 1, 2, . . . 10, and reading the balances.
>
> Now imagine the point of attachment of 5 on the frame to be moving toward b, all other points of attachment remaining unchanged. What will happen? Consider A. There will be action on A by the path 5, 9, by the path 5, 8, 10, and by the path 5, 8, 7, 6. But in each case these actions do not cease at A, just as they do not previously cease at D. The first, for example, continues along the path 10, 8, and so back to 5. If we try to think of all this as cause and effect we must inevitably reach a state of confusion.

The idea of loose coupling, on the other hand, suggests that an event may or may not trigger a rippling effect. There is an extraordinary variety of variables, forces, groupings,

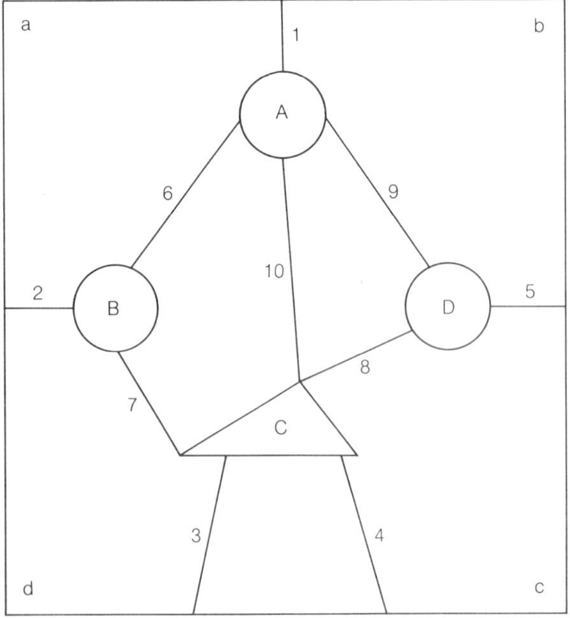

Figure 14-1. System interdependencies

Source: Lawrence J. Henderson, *Pareto's General Sociology* (Cambridge, Mass.: Harvard University Press, 1935), p. 14. Copyright © 1935 by the President & Fellows of Harvard College; renewed 1963 by Lawrence J. Henderson.

actions and counteractions that will dampen out those effects. It is not for nothing that political analysts observe, "Presidents and Cabinet officers arrive with great fanfare and high intentions; however, the bureaucrats remain long after they are gone." Indeed, one is tempted to say that many a well-meaning political knight has broken his lance on bureaucracy's shield. However, the shield metaphor is not quite to the point. The idea of loose coupling informs us that an organization is not a hard, unyielding shield. Rather, it is relatively soft—almost amorphous. In another context, Herbert Marcuse (1964) describes bureaucracy as like a huge, warm marshmallow. This metaphor is better. It reminds us that the organization does have some substance—it is an identifiable "thing." Still, it is not a finely tuned machine, of either the classical or the systems form. Events occur, people come and go, and various effects may or may not be felt.

In summary, there is a developing idea that organizations are collections ("assemblages") of people, resources, and activities. This idea is encouraging many organizational practitioners and analysts to move away from such questions as, "How does function produce form?" toward more active—and less concise—questions such as, "How are loosely coupled activities held together within some identifiable form?" We often get the feeling that organizations work mainly because everyone knows roughly what is supposed to go on. Moreover, everyone knows that everyone also knows what is supposed to go on. This consensus or agreement, these anticipations and understandings, are necessary. No amount of rules, supervision, or other controls could possibly make the whole thing work. Practitioners and analysts therefore need to know how these agreements and understandings—how these loose couplings—are fashioned and how they operate.

SELF-DESIGNING ORGANIZATIONS

There is a third idea that is affecting developing organization thought. In a sense, this idea follows from the preceding two. Specifically, we have suggested that there is a movement afoot to revise the dominant organization-theoretic paradigm in light of a no-growth society. Further, we have indicated that organizations may be much more loosely coupled than heretofore believed. As a consequence of these two developments, many analysts are suggesting that organizations need to learn to design themselves if they are to survive and prosper. In the second article in this chapter, "Designing Organizations to Match Tomorrow," Hedberg, Nystrom, and Starbuck make just such a suggestion.

Basically the idea is this: it is relatively clear that whatever the future holds for organizations, change will be its hallmark. Even, as Scott pointed out earlier, a future of so-called stability or decay will be a fluctuating one. Thus as Hedberg and his colleagues note, the main prerequisite for organizations will be "an ideological commitment to impermanence."

At this stage, one can only speculate as to what is organizationally important to fulfill such a commitment. Hedberg et al. suggested that the following properties are critical: participatory information systems that transmit diverse messages; strategic experimentation that disrupts complacency and stimulates curiosity; and jobs and careers that provide satisfying lives despite changing work environments. To this set we would add the following two requirements.

First, organizations must develop a high level of skill for assessment. This skill would be exercised with respect to both external and internal conditions. As external conditions vary—whether in social, political, technological, or financial arenas—organizations must have the skill to assess those variations and routinely incorporate that assessment into their decision-making processes. And if the decision-making processes themselves need to change as a result of such assessment, that change should be effected with a minimum of organizational trauma.

Similarly, internal assessment will be critical to effective self-design. If Hedberg et al. are correct in predicting that flexibility and temporariness will characterize organizations of the future, then continual—and virtually automatic—monitoring of organizational processes will be necessary. Otherwise inertia sets in, and the organization begins to harden like concrete. Solidified concrete is not the best material to join loosely coupled assemblages of people and activities.

Second, greater attention will have to be paid to creativity. Scott noted that organizations will find themselves moving back and forth along several continua (Growth—Decay, Abundance—Scarcity, Consensus—Conflict). As they experience this movement, they will find it necessary to retain flexibility. In other words, organizations will find it necessary to maintain an environment which facilitates creative thinking. Specifically, as Deutsch (1969) has shown, organizations will need to (a.) encourage and motivate people to question the status quo; (b.) develop conditions that permit reformulation of problems; and (c.) provide opportunities for diverse ideas to meet each other. All these conditions should exist as a normal part of organizational life, with an absence of threat to organizational members.

In summary, as organizations move into their futures, however much they may lurch back and forth, they will have to develop a continuing capacity for redesign. To do so, organizations will have to acquire and process diverse information at all levels. They will also have to develop assessment skills. The organization's position with respect to external conditions, as well as the form and effectiveness of internal actions, need to be examined and evaluated. Otherwise, stagnation is the likely result. Finally, organizations will have to develop an atmosphere in which questioning, experimentation, and change can occur under nonthreatening conditions.

In a nutshell, the issue is simple: our society demands a great number and variety of goods and services. Organizations are the only social instruments available to accommodate those demands. If those instruments are to be effective, their design must be sound in principle and in practice. Therefore their design must be continually assessed, modified, and modified again. To do so is to foster organizational viability. And, like it or not, organizational viability is necessary to a healthy society.

Questions for Review

1. How does Scott see the classical and systems models categorized as modes of governance?
2. Along what dimensions does Scott see the shift from old to new confidences occurring?
3. Scott says that it is possible "to represent the value structure of the radical model as movement either forward or backward along three continua." What are the end points of each of these continua?
4. In what ways do Hedberg et al. see organizations growing inflexible because of benevolence?

5. Hedberg et al. see policymakers with only two basic options open to them in the future. What are these options? In the opinion of the authors, are these options mutually exclusive?
6. Self-designing organizations, according to Hedberg et al., will encounter at least three groups of technical problems. What are they?
7. To fulfill a "commitment to impermanence," several critical properties have been suggested. What are these?
8. What do Hedberg et al. say about living in self-designing organizations?
9. As seen by Scott, what are the operational premises existing in his radical model?
10. Three developments in organizational thought were described. What are they? How do they relate to each other?

Questions for Discussion

1. "The role of management has been socially and legally defined as the stewardship of resources: if the stewardship function is executed successfully, the wealth of an organization is protected and increased; the welfare of the clients and constituents is improved; and the fortunes of the management are advanced." Are Scott's requirements for successful execution of the stewardship function too idealistic? Too high? Can one of these requirements be fulfilled only at the expense of another? What is the usual priority for these functions? Do you know of any organization that currently fulfills all these requirements?
2. "Whether deservedly or not, humanism adapted to the management process has the taint of manipulation," according to Scott. Is this usually deserved or is it not? Why should it be tainted with manipulation? Is there a situation in which "humanistic management" would not be manipulative? What would be the prerequisites for nonmanipulative humanistic management?
3. Scott maintains that ". . . personal satisfaction and organizational efficiency are compatible only at a most superficial level." In your opinion, is this true? Which areas are compatible? Which are not? What future does this suggest for the worker and for management?
4. "The matrix structure requires politicization of structure and behavior in order to work." What does this statement mean to you?
5. Scott asserts that "totalitarianism and federalism are in direct lineage from traditional autocratic and democratic governance modes." What do you understand by the terms *totalitarianism, federalism, autocratic,* and *democratic?* Do you agree with Scott's assertion? Support your argument.
6. "The extant management paradigm is loaded with anomalies." Apart from those already mentioned by Scott, can you think of other anomalies in the present management paradigm? What, if any, are these, and why are they anomalies?
7. According to Hedberg et al., "today's institutions find rapid change stressful largely because of networks of private and public organizations that lack adaptiveness." What examples of this come to your mind? What kind of adaptiveness might be required to lessen the stress?
8. "Occasional failure ought to be every manager's right, and policies and educational programs ought to foster ideological commitments to exploring unknowns rather than to mastering the known," maintain Hedberg et al. Is this view too risky for

organizations? How "occasional" should occasional failure be interpreted? What balance should be maintained between exploring the unknown and mastering the known?

9. Hedberg et al. note that the main prerequisites for organizations will be "an ideological commitment to impermanence." What is your objective reaction to this statement? What is your subjective reaction to this statement? Is there any conflict between your two reactions? If so, does this conflict parallel the external situation for the future?
10. What's wrong with inertia? In an age of scarce resources, should not managers be reluctant—not eager—to move their organizations in new directions? Or should they?

CASE FOR DISCUSSION

CASE: HIGGINS EQUIPMENT COMPANY (B)

In early 1960, the president of the Higgins Equipment Company, John Howard, confided to researchers that he was distressed by company personality problems and by their effects on his organization. Of major recent concern had been the director of engineering's behavior and its effect on relations between the two sections of the engineering department and between both of them and sales and production. The only solution to this problem, the president explained, was to ask Haverstick, the engineering director, to leave; a resolution made all the more difficult by virtue of the man's having been with Higgins for only a year. President Howard said:

> Personalities of Haverstick's type, this conflict type, bother one personally. I dislike strife and I'm always trying to smooth it out. Now Stephen Spencer, the man we have chosen as Haverstick's successor, is peace loving. He's the opposite to what Haverstick was. I'm sure output could be increased by 5 to 10 percent with better cooperation. Haverstick was arrogant and too young. He was trying to tell people in other departments how to run their affairs without having a clean house himself. I find so far that I can turn to Steve, who is very cooperative and very able. I think we'll be able to give him a bonus this year.

About a year later, just as the researchers were concluding their study, Steve Spencer was also discharged. Steve, it was said, "lacked qualifications." Sales and production had been upset by what they saw as a "lack of direction" in engineering. R&D, a subdivision of engineering, felt it was not getting proper technical assistance. New product developments continued to fall behind schedule, while development and expected product costs proved unpredictable.

Company History

The Higgins Equipment Company manufactured a line of electrical testing and radio equipment for industrial and scientific customers. While the vast majority of dollar sales were composed of standard, assembly-line products, an increasing number of orders called for unique specifications, from a particular color of paint to an entirely untried basic design. Historically, the company had passed through three growth stages. Between 1917 and 1927 occurred the "production phase" in which the founder successfully constructed his own prototypes, personally supervised production and arranged for the sale of his products. The period 1927 to 1947 saw an accelerating emphasis on sales. Finally, 1947 to 1960 was an era of explosive growth. R&D became the spearhead of expansion. It was shortly before this last period that Howard became president.

Department Heads

The organization chart (see Exhibit 1) shows Stephen Spencer to be both head of the entire engineering department and of the staff section, engineering services. Engineering services was the result of the growth of auxiliary services which accompanied the enlargement of R&D staff and activities. Originally all of these services had been performed by R&D men or by their personal assistants. In effect, there had never been a decision to establish an

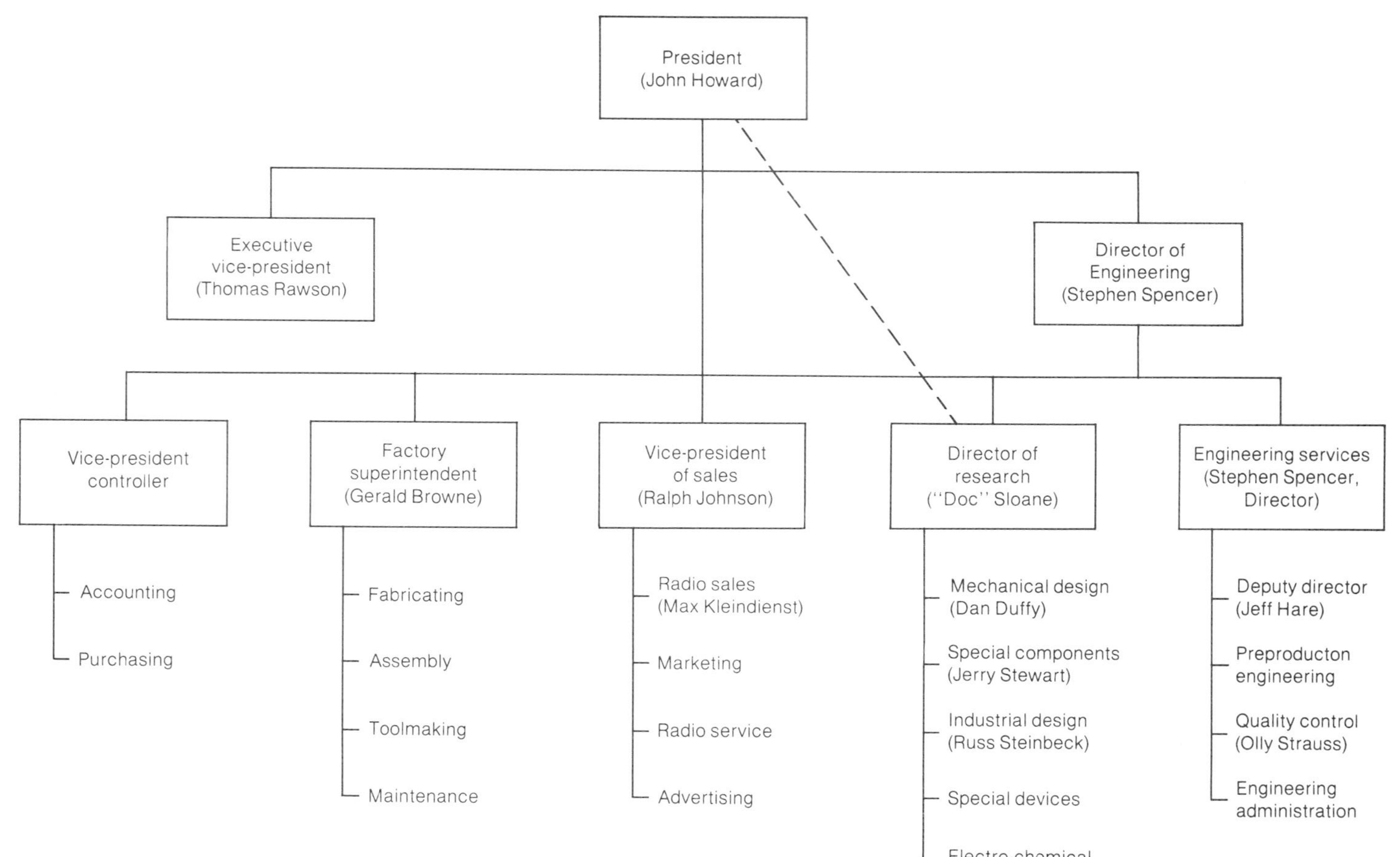

Exhibit 1. Organization chart—1960

engineering services section. It had simply emerged as R&D men freed themselves of what they considered to be details.

The sales department was headed by Ralph Johnson, a vice president and heir apparent to the presidency of the company upon Howard's retirement which was scheduled for 1963. Sales administration problems had been greatly compounded by the addition of the radio line, which required new demands of distribution, sales personnel with entirely new technical and sales skills and, thus, actual sales organization. Growth of the department had never quite caught up with the rapidity of expansion which entry into the radio field brought about.

The production department was headed by Gerald Browne, who had the title of factory superintendent. While sales and engineering both reported directly to the president, the production and control departments reported to the executive vice-president, Thomas Rawson. Because Rawson was relatively inexperienced in both of these areas and because of the dynamic personality of Howard, the production and control departments were not as forcefully represented in top management deliberations as were sales and engineering. The production department was particularly sensitive about this imbalance, despite its deep affection for Rawson.

See Exhibit 2 for personal background data on the central figures in this case.

Roger Sloane (Doc)

In spite of occasional and sometimes frequent friction between department and subdepartment heads, there was one man who never became involved in these disputes. "Doc" Sloane, head of R&D, enjoyed universal admiration among Higgins' employees and officers. "Of course, everyone loves Doc," explained the president. "If you took a vote, I know he'd be the most popular man in the company." The president's interest in Doc's work had personal overtones. He explained, "I started out in development work before devoting myself to sales. I like to think I can still contribute in both arenas." (The researchers noticed that the president's name plate hung on a cubicle door in the R&D department.) "I have always taken pride in the immaculate housing of our equipment and in its high quality, but why is there so much friction in getting our designs into production? A designer I trust asked me this the other day. 'Why should we work so hard when they deliberately foul things up?' We've got good men in R&D but something happens between their efforts and the end product to create problems for us."

Doc always appeared unhurried, contemplative, and candid in his approach to people and problems. His manner of dress and appearance gave the impression of a janitor rather than the most highly educated and renowned electronic designer at Higgins. He described his feelings about his job as follows: "We are a long way from being a research group in the usual sense of the word. There is no kidding ourselves we are anything but a bunch of Rube Goldbergs. But that is where the biggest kick comes from—solving development problems, dreaming up new ways to do things. That's why I so look forward to the special contracts we get involved in. We accept them not for the revenue they represent but for the subsidized basic development work for standard products which they let us do. I like administration the least. The most important thing in the relationships between people is mutual respect, not organizational procedures. Anyway, administrative work takes away from development time." Doc felt that production was resistant. "There are power interests in production which resist change. But you know I'm not a fighting guy. I suppose if I were I might go in there and push my weight around a little. In my view the company's future rests squarely on development engineering. Either we've got it there or we haven't. This is John Howard's conception, too."

Jeff Hare—deputy director of engineering services, 34-years-old, bachelor's degree in engineering, brought to Higgins in 1960 by Stephen Spencer as his assistant. The deputy's job, as such, had not previously existed, although Hare took on some duties previously performed by a newly retired member of the department. Previously worked as engineering assistant in an engineering graduate school. Then had 11 years experience with Spencer's previous employer as junior and senior development engineer.

Preproduction engineer, 39-years-old, technical high school graduate, joined Higgins in 1951. Experienced senior mechanical draftsman—designer and technician. Assumed the newly created post of preproduction engineer in 1954, supervising two engineering school trainees and working closely with the drafting department in fitting into a metal package the separate electronic and mechanical units of Higgins' products.

Olly Strauss—quality control, 38-years-old, high school graduate, joined Higgins in 1949, and worked for eight years on final assembly and testing of equipment before taking over the newly integrated quality control operation. Previous work as a technician in a large engineering school.

Engineering administrator, 34-years-old, undergraduate degree in business administration, joined Higgins in 1955. Experience in engineering scheduling and budgets. First man to fill the office of engineering administrator. With two clerks and a secretary he assembled the data necessary to develop time schedules and cost estimates for development projects. Administered these aspects of projects in progress.

Drafting foreman, 44-years-old, technical high school graduate, in charge of fifteen draftsmen, many capable of mechanical design and electronic detail drafting. Many years experience as senior designer and section manager in drafting department of a large electronics firm.

Technician pool foreman, 36-years-old, with Higgins for 17 years, 10 as assembler and assistant foreman in production, 7 as technician and pool manager in engineering. Administered affairs of and participated in working supervision of 50 technicians working as R&D assistants, pilot-run assemblers, and special devices production force (the latter section run by R&D engineers for the production of nonstandard orders).

Document section manager, 43-years-old, high school graduate, long experience as production and engineering clerk and section supervisor. Joined Higgins in 1956 as engineering change-order clerk. Promoted in 1958 to manage a ten-man group responsible for collecting data for and publishing parts list, blueprints, change orders, and the other large volumes of paper which passed between R&D and production.

Technical writing supervisor, 40-years-old, liberal arts graduate, many years experience as technical writer and supervisor. Came to Higgins in 1954 as supervisor of twelve men and women who wrote and illustrated instructional and promotional material for Higgins' products.

Librarian, 50-years-old, with a great deal of experience in public and school libraries, more recently in industrial libraries. Within a budget, he subscribed to technical journals, purchased books, and collected public data upon the request of R&D personnel.

Exhibit 2

It was Doc's suggestion in 1954 that the company re-enter the radio field, which it had briefly been in during World War II, as well as maintain its position in the test equipment market. This proved a highly profitable venture, both in terms of sales and in terms of technical challenge. ''Although,'' Doc said ruefully, ''it took me further from my own bench.''

R&D Under Doc Sloane

The researchers found evidence to indicate that R&D had high morale and the capacity to accomplish among its interdependent subunits tasks free from the overlay of personal resentment and political intrigue. There seeemed to be a close complementarity between the goals of this department and overall company goals. Central values expressed by members included personal learning, development, and independence. They also felt proud of personal contacts with technically oriented customers, which became increasingly necessary as Higgins' products became more technically specialized and sophisticated. Doc, himself, worked as a part-time sales engineer, consulting with customers.

Sociometric data[1] indicated that the R&D section consisted of three major social groups. These groupings correlated well with measures of individual competence and to some extent with education, experience, and age. The researchers called these three groups the ''Scientists,'' the ''Would-be Scientists,'' and the ''Youngsters.'' Below is a schematic presentation of what the researchers interpreted from their observations and interviews each group was giving to and receiving from each of the others.

Engineering Services Under Steve Spencer

The other section of the engineering department, engineering services, was supposed to provide ancillary services to R&D and to conduct liaison between R&D and other Higgins departments. Top management described the functions of engineering services as, ''establishing and maintaining cooperation with other departments, providing service to development engineers, and freeing more valuable men (R&D designers) from essential activities which are diversions from and beneath their main competence.'' The background and experience of primary engineering services and other key personnel are shown in Exhibit 2.

Sociometric measures revealed that engineering services was not a cohesive group. Many of its members were located in other departments. Its quality control personnel were hardly noticeable in the midst of production's assembly operation. Its technicians, assigned to R&D's development engineers, worked primarily in R&D cubicles or the area devoted to production of special devices. Generally, the remaining engineering services offices were assigned to widespread leftover spaces between elements of R&D.

Among the main functions of engineering services were drafting and provision of technicians from a central pool. Other major functions included: engineering administration, which scheduled and expedited engineering projects; the document section, which compiled parts list and published engineering orders; preproduction engineering, composed of several technicians who pulled together into mechanically compatible packages R&D's individual design components; and finally, quality control, which inspected incoming parts and materials, in-process subassemblies, and finished instruments against predetermined standards.

Researchers compared the interaction patterns *prescribed* (i.e., how people were supposed to behave) for engineering services personnel in their work relationship with R&D

1. Elicited by questions concerning friendship choices and through observations of work and nonwork interactions.

(a) Prescribed interaction-influence patterns*

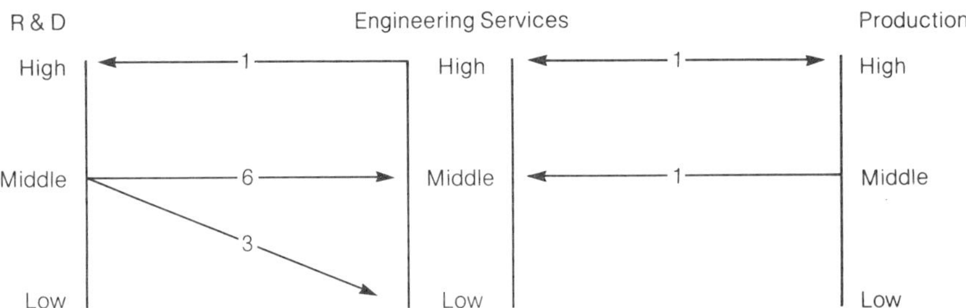

* As described by top management, in response to the question, "Who is supposed to communicate with whom and whose opinion, if either, should dominate?" The vertical lines represent an array of department members, broken into three groups according to job rank, as indicated by title, pay, and responsibilities. Arrows indicate interacting pairs of men. Numbers affixed to arrows represent the number of pairs in interaction. Double-ended arrows indicate a mutual influence, while single-ended arrows depict one-way influence between two men. The interaction recorded in this exhibit refers to personal contact rather than that which may also have occurred through the routine, non-personal, interdepartmental flow of paper.

(b) Observed interaction-influence patterns†

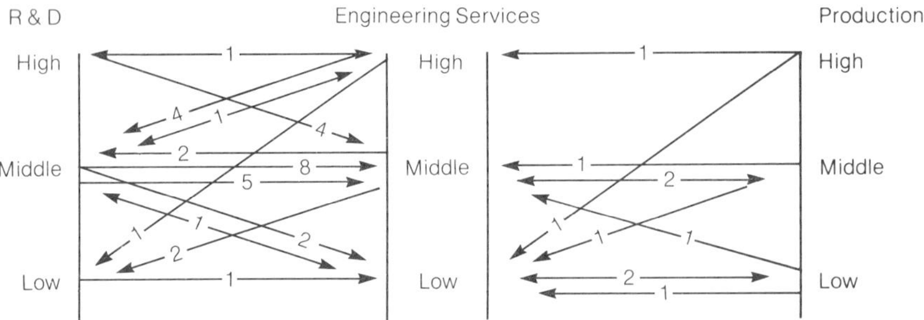

† The researchers developed the chart of observed interaction influence by prolonged observation. Each interaction was recorded and a judgment made concerning the balance of influence between the individuals involved, on the basis of whose point of view tended to dominate most frequently. For example, far more often than not, when Browne was in discussion with Spencer concerning such matters as a production-originated engineering change order, Browne's opinion would carry the day. Or where Spencer and Sloane discussed such things as the budget for a new project, their ideas tended to merge and the decisions emanating from their deliberations tended to reflect the opinions of both men.

Exhibit 3.

and production people with the *actual* patterns of interaction which they observed (see Exhibit 3).

Steve Spencer, when asked about his job, gave the following description:

My role in the company has never really been defined for me. It is complicated by Doc's unique position. In a nebulous way, he works through me and I through him. But he is not the least bit interested in the routines of administration. My relationship with him and his people is somewhat ambiguous. He is highly regarded in this company, and I have a great deal of affection and respect for him myself. But I can't count on him for any responsibility in scheduling projects, checking budgets, or what-have-you. In some senses, I'm in charge of R&D and in others I'm not.

My biggest problem is getting acceptance from the people I work with. I've moved slowly rather than risk antagonism. I saw what happened to Haverstick, and I want to avoid that.

But although his precipitate action had won over a few of the younger R&D men, he certainly didn't have the department's backing. Of course, it was the resentment of other departments which eventually caused his discharge. People have been slow accepting me here. There's nothing really overt, but I get a negative reaction to my ideas.

Browne (production head) is hard to get along with. Before I came and after Haverstick left, there were six months intervening when no one was really doing any scheduling. No work loads were figured, and unrealistic promises were made about releases. This puts us in an awkward position. We've been scheduling way beyond our capacity to manufacture or engineer.

I wish I could be more involved in the technical side. That's been my training, and it's a lot of fun. But in our setup, the technical side is the least necessary for me to be involved in.

Steve went on to explain that:

Certain people within R&D, for instance Russ Steinbeck, head of the radio electronic design section, understand scheduling well and meet project deadlines, but this is not generally true of the rest of the R&D department, especially the mechanical engineers who won't commit themselves. Most of the complaints come from sales and production department heads because items are going to production before they are fully developed, under pressure from sales to get out the unit, and this snags the whole process. Somehow, engineering services should be able to interview and resolve these complaints, but I haven't made much headway so far.

Salespeople were often observed taking their problems directly to designers, while production frequently threw designs back at R&D, claiming they could not be produced and demanding the prompt attention of particular design engineers. The latter were frequently observed in conference with production supervisors on the assembly floor.

Steve was asked where he sought help:

I should be able to go to Howard, but he's too busy most of the time and he's only really interested in the electrical test equipment line. Howard sees himself as head of engineering but I have to take the initiative. Doc isn't interested in planning and there are problems the front office just doesn't understand. Jeff Hare (Steve's deputy director) is a big help to me. He's here to help take the load off the development engineers (R&D), but they tend to feel they're losing something when one of us tries to help. They feel it's a reflection on them to have someone take over what they've been doing. They seem to want to carry a project right through the final stages, particularly the replacement boys. On the other hand, production people see themselves as methods and preproduction people and they want to get their hands on the product at an early stage. Consequently, engineering services people are used below their capacity to contribute and our department is denied functions it should be performing. There's not as much use made of engineering services as there could be.

Steve Spencer's technician foreman added his comments:

Production picks out the engineer who'll be the "bum of the month." They pick on every little detail instead of using their heads and making the minor changes that have to be made. The fifteen-to-twenty-year men shouldn't have to prove their ability anymore, but they spend four hours defending themselves and four hours getting the job done. I have no one to go to when I need help. Steve Spencer is afraid. I'm trying to help him but he can't help me at this time. I'm responsible for fifty people and I've got to support them.

Jeff Hare, whom Steve had brought with him to the company as an assistant, gave another view of the situation:

I try to get our people in preproduction to take responsibility, but they're not used to it, and people in other departments don't usually see them as best qualified to solve the problem.

Production always says it is drafting that is making the errors. Well, that isn't fair because all engineering and R&D are involved, not just the last ones to handle the material. But I haven't made much headway in changing that point of view. There's a real barrier for a newcomer here. Gaining people's confidence is hard.

(Hare resigned from Higgins six months after coming to the company, stating, "There just isn't a job for me here).”

Another of Spencer's subordinates gave his view:

If Doc gets a new product idea you can't argue. But he's too optimistic. He judges what others can do by what he does—but there's only one Doc Sloane. We've had 900 production change orders this year—they changed 2,500 drawings. If I were in Steve's shoes I'd put my foot down on all this new development. I'd look at the reworking we're doing and get production set up the way I wanted it. Haverstick was fired when he was doing a good job. He was getting some system in the company's operations. Of course, it hurt some people. But, there is no denying that Doc is the most important person in the company. What gets overlooked is that Howard is a close second, not just politically but in terms of what he contributes technically and in customer relations.

This subordinate explained that he sometimes went out into the production department but that Browne, the production head, resented this. Men in production said that Haverstick had failed to show respect for old-timers and was always meddling in other departments' business. This was why he had been fired, they contended.

Olly Strauss was in charge of quality control. He commented:

I am now much more concerned with administration and less with work. It is one of the evils you get into. There is tremendous detail in this job. I listen to everyone's opinion. Everybody is important. There shouldn't be distinctions—distinctions between people. I'm not sure whether Steve has to be a fireball like Haverstick. I think the real question is whether Spencer is getting the job done. I know my job is essential. I want to supply service to the more talented men and give them information so they can do their jobs better.

R&D's Views of Engineering Services

Said Dan Duffy of the mechanical design department:

In olden days I really enjoyed the work—and the people I worked with. But now there's a lot of irritation. I get my satisfaction from a good design and from finding solutions to troublesome problems. But it's not as satisfying as it used to be. I don't like someone breathing down my neck. You can be hurried into jeopardizing the design.

Russ Steinbeck, head of the electronic design section, was another designer with definite views:

Production engineering is almost nonexistent in this company. Very little is done by the preproduction section in engineering services. Steve Spencer has been trying to get preproduction into the picture, but he won't succeed because you can't start from such an ambiguous position. There have been three directors of engineering in six years. Steve can't hold his own against the others in the company. Haverstick was too aggressive. Perhaps no amount of tact would have succeeded.

Jerry Stewart was head of special components in the R&D department. Like the rest of the department he valued bench work. But he complained of engineering services:

The services don't do things we want them to do. They tell us what they're going to do. I should probably go to Steve, but I don't get any decisions there. I know I should go through Steve, but this holds things up, so I often go direct.

Views of the Sales Department

The researchers talked to representatives of the sales department—first its head, Ralph Johnson. Ralph explained that his reps made promises to customers, only to find the equipment months late in development. He was persistent in trying to get design engineers to conventions so that they could know the customer's point of view. "We shouldn't have to be after the engineers all the time. They should be able to see what problems they create for the company without our telling them." Ralph described himself as "a moderator—a man who settled disputes."

Max Kleindienst was head of radio sales under Johnson. He explained to the researchers that a great number of decisions concerning sales were made by top management. Sales was understaffed, he thought, and had never really been able to get on top of the job.

We have grown further and further away from engineering. The director of engineering does not pass on the information that we give him. We need better relationships with R&D. It is very difficult for us to talk to customers without technical help. We need each other. The whole of engineering is now too isolated from the outside world. The morale of engineering (services) is very low. They're in a bad spot—they're not well organized.

People don't take much to outsiders here. Much of this is because the expectation is built up by top management that jobs will be filled from the bottom. So it's really tough when an outsider like me comes in.

Views of the Production Department

The researchers paid a call on the production department and its head, Gerald Browne. Gerry said he believed in having a self-contained department. "There shouldn't be a lot of other people breathing down your neck." Gerry and his lieutenants universally expressed their preference for "getting new products into production, establishing procedures for getting standard products into the line and then spending our time doping out new methods and processes for getting our job done better."

One of Gerry's rules was that "I never talk to the underling of a department head. I always talk to the head himself. I always go down the line." He objected to final quality control (engineering services) being separated from his department. He felt it should be a continuation of assembly. "Olly Strauss' superiors don't understand Olly's problems. He'd rather work for me; he's told me that many times."

Purchasing should also have been under production, according to Gerry. Only a few days before he had thrown his storeroom master key on the board-room table in front of the president. "Here, I don't want it any more. I've been accused of fouling up inventory control!"

Gerry later explained his feelings about engineering:

> The trouble with engineering is that they are tolerance crazy. They want everything to a millionth of an inch. I'm the only one in the company who's had any experience with actually machining things to a millionth of an inch. We make sure that the things that engineers say on their drawing actually have to be that way and whether they're obtainable from the kind of raw material we buy.

Engineering services "just didn't check drawings properly," Gerry explained. Gerry spent a considerable proportion of his time going over new product drawings, personally returning those which he found to be in error.

> So finally they have to listen to us. Changes have to be made because they didn't listen to us in the first place. Engineering services says we've got to keep our hands off quality control. But, then, something like this happens: Doc comes in here one day, with a sour look on his face, saying there was some burnt wire on the equipment sent to an electronic show. I said, "You just look here. We didn't make that equipment; your technicians did!"

Gerry recounted his pleasure in doing things which engineering had said were impossible. "But I never tell them how we did it. They ought to be as smart as we are out here in production. Of course, the thing that really gets them is that I don't even have a degree."

In the course of their work, the researchers learned that when the men presently in charge of production took control after World War II, they did so as the result of a management turnover occasioned by discovery of illegalities committed by previous production men during the war. Prior to that time, production had controlled purchasing, stock control, and final quality control (where final assembly of products in such cabinets was accomplished). Because of the wartime events, management decided on a check-and-balance system of organization and removed these three departments from production jurisdiction. The new production managers felt they had been unjustly penalized by this reorganization, particularly since they had uncovered the behavior which was detrimental to the company in the first place.

The researchers also talked to Tom Rawson, age 65, executive vice-president of the company. Tom had direct responsibility for Higgins' production department.

> There shouldn't really be a dividing of departments among top management in the company. The president should be czar over all. The production boys ask me to do something for them, and I really can't do it. It creates bad feelings between engineering and production, this special attention that they (R&D) get from Howard. But then Howard likes to dabble in design. Browne feels that production is treated like a poor relation.

As the researchers were concluding their field work at the Higgins Equipment Company, they found an opportunity to discuss the engineering department and its problems with the president, John Howard. He reflected on what he termed "the unhappy necessity of letting Steve Spencer go."

> I can't understand why we have such poor luck with engineering heads. The man in there before Haverstick was technically well qualified. He'd been a good designer for us before we promoted him to be the first head of engineering. But he took to drinking heavily, and we had to relieve him of the responsibility. Then Haverstick seemed so promising. They say he is doing well in his new job at the _____ company. But they operate much differently from the way we do. Then, Steve Spencer—he seemed to have all the qualifications we needed. And he certainly was a gentleman. But he never could get things done. Apparently he couldn't gain the respect of the design boys. So, here we are, looking for a new man. I'm beginning to wonder whether we'll ever find him.

INSTRUCTIONS

1. Summarize your diagnosis of the major problem(s) in this organization.
2. Prepare for Mr. Howard a plan for remedying the problems(s) you have described above.
3. To provide for the implementation of your plan, present the steps which should be taken by some individual(s) responsible for the effective performance of the functions now assigned to Engineering Services.

References/Author Index

Page numbers in **boldface** type indicate places in text where work is cited.

ADAIR, ROSS. 1960. "The Indian Health Worker," *Human Organization*. 19:59–63. **139–40**

ADAMS, J. STACY. 1976. "The Structure and Dynamics of Behavior in Organizational Boundary Roles," in Marvin Dunette (ed.), *Handbook of Organizational and Industrial Psychology*. Chicago: Rand McNally. Pp. 1175–99. **140**

ADORNO, THEODOR W.; E. FRENKEL-BRUNSWIK; D. J. LEVINSON; and R. N. SANFORD. 1950. *The Authoritarian Personality*. New York: Harper. **203**

AGUILER, FRANCIS. 1967. *Scanning the Business Environment*. New York: Macmillan. **144**

AIKEN, MICHAEL, and JERALD HAGE. 1968. "Organizational Interdependence and Intra-Organizational Structure," *American Sociological Review*. 33 (December):912–30. **141**

———. 1972. "Organizational Permeability." Paper presented at the 1972 meetings of the American Sociological Association. **137, 140**

ALDAG, RAMON J., and ARTHUR P. BRIEF. 1975. "Relationships of Job Satisfaction Indices to Interactions of Task Characteristics with Employee Needs, Traits, and Abilities," Working Paper, University of Wisconsin.

———. 1976. "Impact of Individual Differences of Employee Affective Responses to Task Characteristics," *Journal of Business Research*. 3 (October):311–22.

ALDERFER, CLAYTON. 1969. "Job Enlargement and the Organizational Context," *Personnel Psychology*. 22:418–26.

ALDRICH, HOWARD. 1971. "Organizational Boundaries and Interorganizational Conflict," *Human Relations*. 24: 279–87. **137, 143**

———. 1972. "An Organization-Environment Perspective on Cooperation and Conflict Between Organizations in the Manpower Training System," in Anant Negandhi (ed.), *Conflict and Power in Complex Organizations*. Kent, Ohio: Kent State University. **140, 305**

———. 1977. "Organization Sets and Networks: Making the Most of Simplicity," in Paul Nystrom and William Starbuck (eds.), *Handbook of Organizational Design*. Amsterdam: Elsevier. **146**

———, and JEFFREY PFEFFER. 1976. "Environment of Organizations," in A. K. Inkeles (ed.), *Annual Review of Sociology*, vol. II. Palo Alto, Calif.: Annual Review, Inc. Pp. 79–105. **126, 137, 142**

———, and ALBERT J. REISS, Jr. 1971. "Police Officers as Boundary Personnel," in H. Hahn (ed.), *Police in Urban Society*. Beverly Hills, Calif.: Sage Publications, 193–208. **139**

ALLEN, MICHAEL PATRICK. 1974. "The Structure of Interorganizational Elite Co-optation: Interlocking Corporate Directorates," *American Sociological Review* 39:393–406. **133**

ALLEN, STEPHEN A. 1970. "Corporate Divisional Relationships in Highly Diversified Firms." In Jay Lorsch and Paul R. Lawrence (eds.), *Studies in Organizational Design*. Homewood, Ill.: Irwin-Dorsey.

ANDREWS, J. D. W. 1967. "The Achievement Motive and Advancement in Two Types of Organizations," *Journal of Personality and Social Psychology* 6:163–68.

ARGYRIS, CHRIS. 1954. *Organization of a Bank*. New Haven, Conn.: Yale University Press. **167**

———. 1957. "Some Problems in Conceptualizing Organizational Climate: A Case Study of a Bank," *Administrative Science Quarterly* 2:501–20. **252**

———. 1964. *Integrating the Individual and the Organization*. New York: Wiley. **197, 299**

———. 1973. "Personality and Organization Theory Revisited," *Administrative Science Quarterly* 18 (June):141–67.

ARROW, KENNETH J. 1974. *The Limits of Organization*. New York: Norton. Pp. 1–29. **292, 293, 297**

ASHBY, W. ROSS. 1956. *An Introduction to Cybernetics*. London: Chapman and Hall. **13**

ATKINSON, JOHN W. 1964. *An Introduction to Motivation*. Princeton: Van Nostrand Reingold. **197**

BABBAGE, CHARLES. 1835. *On the Economy of Machinery and Manufactures*. London: Charles Knight. **252**

BALES, ROBERT F. 1953. "The Equilibrium Problem in Small Groups," in Talcott Parsons, Robert F. Bales, and Edward A. Shils, (eds.), *Working Papers in the Theory of Action*. Glencoe, Ill.: Free Press. **330**

———. 1958. "Task Roles and Social Roles in Problem-Solving Groups," in Eleanor F. Maccoby; Theodore M. Newcomb; and Eugene L. Hartley (eds.), *Readings in Social Psychology*. New York: Holt. Pp. 437–47. **95**

BARNARD, CHESTER I. 1938. *Functions of the Executive*. Cambridge: Harvard University Press. **6, 15, 98, 296, 323**

———. 1939. *Dilemmas of Leadership in the Democratic Process*. Stafford Little Lectures. Princeton: Princeton University Press. **68**

———. 1951. *Organization and Management*, as quoted in *Harvard Business* Review 29:70. **283**

BARNES, LOUIS B. 1960. *Organizational Systems and Engineering Groups*. Boston: Graduate School of Business Administration, Harvard University. **210**

BARRETT, JON H. 1970. *Individual Goals and Organizational Objectives.* Ann Arbor: University of Michigan Press. **99–101, 229**

BARTLETT, SIR FREDERIC. 1958. *Thinking: An Experimental and Social Study.* New York: Basic Books. **13**

BATY, GORDON B.; WILLIAM M. EVAN; and TERRY W. ROTHERMEL. 1971. "Personnel Flows as Interorganizational Relations," *Administrative Science Quarterly* 16:430–43. **133**

BAUER, RAYMOND AUGUSTINE; ITHIEL DE SOLA POOL; and LEWIS ANTHONY DEXTER. 1968. *American Business and Public Policy.* New York: Atherton. **134**

BAVELAS, ALEX. 1950. "Communication Patterns in Task-Oriented Groups," *Journal of the Statistical Society of America.* 22:725–30.

BECKER, BORIS W., and PATRICK E. CONNOR. 1977. "On Methodology in Organizational Research: Perceptual Scaling," paper presented at the 1977 Meetings of the Academy of Management, Orlando, Florida. **445**

BECKER, HOWARD S.; BLANCHE GEER; EVERETT C. HUGHES; and ANSELM STRAUSS. 1961. *Boys in White: Student Culture in Medical School.* Chicago: University of Chicago Press. **208**

BECKER, SELWYN, and DUNCAN NEUHAUSER. 1975. *The Efficient Organization.* New York: Elsevier. **57**

BECKHARD, RICHARD. 1969. *Organization Development: Strategies and Models.* Reading, Mass.: Addison-Wesley. **79–80, 417–18, 451**

BELKNAP, IVAN. 1956. *The Human Problems of a State Mental Hospital.* New York: McGraw-Hill. **168**

BEM, D. J. 1972. "Self-Perception Theory," in L. Berkowitz (ed.), *Advances in Experimental Social Psychology*, vol. 6. New York: Academic Press. **203**

BENDIX, REINHARD. 1956. *Work and Authority in Industry.* New York: Wiley. **23**

BENNIS, WARREN G. 1959. "Leadership Theory and Administrative Behavior: The Problem of Authority," *Administrative Science Quarterly* 4 (December):259–301.

———. 1966. *Beyond Bureaucracy.* New York: McGraw-Hill. **22, 28, 138**

———. 1969. *Organization Development: Its Nature, Origins, and Prospects.* Reading, Mass.: Addison-Wesley. **22**

———; N. BERKOWITZ; M. AFFINITO; and M. MALONE. 1958. "Reference Groups and Loyalities in the Out-Patient Department," *Administrative Science Quarterly* 2 (March):481–500.

———, and PHILIP E. SLATER. 1968. *The Temporary Society.* New York: Harper & Row. **498**

BENSON, J. KENNETH. 1971. "Models of Structure Selection," Unpublished paper, University of Missouri-Columbia. **143**

BERELSON, BERNARD, and GARY A. STEINER. 1964. *Human Behavior: An Inventory of Scientific Findings.* New York: Harcourt, Brace.

BERKOWITZ, L. 1954. "Group Standards, Cohesiveness, and Productivity," *Human Relations* 7:509–19. **264**

BERLE, A. A., JR., and G. C. MEANS. 1952. "The Control of the Modern Corporation," *Reader in Bureaucracy*, R. Merton et al. (eds.). Glencoe, Ill.: Free Press. **282–83**

BERLEW, DOUGLAS E., and DOUGLAS T. HALL. 1966. "The Socialization of Managers: Effects of Expectations on Performance," *Administrative Science Quarterly* 11 (September):207–23. **230, 234**

———. 1964. "Some Determinants of Early Managerial Success," Working Paper No. 81-64, Alfred P. Sloan School of Management. Cambridge, Mass.: M. I. T. Press. **404**

BERNSTEIN, LEWIS. 1965. "Joint Ventures in the Light of Recent Antitrust Developments," *The Antitrust Bulletin* 10:25–29. **131–32**

BISHOP, R. C., and J. W. HILL. 1971. "Effects of Job Enlargement and Job Change on Contiguous But Nonmanipulated Jobs as a Function of Workers' Status," *Journal of Applied Psychology* 55:175–81.

BJØRN-ANDERSEN, NIELS, AND BO L. T. HEDBERG. 1977. 'Designing Information Systems in an Organizational Perspective," *North-Holland/TIMS Studies in the Management Sciences* 5:125–42. Amsterdam: North Holland. **487, 488**

BLAKE, ROBERT, and JANE MOUTON. 1964. *The Managerial Grid.* Houston: Gulf. **79, 190**

BLAU, PETER M. 1955. *The Dynamics of Bureaucracy.* Chicago: The University of Chicago Press. **168, 293, 345**

———. 1968. "The Hierarchy of Authority in Organizations," *The American Journal of Sociology* 73:453–67. **352, 376, 378**

———. 1970. "A Formal Theory of Differentiation in Organizations," *American Sociological Review* 35 (April):201–18. **160, 353**

———, and MARSHALL W. MEYER. 1971. *Bureaucracy in Modern Society*, 2d ed. New York: Random House. **410**

———, and RICHARD A. SCHOENHERR. 1971. *The Structure of Organizations.* New York: Basic Books. **39, 40, 206, 348, 353, 477**

———, and W. RICHARD SCOTT. 1962. *Formal Organizations.* San Francisco: Chandler. **104, 140, 169, 229, 281, 293, 296, 302, 375**

———; WOLF V. HEYDEBRAND; and ROBERT E. STAUFFER. 1966. "The Structure of Small Bureaucracies," *American Sociological Review* 31:179–91. **376**

BLAUNER, ROBERT. 1964. *Alienation and Freedom: The Factory Worker and His Industry.* Chicago: The University of Chicago Press. **174**

BLOOD, MILTON R. 1969. "Work Values and Job Satisfaction," *Journal of Applied Psychology* 53:456–59.

———, and C. L. HULIN. 1967. "Alienation, Environmental Characteristics and Worker Responses," *Journal of Applied Psychology* 51:284–90. **254**

BONNER, HUBERT. 1968. "Human Relations in Industry," in Manek S. Wadia (ed.), *Management and the Behavioral Sciences.* Boston: Allyn and Bacon. Pp. 150–51. **19, 23**

BOULDING, KENNETH E. 1956. "General Systems Theory—The Skeleton of a Science," *Management Science* 2: 197–208. **24–25, 346**

BOX, GEORGE E. P., and NORMAN R. DRAPER, 1969. *Evolutionary Operation.* New York: Wiley. **505**

BRIEF, ARTHUR, and RAMON ALDAG. 1975. "Employee Reactions to Job Characteristics: A Constructive Replication," *Journal of Applied Psychology* 60:182–86. **271**

———; M. J. WALLACE JR.; and R. J. ALDAG. 1976. "Linear vs. Nonlinear Models of the Formation of Affective Reactions: The Case of Job Enlargement," *Decision Science* 7:1–9.

BRIGHT, JAMES R. 1958. *Automation and Management.* Cambridge, Mass.: Harvard University Press.

BROBST, DONALD A., and WALDEN P. PRATT (eds.). 1973. *United States Mineral Resources.* Geological Survey Professional Paper 820. Washington: U. S. Government Printing Office. **496**

BROWN, D. S. 1966. "Shaping the Organization to Fit People," *Management of Personnel Quarterly* (now titled *Human Resource Management*) 5 (Summer):12–16. **138, 233**

BROWN, MICHAEL. 1969. "Identification and Some Conditions of Organizational Involvement," *Administrative Science Quarterly* 14:346–55. **219**

BROWN, WARREN B. 1966. "Systems, Boundaries, and Information Flow," *Academy of Management Journal* 9:318–27.

BUCHANAN, BRUCE. 1974. "Building Organizational Commitment: The Socialization of Managers in Work Organizations," *Administrative Science Quarterly* 19:533–46. **220, 221, 224**

———. 1975. "To Walk an Extra Mile: The Whats, Whens, and Whys of Organizational Commitment," *Organizational Dynamics* (Spring): 69–80. **200**

BUCKLOW, M. A. 1966. "A New Role for the Work Group," *Administrative Science Quarterly* 11:59–78. **264**

BURNHAM, JAMES. 1941. *The Managerial Revolution.* New York: John Day. **499**

BURNS, TOM, and G. M. STALKER. 1961. *The Management of Innovation.* London: Tavistock. **34, 37, 38, 40, 54, 125, 152, 153, 160, 161, 173, 181, 188, 332, 408, 468**

BUSINESS WEEK. 1977. "The Great Male Cop-Out from the Work Ethic," *Business Week.* November 14, p. 156.

CALAME, B. E. 1973. "Wary Labor Eyes Job Enrichment," *Wall Street Journal,* February 26, p. 12. **278**

CAMPBELL, DONALD T. 1950. "The Indirect Assessment of Social Attitudes," *Psychological Bulletin* 47:15–38. **205**

———. 1969(a). "Reforms as Experiments," *American Psychologist* 24 (April):409–29. **142, 505**

———. 1969(b). "Variation and Selective Retention in Socio-Cultural Evolution," *General Systems* 16:69–85. **138, 142**

CAMPBELL, JOHN P. 1976. "Contributions Research Can Make in Understanding Organizational Effectiveness," *Organization and Administrative Sciences* 7 (Spring/Summer):36–38. **415, 416, 417, 418–22, 446, 451**

———; M. D. DUNNETTE; E. E. LAWLER, III; and K. E. WEICK, JR. 1970. *Managerial Behavior, Performance and Effectiveness.* New York: McGraw-Hill. **189, 395, 396–97, 398, 399–404, 405–406, 411–12**

CARLISLE, ARTHUR ELLIOTT. 1976. "MacGregor," *Organizational Dynamics* 5 (Summer):50–62. **337**

CARLSON, RAE, and NISSIM LEVY. 1970. "Self, Values and Effects: Derivations from Tomkins' Polarity Theory," *Journal of Personality and Social Psychology* 16:338–45. **445–46**

CARROLL, STEPHEN J.; and HENRY L. TOSI. 1970. "Goal Characteristics and Personality Factors in a Management-by-Objectives Program," *Administrative Science Quarterly* 15 (September):295–305. **82**

———. 1973. *Management by Objectives: Applications and Research.* New York: Macmillan. **230**

CAVES, RICHARD E. 1970. "Uncertainty, Market Structure, and Performance: Galbraith as Conventional Wisdom," in J. W. Markham and G. F. Papanek (eds.), *Industrial Organization and Economic Development.* Boston: Houghton Mifflin. **136**

CHAMBERLAIN, NEIL W. 1950. *Management in Motion.* New Haven, Conn.: Labor and Management Center, Yale University. **331**

———. 1968. *Enterprise and Environment.* New York: McGraw-Hill. **72, 147**

CHANDLER, ALFRED D., JR. 1962. *Strategy and Structure.* Cambridge, Mass.: M. I. T. Press. **40, 142, 147, 175**

———. 1966. *Strategy and Structure.* Garden City, N. Y.: Doubleday Anchor. **147**

CHILD, JOHN. 1969. *The Business Enterprise in Modern Industrial Society.* London: Collier Macmillan. **138**

———. 1973. "Parkinson's Progress: Accounting for the Number of Specialists in Organizations," *Administrative Science Quarterly* 18:328–48. **140**

———. In press. "Participation, Organization and Social Cohesion," *Human Relations.* **140**

CHURCHMAN, C. WEST. 1961. *Prediction and Optimal Decision: Philosophical Issues of a Science of Values.* Englewood Cliffs, N. J.: Prentice-Hall. **206**

CLARK, BURTON R. 1956. *Adult Education in Transition.* Berkeley, Calif.: University of California Press. **15**

———. 1970. *The Distinctive College: Antioch, Reed, and Swarthmore.* Chicago: Aldine. **294**

———. 1972. "The Organizational Saga in Higher Education," *Administrative Science Quarterly* 17 (June):178–84. **502**

CLARK, JAMES V. 1961. "Motivation in Work Groups: A Tentative View," *Human Organization* 19:199–208. **269**

CLARKSON, G. P. E. 1963. "A Model of Trust Investment Behavior," in Richard M. Cyert and James G. March, *A Behavioral Theory of the Firm.* Englewood Cliffs, N. J.: Prentice-Hall. **86**

COHEN, MICHAEL D.; JAMES G. MARCH; and JOHAN P. OLSEN. 1972. "A Garbage Can Model of Organizational Choice," *Administrative Science Quarterly* 17 (March):1–25. **305**

COLE, H. S. D.; CHRISTOPHER FREEMAN; MARIE JAHODA; and K. L. R. PAVITT. (eds.). 1973. *Models of Doom: A Critique of the Limits to Growth.* New York: Universe. **501**

COLEMAN, JAMES. 1957. *Community Conflict.* Glencoe, Ill.: Free Press. **330**

CONNOR, PATRICK E. 1977. "A Critical Inquiry into Some Assumptions and Values Characterizing OD," *Academy of Management Review* 2 (October):635–44. **22, 27**

———. 1978. *Dimensions in Modern Management,* 2d. ed. Boston: Houghton Mifflin.

———, and BORIS W. BECKER. 1974. "Values and Comparative Organizational Research," *Proceedings of the Academy of Management* 88–94. **211**

———, 1975. "Values and the Organization: Suggestions for Research," *Academy of Management Journal* 18:550–61. **24, 26–27, 50, 51, 204, 205–11, 236, 445, 447**

———, and STEFAN D. BLOOMFIELD. 1977. "A Goal Approach to Organization Design," *North-Holland/TIMS Studies in the Management Sciences* 5:99–110. **53, 98, 102, 398, 465–66, 477–84, 490**

———; DOUGLAS M. EGAN; and BARBARA KARMEL. 1973. "Organizational Relationships: Context, Action, and Effectiveness," *Proceedings of the Mountain-Plains Management Association,* 15th annual meeting. **207, 208, 210, 338, 447**

COOPER, R., and R. PAYNE. 1967. 'Extraversion and Some Aspects of Work Behavior," *Personnel Psychology* 20:45–57. **203**

CORDINER, RALPH J. 1956. *New Frontiers for Professional Managers.* New York: McGraw-Hill. **474**

COSER, ROSE L. 1958. "Authority and Decision-Making in a Hospital," *American Sociological Review.* 23 (February):56–63. **172, 332**

COUGHLAN, ROBERT J. 1969. "An Assessment of Teacher Work Values," *Educational Administrative Quarterly* 5:53–73. **209**

———. 1971. "Job Satisfaction in Relatively Closed and Open Schools," *Educational Administrative Quarterly* 7:40–59. **210**

CRECINE, JOHN P. 1969. *Governmental Problem Solving.* Chicago: Rand McNally. **502**

CROZIER, MICHEL. 1964. *The Bureaucratic Phenomenon.* Chicago: The University of Chicago Press. **16, 76, 172**

CUMMINGS, THOMAS, and E. S. MOLLOY. 1977. *Improving Productivity and the Quality of Work Life.* New York: Praeger. **276–77**

———, and S. SRIVASTRA. 1976. *Management of Work: A Socio-Technical Systems Approach.* Kent, O.: Comparative Administration Research Institute and Kent State University Press. **276**

CYERT, RICHARD M., and JAMES G. MARCH. 1963. *A Behavioral Theory of the Firm.* Englewood Cliffs, N. J.: Prentice-Hall. **16, 44, 67, 71, 73–74, 84, 92, 93–94, 98, 100, 138**

———; HERBERT A. SIMON; and D. B. TROW. 1956. "Observation of a Business Decision," *Journal of Business* 29:237–48. **314**

DAHRENDORF, ROLF. 1959. *Class and Class Conflict in Industrial Society.* Stanford, Calif.: Stanford University Press. **495**

DAILEY, ROBERT C. 1977. "The Effects of Cohesiveness and Collaboration on Work Groups: A Theoretical Model," *Groups and Organization Studies* 2:461–69. **277**

DALTON, MELVILLE. 1950. "Conflicts Between Staff and Line Managerial Officers," *American Sociological Review* 15 (June):342–51. **329**

———. 1959. *Men Who Manage.* New York: Wiley.

DAVIS, J. H.; N. L. KERR; R. S. ATKIN; R. HOLT; and D. MEEK. 1975. "The Decision Processes of 6- and 12-person Mock Juries Assigned Unanimous and Two-Thirds Majority Rules," *Journal of Personality and Social Psychology* 32:1–14. **339**

DAVIS, L. E. 1966. "The Design of Jobs," *Industrial Relations* 6: 21–45. **264**

———, and E. L. TRIST. 1974. "Improving the Quality of Work Life: Sociotechnical Case Studies," in J. O'Toole (ed.), *Work and the Quality of Life.* Cambridge, Mass.: M. I. T. Press. **264, 277**

DAVIS, R. V.; G. W. ENGLAND; and L. H. LOFQUIST. 1968. "A Theory of Work Adjustment," *Minnesota Studies in Vocational Rehabilitation.* Bulletin 47. **255**

DAVIS, STANLEY M. 1974. "Two Models of Management: Unity of Command versus Balance of Power," *Sloan Management Review* 16: 29–40. **474**

———, and PAUL R. LAWRENCE. 1978. *Matrix.* Reading, Mass.: Addison-Wesley. **227, 232, 294, 306**

DEARBORN, D. C.; and H. A. SIMON. 1958. "Selective Perception: A Note on the Departmental Identifications of Executives," *Sociometry* 21: 140–44. **89**

DEARDEN, JOHN. 1967. "The Case against R&I Control," *Harvard Business Review.* **476**

DELBECQ, ANDRE L.; FREMONT A. SHULL; ALAN C. FILLEY; ANDREW J. GRIMES. 1969. "Matrix Organization: A Conceptual Guide to Organizational Variation," *Wisconsin Business Papers.* No. 2 (September). **182**

DESALVIA, DONALD N.; and GARY R. GEMILL. 1971. "An Exploratory Study of the Personal Value Systems of College Students and Managers," *Academy of Management Journal* 14:227–38. **203, 208**

DEUTSCH, KARL, et al. 1957. *Political Community and the North Atlantic Area.* Princeton: Princeton University Press. **327–28**

DEUTSCH, MORTON. 1969. "Conflicts: Productive and Destructive," *Journal of Social Issues* 25 (January):7–41. **512**

DEWEY, JOHN. 1910. *How We Think.* Lexington, Mass.: Heath. Chapter 8. **315**

DIETERLY, D., AND B. SCHNEIDER. 1974. "The Effect of Organizational Environment on Perceived Power and Climate: A Laboratory Study," *Organizational Behavior and Human Performance* 11: 316–37. **410, 411**

DILL, WILLIAM R. 1958. "Environment as an Influence on Managerial Autonomy," *Administrative Science Quarterly* 2 (March):409–33.

———. 1962. "The Impact of Environment on Organizational Development," in Sidney Mailick, and Edward H. Van Ness (eds.), *Concepts and Issues in Administrative Behavior.* Englewood Cliffs. N. J.: Prentice-Hall. Pp. 94–109. **137**

———. 1964. "Desegregation or Integration? Comments about Contemporary Research on Organizations," in W. W. Cooper; Harold J. Leavitt; and Maynard W. Shelly II (eds.), *New Perspectives in Organization Research.* New York: Wiley. **13**

———; THOMAS L. HILTON; and WALTER R. REITMAN. 1962. *The New Managers.* Englewood Cliffs, N. J.: Prentice-Hall. **208**

DORE, RONALD. 1973. *British Factory–Japanese Factory.* Berkeley, Calif.: University of California Press. **294**

DORNBUSCH, SANFORD M. 1955. "The Military Academy as an Assimilating Institution," *Social Forces* 33 (May):316–21. **166**

DRAKE, JOHN W. 1973. "The Backgrounds and Value Systems of Transportation Modeling Project Participants and Their Effects on Project Success," *Transportation Research Forum Proceedings*, pp. 659–72. **209**

DRUCKER, PETER F. 1946. *The Concept of the Corporation.* New York: John Day. **475**

DRUCKER 1954 **81**

DUBIN, ROBERT. 1961. *Human Relations in Administration.* Englewood Cliffs, N.J.: Prentice-Hall. **157, 328**

———. 1957. "Power and Union-Management Relations," *Administrative Science Quarterly* 2 (June). **331**

———; JOSEPH E. CHAMPOUX; and LYMAN W. PORTER. 1975. "Central Life Interests and Organizational Commitment of Blue-collar and Clerical Workers," *Administrative Science Quarterly* 20:411–21. **219**

DUNCAN, ROBERT B. 1971. "The Effects of Perceived Environmental Uncertainty on Organizational Decision Unit Structure: A Cybernetic Model," Ph.D. Dissertation, Yale University. **40**

———. 1972. "Characteristics of Organizational Environments and Perceived Environmental Uncertainty," *Administrative Science Quarterly* 17:313–27. **126, 468**

DUNHAM, RANDALL B. 1977. "Reactions to Job Characteristics: Moderating Effects of the Organization," *Academy of Management Journal* 20:42–65. **271**

———; R. J. ALDAG; and A. P. BRIEF. In press. "Dimensionality of Task Design as Measured by the Job Diagnosis Survey," *Academy of Management Journal.* **254**

DURKHEIM, EMILE. 1951. *Suicide*, trans. by J. A. Spaulding and George Simpson. Glencoe, Ill.: Free Press. **328**

ELBING, A.; H. GACLON; and J. GORDON. 1975. "Flexible Working Hours: The Missing Link," *California Management Review* 17:50–57. **276**

ELLUL, JACQUES. 1964. *The Technological Society.* New York: Knopf. **499**

EMERY, FRED, and EINAR THORSRUD. 1969. *New Designs for Work Organization.* Oslo, Norway: Tannum Press. **233**

———, and E. L. TRIST. 1965. "The Causal Texture of Organizational Environment," *Human Relations* 18 (February):21–31. **125–26, 143**

ENGLAND, GEORGE W. 1967. "Organizational Goals and Expected Behavior of American Managers," *Academy of Management Journal* 10: 107–17. **206**

———. 1974. "Personal Value Systems of Managers and Administrators," *Proceedings of the Academy of Management* 81–88. **206**

EPSTEIN, EDWIN M. 1969. *The Corporation in American Politics.* Englewood Cliffs, N. J.: Prentice-Hall. **134**

ERIKSON, ERIK H. 1960. "The Problem of Ego Identity," in *Identity and Anxiety.* Glencoe, Ill.: Free Press. **470**

———. 1964. *Insight and Responsibility.* New York: Norton. **199**

ETZIONI, AMITAI W. 1960a. "New Directions in the Study of Organizations and Society," *Social Research* 27:223–28. **100**

———. 1960b. "Two Approaches to Organizational Analysis: A Critique and a Suggestion," *Administrative Science Quarterly* 5 (September): 257–78. **100, 415, 416, 477, 478**

———. 1961. *A Comparative Analysis of Complex Organizations*. New York: Free Press. **66, 92, 93, 169**

———. 1964. *Modern Organizations*. Englewood Cliffs, N. J.: Prentice-Hall. **72, 77, 97**

———. 1965. "Organizational Control Structure," in March, James G. (ed.), *Handbook of Organizations*. Chicago: Rand McNally. Pp. 650–77. **280–81, 294, 300, 302**

———. 1973. "The Third Sector and Domestic Missions," *Public Administration Review* 33 (July–August):314–23. **415**

———. 1975. *A Comparative Analysis of Complex Organizations*, rev. ed. New York: Free Press. **229**

EULAU, HEINZ; S. ELDERSVELD; and M. JANOWITZ, (eds.). 1956. *Political Behavior*. Glencoe, Ill.: Free Press. **331**

EVAN, WILLIAM M. 1966. "The Organization-Set: Toward a Theory of Interorganizational Relations," in Thompson, James D. (ed.), *Approaches to Organizational Design*. Pittsburgh, Pa.: University of Pittsburgh Press. **305, 306**

———. 1976. "Organization Theory and Organizational Effectiveness: An Exploratory Analysis," *Organizational and Administrative Sciences* 7 (Spring/Summer):15–28. **417, 422–23, 424, 447, 451**

EYSENCK, H. J. 1954. *The Psychology of Politics*. London: Routtedge and Kegan Paul. **203**

———. 1967. *The Biological Basis of Personality*. Springfield, Ill.: Thomas. **202**

———. 1973. *Eysenck on Etraversion*. New York: Wiley. **202**

FAYOL, HENRI. 1916. *General and Industrial Management*. London: Pitman. **252**

———. 1949. *General and Industrial Management*. London: Pitman **19, 23**

FARRIS, G. E. 1969. "Organizational Factors and Individual Performance: A Longitudinal Study," *Journal of Applied Psychology* 53:87–92. **255**

FEIN, M. 1974. "Jfeent: A Reevaluation," *Sloan Management Review* 15:69–88. **277**

FELDMAN, D. C. 1976. "A Practical Program for Employee Socialization," *Organizational Dynamics* (August):64–80. **229**

FESTINGER, LEON. 1950. "Informal Social Communication," *Psychological Review* 57 (September):271–92. **325**

FIEDLER, FRED E. 1976. "The Leadership Game: Matching the Man to the Situation," *Organizational Dynamics* (Winter):6–16. **235**

FILLEY, ALLEN C.; ROBERT J. HOUSE; and STEVEN KERR. 1976. *Managerial Process and Organizational Behavior*, 2d ed. Glenview, Ill.: Scott, Foresman. **229**

FISHBEIN, MARTIN. 1967. "Attitude and the Prediction of Behavior," in Martin Fishbein (ed.), *Readings in Attitude Theory and Measurement*. New York: Wiley. Pp. 477–92. **225**

FORD, R. N. 1969. *Motivation through the Work Itself*. New York: American Management Association. **252, 263**

———. 1973. "Job Enrichment Lesson from AT&T," *Harvard Business Review* (January–February):96–106. **252, 275**

FOREHAND, G. A., and B. VON H. GILMER. 1964. "Environmental Variation in Studies of Organizational Behavior," *Psychological Bulletin* 62: 361–82. **396, 400, 401**

FORRESTER, JAY W. 1971. *World Dynamics*. Cambridge, Mass.: Wright-Allen. **501**

FOURAKER, LAWRENCE; and J. M. STOPFORD. 1968. "Organizational Structure and Multinational Strategy," *Administrative Science Quarterly* 13 (June):47–64. **147**

FREDERIKSEN, N. 1966. "Some Effects of Organizational Climates on Administrative Performance," *Research Memorandum RM-66-21*. Princeton, N. J.: Educational Testing Service. **404**

———. 1963. "Administrative Performance in Relation to Organizational Climate," Paper presented at a symposium on Measuring Managerial Effectiveness. American Psychological Association, San Francisco (September) **404**

FRENCH, J. R. P., JR. 1960. "The Effects of the Industrial Environment on Mental Health: A Theoretical Approach." Paper presented at the meetings of the American Psychological Association.

———; W. ROGERS; and S. COBB. 1971. "Adjustment as Person-Environment Fit," mimeographed paper. Ann Arbor: Institute for Social Research, University of Michigan. **276**

FRENCH, WENDELL L., and CECIL H. BELL. 1973. *Organization Development*. Englewood Cliffs, N. J.: Prentice-Hall. **22, 26, 27, 28**

FROST, PETER, and THOMAS MAHONEY. 1974. "The Role of Technology in Models of Organizational Effectiveness," *Organizational Behavior and Human Performance* 11:122–38. **161**

FULLAN, MICHAEL. 1970. "Industrial Technology and Worker Integration in the Organization," *American Sociological Review* 35 (December): 1028–39. **157, 160, 190**

FUNKENSTEIN, D. H. 1962. "Failure to Graduate from Medical School," *Journal of Medical Education* 37:585–603.

GALBRAITH, JAY R. 1970. "Environmental and Technological Determinants of Organization Design" in Jay Lorsch and Paul R. Lawrence (eds.), *Studies In Organization Design*. Homewood, Ill.: Irwin. **40, 49, 363**

———. 1971. "Designing Matrix Organizations," *Business Horizons* (February):29–40. **48, 353, 355–64, 378–79, 384**

———. 1973. *Designing Complex Organizations*. Reading, Mass.: Addison-Wesley. **39–40, 47, 57, 281, 296, 469, 486, 505**

———. 1974. "Organization Design: An Information Processing View," *Interfaces* 4:28–36. **34–35, 43–49, 232, 486**

———. 1977. *Organization Design*. Reading, Mass.: Addison-Wesley. **232, 486**

GAMSON, ZELDA F. 1968. "Organizational Responses to Members," *The Sociological Quarterly* 9 (Spring):139–49. **232, 233**

GELLERMAN, SAUL W. 1959. "The Company Personality," *Management Review* 48:69–76. **401**

GEORGIOU, PETRO. 1973. "The Goal Paradigm and Notes Toward a Counter Paradigm," *Administrative Science Quarterly* 18:291–310. **66, 494**

GEORGOPOULOS, B. S. 1965. "Normative Structure Variables and Organizational Behavior," *Human Relations* 18:115–70. **401**

GIBSON, JAMES L.; JOHN M. IVANCEVICH; and JAMES H. DONNELLY, JR., 1976. *Organizations: Behavior, Structure, Processes*, rev. ed. Dallas, Texas: Business Publications. **416**

GIES, FREDERICK JOHN, and B. CHARLES LEONARD. 1971. "The Relationship Between Teacher Perception of Organizational Climate and Values Concerning Disadvantaged Pupils," *Negro Educational Review* 22: 152–59. **210**

GILBRETH, FRANK B., and LILLIAN M. GILBRETH. 1917. *Applied Motion Study*. New York: Sturgis and Walton. **23**

GLASER, E. M. 1975. *Improving the Quality of Worklife . . . And in the Process, Improving Productivity*. Los Angeles: Human Interaction Research Institute. **263**

GLASSMAN, R. B. 1973. "Persistence and Loose Coupling in Living Systems." *Behavioral Science* 18:83–98. **509**

GOFFMAN, ERVING. 1961. "On the Characteristics of Total Institutions," in Donald Cressey (ed.), *The Prison*. New York: Holt, Rinehart, and Winston. **141, 208**

GOGGIN, WILLIAM. 1974. "The Multidimensional Structure at Dow Corning," *Harvard Business Review* 54–55. **472**

GOLEMBIEWSKI, ROBERT T. 1972. *Renewing Organizations.* Itasca, Ill.: Peacock. **22, 27, 411**

GOMBERG, WILLIAM. 1973. "Job Satisfaction: Sorting Out the Nonsense," *AFL-CIO American Federationist* (June). **277**

GORDON, GERALD; CHRISTIAN TANON; and EDWARD MORSE V. 1974. *Hospital Structure, Costs, and Innovation.* Ithaca, N. Y.: Cornell University. **504**

GORDON, W. J. J. 1961. *Synetics.* New York: Harper. **187**

GORE, WILLIAM J. 1964. *Administrative Decision-Making.* New York: Wiley. **70**

GOULD, JULIUS, and WILLIAM L. KOLB (eds.). 1964. *A Dictionary of the Social Sciences.* New York: Free Press. **205**

GOULDNER, ALVIN W. 1954. *Patterns of Industrial Bureaucracy.* New York: Free Press. **293, 345**

———. 1957. "Cosmopolitans and Locals: Toward an Analysis of Latent Social Roles—I," *Administrative Science Quarterly* 2 (December):281–306. **56**

———. 1959. "Organizational Analysis," in R. K. Merton; L. Broom; and L. S. Cottrell (eds.), *Sociology Today.* New York: Basic Books, Pp. 400–28. **13, 53, 415, 477**

———. 1961. "The Norm of Reciprocity," *American Sociological Review* 25: 161–79. **293**

GRAICUNAS, V. A. 1937. "Relationship in Organization," in Luther Gulick and L. Urwick (eds.), *Papers on the Science of Administration.* New York: Institute of Public Administration. Pp. 181–87. **350**

GREGORY, R. H., and VAN HORN, R. L. 1960. *Automatic Data-Processing Systems.* Belmont, Calif.: Wadsworth. **315**

GRIMES, A. J., and S. M. KLEIN. 1973. "The Technological Imperative: The Relative Impact of Task Unit, Modal Technology, and Hierarchy on Structure," *Academy of Management Journal.* Pp. 596–97. **182**

GRINYER, PETER H., and DAVID NORBURN. 1975. "Planning for Existing Markets: Perceptions of Executives and Financial Performance," *Journal of the Royal Statistical Society,* (series A). 138 (part 1):70–97. **504, 505**

GROSS, BERTRAM. 1965. "What Are Your Organization's Objectives? A General-Systems Approach to Planning," *Human Relations* 18. **92, 94–95, 477–78, 479**

GROSS, EDWARD. 1968. "Universities as Organizations: A Research Approach," *American Sociological Review* 33 (August):518–44. **480**

———. 1969. "The Definition of Organizational Goals," *British Journal of Sociology* 20 (September):277–94. **53, 57, 92, 95, 96, 97, 98, 102, 103, 417, 465, 477, 478, 479**

———, and PAUL V. GRAMBSCH. 1974. *Changes in University Organization, 1964-1971.* New York: McGraw-Hill.

GROSS, NEAL; WARD S. MASON; and ALEXANDER W. MCEACHERN. 1958. *Explorations in Role Analysis.* New York: Wiley. **208**

GRUSKY, OSCAR. 1966. "Career Mobility and Organizational Commitment." *Administrative Science Quarterly.* 10:488–503. **220**

GUETZKOW, HAROLD. 1966. "Relations Among Organizations," in Raymond V. Bowers (ed.), *Studies on Behavior in Organizations.* Athens, Ga.: University of Georgia Press. **144, 145**

GULICK, L. H. 1937. "Notes on the Theory of Organizations," in *Papers on the Science of Administration,* L. Gulick and L. Urwick (eds.). New York: Columbia University Press. Pp. 15–30.

———, and L. URWICK (eds.). 1937. *Papers on the Science of Administration.* New York: Institute of Public Administration, Columbia University Press. **13, 19, 345, 347, 477**

GULOWSEN, J. A. 1972. "A Measure of Work Group Autonomy," in L. E. Davis and J. C. Taylor (eds.), *Design of Jobs.* Middlesex, England: Penguin. **264, 267**

HABERSTROH, CHADWICK J. 1966. "Control as an Organizational Process," in Albert H. Rubenstein, and Chadwick J. Haberstroh (eds.), *Some Theories of Organization.* Homewood, Ill.: The Dorsey Press, 513–18. **23**

HACKMAN, J. RICHARD, and EDWARD E. LAWLER, III. 1971. "Employee Reactions to Job Characteristics," *Journal of Applied Psychology,* 55 (June):259–86. **221, 233, 254, 256, 258**

———. 1975. "On the Coming Demise of Job Enrichment," in E. L. Cass and F. G. Zimmer (eds.), *Man and Work in Society.* New York: Van Nostrand Reinhold. **274**

———; GREG OLDHAM; RICHARD JANSON; and KEN PURDY. 1975. "A New Strategy for Job Enrichment," *California Management Review* 17:4. Pp. 57–71. **217, 233, 256, 261**

———. 1976. "Group Influences on Individuals in Organizations," in Marvin D. Dunnette (ed.), *Handbook of Industrial and Organizational Psychology.* Chicago: Rand McNally. **264**

———. 1977. "Work Design," in J. R. Hackman and J. L. Suttle (eds.), *Improving Life at Work.* Santa Monica, Calif.: Goodyear. **256, 278**

———, and C. G. MORRIS. 1975. "Group Tasks, Group Interaction Process, and Group Performance Effectiveness: A Review and Proposed Integration," in L. Berkowitz (ed.), *Advances in Experimental Social Psychology.* vol 8. New York: Academic Press. **265, 266, 267**

———, and GREG R. OLDHAM. 1975. "Development of the Job Diagnostic Survey," *Journal of Applied Psychology,* 60:159–70. **254, 256, 259**

———. 1976. "Motivation Through the Design of Work: Test of a Theory," *Organizational Behavior and Human Performance,* 16:250–79. **254, 256, 258–59**

HAGE, JERALD. 1965. "An Axiomatic Theory of Organizations," *Administrative Science Quarterly,* 10 (December):289–320. **191, 349, 350–51, 375**

———, and MICHAEL AIKEN. 1967. "Program Change and Organizational Properties: A Comparative Analysis," *American Journal of Sociology,* 72 (March):503–19. **376**

———. 1969. "Routine Technology, Social Structure, and Organizational Goals," *Administrative Science Quarterly,* 14:366–76. **157, 161, 188**

———. 1970. *Social Change in Complex Organizations.* New York: Random House. **138**

———, and ROBERT DEWAR. 1973. "Elite Values Versus Organization Structure in Predicting Innovation," *Administrative Science Quarterly,* 18: 279–90. **208**

HAIMANN, THEO; WILLIAM G. SCOTT; and PATRICK E. CONNOR. 1978. *Managing the Modern Organization* (3rd ed.), Boston: Houghton Mifflin. **54, 55, 311, 312–13, 339, 350**

HALBERSTAM, DAVID. 1972. *The Best and the Brightest.* New York: Random House.

HALL, DOUGLAS T. 1971. "A Theoretical Model of Career Subidentity Development in Organizational Settings," *Organizational Behavior and Human Performance,* 6:50–76. **197, 201**

———, and EDWARD E. LAWLER. 1970. "Job Characteristics and Pressures and the Organizational Integration of Professionals," *Administrative Science Quarterly,* 15 (September):271–81.

———. 1976. "Humanizing Organizations: The Potential Impact of New People and Emerging Values upon Organizations," in H. Meltzer and F. R. Wickert, *Humanizing Organizational Behavior.* Springfield, Ill.: Charles C. Thomas. **200**

———, and FRANCINE S. HALL. 1976. "What's New in Career Management," *Organizational Dynamics*, Summer:17–33. **230, 231**

———, and MARILYN A. MORGAN. 1977. "Career Development and Planning," in W. C. Hamner and F. L. Schmidt, *Contemporary Problems in Personnel*. Chicago: St. Clair Press, 206. **198, 230, 231, 234**

———, and BENJAMIN SCHNEIDER. 1972. "Correlates of Organizational Identification as a Function of Career Pattern and Organizational Type," *Administrative Science Quarterly*. 17:340–50. **220, 224**

———, BENJAMIN SCHNEIDER, and H. T. NYGREN. 1970. "Personal Factors in Organizational Identification." *Administrative Science Quarterly*, 15:176–89. **219**

HALL, JAMES L., and JOEL K. LEIDECKER. 1978. "A Review of Vertical and Lateral Relations: A New Perspective for Managers," in Patrick E. Connor (ed.), *Dimensions in Modern Management*, 2nd ed. Pp. 141–49. **349**

HALL, RICHARD H. 1962. "Intraorganizational Structural Variation: Application of The Bureaucratic Model," *Administrative Science Quarterly*, 7 (December):295–308. **161**

———. 1972. *Organizations: Structure and Processes*. Englewood Cliffs, N.J.: Prentice-Hall. **206–7, 211, 477**

———, 1977. *Organizations: Structure and Process* (2nd ed.). Englewood Cliffs, N.J.: Prentice-Hall. **188, 229, 349, 374, 375**

HAMNER, W. CLAY. 1977. "Reinforcement Theory," in Henry L. Tosi, and W. Clay Hamner (eds.), *Organizational Behavior and Management: A Contingency Approach*. Chicago: St. Clair Press, rev. ed., 93–112. **230**

———, and ELLEN P. HAMNER. 1976. "Behavior Modification on the Bottom Line," *Organizational Dynamics*, 4 (Spring):2–21. **230**

———, and DENNIS W. ORGAN. 1978. *Organizational Behavior: An Applied Psychological Approach*, Dallas: Business Publications, Pp. 170, 323. **195, 201, 202, 203, 396**

HANNAN, MICHAEL T., and JOHN H. FREEMAN. 1977. "The Population Ecology of Organizations," *American Journal of Sociology*, 82 March:929–64. **305**

HARRISON, MICHAEL. 1972. "The Adjustment of a Social Movement to its Organizational Environment," unpublished paper, Department of Sociology, SUNY, Stony Brook. **140**

HASENFELD, YEHESKEL. 1972. "People Processing Organizations: An Exchange Approach," *American Sociological Review* 37:256–63. **141**

HAWKES, ROBERT W. 1962. "Physical Psychiatric Rehabilitation Models Compared," paper presented to the Ohio Valley Sociological Society. **163**

HEDBERG, BO L. T. 1973. *Organizational Stagnation and Choice of Strategy*. Berlin: International Institute of Management. **502**

———; PAUL C. NYSTROM; and WILLIAM H. STARBUCK. 1976. "Camping on Seesaws: Prescriptions for a Self-Designing Organization," *Administrative Science Quarterly*, 21 (March):41–65. **503**

HEFFERMAN, ESTHER. 1972. *Making It in Prison: The Square, the Cool, and the Life*. New York: Wiley. **208**

HEILBRONER, ROBERT L. 1959. *The Future as History*. New York: Harper. **494, 495, 496**

HELLRIEGEL, DON, and JOHN W. SLOCUM, JR. 1974. "Organizational Climate: Measures, Research, and Contingencies," *Academy of Management Journal*, 17:255–80. **411**

———. 1976. *Organizational Behavior: Contingency Views*. St. Paul, Minn.: West Publishing. **57, 396**

HENDERSON, LAWRENCE J. 1935. *Pareto's General Sociology*. Cambridge, Mass.: Harvard University Press. **25–26, 510**

HEROLD, D. M. in press. "Group Effectiveness as a Function of Task-Appropriate Interaction Processes," in J. L. Livingstone (ed.), *Managerial Accounting: The Behavioral Foundations*. Columbus, Ohio: Grid Publishers. **265**

HERSEY, PAUL, and KENNETH H. BLANCHARD. 1977. *Management of Organizational Behavior*, 3rd. ed. Englewood Cliffs, N. J.: Prentice-Hall. **200, 235**

HERZBERG, FREDERICK. 1966. *Work and Nature of Man*. Cleveland: World Publishing. **21**

———. 1974. "The Wise Old Turk," *Harvard Business Review* (September–October):70–90. **252, 263**

———; B. MAUSNER; and B. SNYDERMAN. 1959. *The Motivation to Work*. New York: Wiley. **252**

HESEL, RAY. 1971. "Value Orientation and Pupil Control Ideology of Public School Educators," *Education Administration Quarterly*, 7:24–33. **209**

HICKSON, D. J. 1966. "A Convergence in Organization Theory," *Administrative Science Quarterly*, 11 (September):225–37. **144**

———; D. S. PUGH; and DIANA PHESEY. 1969. "Operations Technology and Organization Structure: An Empirical Reappraisal," *Administrative Science Quarterly*, 14 (September):378–97. **157, 160, 161**

HIRSCH, PAUL. 1972. "Processing Fads and Fashions: An Organizational Set Analysis of Cultural Industry Systems," *American Journal of Sociology*, 77:639–59. **141, 142**

HODGKINSON, CHRISTOPHER. 1971. "Organizational Influence on Value Systems," *Educational Administration Quarterly*, 7:46–55. **209, 210**

HOPWOOD, ANTHONY G. 1973. "Problems with Using Accounting Information in Performance Evaluation," *Management International Review*, 13, (2-3):83–98. **504**

HOUSE OF REPRESENTATIVES, Staff Report to the Antitrust Subcommittee of the Committee on the Judiciary. 1965. *Interlocks in Corporate Management*. Washington, D.C.: U.S. Government Printing Office. **132**

HREBINIAK, LAWRENCE G. 1974. "Effects of Job Level and Participation on Employee Attitudes and Perceptions of Influence." *Academy of Management Journal*, 17:649–62. **219, 220**

———. 1978. *Complex Organizations*. St. Paul: West Publishing Co. **445**

———, and JOSEPH A. ALUTTO. 1972. "Personal and Role-related Factors in the Development of Organizational Commitment." *Administrative Science Quarterly*, 17:555–72. **219, 223, 224**

HULIN, CHARLES L. 1973. "Worker Background and Job Satisfaction: A Reply," *Industrial and Labor Relations Review*, 26:853–55.

———. and MILTON R. BLOOD. 1968. "Job Enlargement, Individual Differences, and Worker Responses," *Psychological Bulletin*, 69:41–55. **277**

HUSE, EDGAR F. 1975. *Organization Development and Change*. St. Paul: West Publishing Co. **22**

HUXLEY, ALDOUS. 1950. *Brave New World*. New York: Harper & Row. **288**

INDIK, BERNARD P. 1965. "Organizational Size and Member Participation: Some Empirical Tests of Alternative Explanations," *Human Relations*, 18:339–50. **397**

IVANCEVICH, JOHN, and JAMES H. DONNELLY, JR. 1975. "Relation of Organizational Structure to Job Satisfaction, Anxiety-Stress, and Performance," *Administrative Science Quarterly*, 20:2 (June) 272–80. **227**

JACOBS, DAVID. 1974. "Dependency and Vulnerability: An Exchange Approach to the Control of Organizations," *Administrative Science Quarterly*, 19:45–59. **130**

JAMES, L. R., and A. P. JONES. 1974. "Organizational Climate: A Review of Theory and Research," *Psychological Bulletin*, 81:1096–1112. **396, 397**

JANOWITZ, MORRIS. 1959. "Changing Patterns of Organizational Authority: The Military Establishment," *Administrative Science Quarterly*, 3 (March):473–93. **165**

JAQUES, ELIOT. 1959. *The Measurement of Responsibility*. Cambridge, Mass.: Harvard University Press. **172**

JENNINGS, E. E. 1971. *Renter to the Executive Suite*. New York: McGraw-Hill. **230, 234**

JONES, EDWARD E., and HAROLD B. GARARD. 1967. *Foundations of Social Psychology*. New York: Wiley. **335**

JORDAN, WILLIAM A. 1970. *Airline Regulation in America: Effects and Imperfections*. Baltimore, Md.: The Johns Hopkins University Press. **134**

———. 1972. "Producer Protection, Prior Market Structure, and the Effects of Government Regulation," *Journal of Law and Economics*, 15:151–76. **130, 134**

KAHN, HERMAN, and ANTHONY J. WIENER. 1967. *The Year 2000*. New York: Macmillan.

———; WILLIAM BROWN; and LEON MARTEL. 1976. *The Next 2000 Years: A Scenario for America and the World*. New York: Gilliam Morrow & Co. **501**

KAHN, ROBERT L. 1974. "The Work Module: A Proposal for the Humanization of Work," in James O'Toole (ed.), *Work and the Quality of Life*. Cambridge, Mass.: M. I. T. Press. **274, 276**

KAHN, ROBERT; DONALD M. WOLFE; ROBERT P. QUINN; J. DIEDRICK SNOEK; and ROBERT A. ROSENTHAL. 1964. *Organizational Stress*. New York: Wiley. **402, 403**

KAST, FREMONT E. 1974. "Organizational and Individual Objectives," in Joseph W. McGuire (ed.), *Contemporary Management: Issues and Viewpoints*. Englewood Cliffs, N.J.: Prentice-Hall, pp. 150–80. **67, 69–83, 147**

———, and JAMES E. ROSENZWEIG. 1973. *Contingency Views of Organization and Management*. Chicago: Science Research Associates. **408, 495, 498**

———. 1974. *Organization and Management Theory: A Systems Approach*, 2nd ed. New York: McGraw-Hill. **21, 207, 422**

KATZ, DANIEL. 1964. "The Motivational Basis of Organizational Behavior," *Behavioral Science*, vol. 9 (April). **196**

———, and ROBERT L. KAHN. 1966. *The Social Psychology of Organizations*. New York: Wiley. **50, 73, 92, 94, 130, 146, 207, 226, 306, 346, 422, 477**

———, and EZRA STOTLAND. 1959. "A Preliminary Statement to a Theory of Attitude Structure and Change," in S. Koch (ed.), *Psychology: A Study of a Science*. New York: McGraw-Hill. Pp. 423–75. **205, 208**

KATZELL, R. A., D. YANKELOVICH, et al. 1975. *Work, Productivity, and Job Satisfaction*. New York: The Psychology Corporation. **263, 277, 278**

KAUFMAN, HERBERT. 1967. *The Forest Ranger: A Study in Administrative Behavior*. Baltimore, Md.: The Johns Hopkins University Press. **294**

KEESING, F. M., and M. M. KEESING. 1956. *Elite Communication in Samoa*. Stanford, Calif.: Stanford University Press. **331**

KELLER, ROBERT, and WINFORD HOLLAND. 1975. "Boundary-Spanning Roles in a Research and Development Organization: An Empirical Investigation," *Academy of Management Journal*, 18:388–93. **145**

———; ANDREW SZILAGYI; and WINFORD HOLLAND. In press. "Boundary-Spanning Activity and Employee Reactions: An Empirical Study," *Human Relations*. **141**

KELMAN, HERBERT C. 1958. "Compliance, Identification, and Internalization; Three Processes of Attitude Change," *Journal of Conflict Resolution*, 2 (March): 51–60. **300, 301**

KHANDWALLA, PRADIP N. 1972. "Environment and its Impact on the Organization," *International Studies of Management and Organizations*, 2: 297–313. **126**

———. 1974. "Mass Output Orientation of Operations Technology and Organization Structure," *Administrative Science Quarterly*, 19 (March): 74–97. **505**

———. 1977. *The Design of Organizations*. New York: Harcourt Brace Jovanovich. **153, 232**

KIMBERLY, JOHN R. 1975. "Environmental Constraint and Organizational Structure: A Comparative Analysis of Rehabilitation Organizations," *Administrative Science Quarterly*, 20 (March):1–9. **126**

KINGDON, DONALD R. 1973. *Matrix Organization: Managing Information Technologies*. London: Tavistock. **39**

KLOPFER, FREDERICK J. 1975. "Decision Rules and Decision Consequence in Group Decision Making," unpublished doctoral dissertation, Texas Tech University. **339**

KLUCKHOLN, CLYDE, et al. 1962. "Values and Value-Orientations in the Theory of Action," in Talcott Parsons, and Edward A. Shils (eds.), *Toward a General Theory of Action*. New York; Harper and Row, 388–433. **205, 206**

KNUDSON, HARRY R.; ROBERT T. WOODWORTH; and CECIL H. BELL. 1973. *Management: An Experiential Approach*. New York: McGraw-Hill. **336**

KOCH, JAMES L., and RICHARD M. STEERS. 1976. "Job Attachment, Satisfaction, and Turnover among Public Employees." Technical Report No. 6, Office of Naval Research, University of Oregon. **219, 224**

KOCHAN, THOMAS. 1975. "Determinants of the Power of Boundary Units in an Interorganizational Bargaining Relation," *Administrative Science Quarterly*, 20:434–52. **139, 142**

KORMAN, ABRAHAM K. 1977. *Organizational Behavior*. Englewood Cliffs, N. J.: Prentice-Hall. **228**

KOTTER, JOHN P. 1974. "Organizational Design," Copyright held by the President and Fellows of Harvard College. **470**

KOVNER, ANTHONY. 1966. "The Nursing Unit: A Technological Perspective." Unpublished Ph.D. dissertation, University of Pittsburgh. **172**

KUHN, THOMAS S. 1962. *The Structure of Scientific Revolutions*. Chicago: University of Chicago Press. **494**

LANDAU, MARTIN. 1973. "On the Concept of the Self-Correcting Organization," *Public Administration Review*, 33 (November–December):533–42. **503**

LANDSBERGER, HENRY A. 1961. "The Horizontal Dimension in Bureaucracy," *Administrative Science Quarterly*, 6 (December):299–322. **349**

LATHAN, E. 1952. *The Group Basis of Politics*. Ithaca, N. Y.: Cornell University Press. **331**

LAWLER, EDWARD E. III. 1969. "Job Design and Employee Motivation," *Personnel Psychology*, 22 (Winter):426–35. **252, 254**

———. 1971. *Pay and Organizational Effectiveness: A Psychological View*. New York: McGraw-Hill. **216, 470**

———. 1973. *Motivation in Work Organizations*. Belmont, Calif.: Wadsworth. **215**

———. 1974. "The Individualized Organization: Problems and Promise," *California Management Review*, 17:2, 31-39. **218, 228, 236**

———. 1976. "Individualizing Organizations: A Needed Emphasis in Organizational Psychology," in Meltzer and Wickert, *Humanizing Organization Behavior*, 201–10. **236**

———, and C. CAMMANN. 1972. "What Makes a Work Group Successful?" in A. J. Marrow (ed.), *The Failure of Success*. New York: Amacom. **264**

———; J. RICHARD HACKMAN; and S. KAUFMAN. "Effects of Job Redesign: A Field Experiment," *Journal of Applied Social Psychology*, 3: 49–62.

———, and DOUGLAS T. HALL. 1970. "The Relationship of Job Characteristics to Job Involvement, Satisfaction, and Intrinsic Motivation," *Journal of Applied Psychology*, 54:305–12. **258**

———; W. J. KULECH; J. G. RHODE; and J. E. SORENSON. 1975. "Job Choice and Post-Decision Dissonance," *Organizational Behavior and Human Performance*, 13:133–45.

LAWRENCE, PAUL R., and JAY W. LORSCH. 1967a. "Differentiation and Integration in Complex Organizations," *Administrative Science Quarterly*, 12 (June):1–47. **34, 38, 40, 54, 55, 149, 150, 151, 152, 160, 161, 306, 347, 359, 408, 468, 469, 486**

———. 1967b. "New Management Job: The Integrator," *Harvard Business Review* (November–December):142–51. **34, 38, 39, 40, 47, 54, 55, 149, 150, 151, 152, 160, 161, 354, 359, 365–73, 380, 384, 408, 468**

———. 1967c. *Organization and Environment*. Boston: Graduate School of Business Administration, Harvard University. **34, 38, 39, 40, 48–49, 54, 55, 75, 160, 161, 188, 296, 366, 408, 467, 468, 469**

———. 1969. *Organization and Environment: Managing Differentiation and Integration*. Homewood, Ill.: Irwin. **48–49, 126, 181, 467, 478, 480**

LEAVITT, HAROLD J. 1958a. *Managerial Psychology*. Chicago: University of Chicago Press. **21, 24**

———. 1958b. "Some Effects of Certain Communication Patterns on Group Performance," in *Readings in Social Psychology*, Eleanor Maccoby, et al. (eds.). New York: Holt, Rinehart & Winston. Pp. 546–63.

———; WILLIAM R. DILL; and H. B. EYRING. 1973. *The Organizational World*. New York; Harcourt, Brace Jovanovich. **197**

———, and THOMAS L. WHISLER. 1958. "Management in the 1980's," *Harvard Business Review*, 36, 6 (November–December):41–48.

LEE, SANG M. 1971. "An Empirical Analysis of Organizational Identification." *Academy of Management Journal*. 14:213–26. **219**

LEVINE, SOL, and PAUL E. WHITE. 1961. "Exchange as a Conceptual Framework for the Study of Interorganizational Relationships," *Administrative Science Quarterly*, 5 (March):583–601. **123**

LEVINSON, DANIEL J. 1978. "Growing Up with the Dream," *Psychology Today*, 89:20–31. **199**

———; C. DARROW; M. LEVINSON EIKLEIN; and B. MCKEE. 1974. "The Psychological Development of Men in Early Adulthood and the Mid-Life Transition," in D. F. Hicks, A. Memeo, and M. Roffs (eds.), *Life History Research in Psychopathology*, vol. 3, Minneapolis: University of Minnesota. **199**

LEVINSON, HARRY. 1965. "Reciprocation; The Relationship between Man and Organization," *Administrative Science Quarterly*, 9 (March): 370–90. **78**

LEVY, MARION J. JR. 1966. *Modernization and Structure of Societies*. Princeton, N. J.: Princeton University Press. **352**

LIGHT, IVAN H. 1972. *Ethnic Enterprise in America*. Berkeley, Calif.: University of California Press. **298**

LIKERT, RENSIS. 1960. "Influence and National Sovereignty," *Festschrift for Gardner Murphy*, J. G. Peatman and E. L. Hartley, (eds.), New York. **285**

———. 1961. *New Patterns of Management*. New York: McGraw-Hill. **285, 287**

———. 1967. *The Human Organization*. New York: McGraw-Hill. **80, 299, 405, 406, 407, 446**

LINDBLOM, CHARLES E. 1959. "The Science of Muddling Through," *Public Administration Review*, 19 (Spring):79–88. **505**

LIPSET, SEYMOUR; MARTIN TROW; and JAMES COLEMAN. 1956. *Union Democracy*. Glencoe, Ill.: Free Press. **293–94, 345**

LITTERER, JOSEPH A. 1973. *The Analysis of Organizations* (2nd ed.) New York: John Wiley and Sons. **378, 379–80**

LITWIN, G. H., and R. STRINGER. 1966. "The Influence of Organizational Climate on Human Motivation." Paper presented at a conference on Organizational Climate, Foundation for Research on Human Behavior, Ann Arbor, Mich. (March). **400, 401, 403, 404, 405**

LOCKE, EDWIN A. 1970. "Job Satisfaction and Job Performance: A Theoretical Analysis," *Organizational Behavior and Human Performance*, 5: 484–500. **206**

LORSCH, JAY W. 1965. *Product Innovation and Organization*. New York: Macmillan. **55, 149**

LORSCH, JAY W. 1970. "Introduction to the Structural Design of Organizations". In Gene W. Dalton, Paul R. Lawrence, and Jay W. Lorsch (eds.), *Organizational Structure and Design*. Homewood, Ill.: Irwin, p. 13. **150–51**

———. 1971. "Matrix Organization and Technical Innovations" in Jay Galbraith (ed.), *Matrix Organizations: Organization Design for High Technology*. Cambridge, Mass.: The M. I. T. Press. **360**

———, and STEPHEN A. ALLEN. 1972. *Managing Diversity and Interdependence*. Boston: Division of Research, Harvard Business School. **467, 468, 469, 474**

———, and PAUL R. LAWRENCE. 1968. "Environmental Factors and Organization Integration," paper read at the Annual Meeting of the American Sociological Association, Boston, Mass.

———, and PAUL R. LAWRENCE (eds.). 1970. *Studies in Organization Design*. Homewood, Ill.: Irwin-Dorsey. **55, 149**

———, and JOHN J. MORSE. 1974. *Organizations and Their Members: A Contingency Approach*. New York: Harper & Row. **467, 468, 469, 470**

LUNDBERG, CRAIG C. 1974. "Organization Development: Current Perspectives and Future Issues," in Laurence J. Moore and Sang M. Lee (eds.) *Scientific and Behavioral Foundation Division Analysis*. Atlanta, Ga.: AIDS. **28**

MACAULAY, STEWART. 1963. "Non-contractual Relations in Business: A Preliminary Study," *American Sociological Review*, 28:55–67. **139**

MACAVOY, PAUL W. 1965. *The Economic Effects of Regulation*. Cambridge, Mass.: M. I. T. Press. **134**

MACRAE, DUNCAN. 1958. "Factors in the French Vote," *American Journal of Sociology* (November). **331**

MAHER, J. R. 1971. "Job Enrichment, Performance and Morale in a Simulated Factory," in J. R. Maher (ed.), *New Perspectives in Job Enrichment*. New York: Van Nostrand Reinhold.

———, and W. B. OVERBAGH. 1971. "Better Inspection Performance Through Job Enrichment," in J. R. Maher (ed.), *New Perspectives in Job Enrichment*. New York: Van Nostrand Reinhold. **255**

MAIER, NORMAN R. F. 1963. *Problem Solving Discussions and Conferences: Leadership Methods and Skills*. New York: McGraw-Hill. **187**

———. 1973. *Psychology in Industrial Organizations*, 4th ed. Boston: Houghton Mifflin. **228**

MANN, FLOYD C., and L. R. HOFFMAN. 1960. *Automation and the Worker*. New York: Holt, Rinehart & Winston. **286**

MARCH, JAMES G. (ed.). 1965. *Handbook of Organizations*. Chicago: Rand McNally. **13, 52–53**

———, and HERBERT A. SIMON. 1958. *Organizations*. New York: Wiley. **16, 23, 43, 44, 68, 74, 77–78, 88, 98, 100, 102, 138, 145, 170, 172, 223, 299, 314, 316, 410, 449**

MARCUSE, HERBERT. 1964. *One-Dimensional Man*. Boston: Beacon Press. **511**

MARGULIES, NEWTON, and ANTHONY P. RAIA. 1972. *Organization Development: Values, Process and Technology*. New York: McGraw-Hill. **22, 27, 28**

MARSCHAK, JACOB. 1954. *Mathematical Thinking in the Social Sciences*, Paul Lazarsfeld (ed.). Glencoe, Ill.: The Free Press. **324**

MASLOW, A. H. 1943. "A Theory of Human Motivation," *Psychological Review*. 50:370–96. **21**

MASLOW, ABRAHAM. 1964. *Motivation and Personality*. New York: Harper & Row. **497**

MASSIE, JOSEPH L. 1965. "Management Theory," in James G. March (ed.), *Handbook of Organizations*. Chicago: Rand McNally. **271**

MATHIESON, THOMAS. 1972. *Across The Boundaries of Organizations*. Calif.: Glendessary Press. **138, 144, 146**

MATTHEWS, DONALD R. 1960. *U. S. Senators and Their World*. Chapel Hill: University of North Carolina Press. **297**

MCCLELLAND, DAVID C. 1961. *The Achieving Society*. Princeton: Van Nostrand Reingold. **197, 198, 372**

———, C.; J. W. ATKINSON; R. A. CLARK; and E. L. LOWELL. 1953. *The Achievement Motive*. New York: Appleton-Century-Crofts. **21**

MCCORMICK, G. J.; J. W. CUNNINGHAM; and G. G. GORDON. "Job Dimensions Based on Factor Analysis of Work-Oriented Job Variables," *Personnel Psychology*, 20:417–30. **255**

MCGREGOR, DOUGLAS. 1960. *The Human Side of Enterprise*. New York: McGraw-Hill. **20, 21, 252**

MCKELVEY, BILL. 1975. "Guidelines for the Empirical Classification of Organizations," *Administrative Science Quarterly*, 20 (December):509–25. **478**

———, 1976. "Toward More Comprehensive Organization Design Objectives," in Ralph H. Kilmann, Louis R. Pondy, and Dennis P. Slevin (eds.), *The Management of Organization Design—I*: 27–51. **485**

———, and RALPH H. KILMANN. 1975. "Organization Design: A Participative Multivariate Approach," *Administrative Science Quarterly*, 20 (March):24–36. **478, 485, 486–87, 488**

MEADOWS, DONELLA; DENNIS L. MEADOWS; JØRGEN RANDERS; and WILLIAM W. BEHRENS, III. 1972. *The Limits of Growth: A Report for The Club of Rome's Project on the Predicament of Mankind*. New York: Universe. **496, 501**

MEE, JOHN F. 1964. "Matrix Organization," *Business Horizons* (Summer):70. **355**

MEIER, RICHARD L. 1963. "Communications Overload," *Administrative Science Quarterly*, 7 (March):521–44. **168**

———, 1965. "Information Input Overload," in Fred Massarik and P. Ratoosh (eds.), *Mathematical Explorations in Behavioral Sciences*. Homewood, Ill.: Irwin. **138**

MERRENS, M. R., and J. B. GARRETT. 1975. "The Protestant Ethic Scale as a Predictor of Repetitive Work Performance," *Journal of Applied Psychology*, 60:125–27.

MERTON, ROBERT K. 1957. "Bureaucratic Structure and Personality," in Robert K. Merton, *Social Theory and Social Structure*. New York: The Free Press of Glencoe. **76, 95, 164, 226**

———, 1968. *Social Theory and Social Structure* (rev. ed.). New York: Free Press. **56**

———; LEONARD BROOM; and LEONARD S. COTTRELL, JR. (eds.) 1958. *Sociology Today*. New York: Basic Books. **332**

———; GEORGE READER; and PATRICIA L. KENDALL (eds.) 1957, *The Student Physician*. Cambridge, Mass.: Harvard University Press. **208**

MESAROVIC, MIHAJLO, and EDUARD PESTEL. 1974. *Mankind at the Turning Point: The Second Report of The Club of Rome*. New York: Dutton. **501**

MEYER, H. H. 1967. "Differences in Organizational Climate in Outstanding and Average Sales Offices: A Summary Report," General Electric, Behavioral Research Service and Public Relations Personnel Service. **401**

MEYER, JOHN W., and BRIAN ROWAN. 1977. "Institutionalized Organizations: Formal Structure as Myth and Ceremony," *American Journal of Sociology*, vol. 83, no. 2, September:340–63. **294, 305, 306**

MEYER, MARSHAL W. 1968. "Two Authority Structures of Bureaucratic Organization," *Administrative Science Quarterly*, 13 (September): 211–28. **352, 376, 378**

———; 1972. *Bureaucratic Structure and Authority*. Harper & Row. **157**

———; 1975. "Organizational Domains," *American Sociological Review*, vol. 40, no. 5 (October):599–615. **126**

MICHELS, ROBERT. 1949. *Political Parties*. New York: The Free Press. **76, 345**

MILES, RAYMOND E. 1975. *Theories of Management: Implications for Organizational Behavior and Development*. New York: McGraw-Hill. **22, 27, 28, 268**

———; CHARLES C. SNOW; and JEFFREY PFEFFER. 1974. "Organization-Environment Concepts and Issues," *Industrial Relations*, 13, (October):244–64. **122, 123, 147, 148**

MILLER, ERIC. 1959. "Technology, Time, and Territory," *Human Relations*, 12: 243–72. **471**

MILLS, THEODORE M. 1967. *The Sociology of Small Groups*. Englewood Cliffs, N. J.: Prentice-Hall. **411**

MINDLIN, SERGIO, and HOWARD ALDRICH. 1975. "Interorganizational Dependence: A Review of the Concept and a Reexamination of the Findings of the Aston Group," *Administrative Science Quarterly*, 20: 382–92. **146**

MINTZBERG, HENRY. 1973. *The Nature of Managerial Work*. New York: Harper & Row. **129, 146**

MITCHELL, TERENCE R. 1974. "Expectancy Models of Job Satisfaction, Occupational Preference and Effort: A Theoretical, Methodological, and Empirical Appraisal," *Psychological Bulletin*, 81 (December):1053–77. **215**

MITROFF, IAN I., and TOM R. FEATHERINGHAM. 1974. "On Systematic Problem Solving and the Error of the Third Kind," *Behavioral Science*, 19:383–93. **506**

———, and RALPH H. KILMANN. 1976. "On Organization Stories: An Approach to the Design and Analysis of Organizations Through Myths and Stories," in Ralph H. Kilmann, Louis R. Pondy, and Dennis P. Slevin (eds.) *The Management of Organization Design: Volume I, Strategies and Implementation*. New York: Elsevier North Holland. Pp. 189–207. **502**

MOONEY, JAMES D., and ALAN C. REILEY. 1931. *Onward Industry!* New York: Harper. **19**

MOORE, WILBERT E. 1970. *The Professions: Roles and Rules*. New York: Russell Sage Foundation. **208**

MORSE, JOHN J., and JAY W. LORSCH. 1970. "Beyond Theory Y," *Harvard Business Review* (May–June):61–68. **255**

MOWDAY, RICHARD T.; LYMAN W. PORTER; and ROBERT DUBIN. 1974. "Unit Performance, Situational Factors, and Employee Attitudes in Spatially Separated Work Units," *Organizational Behavior and Human Performance*, 12:231–48. **219**

MUMFORD, ENID, and HAROLD SACKMAN (eds.). 1975. *Human Choice and Computers*. Amsterdam: North Holland. **504**

MYERS, M. SCOTT, and S. S. MYERS. 1974. "Toward Understanding the Changing Work Ethic," *California Management Review*, Spring:7–19. **200**

NADEL, MARK. 1971. *The Politics of Consumer Protection*. Indianapolis: Bobbs-Merrill. **142**

NADLER, DAVID A. 1977. *Feedback and Organizational Development: Using Data-Based Methods*. Reading, Mass.: Addison-Wesley. **217**

NAKANE, CHIE. 1973. *Japanese Society*. Middlesex, England: Penguin. **294**

NEMIROFF, PAUL M., and DAVID L. FORD, JR. 1976. "Task Effectiveness and Human Fulfillment in Organizations: A Review and Development of a Conceptual Contingency Model," *Academy of Management Review*, October:69–82. **408**

NIVEN, LARRY, and JERRY POURNELLE. 1974. *The Mote in God's Eye*. New York: Simon & Schuster. **311**

NYSTROM, PAUL C. 1975. "Input-Output Processes of the Federal Trade Commission," *Administrative Science Quarterly*, 20 (March):104–13. **504**

———; BO L. T. HEDBERG; and WILLIAM H. STARBUCK. 1976. "Interacting Processes as Organization Designs," in Ralph H. Kilmann, Louis R. Pondy, and Dennis Slevin (eds.), *The Management of Organization Design: Volume I, Strategies and Implementation*. New York: Elsevier North-Holland. **502, 504**

OLDHAM, GREG R. 1976. "Job Characteristics and Internal Motivation: The Moderating Effect of Interpersonal and Individual Variables," *Human Relations*, 29:559–69. **261**

———. "Job Characteristics and Internal Motivation: The Moderating Effect of Interpersonal and Individual Variables," *Human Relations*, in press. **254**

———; J. R. HACKMAN; and J. L. PEARCE. 1976. "Conditions Under Which Employees Respond Positively to Enriched Work," *Journal of Applied Psychology*, 61:395–403. **261**

OLTMANS, WILLEM L. 1974. *On Growth*. New York: Putnam. **501**

ONDRACK, D. A. 1971. "Attitudes Toward Authority," *Personnel Administration*, 34:8–17. **203**

———. 1973. "Emerging Occupational Values: A Review and Some Findings," *Academy of Management Journal*, 16:423–32. **197, 203**

ORGAN, DENNIS W. 1971. "Linking Pins Between Organizations and Environment," *Business Horizons*, 14 (December):73–80. **146**

———. 1975. "Extraversion, Locus of Control, and Individual Differences in Conditionability in Organizations," *Journal of Applied Psychology*, 60 (June):401–04. **203**

OSBORN, RICHARD N., and JAMES G. HUNT. 1974. "Environment and Organizational Effectiveness," *Administrative Science Quarterly*, 19: 231–46. **126**

OUCHI, WILLIAM G. 1977. "The Relationship Between Organizational Structure and Organizational Control", *Administrative Science Quarterly*, 22, March:95–111. **305**

———. 1978. "The Transmission of Control Through Organizational Hierarchy," *Academy of Management Journal*, 21 (June):173–92. **305**

———, and REUBEN T. HARRIS. 1976. "Structure, Technology, and Environment," in George Strauss, Raymond E. Miles, Charles C. Snow, and Arnold S. Tannenbaum (eds.), *Organizational Behavior*. Belmont, Calif.: Wadsworth. Pp. 107–40. **147, 147**

———, and M. A. MAGUIRE. 1975. "Organizational Control; Two Functions," *Administrative Science Quarterly*, 20 (December):559–69. **281, 297, 305**

PALEN, J. JOHN. 1972. "The Education of the Senior Military Decision-Maker," *Sociological Quarterly*, 13:145–60. **208**

PARSONS, TALCOTT. 1951. *The Social System*. Glencoe, Ill.: Free Press. **72**

———. 1956. "Suggestions for a Sociological Approach to the Theory of Organizations, I and II," *Administrative Science Quarterly*, 1 (June and September):63–85, 225–39. **26, 72, 92–93, 95, 138, 207**

———. 1960. *Structure and Process in Modern Society*. Glencoe, Ill.: Free Press. **17, 23, 75, 92–93, 95, 129, 169, 299, 305, 480**

PATCHEN, MARTIN. 1970. *Participation, Achievement, and Involvement on the Job*. Englewood, N. J.: Prentice-Hall. **219, 220**

PAUL, W. J.; K. B. ROBERTSON; and F. HERZBERG. 1969. "Job Enrichment Pays Off," *Harvard Business Review* (March–April):61–78. **276**

PAVALKO, RONALD M. 1971. *Sociology of Occupations and Professions*. Itasca, Ill.: F. E. Peacock Publishers. **229**

PAYNE, ROY L., and DEREK S. PUGH. 1975. "Organization Structure and Organization Climate," in Marvin Dunnette (ed.), *Handbook of Industrial and Organizational Psychology*. Chicago: Rand McNally. pp. 1125–73. **396, 397, 405, 406–408**

———. 1975. "Organizational Structure and Climate," in Marvin D. Dunnette *Handbook of Industrial and Organizational Psychology*. Chicago: Rand McNally, Pp. 1125–73.

PEERY, NEWMAN S. JR. 1972. "General Systems Theory: An Inquiry into Its Social Philosophy," *Academy of Management Journal*, 15:495–510.

———. 1973. "General Systems Theory: A Critique of Its Use in Administrative Theory," *Proceedings of the Mountain-Plains Management Association*. **207**

PELZ, DONALD C. 1952. "Influence: A Key to Effective Leadership in the First-Line Supervisor," *Personnel*, 29 (November):209–17. **284**

PENNINGS, JOHANNES M. 1970. "Work Value Systems of White-Collar Workers," *Administrative Science Quarterly*, 15:397–405. **209**

PERROW, CHARLES. 1960. "Authority, Goals, and Prestige in a General Hospital," unpublished Ph.D. Dissertation, Berkeley, Calif.: University of California. **105**

———. 1961a. "The Analysis of Goals in Complex Organizations," *American Sociological Review*, 26 (April):854–66. **57, 70, 172**

———. 1961b. "Organizational Prestige, Some Functions and Dysfunctions," *American Journal of Sociology*, 66 (January):335–41. **70, 175, 176**

———. 1966. "Reality Adjustment: A Young Institution Settles for Humane Care," *Social Problems*, 14 (Summer):69–79. **33, 208**

———. 1967. "A Framework for the Comparative Analysis of Organizations," *American Sociological Review*, 32 (April):194–208. **157, 159–60, 161–62, 169–76, 178–79, 192**

———. 1968. "Organizational Goals," *International Encyclopedia of the Social Sciences* (rev. ed.). New York: Macmillan, 11:305–11. **66, 175**

———. 1970. *Organizational Analysis: A Sociological View*, Belmont, Calif.: Wadsworth. **33–34, 70–71, 72, 92, 95–96, 97, 100, 126, 144, 148–49, 229, 477, 478, 479**

———. 1972. *Complex Organizations: A Critical Essay*. Glenview, Ill.: Scott, Foresman. **281, 294, 299**

PERVIN, L. A. 1967. "A Twenty-College Study of Student Plus College Interactions Using TAPE (transactional analysis of personality and environment): Rationale, Reliability, and Validity," *Journal of Educational Psychology*, 58:290–302.

———. 1968. "Performance and Satisfaction as a Function of Individual-Environmental Fit," *Psychological Bulletin*, 69:56–68.

PFEFFER, JEFFREY. 1972a. "Size and Composition of Corporate Boards of Directors: The Organization and Its Environment," *Administrative Science Quarterly*. 17 (June):218–28. **141, 143, 147**

———. 1972b. "Merger as a Response to Organization Interdependence," *Administrative Science Quarterly*, 17 (September):387–94. **130, 131, 147**

———. 1973. "Size, Composition and Function of Hospital Boards of Directors: A Study of Organization-Environment Linkage," *Administrative Science Quarterly*, 18:349–64. **133, 147**

———. 1974a. "Administrative Regulation and Licensing: Social Problem or Solution?" *Social Problems*, 21:468–79. **130, 134**

———. 1974b. "Co-optation and the Composition of Electric Utility Boards of Directors," *Pacific Sociological Review*, 17:333–63. **133**

———. 1976. "Beyond Management and the Worker: The Institutional Function of Management," *Academy of Management Review*, 1:36–46. **127, 129–36, 305**

———, and HUSEYIN LEBLEBICI. 1973a. "The Effect of Competition on Some Dimensions of Organizational Structure," *Social Forces*, 52:268–79. **142, 147**

———, and HUSEYIN LEBLEBICI. 1973b. "Executive Recruitment and the Development of Interfirm Organizations," *Administrative Science Quarterly*, 18 (December):449–61. **133, 141, 143**

———, and PHILLIP NOWAK. "Organizational Context and Interorganizational Linkages Among Corporations." Unpublished ms., Berkeley, Calif.: University of California. **129, 132**

PHILLIPS, ALMARIN. 1960. "A Theory of Interfirm Organization," *Quarterly Journal of Economics*, 74 (November):602–13. **148**

PHILLIPS, D. C. 1972. "The Methodological Basis of Systems Theory," *Academy of Management Journal*, 15:469–77.

PIERCE, JON L. and RANDALL R. DUNHAM. 1976. "Task Design: A Literature Review," *Academy of Management Journal*, October:83–97. **248–50, 252–55, 268, 269, 271, 277**

PONDY, LOUIS R. 1969. "Effects of Size, Complexity, and Ownership on Administrative Intensity," *Administrative Science Quarterly*, 14 (March): 47–60. **502**

PORTER, LYMAN W., and EDWARD E. LAWLER III. 1965. "Properties of Organization Structure in Relation to Job Attitudes and Behavior," *Psychological Bulletin*, 64:25–51. **205**

———. 1968a. *Managerial Attitudes and Performance*. Homewood, Ill.: Irwin. **225, 470**

———. 1968b. "What Job Attitudes Tell about Motivation," *Harvard Business Review*, pp. 118–26. **225, 470**

———; and J. RICHARD HACKMAN. 1975. *Behavior in Organizations*. New York: McGraw-Hill. **195, 197**

———, and RICHARD M. STEERS. 1973. "Organizational Work and Personal Factors in Employee Turnover and Absenteeism." *Psychological Bulletin*, 80:161–76. **220**

———; RICHARD T. MOWDAY; and PAUL V. BOULIAN. 1974. "Organizational Commitment, Job Satisfaction, and Turnover Among Psychiatric Technicians." *Journal of Applied Psychology*, 59:603–9. **219, 220, 221, 224**

POSNER, RICHARD A. 1974. "Theories of Economic Regulation," *Bell Journal of Economics and Management Science*, 5:335–58. **130, 134**

POUNDS, WILLIAM F. 1963. "The Scheduling Environment," in J. F. Muth and G. Thompson (eds.) *Industrial Scheduling*. Englewood Cliffs, N. J.: Prentice-Hall. **44**

PRESTHUS, ROBERT. 1965. *The Organizational Society*. New York: Vintage Books. **229**

PRICE, JAMES L. 1963. "The Impact of Governing Boards on Organizational Effectiveness and Morale," *Administrative Science Quarterly*, 8: 361–68. **133, 143**

PRITCHARD, R. D., and L. H. PETERS. 1974. "Job Duties and Job Interests as Predictors of Intrinsic and Extrinsic Satisfaction," *Organization Behavior and Human Performance*, vol. 12, no. 3, 315–30. **255**

PUGH, D. S.; D. J. HICKSON; C. R. HININGS; K. M. MACDONALD; C. TURNER; and T. LUPTON. 1963. "A Conceptual Scheme for Organizational Analysis," *Administrative Science Quarterly*, 8 (December): 289–315. **104, 350, 352**

PUGH, D. S.; D. J. HICKSON; C. R. HININGS; and C. TURNER. 1968. "Dimensions of Organizational Structure," *Administrative Science Quarterly*, 13 (June):65–105. **348, 349, 350, 353**

PUGH, D. S.; D. J. HICKSON; and C. R. HININGS. 1969. "An Empirical Taxonomy of Structures of Work Organizations," *Administrative Science Quarterly*, 14 (March):115–26. **126, 188, 477**

REEVES, T. KYNASTON, and JOAN WOODWARD. 1970. "The Study of Managerial Control," in Joan Woodward (ed.), *Industrial Organization: Behavior and Control*. London: Oxford University Press. **281**

REICH, CHARLES A. 1970. *The Greening of America*. New York: Random House. **497**

REID, SAMMUEL R. 1968. *Mergers, Managers, and the Economy*. New York: McGraw-Hill. **131**

REIF, W. E., and F. LUTHANS. 1972. "Does Job Enrichment Really Pay Off?" *California Management Review*, 15:30–37. **267**

REISS, ALBERT J. 1971. *The Police and the Public*. New Haven, Conn.: Yale University Press. **141**

REITZ, H. JOSEPH. 1977. *Behavior in Organizations*. Homewood, Ill.: Richard D. Irwin. **226, 228**

RIDGWAY, VALENTINE F. 1957. "Administration of Manufacturer-Dealer Systems," *Administrative Science Quarterly*, March. **332**

ROBEY, DANIEL. 1974. "Task Design, Work Values, and Worker Response: An Experimental Test," *Organization Behavior and Human Performance*, 12:264–73.

ROBINSON, JOHN P., and PHILLIP R. SHAVER (eds.). 1969. *Measures of Social Psychological Attitudes*, Ann Arbor: Institute for Social Research, University of Michigan. **211**

ROBY, T. B.; E. H. NICOL; and F. M. FARRELL. 1963. "Group Problem Solving under Two Types of Executive Structure," *Journal of Abnormal and Social Psychology*, 67:550–56. **404**

ROETHLISBERGER, FRITZ J. 1956. *Management and Morale*. Cambridge, Mass.: Harvard University Press.

———. 1968. "Efficiency and Cooperative Behavior," in Fritz J. Roithlesberger, *Man-in-Organization*. Cambridge, Mass.: The Belknap Press of Harvard University, Pp. 95–108. **24**

———, and WILLIAM J. DICKSON. 1939. *Management and the Worker*. Cambridge, Mass.: Harvard University Press. **6, 15, 293**

ROGERS, ROLF E. 1975. *Organizational Theory*. Boston: Allyn and Bacon. **203**

ROHLEN, THOMAS P. 1974. *For Harmony and Strength: Japanese White-Collar Organization in Anthropological Perspective*. Berkeley, Calif.: University of California Press. **294**

ROKEACH, MILTON. 1960. *The Open and Closed Mind*. New York: Basic Books. **203**

———. 1968. *Beliefs, Attitudes, and Values*, San Francisco: Jossey-Bass. **205**

———. 1969. "The Role of Values in Public Opinion Research," *Public Opinion Quarterly*, 32:547–59. **211**

ROSS, I. C., and ALVIN ZANDER. 1957. "Need Satisfaction and Employee Turnover." *Personnel Psychology*, 10:327–38. **220**

ROSS, JOEL E., and ROBERT G. MURDICK. 1973. "People, Productivity, and Management Structure," *Personnel* (September–October):9–16.

ROTTER, J. B. 1966. "Generalized Expectancies for Internal versus External Control of Reinforcement," *Psychological Monographs*, vol. 80, (1, whole no. 609). **203**

———. 1971a. "Generalized Expectancies for Interpersonal Trust," *American Psychology*, 26:443–52. **203**

———. 1971b. "External Control and Internal Control," *Psychology Today*, 5:37–42, 58–59. **203**

RUSSELL, J. A., and A. MEHRABIAN. 1975. "Task Setting and Personality Variables Affecting the Desire to Work," *Journal of Applied Psychology*, 60:518–20.

SAYLES, LEONARD. 1964. *Managerial Behavior*. New York: McGraw-Hill. **349**

SCHACHTER, S.; N. ELLERTSON; D. MCBRIDE; and D. GREGORY. 1951. "An Experimental Test of Cohesiveness and Productivity," *Human Relations*, 4:229–38. **264**

SCHEIN, EDGAR H. 1964. "How to Break In the College Graduate," *Harvard Business Review*, 42:68–76. **197, 230**

SCHEIN, EDGAR H. 1968. "Organizational Socialization and the Profession of Management," *Industrial Management Review* (Winter). **230**

SCHEIN, EDGAR. 1970. *Organizational Psychology*. Englewood Cliffs, N. J.: Prentice-Hall. **77, 219**

SCHEIN, EDGAR H. 1975. "Career Anchors Hold Executives to Their Career Paths," *Personnel*, 52:11–24. **199**

SCHNEIDER, B., and C. J. BARTLETT. 1968. "Individual Differences and Organizational Climate, I: The Research Plan and Questionnaire Development," *Personnel Psychology*, 21:323–33. **401–402, 403, 405**

———. 1970. "Individual Differences and Organizational Climate, II: Measurement of Organizational Climate by the Multitrait-Multirater Matrix," *Personnel Psychology*, 23:493–512. **397**

SCHULER, RANDALL S. 1979. "Worker Background and Job Satisfaction: A Comment," *Industrial and Labor Relations Review*, 26:851–53.

———. 1977. "Modernizing Effects of Job Involvement and Growth Need Strength on Task-Outcome Relationships," *Journal of Business Research*, vol. 5, no. 4, 293–304. **271**

SCHUMACHER, ERNST FRIEDRICH. 1973. *Small is Beautiful: A Study of Economics as if People Mattered*. London: Blond and Briggs. **502**

SCHWAB, DONALD P., and LARRY L. CUMMINGS. 1976. "Impact of Task Scope on Employee Productivity: An Evaluation Using Expectancy Theory," *Academy of Management Review*, vol. 1 (no. 2, April):23–35. **255**

SCOTT, WILLIAM A. 1956. *Values and Organizations*. Chicago: Rand McNally. **205**

SCOTT, WILLIAM E. JR. 1966. "Activation Theory and Task Design," *Organizational Behavior and Human Performance*, 1:3–30. **202**

SCOTT, WILLIAM E. JR., and LARRY L. CUMMINGS (eds.) 1973. *Readings in Organizational Behavior and Human Performance*. Homewood, Ill.: Richard D. Irwin. **205**

SCOTT, WILLIAM G. 1961. "Organization Theory: An Overview and an Appraisal," *Academy of Management Journal*, 4:7–26. **494**

———. 1969. "Organization Government: The Prospects for a Truly Participative System," *Public Administration Review*, 29:43–53. **26**

———, and TERENCE R. MITCHELL. 1972. *Organization Theory: A Structural and Behavioral Analysis* (rev. ed.). Homewood, Ill.: Irwin-Dorsey. **21, 24, 495**

SCOTT, W. RICHARD. 1964. "Theory of Organizations," in Faris, Robert E. L. (ed.), *Handbook of Modern Sociology*. Chicago: Rand McNally. **53, 96, 104, 185, 477, 478**

———. 1975. "Organizational Structure," In Alex Inkeles, James Coleman, and Neil Smelser (eds.), *Annual Review of Sociology*, 1:1–20. Palo Alto, Calif.: Annual Reviews. **346**

SEASHORE, STANLEY E. 1954. *Group Cohesiveness in the Industrial Work Group*. Ann Arbor, Mich.: University of Michigan. **264**

———, and EPHRAIM YUCHTMAN. 1967. "Factorial Analysis of Organizational Performance," *Administrative Science Quarterly*, XII (December):393. **147**

SEEMAN, MELVIN. 1959. "On the Meaning of Alienation," *American Sociological Review*, 24 (December):783–91.

SELLS, S. B. (ed.) 1963. *Stimulus Determinants of Behavior*. New York: Ronald Press. **401**

SELZNICK, PHILIP. 1949. *TVA and the Grass Roots*. Berkeley, Calif.: University of California Press. **15, 147, 293, 345**

SHELDON, MARY E. 1971. "Investments and Involvements as Mechanisms Producing Commitment to the Organization." *Administrative Science Quarterly*, 16:142–50. **219, 220**

SHEPARD, JON M. 1970. "Functional Specialization, Alienation, and Job Satisfaction," *Industrial and Labor Relations Review*, 23 (January):207–19.

———. 1973. "Worker Background and Job Satisfaction: Reply," *Industrial and Labor Relations Review*, 26:856–59.

———, A. 1964. "On the Concept of Organizational Goal," *Administrative Science Quarterly*, 9 (June): 1–22.

———. 1973a. "Applying Information Technology to Organizational Design," *Public Administration Review*, 33 (May–June):268–78.

———. 1973b. "The Structure of Ill-Structured Problems." *Artificial Intelligence*. New York: Free Press. 4:181–202.

———. *Administrative Behavior* (3rd ed.). New York: The Free Press.

SIMS, HENRY P., and A. D. SZILAGYI. 1975. "Individual Moderators of Job Characteristic Relationships," *Academy of Management Proceedings*.

———; and R. J. KELLER. "The Measurement of Job Characteristics," *Academy of Management Journal* (in press).

SLATER, PHILLIP. 1970. *The Pursuit of Loneliness: American Culture at the Breaking Point*. Boston: Beacon Press. **203**

SLOAN, ALFRED P. 1964. *My Years at General Motors*. Garden City, N. Y.: Doubleday. **474**

SMITH, ADAM. 1776. *The Wealth of Nations*. New York: Modern Library.

SMITH, C. G.; O. ARI; and A. S. TANNENBAUM. 1962. "The Relationship of Patterns of Control to Norms in a Service Organization," unpublished report. **289**

SHERWIN, DOUGLAS S. 1977. "The Meaning of Control," in M. T. Matteson and J. M. Ivancevich, (eds.), *Management Classics*. Santa Monica, Calif.: Goodyear. Pp. 265–71. **281**

SHORTELL, STEPHEN M. 1975. "A Configurational Theory of Organizations." Paper presented to Pacific Sociological Association, Victoria, B. C. (April). **127**

———. 1977. "The Role of Environment in a Configurational Theory of Organizations," *Human Relations*, 30: 275–302. **126**

SIEBER, SAM. 1974. "Toward a Theory of Role Accumulation," *American Sociological Review*, 39:567–78. **146**

SIKULA, ANDREW F. 1971. "Values and Value Systems: Relationship to Personal Goals," *Personnel Journal*, 50:310–12. **208**

SILLS, DAVID L. 1970. "Preserving Organizational Goals," in Oscar Grusky and George A. Miller (eds.), *The Sociology of Organizations*. New York: Free Press. Pp. 227–36. **76**

SIMON, HERBERT A. 1945. *Administrative Behavior*. New York: Macmillan. **324**

———. 1955. "A Behavioral Model of Rational Choice," *Quarterly Journal of Economics* 69 (February): 99–118. **323**

———. 1957a. *Administrative Behavior* (2d ed.). New York: Macmillan. **16, 67, 74, 323**

———. 1957b. *Models of Man: Social and Rational*. New York: Wiley. **16, 86**

———. 1958. "The Role of Expectations," in C. F. Carter, G. P. Meredith, and G. L. S. Shackle (eds.), *Expectations, Uncertainly and Business Behavior*. New York: Social Science Research Council.

———. 1960a. "The Corporation: Will it be Managed by Machines?", in M. Anshen and G. L. Bach (eds.), *Management and Corporations*, McGraw-Hill, Pp. 17–55. **36**

———. 1960b. *The New Science of Management Decision*, New York: Harper & Row. **36, 312–13, 314–22, 351, 446**

———. 1962. "The Architecture of Complexity," *Proceedings of the American Philosophical Society*, 106, December: 467–82. **305**

SIMON. 1947. **98**

SIMON. 1953. **324**

SIMON. 1959. **78**

SIMON. 1964. **67, 68, 78, 84–91, 97, 98, 100, 305, 306**

SIMON. 1973. **504**

SIMON. 1976. **312, 334–35**

SNYDER, RICHARD C. 1958. *Approaches to the Study of Politics*, Roland Young (ed.). Evanston, Ill.: Northwestern University Press. **324**

STARBUCK, WILLIAM H. 1974. "Systems Optimization with Unknown Criteria," Proceedings of the 1974 International Conference on Systems, Man, and Cybernetics. New York: Institute of Electrical and Electronics Engineers, Pp. 67–76. **505**

———. 1976. "Organizations and Their Environments," in Marvin D. Dunnette (ed.), *Handbook of Organizational and Industrial Psychology*. Chicago: Rand McNally, 1069–1124. **122, 143**

———, and JOHN M. DUTTON. 1973. "Designing Adaptive Organizations," *Journal of Business Policy*. vol. 3 (Summer), 21–28. **505**

STEERS, RICHARD M. 1975. "Problems in the Measurement of Organizational Effectiveness." *Administrative Science Quarterly*, 20:546–558. **219, 437**

———. 1977. *Organizational Effectiveness: A Behavioral View*. Santa Monica, Calif.: Goodyear. **225**

———, and DANIEL N. BRAUNSTEIN. 1976. "A Behaviorally Based Measure of Manifest Needs in Work Settings." *Journal of Vocational Behavior*, 9:251–66.

———, and LYMAN W. PORTER. 1975. *Motivation and Work Behavior*. New York: McGraw-Hill. **21, 225, 398**

STERN, G. G. 1962. "Environments for Learning," in N. Stanford (ed.), *The American College*. New York: Wiley.

STERN, LOUIS W.; BRIAN STERNTHAL; and C. SAMUEL CRAIG. 1973. "Managing Conflict in Distribution Channels: A Laboratory Study," *Journal of Marketing Research*, 10:169–79. **133**

STIGLER, GEORGE J. 1971. "The Theory of Economic Regulation," *Bell Journal of Economics and Management Science*, 2:3–21. **134**

STINCHOMBE, ARTHUR L. 1959. "Bureaucratic and Craft Administration of Production: A Comparative Study," *Administrative Science Quarterly*, 4 (September):168–87. **164**

———. 1965. "Social Structure and Organizations," in James G. March (ed.), *Handbook of Organizations*. Chicago: Rand McNally. Pp. 142–93. **69, 175**

STOGDILL, RALPH, and COONS H. 1957. *Leader Behavior: Its Description and Measurement*. Columbus, Ohio: Ohio State University. **190**

STONE, EUGENE F. 1974. "Job Scope, Job Satisfaction, and the Protestant Ethic: A Study of Enlisted Men in the U. S. Navy," *Technical Report No. 27*. Irvine, Calif.: University of California Press.

———, and LYMAN W. PORTER. 1973. "Job Scope and Job Satisfaction: A Study of Urban Workers," *Technical Report No. 22*. Irvine, Calif.: University of California Press.

———. 1975. "Job Characteristics and Job Attitudes: A Multivariate Study," *Journal of Applied Psychology*, 60:57–64. **220**

STRAUSS, GEORGE W. 1962. "Tactics of Lateral Relationship: The Purchasing Agent," *Administrative Science Quarterly*, 7 (September): 161–86. **139, 349**

STREET, DAVID; ROBERT VINTER; and CHARLES PERROW. 1966. *Organization for Treatment: A Comparative Study of Institutions for Delinquents*. New York: Free Press. **171, 173, 175**

STRODTBECK, F. L.; RITA M. JAMES; and C. HAWKINS. "Social Status in Jury Deliberations," *American Sociological Review* (December). **329**

SUDNOW, DAVID. 1965. "Normal Crimes: Sociological Features of the Penal Code in a Public Defender Office," *Social Problems*, 12 (Winter). **171**

SUPER, D. E. 1957. *The Psychology of Careers*. New York: Harper & Row. **199**

———, and M. J. BOHN JR. 1970. *Occupational Psychology*. Belmont, Calif.: Wadsworth. **199**

SUSMAN, GERALD I. 1970. "The Impact of Automation on Work Group Autonomy and Task Specialization," *Human Relations*, 23:567–77. **266**

———. 1972. "Process Design Automation and Worker Alienation," *Industrial Relations*, 11:34–35.

———. 1973. "Job Enlargement: Effects of Culture on Worker Responses," *Industrial Relations*, 12:1–15.

TAGUIRI, RENATO. 1966. "Comments on Organizational Climate." Paper presented at a conference on Organizational Climate, Foundation for Research on Human Behavior, Ann Arbor, Mich. (March). **402, 403, 405**

TANNENBAUM, ARNOLD S. 1955. "One Man's Meat," *Adult Leadership*, 3:22–23.

———. 1956. "Control Structure and Union Functions," *American Journal of Sociology*, 61:536–45. **285**

———. 1957. "Personality Change as a Result of an Experimental Change of Environmental Conditions," *Journal of Abnormal and Social Psychology*, 55, 404–6. **288**

———. 1961. "Control and Effectiveness in a Voluntary Organization," *American Journal of Sociology*, 67, 33–46. **287**

———. 1968. *Control in Organizations*. New York: McGraw-Hill. **280, 299**

———, and FLOYD H. ALLPORT. 1956. "Personality Structure and Group Structure: An Interpretive Study of Their Relationship Through an Event-Structure Hypothesis," *Journal of Abnormal and Social Psychology*, vol. 53 (November): 272–80.

———, and ROBERT L. KAHN. 1958. *Participation in Union Locals*. Evanston, Ill.: Row, Peterson. **285, 289**

TANNENBAUM, ROBERT, and SHELDON A. DAVIS. 1969. "Values, Man, and Organizations," *Industrial Management Review*, 10:67–86. **22**

———, and FRED MASSARIK. 1950. "Participation by Subordinates in the Managerial Decision Making Process," *Canadian Journal of Economics and Political Science* (August). **323**

———, and WARREN H. SCHMIDT. 1958. "How to Choose a Leadership Pattern," *Harvard Business Review* (March–April):95–101. **338, 341**

TAYLOR, FREDERICK W. 1911. *Scientific Management*. New York: Harper & Row. **13, 19, 20, 23, 252**

TAYLOR, J. C. 1971. "Some Effects of Technology in Organizational Change," *Human Relations*, 24:105–23. **265–66**

TERREBERRY, SHIRLEY. 1968. "The Evolution of Organizational Environments," *Administrative Science Quarterly*, 12 (March):590–613. **126, 137, 143**

THAYER, FREDERICK. 1972. "General System(s) Theory: The Promise that Could Not be Kept," *Academy of Management Journal*, 15:481–93.

THEODORSON, GEORGE A., and ACHILLES G. THEODORSON. 1969. *A Modern Dictionary of Sociology*. New York: Cromwell. **205, 346–47**

THOMAS, CHARLES W., and SAMUEL C. FOSTER. 1973. "Importation Model of Inmate Social Roles," *Sociological Quarterly*, 14:226–34. **208**

THOMPSON, JAMES D. 1962. "Organizations and Output Transactions," *American Journal of Sociology*, 68 (November):309–24. **137**

———. 1964. "Decision-Making, the Firm, and the Market," in W. W. Cooper et al. (eds.), *New Perspectives in Organization Research*. New York: Wiley. **18**

———. 1967. *Organizations in Action*. New York: McGraw-Hill. **4, 13–18, 26, 38, 66–67, 75, 81, 98, 104, 123, 124, 126, 130, 141, 142, 144, 145, 147, 158–59, 161, 163–68, 177–78, 179, 191, 207, 226, 281, 306, 346, 381, 422, 468, 475, 477, 485–86**

———, and FREDERICK L. BATES. 1957. "Technology, Organization, and Administration," *Administrative Science Quarterly*, 2 (December):325–42. **157**

———, and WILLIAM J. MCEWEN. 1958. "Organizational Goals and Environment: Goal-Setting as an Interaction Process," *American Sociological Review*, 23 (February):23–31. **122, 147, 480**

———, and ARTHUR TUDEN. 1959. "Strategies, Structures and Processes of Organizational Decision," in James D. Thompson, et al. (eds.), *Comparative Studies in Administration*. Pittsburgh, Pa.: University of Pittsburgh Press. **186, 313, 323–33**

TOFFLER, ALVIN. 1970. *Future Shock*. New York: Random House. **498**

TOSI, HENRY L., and STEPHEN J. CARROLL. 1976. *Management: Contingencies, Structure, and Process*. Chicago: St. Clair Press. **227, 229**

TRIST, ERIC L., and E. K. BAMFORTH. 1951. "Some Social and Psychological Consequences of the Long-Wall Method of Goal-Getting," *Human Relations*, 4:3–38. **294**

———; G. W. HIGGIN; H. MURRAY; and A. B. POLLOCK. 1963. *Organizational Choice*. London: Tavistock Publications. **264**

TURNER, ARTHUR N., and PAUL R. LAWRENCE. 1965. "The Town-City Difference," in *Industrial Worker: An Investigation of Response of Task Attributes*, Boston: Harvard Univ., Div. of Research, Graduate School of Business Administration. **254, 269**

TYLER, WILLIAM B. 1973. "Measuring Organizational Specialization; The Concept of Role Variety." *Administrative Science Quarterly*, 18: 383–92. **351**

UDY, STANLEY H. JR. 1958. "Bureaucratic Elements in Organizations: Some Research Findings." *American Sociological Review*, 415–18. **161**

———. 1959. *Organization of Work*. New Haven, Conn.: Human Relations Area Files Press. **346**

———. 1962. "Administrative Rationality, Social Setting, and Organizational Development," *American Journal of Sociology*, 68 (November):299–308. **306**

URWICK, LYNDALL F. 1937. "Organization as a Technical Problem," in L. Gulick and L. Urwick (eds.), *Papers on the Science of Administration*. New York: Institute of Public Administration. Pp. 47–88. **23, 347, 353**

VAN DE VEN, ANDREW H. 1976. "A Framework for Organization Assessment." *Academy of Management Review*, 1:64–78. **57**

———, and ANDRÉ L. DELBECQ. 1971. "Nominal and Interacting Group Processes for Committee Decision-Making Effectiveness." *Academy of Management Journal*, 14 (June):203–12. **187**

———. 1974. "A Task Contingent Model of Work-Unit Structure," *Administrative Science Quarterly*, 19 (June):183–97. **161**

VANCIL, RICHARD F. 1975. "What Kind of Management Control Do You Need?" in *Harvard Business Review—On Management*. New York: Harper & Row. Pp. 464–81. **297**

VAN MAANEN J., and EDGAR H. SCHEIN. 1977. "Career Development," in J. Richard Hackman and J. L. Suttle, (eds.), *Improving Life at Work*. Santa Monica, Calif.: Goodyear, Pp. 30–95. **198, 199, 231, 234**

VICKERS, GEOFFREY. 1957. "Control Stability and Choice," reprinted in *General Systems, Yearbook of the Society for General Systems*, 2:1–8. **37, 288, 289**

VIOLA, R. H. 1977. *Organizations in a Changing Society: Administration and Human Values*. Philadelphia: W. B. Saunders. **198, 237**

VOLLMER, HOWARD M. and DONALD L. MILLS; eds. 1966. *Professionalization*. Englewood Cliffs, N. J.: Prentice-Hall. **79, 208, 229**

VON BERTALANFFY, LUDWIG. 1951. "Problems of General System Theory," *Human Biology*, 23:302–12. **346**

———. 1952. *Problems of Life*. London: Watts. **494**

VROOM, VICTOR H. 1960. *Some Personality Determinants of the Effects of Participation*. Englewood Cliffs, N. J.: Prentice-Hall.

———. 1964. *Work and Motivation*. New York: Wiley. **21, 225, 338**

———. 1969. "Industrial Social Psychology," in G. Lindzey and E. Aronson (eds.), *Handbook of Social Psychology* (2nd ed.). Reading, Mass.: Addison-Wesley. **264**

———. 1973. "A New Look at Managerial Decision Making," *Organizational Dynamics*, 1 (Spring):66–80. **339**

WALKER, ARTHUR H., and JAY W. LORSCH. 1968. "Organizational Choice: Product versus Function," *Harvard Business Review* (November–December):129–38. **467, 471**

WALKER, C. R. 1950. "The Problem of the Repetitive Job," *Harvard Business Review*, 28 (May):54–58. **252**

WALTERS, R. W., AND ASSOCIATES. 1975. *Job Enrichment for Results*. Reading, Mass.: Addison-Wesley. **261**

WALTON, RICHARD E. 1975. "From Hawthorne to Topeka and Kalmar," in E. L. Cass and F. G. Zimmer (eds.), *Man and Work in Society*. New York: Van Nostrand Reinhold. **266, 277**

WANOUS, J. P. 1974. "Individual Differences and Reactions to Job Characteristics," *Journal of Applied Psychology*, 59:616–22.

———. 1976. "Organizational Entry: From Naive Expectations to Realistic Beliefs," *Journal of Applied Psychology*, 61:22–29. **228, 229**

———. 1977. "Organizational Entry: Newcomers Moving from Outside to Inside," *Psychological Bulletin*, 84, 4 (July):601–18. **228, 229**

WARNER, KEITH W., and A. EUGENE HAVENS. 1968. "Goal Displacement and the Intangibility of Organizational Goals," *Administrative Science Quarterly*, 12 (March):539–55. **76**

WAYS, MAX. 1970. "More Power to Everybody." *Fortune*, 8 (May). **82**

WEBER, MAX. 1946. *Essays in Sociology*. New York: Oxford University Press. **345, 347, 353**

———. 1947. *The Theory of Social and Economic Organization*, trans. by A. M. Henderson and T. Parsons. New York: Oxford University Press. **13, 164, 281**

———. 1958. *From Max Weber: Essays in Sociology*. H. H. Gerth and C. Wright Mills, (eds.). New York: Oxford University Press. **19, 23, 327, 477**

WEICK, KARL E. 1969. *The Social Psychology of Organizing*. Reading, Mass.: Addison-Wesley. **123**

———. 1976. "Educational Organizations As Loosely Coupled Systems," *Administrative Science Quarterly*, 21 (March):1–19. **303, 509**

WEED, E. D. 1971. "Job Enrichment 'Cleans Up' at Texas Instruments," in J. R. Maher (ed.), *New Perspectives in Job Enrichment*. New York: Van Nostrand Reinhold Corporation.

WHITE, ORION F. JR. 1969. "The Dialectical Organization—An Alternative to Bureaucracy," *Public Administration Review*, 29 (January–February):32–42. **503**

WHYTE, WILLIAM F. 1955. *Street Corner Society*. Chicago: University of Chicago Press. **129**

WILCOX, HERBERT G. 1969. "Hierarchy, Human Nature and the Participative Panacea," *Public Administration Review*, 29:53–63. **28**

WILD, RAY, and R. KEMPNER. 1972. "Influence of Community and Plant Characteristics in Job Attitudes of Manual Workers," *Journal of Applied Psychology*, 56 (April):106–13.

WILDAVSKY, AARON B. 1972. "The Self-Evaluating Organization," *Public Administration Review*, 32 (September–October):509–20. **477, 503, 505, 506**

WILENSKY, HAROLD L. 1967. *Organizational Intelligence*. New York: Basic Books. **143, 145**

WILLIAMSON, OLIVER A. 1975. *Markets and Hierarchies: Analysis and Antitrust Implications*. New York: Free Press. **292, 295, 297, 300, 305**

WILSON, JAMES Q. 1966. "Innovation in Organization: Notes Toward a Theory," in James D. Thompson (ed.), *Approaches to Organizational Design*. Pittsburgh, Pa.: University of Pittsburgh Press. **229**

———. 1973. *Political Organizations*. New York: Basic Books. **138, 142**

WISPE, L. G., and K. E. LLOYD. 1955. "Some Situational and Psychological Determinants of the Desire for Structured Interpersonal Relations," *Journal of Abnormal and Social Psychology*, 51:57–60.

WITTREICH, W. J., and K. B. RADCLIFFE JR. 1956. "Differences in the Perception of an Authority Figure and a Nonauthority Figure by Navy Recruits," *Journal of Abnormal and Social Psychology*, 53:383–84.

WOODWARD, JOAN. 1965. *Industrial Organization: Theory and Practice*. London: Oxford University Press. **40, 158, 163, 173, 176, 178–79, 188, 191, 209, 306, 468**

WRIGHTSMAN, L. S., and N. J. BAKER. 1969. "Where Have all the Idealistic Imperturable Freshmen Gone?" *Proceedings* of the 77th Annual Convention of the American Psychological Association, 4, Summary: 299–300. **203**

YANKELOVICH, DANIEL. 1974a. "The Meaning of Work," in Jerry M. Rosow (ed.), *The Worker and the Job*. Englewood Cliffs, N. J.: Prentice-Hall. **198, 203**

———. 1974b. *The New Morality*. New York: McGraw-Hill. **197**

YUCHTMAN, EPHRAIM, and STANLEY E. SEASHORE. 1967. "A System Resource Approach to Organizational Effectiveness," *American Sociological Review*, 32 (December):891–903. **80**

ZALD, MAYER N. 1963. "Comparative Analysis and Measurement of Organizational Goals: The Case of Correctional Institutions for Delinquents," *Sociological Quarterly*, 4 (Summer). **208**

———. 1967. "Urban Differentiation, Characteristics of Boards of Directors and Organizational Effectiveness," *American Journal of Sociology*, 73: 261–72. **133**

———. 1969. "The Power and Functions of Boards of Directors," *American Journal of Sociology*, 75:97–111. **143**

ZWERMAN, WILLIAM L. 1970. *New Perspectives on Organization Theory*. Westport, Conn.: Greenwood. **160**

SUBJECT INDEX